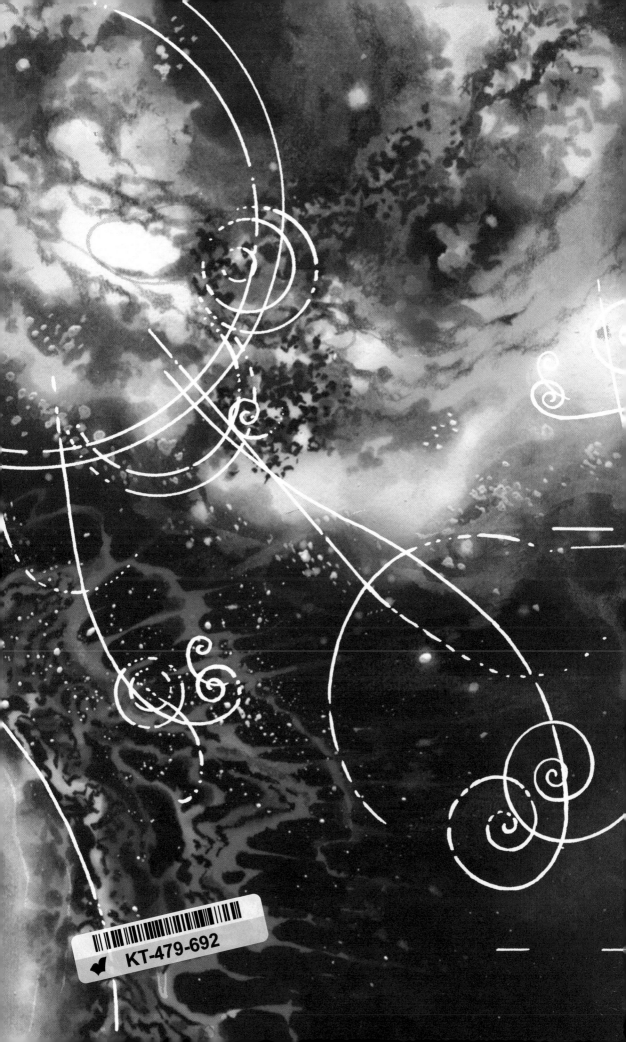

KT-479-692

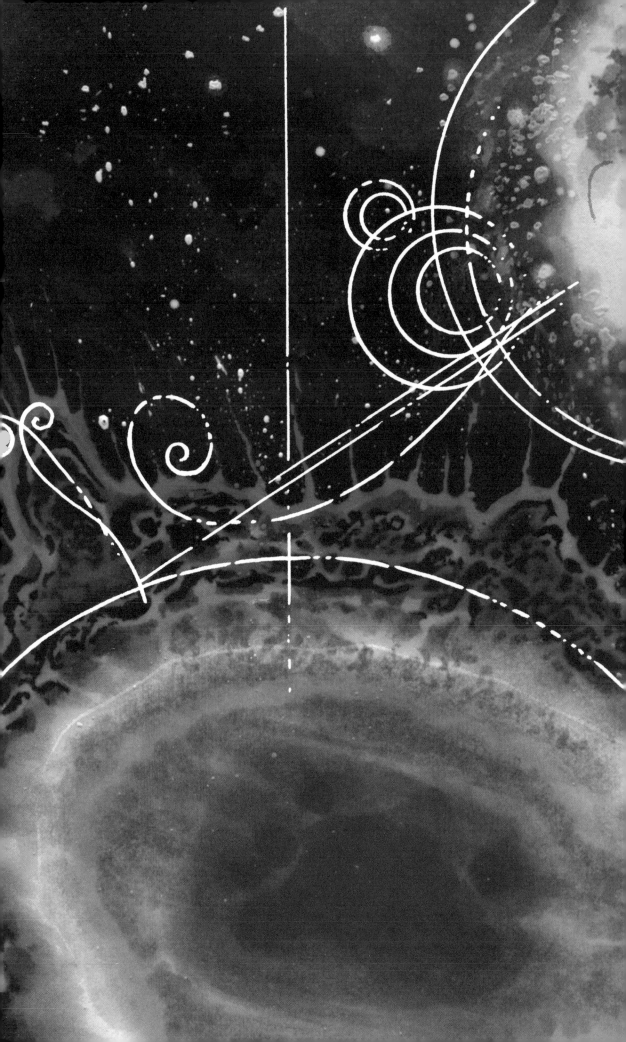

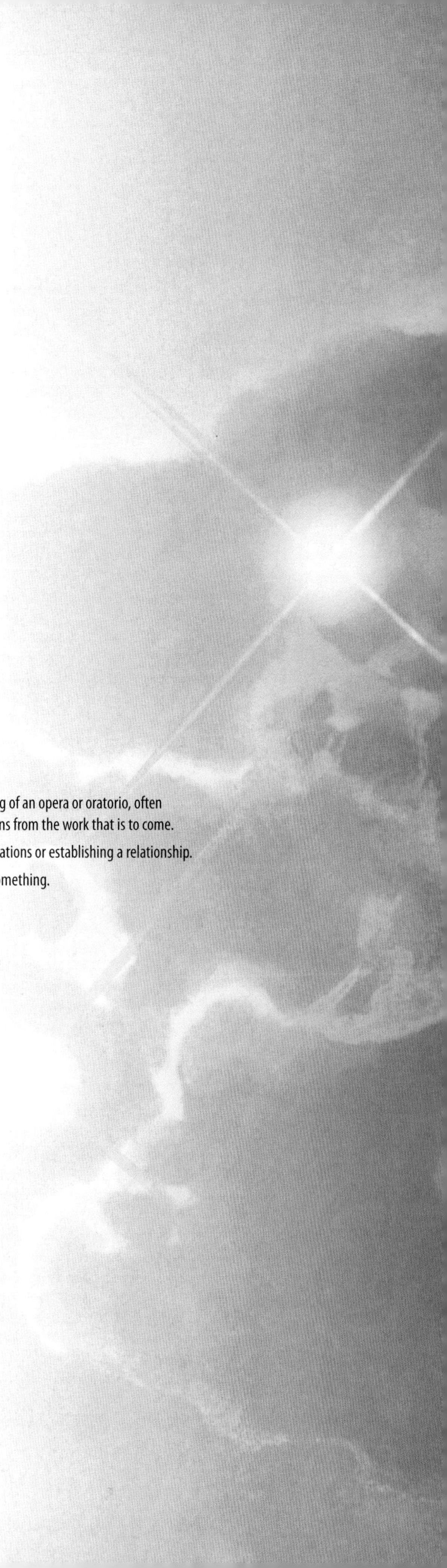

OVERTURE

noun

1. A piece of orchestral music played at the beginning of an opera or oratorio, often containing the main themes of the work or quotations from the work that is to come.
2. Approaches made with the aim of opening negotiations or establishing a relationship.
3. The first part of an event. The very beginning of something.

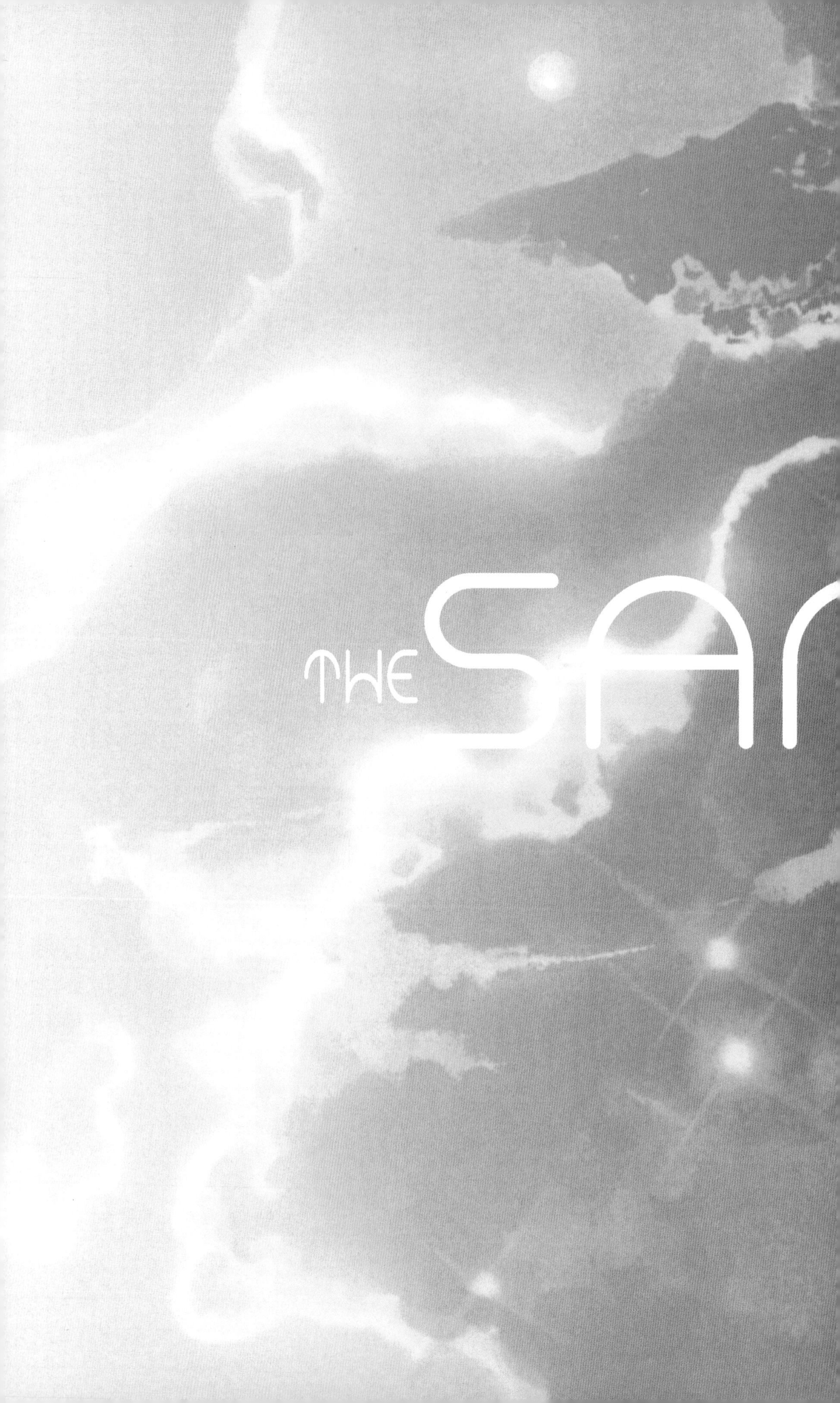
THE SA

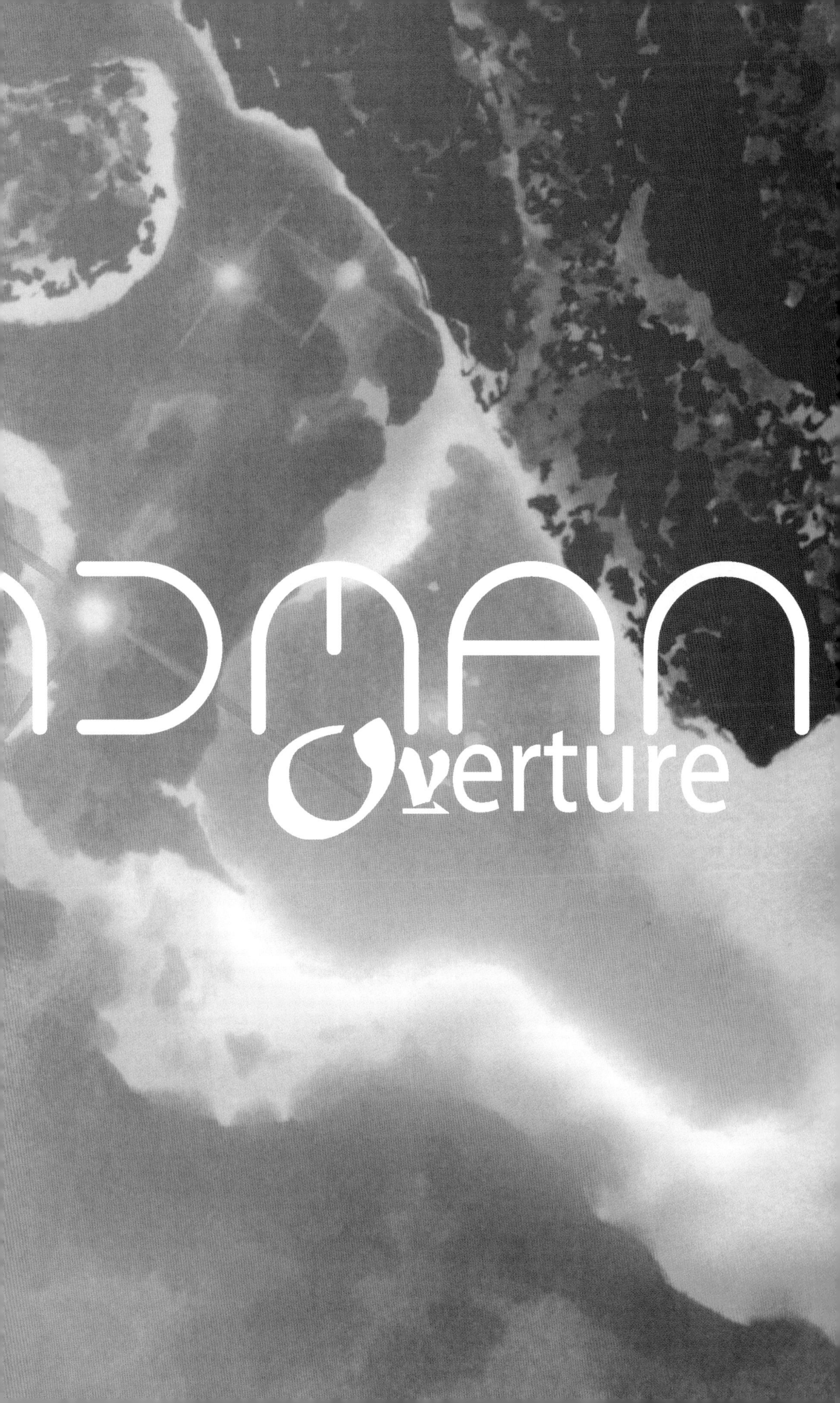
Overture

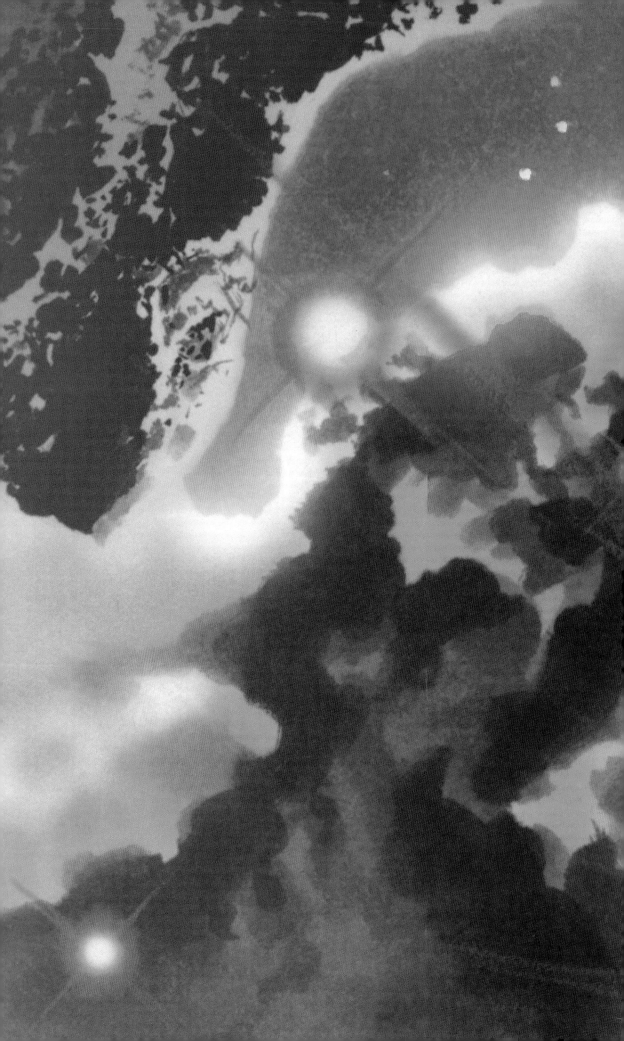

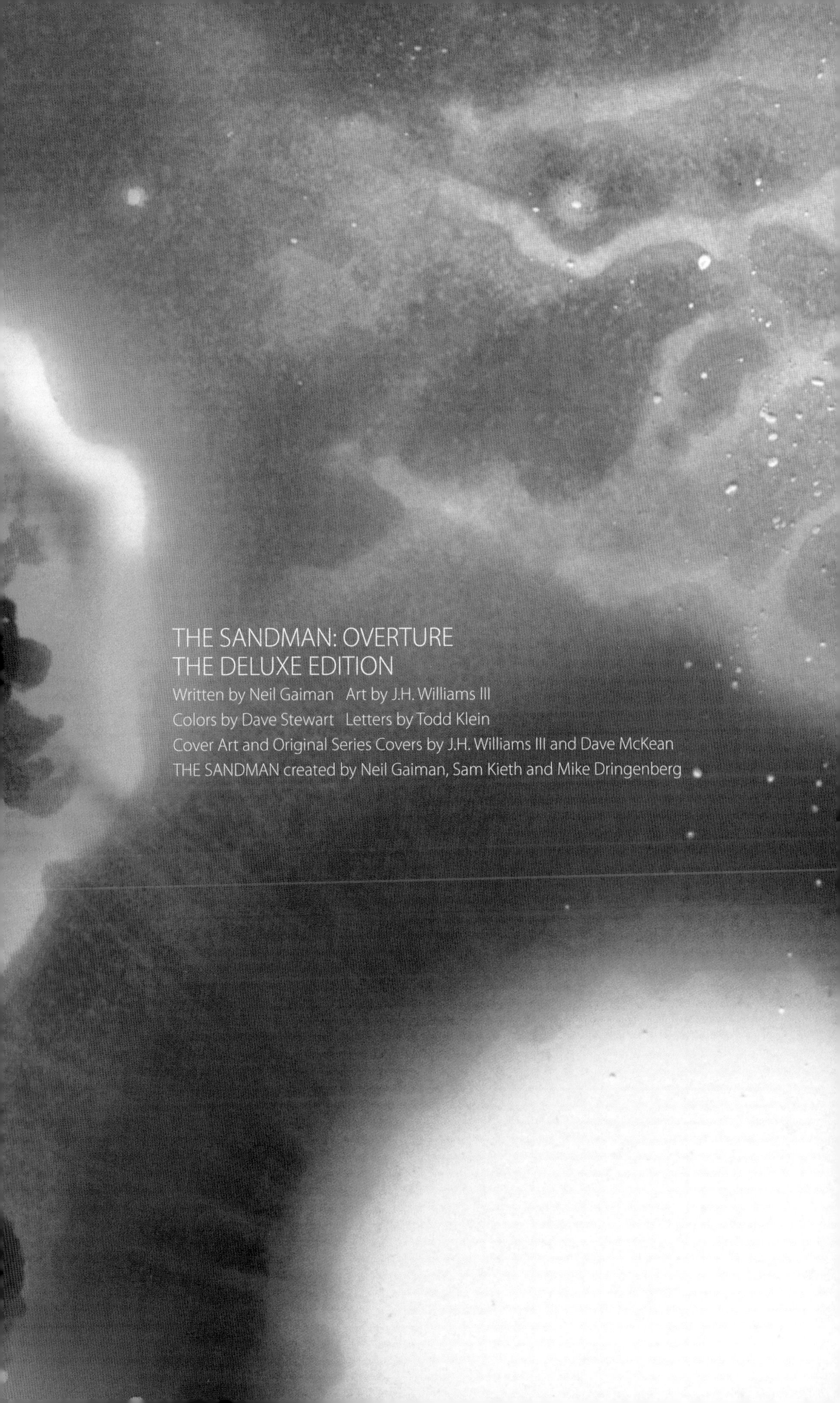

THE SANDMAN: OVERTURE
THE DELUXE EDITION

Written by Neil Gaiman   Art by J.H. Williams III

Colors by Dave Stewart   Letters by Todd Klein

Cover Art and Original Series Covers by J.H. Williams III and Dave McKean

THE SANDMAN created by Neil Gaiman, Sam Kieth and Mike Dringenberg

Shelly Bond Karen Berger Editors – Original Series Gregory Lockard Rowena Yow Associate Editors – Original Series Sara Miller Assistant Editor – Original Series
Jamie Rich Group Editor – Vertigo Comics Jeb Woodard Group Editor – Collected Editions Scott Nybakken Editor – Collected Edition Steve Cook Design Director – Books
Louis Prandi Publication Design

Diane Nelson President Dan DiDio Publisher Jim Lee Publisher Geoff Johns President & Chief Creative Officer
Amit Desai Executive VP – Business & Marketing Strategy, Direct to Consumer & Global Franchise Management Sam Ades Senior VP – Direct to Consumer Bobbie Chase VP – Talent Development
Mark Chiarello Senior VP – Art, Design & Collected Editions John Cunningham Senior VP – Sales & Trade Marketing Anne DePies Senior VP – Business Strategy, Finance & Administration
Don Falletti VP – Manufacturing Operations Lawrence Ganem VP – Editorial Administration & Talent Relations Alison Gill Senior VP – Manufacturing & Operations
Hank Kanalz Senior VP – Editorial Strategy & Administration Jay Kogan VP – Legal Affairs Thomas Loftus VP – Business Affairs Jack Mahan VP – Business Affairs
Nick J. Napolitano VP – Manufacturing Administration Eddie Scannell VP – Consumer Marketing Courtney Simmons Senior VP – Publicity & Communications
Jim (Ski) Sokolowski VP – Comic Book Specialty Sales & Trade Marketing Nancy Spears VP – Mass, Book, Digital Sales & Trade Marketing

THE SANDMAN: OVERTURE — THE DELUXE EDITION

Published by DC Comics. Compilation Copyright © 2015 DC Comics. All Rights Reserved.

Originally published in single magazine form in THE SANDMAN: OVERTURE 1-6. Copyright © 2013, 2014, 2015
DC Comics. All Rights Reserved. All characters, their distinctive likenesses and related elements featured in this publication are trademarks
of DC Comics. VERTIGO is a trademark of DC Comics. The stories, characters and incidents featured in this publication are entirely fictional.
DC Comics does not read or accept unsolicited submissions of ideas, stories or artwork.
DC Comics, 2900 W. Alameda Avenue, Burbank, CA 91505. Printed in Canada. Second Printing.
ISBN: 978-1-4012-4896-3 (J.H. Williams III dustjacket) ISBN: 978-1-4012-6205-1 (Dave McKean dustjacket)

Library of Congress Cataloging-in-Publication Data

Gaiman, Neil.
  The Sandman : overture deluxe edition / Neil Gaiman ; illustrated by J.H. Williams III.
    pages cm
  ISBN 978-1-4012-4896-3 (hardback)
  1. Graphic novels. I. Williams, J.H., III. II. Title.
  PN6728.S26G4 2015
  741.5'973—dc23
                    2015028077

PEFC Certified
Printed on paper from
sustainably managed
forests and controlled
sources
PEFC/01-31-106 www.pefc.org

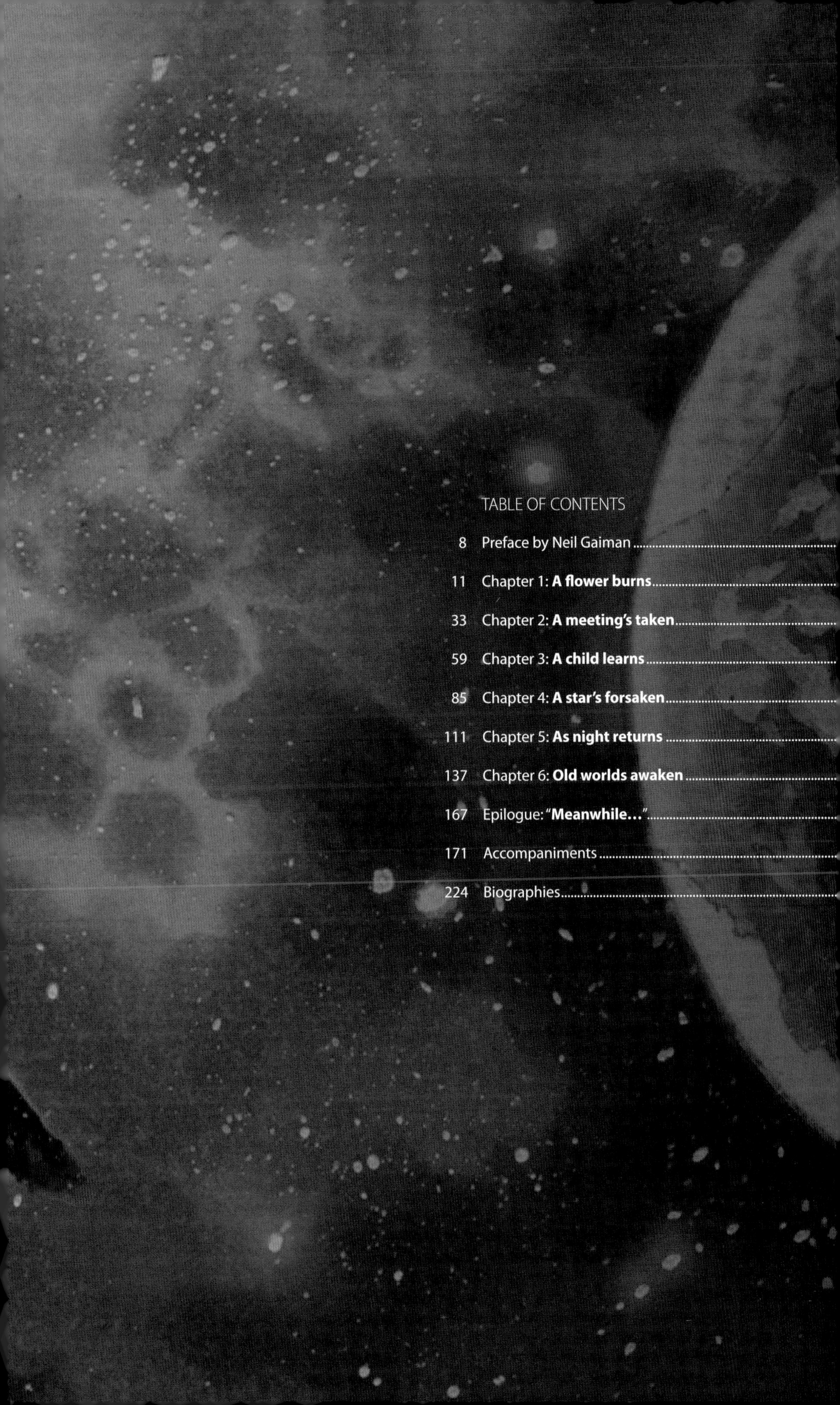

TABLE OF CONTENTS

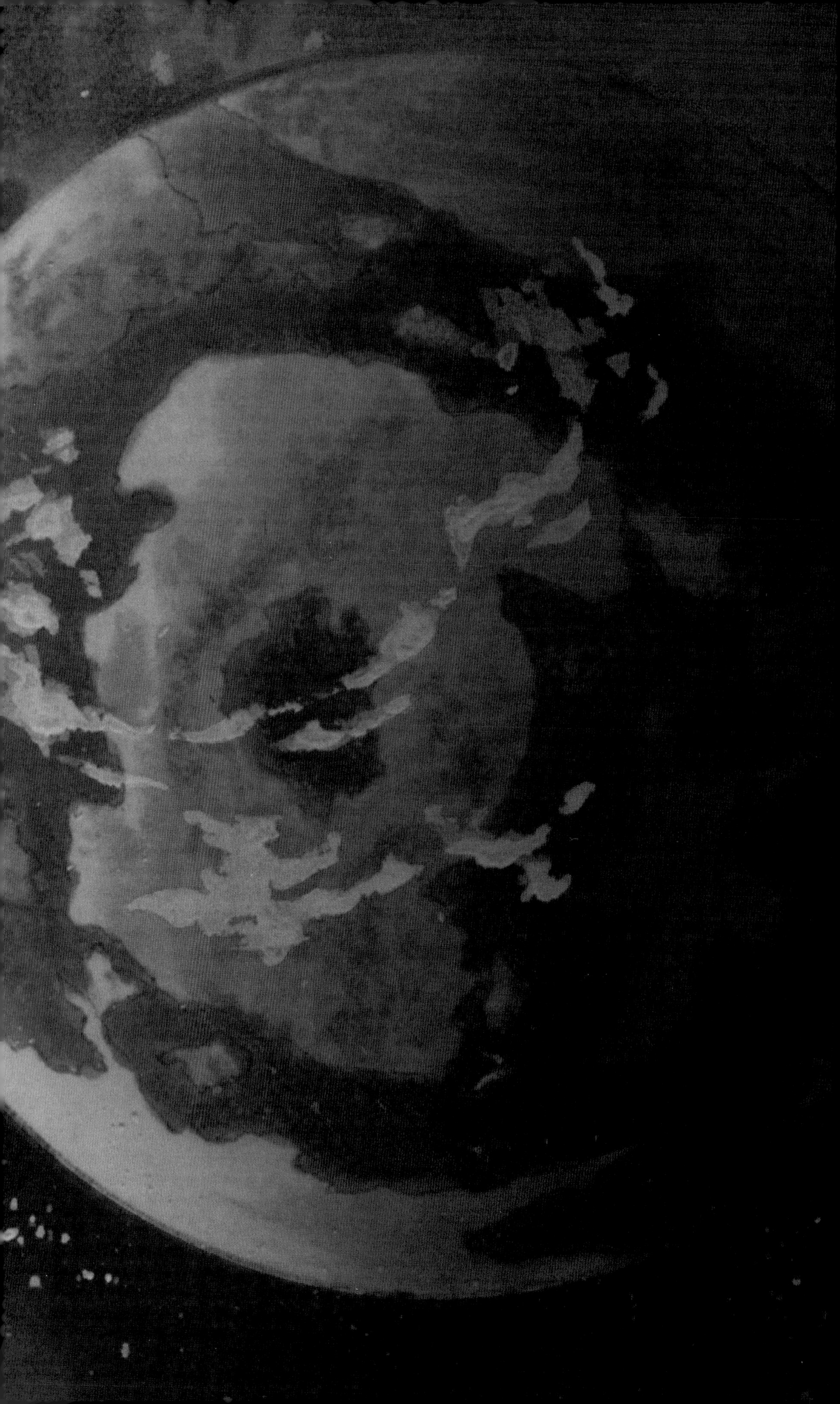

FOREWORD IS FOREWARNED

I woke a few moments ago from a fever and a host of interlocking fever dreams, one after the next. There was one where I was in London, walking through old abandoned formerly beautiful buildings, all of them about to be demolished. Sometimes I'd find myself walking past the enormous line of people waiting to attend the television memorial for a dead author friend of mine, but his memorial was a television spectacular with comedians and big band music. There was the one where I had accidentally connected my bank card to a portable printer and the little printer kept printing cash, but on the wrong paper and at the wrong size, so my money had huge, incredibly detailed faces on it, works of art that could not be spent. Then I woke from one dream into another: I was asleep in the passenger seat of the car, and saw that we were driving through a densely populated town, and that the driver was also asleep. I tried hard to wake her up and failed, and knew that no one was in control, no one was at the wheel, and soon someone was going to be killed, and I was shouting and calling without effect; but I whimpered and snuffled enough in the real world that my wife stroked my face and said, "Honey? You're having a nightmare," and, finally, I woke for real.

But I woke into a world in which, somewhere, I am still being driven through my life by a sleeping driver, in which money is only good as art, in which we can write the finest books but at the end the crowds will come out and say good-bye for the entertainment, in which the buildings and cities we inhabit will relentlessly be destroyed by progress and time: a world colored by dreams and illuminated by them, too.

Today I write this introduction for THE SANDMAN: OVERTURE, which, in the way of these things, is also its tombstone: the last thing I will type, the first thing you will read. It seems peculiarly final — the story, after all, has been living in my head for over 25 years: a strange and colorful journey to a distant galaxy that would have explained a host of things that were implied or hinted at in the body of THE SANDMAN itself.

My working title for it was SANDMAN ZERO, because it showed you what had happened before the first issue of THE SANDMAN, which began with Dream being captured.

We were told that he was returning from a distant galaxy, "tired beyond reckoning and tried beyond all endurance," in triumph of a sort, but we never learned why he was so exhausted, or why he had gone so far. It was a story I had wanted to tell, but it simply didn't fit in the story that began in THE SANDMAN #1 and finished in THE SANDMAN #75.

There were scenes I had wanted to write for so long, visions in my head that had lived with me for 20 years. I was fortunate in finding J.H. Williams III as my collaborator — I would write things that were impossible to draw, and he would draw them, impossible though they were. Dave Stewart colored those parts that JHW3 didn't, and the whole is seamless.

Todd Klein has been putting the words into my characters' mouths for 28 years now. He is unique, and his contributions are impossible to underestimate.

Karen Berger, for many years my editor, never lost faith. Shelly Bond, who came on board in 1992 and never left, has been a pillar and a rock. Dave McKean came back and made the covers. DC Comics' co-publishers, Dan DiDio and Jim Lee, and DC's queen, Diane Nelson, made this happen.

If you have never read THE SANDMAN before (and everyone has to start somewhere), this volume comes after the final SANDMAN story, THE WAKE, and after ENDLESS NIGHTS, a book of shorter stories (one for each of the Endless), and it comes before the first volume, PRELUDES AND NOCTURNES. I hope that, even if you are familiar with the 10 volumes of THE SANDMAN and ENDLESS NIGHTS, reading this volume will change the way that you encounter scenes that might have been familiar.

I wrote the first outline for THE SANDMAN in October 1987. I write this preface in September 2015, almost 28 years later.

Dreams still fascinate me: the way they color our lives, what they tell us about ourselves and the world we inhabit. And Dream still fascinates me: what he lets himself feel and know, how he lies to himself, how he keeps going. I do not recall ever enjoying myself more as a writer than in Chapter Two of this book, when Dream was finally able to talk to himself (and itself and herself and themselves and a cat).

I hope that this book answers some of your questions. That it may raise more questions than it answers is, I'm afraid, just part of the nature of things SANDMAN.

And questions are, I suspect, all we will take with us on our final journeys through Time and into Night.

Sleep safely,

Neil Gaiman
September 2015

For Karen Berger. You made it happen.

And for the SANDMAN periodical editorial team, who scribbled
down my corrections and caught up with me in strange places
between 1988 and 2015: Art Young, Tom Peyer, Alisa Kwitney,
Lisa Aufenanger, Shelly Bond, Jenny Lee, and Shelly Bond again.

You were the dream team, and you did your work in the
shadows. I'm grateful.

Neil

I dedicate the work in this book to my ever-enchanting wife,
Wendy Williams. Many have little understanding that such a
thing as SANDMAN: OVERTURE could not possibly exist as you
see it here without her.

She is the stuff of dreams.

J.H.

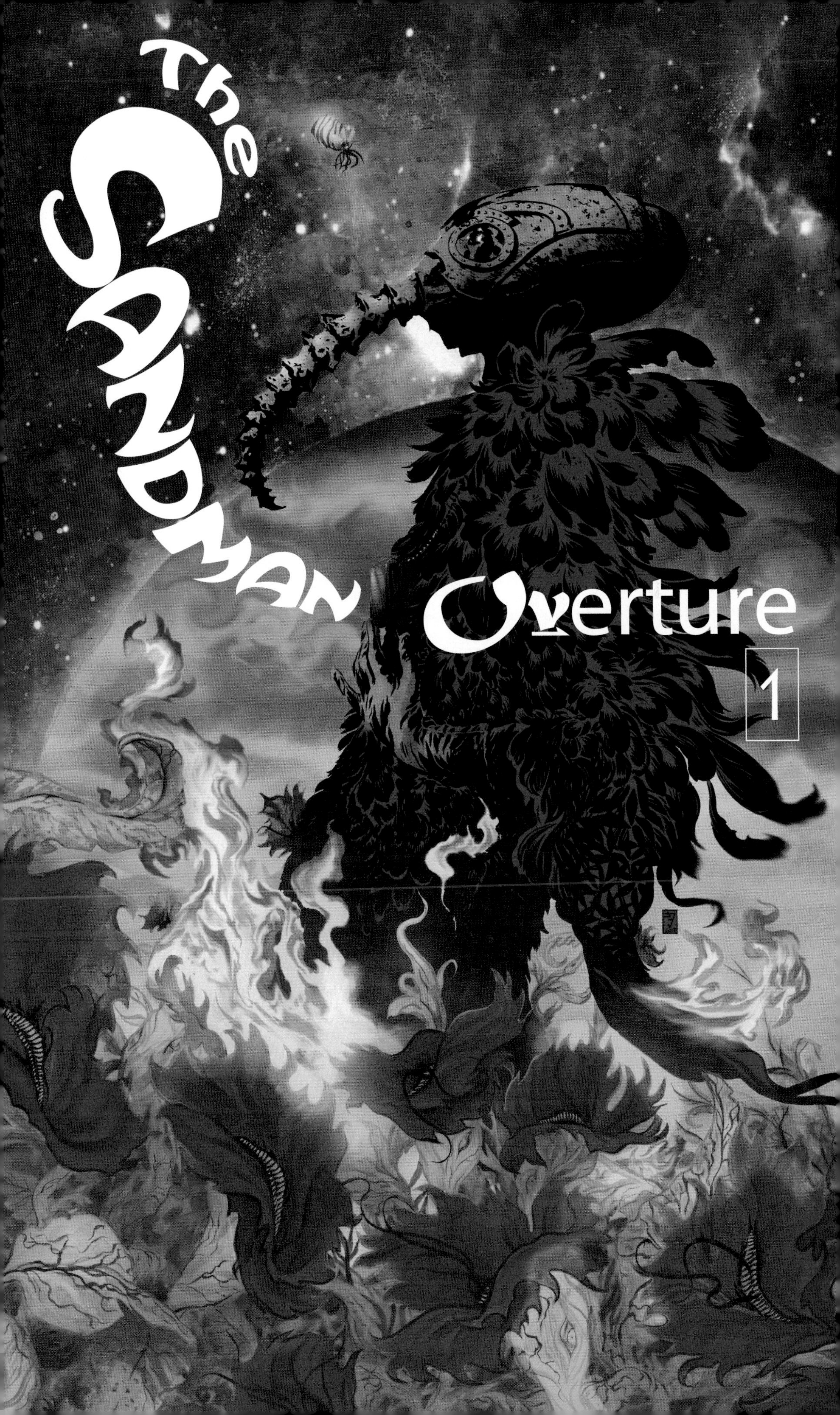
The SANDMAN
Overture
1

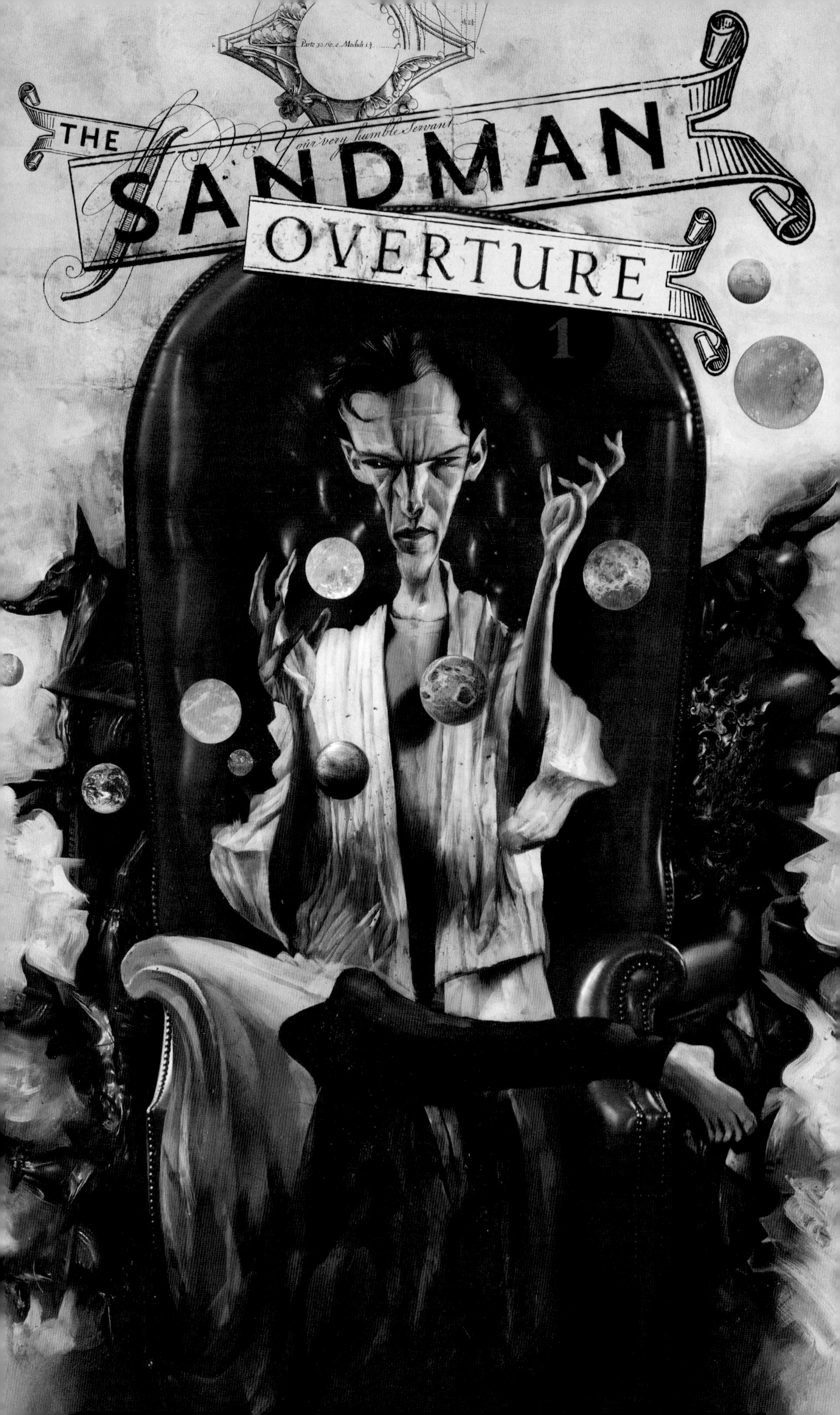
THE SANDMAN
OVERTURE
1
Your very humble Servant

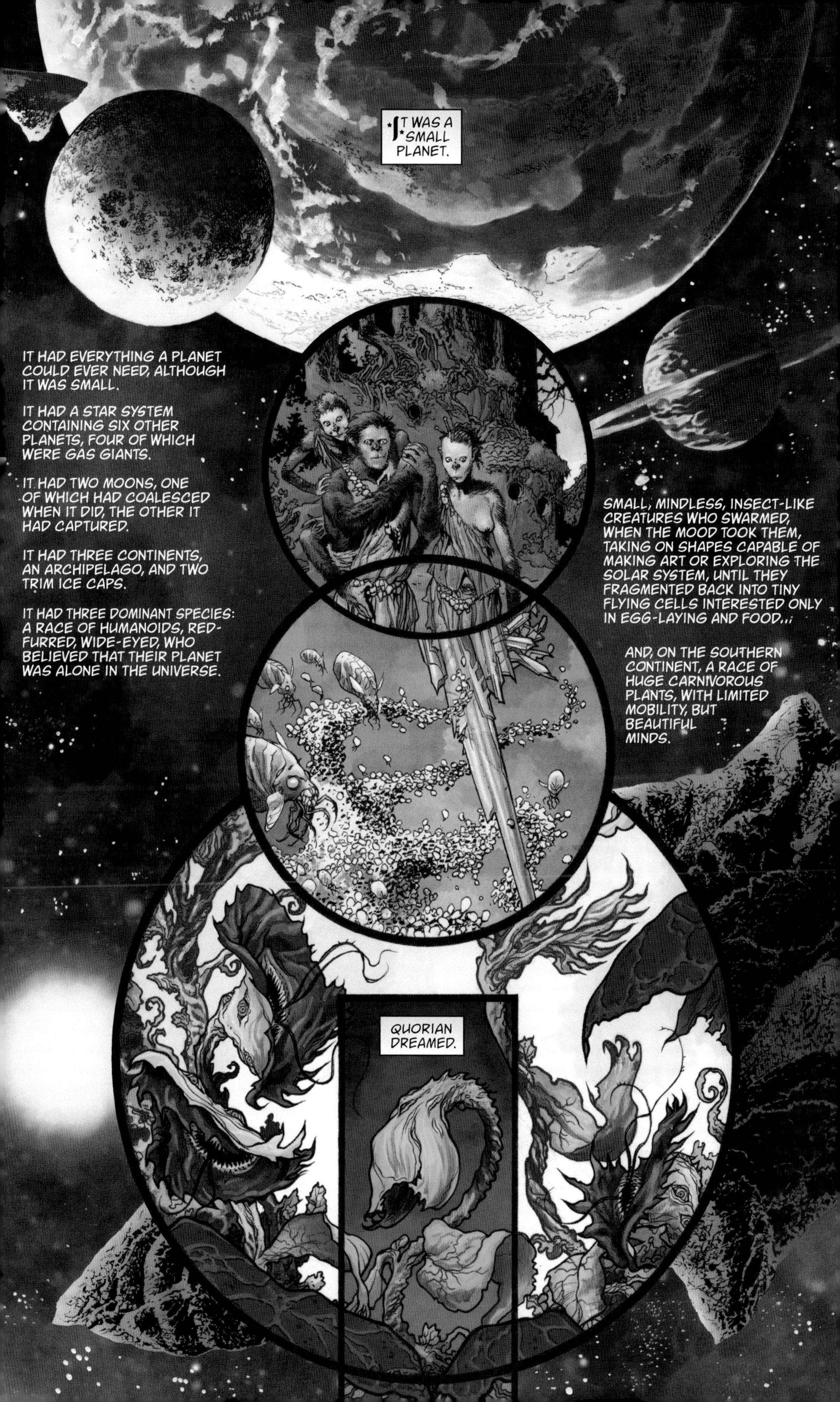
IT WAS A SMALL PLANET.
IT HAD EVERYTHING A PLANET COULD EVER NEED, ALTHOUGH IT WAS SMALL.
IT HAD A STAR SYSTEM CONTAINING SIX OTHER PLANETS, FOUR OF WHICH WERE GAS GIANTS.
IT HAD TWO MOONS, ONE OF WHICH HAD COALESCED WHEN IT DID, THE OTHER IT HAD CAPTURED.
IT HAD THREE CONTINENTS, AN ARCHIPELAGO, AND TWO TRIM ICE CAPS.
IT HAD THREE DOMINANT SPECIES: A RACE OF HUMANOIDS, RED-FURRED, WIDE-EYED, WHO BELIEVED THAT THEIR PLANET WAS ALONE IN THE UNIVERSE.
SMALL, MINDLESS, INSECT-LIKE CREATURES WHO SWARMED, WHEN THE MOOD TOOK THEM, TAKING ON SHAPES CAPABLE OF MAKING ART OR EXPLORING THE SOLAR SYSTEM, UNTIL THEY FRAGMENTED BACK INTO TINY FLYING CELLS INTERESTED ONLY IN EGG-LAYING AND FOOD...;
AND, ON THE SOUTHERN CONTINENT, A RACE OF HUGE CARNIVOROUS PLANTS, WITH LIMITED MOBILITY, BUT BEAUTIFUL MINDS.
QUORIAN DREAMED.

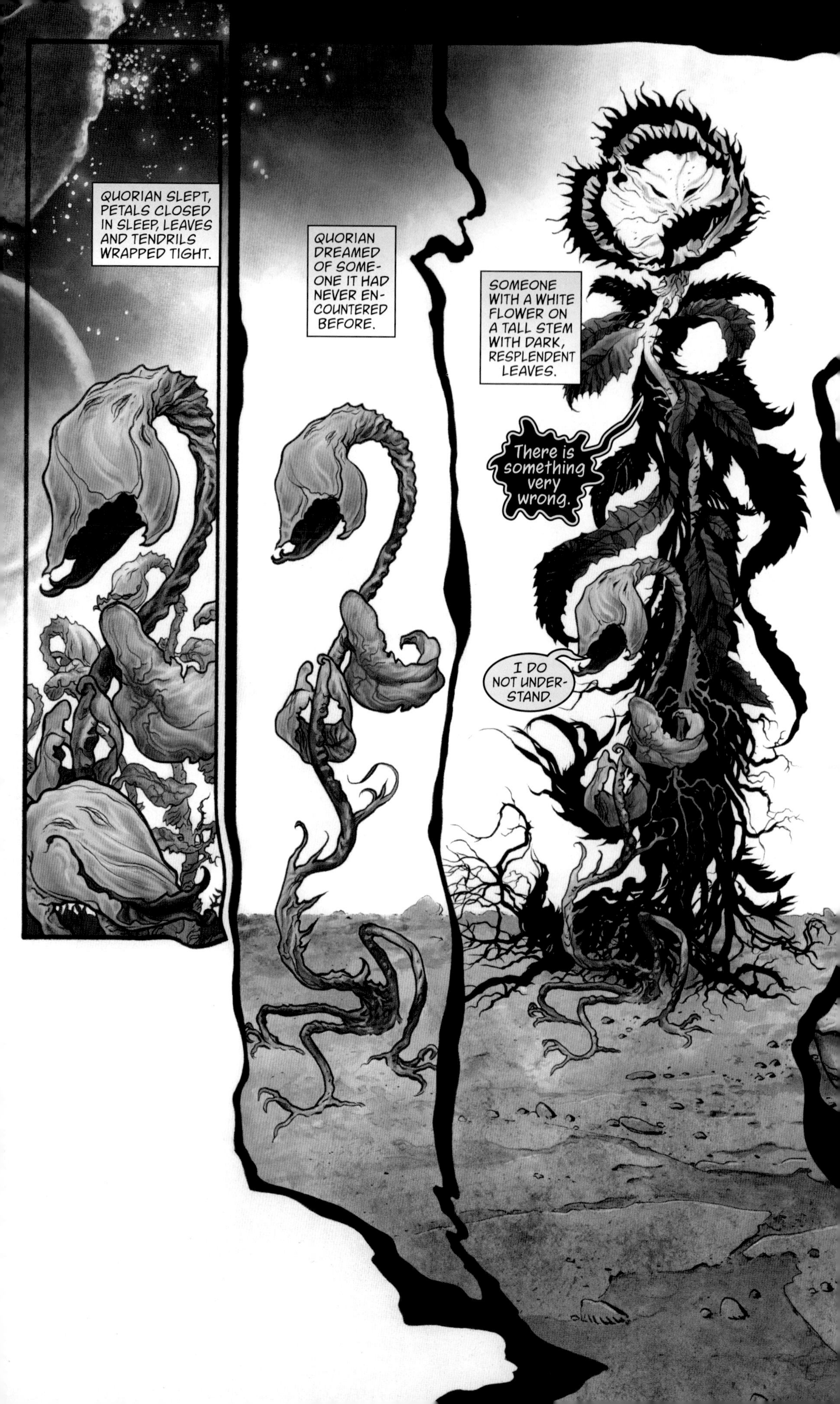
QUORIAN SLEPT, PETALS CLOSED IN SLEEP, LEAVES AND TENDRILS WRAPPED TIGHT.
QUORIAN DREAMED OF SOME-ONE IT HAD NEVER EN-COUNTERED BEFORE.
SOMEONE WITH A WHITE FLOWER ON A TALL STEM WITH DARK, RESPLENDENT LEAVES.
There is something very wrong.
I DO NOT UNDER-STAND.

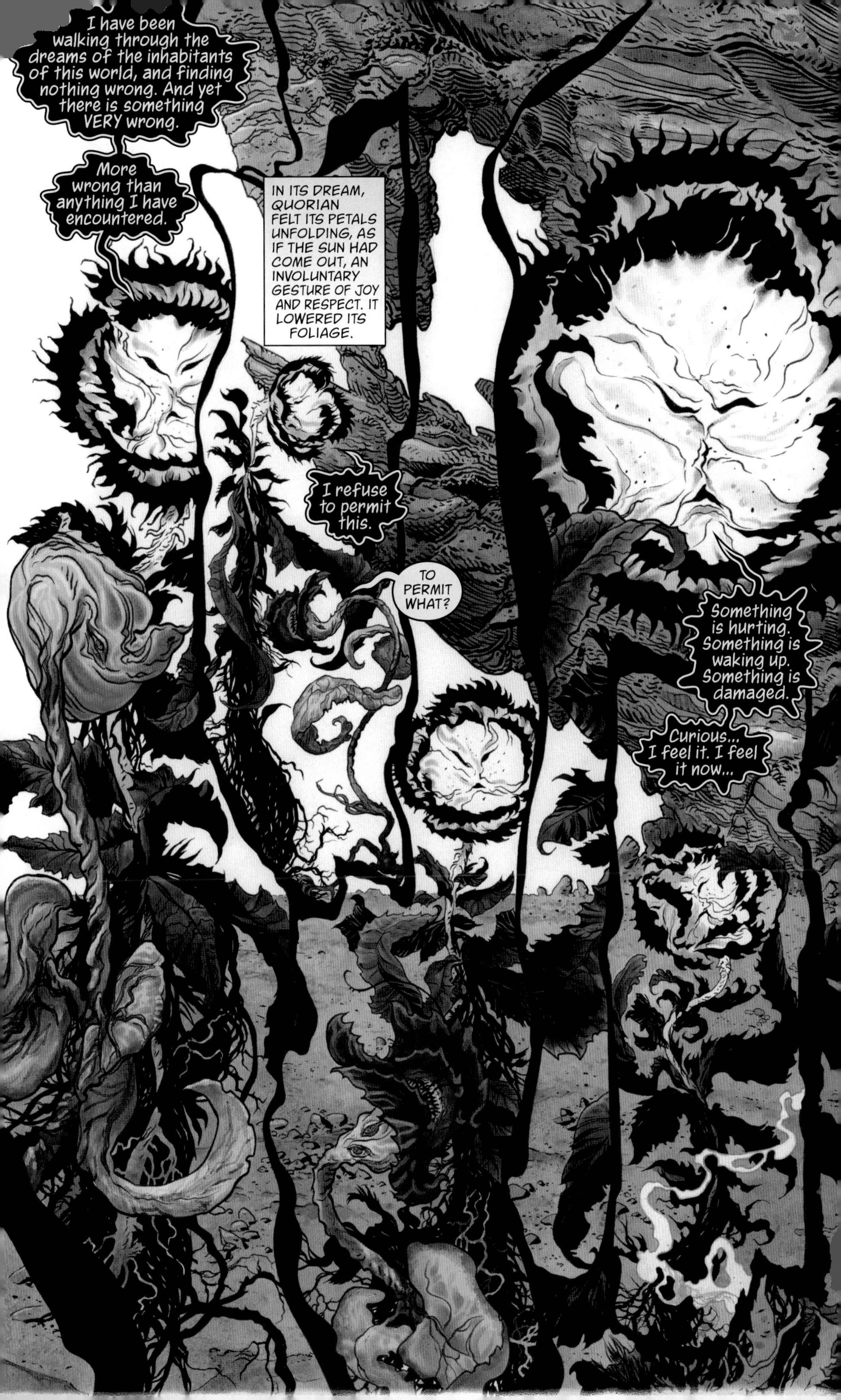
I have been walking through the dreams of the inhabitants of this world, and finding nothing wrong. And yet there is something VERY wrong.
More wrong than anything I have encountered.
IN ITS DREAM, QUORIAN FELT ITS PETALS UNFOLDING, AS IF THE SUN HAD COME OUT, AN INVOLUNTARY GESTURE OF JOY AND RESPECT. IT LOWERED ITS FOLIAGE.
I refuse to permit this.
TO PERMIT WHAT?
Something is hurting. Something is waking up. Something is damaged.
Curious... I feel it. I feel it now...

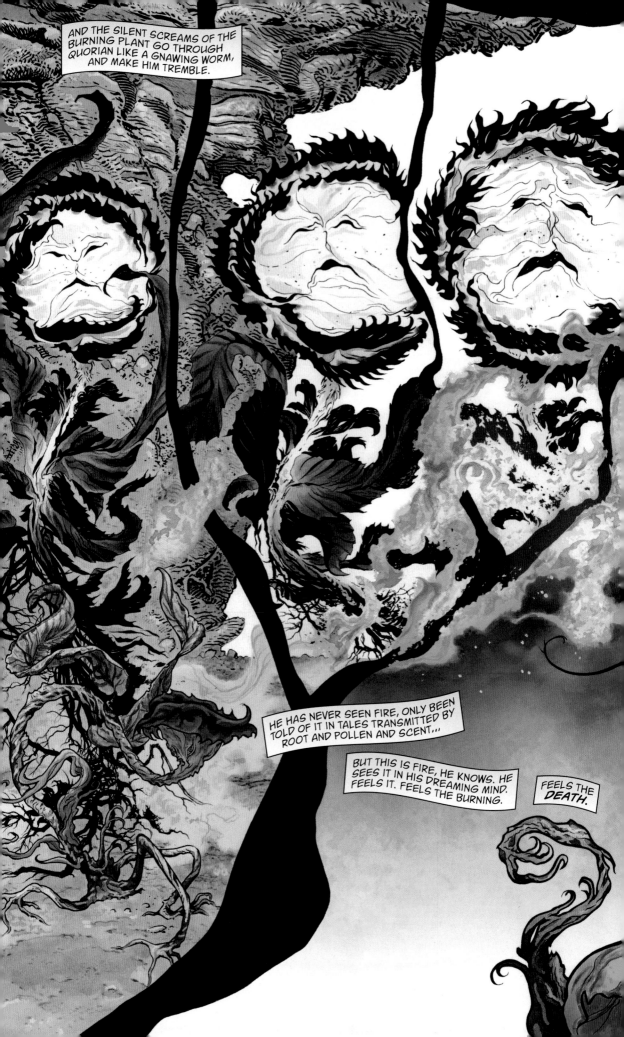

AND THE SILENT SCREAMS OF THE
BURNING PLANT GO THROUGH
QUORIAN LIKE A GNAWING WORM,
AND MAKE HIM TREMBLE.

HE HAS NEVER SEEN FIRE, ONLY BEEN
TOLD OF IT IN TALES TRANSMITTED BY
ROOT AND POLLEN AND SCENT...

BUT THIS IS FIRE, HE KNOWS. HE
SEES IT IN HIS DREAMING MIND. HE
FEELS IT. FEELS THE BURNING.

FEELS THE
DEATH.

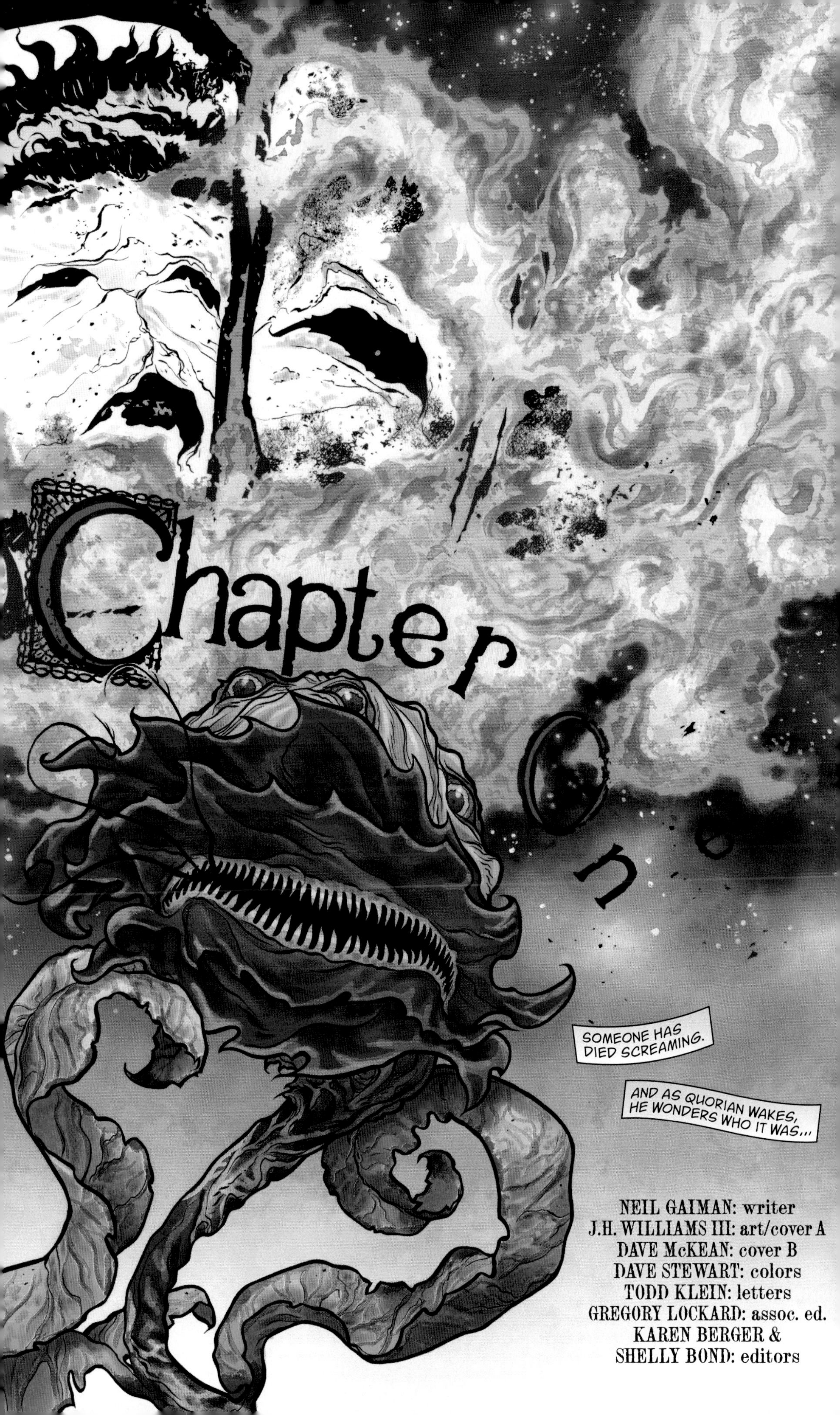
Chapter One
SOMEONE HAS DIED SCREAMING.
AND AS QUORIAN WAKES, HE WONDERS WHO IT WAS...
NEIL GAIMAN: writer
J.H. WILLIAMS III: art/cover A
DAVE McKEAN: cover B
DAVE STEWART: colors
TODD KLEIN: letters
GREGORY LOCKARD: assoc. ed.
KAREN BERGER &
SHELLY BOND: editors

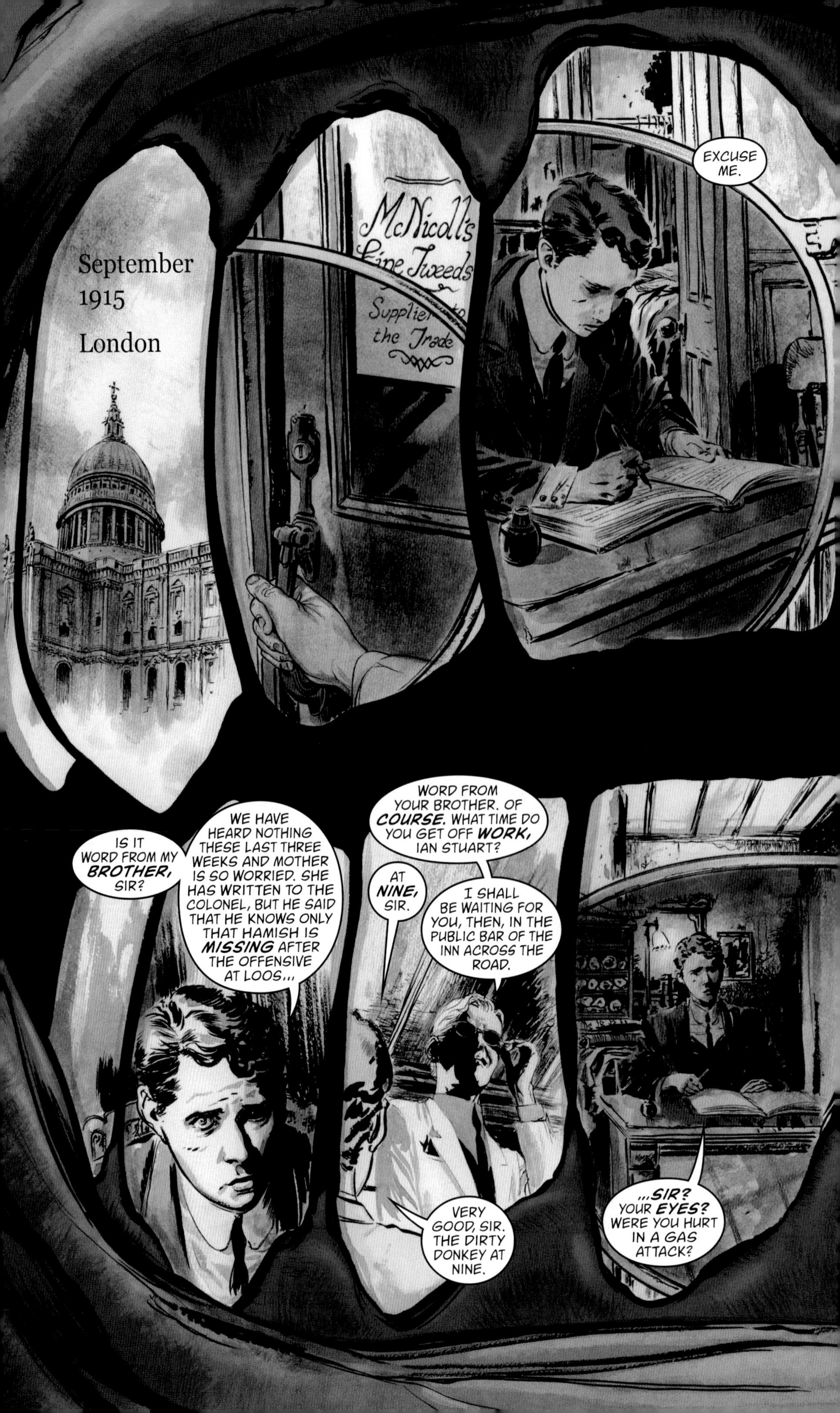
September 1915 London
McNicoll's Fine Tweeds Suppliers to the Trade
EXCUSE ME.
IS IT WORD FROM MY BROTHER, SIR?
WE HAVE HEARD NOTHING THESE LAST THREE WEEKS AND MOTHER IS SO WORRIED. SHE HAS WRITTEN TO THE COLONEL, BUT HE SAID THAT HE KNOWS ONLY THAT HAMISH IS MISSING AFTER THE OFFENSIVE AT LOOS...
WORD FROM YOUR BROTHER. OF COURSE. WHAT TIME DO YOU GET OFF WORK, IAN STUART?
AT NINE, SIR.
I SHALL BE WAITING FOR YOU, THEN, IN THE PUBLIC BAR OF THE INN ACROSS THE ROAD.
VERY GOOD, SIR. THE DIRTY DONKEY AT NINE.
...SIR? YOUR EYES? WERE YOU HURT IN A GAS ATTACK?

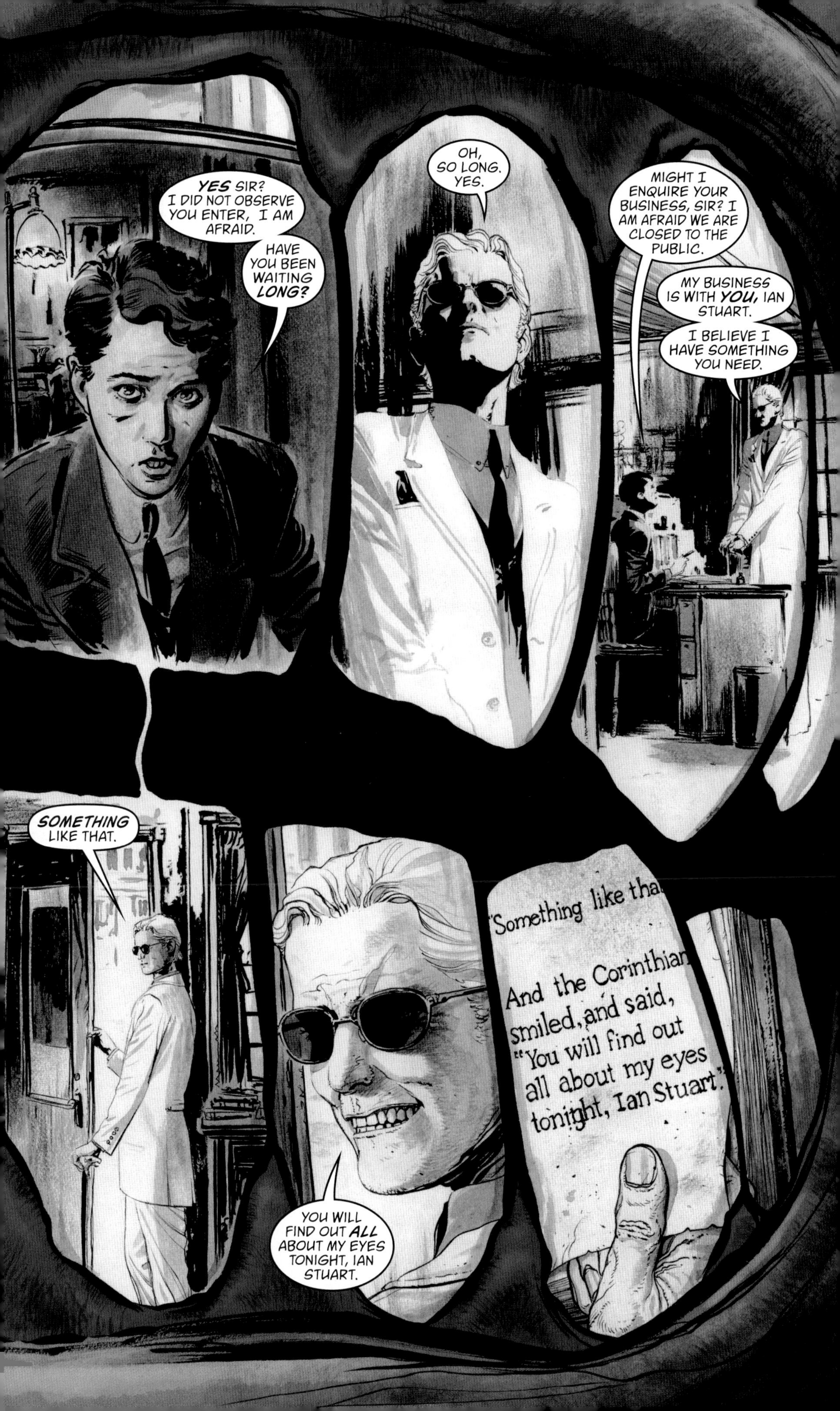
YES SIR? I DID NOT OBSERVE YOU ENTER, I AM AFRAID.
HAVE YOU BEEN WAITING LONG?
OH, SO LONG. YES.
MIGHT I ENQUIRE YOUR BUSINESS, SIR? I AM AFRAID WE ARE CLOSED TO THE PUBLIC.
MY BUSINESS IS WITH YOU, IAN STUART.
I BELIEVE I HAVE SOMETHING YOU NEED.
SOMETHING LIKE THAT.
YOU WILL FIND OUT ALL ABOUT MY EYES TONIGHT, IAN STUART.
"Something like tha
And the Corinthian smiled, and said, "You will find out all about my eyes tonight, Ian Stuart".

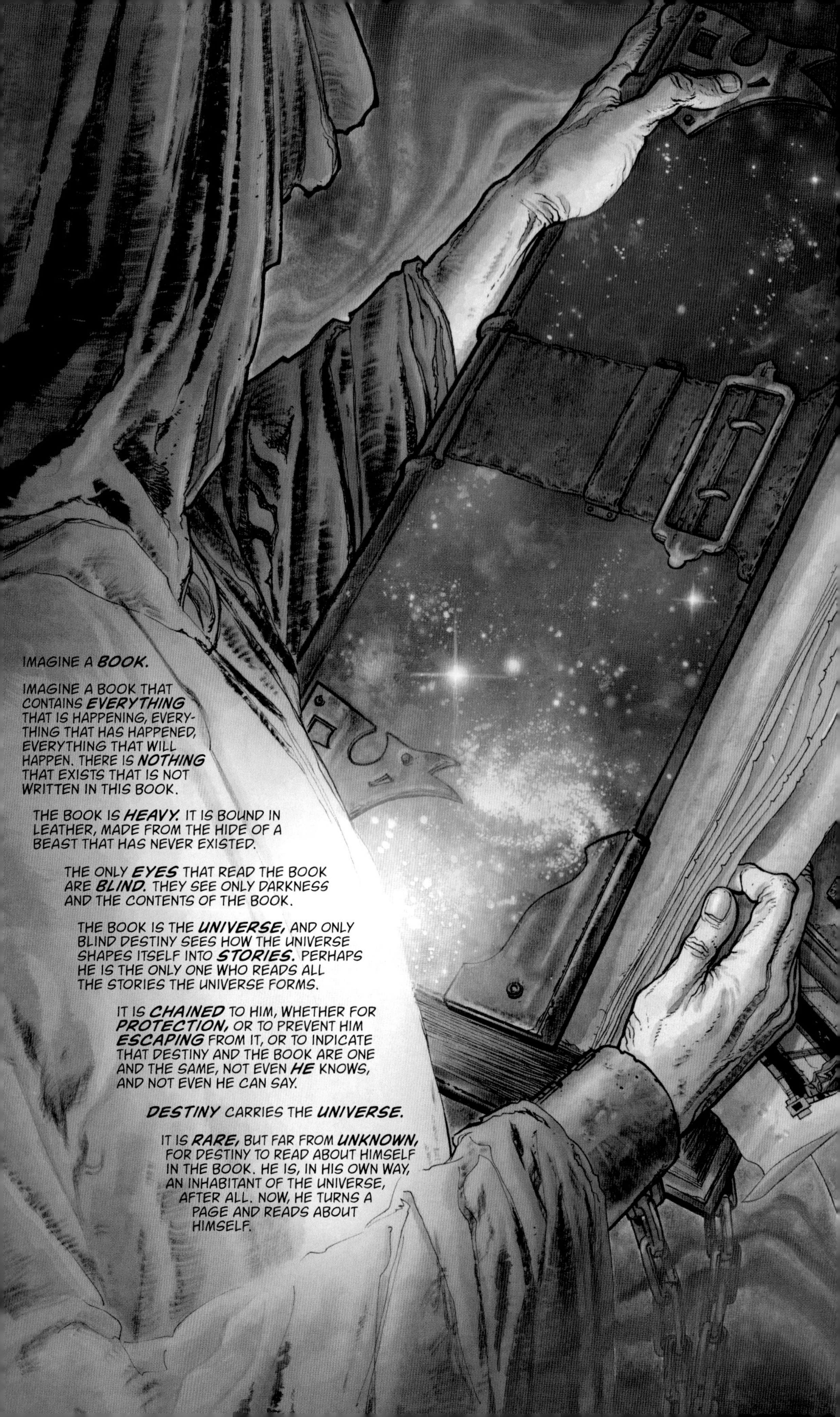
IMAGINE A BOOK.
IMAGINE A BOOK THAT CONTAINS EVERYTHING THAT IS HAPPENING, EVERYTHING THAT HAS HAPPENED, EVERYTHING THAT WILL HAPPEN. THERE IS NOTHING THAT EXISTS THAT IS NOT WRITTEN IN THIS BOOK.
THE BOOK IS HEAVY. IT IS BOUND IN LEATHER, MADE FROM THE HIDE OF A BEAST THAT HAS NEVER EXISTED.
THE ONLY EYES THAT READ THE BOOK ARE BLIND. THEY SEE ONLY DARKNESS AND THE CONTENTS OF THE BOOK.
THE BOOK IS THE UNIVERSE, AND ONLY BLIND DESTINY SEES HOW THE UNIVERSE SHAPES ITSELF INTO STORIES. PERHAPS HE IS THE ONLY ONE WHO READS ALL THE STORIES THE UNIVERSE FORMS.
IT IS CHAINED TO HIM, WHETHER FOR PROTECTION, OR TO PREVENT HIM ESCAPING FROM IT, OR TO INDICATE THAT DESTINY AND THE BOOK ARE ONE AND THE SAME, NOT EVEN HE KNOWS, AND NOT EVEN HE CAN SAY.
DESTINY CARRIES THE UNIVERSE.
IT IS RARE, BUT FAR FROM UNKNOWN, FOR DESTINY TO READ ABOUT HIMSELF IN THE BOOK. HE IS, IN HIS OWN WAY, AN INHABITANT OF THE UNIVERSE, AFTER ALL. NOW, HE TURNS A PAGE AND READS ABOUT HIMSELF.

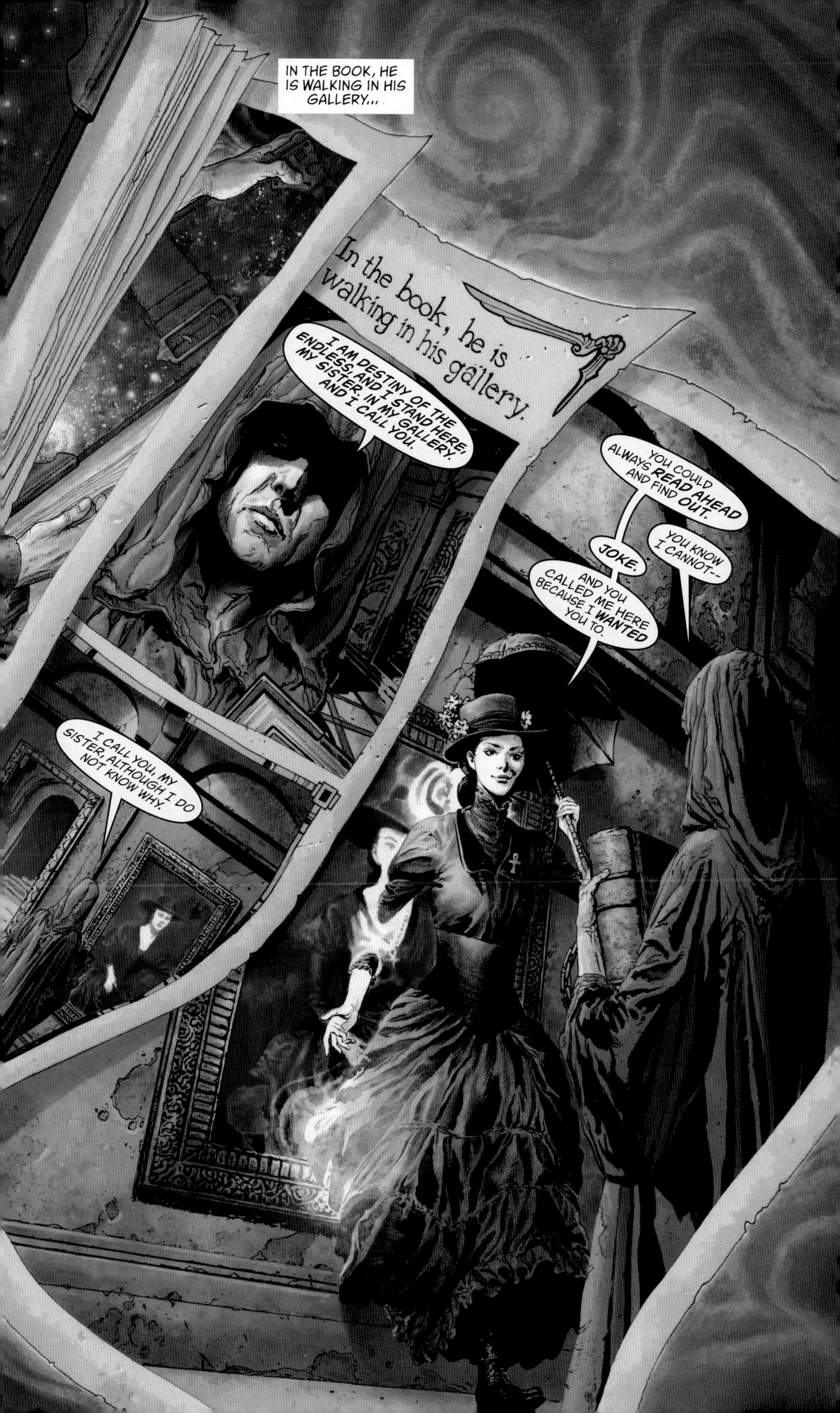
IN THE BOOK, HE IS WALKING IN HIS GALLERY...
In the book, he is walking in his gallery.
I AM DESTINY OF THE ENDLESS, AND I STAND HERE, MY SISTER, IN MY GALLERY, AND I CALL YOU.
I CALL YOU, MY SISTER, ALTHOUGH I DO NOT KNOW WHY.
YOU COULD ALWAYS READ AHEAD AND FIND OUT.
YOU KNOW I CANNOT--
JOKE.
AND YOU CALLED ME HERE BECAUSE I WANTED YOU TO.

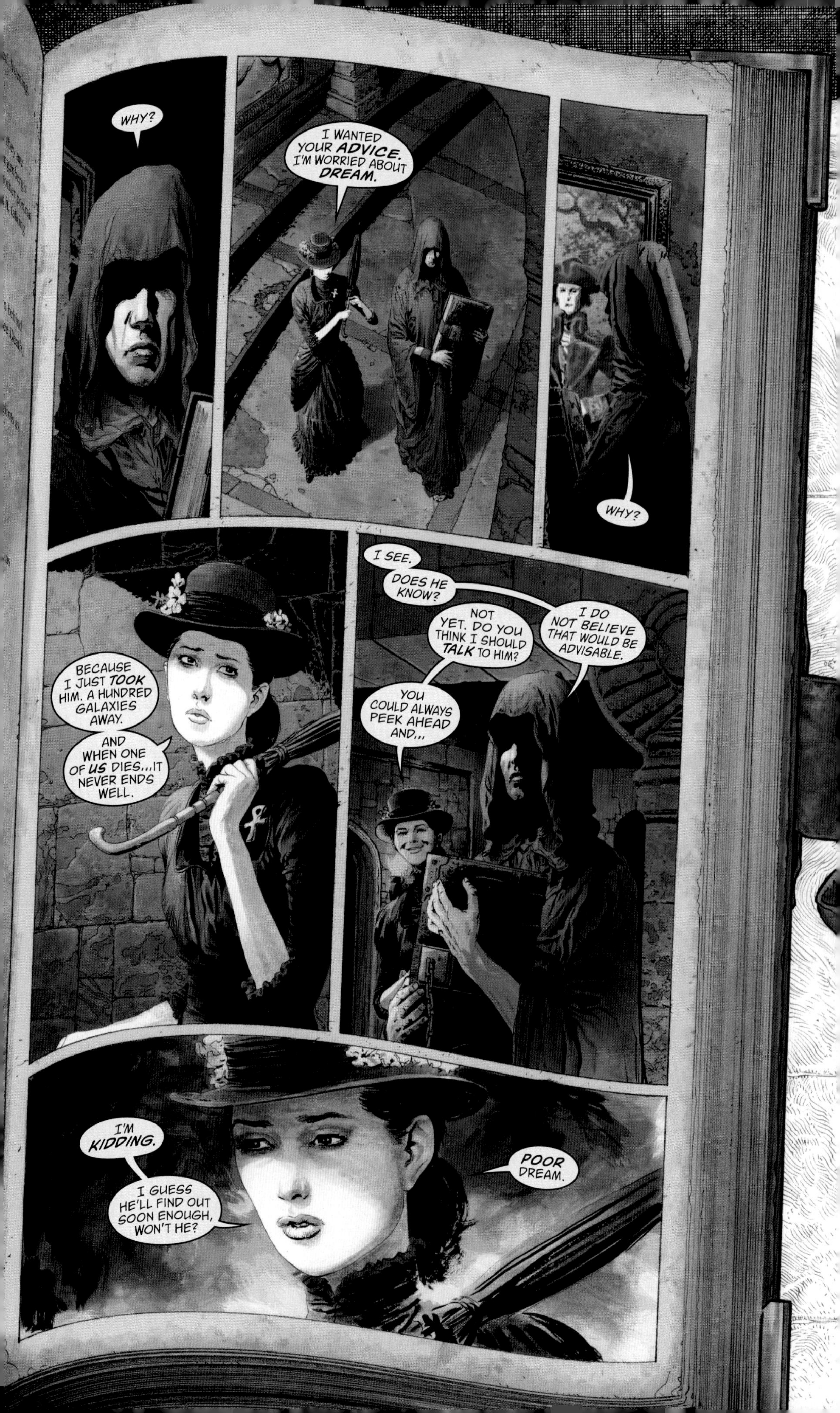
WHY?
I WANTED YOUR ADVICE. I'M WORRIED ABOUT DREAM.
WHY?
BECAUSE I JUST TOOK HIM. A HUNDRED GALAXIES AWAY.
AND WHEN ONE OF US DIES...IT NEVER ENDS WELL.
I SEE.
DOES HE KNOW?
NOT YET. DO YOU THINK I SHOULD TALK TO HIM?
I DO NOT BELIEVE THAT WOULD BE ADVISABLE.
YOU COULD ALWAYS PEEK AHEAD AND...
I'M KIDDING.
I GUESS HE'LL FIND OUT SOON ENOUGH, WON'T HE?
POOR DREAM.

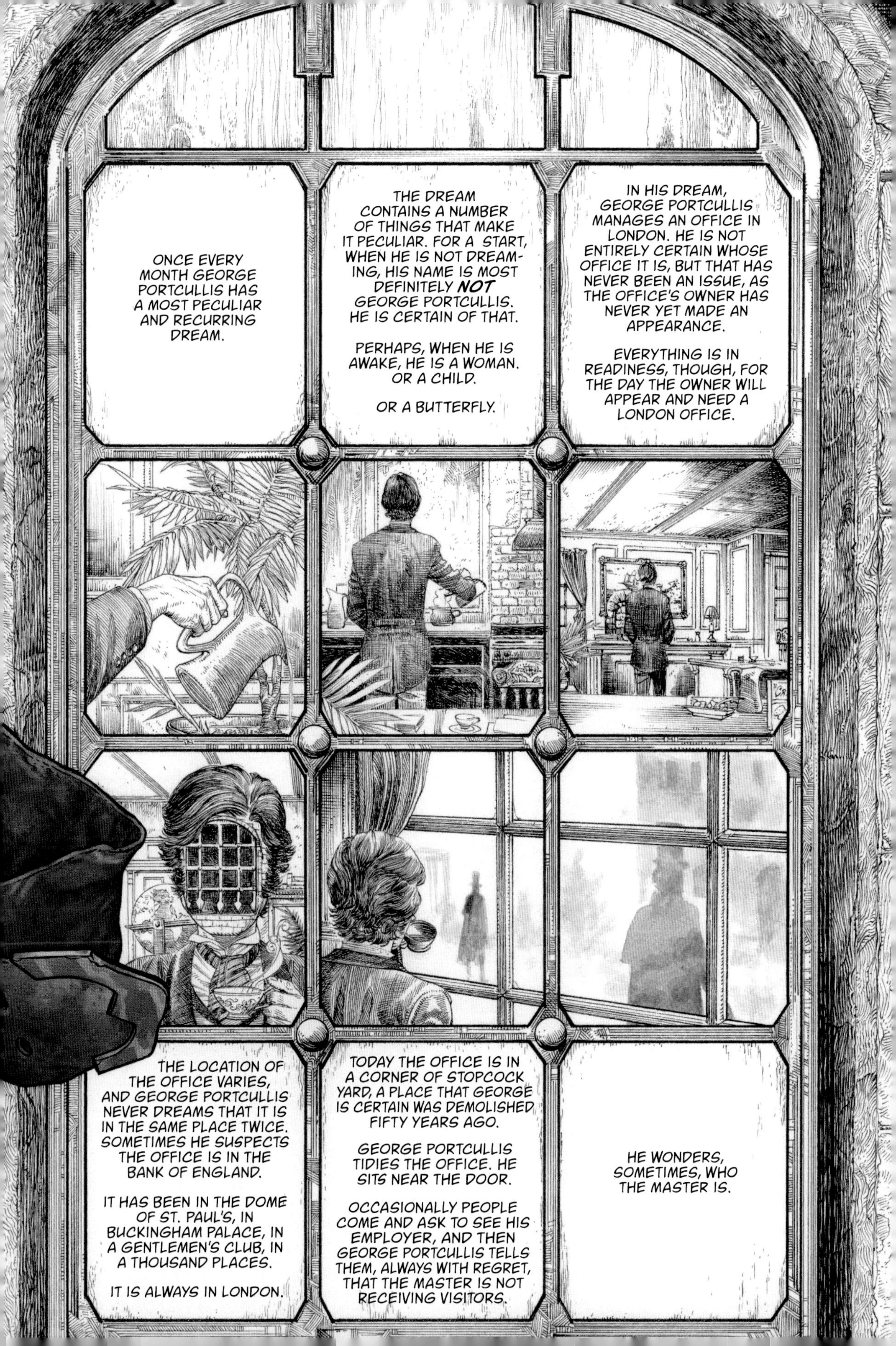
ONCE EVERY MONTH GEORGE PORTCULLIS HAS A MOST PECULIAR AND RECURRING DREAM.
THE DREAM CONTAINS A NUMBER OF THINGS THAT MAKE IT PECULIAR. FOR A START, WHEN HE IS NOT DREAMING, HIS NAME IS MOST DEFINITELY ***NOT*** GEORGE PORTCULLIS. HE IS CERTAIN OF THAT.
PERHAPS, WHEN HE IS AWAKE, HE IS A WOMAN. OR A CHILD.
OR A BUTTERFLY.
IN HIS DREAM, GEORGE PORTCULLIS MANAGES AN OFFICE IN LONDON. HE IS NOT ENTIRELY CERTAIN WHOSE OFFICE IT IS, BUT THAT HAS NEVER BEEN AN ISSUE, AS THE OFFICE'S OWNER HAS NEVER YET MADE AN APPEARANCE.
EVERYTHING IS IN READINESS, THOUGH, FOR THE DAY THE OWNER WILL APPEAR AND NEED A LONDON OFFICE.
THE LOCATION OF THE OFFICE VARIES, AND GEORGE PORTCULLIS NEVER DREAMS THAT IT IS IN THE SAME PLACE TWICE. SOMETIMES HE SUSPECTS THE OFFICE IS IN THE BANK OF ENGLAND.
IT HAS BEEN IN THE DOME OF ST. PAUL'S, IN BUCKINGHAM PALACE, IN A GENTLEMEN'S CLUB, IN A THOUSAND PLACES.
IT IS ALWAYS IN LONDON.
TODAY THE OFFICE IS IN A CORNER OF STOPCOCK YARD, A PLACE THAT GEORGE IS CERTAIN WAS DEMOLISHED FIFTY YEARS AGO.
GEORGE PORTCULLIS TIDIES THE OFFICE. HE SITS NEAR THE DOOR.
OCCASIONALLY PEOPLE COME AND ASK TO SEE HIS EMPLOYER, AND THEN GEORGE PORTCULLIS TELLS THEM, ALWAYS WITH REGRET, THAT THE MASTER IS NOT RECEIVING VISITORS.
HE WONDERS, SOMETIMES, WHO THE MASTER IS.

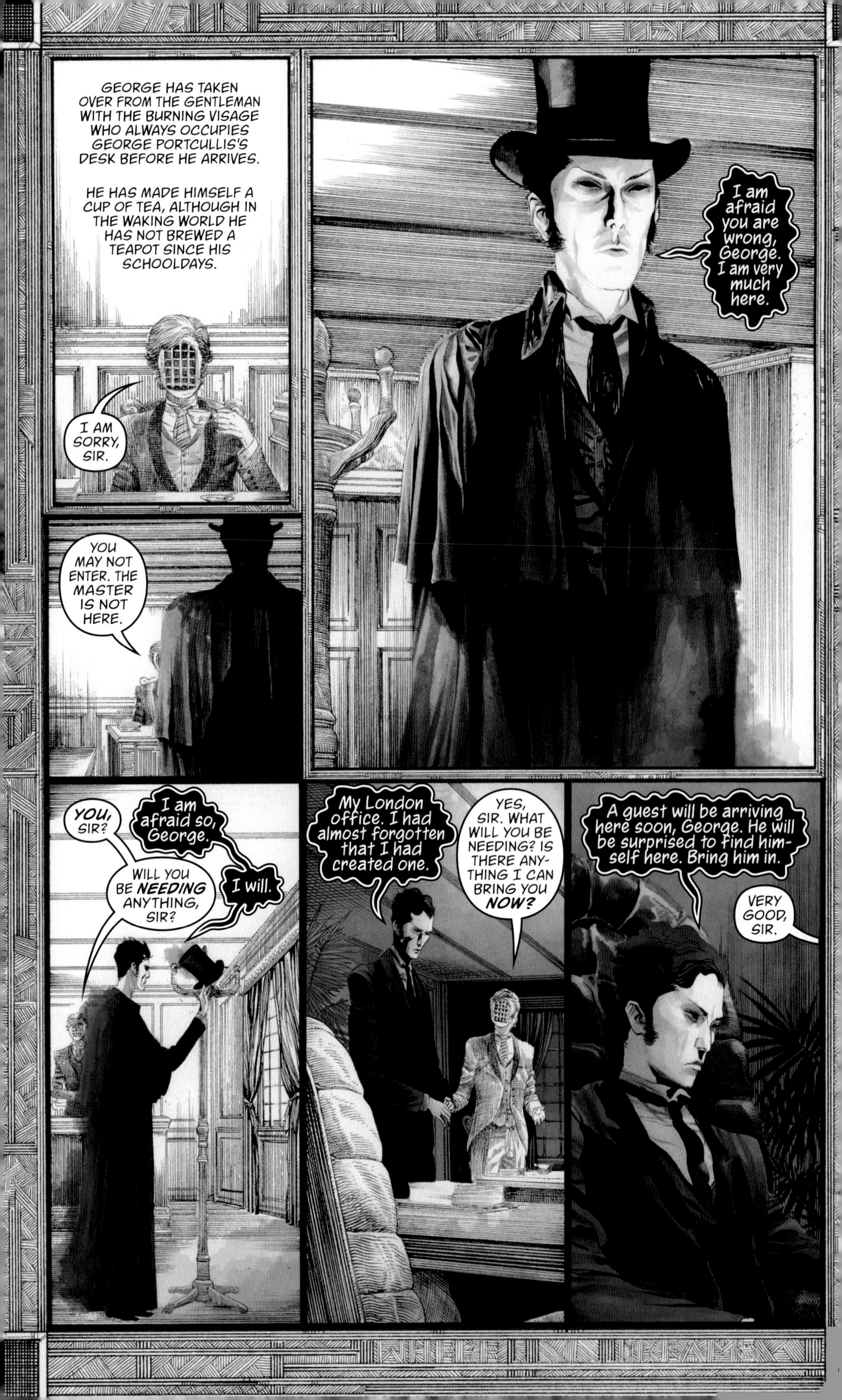

GEORGE HAS TAKEN OVER FROM THE GENTLEMAN WITH THE BURNING VISAGE WHO ALWAYS OCCUPIES GEORGE PORTCULLIS'S DESK BEFORE HE ARRIVES.
HE HAS MADE HIMSELF A CUP OF TEA, ALTHOUGH IN THE WAKING WORLD HE HAS NOT BREWED A TEAPOT SINCE HIS SCHOOLDAYS.
I AM SORRY, SIR.
YOU MAY NOT ENTER. THE MASTER IS NOT HERE.
I am afraid you are wrong, George. I am very much here.
YOU, SIR?
I am afraid so, George.
WILL YOU BE NEEDING ANYTHING, SIR?
I will.
My London office. I had almost forgotten that I had created one.
YES, SIR. WHAT WILL YOU BE NEEDING? IS THERE ANYTHING I CAN BRING YOU NOW?
A guest will be arriving here soon, George. He will be surprised to find himself here. Bring him in.
VERY GOOD, SIR.

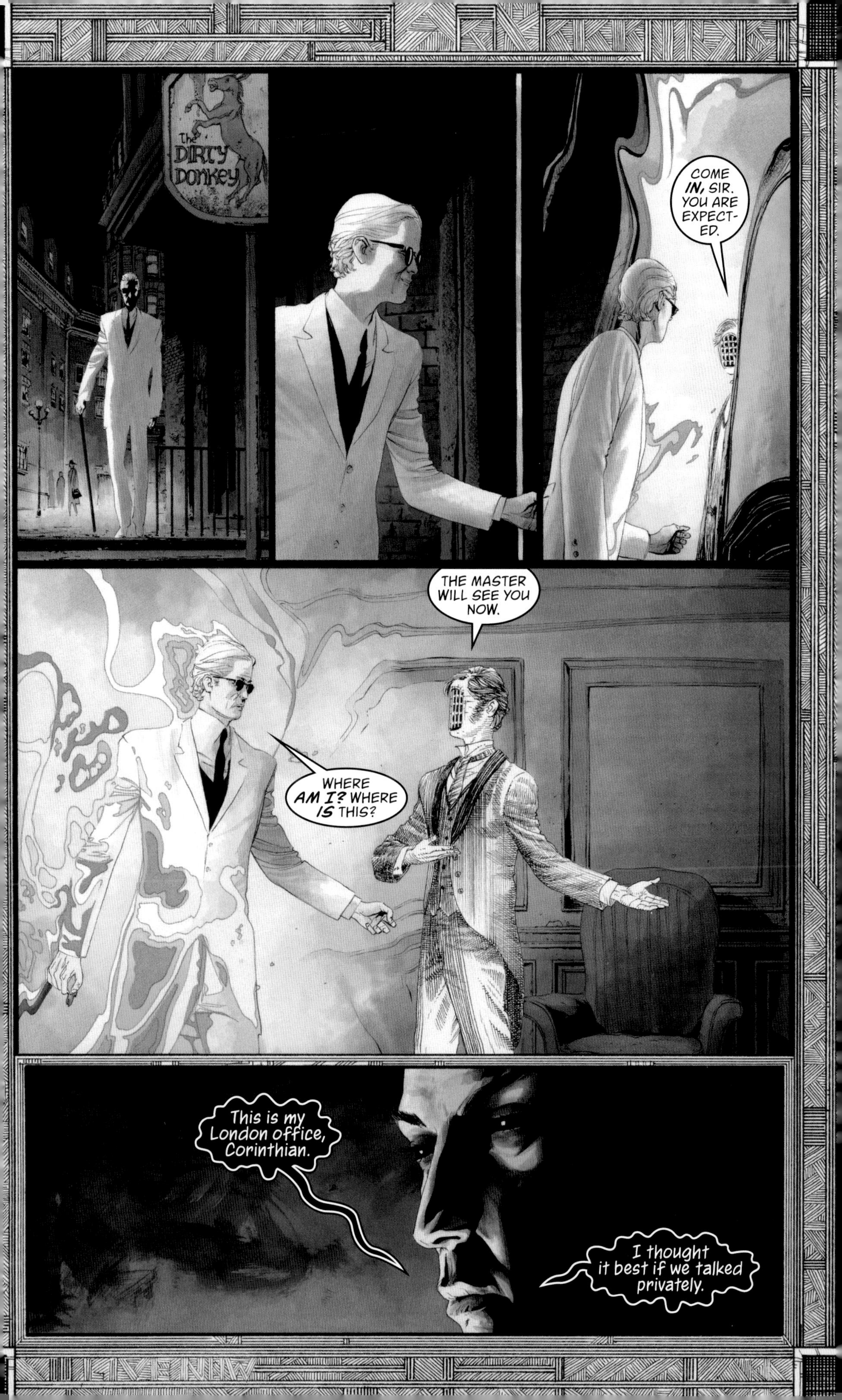
The DIRTY DONKEY
COME IN, SIR. YOU ARE EXPECTED.
THE MASTER WILL SEE YOU NOW.
WHERE AM I? WHERE IS THIS?
This is my London office, Corinthian.
I thought it best if we talked privately.

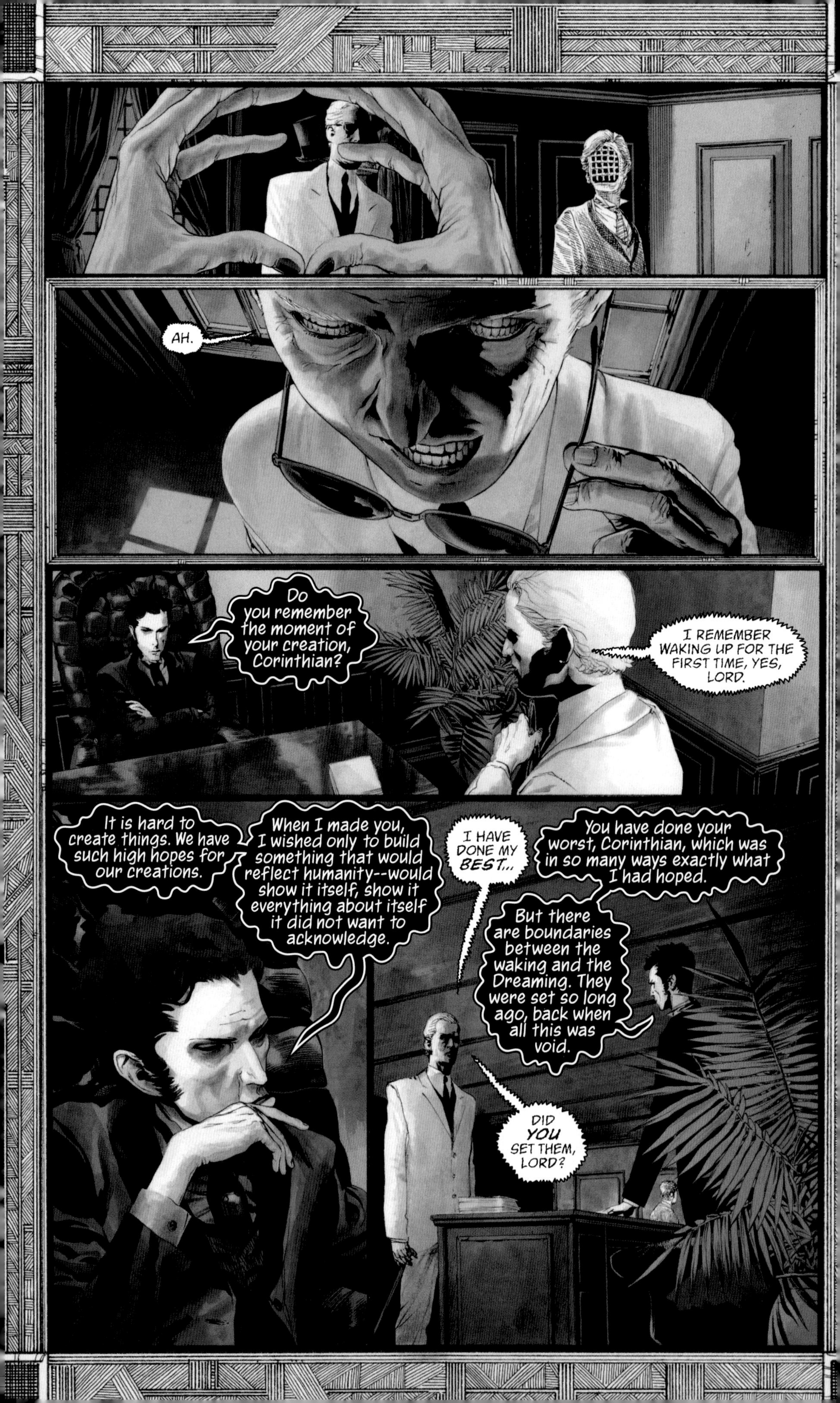
AH.
Do you remember the moment of your creation, Corinthian?
I REMEMBER WAKING UP FOR THE FIRST TIME, YES, LORD.
It is hard to create things. We have such high hopes for our creations.
When I made you, I wished only to build something that would reflect humanity--would show it itself, show it everything about itself it did not want to acknowledge.
I HAVE DONE MY BEST...
You have done your worst, Corinthian, which was in so many ways exactly what I had hoped.
But there are boundaries between the waking and the Dreaming. They were set so long ago, back when all this was void.
DID YOU SET THEM, LORD?

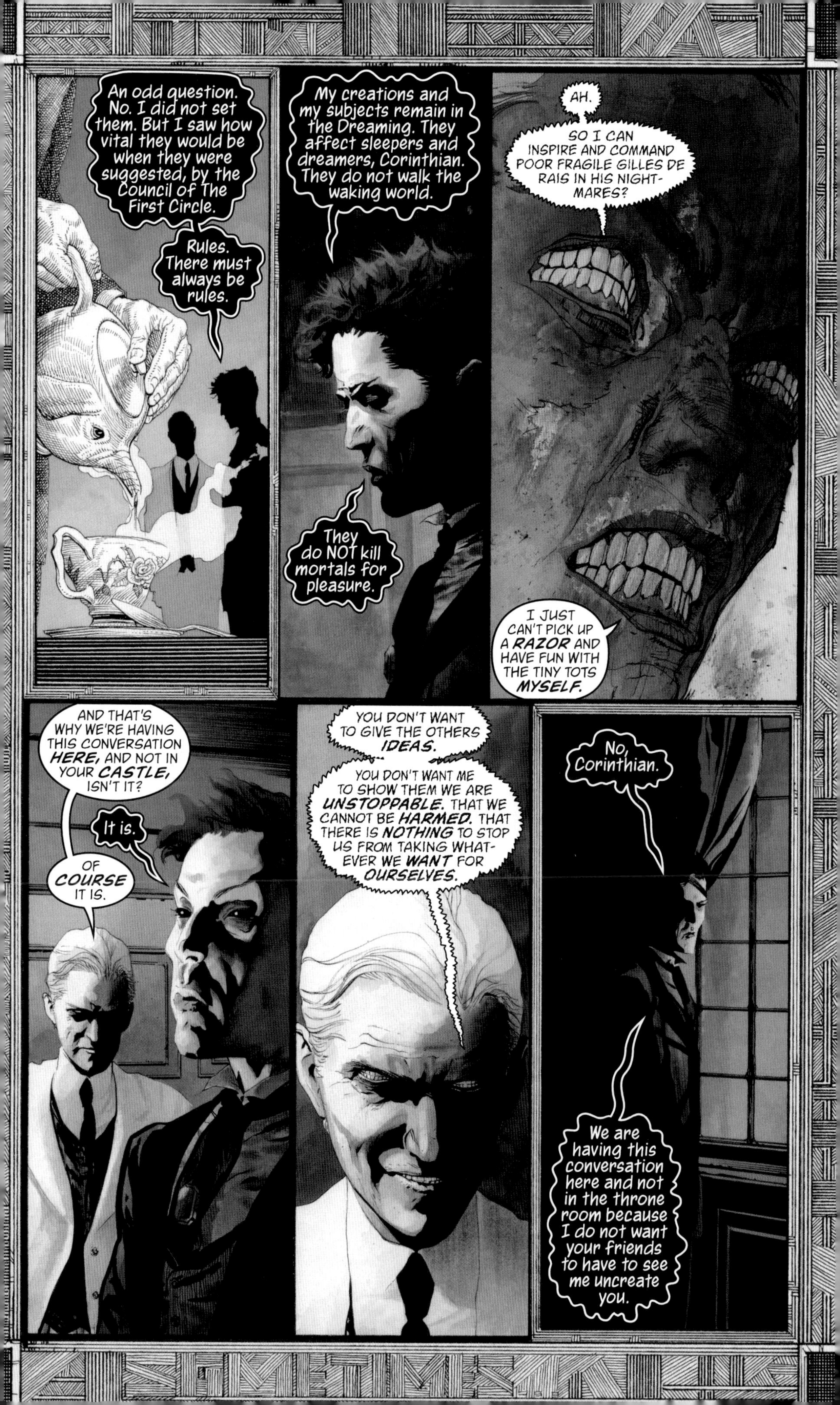

An odd question. No. I did not set them. But I saw how vital they would be when they were suggested, by the Council of The First Circle.
Rules. There must always be rules.
My creations and my subjects remain in the Dreaming. They affect sleepers and dreamers, Corinthian. They do not walk the waking world.
They do NOT kill mortals for pleasure.
AH.
SO I CAN INSPIRE AND COMMAND POOR FRAGILE GILLES DE RAIS IN HIS NIGHT-MARES?
I JUST CAN'T PICK UP A RAZOR AND HAVE FUN WITH THE TINY TOTS MYSELF.
AND THAT'S WHY WE'RE HAVING THIS CONVERSATION HERE, AND NOT IN YOUR CASTLE, ISN'T IT?
It is.
OF COURSE IT IS.
YOU DON'T WANT TO GIVE THE OTHERS IDEAS.
YOU DON'T WANT ME TO SHOW THEM WE ARE UNSTOPPABLE. THAT WE CANNOT BE HARMED. THAT THERE IS NOTHING TO STOP US FROM TAKING WHAT-EVER WE WANT FOR OURSELVES.
No, Corinthian.
We are having this conversation here and not in the throne room because I do not want your friends to have to see me uncreate you.

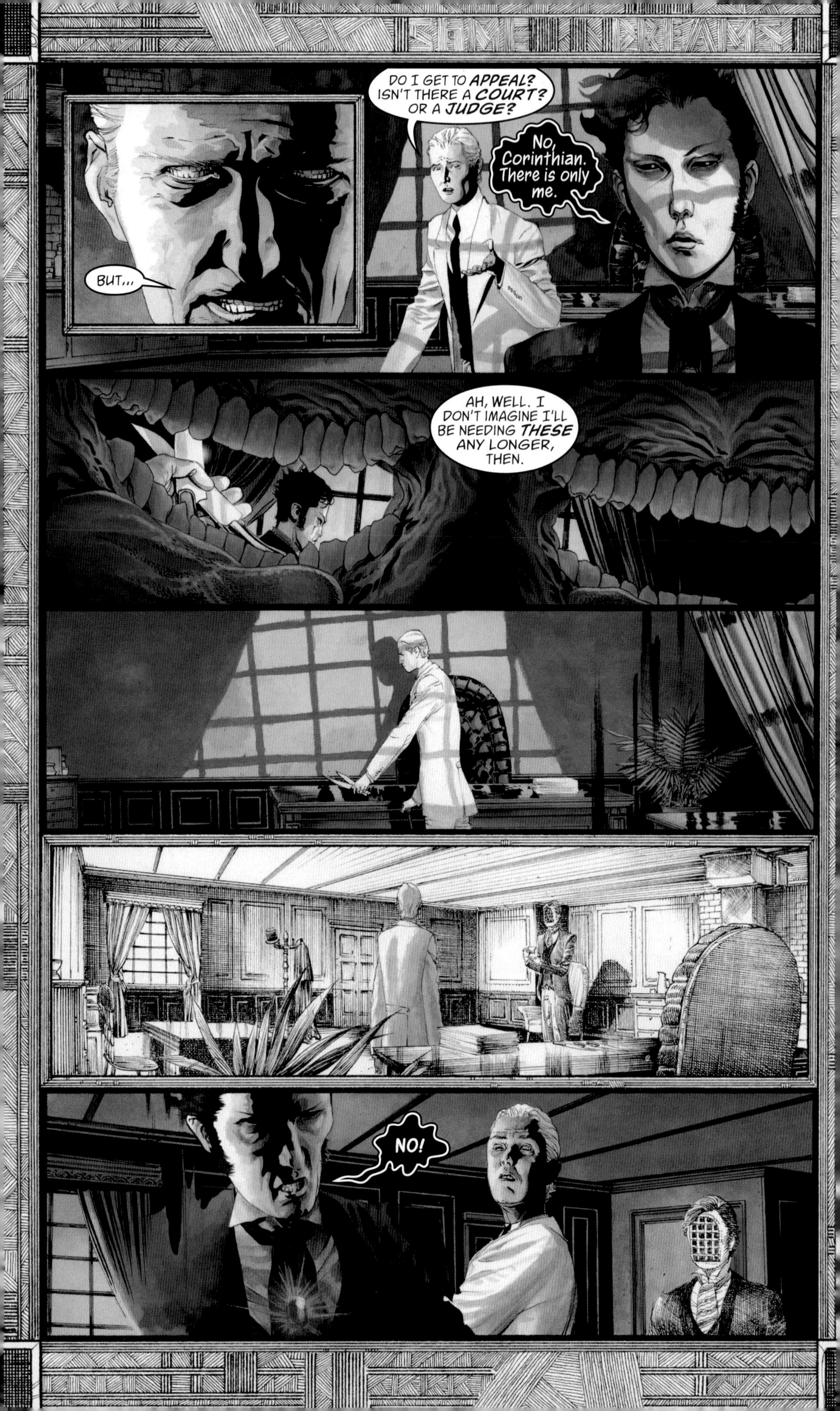
SOME DREAMS
DO I GET TO APPEAL? ISN'T THERE A COURT? OR A JUDGE?
BUT...
No, Corinthian. There is only me.
AH, WELL. I DON'T IMAGINE I'LL BE NEEDING THESE ANY LONGER, THEN.
NO!

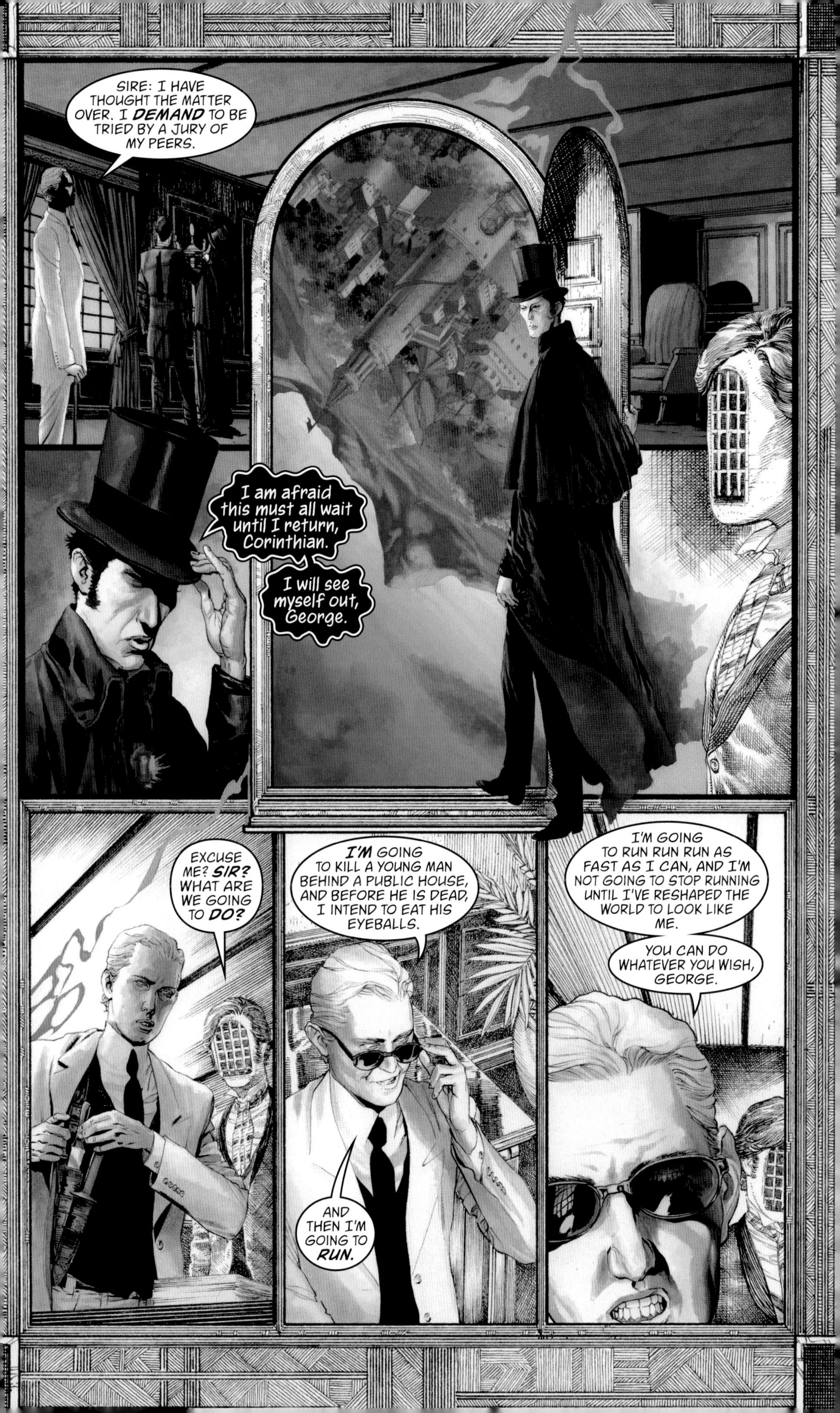
SIRE: I HAVE THOUGHT THE MATTER OVER. I DEMAND TO BE TRIED BY A JURY OF MY PEERS.
I am afraid this must all wait until I return, Corinthian.
I will see myself out, George.
EXCUSE ME? SIR? WHAT ARE WE GOING TO DO?
I'M GOING TO KILL A YOUNG MAN BEHIND A PUBLIC HOUSE, AND BEFORE HE IS DEAD, I INTEND TO EAT HIS EYEBALLS.
AND THEN I'M GOING TO RUN.
I'M GOING TO RUN RUN RUN AS FAST AS I CAN, AND I'M NOT GOING TO STOP RUNNING UNTIL I'VE RESHAPED THE WORLD TO LOOK LIKE ME.
YOU CAN DO WHATEVER YOU WISH, GEORGE.

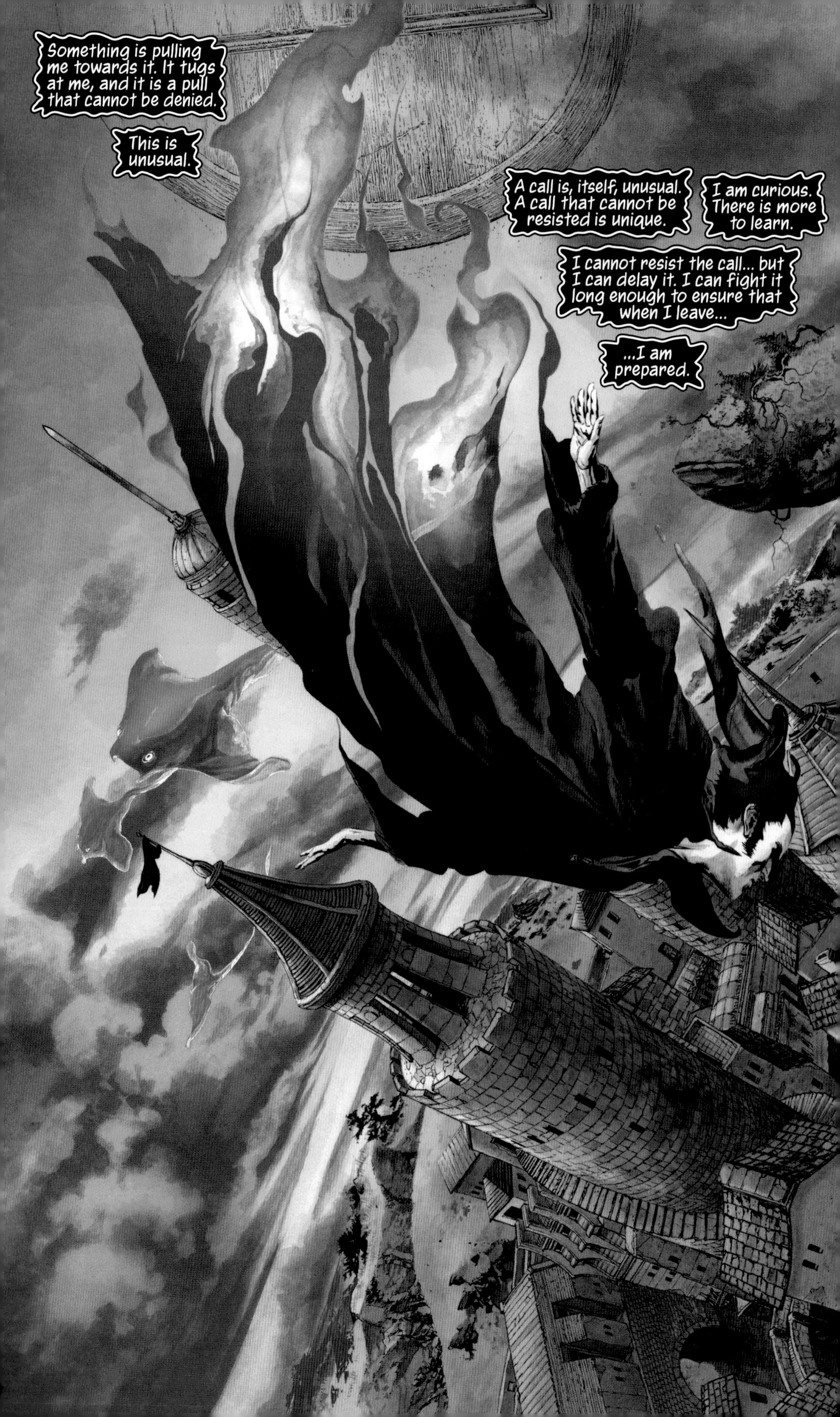
Something is pulling me towards it. It tugs at me, and it is a pull that cannot be denied.
This is unusual.
A call is, itself, unusual. A call that cannot be resisted is unique.
I am curious. There is more to learn.
I cannot resist the call... but I can delay it. I can fight it long enough to ensure that when I leave...
...I am prepared.

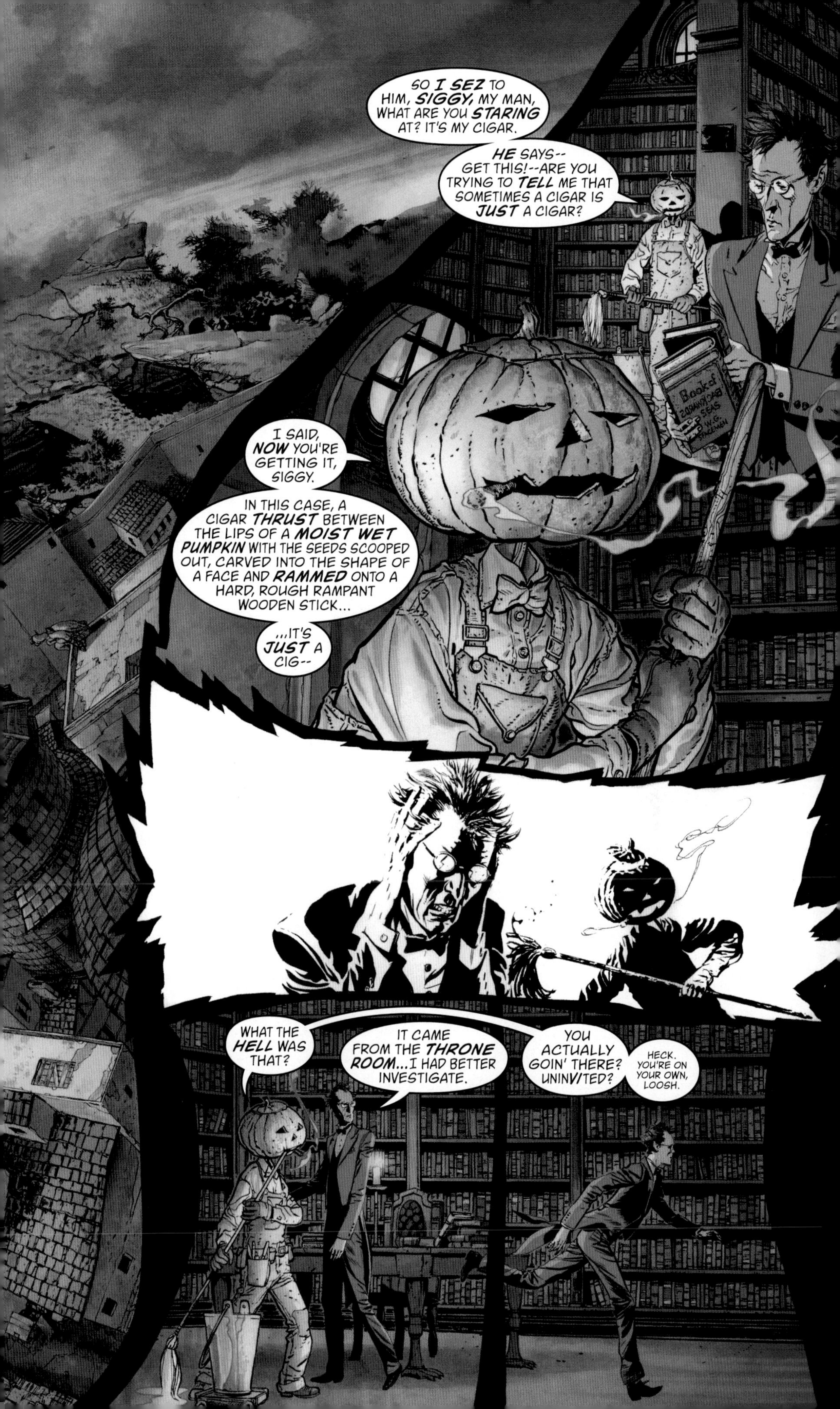
SO I SEZ TO HIM, SIGGY, MY MAN, WHAT ARE YOU STARING AT? IT'S MY CIGAR.
HE SAYS-- GET THIS!--ARE YOU TRYING TO TELL ME THAT SOMETIMES A CIGAR IS JUST A CIGAR?
I SAID, NOW YOU'RE GETTING IT, SIGGY.
IN THIS CASE, A CIGAR THRUST BETWEEN THE LIPS OF A MOIST WET PUMPKIN WITH THE SEEDS SCOOPED OUT, CARVED INTO THE SHAPE OF A FACE AND RAMMED ONTO A HARD, ROUGH RAMPANT WOODEN STICK...
...IT'S JUST A CIG--
WHAT THE HELL WAS THAT?
IT CAME FROM THE THRONE ROOM...I HAD BETTER INVESTIGATE.
YOU ACTUALLY GOIN' THERE? UNINVITED?
HECK. YOU'RE ON YOUR OWN, LOOSH.

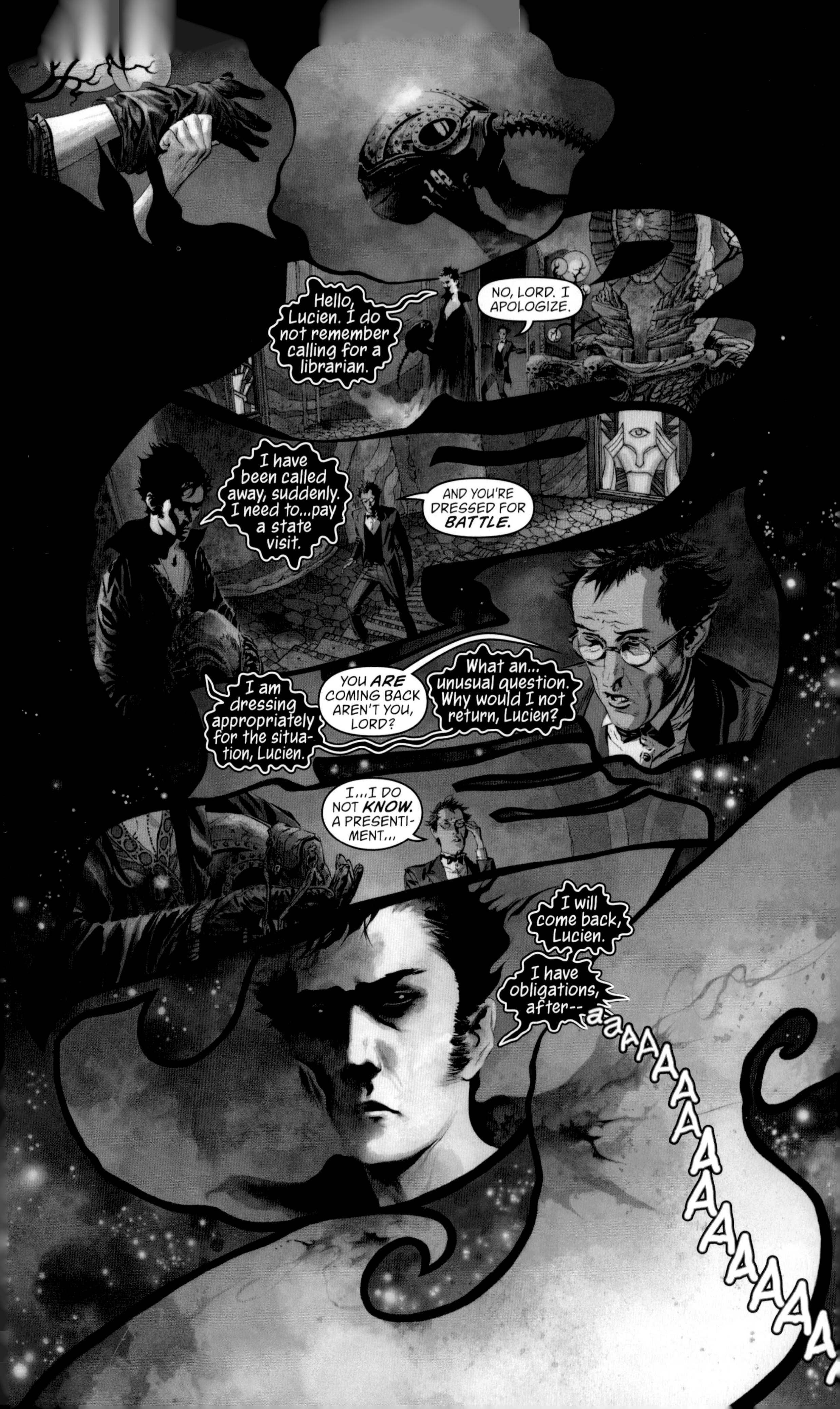
Hello, Lucien. I do not remember calling for a librarian.
NO, LORD. I APOLOGIZE.
I have been called away, suddenly. I need to...pay a state visit.
AND YOU'RE DRESSED FOR BATTLE.
I am dressing appropriately for the situation, Lucien.
YOU ARE COMING BACK AREN'T YOU, LORD?
What an... unusual question. Why would I not return, Lucien?
I...I DO NOT KNOW. A PRESENTIMENT...
I will come back, Lucien.
I have obligations, after--
aaAAAAAAAAAAAA

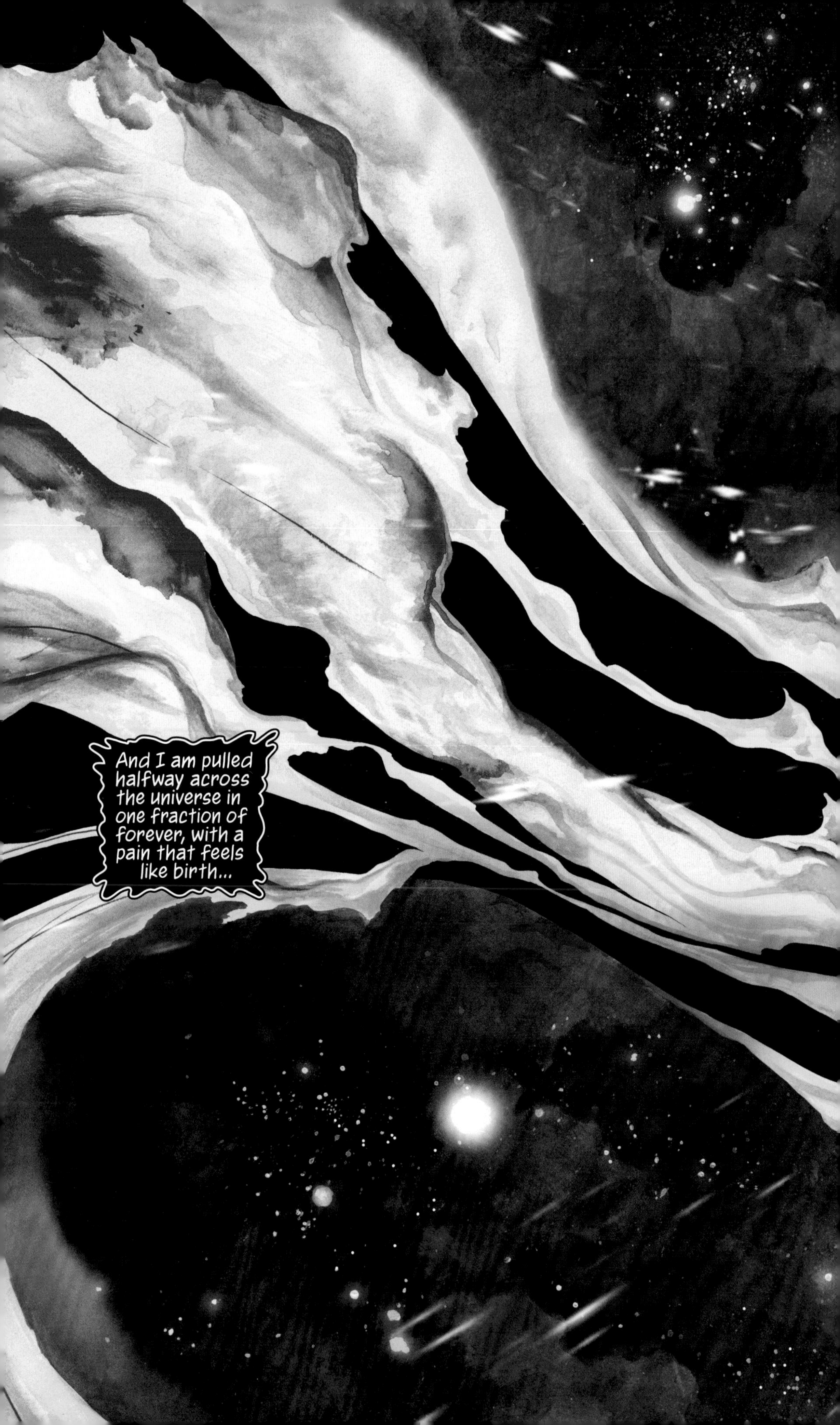
And I am pulled halfway across the universe in one fraction of forever, with a pain that feels like birth...

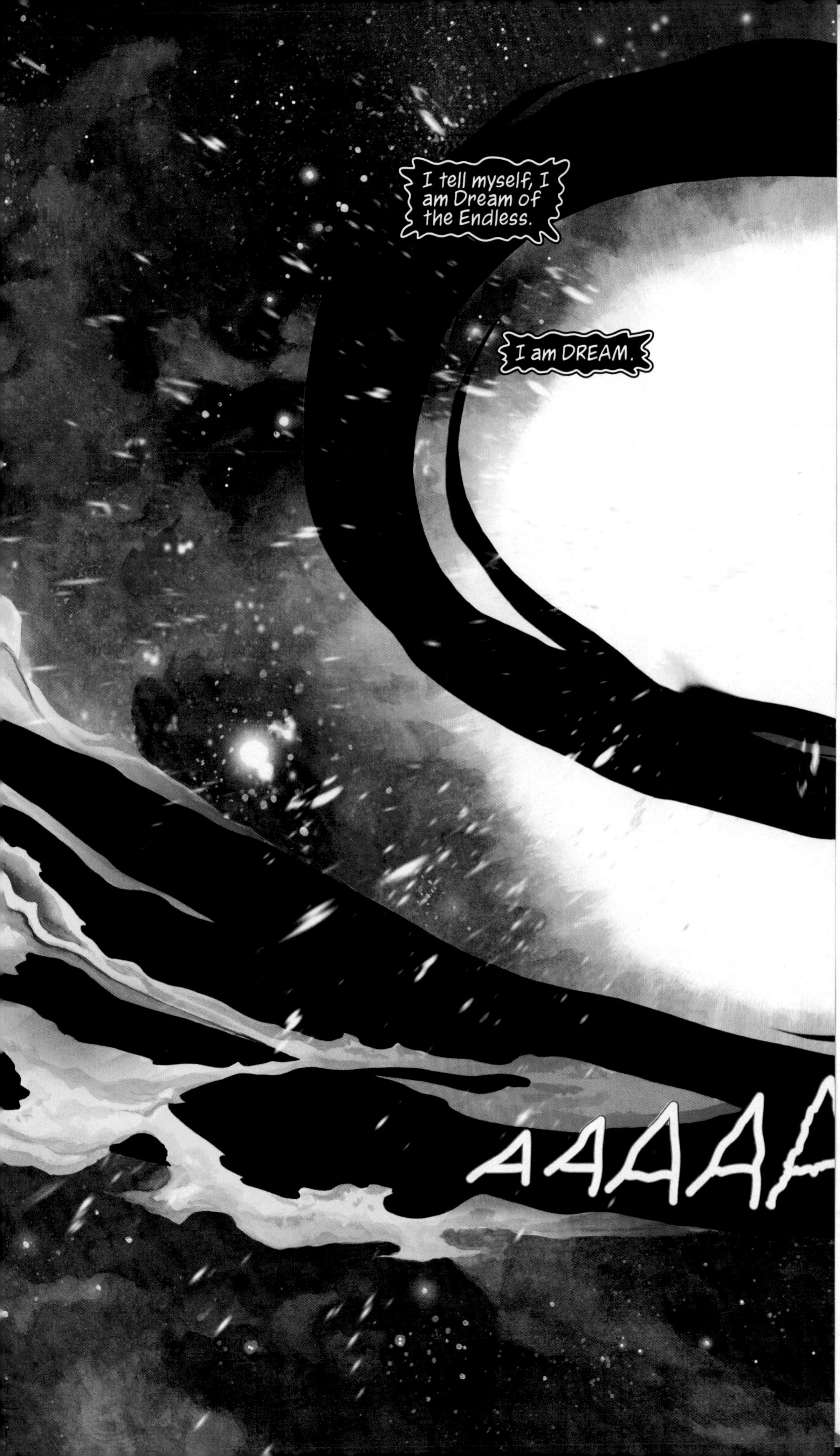
I tell myself, I am Dream of the Endless.
I am DREAM.
AAAAA

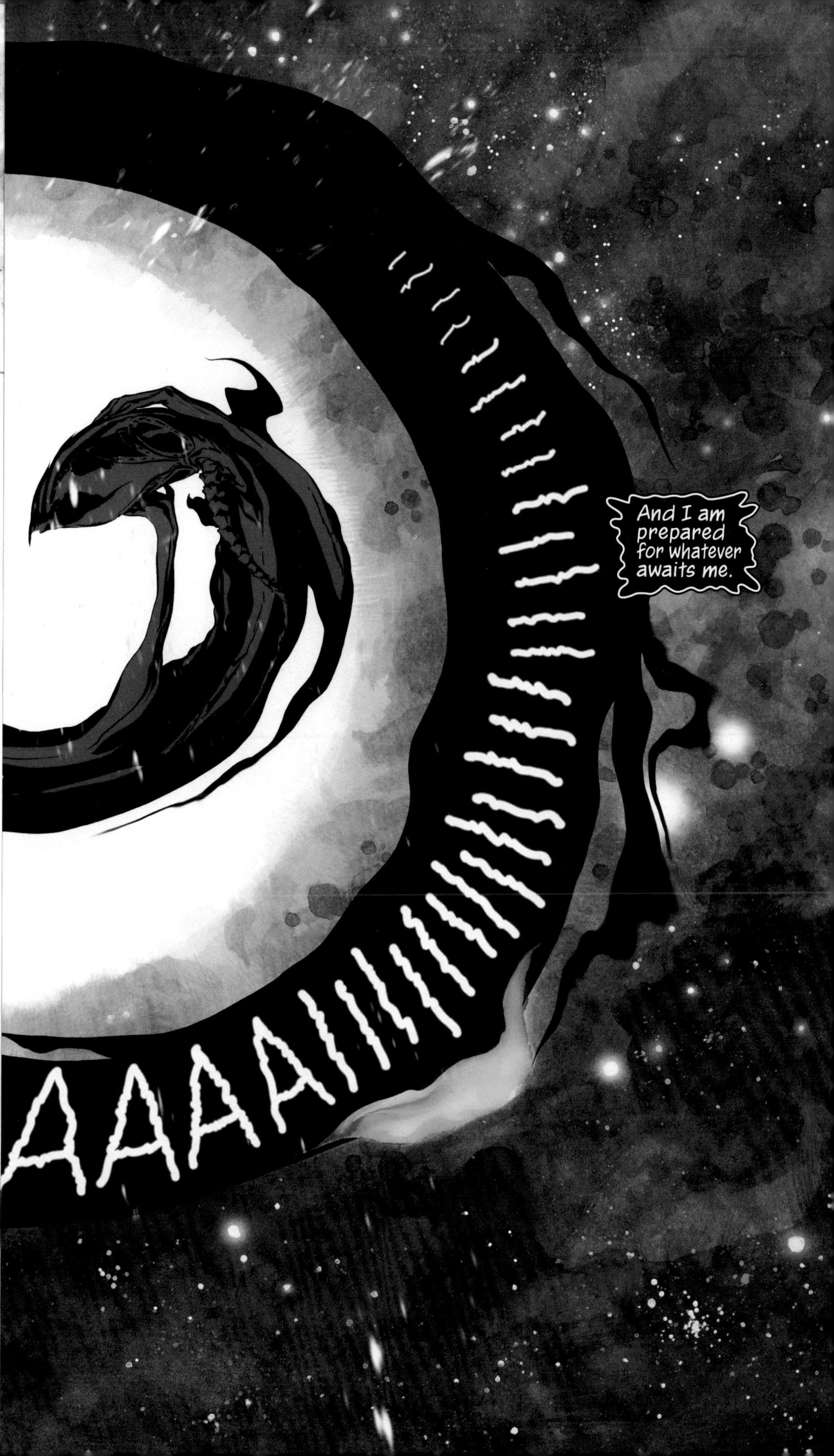
And I am prepared for whatever awaits me.
AAAAIIIIIIIIIIIIIIIIIIIIIIIIIIIIIIIII

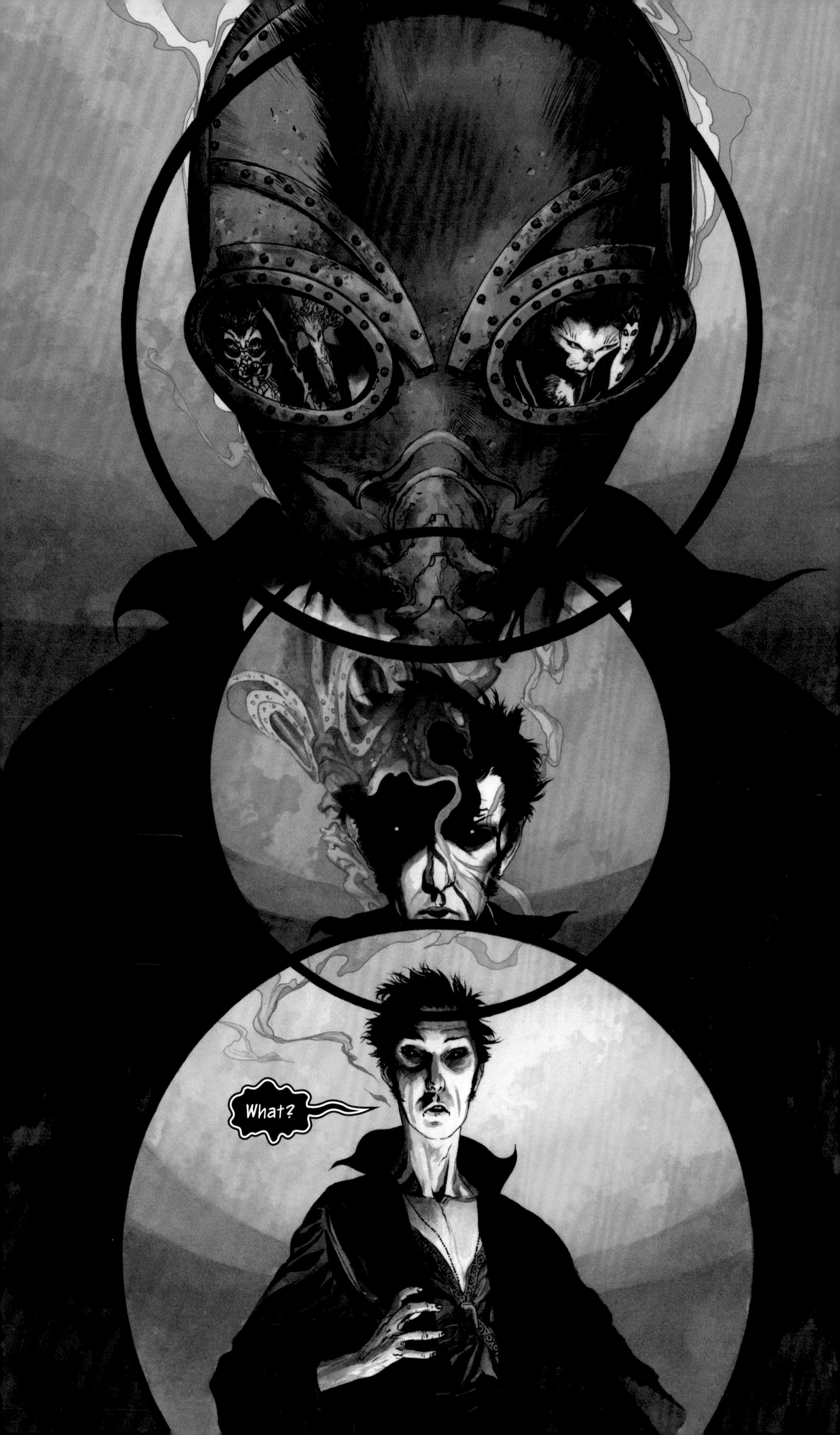
What?

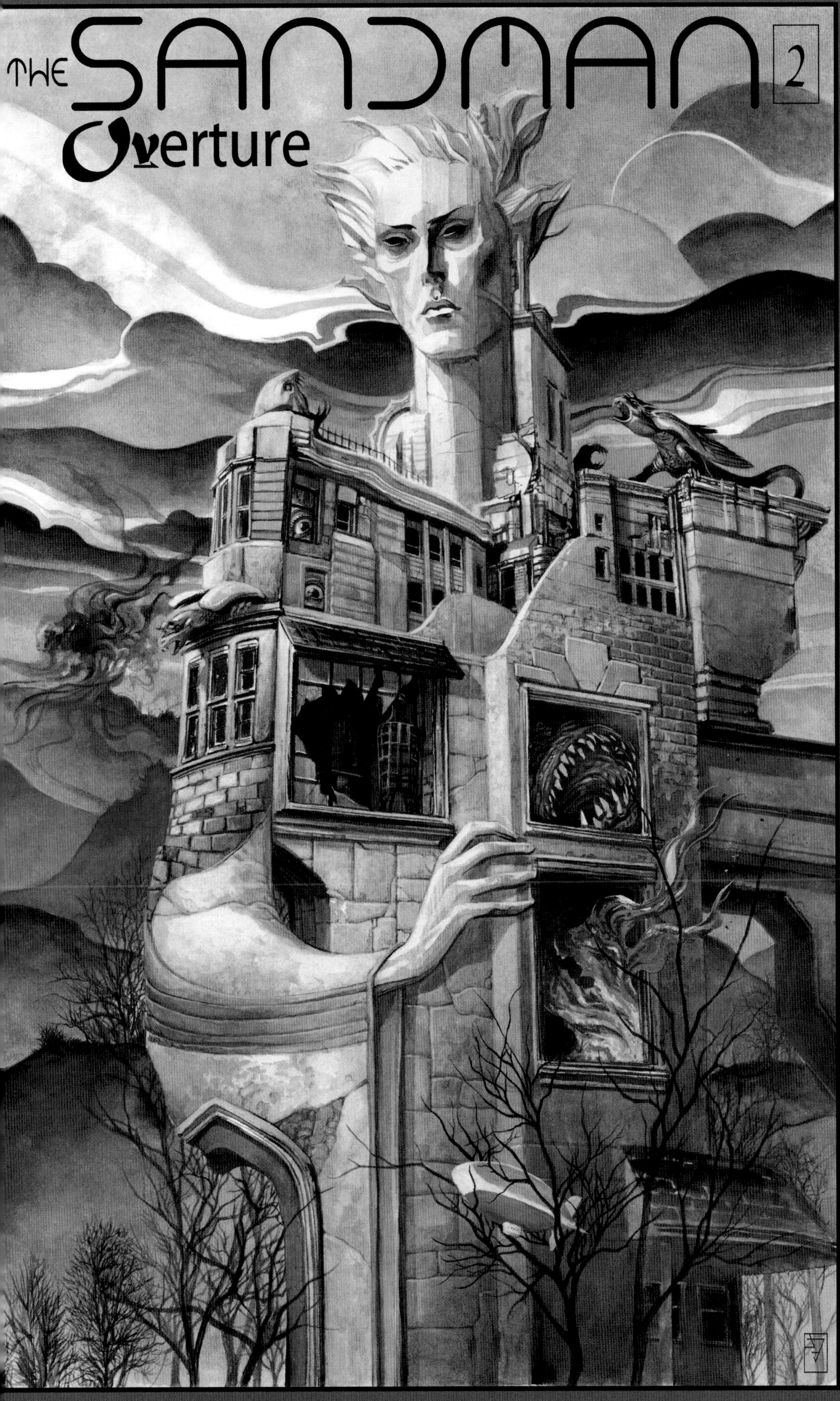
THE SANDMAN
2
Overture

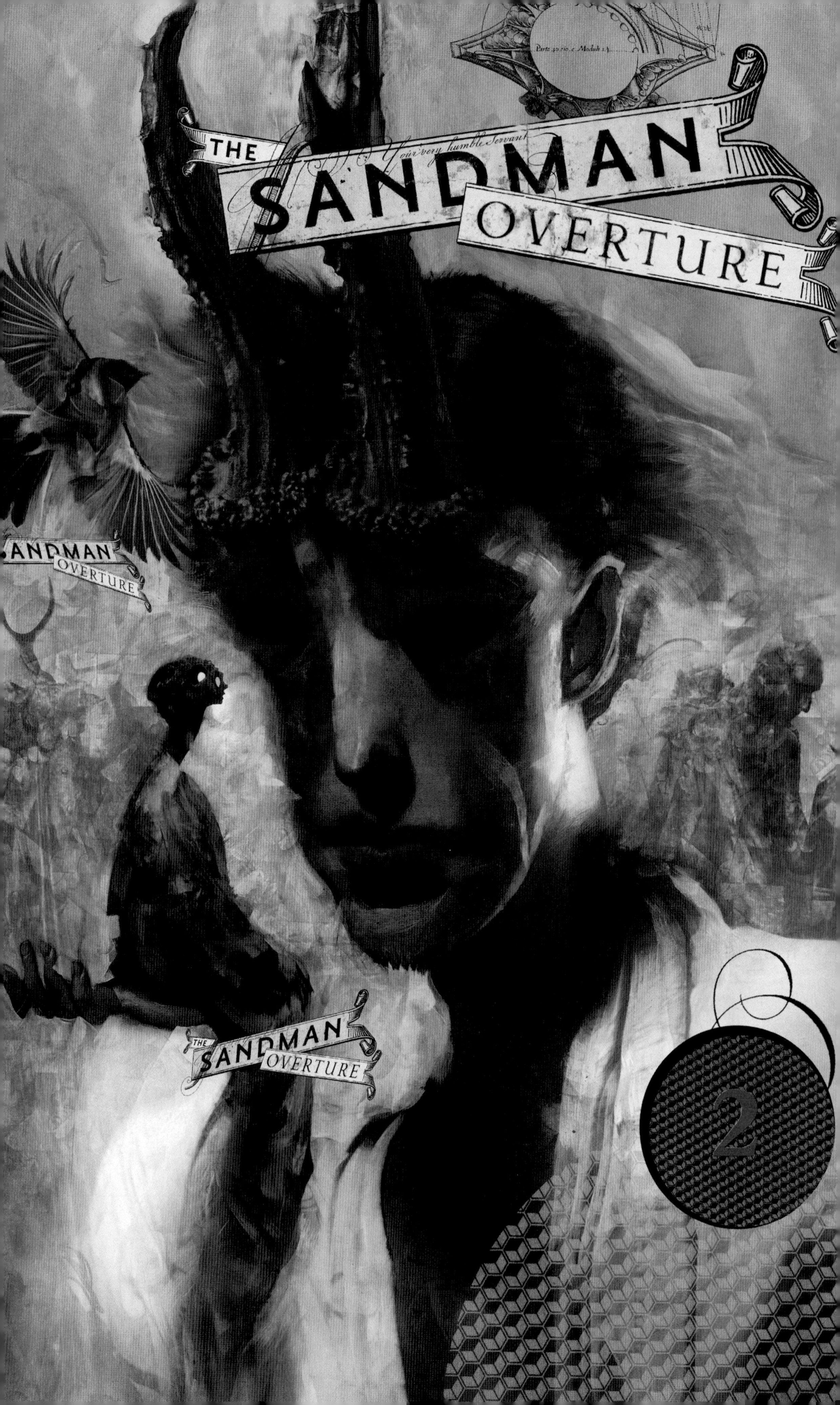
THE SANDMAN OVERTURE
Your very humble Servant
SANDMAN OVERTURE
THE SANDMAN OVERTURE
2

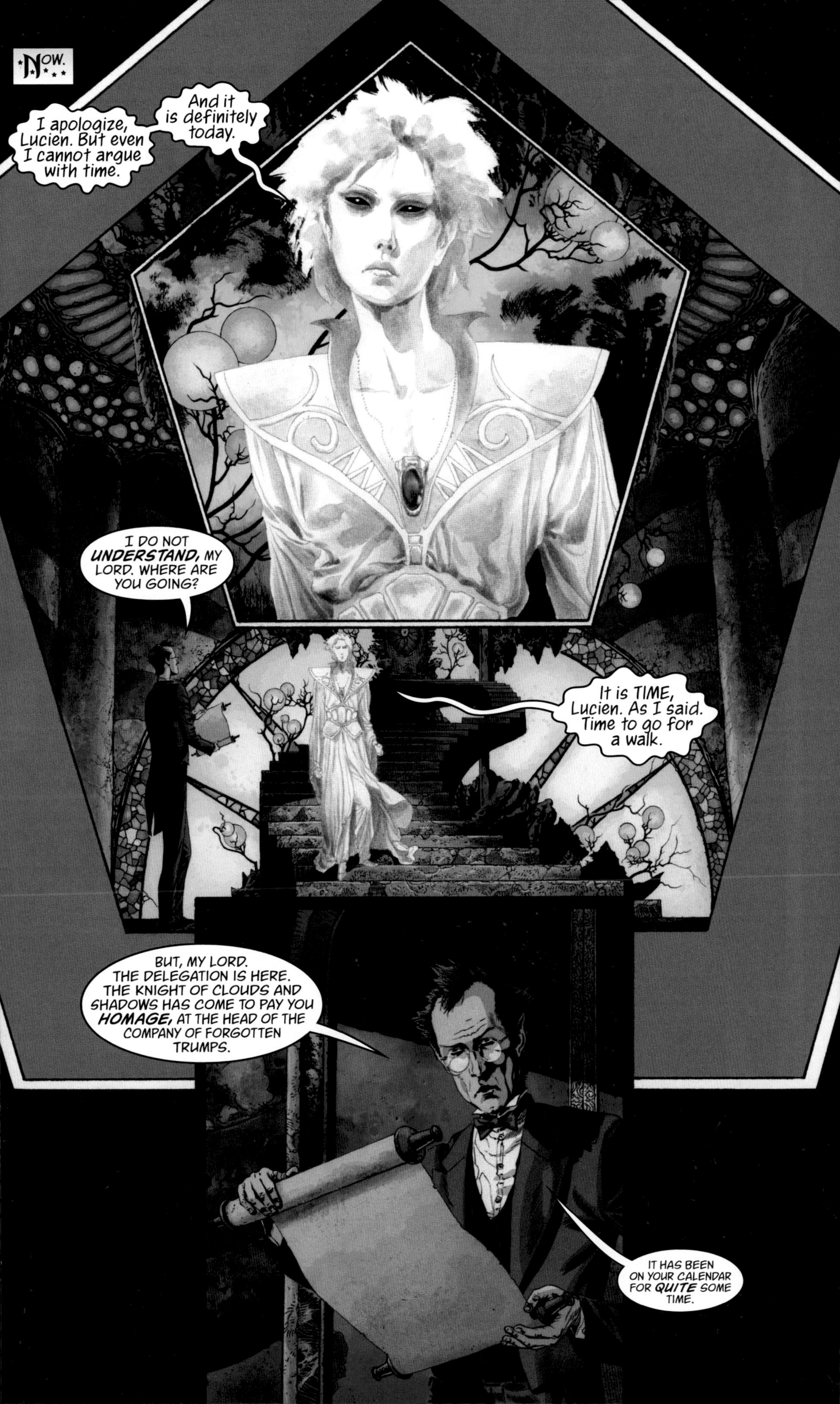
NOW.
I apologize, Lucien. But even I cannot argue with time.
And it is definitely today.
I DO NOT UNDERSTAND, MY LORD. WHERE ARE YOU GOING?
It is TIME, Lucien. As I said. Time to go for a walk.
BUT, MY LORD. THE DELEGATION IS HERE. THE KNIGHT OF CLOUDS AND SHADOWS HAS COME TO PAY YOU HOMAGE, AT THE HEAD OF THE COMPANY OF FORGOTTEN TRUMPS.
IT HAS BEEN ON YOUR CALENDAR FOR QUITE SOME TIME.

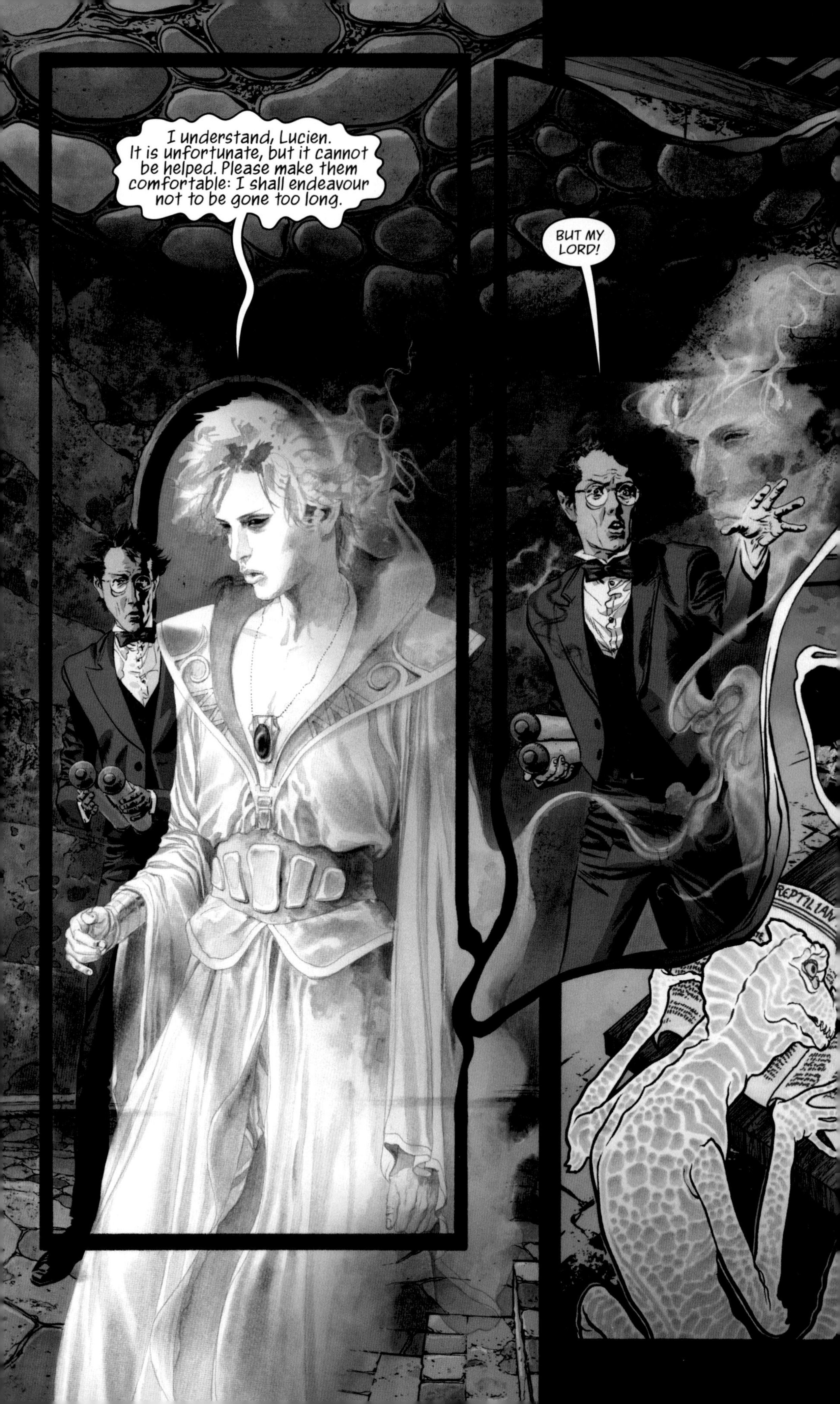
I understand, Lucien. It is unfortunate, but it cannot be helped. Please make them comfortable: I shall endeavour not to be gone too long.
BUT MY LORD!
REPTILIAN

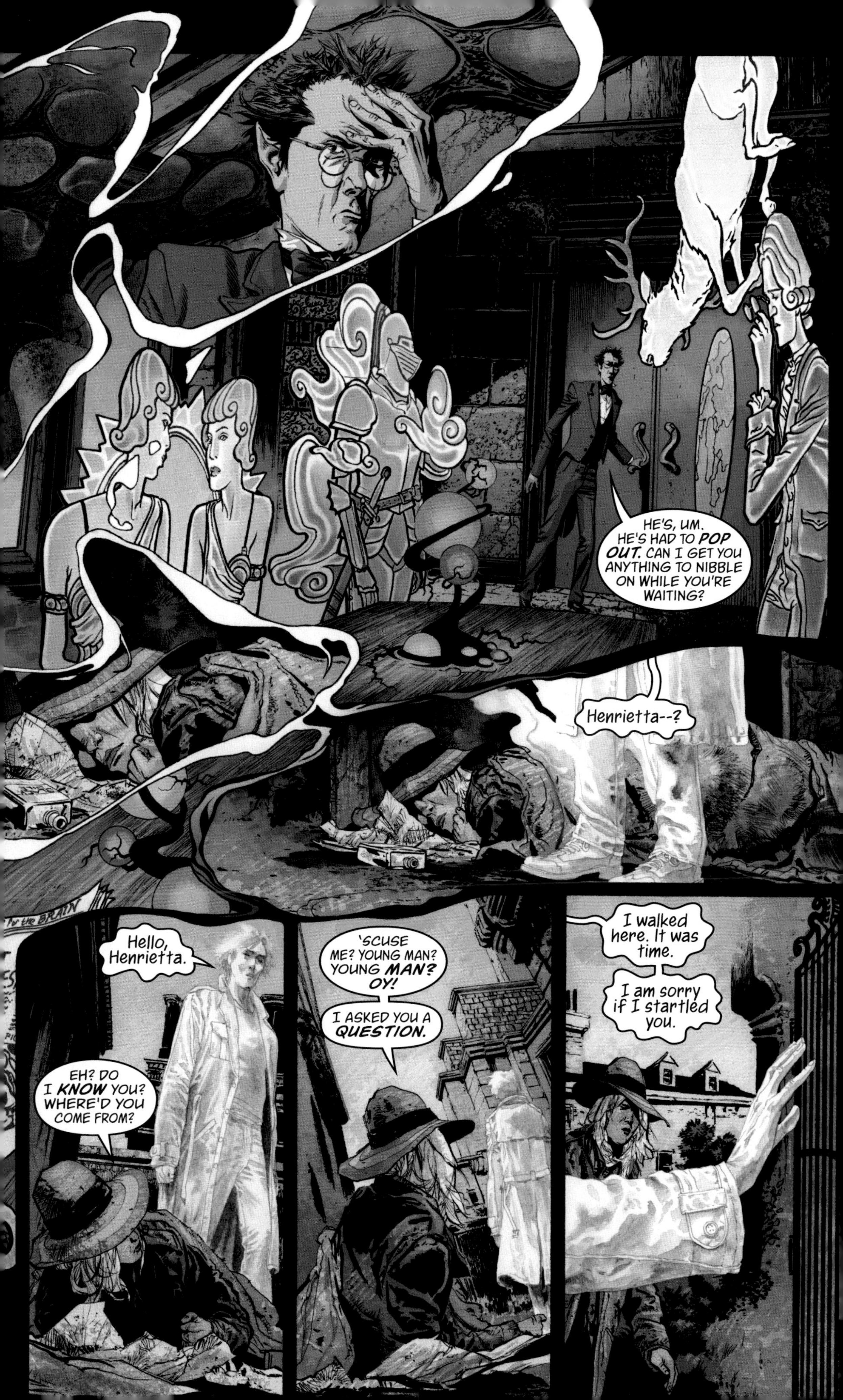
HE'S, UM. HE'S HAD TO **POP OUT.** CAN I GET YOU ANYTHING TO NIBBLE ON WHILE YOU'RE WAITING?
Henrietta--?
Hello, Henrietta.
EH? DO I **KNOW** YOU? WHERE'D YOU COME FROM?
'SCUSE ME? YOUNG MAN? YOUNG **MAN?** **OY!**
I ASKED YOU A **QUESTION.**
I walked here. It was time.
I am sorry if I startled you.

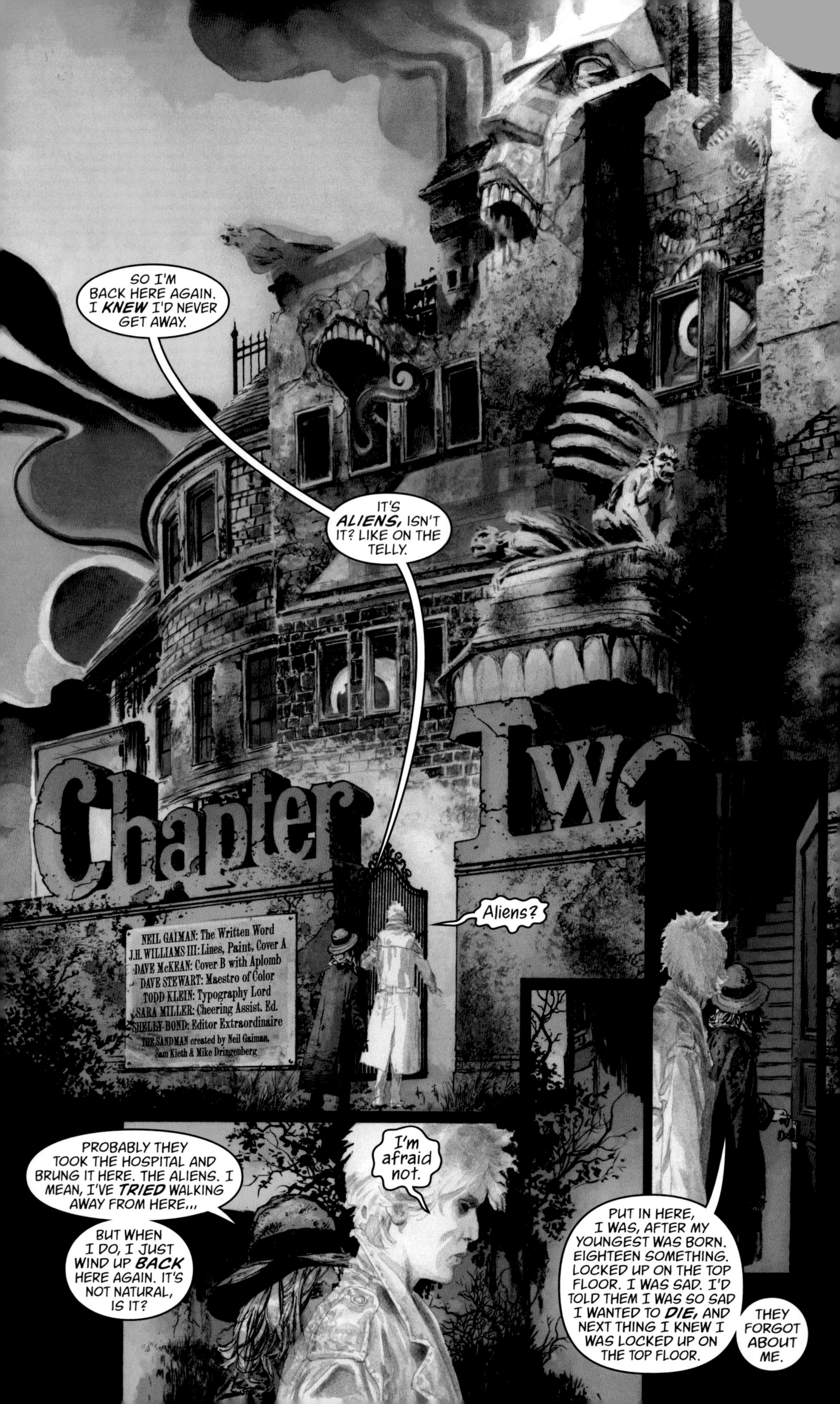
SO I'M BACK HERE AGAIN. I KNEW I'D NEVER GET AWAY.
IT'S ALIENS, ISN'T IT? LIKE ON THE TELLY.
Chapter Two
Aliens?
NEIL GAIMAN: The Written Word
J.H. WILLIAMS III: Lines, Paint, Cover A
DAVE McKEAN: Cover B with Aplomb
DAVE STEWART: Maestro of Color
TODD KLEIN: Typography Lord
SARA MILLER: Cheering Assist. Ed.
SHELLY BOND: Editor Extraordinaire
THE SANDMAN created by Neil Gaiman, Sam Kieth & Mike Dringenberg
PROBABLY THEY TOOK THE HOSPITAL AND BRUNG IT HERE. THE ALIENS. I MEAN, I'VE TRIED WALKING AWAY FROM HERE...
BUT WHEN I DO, I JUST WIND UP BACK HERE AGAIN. IT'S NOT NATURAL, IS IT?
I'm afraid not.
PUT IN HERE, I WAS, AFTER MY YOUNGEST WAS BORN. EIGHTEEN SOMETHING. LOCKED UP ON THE TOP FLOOR. I WAS SAD. I'D TOLD THEM I WAS SO SAD I WANTED TO DIE, AND NEXT THING I KNEW I WAS LOCKED UP ON THE TOP FLOOR.
THEY FORGOT ABOUT ME.

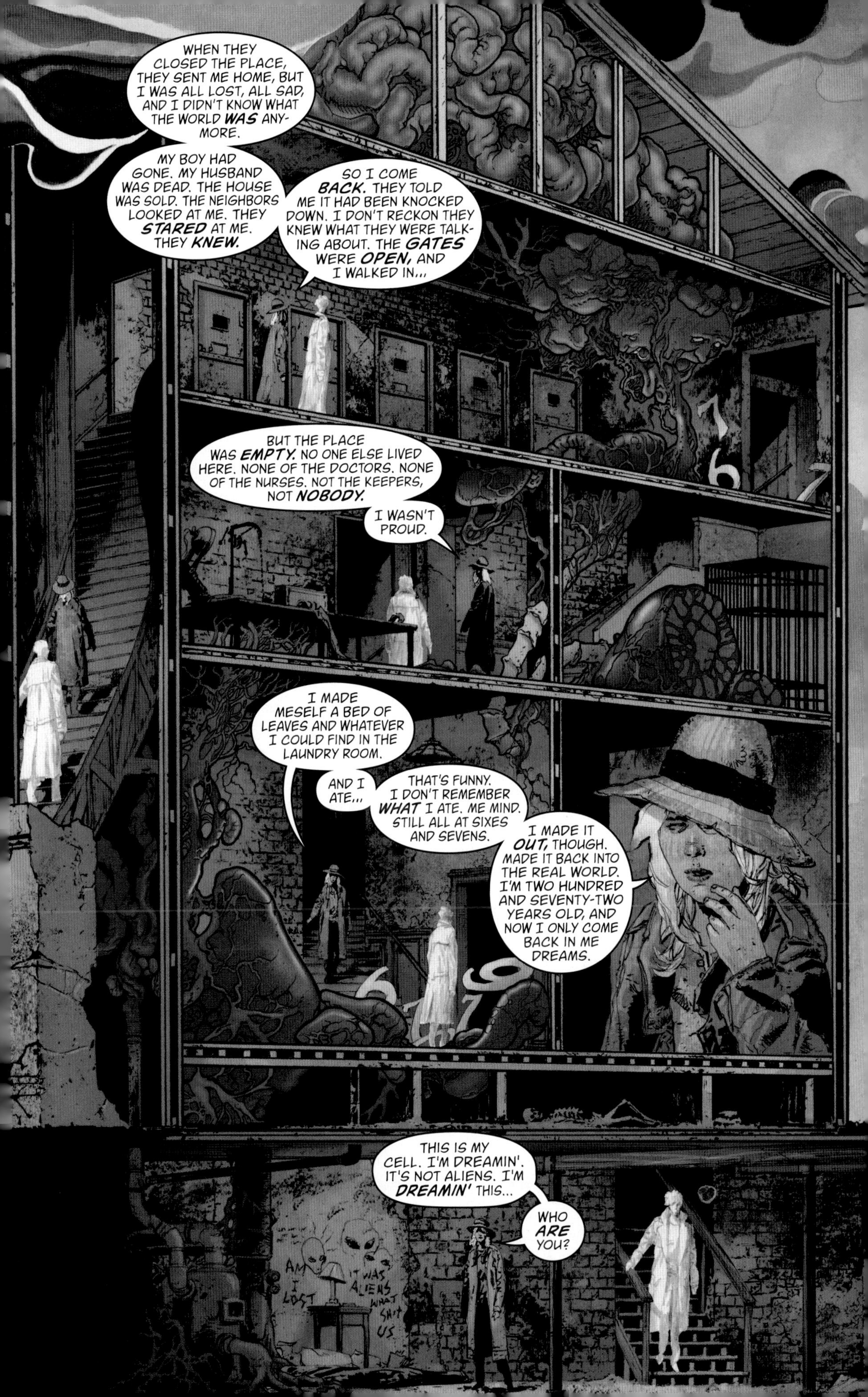
WHEN THEY CLOSED THE PLACE, THEY SENT ME HOME, BUT I WAS ALL LOST, ALL SAD, AND I DIDN'T KNOW WHAT THE WORLD WAS ANYMORE.
MY BOY HAD GONE. MY HUSBAND WAS DEAD. THE HOUSE WAS SOLD. THE NEIGHBORS LOOKED AT ME. THEY STARED AT ME. THEY KNEW.
SO I COME BACK. THEY TOLD ME IT HAD BEEN KNOCKED DOWN. I DON'T RECKON THEY KNEW WHAT THEY WERE TALKING ABOUT. THE GATES WERE OPEN, AND I WALKED IN...
BUT THE PLACE WAS EMPTY. NO ONE ELSE LIVED HERE. NONE OF THE DOCTORS. NONE OF THE NURSES. NOT THE KEEPERS, NOT NOBODY.
I WASN'T PROUD.
I MADE MESELF A BED OF LEAVES AND WHATEVER I COULD FIND IN THE LAUNDRY ROOM.
AND I ATE...
THAT'S FUNNY. I DON'T REMEMBER WHAT I ATE. ME MIND. STILL ALL AT SIXES AND SEVENS.
I MADE IT OUT, THOUGH. MADE IT BACK INTO THE REAL WORLD. I'M TWO HUNDRED AND SEVENTY-TWO YEARS OLD, AND NOW I ONLY COME BACK IN ME DREAMS.
THIS IS MY CELL. I'M DREAMIN'. IT'S NOT ALIENS. I'M DREAMIN' THIS...
WHO ARE YOU?
AM I LOST
IT WAS ALIENS WHAT SHOT US

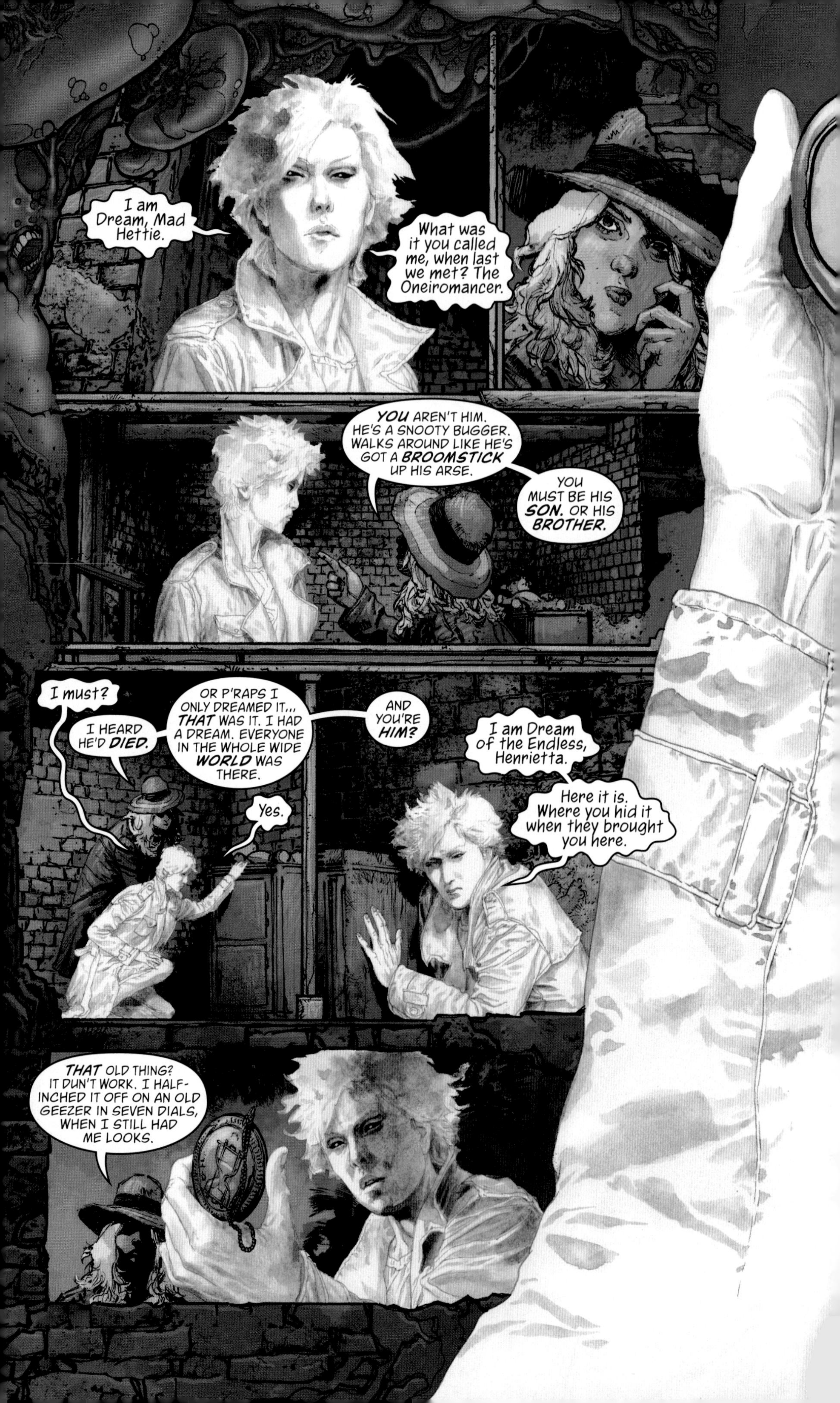

I am Dream, Mad Hettie.
What was it you called me, when last we met? The Oneiromancer.
YOU AREN'T HIM. HE'S A SNOOTY BUGGER. WALKS AROUND LIKE HE'S GOT A BROOMSTICK UP HIS ARSE.
YOU MUST BE HIS SON. OR HIS BROTHER.
I must?
I HEARD HE'D DIED.
OR P'RAPS I ONLY DREAMED IT... THAT WAS IT. I HAD A DREAM. EVERYONE IN THE WHOLE WIDE WORLD WAS THERE.
AND YOU'RE HIM?
Yes.
I am Dream of the Endless, Henrietta.
Here it is. Where you hid it when they brought you here.
THAT OLD THING? IT DUN'T WORK. I HALF-INCHED IT OFF ON AN OLD GEEZER IN SEVEN DIALS, WHEN I STILL HAD ME LOOKS.

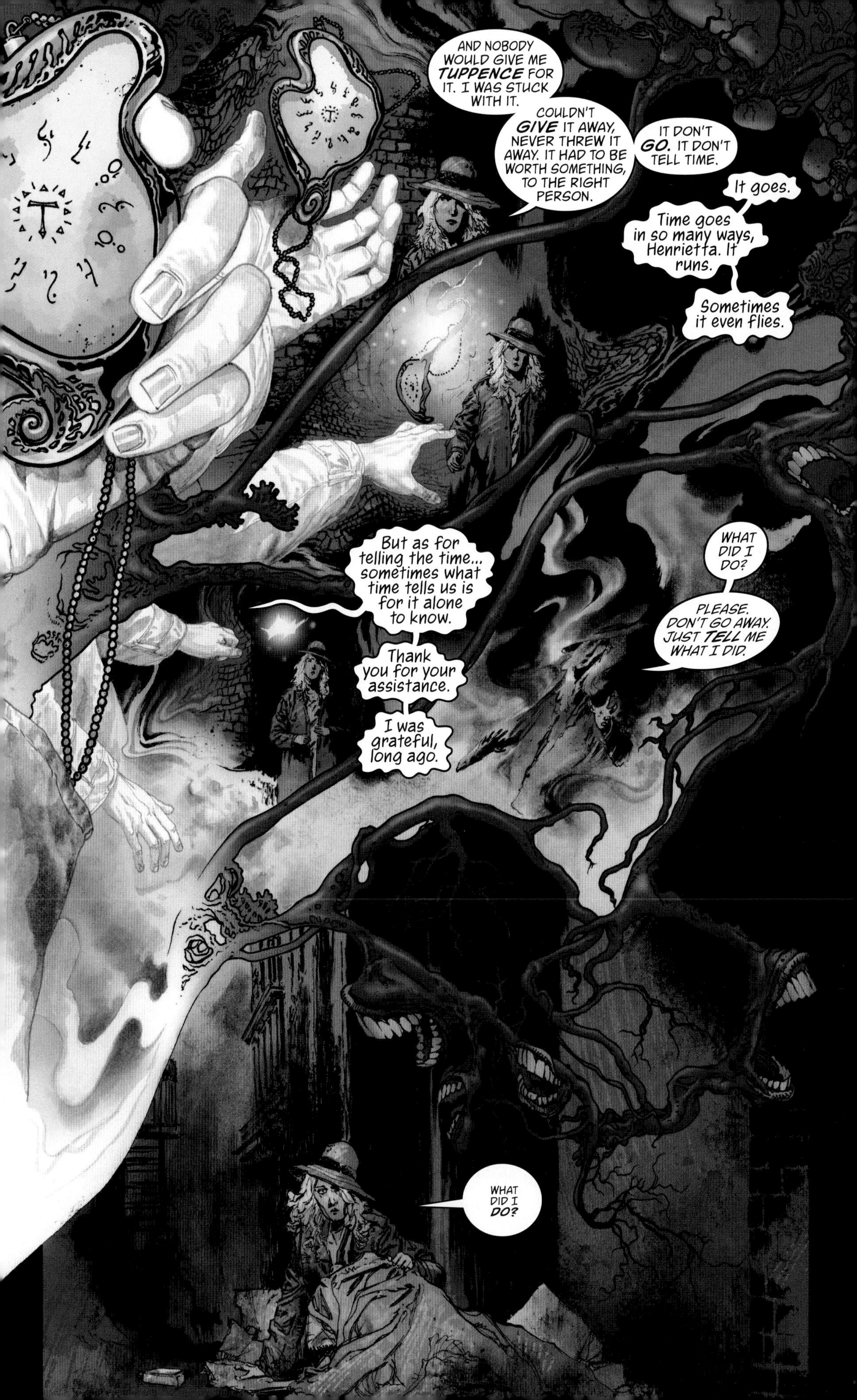
AND NOBODY WOULD GIVE ME TUPPENCE FOR IT. I WAS STUCK WITH IT.
COULDN'T GIVE IT AWAY, NEVER THREW IT AWAY. IT HAD TO BE WORTH SOMETHING, TO THE RIGHT PERSON.
IT DON'T GO. IT DON'T TELL TIME.
It goes.
Time goes in so many ways, Henrietta. It runs.
Sometimes it even flies.
But as for telling the time... sometimes what time tells us is for it alone to know.
Thank you for your assistance.
I was grateful, long ago.
WHAT DID I DO?
PLEASE. DON'T GO AWAY. JUST TELL ME WHAT I DID.
WHAT DID I DO?

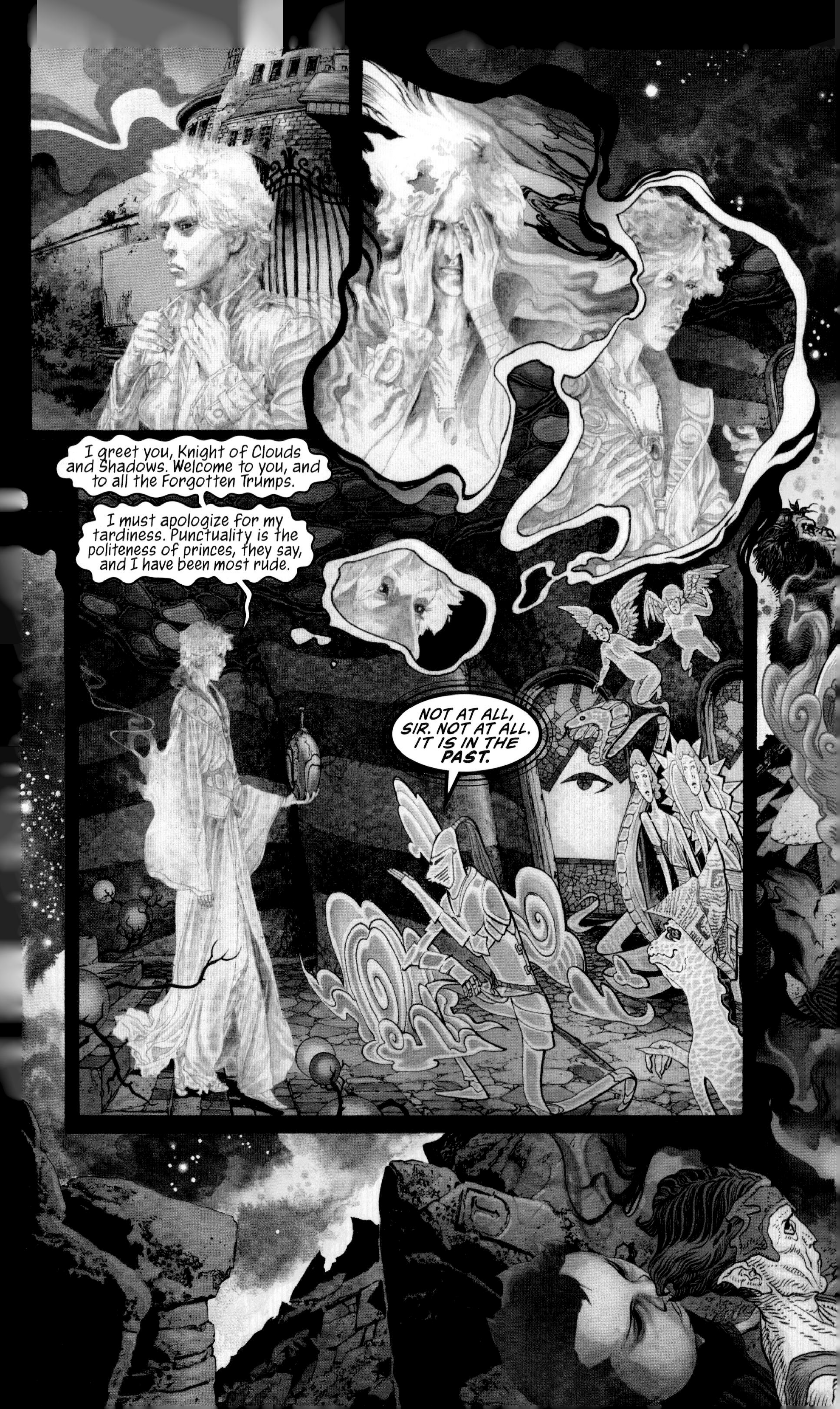

I greet you, Knight of Clouds and Shadows. Welcome to you, and to all the Forgotten Trumps.
I must apologize for my tardiness. Punctuality is the politeness of princes, they say, and I have been most rude.
NOT AT ALL, SIR. NOT AT ALL. IT IS IN THE PAST.

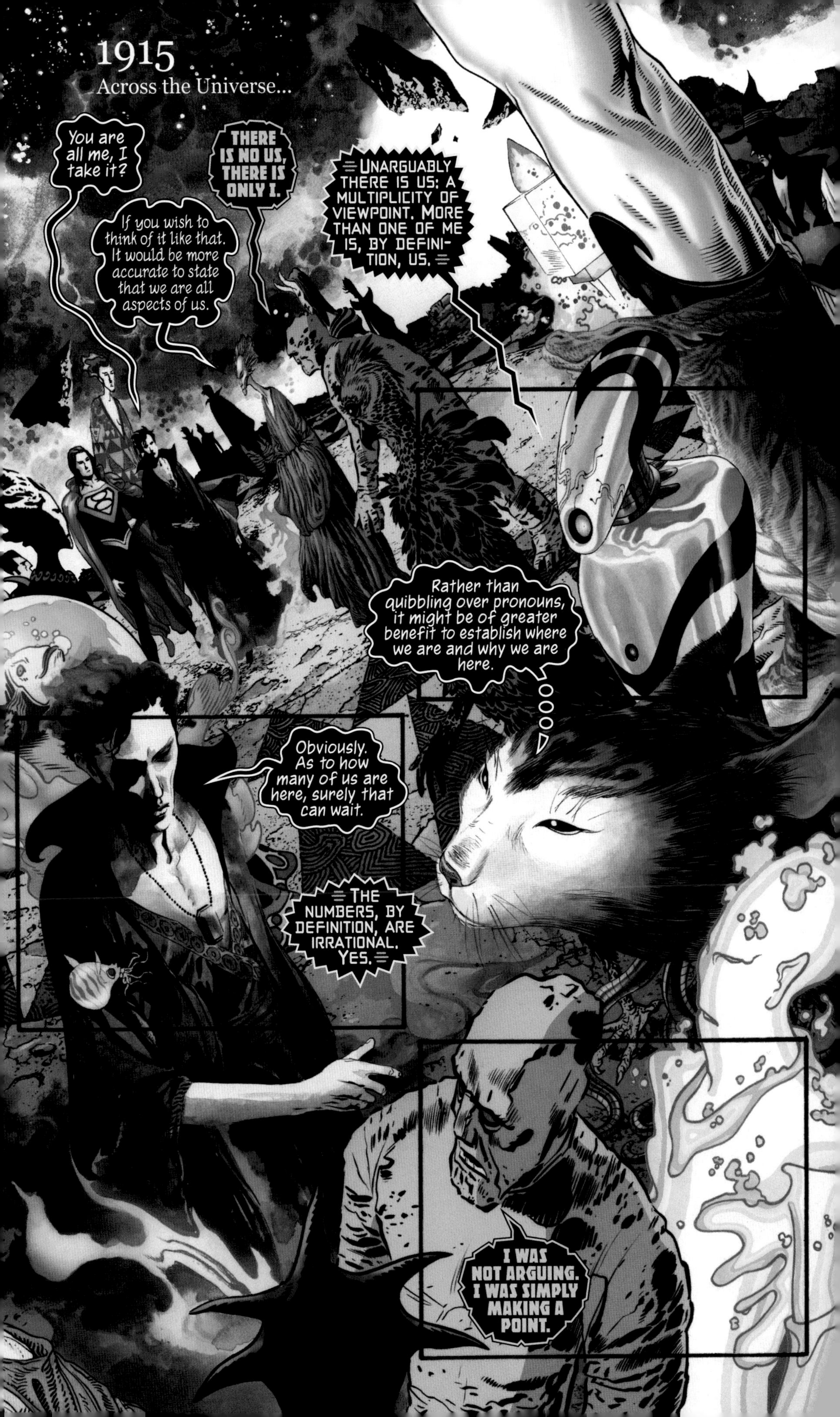
1915
Across the Universe...
You are all me, I take it?
If you wish to think of it like that. It would be more accurate to state that we are all aspects of us.
THERE IS NO US, THERE IS ONLY I.
UNARGUABLY THERE IS US: A MULTIPLICITY OF VIEWPOINT. MORE THAN ONE OF ME IS, BY DEFINITION, US.
Rather than quibbling over pronouns, it might be of greater benefit to establish where we are and why we are here.
Obviously. As to how many of us are here, surely that can wait.
THE NUMBERS, BY DEFINITION, ARE IRRATIONAL. YES.
I WAS NOT ARGUING. I WAS SIMPLY MAKING A POINT.

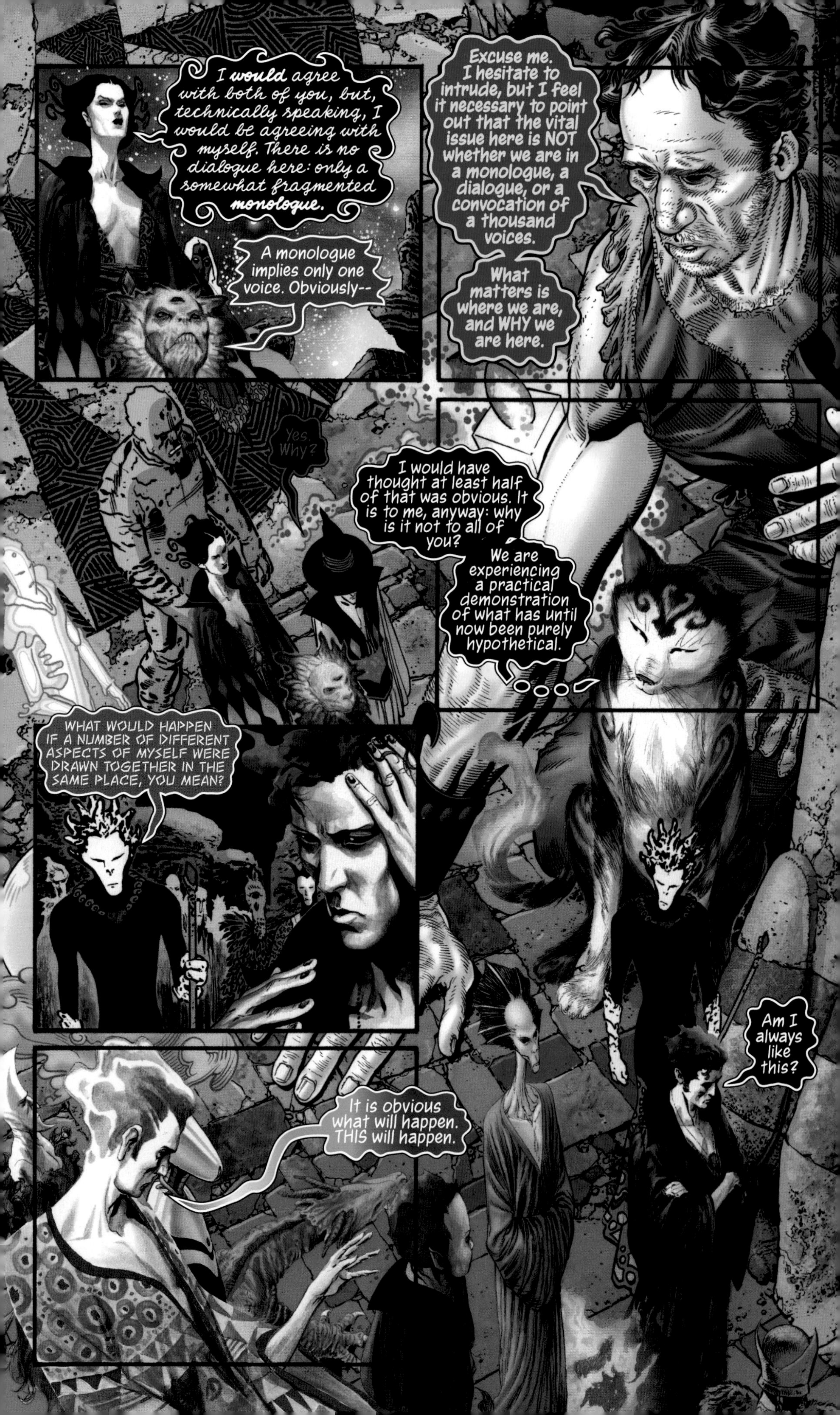
I **would** agree with both of you, but, technically speaking, I would be agreeing with myself. There is no dialogue here: only a somewhat fragmented **monologue.**
A monologue implies only one voice. Obviously--
Excuse me. I hesitate to intrude, but I feel it necessary to point out that the vital issue here is NOT whether we are in a monologue, a dialogue, or a convocation of a thousand voices.
What matters is where we are, and WHY we are here.
Yes. Why?
I would have thought at least half of that was obvious. It is to me, anyway: why is it not to all of you?
We are experiencing a practical demonstration of what has until now been purely hypothetical.
WHAT WOULD HAPPEN IF A NUMBER OF DIFFERENT ASPECTS OF MYSELF WERE DRAWN TOGETHER IN THE SAME PLACE, YOU MEAN?
Am I always like this?
It is obvious what will happen. THIS will happen.

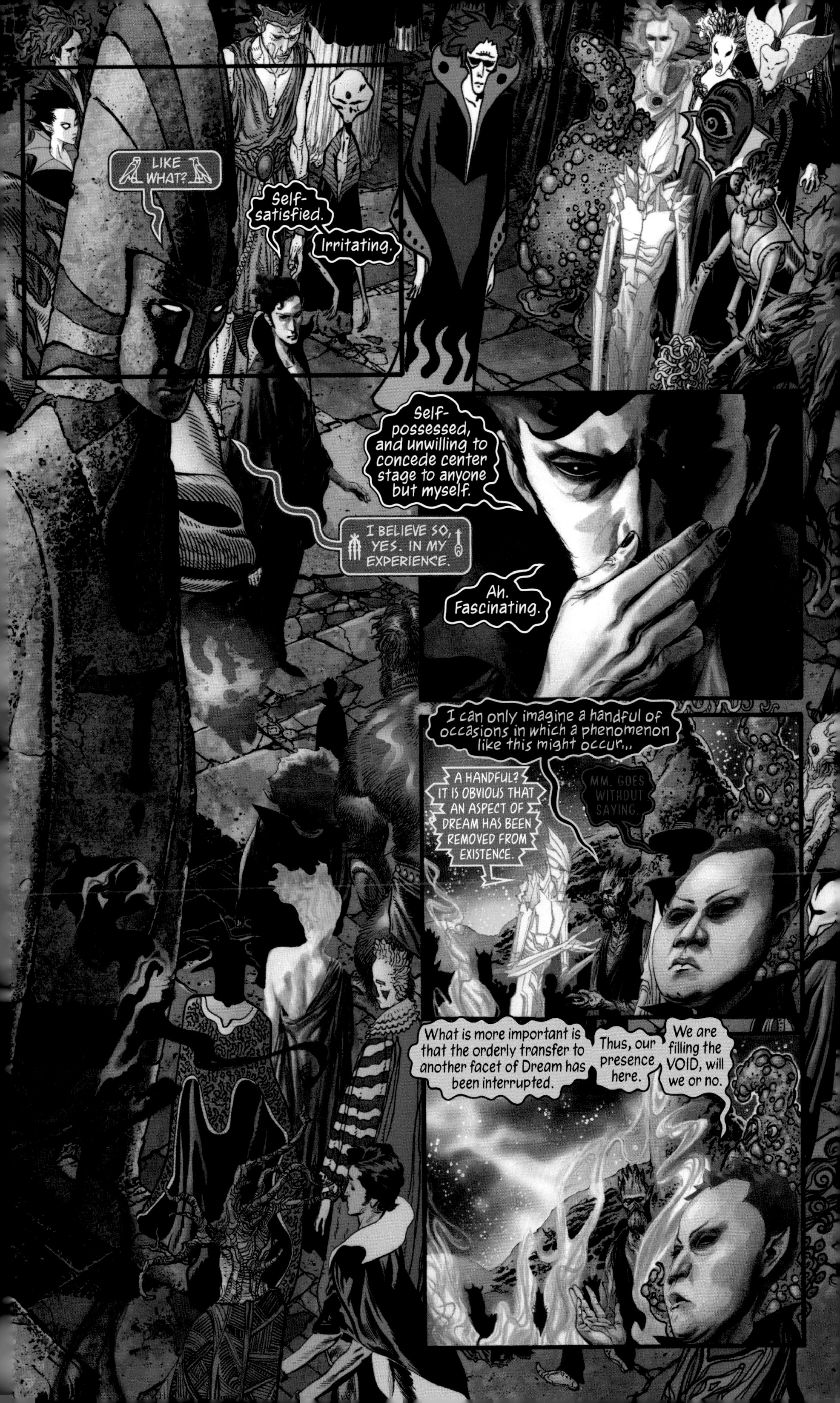

LIKE WHAT?
Self-satisfied.
Irritating.
Self-possessed, and unwilling to concede center stage to anyone but myself.
I BELIEVE SO, YES. IN MY EXPERIENCE.
Ah. Fascinating.
I can only imagine a handful of occasions in which a phenomenon like this might occur...
A HANDFUL? IT IS OBVIOUS THAT AN ASPECT OF DREAM HAS BEEN REMOVED FROM EXISTENCE.
MM. GOES WITHOUT SAYING.
What is more important is that the orderly transfer to another facet of Dream has been interrupted.
Thus, our presence here.
We are filling the VOID, will we or no.

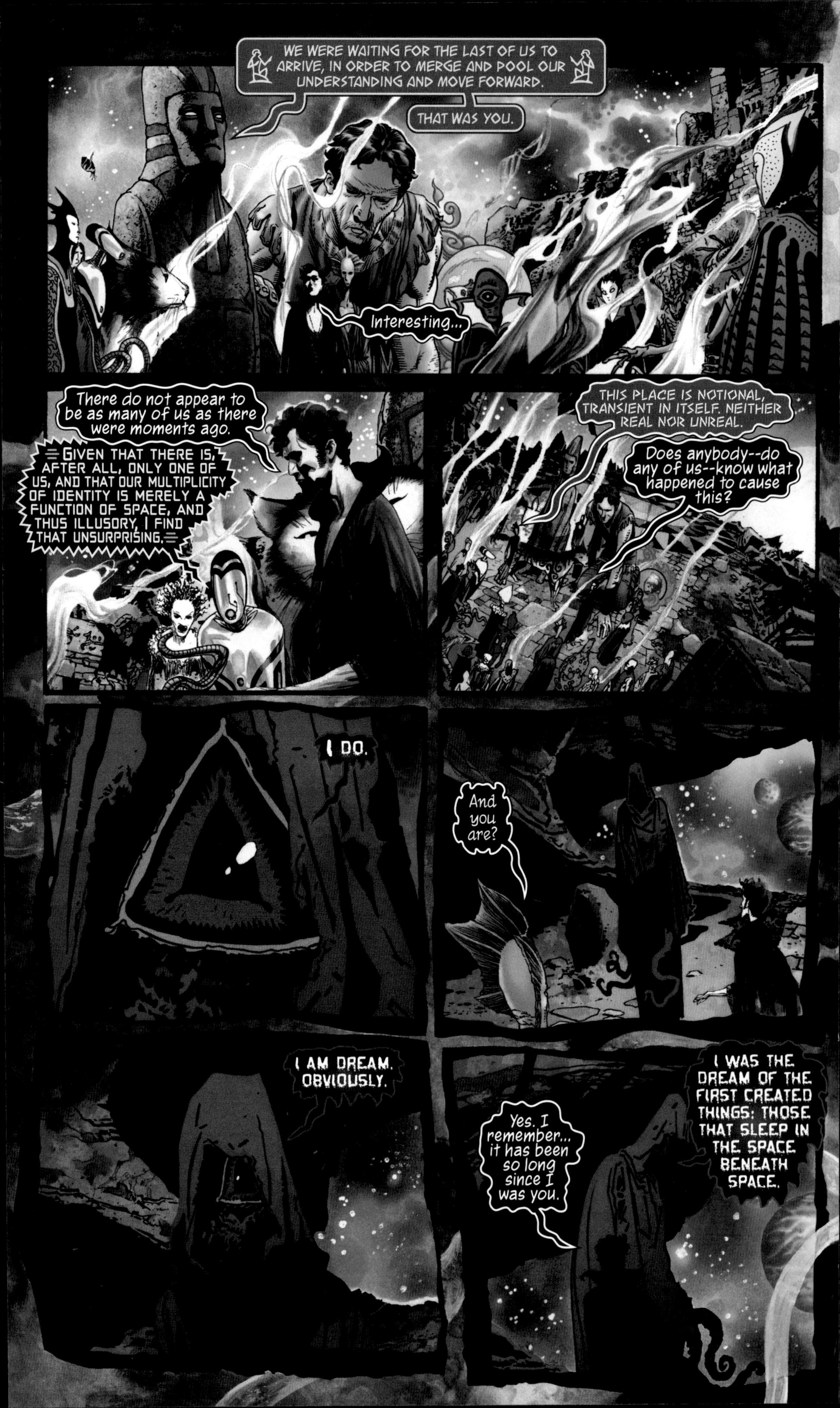

WE WERE WAITING FOR THE LAST OF US TO ARRIVE, IN ORDER TO MERGE AND POOL OUR UNDERSTANDING AND MOVE FORWARD.
THAT WAS YOU.
Interesting...
There do not appear to be as many of us as there were moments ago.
GIVEN THAT THERE IS, AFTER ALL, ONLY ONE OF US, AND THAT OUR MULTIPLICITY OF IDENTITY IS MERELY A FUNCTION OF SPACE, AND THUS ILLUSORY, I FIND THAT UNSURPRISING.
THIS PLACE IS NOTIONAL, TRANSIENT IN ITSELF. NEITHER REAL NOR UNREAL.
Does anybody--do any of us--know what happened to cause this?
I DO.
And you are?
I AM DREAM. OBVIOUSLY.
Yes. I remember... it has been so long since I was you.
I WAS THE DREAM OF THE FIRST CREATED THINGS: THOSE THAT SLEEP IN THE SPACE BENEATH SPACE.

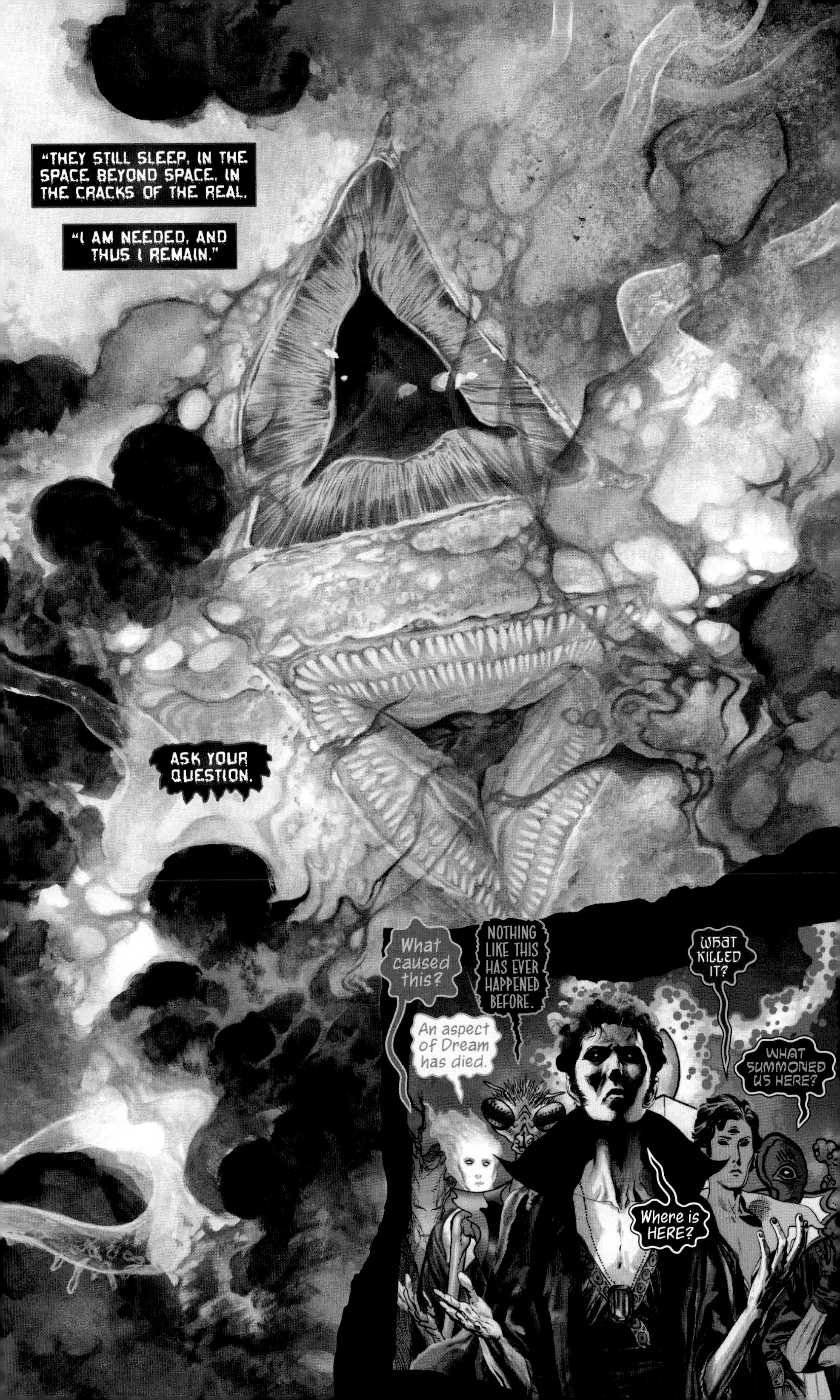
"THEY STILL SLEEP, IN THE SPACE BEYOND SPACE, IN THE CRACKS OF THE REAL.
"I AM NEEDED, AND THUS I REMAIN."
ASK YOUR QUESTION.
What caused this?
NOTHING LIKE THIS HAS EVER HAPPENED BEFORE.
WHAT KILLED IT?
An aspect of Dream has died.
WHAT SUMMONED US HERE?
Where is HERE?

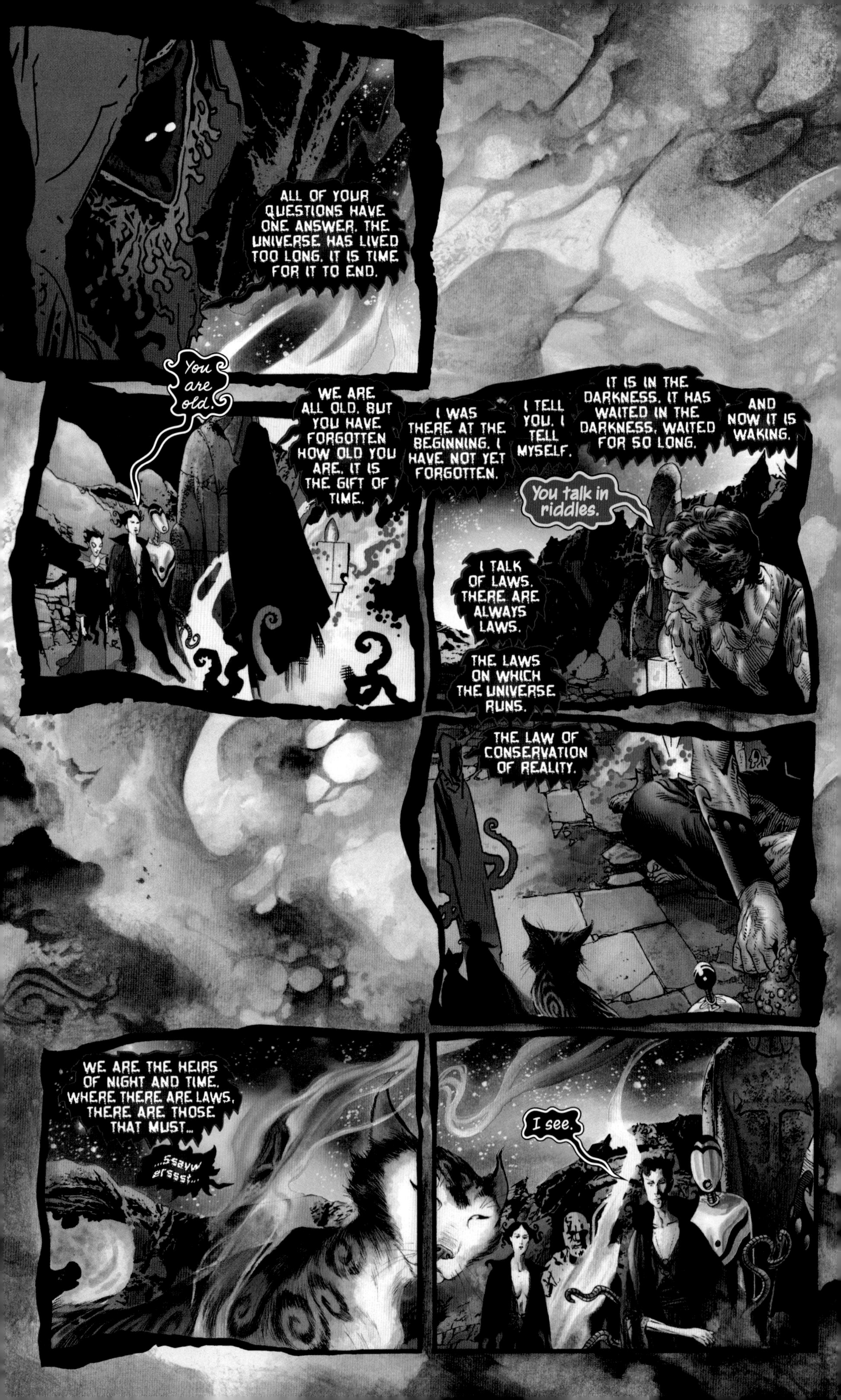
ALL OF YOUR QUESTIONS HAVE ONE ANSWER. THE UNIVERSE HAS LIVED TOO LONG. IT IS TIME FOR IT TO END.
You are old.
WE ARE ALL OLD. BUT YOU HAVE FORGOTTEN HOW OLD YOU ARE. IT IS THE GIFT OF TIME.
I WAS THERE AT THE BEGINNING. I HAVE NOT YET FORGOTTEN.
I TELL YOU. I TELL MYSELF.
IT IS IN THE DARKNESS. IT HAS WAITED IN THE DARKNESS. WAITED FOR SO LONG.
AND NOW IT IS WAKING.
You talk in riddles.
I TALK OF LAWS. THERE ARE ALWAYS LAWS.
THE LAWS ON WHICH THE UNIVERSE RUNS.
THE LAW OF CONSERVATION OF REALITY.
WE ARE THE HEIRS OF NIGHT AND TIME. WHERE THERE ARE LAWS, THERE ARE THOSE THAT MUST...
...Ssayw erssst...
I see.

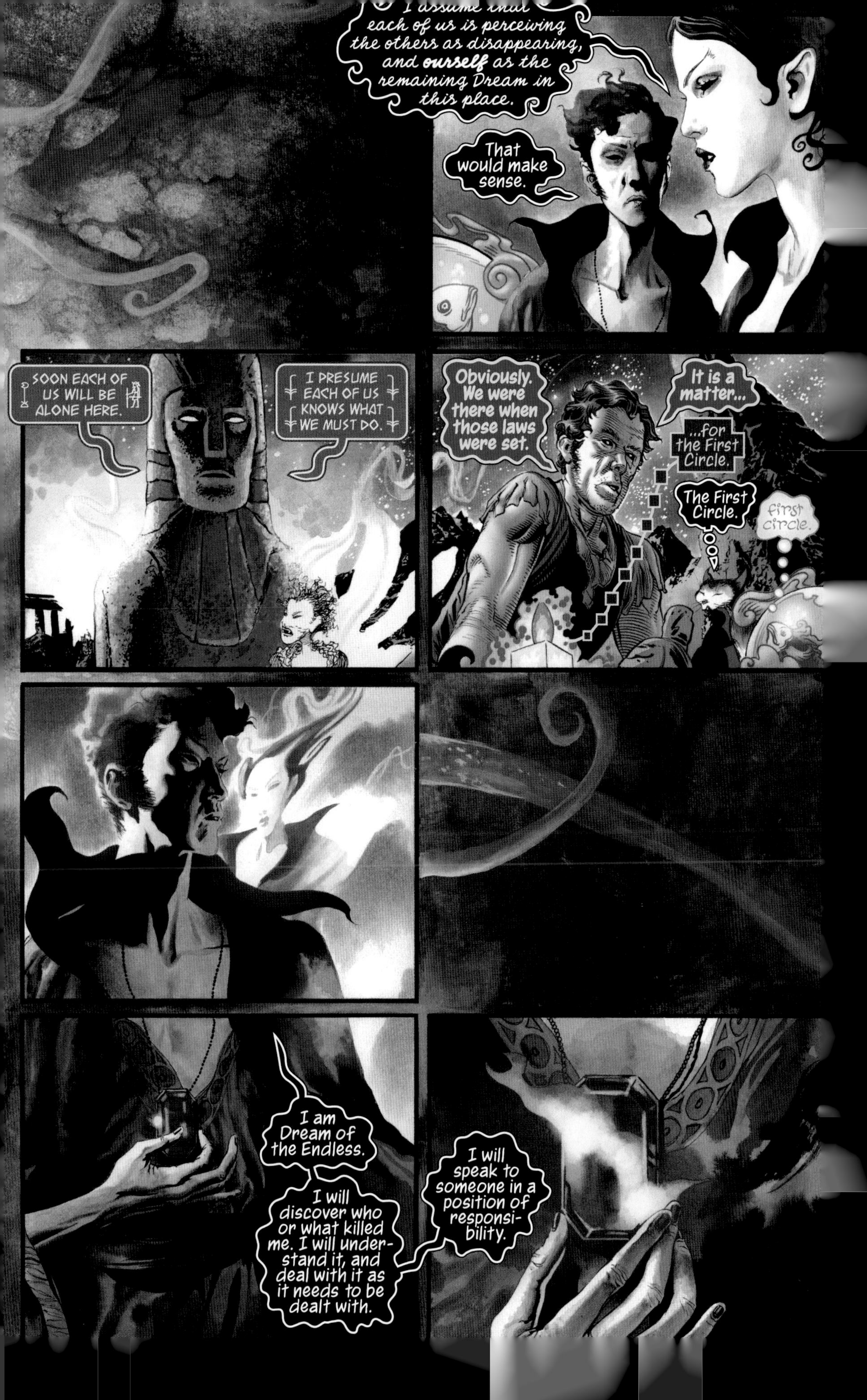
I assume that each of us is perceiving the others as disappearing, and **ourself** as the remaining Dream in this place.
That would make sense.
SOON EACH OF US WILL BE ALONE HERE.
I PRESUME EACH OF US KNOWS WHAT WE MUST DO.
Obviously. We were there when those laws were set.
It is a matter...
...for the First Circle.
The First Circle.
first circle.
I am Dream of the Endless.
I will discover who or what killed me. I will understand it, and deal with it as it needs to be dealt with.
I will speak to someone in a position of responsibility.

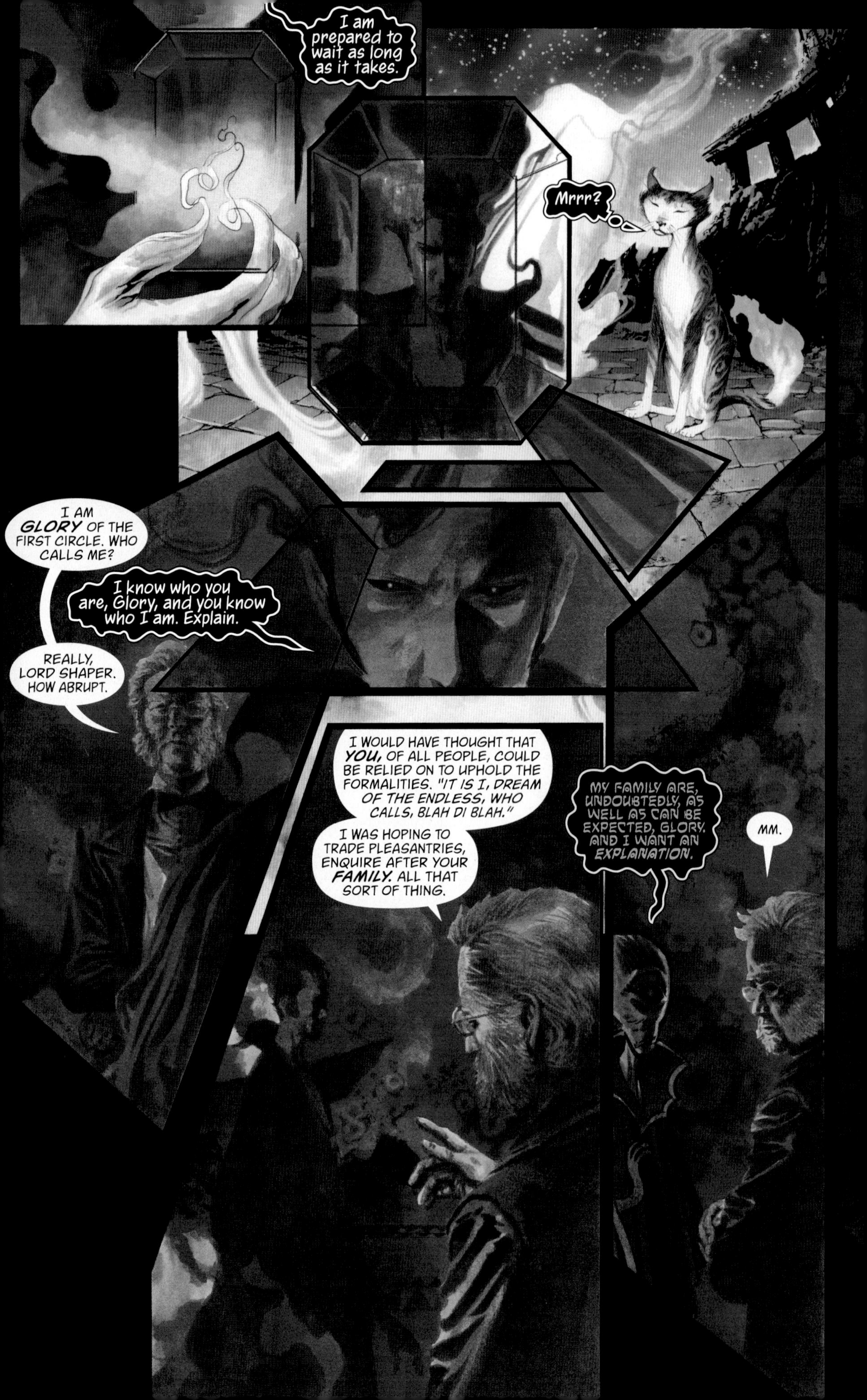
I am prepared to wait as long as it takes.
Mrrr?
I AM GLORY OF THE FIRST CIRCLE. WHO CALLS ME?
I know who you are, Glory, and you know who I am. Explain.
REALLY, LORD SHAPER. HOW ABRUPT.
I WOULD HAVE THOUGHT THAT YOU, OF ALL PEOPLE, COULD BE RELIED ON TO UPHOLD THE FORMALITIES. "IT IS I, DREAM OF THE ENDLESS, WHO CALLS, BLAH DI BLAH."
I WAS HOPING TO TRADE PLEASANTRIES, ENQUIRE AFTER YOUR FAMILY. ALL THAT SORT OF THING.
MY FAMILY ARE, UNDOUBTEDLY, AS WELL AS CAN BE EXPECTED, GLORY. AND I WANT AN EXPLANATION.
MM.

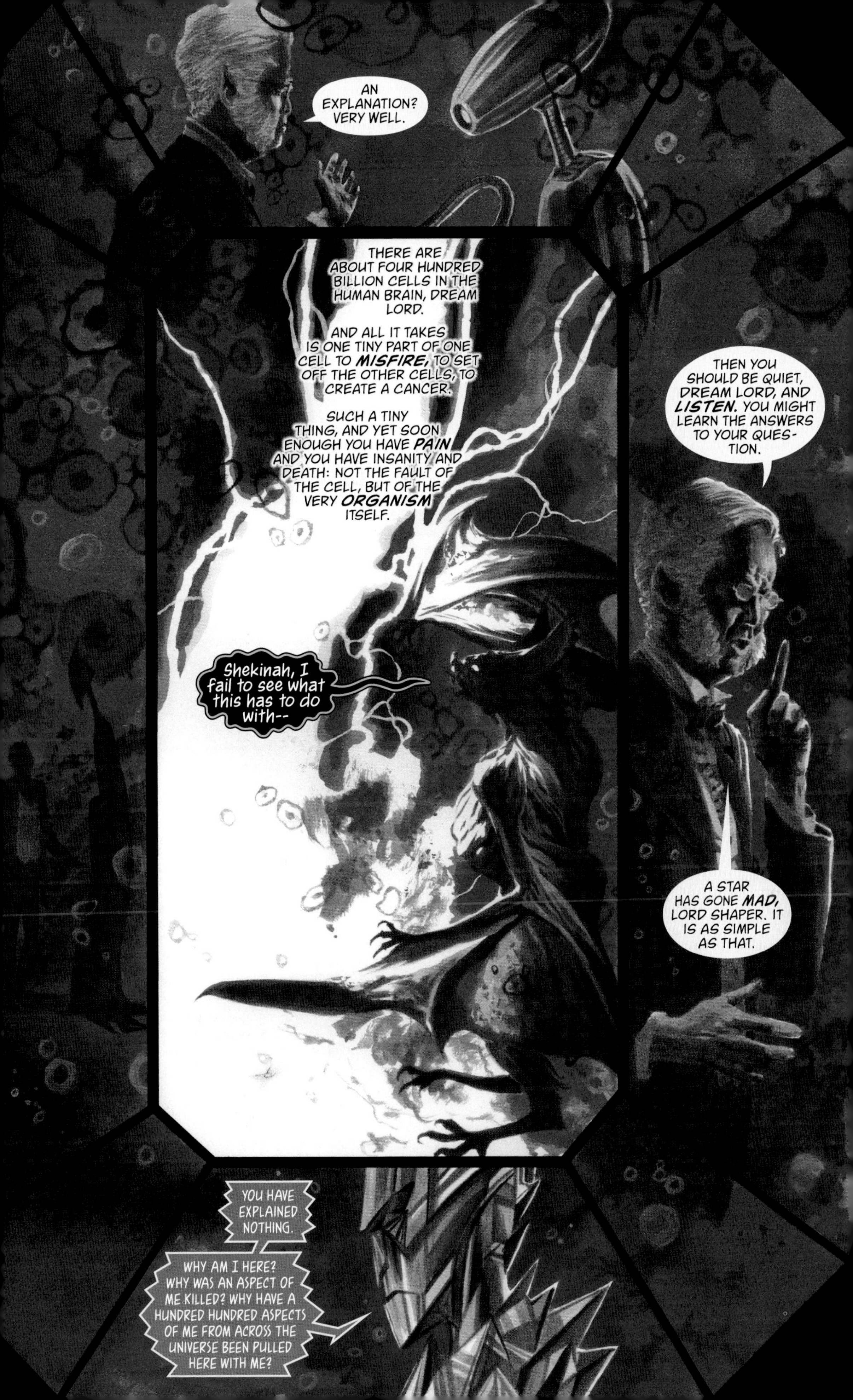
AN EXPLANATION? VERY WELL.
THERE ARE ABOUT FOUR HUNDRED BILLION CELLS IN THE HUMAN BRAIN, DREAM LORD.
AND ALL IT TAKES IS ONE TINY PART OF ONE CELL TO MISFIRE, TO SET OFF THE OTHER CELLS, TO CREATE A CANCER.
SUCH A TINY THING, AND YET SOON ENOUGH YOU HAVE PAIN AND YOU HAVE INSANITY AND DEATH: NOT THE FAULT OF THE CELL, BUT OF THE VERY ORGANISM ITSELF.
Shekinah, I fail to see what this has to do with--
THEN YOU SHOULD BE QUIET, DREAM LORD, AND LISTEN. YOU MIGHT LEARN THE ANSWERS TO YOUR QUES-TION.
A STAR HAS GONE MAD, LORD SHAPER. IT IS AS SIMPLE AS THAT.
YOU HAVE EXPLAINED NOTHING.
WHY AM I HERE? WHY WAS AN ASPECT OF ME KILLED? WHY HAVE A HUNDRED HUNDRED ASPECTS OF ME FROM ACROSS THE UNIVERSE BEEN PULLED HERE WITH ME?

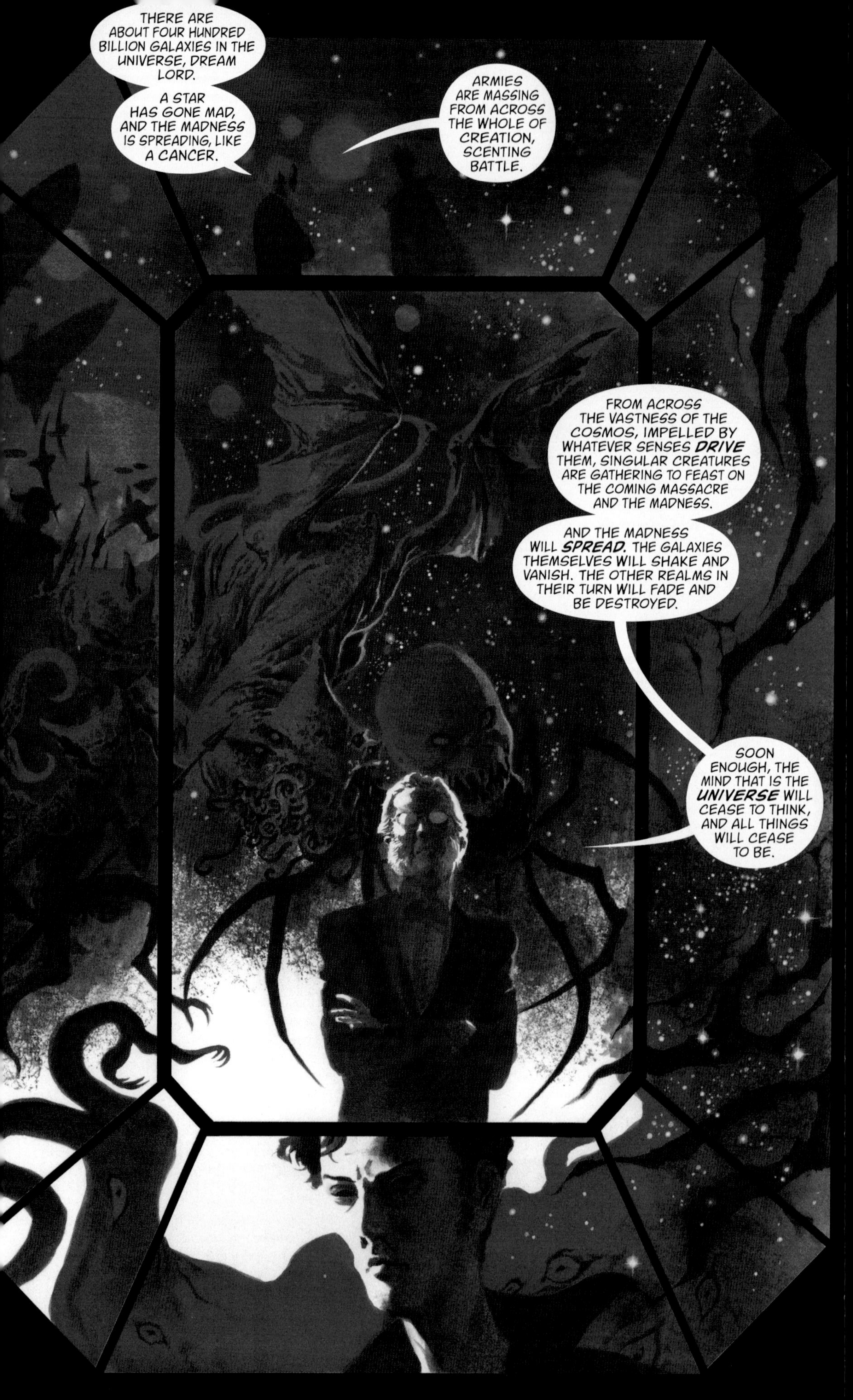
THERE ARE ABOUT FOUR HUNDRED BILLION GALAXIES IN THE UNIVERSE, DREAM LORD.
A STAR HAS GONE MAD, AND THE MADNESS IS SPREADING, LIKE A CANCER.
ARMIES ARE MASSING FROM ACROSS THE WHOLE OF CREATION, SCENTING BATTLE.
FROM ACROSS THE VASTNESS OF THE COSMOS, IMPELLED BY WHATEVER SENSES DRIVE THEM, SINGULAR CREATURES ARE GATHERING TO FEAST ON THE COMING MASSACRE AND THE MADNESS.
AND THE MADNESS WILL SPREAD. THE GALAXIES THEMSELVES WILL SHAKE AND VANISH. THE OTHER REALMS IN THEIR TURN WILL FADE AND BE DESTROYED.
SOON ENOUGH, THE MIND THAT IS THE UNIVERSE WILL CEASE TO THINK, AND ALL THINGS WILL CEASE TO BE.

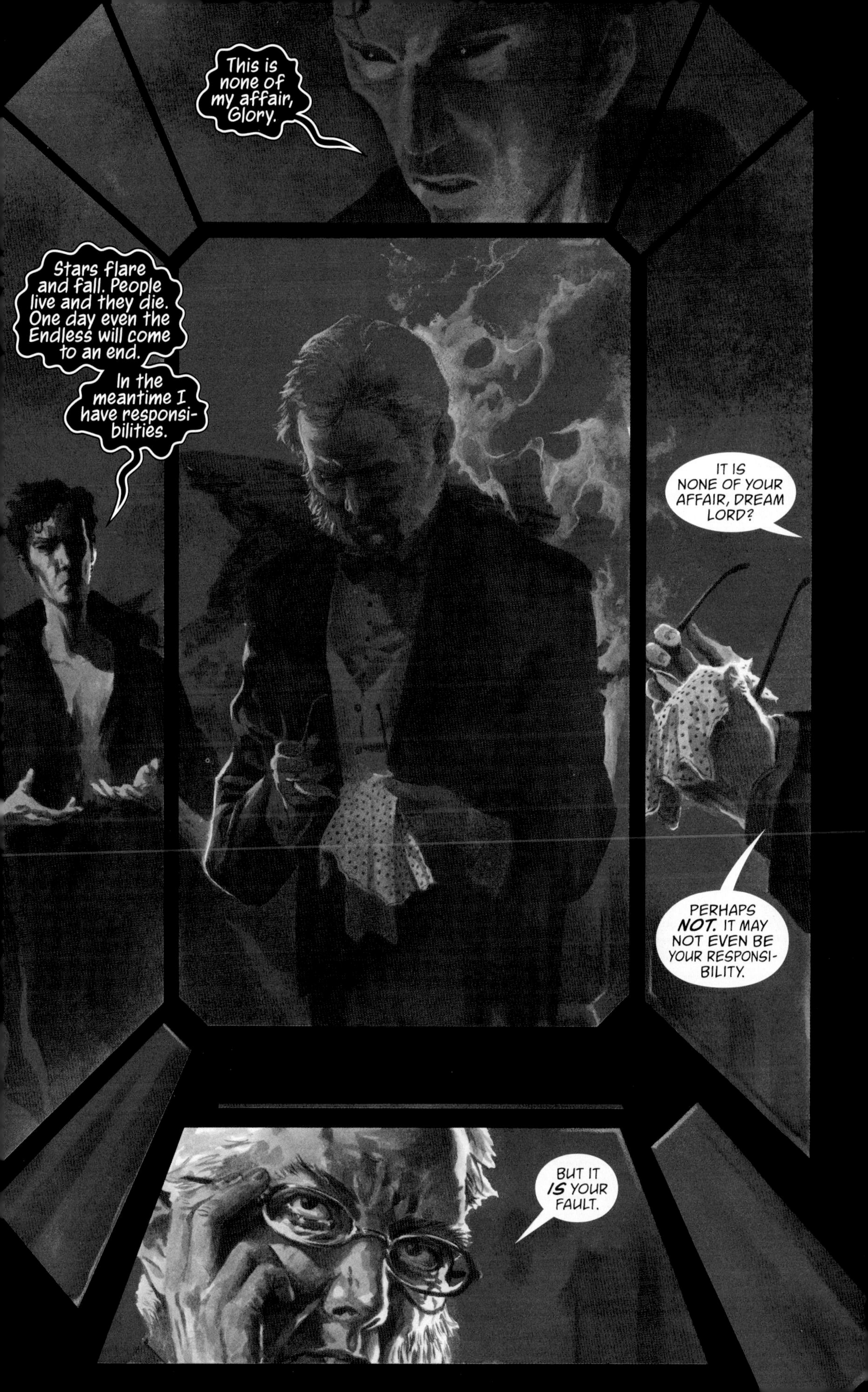
This is none of my affair, Glory.
Stars flare and fall. People live and they die. One day even the Endless will come to an end.
In the meantime I have responsi-bilities.
IT IS NONE OF YOUR AFFAIR, DREAM LORD?
PERHAPS *NOT.* IT MAY NOT EVEN BE YOUR RESPONSI-BILITY.
BUT IT *IS* YOUR FAULT.

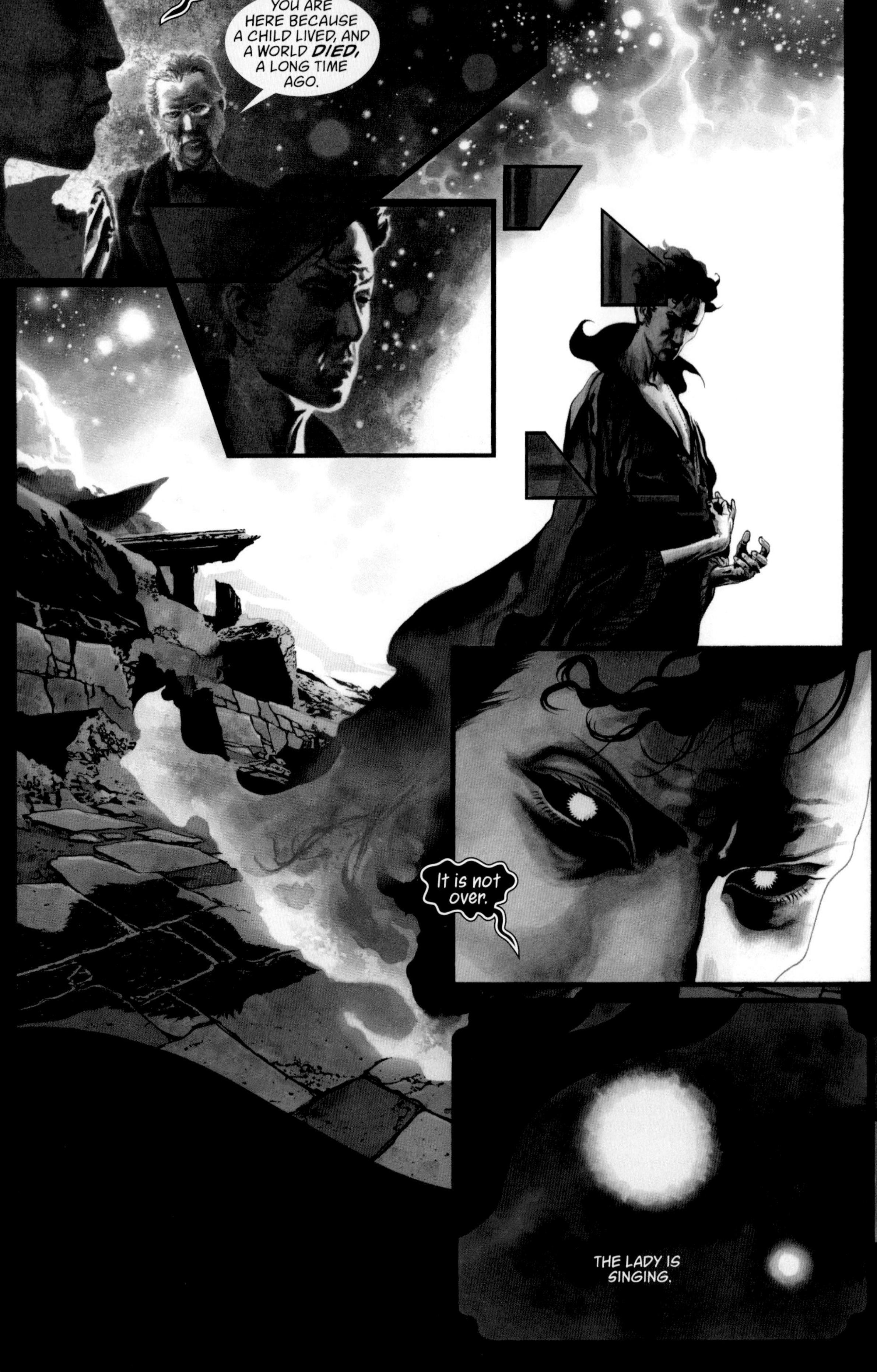
YOU ARE HERE BECAUSE A CHILD LIVED, AND A WORLD ***DIED,*** A LONG TIME AGO.
It is not over.
THE LADY IS SINGING.

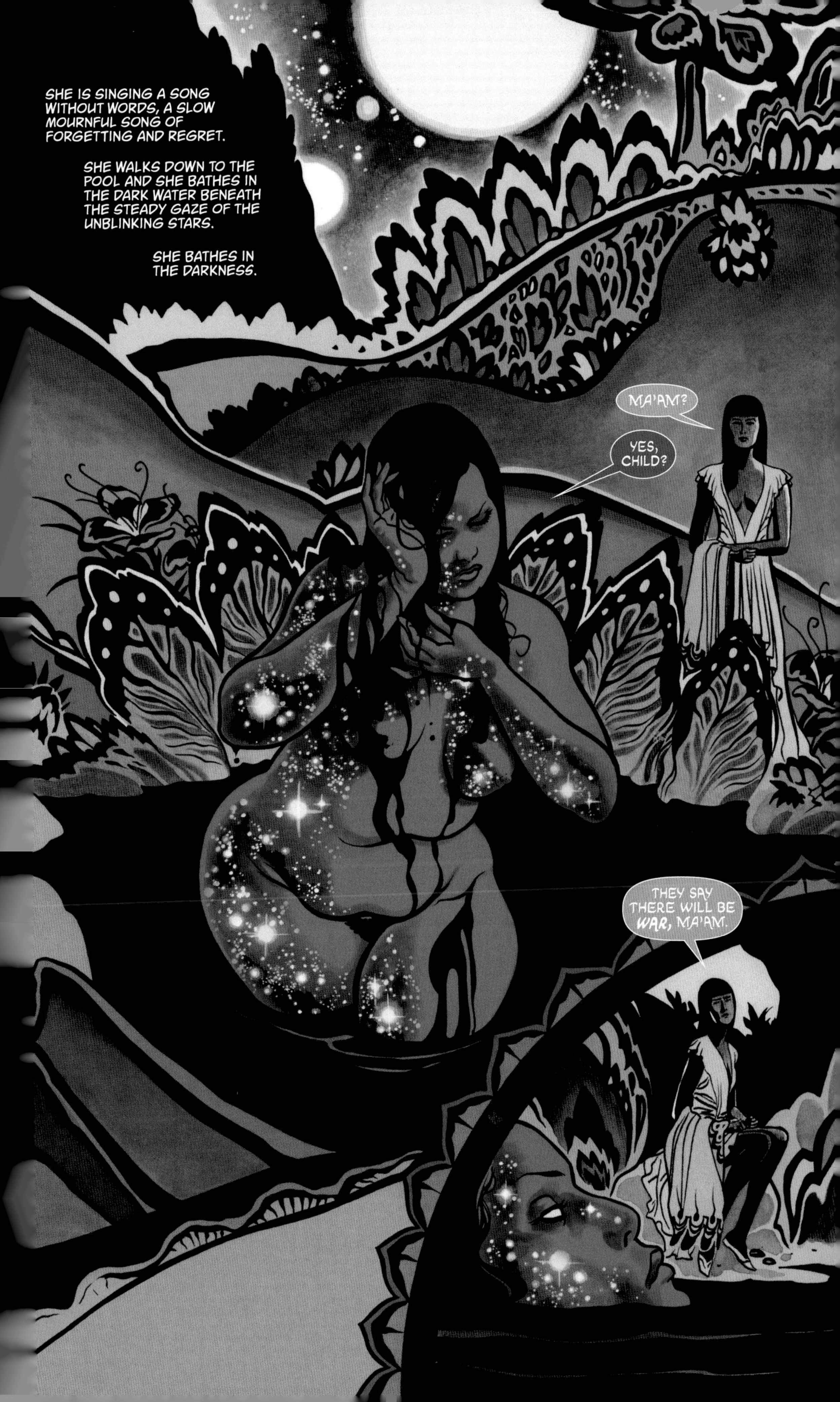
SHE IS SINGING A SONG WITHOUT WORDS, A SLOW MOURNFUL SONG OF FORGETTING AND REGRET.
SHE WALKS DOWN TO THE POOL AND SHE BATHES IN THE DARK WATER BENEATH THE STEADY GAZE OF THE UNBLINKING STARS.
SHE BATHES IN THE DARKNESS.
MA'AM?
YES, CHILD?
THEY SAY THERE WILL BE WAR, MA'AM.

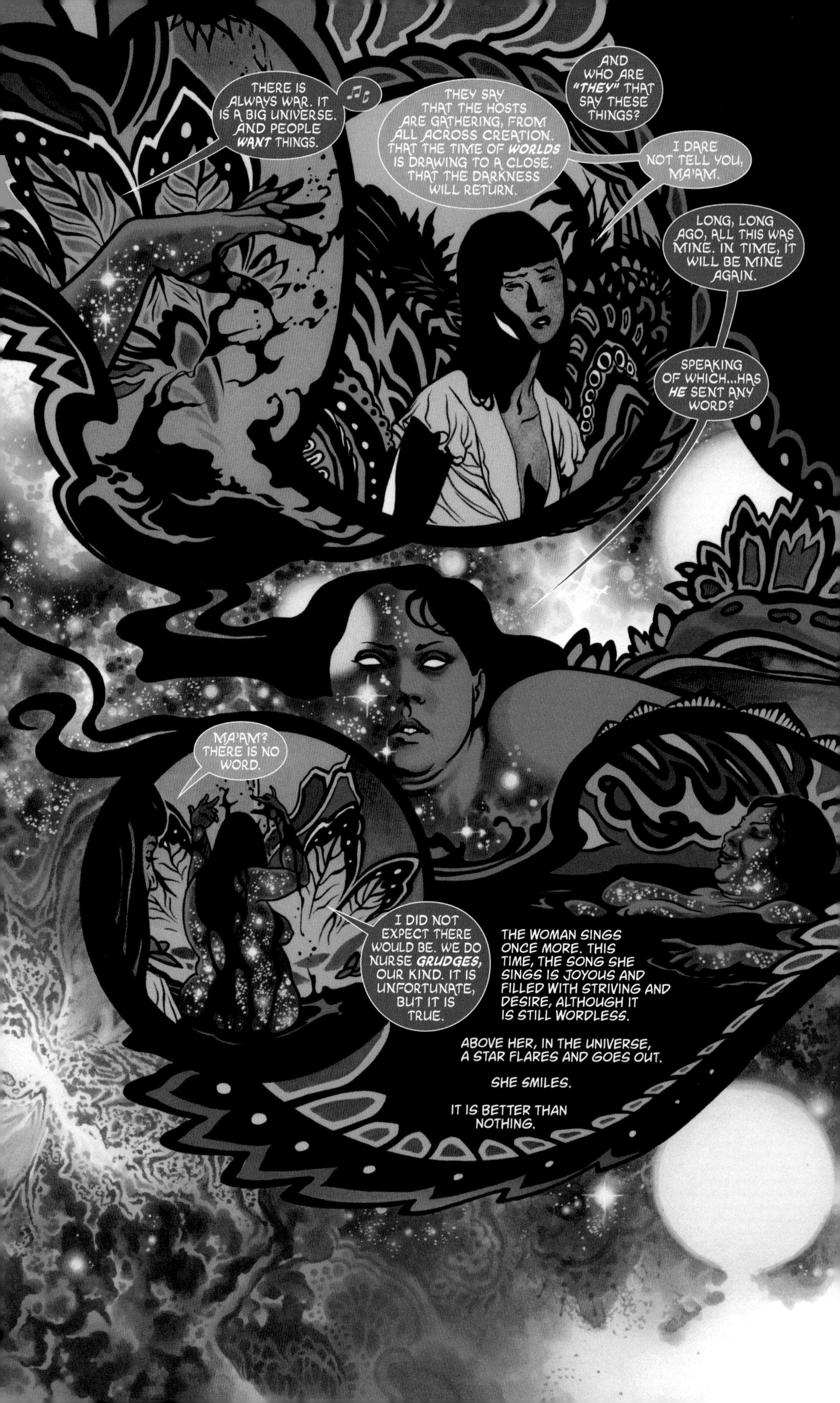
THERE IS ALWAYS WAR. IT IS A BIG UNIVERSE. AND PEOPLE WANT THINGS.
THEY SAY THAT THE HOSTS ARE GATHERING, FROM ALL ACROSS CREATION. THAT THE TIME OF WORLDS IS DRAWING TO A CLOSE. THAT THE DARKNESS WILL RETURN.
AND WHO ARE "THEY" THAT SAY THESE THINGS?
I DARE NOT TELL YOU, MA'AM.
LONG, LONG AGO, ALL THIS WAS MINE. IN TIME, IT WILL BE MINE AGAIN.
SPEAKING OF WHICH...HAS HE SENT ANY WORD?
MA'AM? THERE IS NO WORD.
I DID NOT EXPECT THERE WOULD BE. WE DO NURSE GRUDGES, OUR KIND. IT IS UNFORTUNATE, BUT IT IS TRUE.
THE WOMAN SINGS ONCE MORE. THIS TIME, THE SONG SHE SINGS IS JOYOUS AND FILLED WITH STRIVING AND DESIRE, ALTHOUGH IT IS STILL WORDLESS.
ABOVE HER, IN THE UNIVERSE, A STAR FLARES AND GOES OUT.
SHE SMILES.
IT IS BETTER THAN NOTHING.

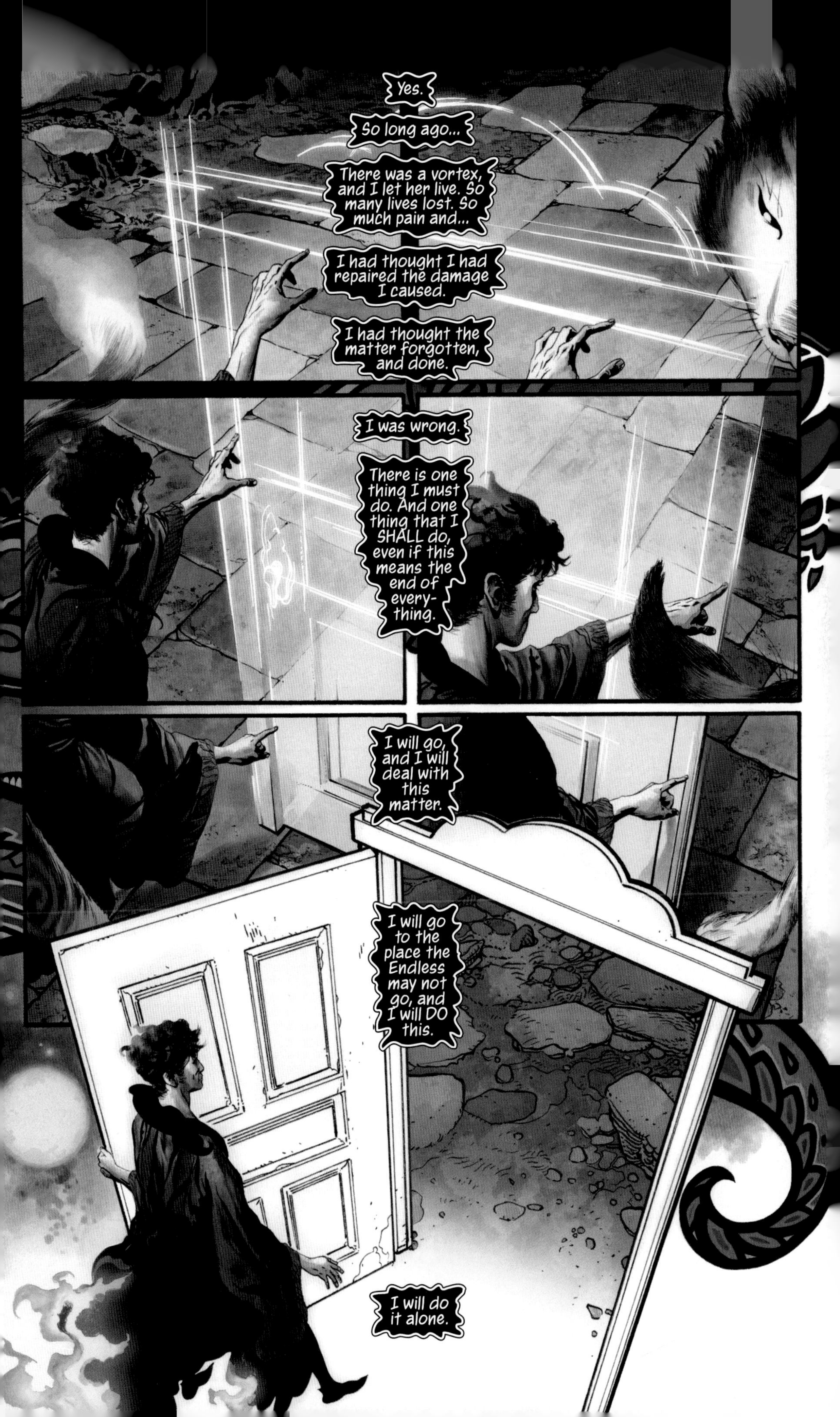
Yes.
So long ago...
There was a vortex, and I let her live. So many lives lost. So much pain and...
I had thought I had repaired the damage I caused.
I had thought the matter forgotten, and done.
I was wrong.
There is one thing I must do. And one thing that I SHALL do, even if this means the end of every-thing.
I will go, and I will deal with this matter.
I will go to the place the Endless may not go, and I will DO this.
I will do it alone.

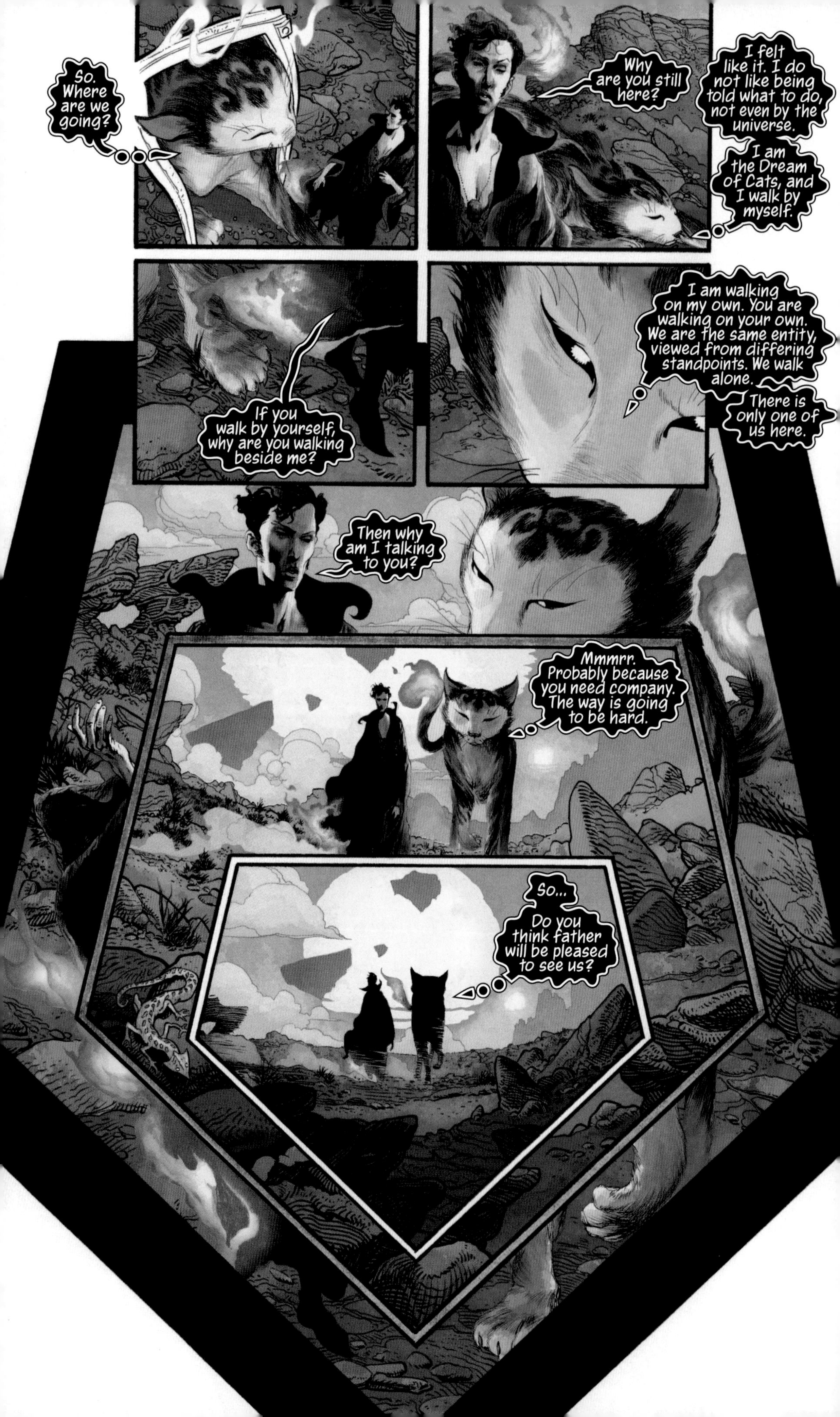
So. Where are we going?
Why are you still here?
I felt like it. I do not like being told what to do, not even by the universe.
I am the Dream of Cats, and I walk by myself.
If you walk by yourself, why are you walking beside me?
I am walking on my own. You are walking on your own. We are the same entity, viewed from differing standpoints. We walk alone.
There is only one of us here.
Then why am I talking to you?
Mmmrr. Probably because you need company. The way is going to be hard.
So...
Do you think father will be pleased to see us?

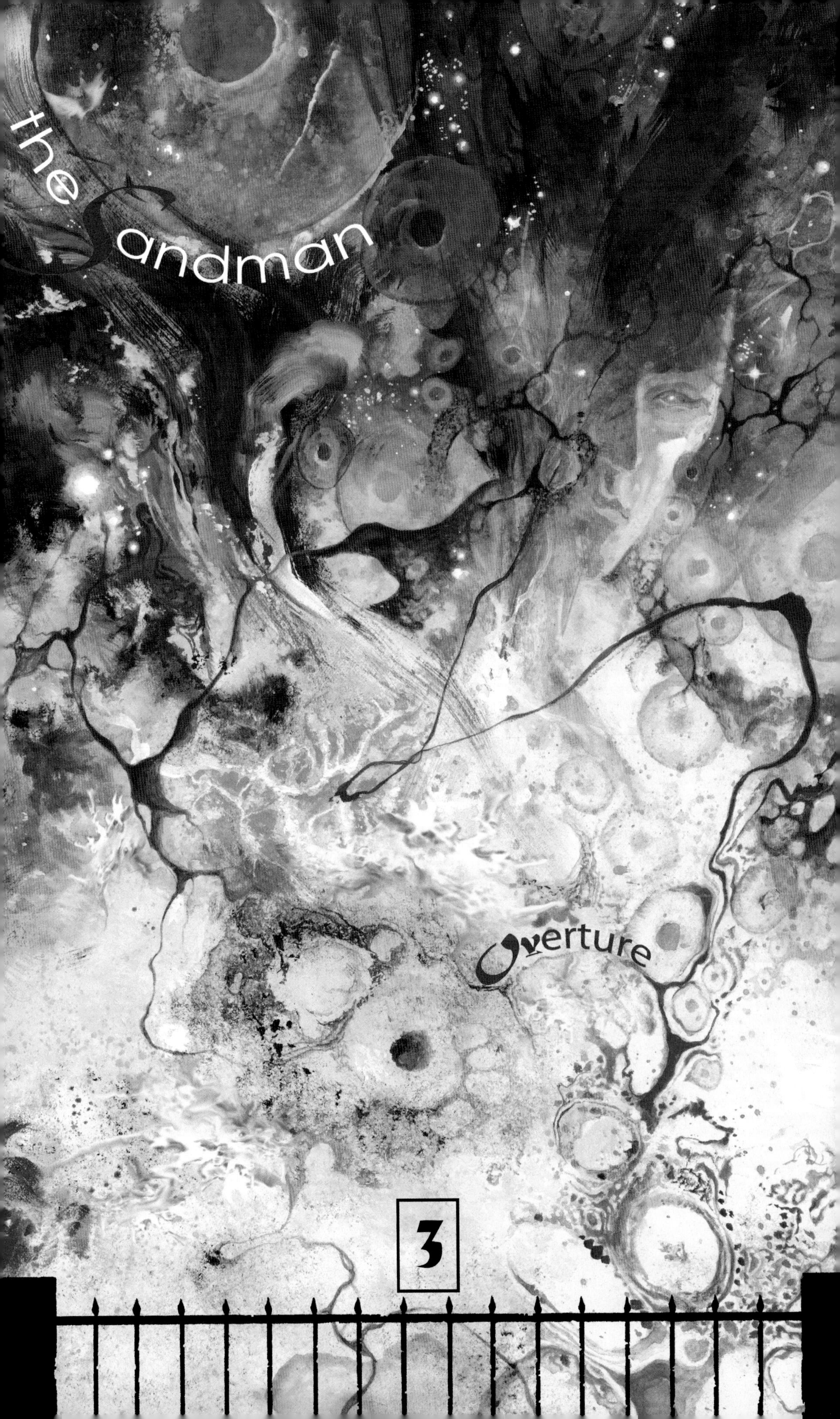
the Sandman
Overture
3

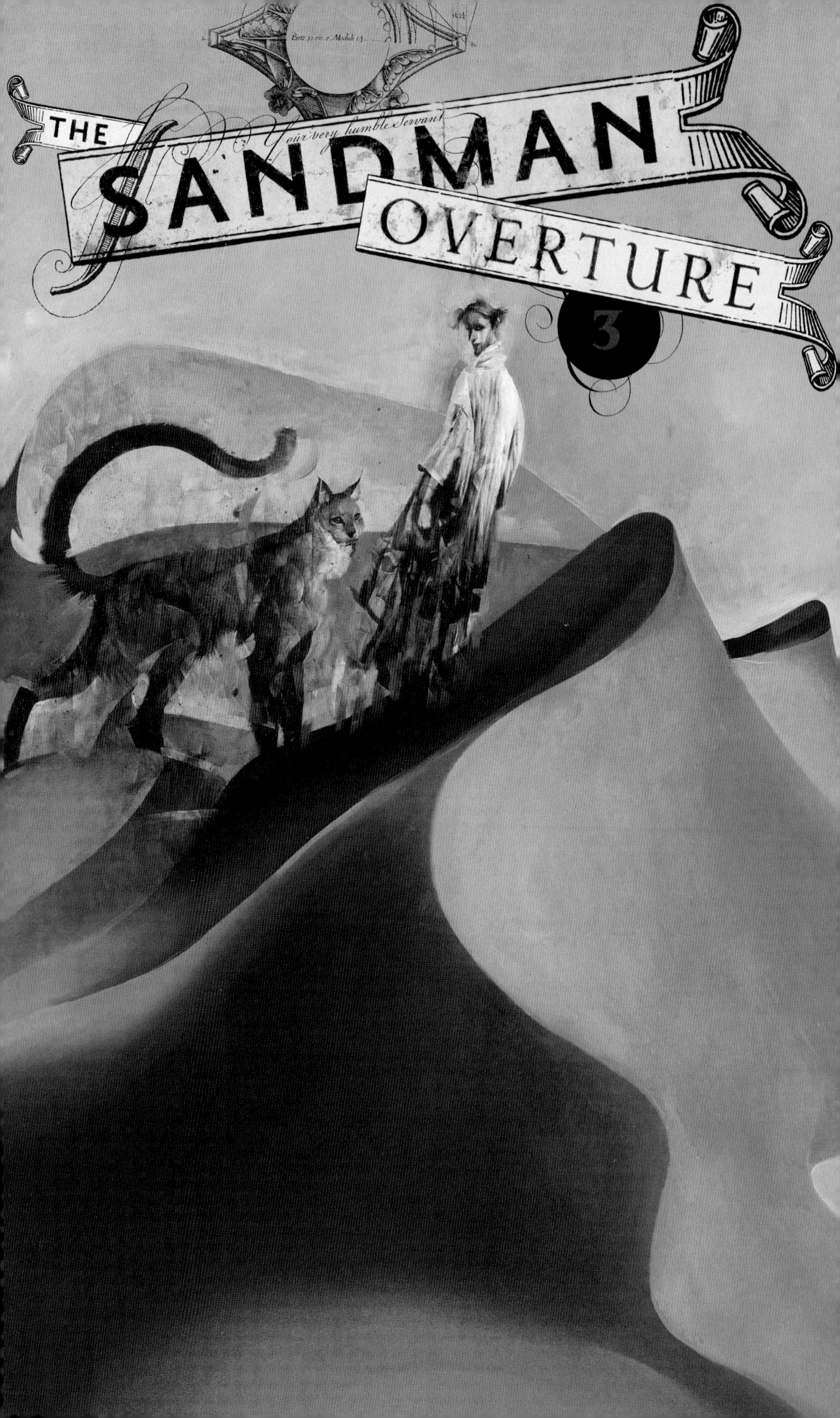
THE
SANDMAN
OVERTURE
3
Your very humble Servant
Parte 30 e Moduli 13

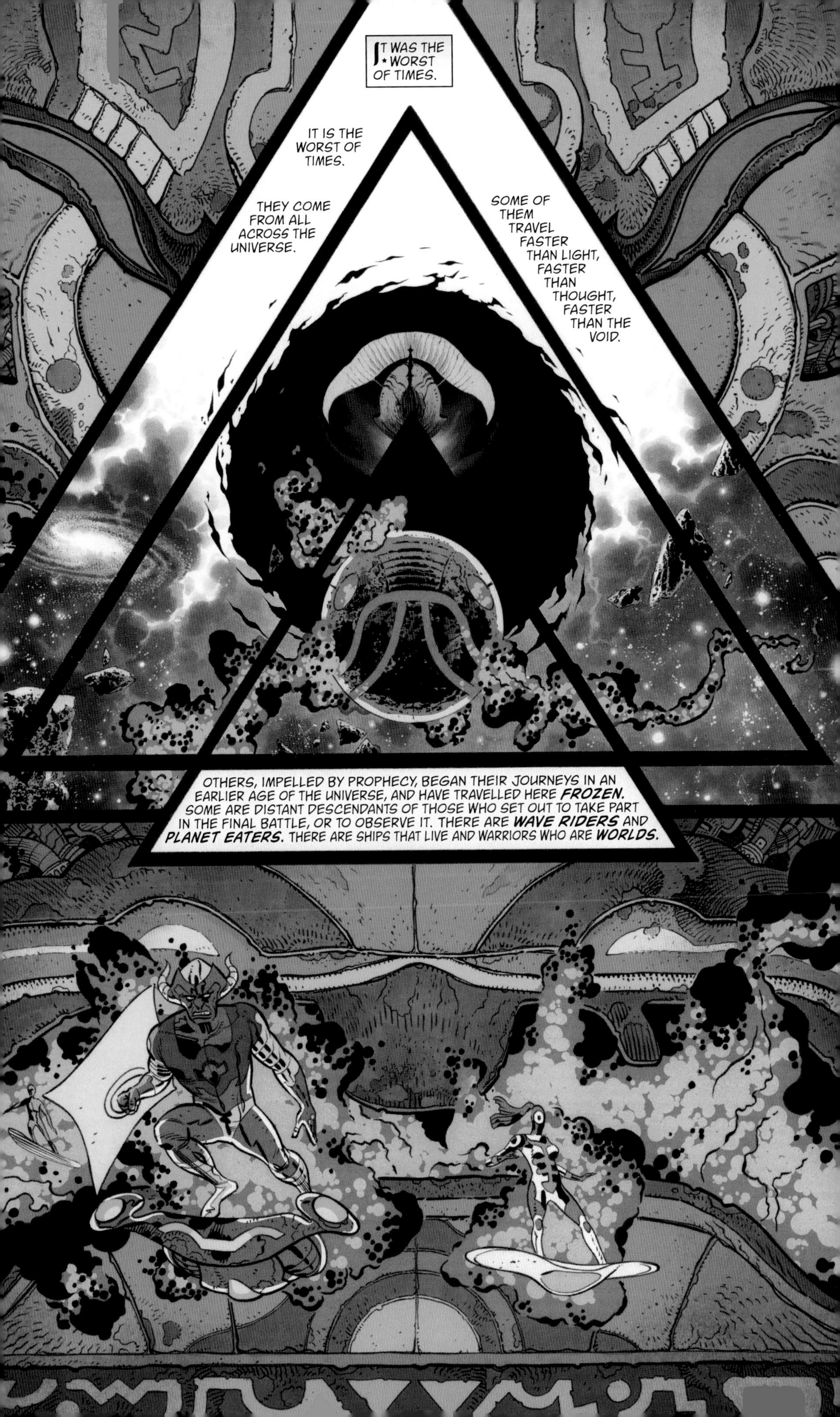
IT WAS THE WORST OF TIMES.
IT IS THE WORST OF TIMES.
THEY COME FROM ALL ACROSS THE UNIVERSE.
SOME OF THEM TRAVEL FASTER THAN LIGHT, FASTER THAN THOUGHT, FASTER THAN THE VOID.
OTHERS, IMPELLED BY PROPHECY, BEGAN THEIR JOURNEYS IN AN EARLIER AGE OF THE UNIVERSE, AND HAVE TRAVELLED HERE FROZEN. SOME ARE DISTANT DESCENDANTS OF THOSE WHO SET OUT TO TAKE PART IN THE FINAL BATTLE, OR TO OBSERVE IT. THERE ARE WAVE RIDERS AND PLANET EATERS. THERE ARE SHIPS THAT LIVE AND WARRIORS WHO ARE WORLDS.

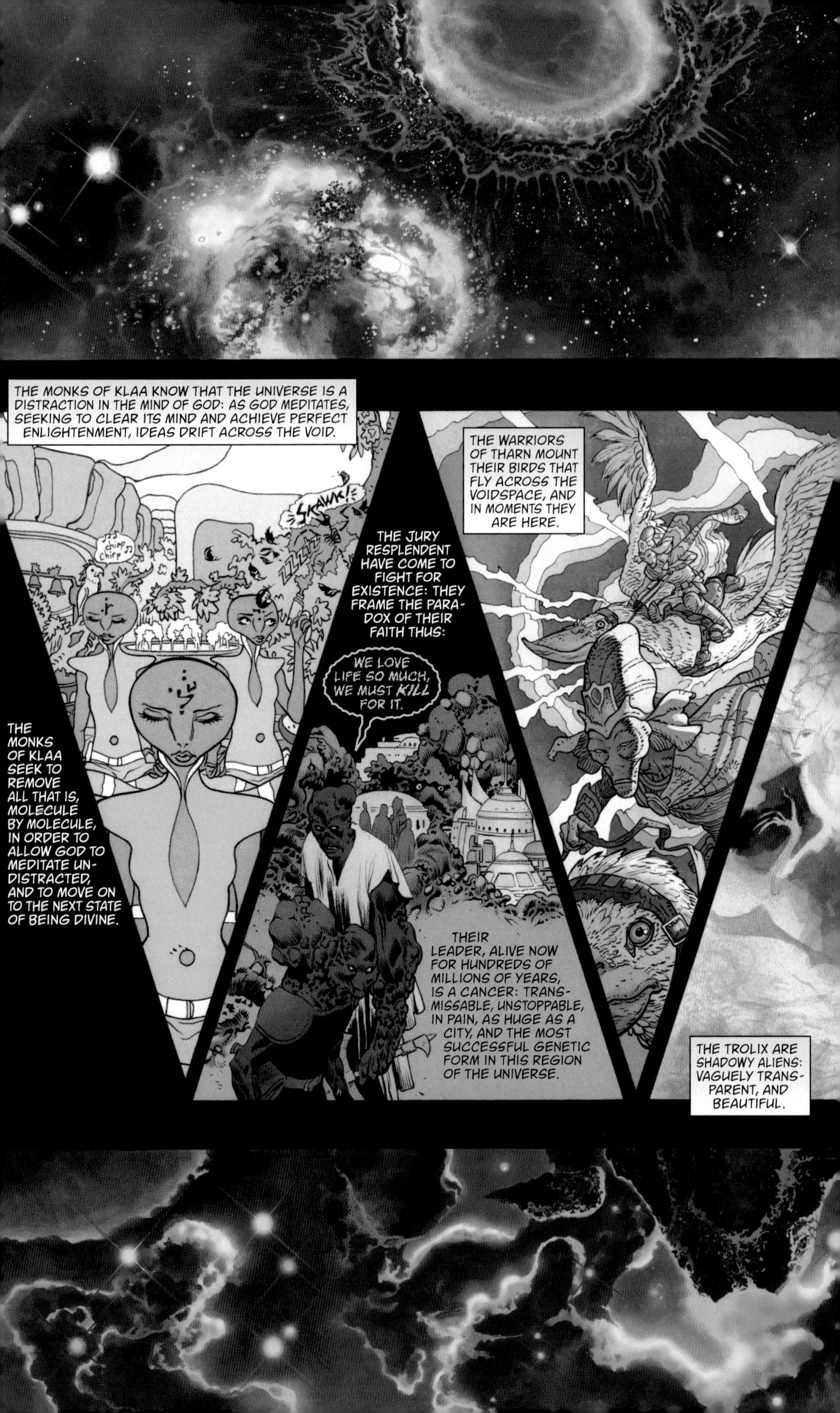
THE MONKS OF KLAA KNOW THAT THE UNIVERSE IS A DISTRACTION IN THE MIND OF GOD: AS GOD MEDITATES, SEEKING TO CLEAR ITS MIND AND ACHIEVE PERFECT ENLIGHTENMENT, IDEAS DRIFT ACROSS THE VOID.
SKAWK!
chirp Chirp
THE MONKS OF KLAA SEEK TO REMOVE ALL THAT IS, MOLECULE BY MOLECULE, IN ORDER TO ALLOW GOD TO MEDITATE UN-DISTRACTED, AND TO MOVE ON TO THE NEXT STATE OF BEING DIVINE.
THE JURY RESPLENDENT HAVE COME TO FIGHT FOR EXISTENCE: THEY FRAME THE PARA-DOX OF THEIR FAITH THUS:
WE LOVE LIFE SO MUCH, WE MUST KILL FOR IT.
THEIR LEADER, ALIVE NOW FOR HUNDREDS OF MILLIONS OF YEARS, IS A CANCER: TRANS-MISSABLE, UNSTOPPABLE, IN PAIN, AS HUGE AS A CITY, AND THE MOST SUCCESSFUL GENETIC FORM IN THIS REGION OF THE UNIVERSE.
THE WARRIORS OF THARN MOUNT THEIR BIRDS THAT FLY ACROSS THE VOIDSPACE, AND IN MOMENTS THEY ARE HERE.
THE TROLIX ARE SHADOWY ALIENS: VAGUELY TRANS-PARENT, AND BEAUTIFUL.

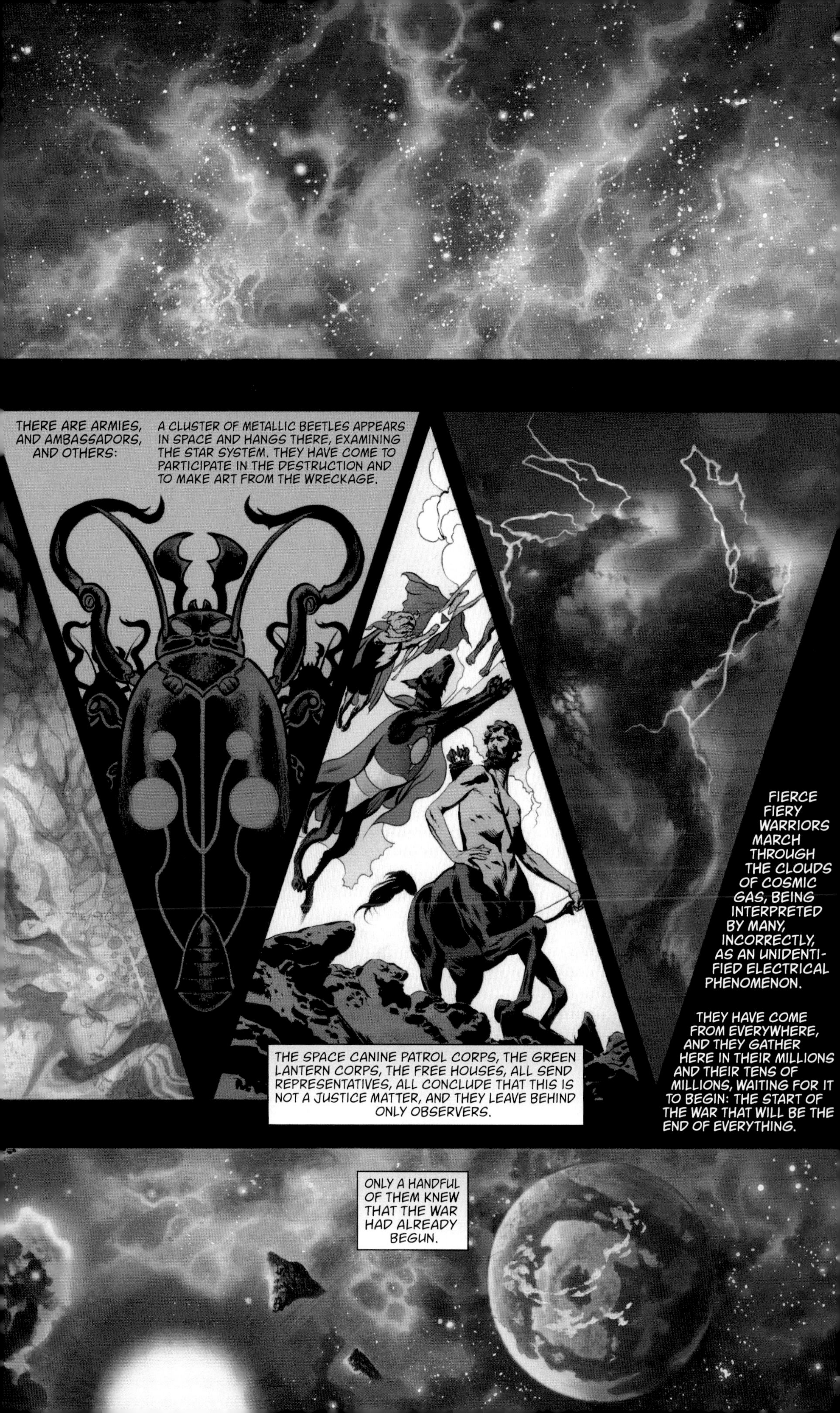
THERE ARE ARMIES, AND AMBASSADORS, AND OTHERS:
A CLUSTER OF METALLIC BEETLES APPEARS IN SPACE AND HANGS THERE, EXAMINING THE STAR SYSTEM. THEY HAVE COME TO PARTICIPATE IN THE DESTRUCTION AND TO MAKE ART FROM THE WRECKAGE.
THE SPACE CANINE PATROL CORPS, THE GREEN LANTERN CORPS, THE FREE HOUSES, ALL SEND REPRESENTATIVES, ALL CONCLUDE THAT THIS IS NOT A JUSTICE MATTER, AND THEY LEAVE BEHIND ONLY OBSERVERS.
FIERCE FIERY WARRIORS MARCH THROUGH THE CLOUDS OF COSMIC GAS, BEING INTERPRETED BY MANY, INCORRECTLY, AS AN UNIDENTIFIED ELECTRICAL PHENOMENON.
THEY HAVE COME FROM EVERYWHERE, AND THEY GATHER HERE IN THEIR MILLIONS AND THEIR TENS OF MILLIONS, WAITING FOR IT TO BEGIN: THE START OF THE WAR THAT WILL BE THE END OF EVERYTHING.
ONLY A HANDFUL OF THEM KNEW THAT THE WAR HAD ALREADY BEGUN.

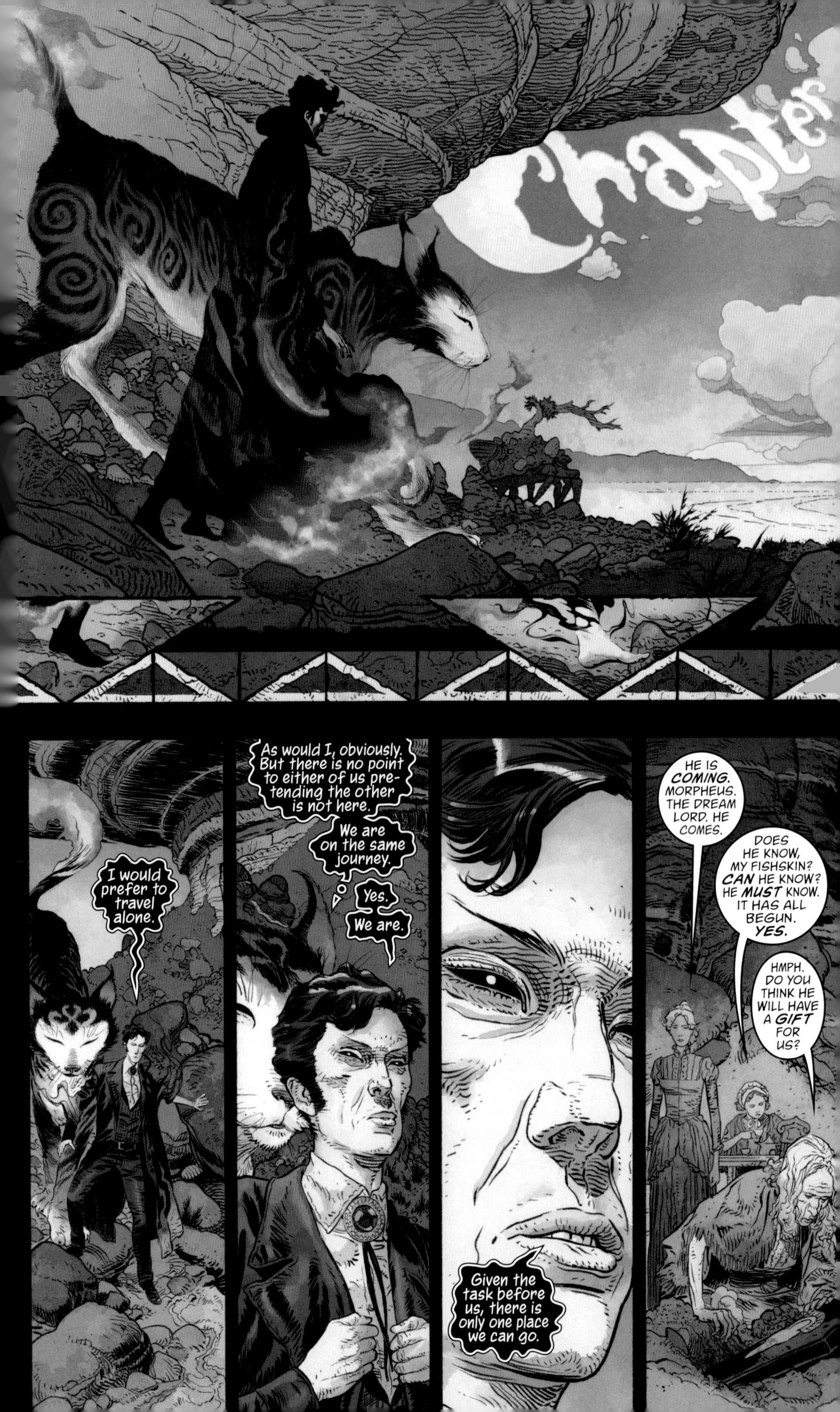

Chapter
I would prefer to travel alone.
As would I, obviously. But there is no point to either of us pretending the other is not here.
We are on the same journey.
Yes.
We are.
Given the task before us, there is only one place we can go.
HE IS COMING. MORPHEUS. THE DREAM LORD. HE COMES.
DOES HE KNOW, MY FISHSKIN? CAN HE KNOW? HE MUST KNOW. IT HAS ALL BEGUN. YES.
HMPH. DO YOU THINK HE WILL HAVE A GIFT FOR US?

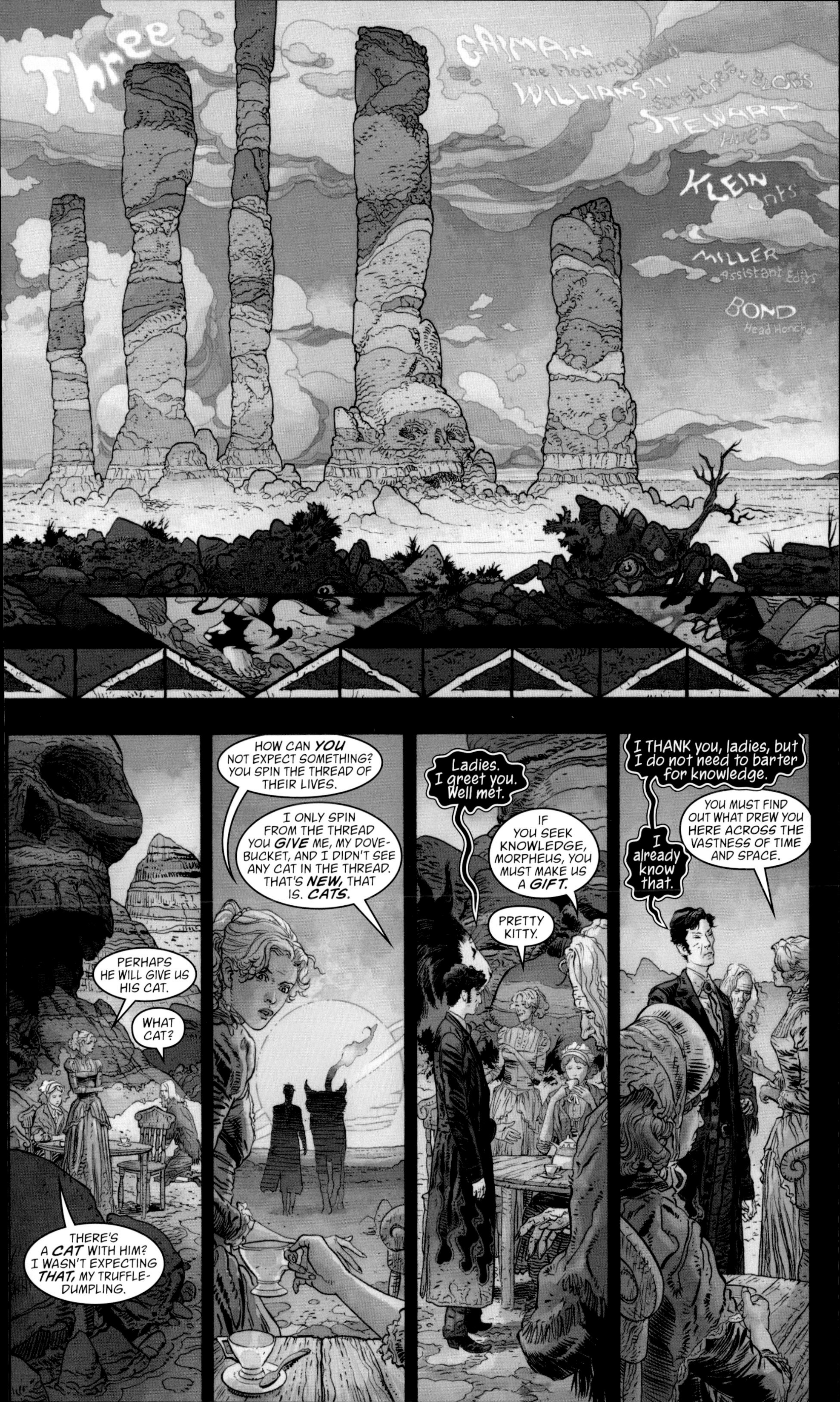
Three
GAIMAN
The Floating Island
WILLIAMS III
Scratches & BLOBS
STEWART
Hues
KLEIN
Fonts
MILLER
Assistant Edits
BOND
Head Honcho
PERHAPS HE WILL GIVE US HIS CAT.
WHAT CAT?
THERE'S A CAT WITH HIM? I WASN'T EXPECTING THAT, MY TRUFFLE-DUMPLING.
HOW CAN YOU NOT EXPECT SOMETHING? YOU SPIN THE THREAD OF THEIR LIVES.
I ONLY SPIN FROM THE THREAD YOU GIVE ME, MY DOVE-BUCKET, AND I DIDN'T SEE ANY CAT IN THE THREAD. THAT'S NEW, THAT IS. CATS.
Ladies. I greet you. Well met.
IF YOU SEEK KNOWLEDGE, MORPHEUS, YOU MUST MAKE US A GIFT.
PRETTY KITTY.
I THANK you, ladies, but I do not need to barter for knowledge.
YOU MUST FIND OUT WHAT DREW YOU HERE ACROSS THE VASTNESS OF TIME AND SPACE.
I already know that.

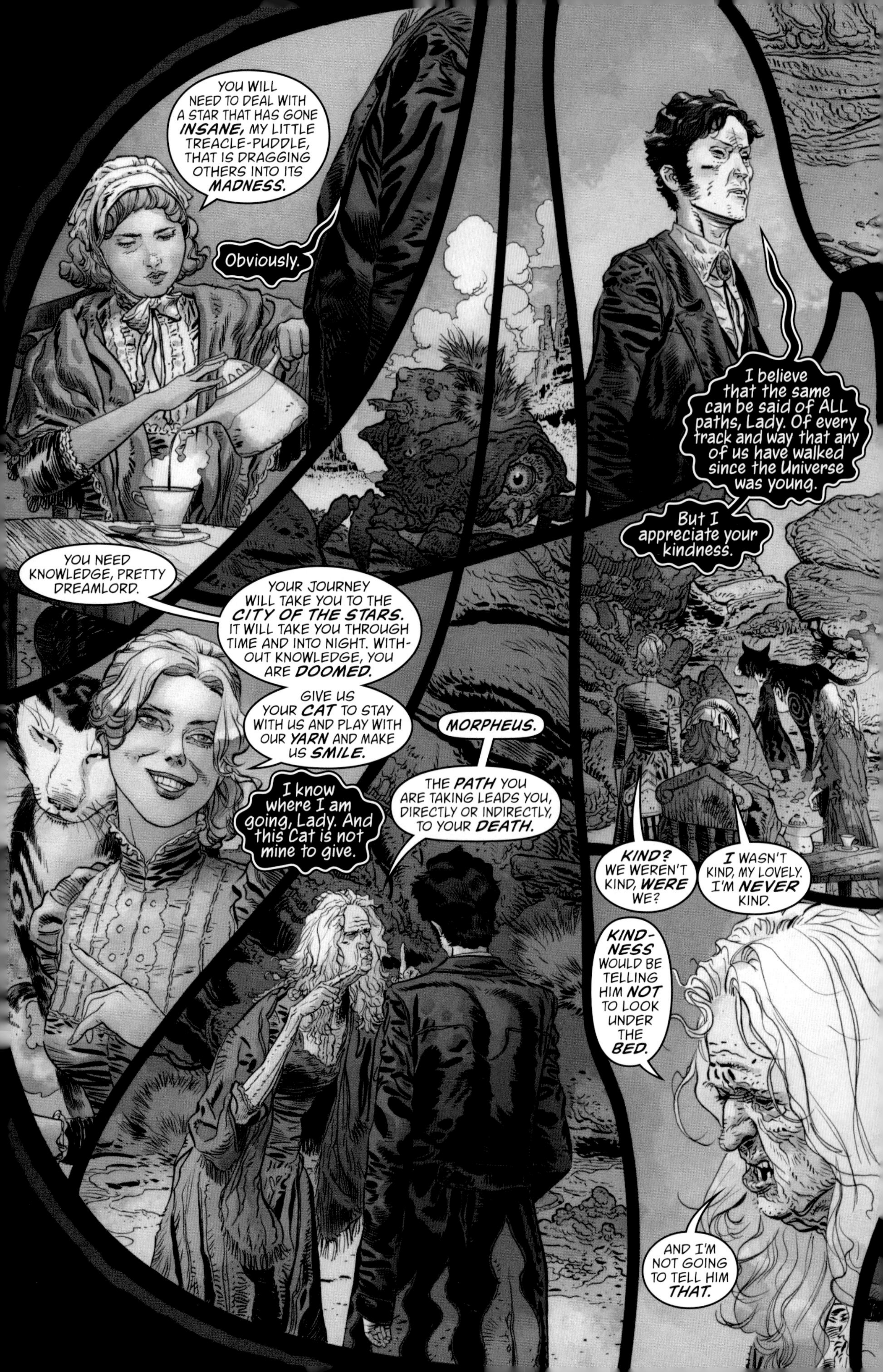
YOU WILL NEED TO DEAL WITH A STAR THAT HAS GONE INSANE, MY LITTLE TREACLE-PUDDLE, THAT IS DRAGGING OTHERS INTO ITS MADNESS.
Obviously.
I believe that the same can be said of ALL paths, Lady. Of every track and way that any of us have walked since the Universe was young.
But I appreciate your kindness.
YOU NEED KNOWLEDGE, PRETTY DREAMLORD.
YOUR JOURNEY WILL TAKE YOU TO THE CITY OF THE STARS. IT WILL TAKE YOU THROUGH TIME AND INTO NIGHT. WITH-OUT KNOWLEDGE, YOU ARE DOOMED.
GIVE US YOUR CAT TO STAY WITH US AND PLAY WITH OUR YARN AND MAKE US SMILE.
I know where I am going, Lady. And this Cat is not mine to give.
MORPHEUS.
THE PATH YOU ARE TAKING LEADS YOU, DIRECTLY OR INDIRECTLY, TO YOUR DEATH.
KIND? WE WEREN'T KIND, WERE WE?
I WASN'T KIND, MY LOVELY. I'M NEVER KIND.
KINDNESS WOULD BE TELLING HIM NOT TO LOOK UNDER THE BED.
AND I'M NOT GOING TO TELL HIM THAT.

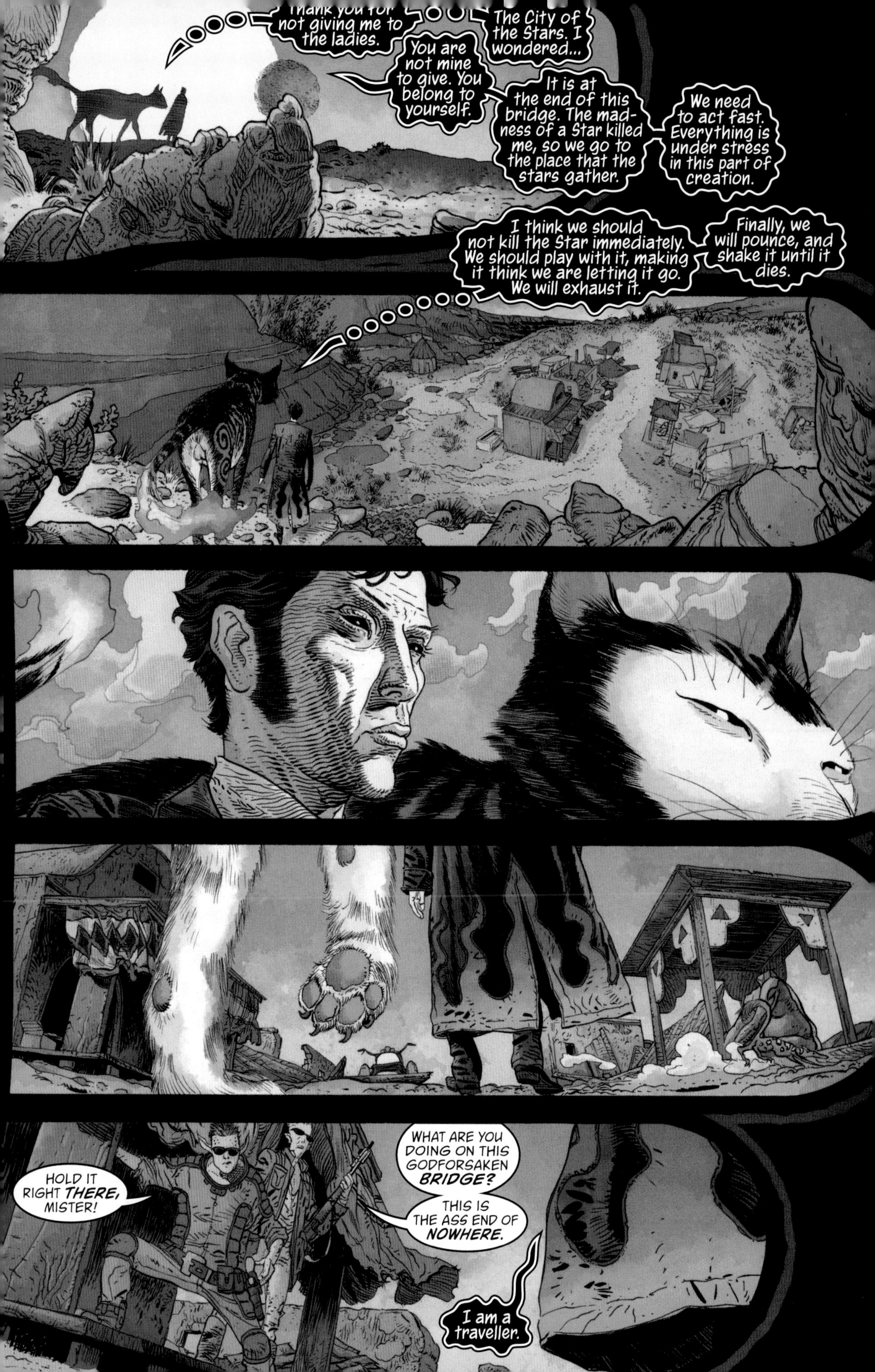
Thank you for not giving me to the ladies.
The City of the Stars. I wondered...
You are not mine to give. You belong to yourself.
It is at the end of this bridge. The madness of a Star killed me, so we go to the place that the stars gather.
We need to act fast. Everything is under stress in this part of creation.
I think we should not kill the Star immediately. We should play with it, making it think we are letting it go. We will exhaust it.
Finally, we will pounce, and shake it until it dies.
HOLD IT RIGHT THERE, MISTER!
WHAT ARE YOU DOING ON THIS GODFORSAKEN BRIDGE?
THIS IS THE ASS END OF NOWHERE.
I am a traveller.

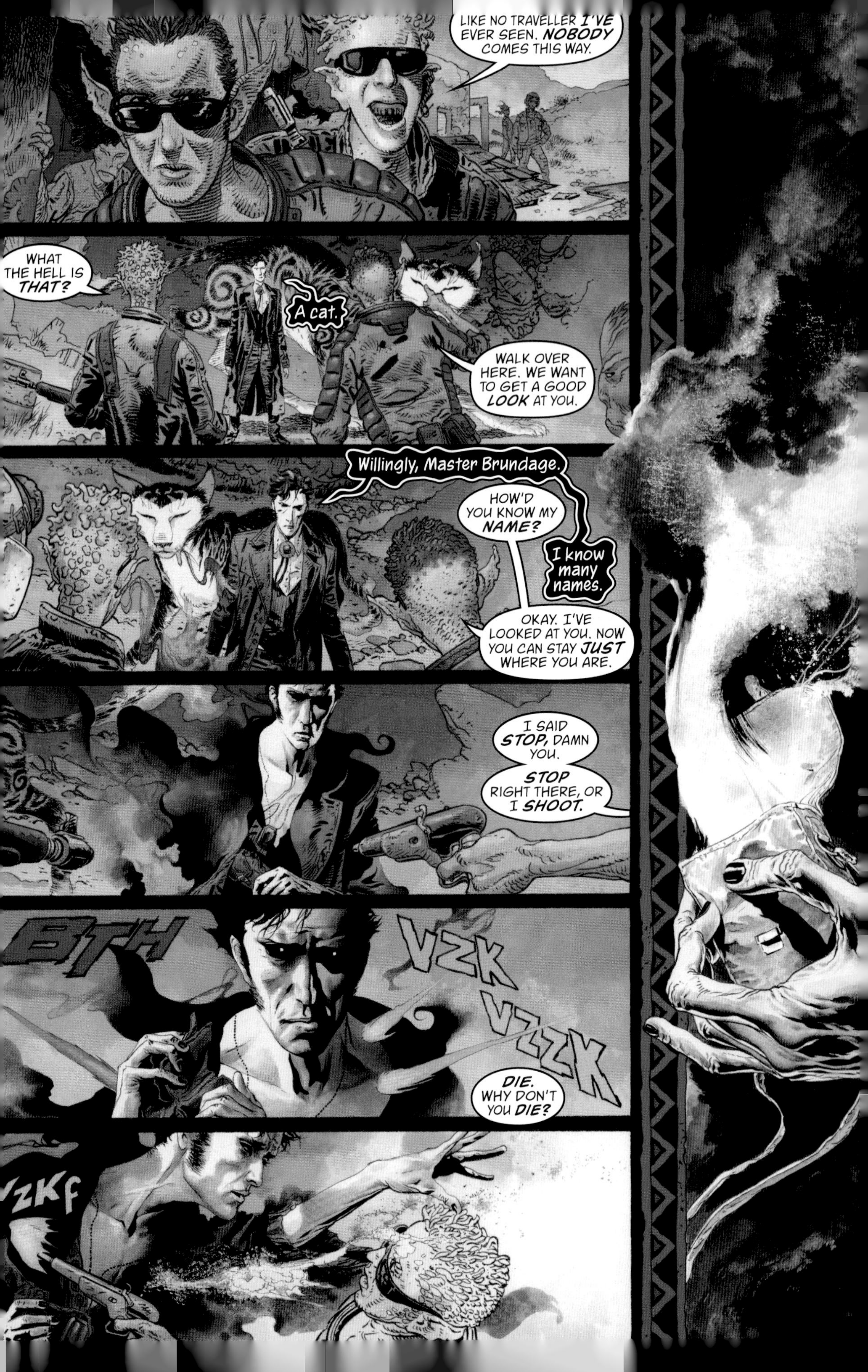
LIKE NO TRAVELLER I'VE EVER SEEN. NOBODY COMES THIS WAY.
WHAT THE HELL IS THAT?
A cat.
WALK OVER HERE. WE WANT TO GET A GOOD LOOK AT YOU.
Willingly, Master Brundage.
HOW'D YOU KNOW MY NAME?
I know many names.
OKAY. I'VE LOOKED AT YOU. NOW YOU CAN STAY JUST WHERE YOU ARE.
I SAID STOP, DAMN YOU.
STOP RIGHT THERE, OR I SHOOT.
BTH
VZK
VZZK
DIE. WHY DON'T YOU DIE?
VZKF

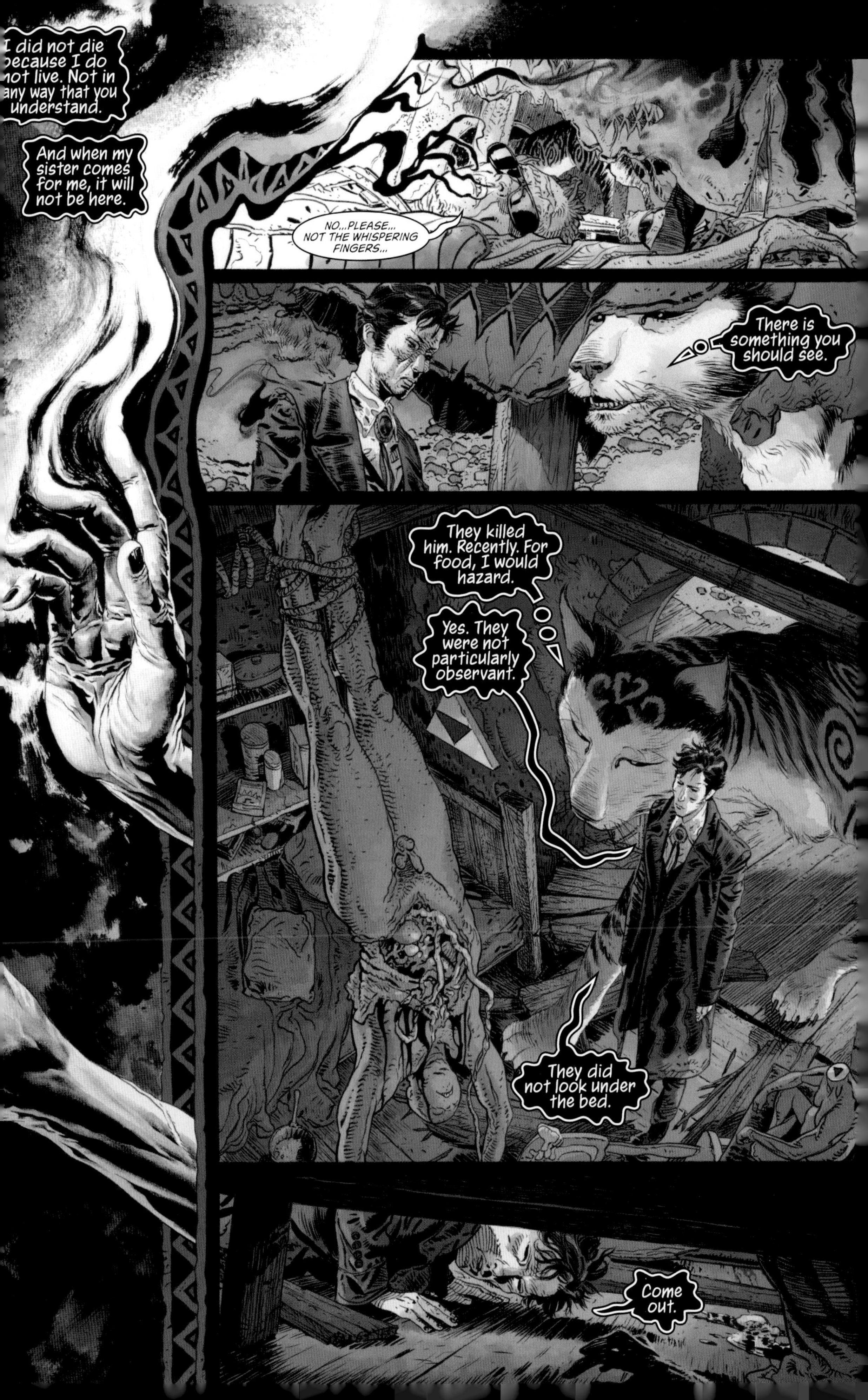
I did not die because I do not live. Not in any way that you understand.
And when my sister comes for me, it will not be here.
NO... PLEASE... NOT THE WHISPERING FINGERS...
There is something you should see.
They killed him. Recently. For food, I would hazard.
Yes. They were not particularly observant.
They did not look under the bed.
Come out.

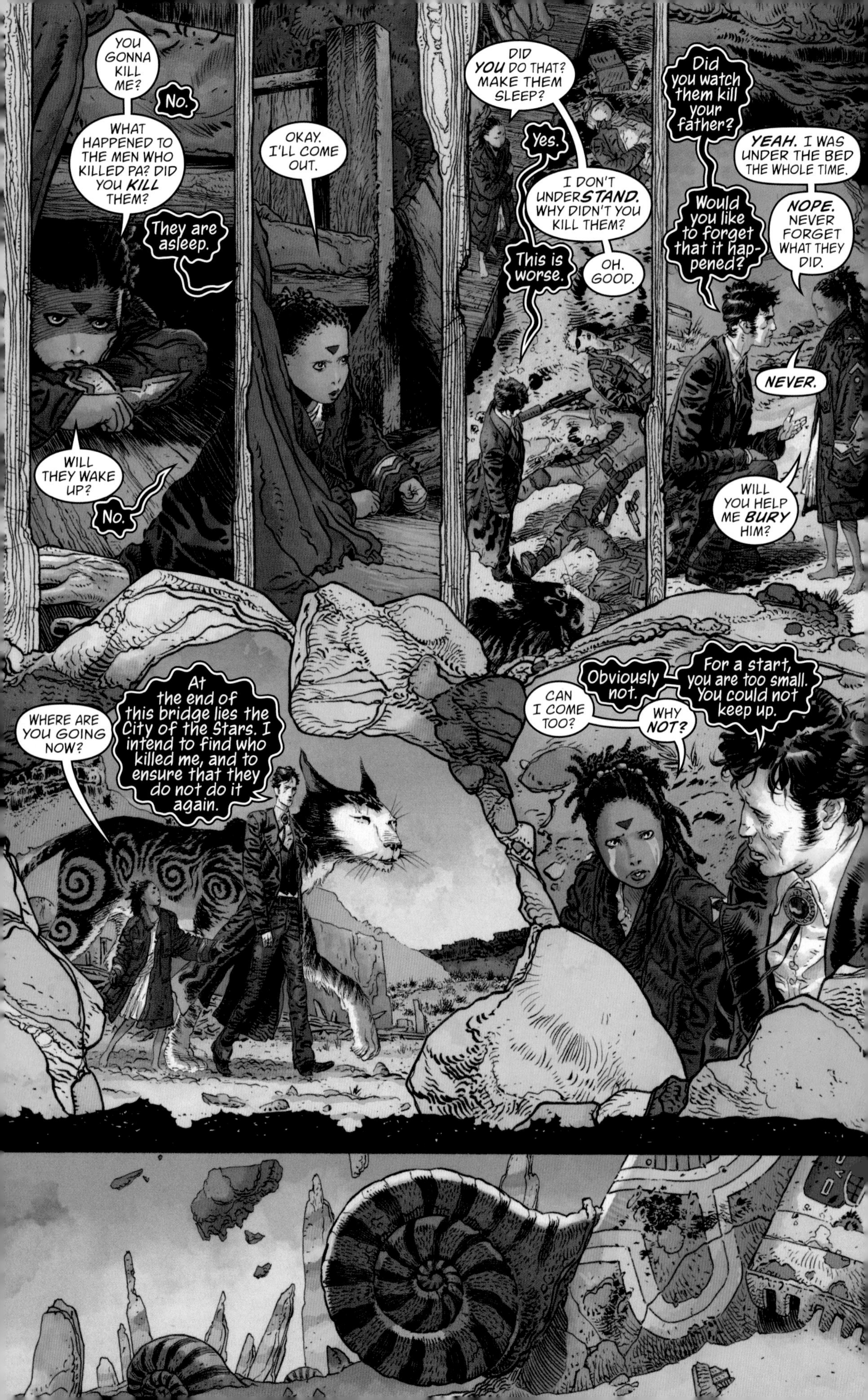
YOU GONNA KILL ME?
No.
WHAT HAPPENED TO THE MEN WHO KILLED PA? DID YOU KILL THEM?
They are asleep.
WILL THEY WAKE UP?
No.
OKAY. I'LL COME OUT.
DID YOU DO THAT? MAKE THEM SLEEP?
Yes.
I DON'T UNDERSTAND. WHY DIDN'T YOU KILL THEM?
This is worse.
OH. GOOD.
Did you watch them kill your father?
YEAH. I WAS UNDER THE BED THE WHOLE TIME.
Would you like to forget that it happened?
NOPE. NEVER FORGET WHAT THEY DID.
NEVER.
WILL YOU HELP ME BURY HIM?
WHERE ARE YOU GOING NOW?
At the end of this bridge lies the City of the Stars. I intend to find who killed me, and to ensure that they do not do it again.
CAN I COME TOO?
Obviously not.
WHY NOT?
For a start, you are too small. You could not keep up.

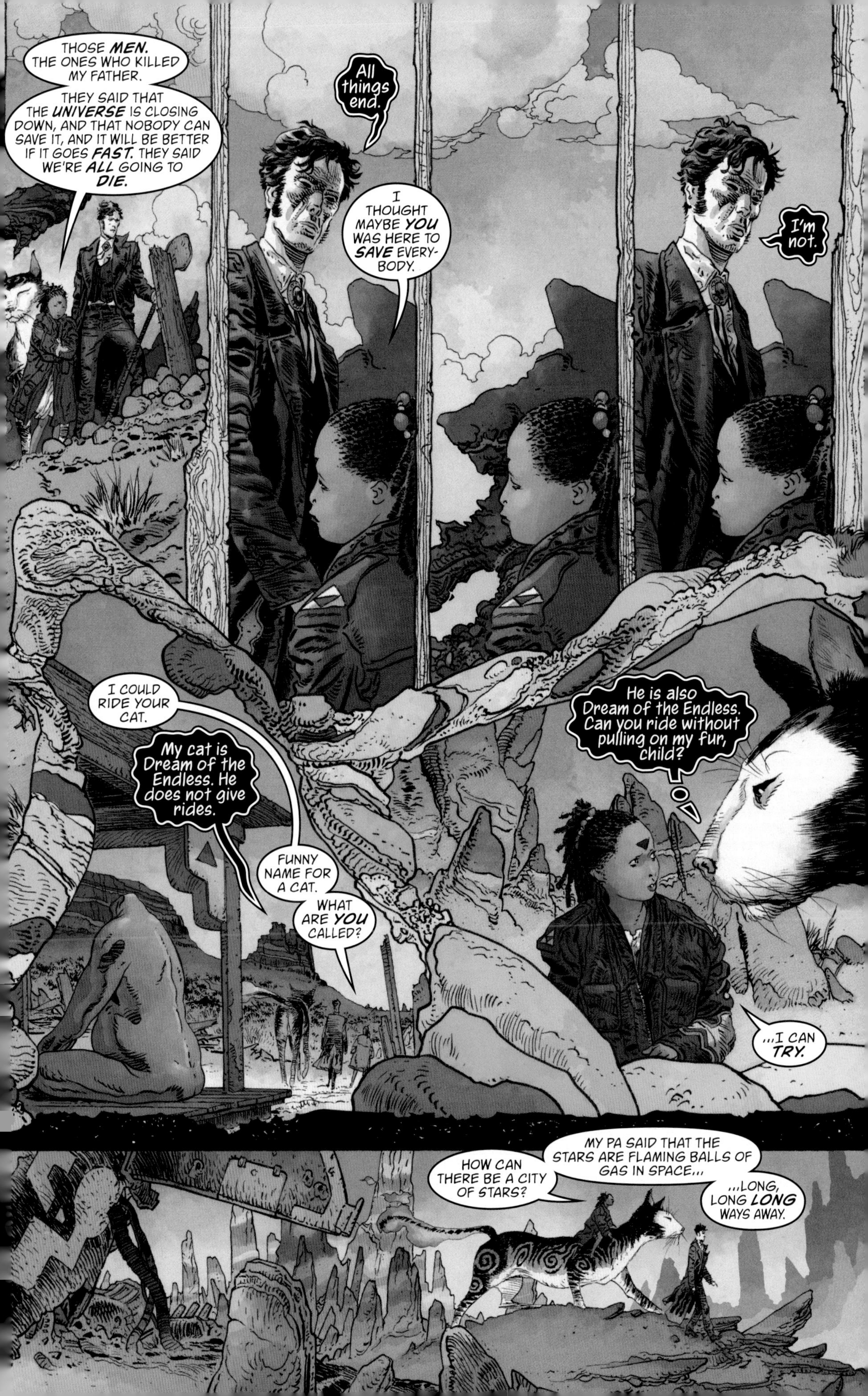
THOSE MEN. THE ONES WHO KILLED MY FATHER.
THEY SAID THAT THE UNIVERSE IS CLOSING DOWN, AND THAT NOBODY CAN SAVE IT, AND IT WILL BE BETTER IF IT GOES FAST. THEY SAID WE'RE ALL GOING TO DIE.
All things end.
I THOUGHT MAYBE YOU WAS HERE TO SAVE EVERY-BODY.
I'm not.
I COULD RIDE YOUR CAT.
My cat is Dream of the Endless. He does not give rides.
FUNNY NAME FOR A CAT.
WHAT ARE YOU CALLED?
He is also Dream of the Endless. Can you ride without pulling on my fur, child?
...I CAN TRY.
HOW CAN THERE BE A CITY OF STARS?
MY PA SAID THAT THE STARS ARE FLAMING BALLS OF GAS IN SPACE...
...LONG, LONG LONG WAYS AWAY.

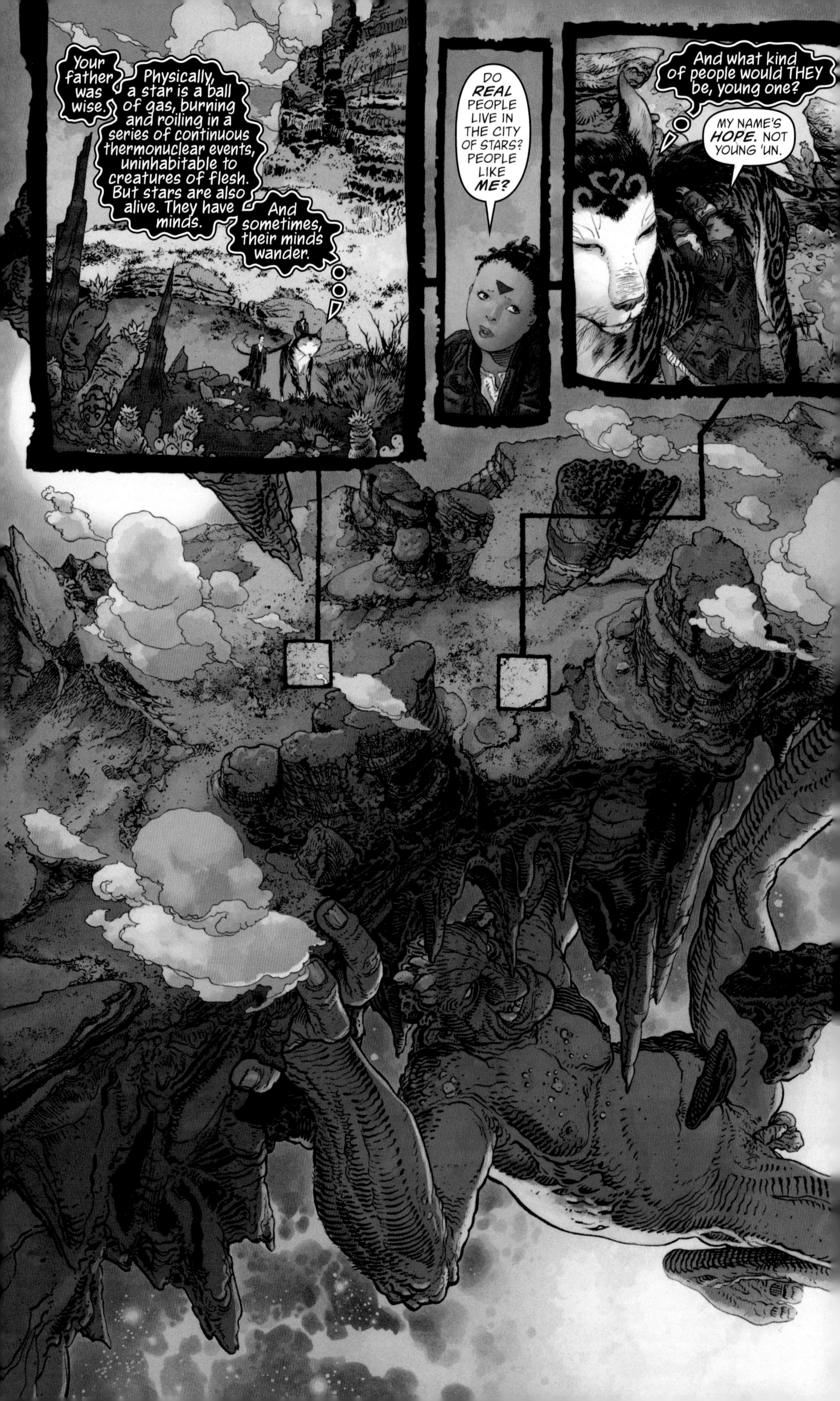
Your father was wise.
Physically, a star is a ball of gas, burning and roiling in a series of continuous thermonuclear events, uninhabitable to creatures of flesh. But stars are also alive. They have minds.
And sometimes, their minds wander.
DO REAL PEOPLE LIVE IN THE CITY OF STARS? PEOPLE LIKE ME?
And what kind of people would THEY be, young one?
MY NAME'S HOPE. NOT YOUNG 'UN.

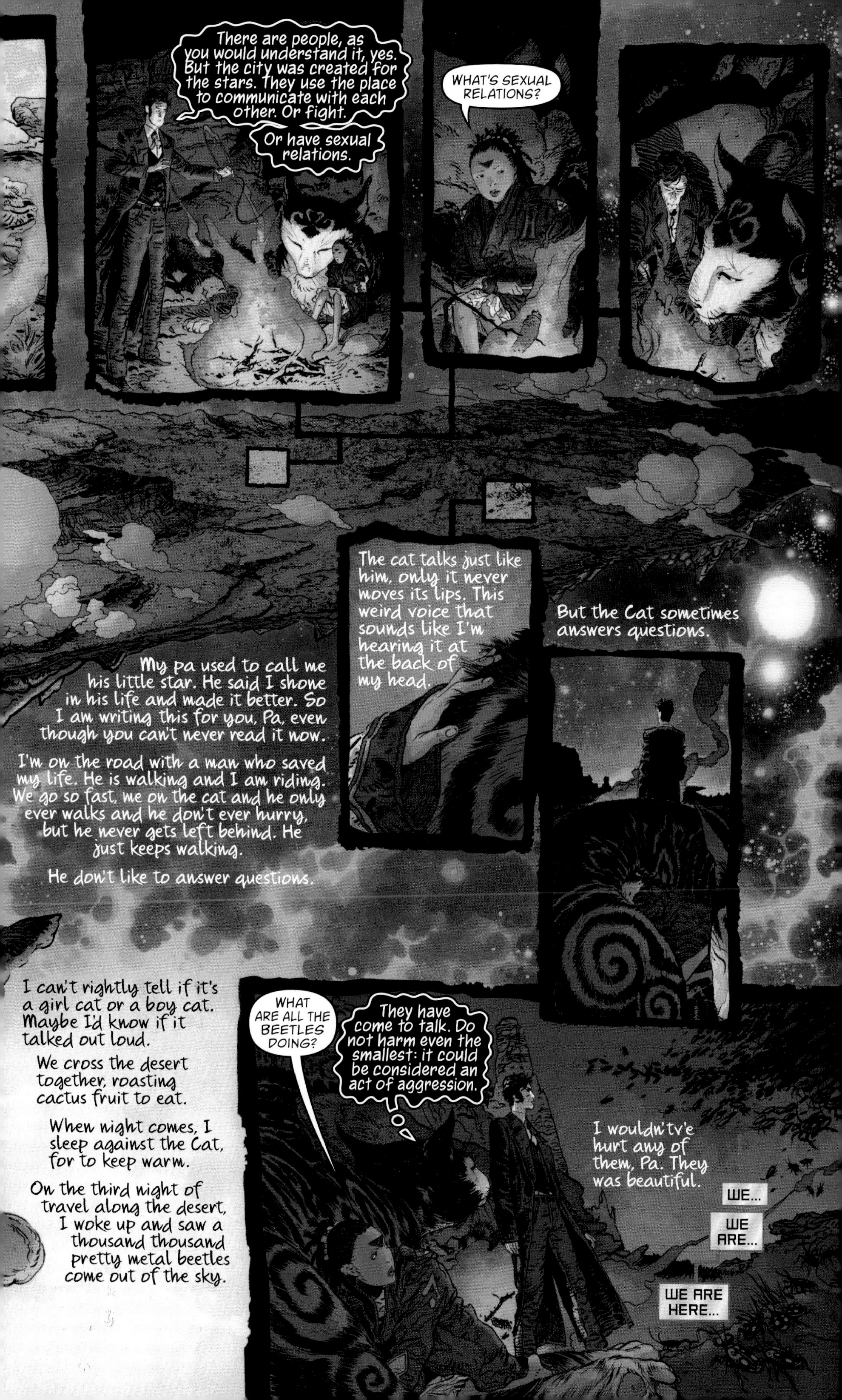
There are people, as you would understand it, yes. But the city was created for the stars. They use the place to communicate with each other. Or fight.
Or have sexual relations.
WHAT'S SEXUAL RELATIONS?
My pa used to call me his little star. He said I shone in his life and made it better. So I am writing this for you, Pa, even though you can't never read it now.
I'm on the road with a man who saved my life. He is walking and I am riding. We go so fast, me on the cat and he only ever walks and he don't ever hurry, but he never gets left behind. He just keeps walking.
He don't like to answer questions.
The cat talks just like him, only it never moves its lips. This weird voice that sounds like I'm hearing it at the back of my head.
But the Cat sometimes answers questions.
I can't rightly tell if it's a girl cat or a boy cat. Maybe I'd know if it talked out loud.
We cross the desert together, roasting cactus fruit to eat.
When night comes, I sleep against the Cat, for to keep warm.
On the third night of travel along the desert, I woke up and saw a thousand thousand pretty metal beetles come out of the sky.
WHAT ARE ALL THE BEETLES DOING?
They have come to talk. Do not harm even the smallest: it could be considered an act of aggression.
I wouldn'tv'e hurt any of them, Pa. They was beautiful.
WE...
WE ARE...
WE ARE HERE...

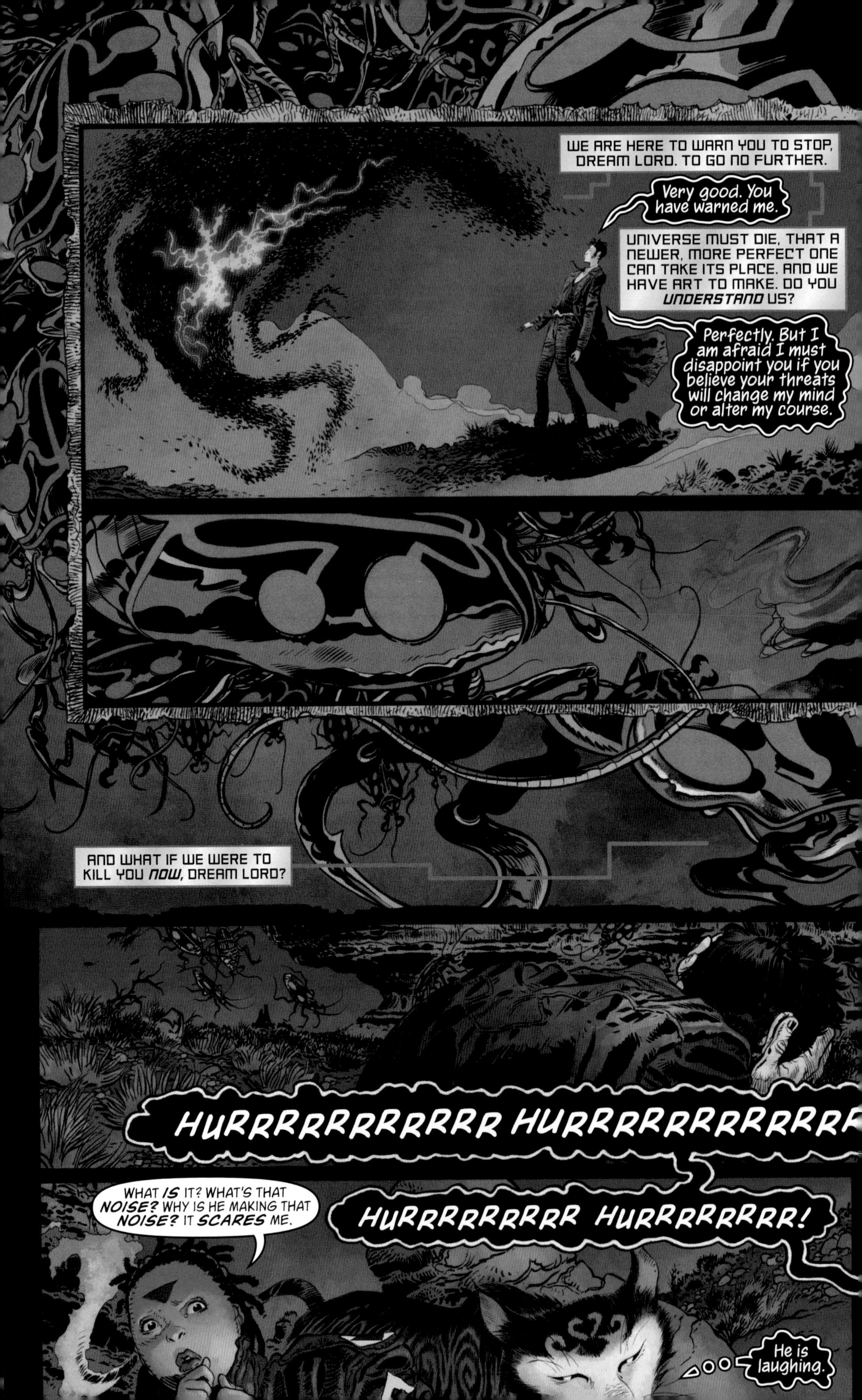
WE ARE HERE TO WARN YOU TO STOP, DREAM LORD. TO GO NO FURTHER.
Very good. You have warned me.
UNIVERSE MUST DIE, THAT A NEWER, MORE PERFECT ONE CAN TAKE ITS PLACE. AND WE HAVE ART TO MAKE. DO YOU UNDERSTAND US?
Perfectly. But I am afraid I must disappoint you if you believe your threats will change my mind or alter my course.
AND WHAT IF WE WERE TO KILL YOU NOW, DREAM LORD?
HURRRRRRRRRRR HURRRRRRRRRRRR
WHAT IS IT? WHAT'S THAT NOISE? WHY IS HE MAKING THAT NOISE? IT SCARES ME.
HURRRRRRRRRR HURRRRRRRRR!
He is laughing.

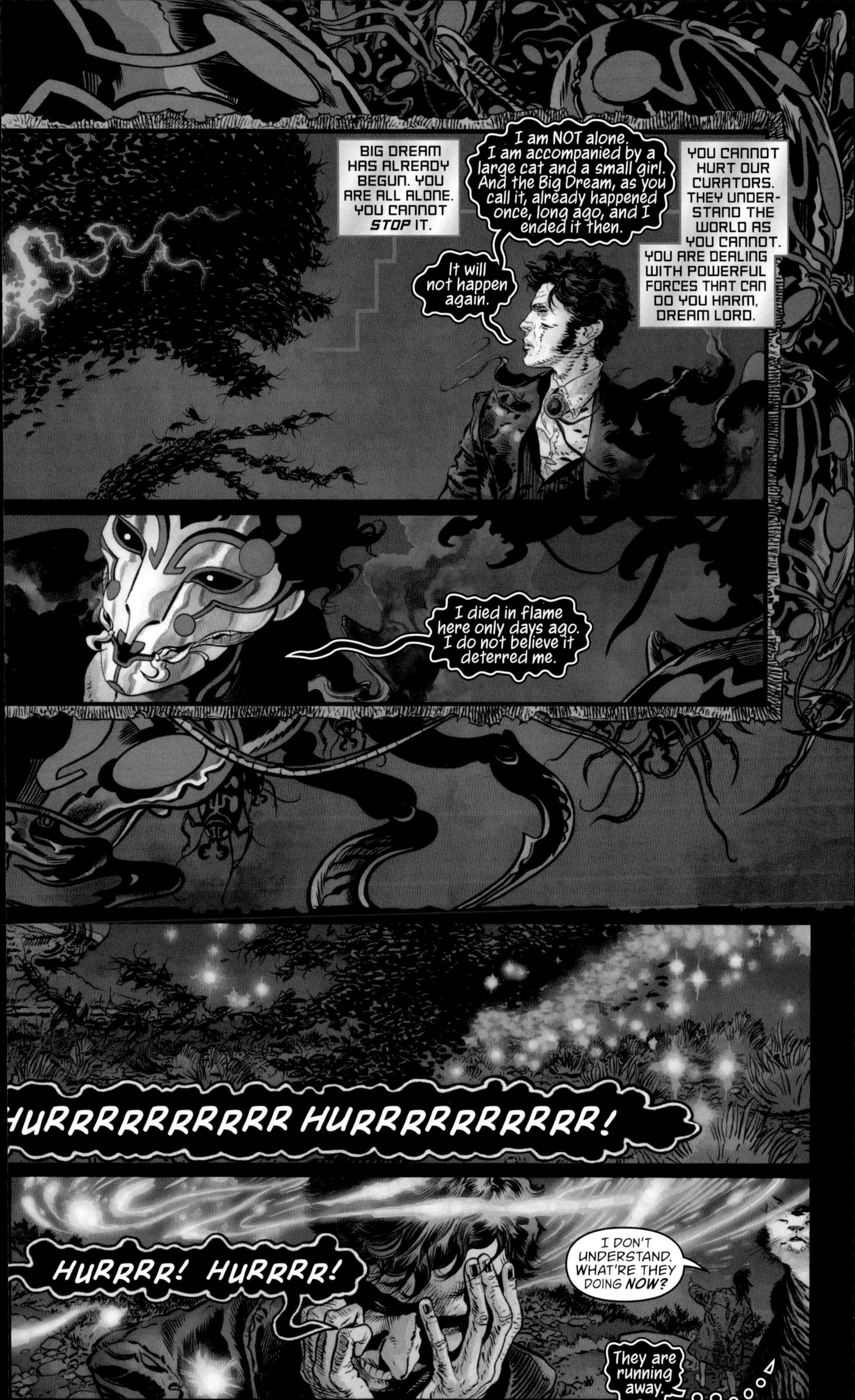

BIG DREAM HAS ALREADY BEGUN. YOU ARE ALL ALONE. YOU CANNOT STOP IT.
I am NOT alone. I am accompanied by a large cat and a small girl. And the Big Dream, as you call it, already happened once, long ago, and I ended it then.
It will not happen again.
YOU CANNOT HURT OUR CURATORS. THEY UNDER-STAND THE WORLD AS YOU CANNOT.
YOU ARE DEALING WITH POWERFUL FORCES THAT CAN DO YOU HARM, DREAM LORD.
I died in flame here only days ago. I do not believe it deterred me.
HURRRRRRRRRR HURRRRRRRRRRR!
HURRRR! HURRRR!
I DON'T UNDERSTAND. WHAT'RE THEY DOING NOW?
They are running away.

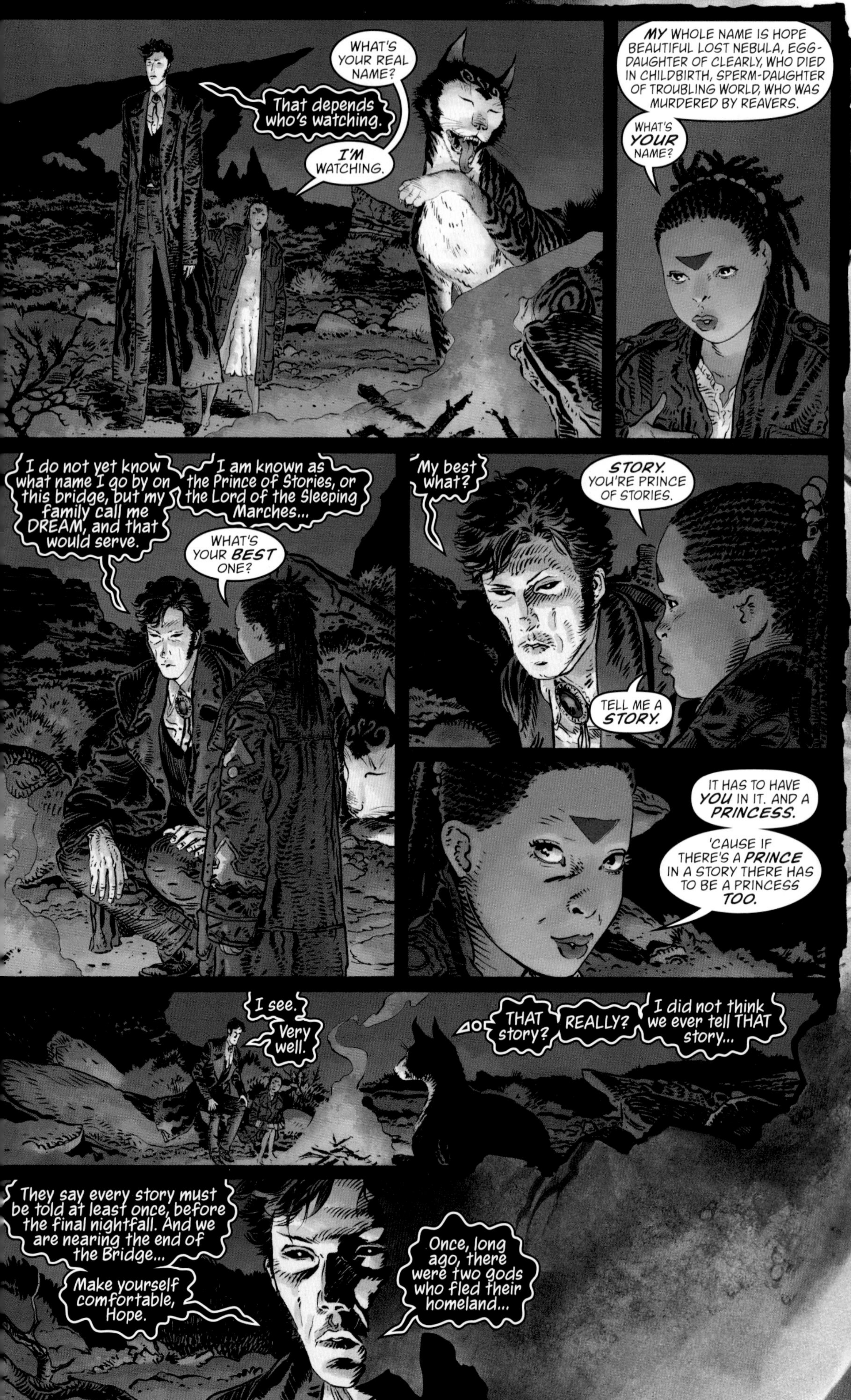
WHAT'S YOUR REAL NAME?
That depends who's watching.
I'M WATCHING.
MY WHOLE NAME IS HOPE BEAUTIFUL LOST NEBULA, EGG-DAUGHTER OF CLEARLY, WHO DIED IN CHILDBIRTH, SPERM-DAUGHTER OF TROUBLING WORLD, WHO WAS MURDERED BY REAVERS.
WHAT'S YOUR NAME?
I do not yet know what name I go by on this bridge, but my family call me DREAM, and that would serve.
I am known as the Prince of Stories, or the Lord of the Sleeping Marches...
WHAT'S YOUR BEST ONE?
My best what?
STORY. YOU'RE PRINCE OF STORIES.
TELL ME A STORY.
IT HAS TO HAVE YOU IN IT. AND A PRINCESS.
'CAUSE IF THERE'S A PRINCE IN A STORY THERE HAS TO BE A PRINCESS TOO.
I see.
Very well.
THAT story?
REALLY?
I did not think we ever tell THAT story...
They say every story must be told at least once, before the final nightfall. And we are nearing the end of the Bridge...
Make yourself comfortable, Hope.
Once, long ago, there were two gods who fled their homeland...

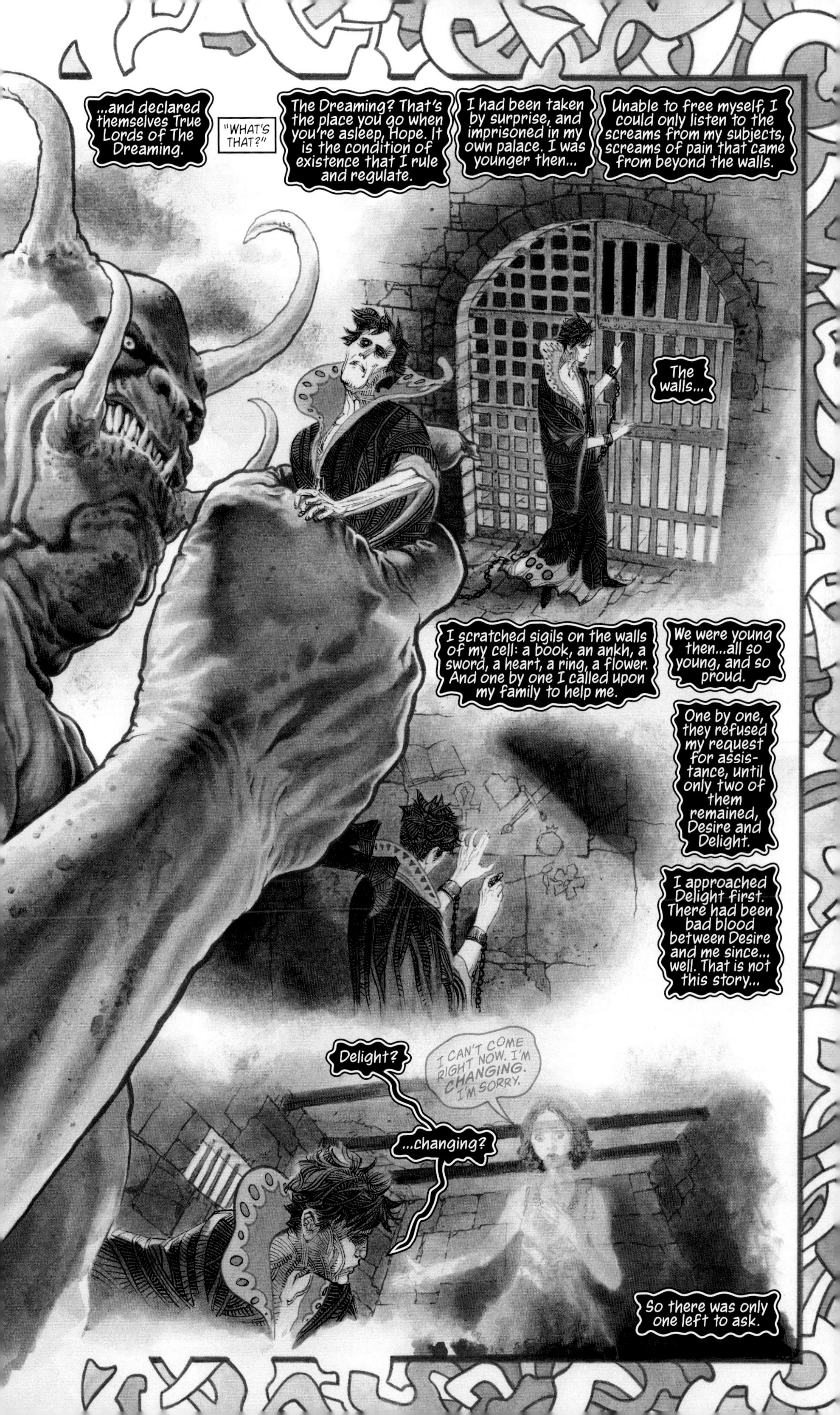
...and declared themselves True Lords of The Dreaming.
"WHAT'S THAT?"
The Dreaming? That's the place you go when you're asleep, Hope. It is the condition of existence that I rule and regulate.
I had been taken by surprise, and imprisoned in my own palace. I was younger then...
Unable to free myself, I could only listen to the screams from my subjects, screams of pain that came from beyond the walls.
The walls...
I scratched sigils on the walls of my cell: a book, an ankh, a sword, a heart, a ring, a flower. And one by one I called upon my family to help me.
We were young then...all so young, and so proud.
One by one, they refused my request for assistance, until only two of them remained, Desire and Delight.
I approached Delight first. There had been bad blood between Desire and me since... well. That is not this story...
Delight?
I CAN'T COME RIGHT NOW. I'M CHANGING. I'M SORRY.
...changing?
So there was only one left to ask.

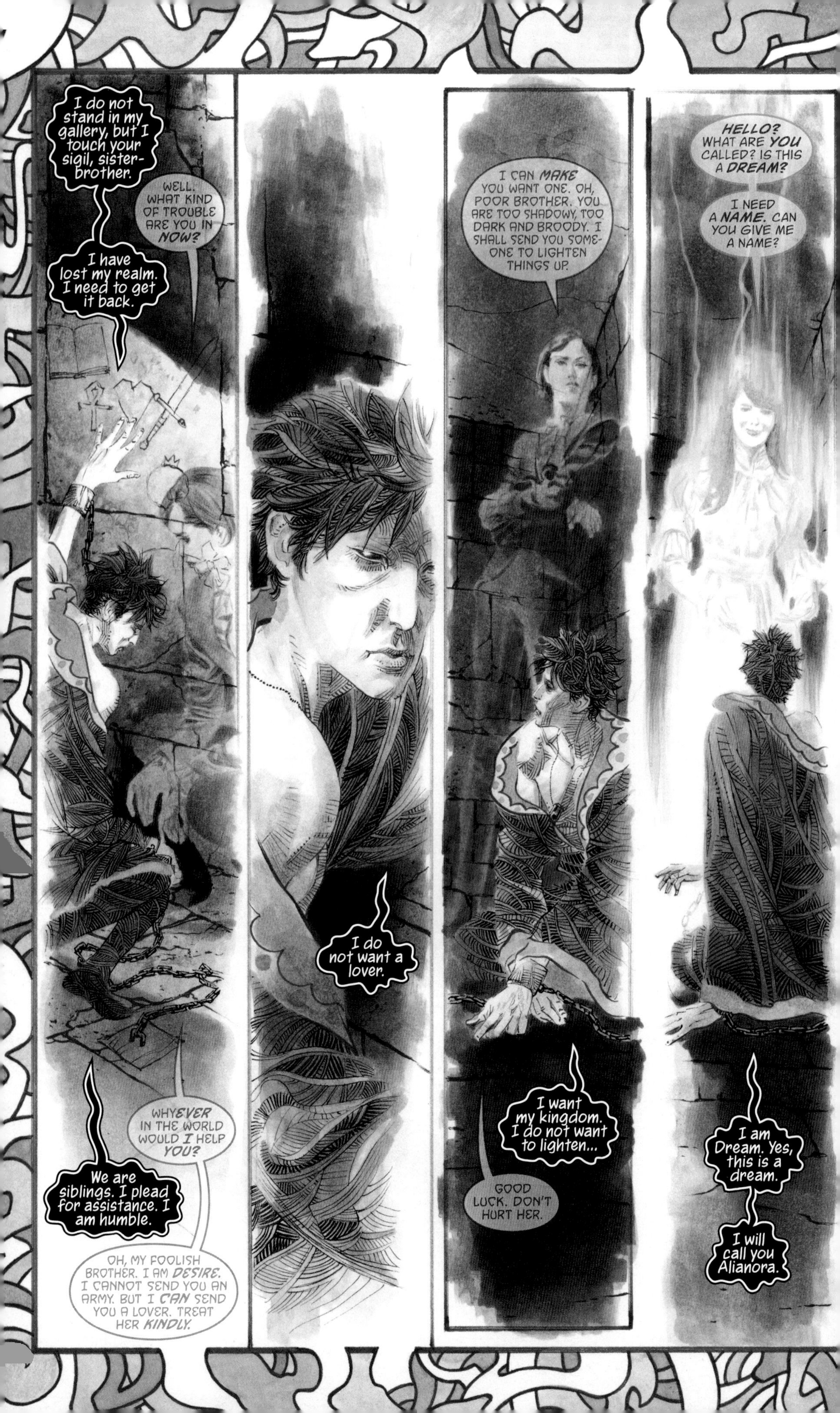

I do not stand in my gallery, but I touch your sigil, sister-brother.
WELL. WHAT KIND OF TROUBLE ARE YOU IN NOW?
I have lost my realm. I need to get it back.
WHYEVER IN THE WORLD WOULD I HELP YOU?
We are siblings. I plead for assistance. I am humble.
OH, MY FOOLISH BROTHER. I AM DESIRE. I CANNOT SEND YOU AN ARMY. BUT I CAN SEND YOU A LOVER. TREAT HER KINDLY.
I do not want a lover.
I CAN MAKE YOU WANT ONE. OH, POOR BROTHER. YOU ARE TOO SHADOWY, TOO DARK AND BROODY. I SHALL SEND YOU SOME-ONE TO LIGHTEN THINGS UP.
I want my kingdom. I do not want to lighten...
GOOD LUCK. DON'T HURT HER.
HELLO? WHAT ARE YOU CALLED? IS THIS A DREAM?
I NEED A NAME. CAN YOU GIVE ME A NAME?
I am Dream. Yes, this is a dream.
I will call you Alianora.

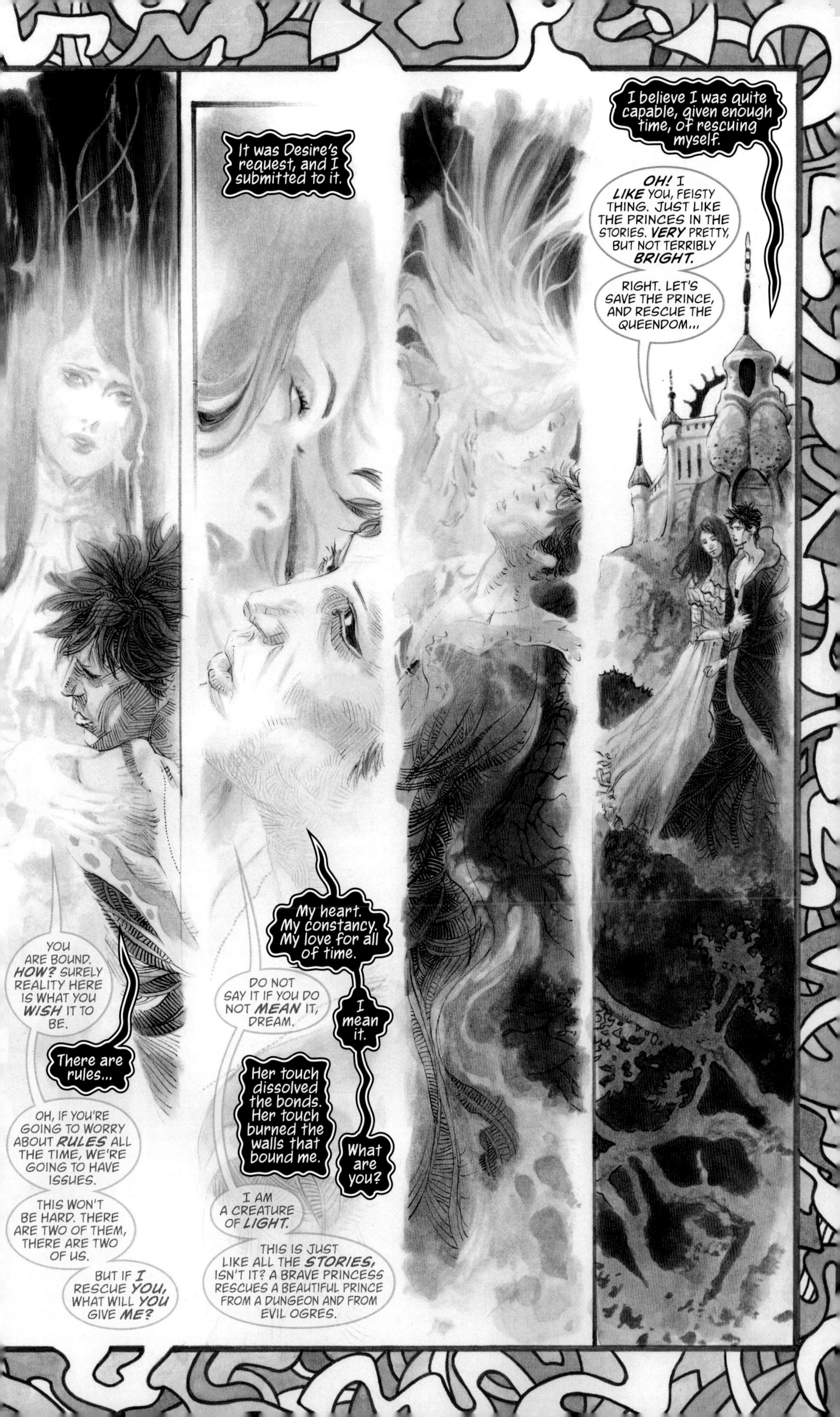

It was Desire's request, and I submitted to it.
My heart. My constancy. My love for all of time.
DO NOT SAY IT IF YOU DO NOT MEAN IT, DREAM.
I mean it.
Her touch dissolved the bonds. Her touch burned the walls that bound me.
What are you?
I AM A CREATURE OF LIGHT.
YOU ARE BOUND. HOW? SURELY REALITY HERE IS WHAT YOU WISH IT TO BE.
There are rules...
OH, IF YOU'RE GOING TO WORRY ABOUT RULES ALL THE TIME, WE'RE GOING TO HAVE ISSUES.
THIS WON'T BE HARD. THERE ARE TWO OF THEM, THERE ARE TWO OF US.
BUT IF I RESCUE YOU, WHAT WILL YOU GIVE ME?
THIS IS JUST LIKE ALL THE STORIES, ISN'T IT? A BRAVE PRINCESS RESCUES A BEAUTIFUL PRINCE FROM A DUNGEON AND FROM EVIL OGRES.
I believe I was quite capable, given enough time, of rescuing myself.
OH! I LIKE YOU, FEISTY THING. JUST LIKE THE PRINCES IN THE STORIES. VERY PRETTY, BUT NOT TERRIBLY BRIGHT.
RIGHT. LET'S SAVE THE PRINCE, AND RESCUE THE QUEENDOM...

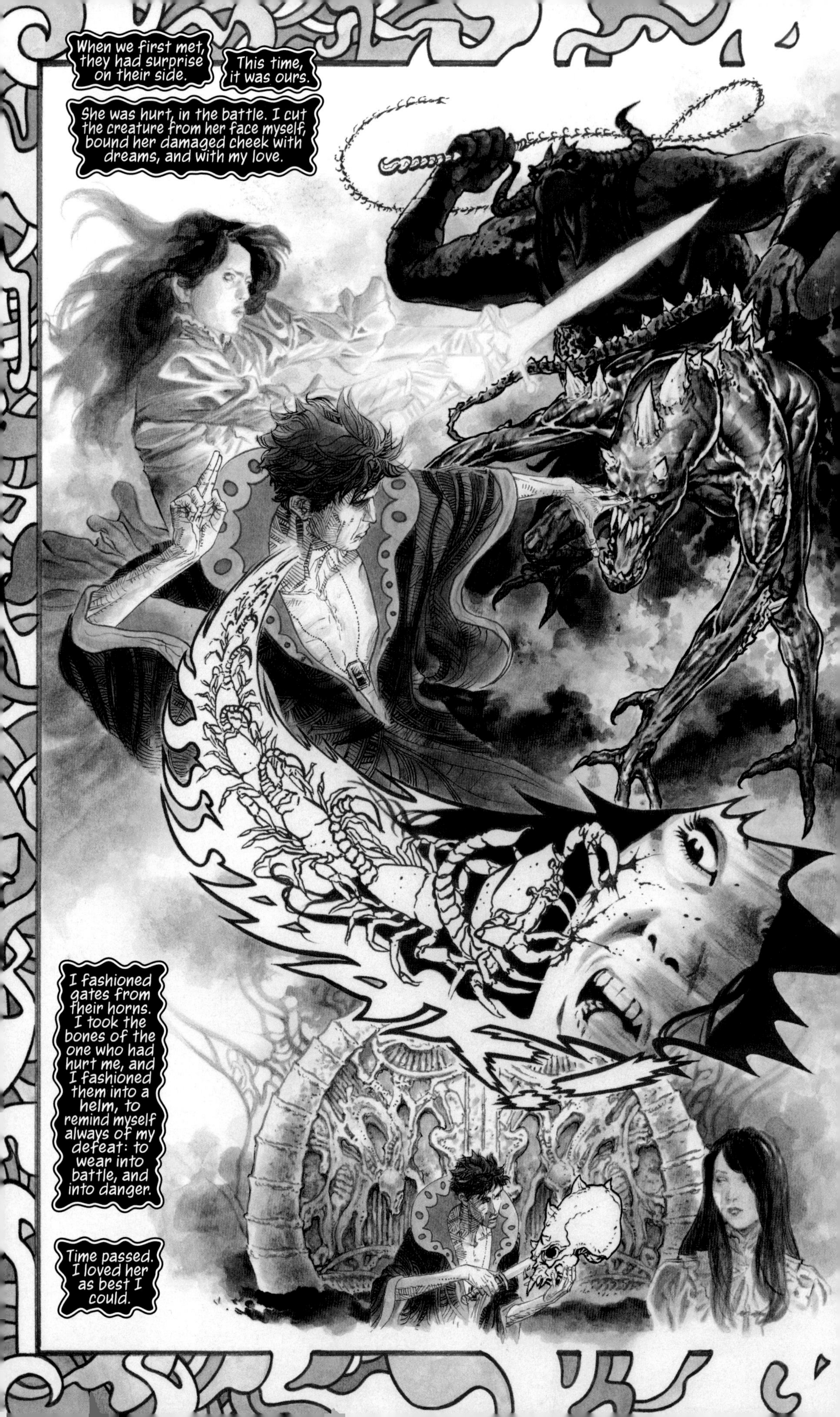
When we first met, they had surprise on their side.
This time, it was ours.
She was hurt, in the battle. I cut the creature from her face myself, bound her damaged cheek with dreams, and with my love.
I fashioned gates from their horns. I took the bones of the one who had hurt me, and I fashioned them into a helm, to remind myself always of my defeat: to wear into battle, and into danger.
Time passed. I loved her as best I could.

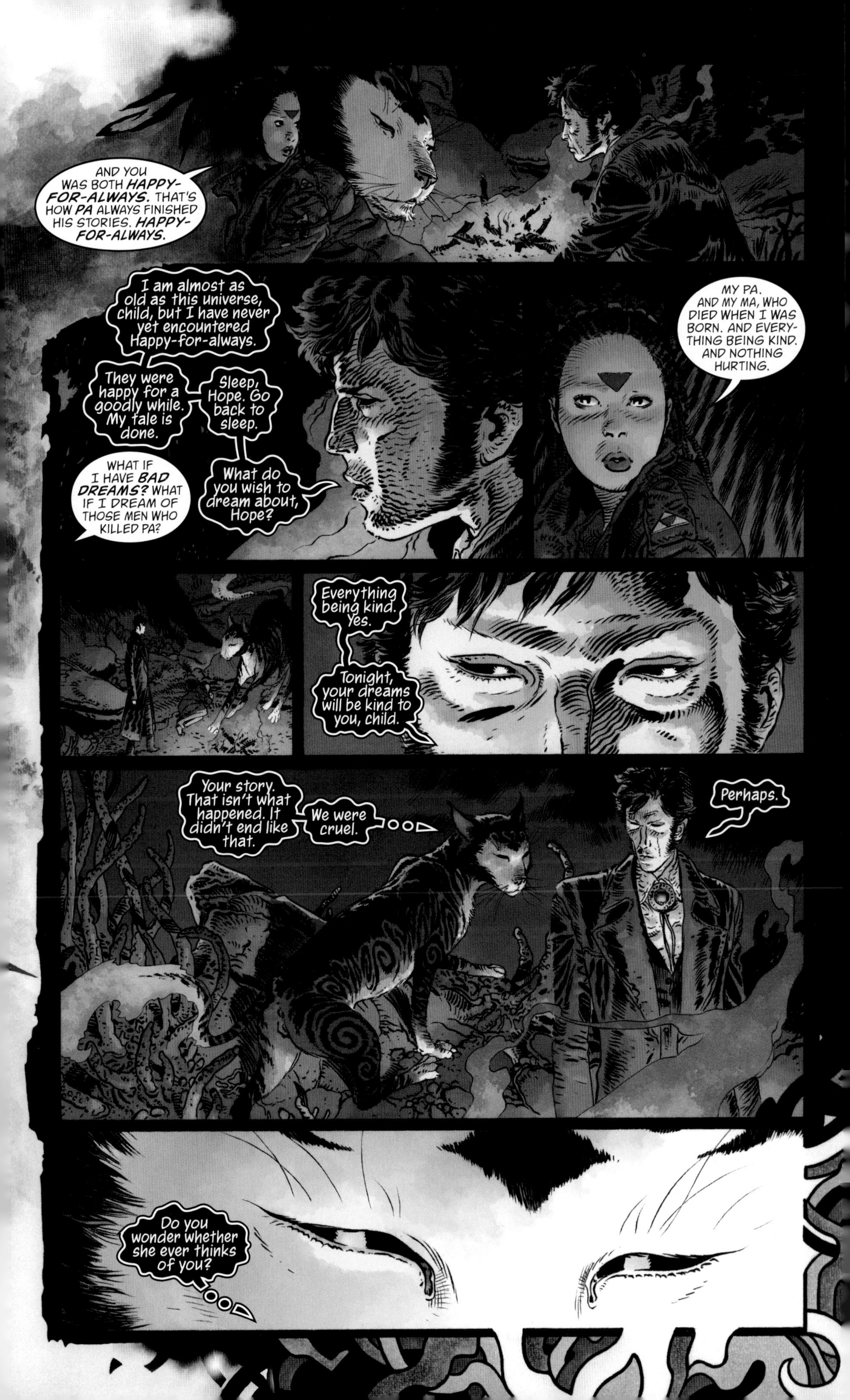
AND YOU WAS BOTH HAPPY-FOR-ALWAYS. THAT'S HOW PA ALWAYS FINISHED HIS STORIES. HAPPY-FOR-ALWAYS.
I am almost as old as this universe, child, but I have never yet encountered Happy-for-always.
They were happy for a goodly while. My tale is done.
Sleep, Hope. Go back to sleep.
WHAT IF I HAVE BAD DREAMS? WHAT IF I DREAM OF THOSE MEN WHO KILLED PA?
What do you wish to dream about, Hope?
MY PA. AND MY MA, WHO DIED WHEN I WAS BORN. AND EVERYTHING BEING KIND. AND NOTHING HURTING.
Everything being kind. Yes.
Tonight, your dreams will be kind to you, child.
Your story. That isn't what happened. It didn't end like that.
We were cruel.
Perhaps.
Do you wonder whether she ever thinks of you?

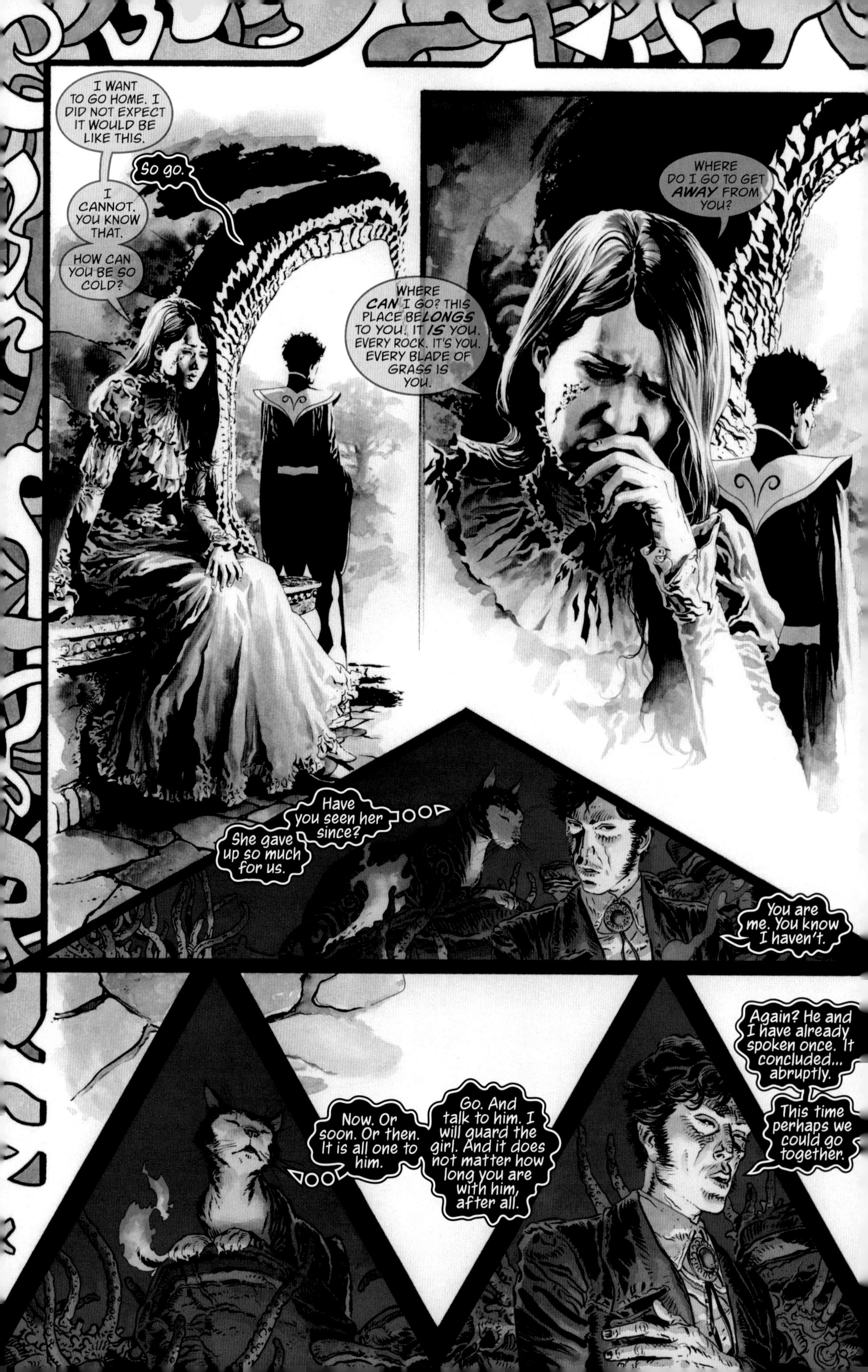
I WANT TO GO HOME. I DID NOT EXPECT IT WOULD BE LIKE THIS.
So go.
I CANNOT. YOU KNOW THAT.
HOW CAN YOU BE SO COLD?
WHERE *CAN* I GO? THIS PLACE BE*LONGS* TO YOU. IT *IS* YOU. EVERY ROCK. IT'S YOU. EVERY BLADE OF GRASS IS YOU.
WHERE DO I GO TO GET *AWAY* FROM YOU?
She gave up so much for us.
Have you seen her since?
You are me. You know I haven't.
Now. Or soon. Or then. It is all one to him.
Go. And talk to him. I will guard the girl. And it does not matter how long you are with him, after all.
Again? He and I have already spoken once. It concluded... abruptly.
This time perhaps we could go together.

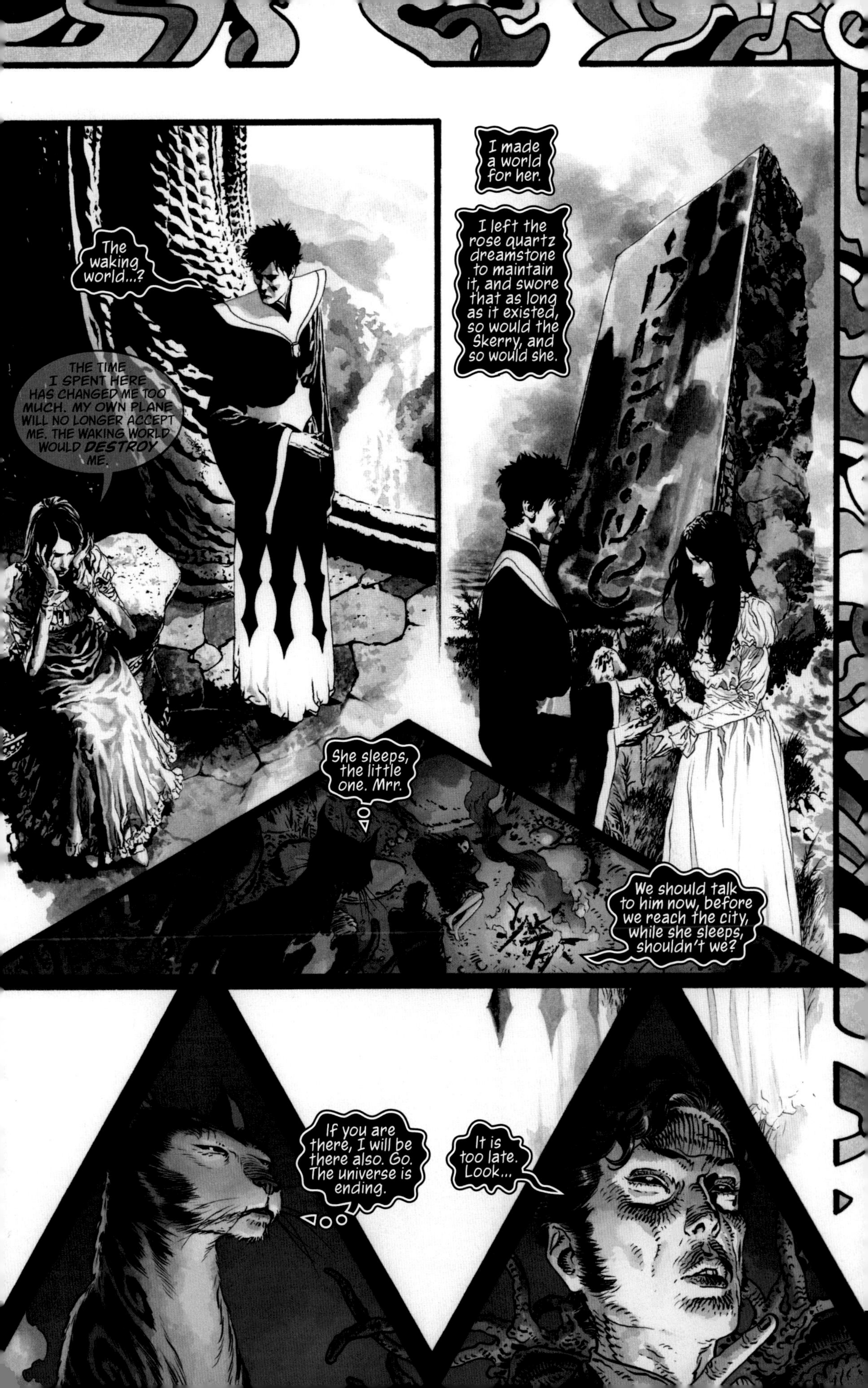

The waking world...?
THE TIME I SPENT HERE HAS CHANGED ME TOO MUCH. MY OWN PLANE WILL NO LONGER ACCEPT ME. THE WAKING WORLD WOULD *DESTROY* ME.
I made a world for her.
I left the rose quartz dreamstone to maintain it, and swore that as long as it existed, so would the Skerry, and so would she.
She sleeps, the little one. Mrr.
We should talk to him now, before we reach the city, while she sleeps, shouldn't we?
If you are there, I will be there also. Go. The universe is ending.
It is too late. Look...

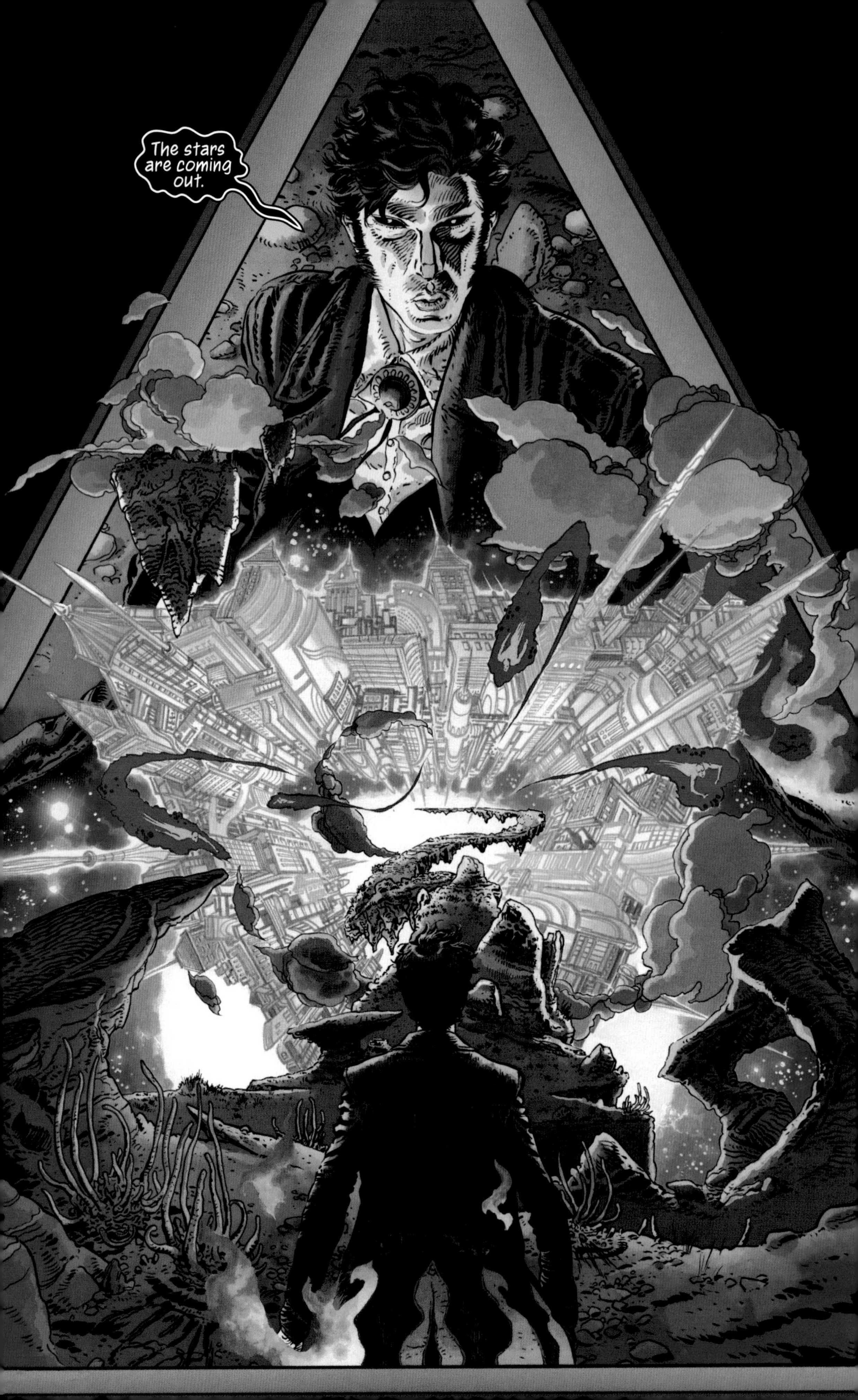
The stars are coming out.

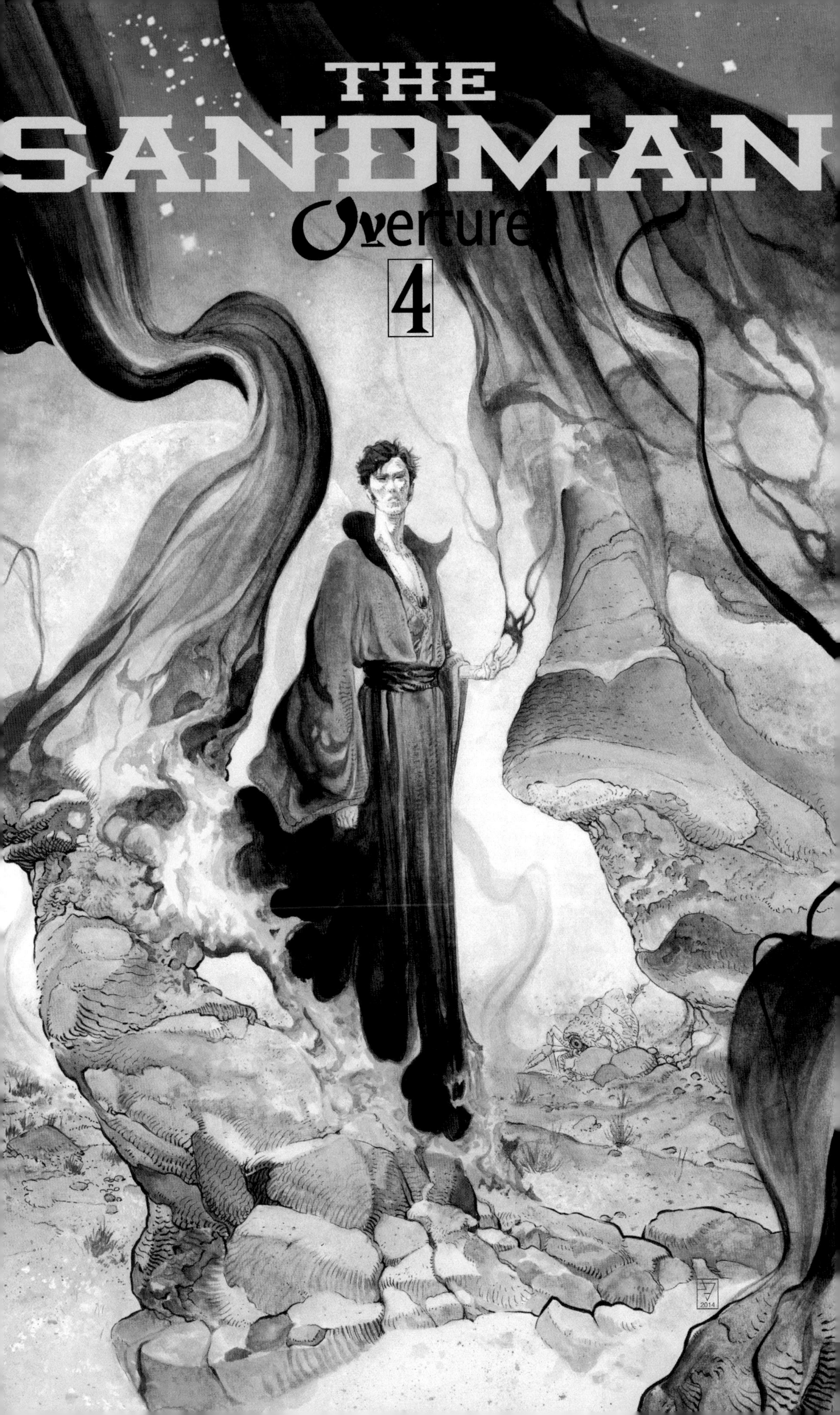
THE SANDMAN
Overture
4
2014

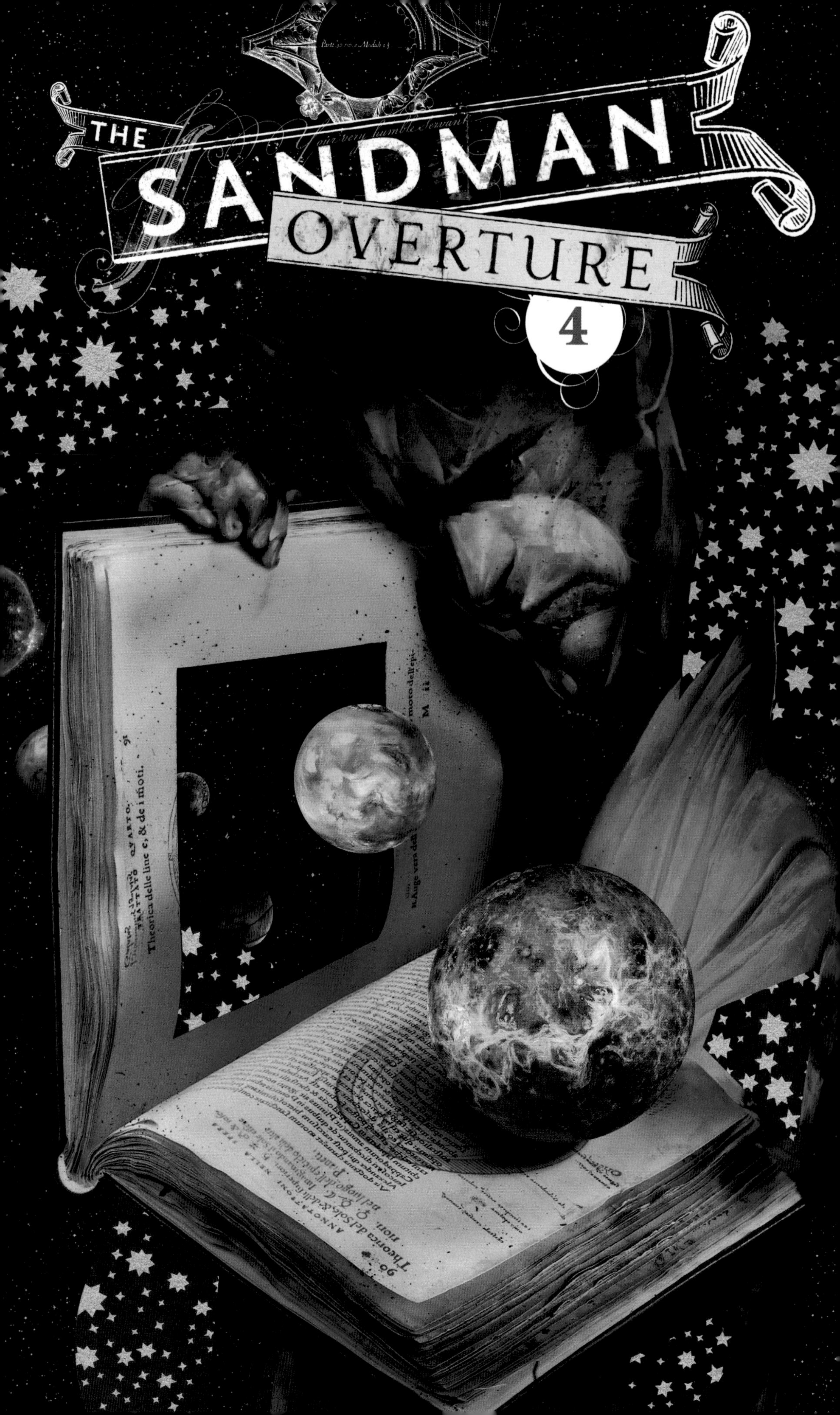
THE
SANDMAN
OVERTURE
4

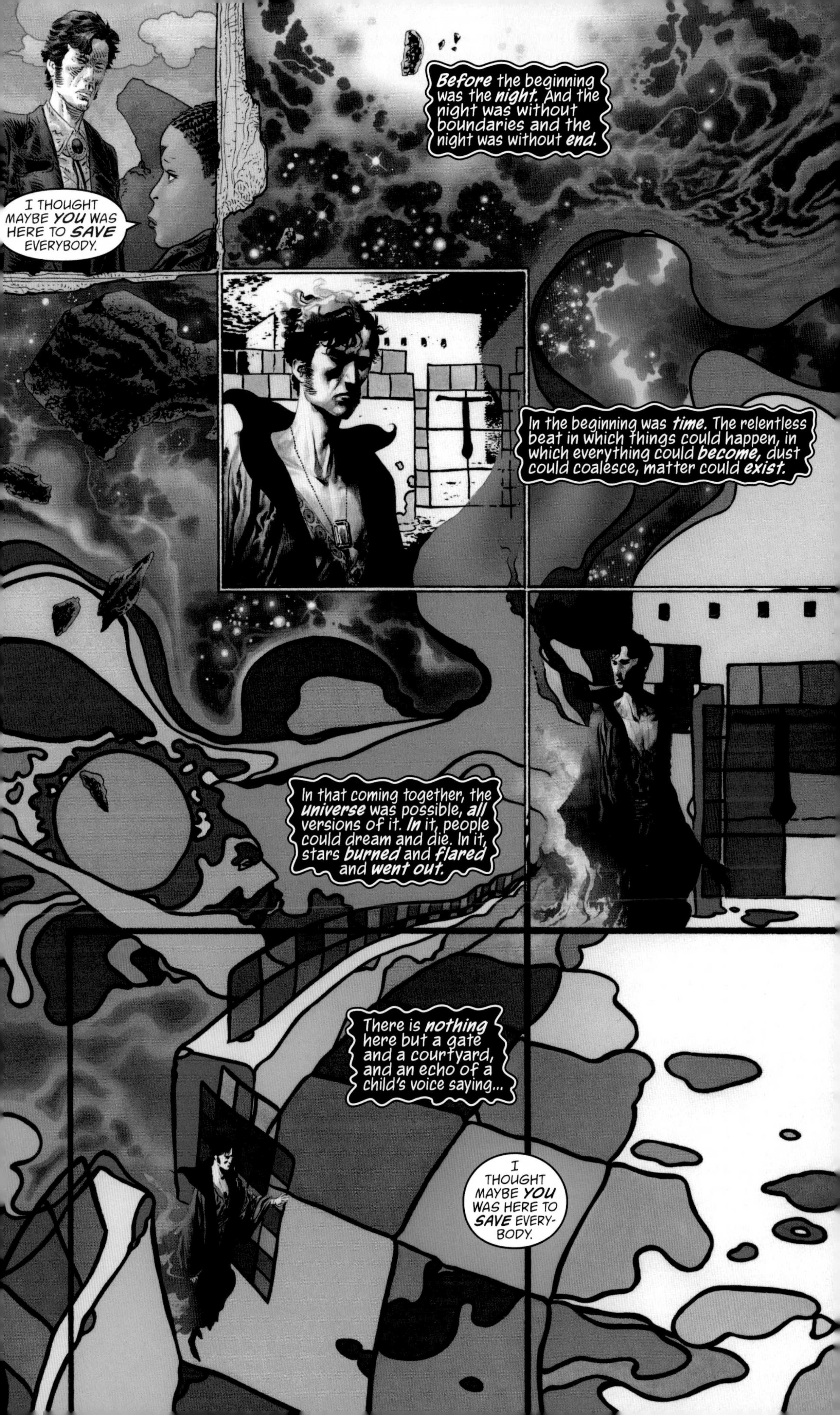

I THOUGHT MAYBE YOU WAS HERE TO SAVE EVERYBODY.
Before the beginning was the night. And the night was without boundaries and the night was without end.
In the beginning was time. The relentless beat in which things could happen, in which everything could become, dust could coalesce, matter could exist.
In that coming together, the universe was possible, all versions of it. In it, people could dream and die. In it, stars burned and flared and went out.
There is nothing here but a gate and a courtyard, and an echo of a child's voice saying...
I THOUGHT MAYBE YOU WAS HERE TO SAVE EVERY-BODY.

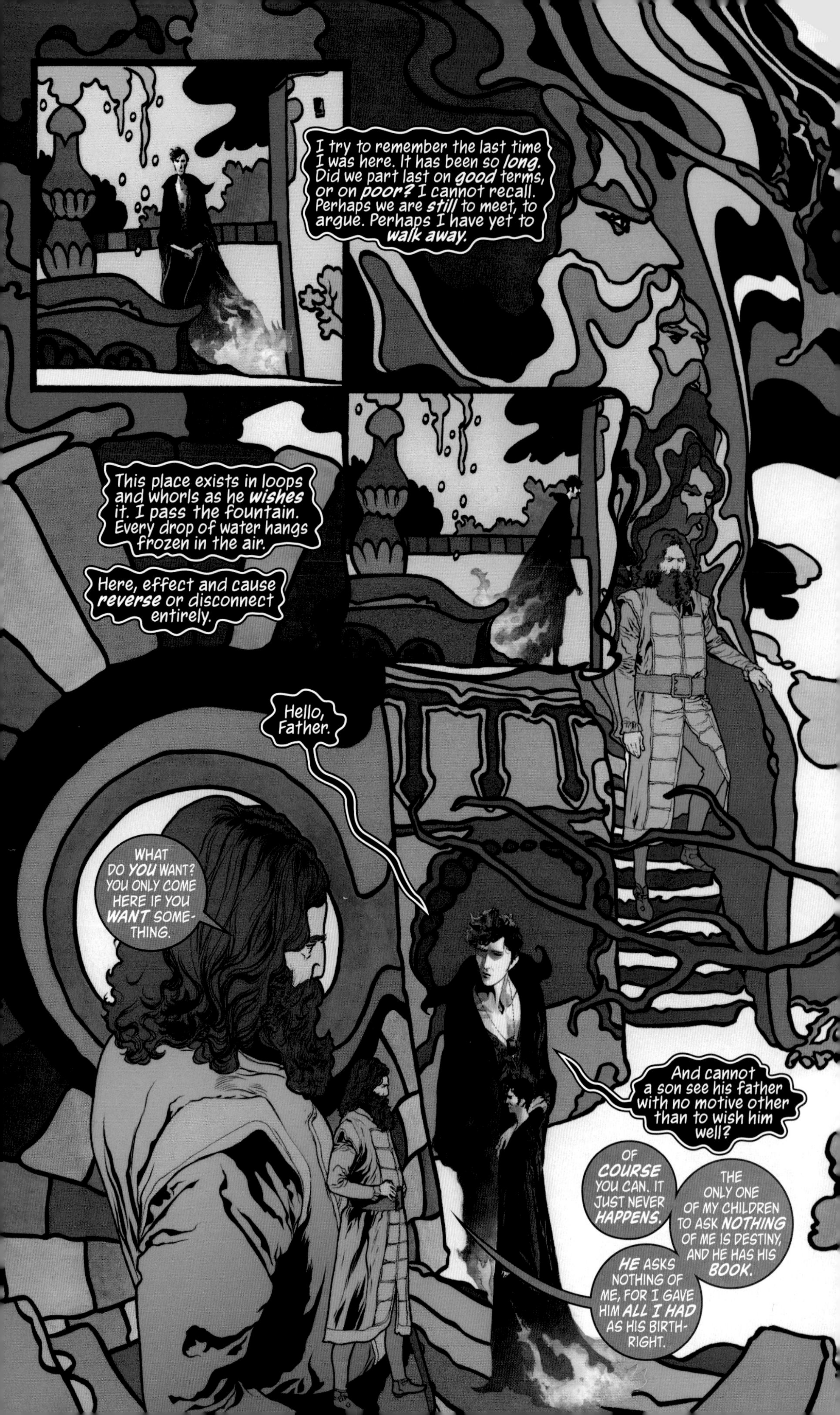

I try to remember the last time I was here. It has been so *long.* Did we part last on *good* terms, or on *poor?* I cannot recall. Perhaps we are *still* to meet, to argue. Perhaps I have yet to *walk away.*
This place exists in loops and whorls as he *wishes* it. I pass the fountain. Every drop of water hangs frozen in the air.
Here, effect and cause *reverse* or disconnect entirely.
Hello, Father.
WHAT DO *YOU* WANT? YOU ONLY COME HERE IF YOU *WANT* SOME-THING.
And cannot a son see his father with no motive other than to wish him well?
OF *COURSE* YOU CAN. IT JUST NEVER *HAPPENS.*
THE ONLY ONE OF MY CHILDREN TO ASK *NOTHING* OF ME IS DESTINY, AND HE HAS HIS *BOOK.*
HE ASKS NOTHING OF ME, FOR I GAVE HIM *ALL I HAD* AS HIS BIRTH-RIGHT.

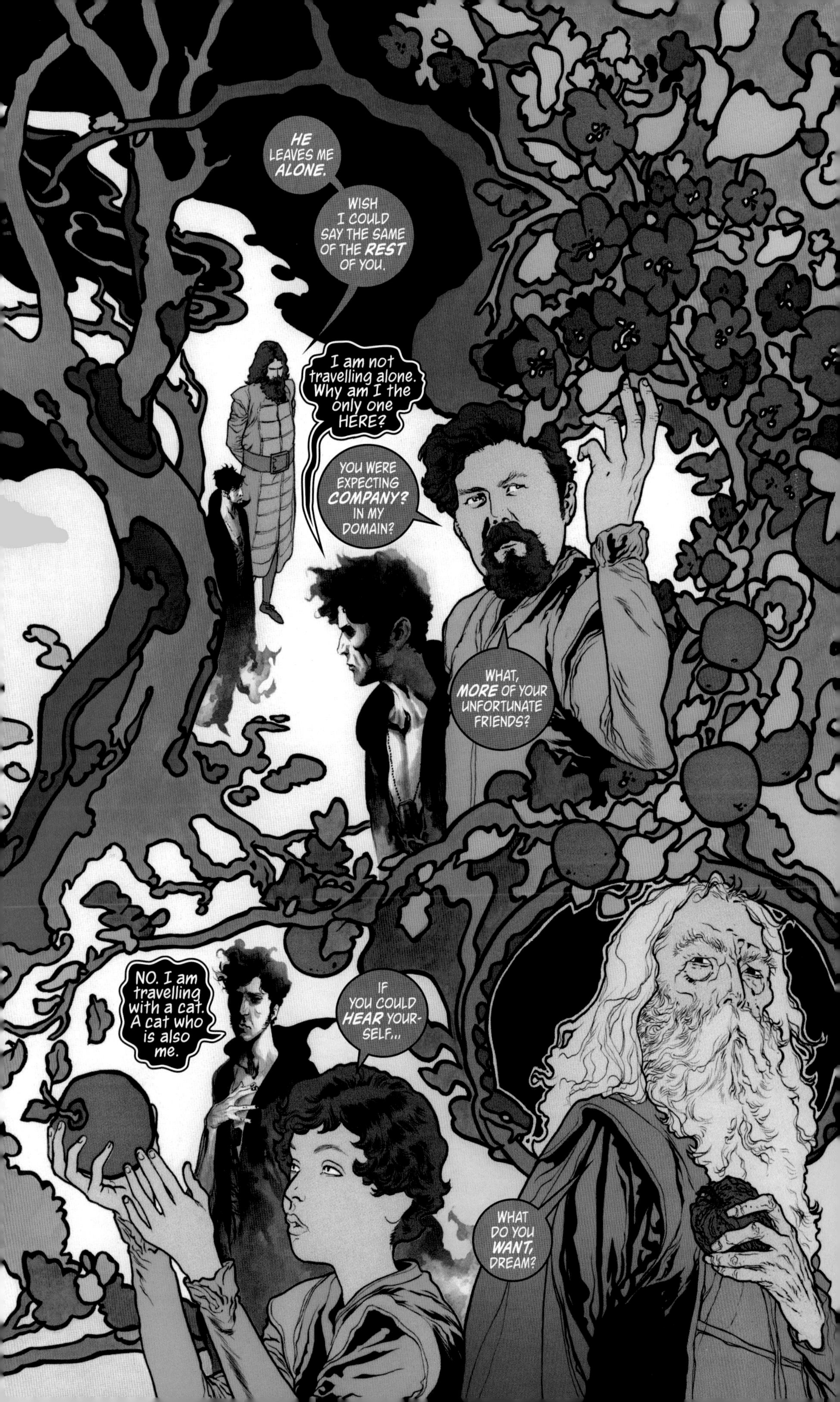
HE LEAVES ME ALONE.
WISH I COULD SAY THE SAME OF THE REST OF YOU.
I am not travelling alone. Why am I the only one HERE?
YOU WERE EXPECTING COMPANY? IN MY DOMAIN?
WHAT, MORE OF YOUR UNFORTUNATE FRIENDS?
NO. I am travelling with a cat. A cat who is also me.
IF YOU COULD HEAR YOURSELF...
WHAT DO YOU WANT, DREAM?

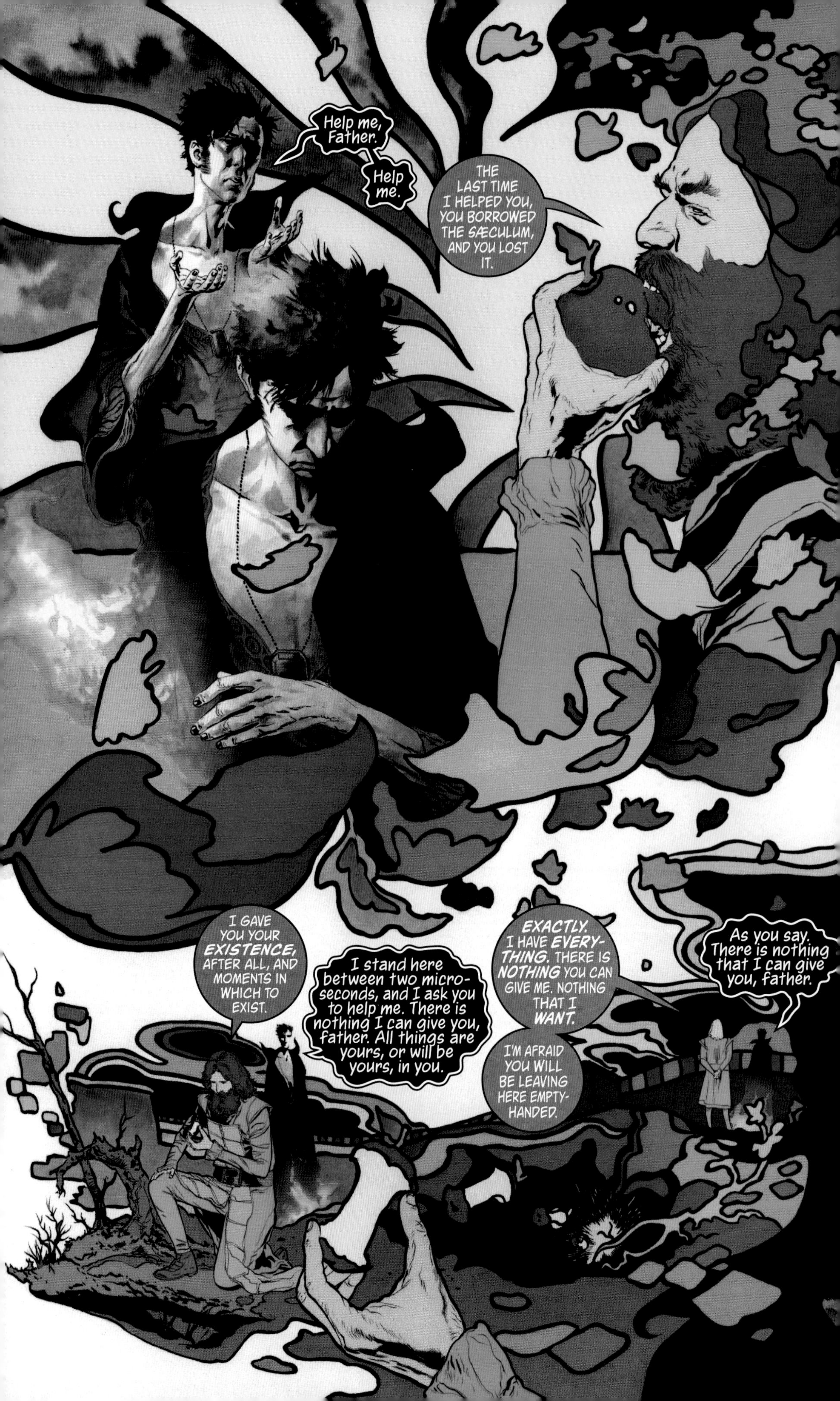
Help me, Father.
Help me.
THE LAST TIME I HELPED YOU, YOU BORROWED THE SÆCULUM, AND YOU LOST IT.
I GAVE YOU YOUR EXISTENCE, AFTER ALL, AND MOMENTS IN WHICH TO EXIST.
I stand here between two micro-seconds, and I ask you to help me. There is nothing I can give you, father. All things are yours, or will be yours, in you.
EXACTLY. I HAVE EVERY-THING. THERE IS NOTHING YOU CAN GIVE ME. NOTHING THAT I WANT.
I'M AFRAID YOU WILL BE LEAVING HERE EMPTY-HANDED.
As you say. There is nothing that I can give you, father.

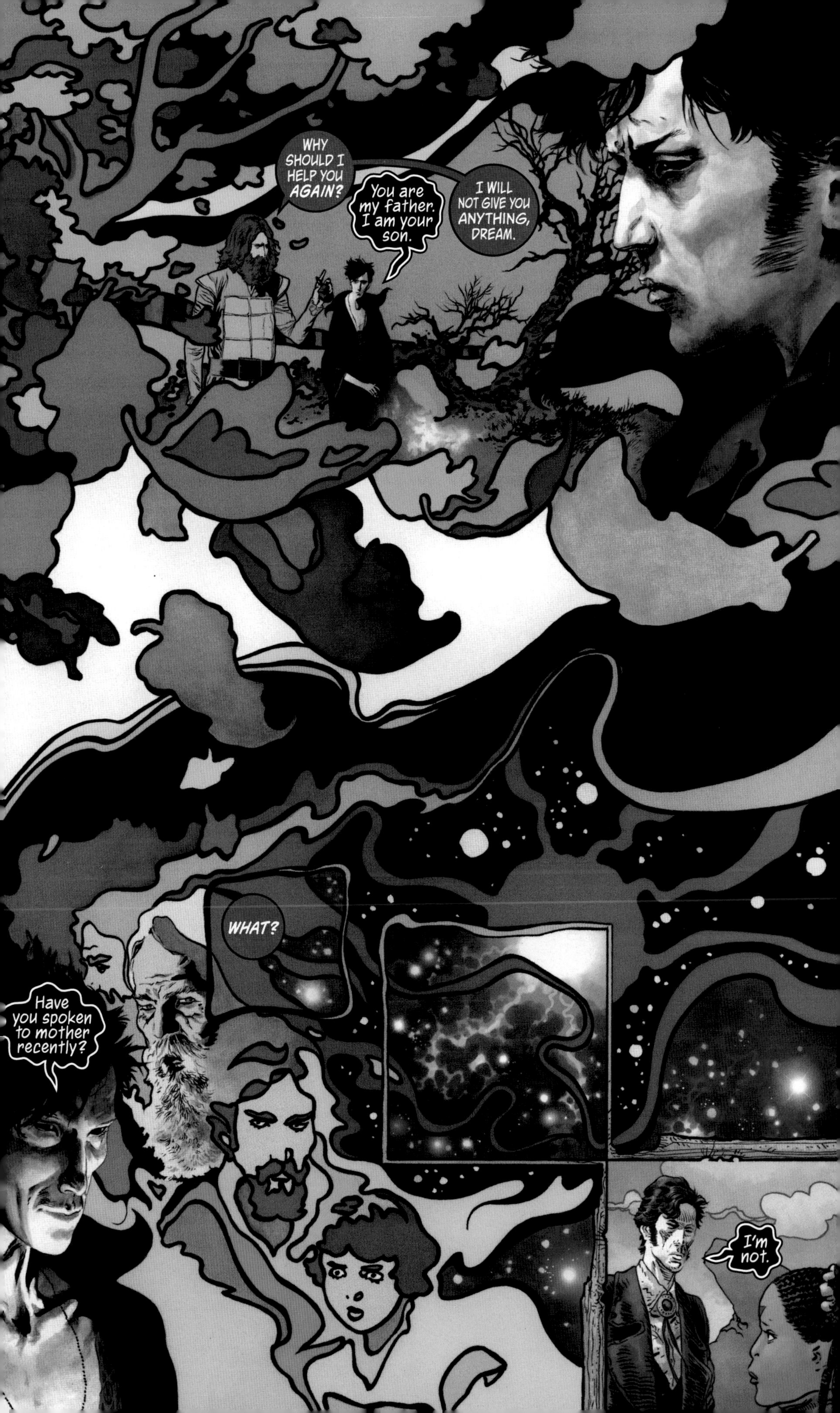
WHY SHOULD I HELP YOU AGAIN?
You are my father. I am your son.
I WILL NOT GIVE YOU ANYTHING, DREAM.
WHAT?
Have you spoken to mother recently?
I'm not.

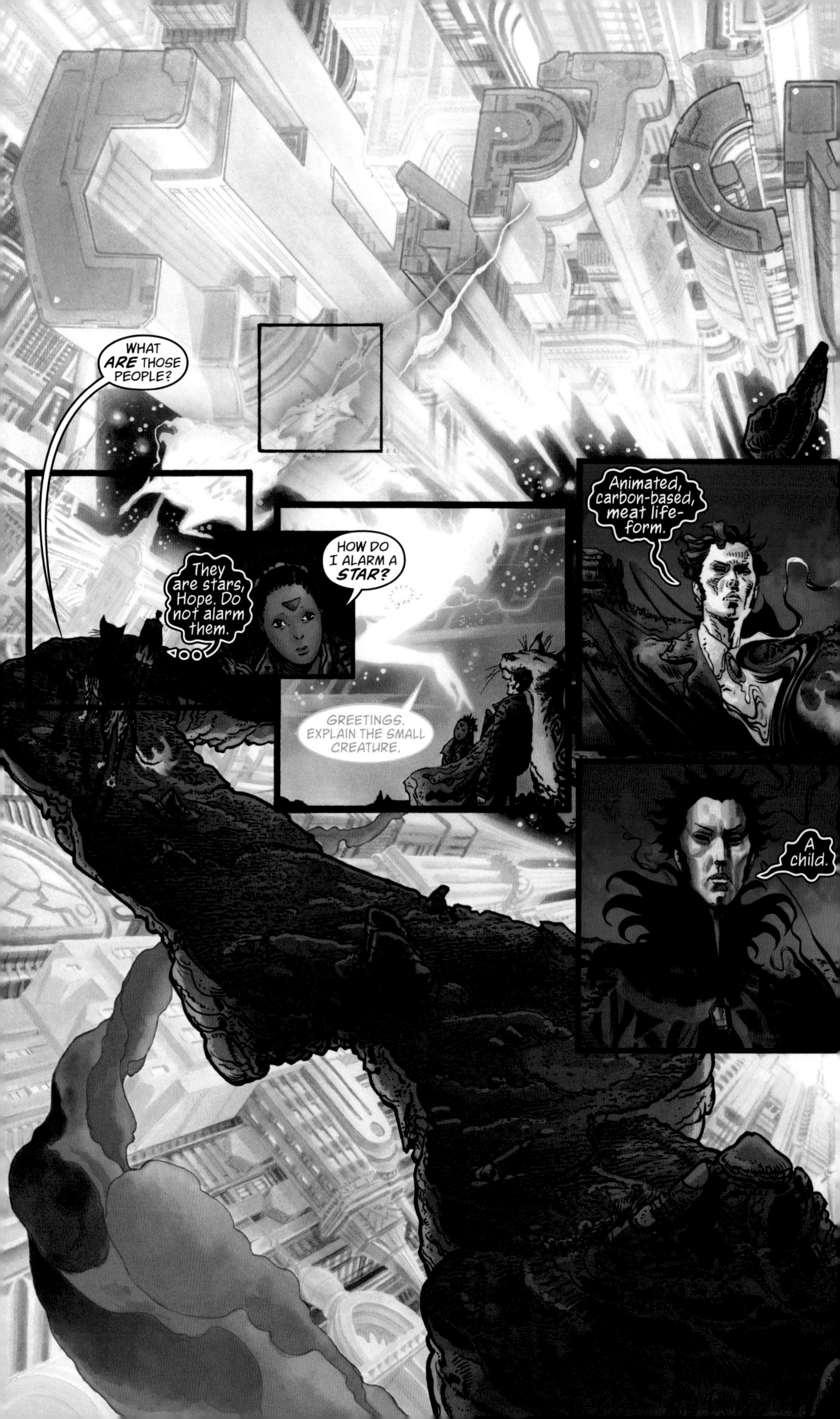
WHAT ARE THOSE PEOPLE?
They are stars, Hope. Do not alarm them.
HOW DO I ALARM A STAR?
GREETINGS. EXPLAIN THE SMALL CREATURE.
Animated, carbon-based, meat life-form.
A child.

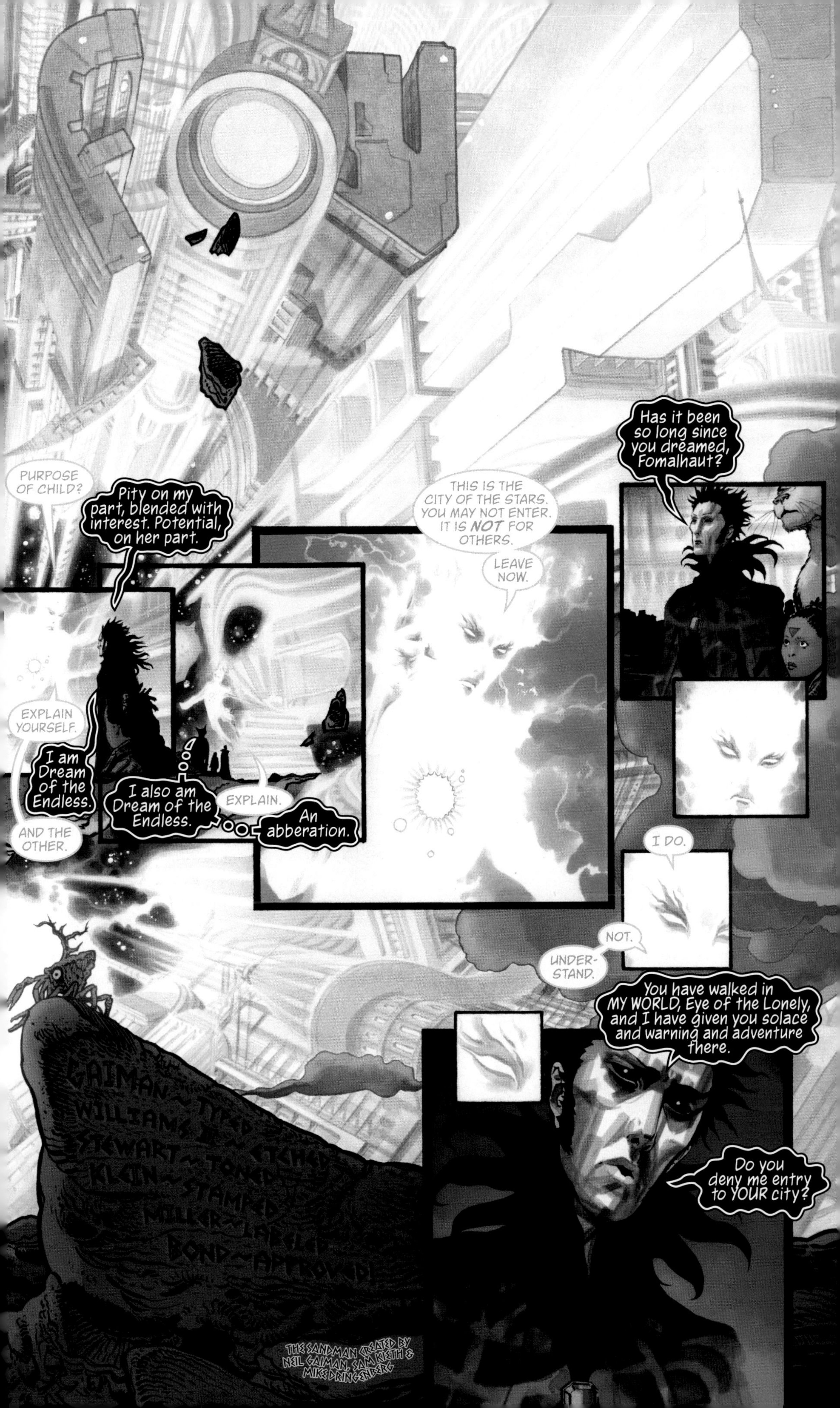
PURPOSE OF CHILD?
Pity on my part, blended with interest. Potential, on her part.
EXPLAIN YOURSELF.
I am Dream of the Endless.
AND THE OTHER.
I also am Dream of the Endless.
EXPLAIN.
An abberation.
THIS IS THE CITY OF THE STARS. YOU MAY NOT ENTER. IT IS **NOT** FOR OTHERS.
LEAVE NOW.
Has it been so long since you dreamed, Fomalhaut?
I DO.
NOT.
UNDER-STAND.
You have walked in MY WORLD, Eye of the Lonely, and I have given you solace and warning and adventure there.
Do you deny me entry to YOUR city?
GAIMAN ~ TYPED
WILLIAMS III ~ ETCHED
STEWART ~ TONED
KLEIN ~ STAMPED
MILLER ~ LABELED
BOND ~ APPROVED
THE SANDMAN CREATED BY NEIL GAIMAN, SAM KIETH & MIKE DRINGENBERG

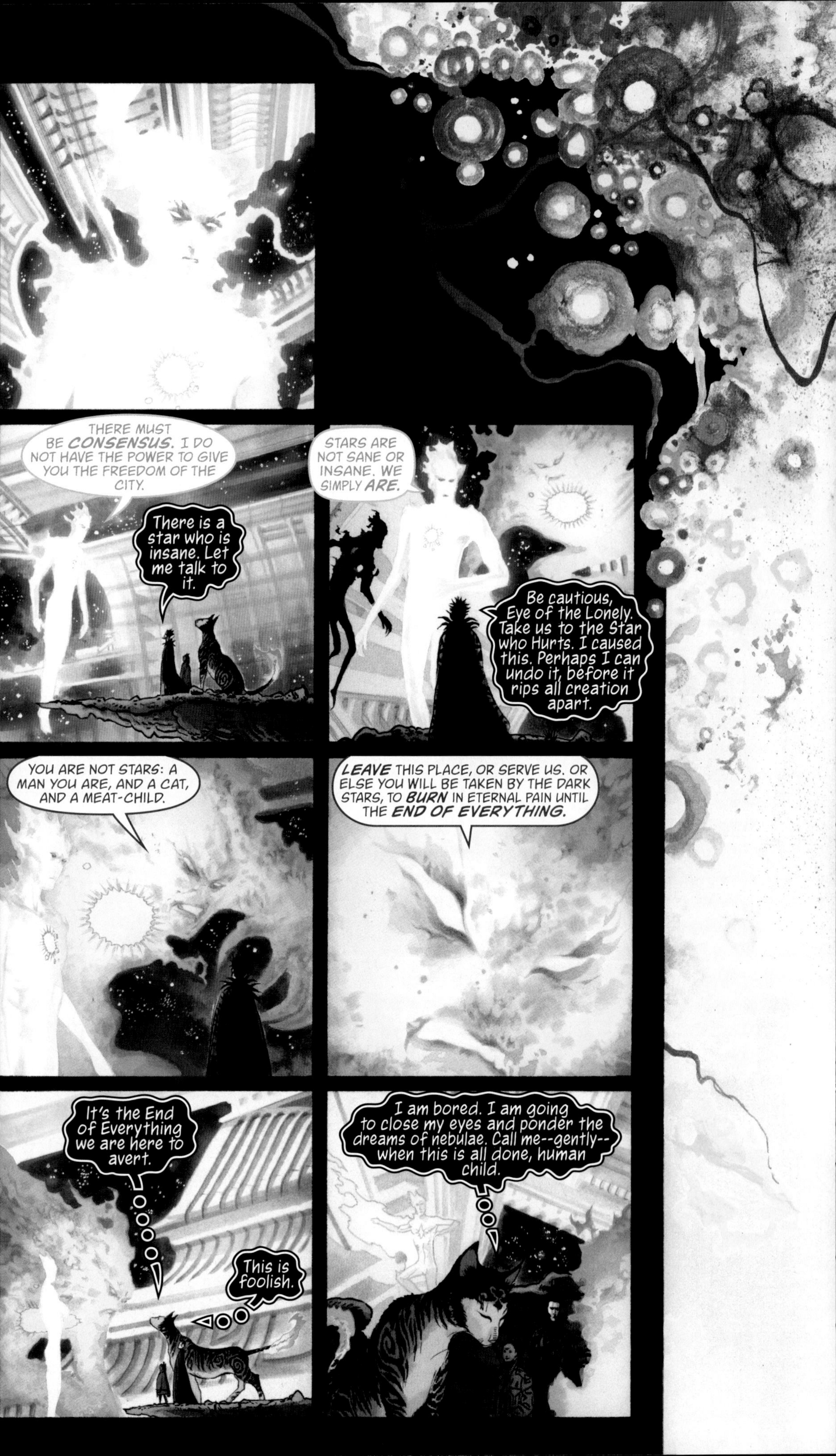
THERE MUST BE CONSENSUS. I DO NOT HAVE THE POWER TO GIVE YOU THE FREEDOM OF THE CITY.
There is a star who is insane. Let me talk to it.
STARS ARE NOT SANE OR INSANE. WE SIMPLY ARE.
Be cautious, Eye of the Lonely. Take us to the Star who Hurts. I caused this. Perhaps I can undo it, before it rips all creation apart.
YOU ARE NOT STARS: A MAN YOU ARE, AND A CAT, AND A MEAT-CHILD.
LEAVE THIS PLACE, OR SERVE US. OR ELSE YOU WILL BE TAKEN BY THE DARK STARS, TO BURN IN ETERNAL PAIN UNTIL THE END OF EVERYTHING.
It's the End of Everything we are here to avert.
This is foolish.
I am bored. I am going to close my eyes and ponder the dreams of nebulae. Call me--gently--when this is all done, human child.

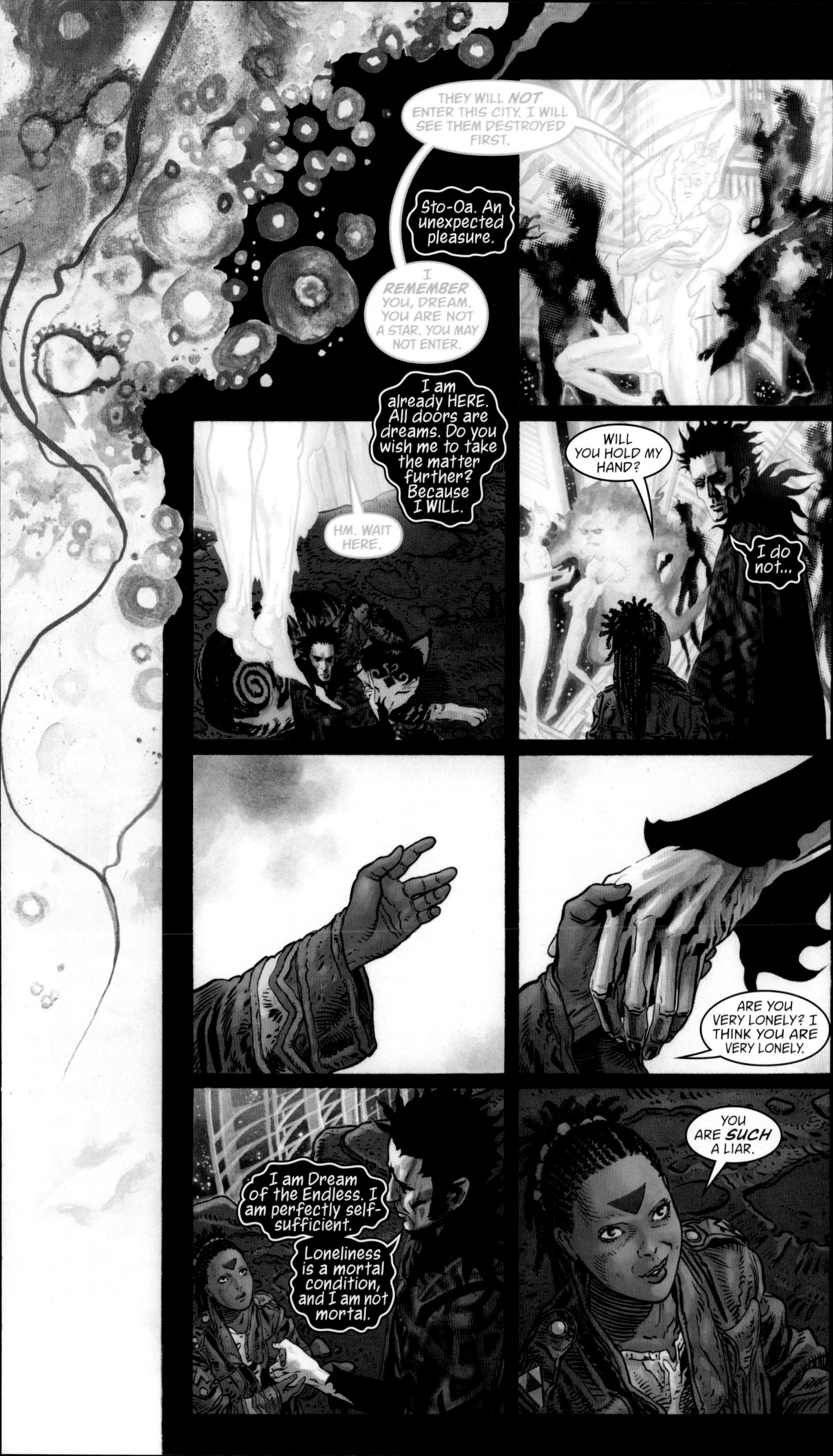
THEY WILL NOT ENTER THIS CITY. I WILL SEE THEM DESTROYED FIRST.
Sto-Oa. An unexpected pleasure.
I REMEMBER YOU, DREAM. YOU ARE NOT A STAR. YOU MAY NOT ENTER.
I am already HERE. All doors are dreams. Do you wish me to take the matter further? Because I WILL.
HM. WAIT HERE.
WILL YOU HOLD MY HAND?
I do not...
ARE YOU VERY LONELY? I THINK YOU ARE VERY LONELY.
I am Dream of the Endless. I am perfectly self-sufficient.
Loneliness is a mortal condition, and I am not mortal.
YOU ARE SUCH A LIAR.

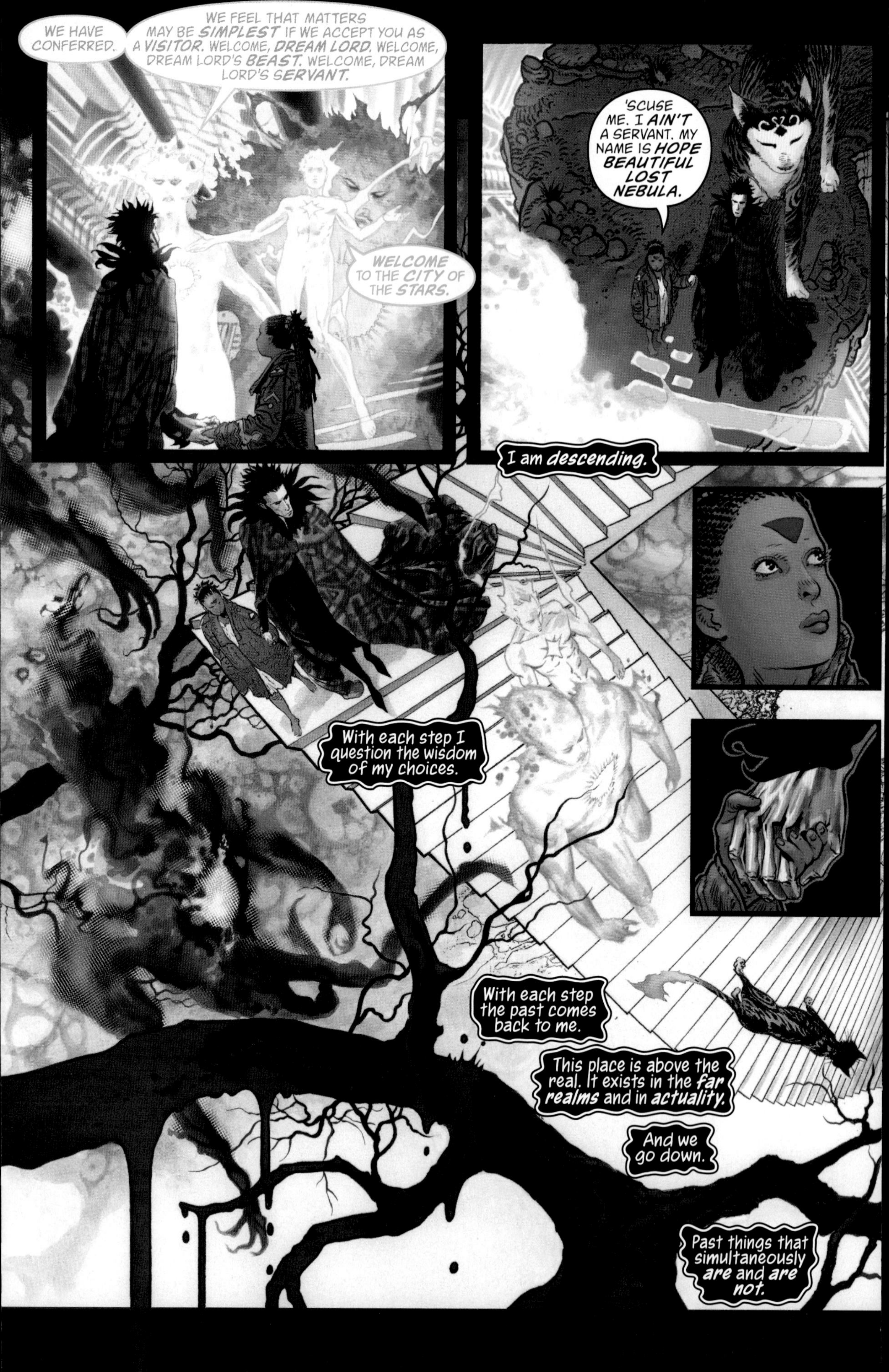
WE HAVE CONFERRED.
WE FEEL THAT MATTERS MAY BE SIMPLEST IF WE ACCEPT YOU AS A VISITOR. WELCOME, DREAM LORD. WELCOME, DREAM LORD'S BEAST. WELCOME, DREAM LORD'S SERVANT.
WELCOME TO THE CITY OF THE STARS.
'SCUSE ME. I AIN'T A SERVANT. MY NAME IS HOPE BEAUTIFUL LOST NEBULA.
I am descending.
With each step I question the wisdom of my choices.
With each step the past comes back to me.
This place is above the real. It exists in the far realms and in actuality.
And we go down.
Past things that simultaneously are and are not.

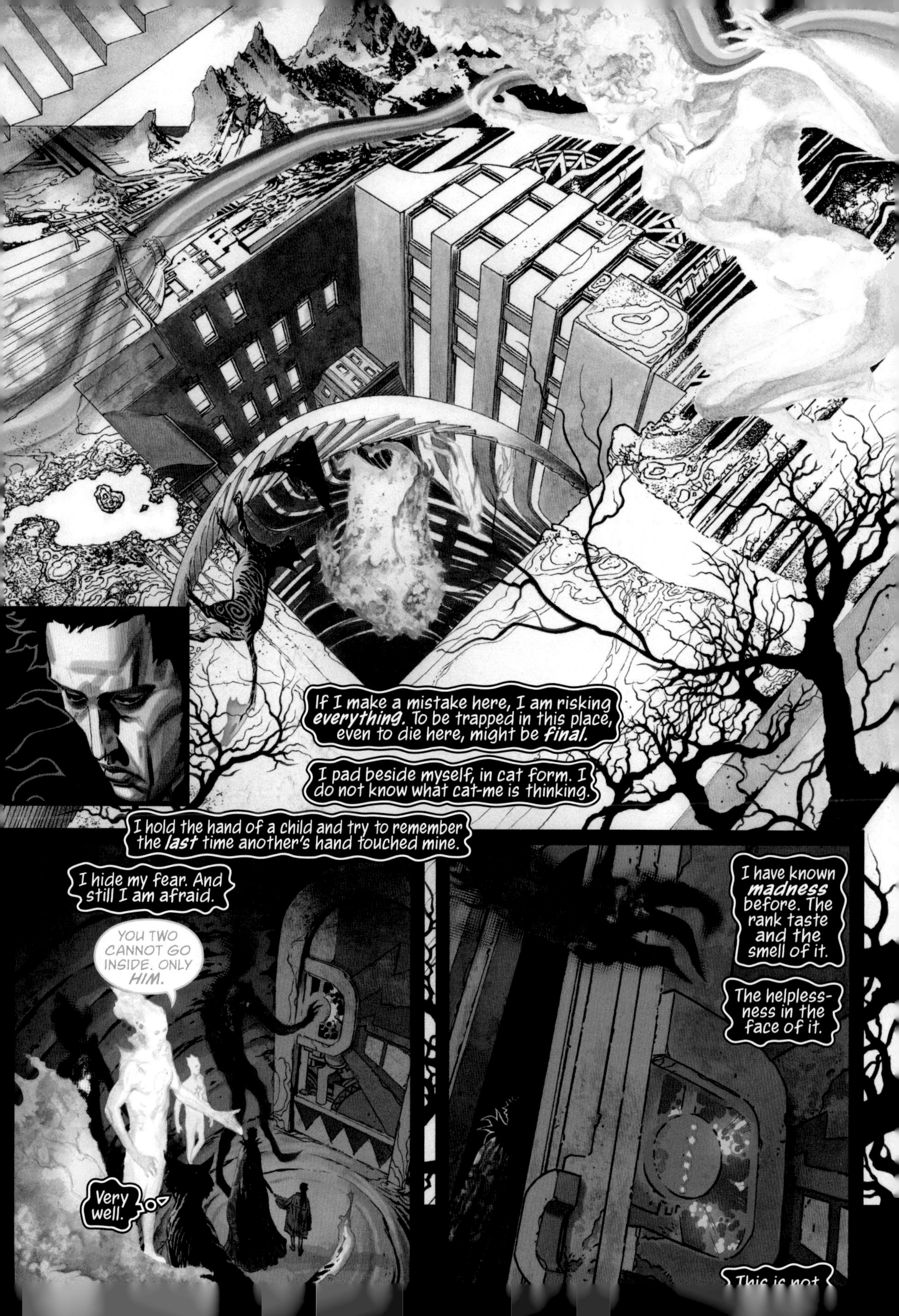

If I make a mistake here, I am risking *everything.* To be trapped in this place, even to die here, might be *final.*
I pad beside myself, in cat form. I do not know what cat-me is thinking.
I hold the hand of a child and try to remember the *last* time another's hand touched mine.
I hide my fear. And still I am afraid.
YOU TWO CANNOT GO INSIDE. ONLY *HIM.*
Very well.
I have known *madness* before. The rank taste and the smell of it.
The helplessness in the face of it.
This is not

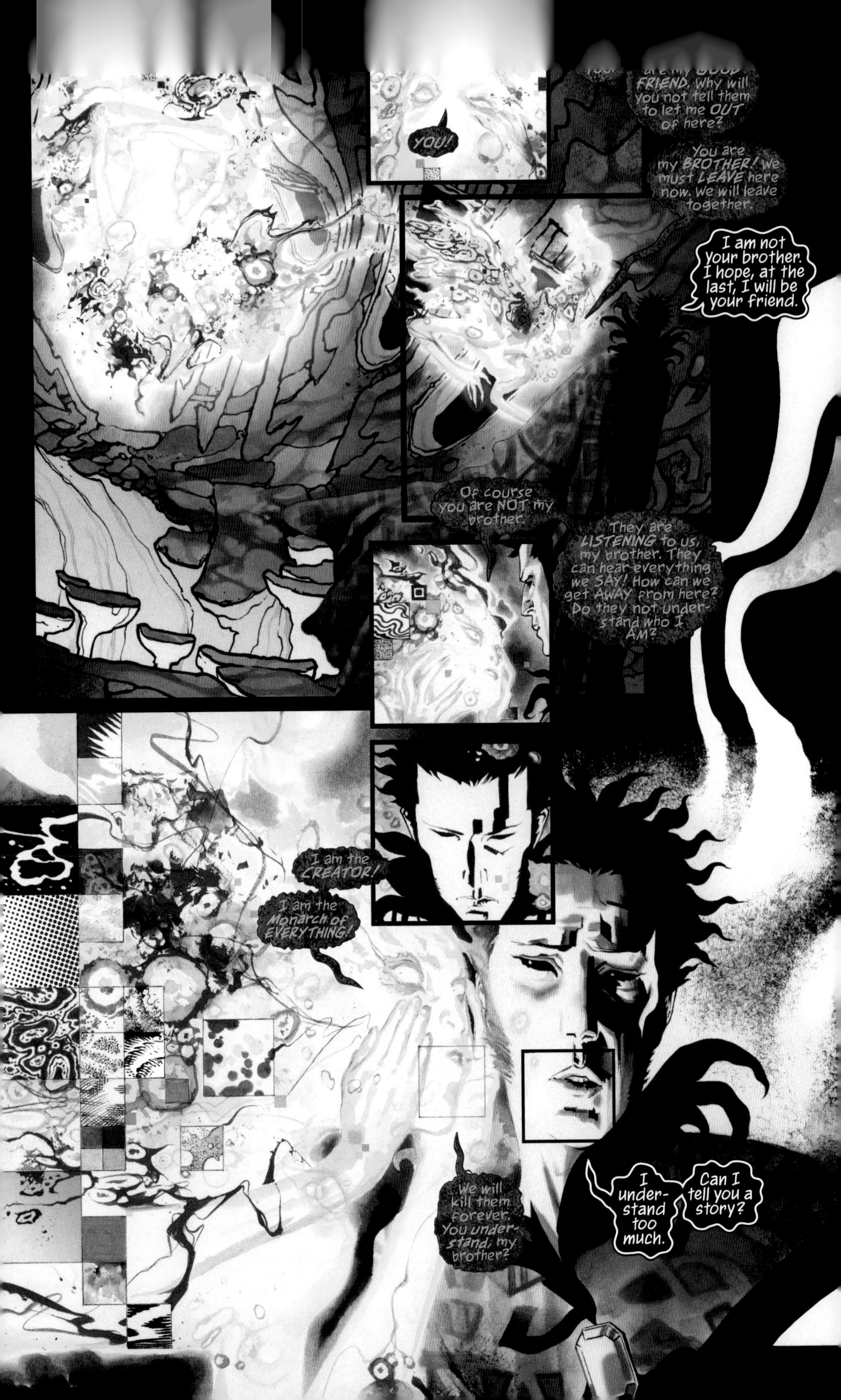

YOU!
FRIEND. Why will you not tell them to let me OUT of here?
You are my BROTHER! We must LEAVE here now. We will leave together.
I am not your brother. I hope, at the last, I will be your friend.
Of course you are NOT my brother.
They are LISTENING to us, my brother. They can hear everything we SAY! How can we get AWAY from here? Do they not understand who I AM?
I am the CREATOR!
I am the Monarch of EVERYTHING!
We will kill them forever. You understand, my brother?
I understand too much.
Can I tell you a story?

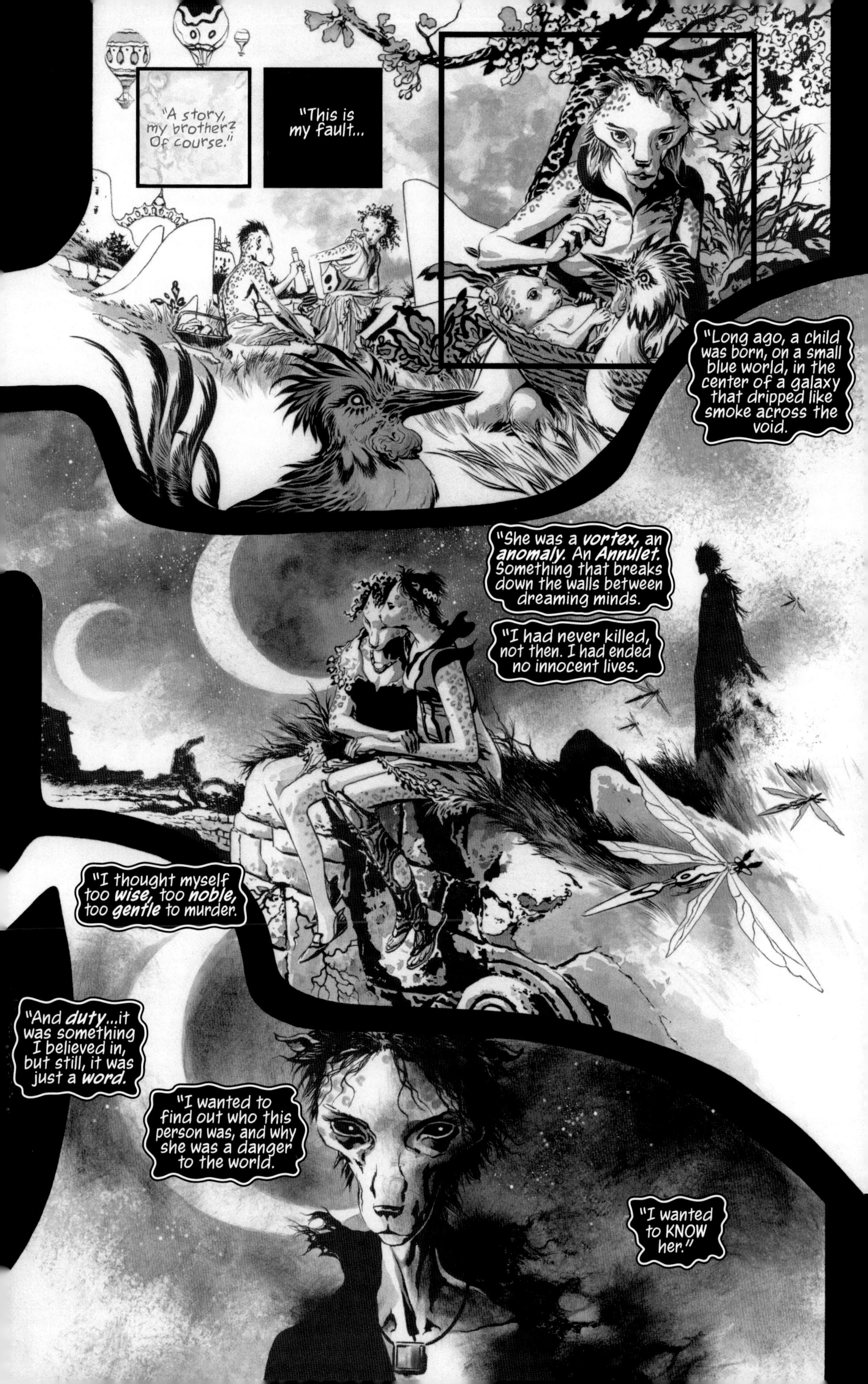
"A story, my brother? Of course."
"This is my fault...
"Long ago, a child was born, on a small blue world, in the center of a galaxy that dripped like smoke across the void.
"She was a *vortex*, an *anomaly*. An *Annulet*. Something that breaks down the walls between dreaming minds.
"I had never killed, not then. I had ended no innocent lives.
"I thought myself too *wise*, too *noble*, too *gentle* to murder.
"And *duty*...it was something I believed in, but still, it was just a *word*.
"I wanted to find out who this person was, and why she was a danger to the world.
"I wanted to KNOW her."

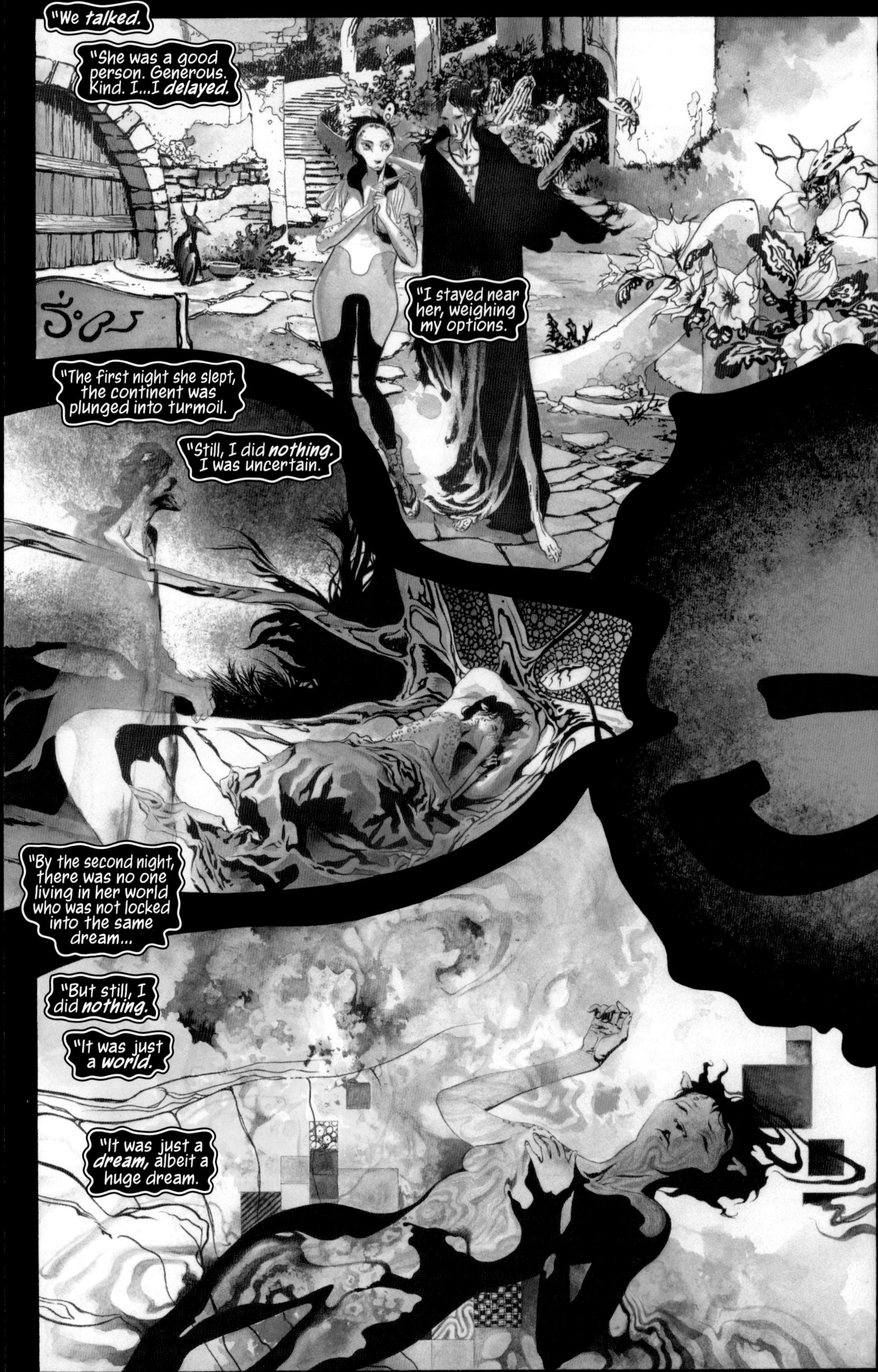
"We *talked.*
"She was a good person. Generous. Kind. I...I *delayed.*
"I stayed near her, weighing my options.
"The first night she slept, the continent was plunged into turmoil.
"Still, I did *nothing.* I was uncertain.
"By the second night, there was no one living in her world who was not locked into the same dream...
"But still, I did *nothing.*
"It was just a *world.*
"It was just a *dream,* albeit a huge dream.

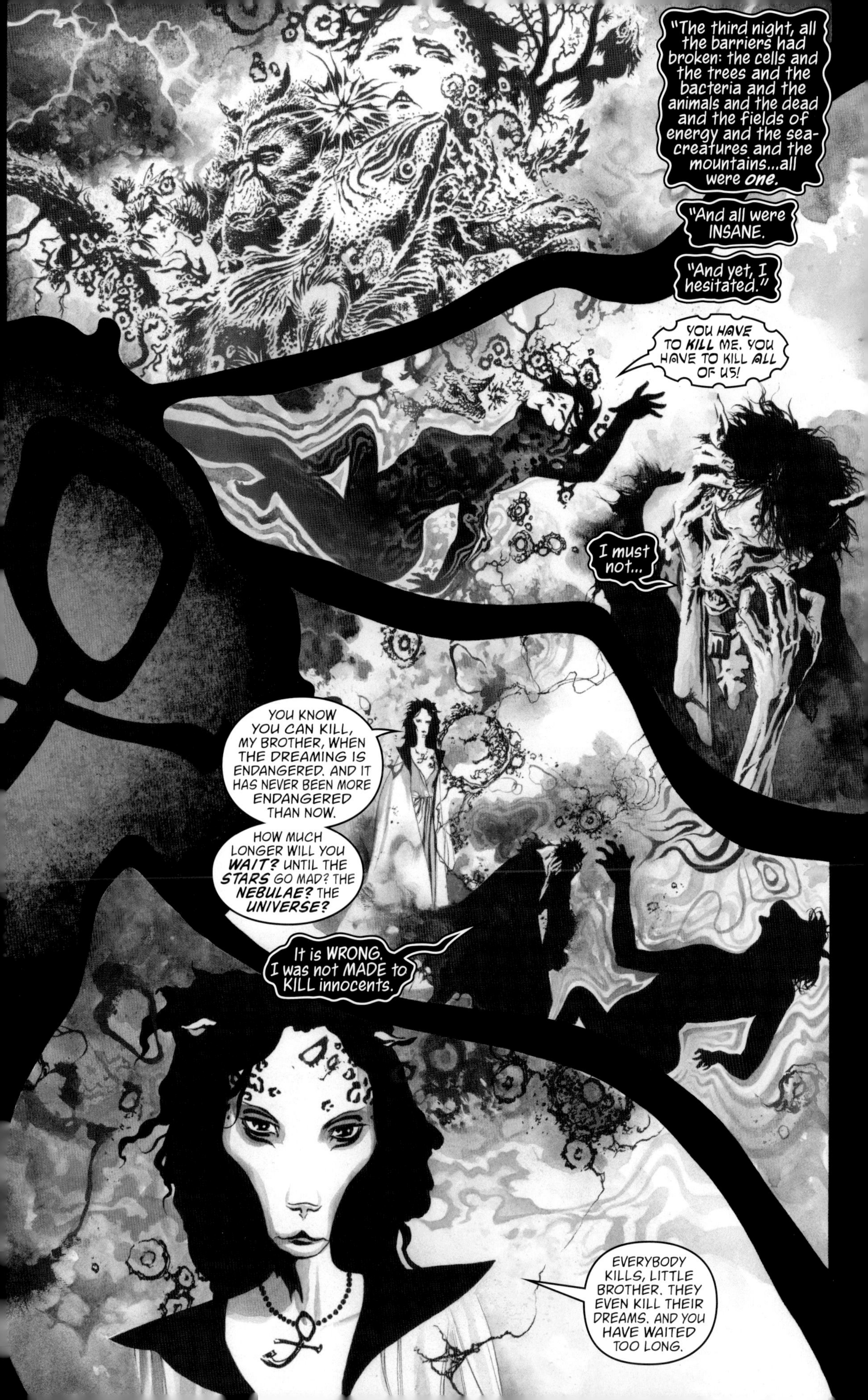
"The third night, all the barriers had broken: the cells and the trees and the bacteria and the animals and the dead and the fields of energy and the sea-creatures and the mountains...all were *one.*
"And all were INSANE.
"And yet, I hesitated."
YOU *HAVE* TO *KILL* ME. YOU HAVE TO KILL *ALL* OF US!
I must not...
YOU KNOW YOU CAN KILL, MY BROTHER, WHEN THE DREAMING IS ENDANGERED. AND IT HAS NEVER BEEN MORE ENDANGERED THAN NOW.
HOW MUCH LONGER WILL YOU *WAIT?* UNTIL THE *STARS* GO MAD? THE *NEBULAE?* THE *UNIVERSE?*
It is WRONG. I was not MADE to KILL innocents.
EVERYBODY KILLS, LITTLE BROTHER. THEY EVEN KILL THEIR DREAMS. AND YOU HAVE WAITED TOO LONG.

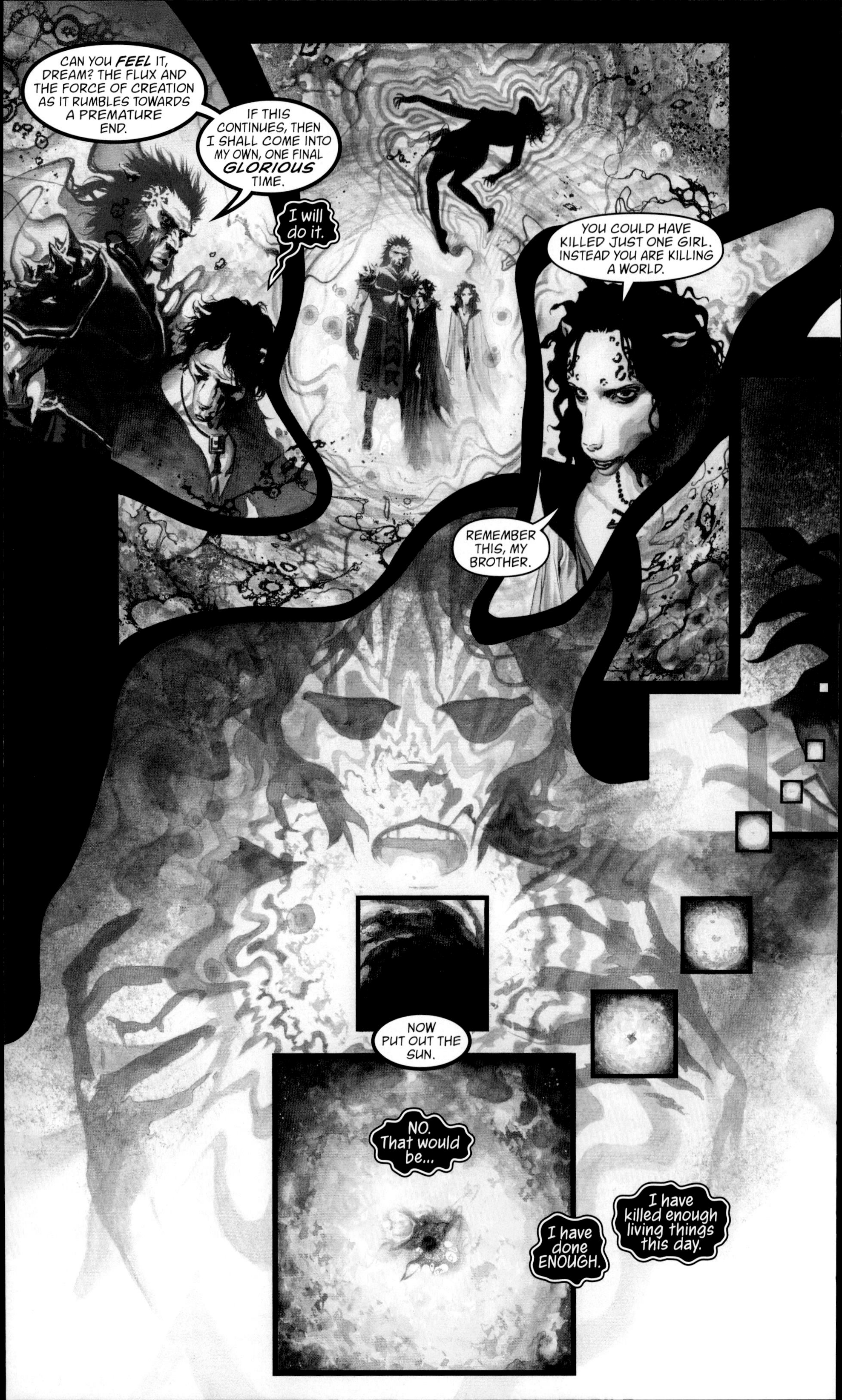
CAN YOU FEEL IT, DREAM? THE FLUX AND THE FORCE OF CREATION AS IT RUMBLES TOWARDS A PREMATURE END.
IF THIS CONTINUES, THEN I SHALL COME INTO MY OWN, ONE FINAL GLORIOUS TIME.
I will do it.
YOU COULD HAVE KILLED JUST ONE GIRL. INSTEAD YOU ARE KILLING A WORLD.
REMEMBER THIS, MY BROTHER.
NOW PUT OUT THE SUN.
NO. That would be...
I have done ENOUGH.
I have killed enough living things this day.

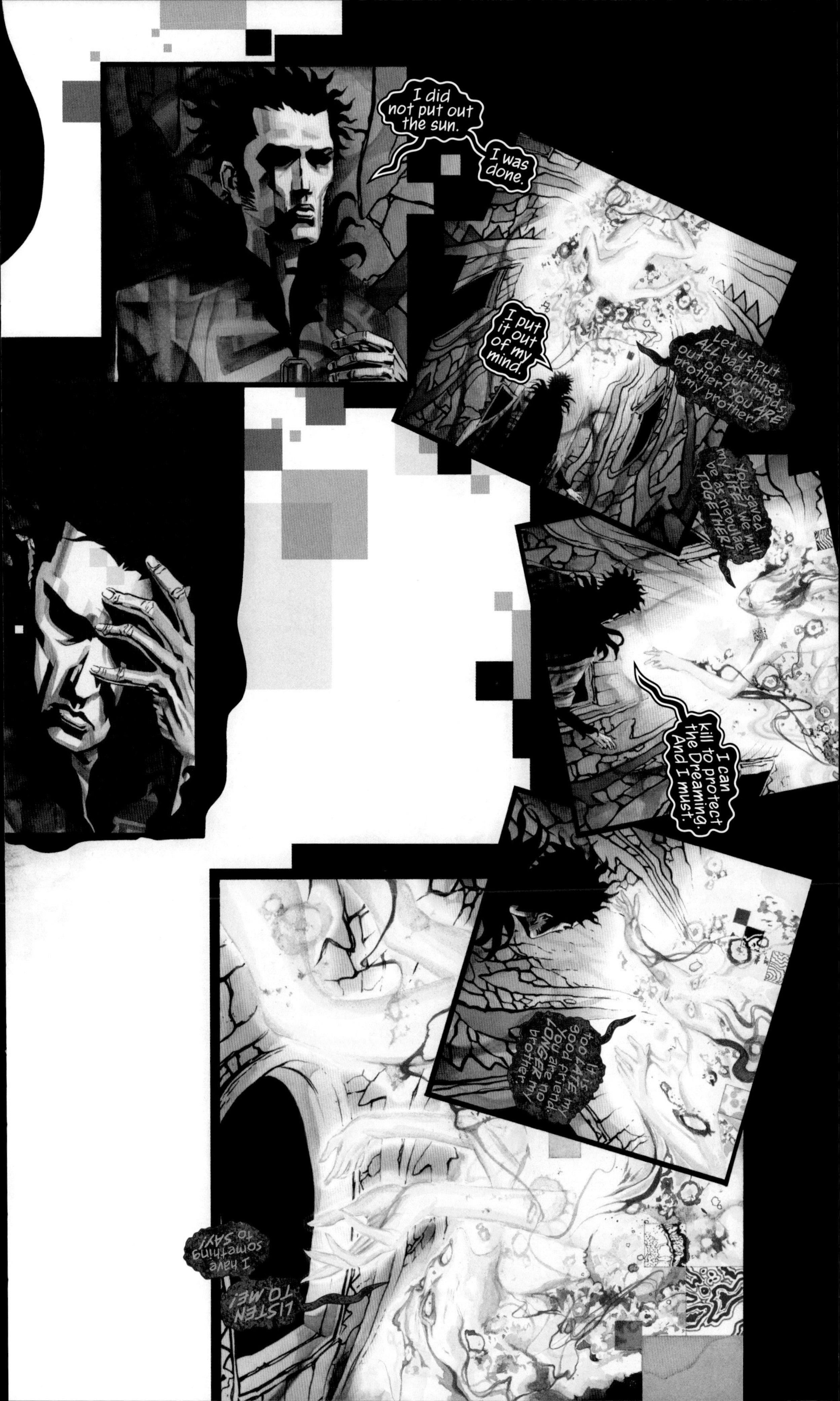

I did not put out the sun.
I was done.
I put it out of my mind.
Let us put ALL bad things out of our minds, brother! You ARE my brother!
You saved my LIFE! We will be as nebulae TOGETHER!
I can kill to protect the Dreaming. And I must.
It's too LATE, my good friend. You are no LONGER my brother.
LISTEN TO ME!
I have something to SAY!

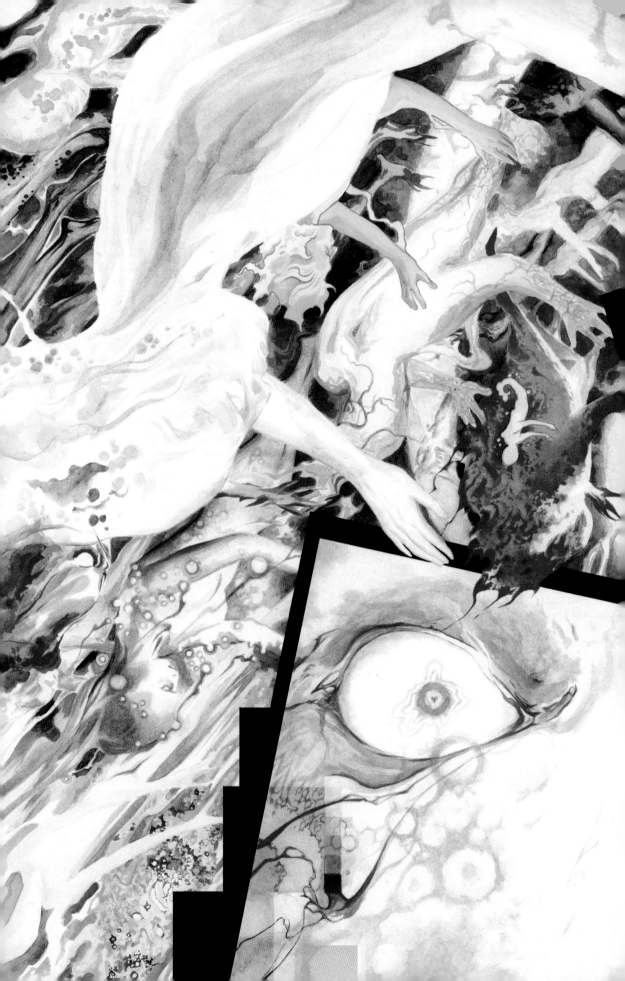

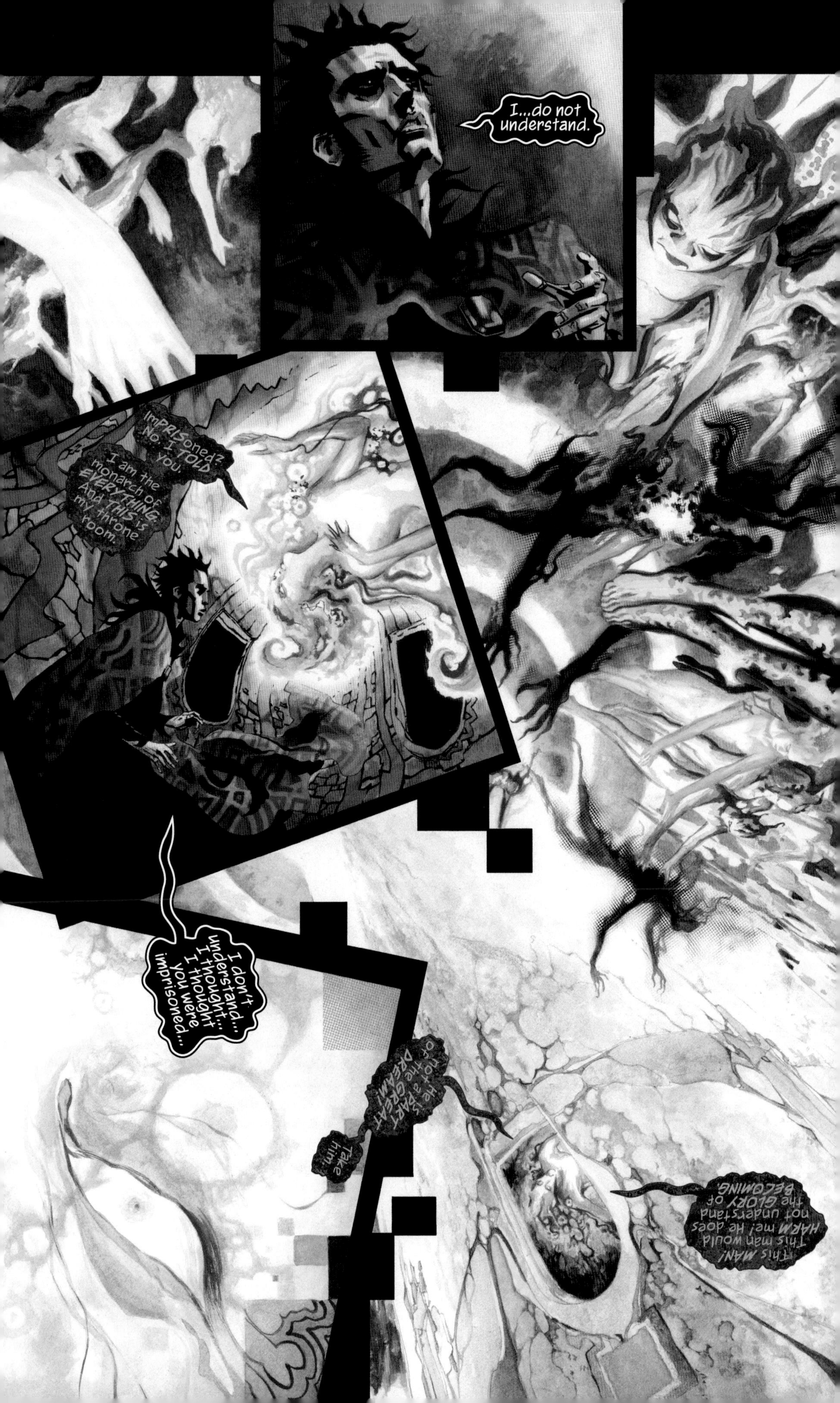

I...do not understand.
ImPRISoned? No. I TOLD you.
I am the monarch of EVERYTHING. And THIS is my throne room.
I don't understand... I thought... I thought you were imprisoned...
He is not a PART of the GREAT DREAM!
Take him!
THIS MAN! This man would HARM me! He does not understand the GLORY of BECOMING.

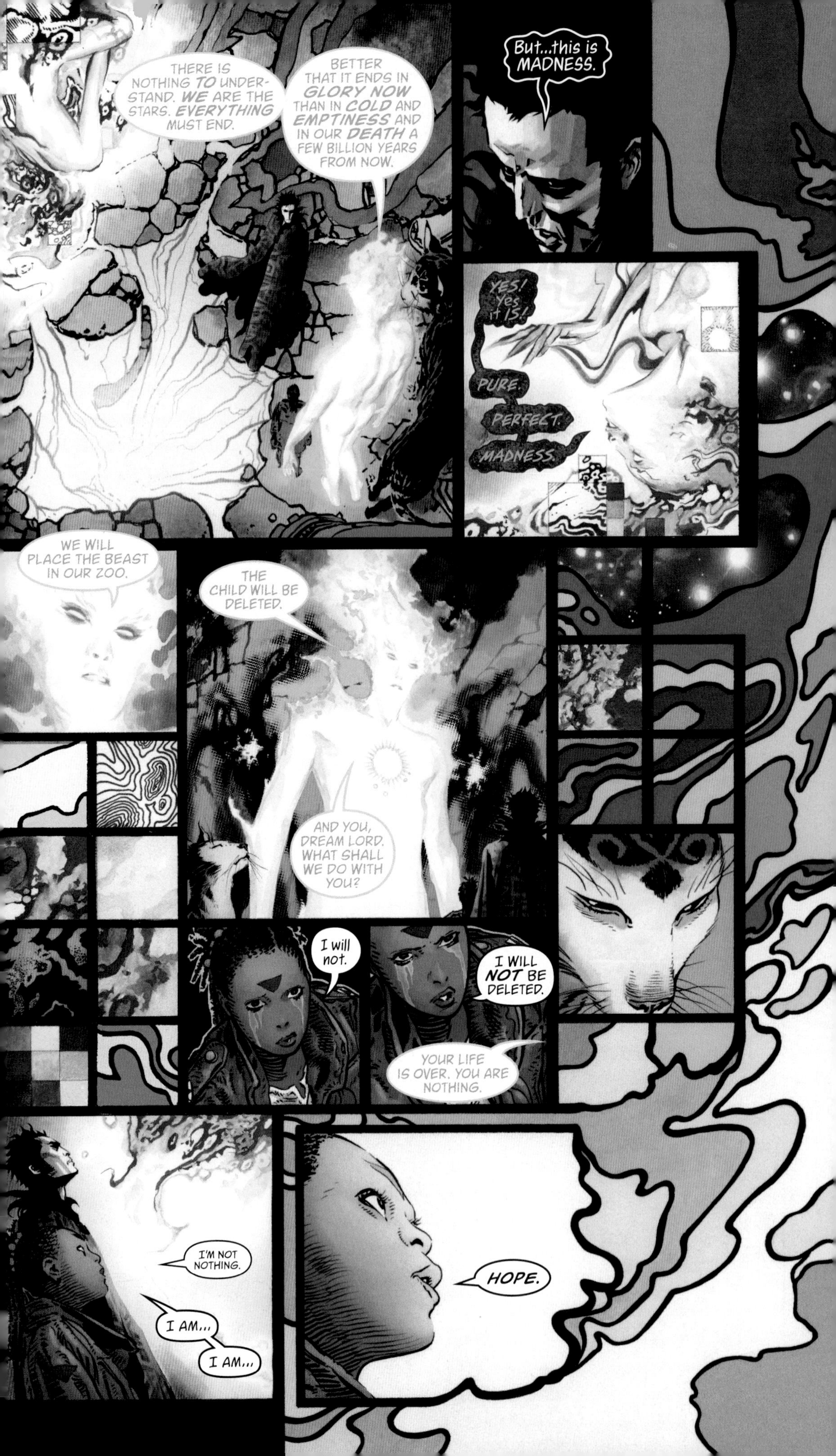
THERE IS NOTHING TO UNDERSTAND. WE ARE THE STARS. EVERYTHING MUST END.
BETTER THAT IT ENDS IN GLORY NOW THAN IN COLD AND EMPTINESS AND IN OUR DEATH A FEW BILLION YEARS FROM NOW.
But...this is MADNESS.
YES! Yes it IS!
PURE.
PERFECT.
MADNESS.
WE WILL PLACE THE BEAST IN OUR ZOO.
THE CHILD WILL BE DELETED.
AND YOU, DREAM LORD. WHAT SHALL WE DO WITH YOU?
I will not.
I WILL NOT BE DELETED.
YOUR LIFE IS OVER. YOU ARE NOTHING.
I'M NOT NOTHING.
I AM...
I AM...
HOPE.

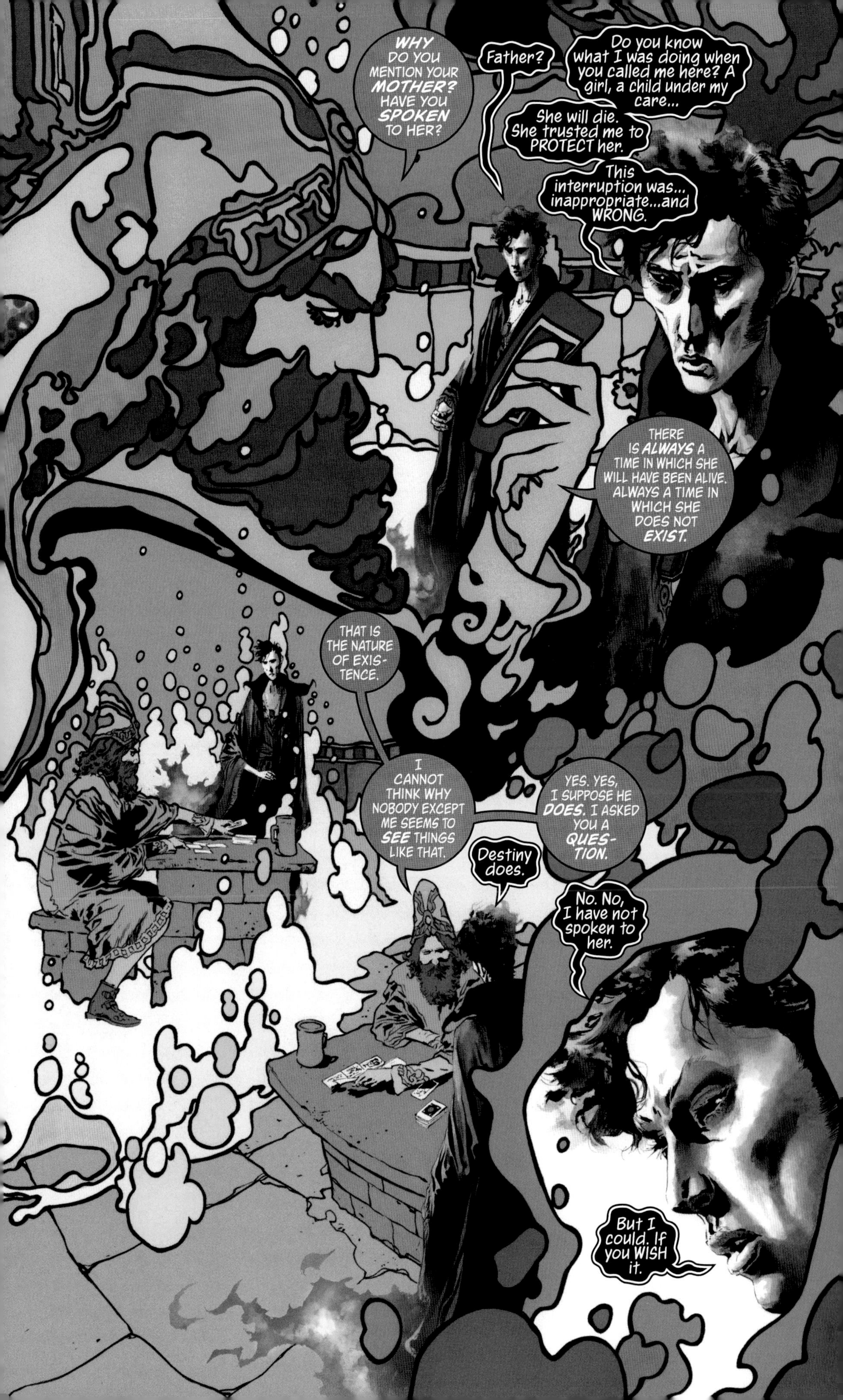
WHY DO YOU MENTION YOUR MOTHER? HAVE YOU SPOKEN TO HER?
Father?
Do you know what I was doing when you called me here? A girl, a child under my care...
She will die. She trusted me to PROTECT her.
This interruption was... inappropriate...and WRONG.
THERE IS ALWAYS A TIME IN WHICH SHE WILL HAVE BEEN ALIVE. ALWAYS A TIME IN WHICH SHE DOES NOT EXIST.
THAT IS THE NATURE OF EXIS-TENCE.
I CANNOT THINK WHY NOBODY EXCEPT ME SEEMS TO SEE THINGS LIKE THAT.
Destiny does.
YES. YES, I SUPPOSE HE DOES. I ASKED YOU A QUES-TION.
No. No, I have not spoken to her.
But I could. If you WISH it.

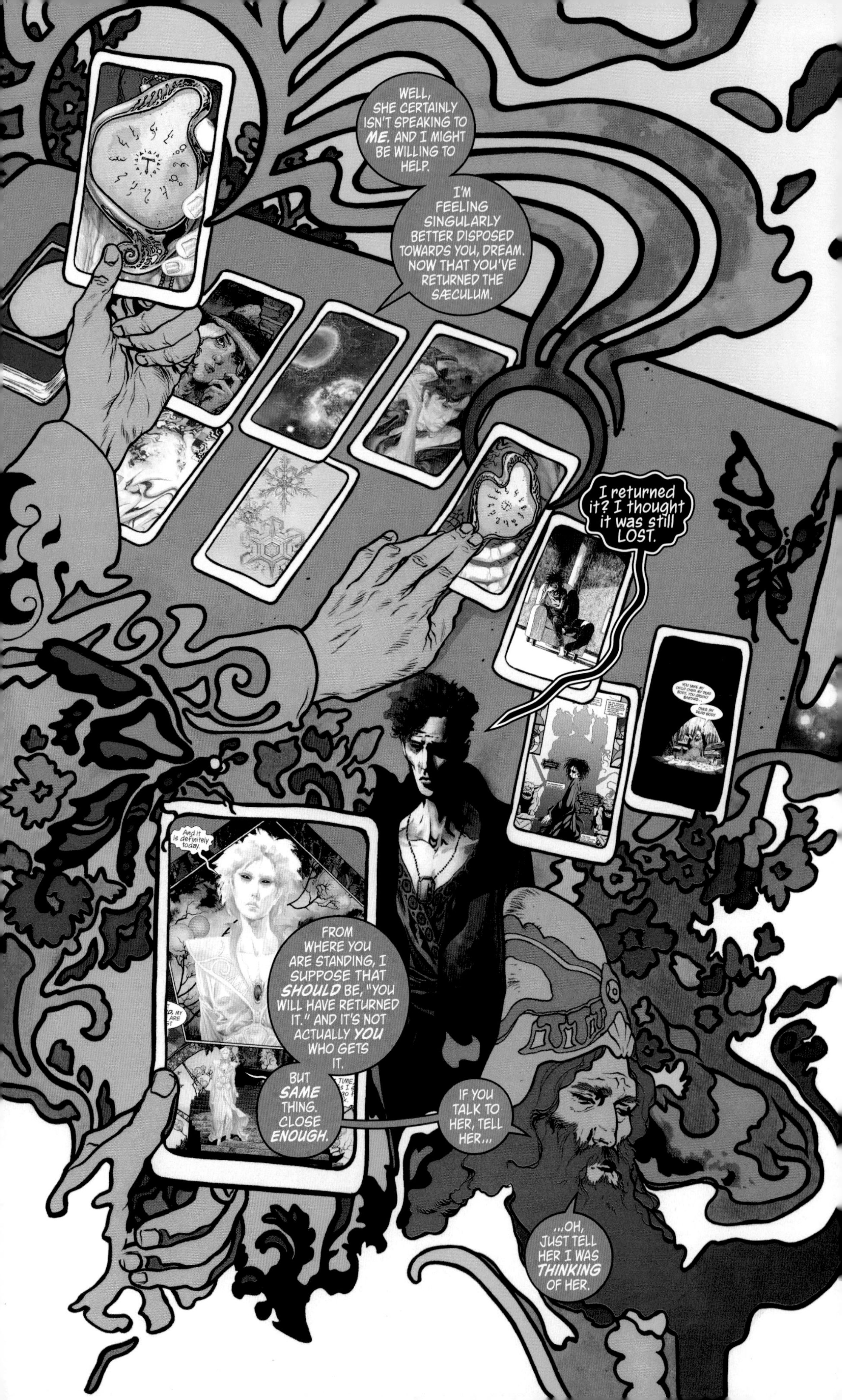
WELL, SHE CERTAINLY ISN'T SPEAKING TO *ME*. AND I MIGHT BE WILLING TO HELP.
I'M FEELING SINGULARLY BETTER DISPOSED TOWARDS YOU, DREAM. NOW THAT YOU'VE RETURNED THE SÆCULUM.
I returned it? I thought it was still LOST.
And it is definitely today.
FROM WHERE YOU ARE STANDING, I SUPPOSE THAT *SHOULD* BE, "YOU WILL HAVE RETURNED IT." AND IT'S NOT ACTUALLY *YOU* WHO GETS IT.
BUT *SAME* THING. CLOSE *ENOUGH*.
IF YOU TALK TO HER, TELL HER...
...OH, JUST TELL HER I WAS *THINKING* OF HER.

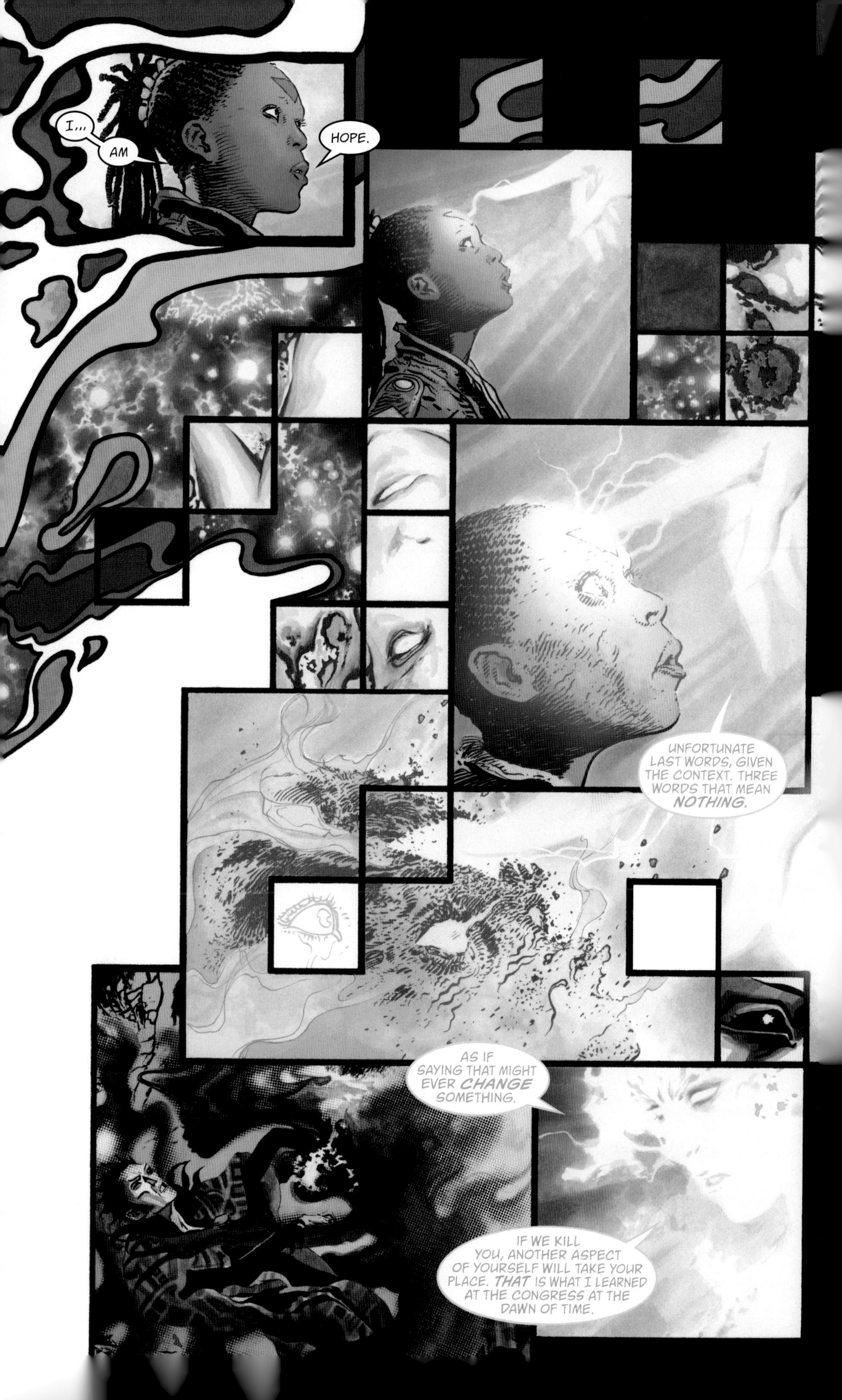
I...
AM
HOPE.
UNFORTUNATE LAST WORDS, GIVEN THE CONTEXT. THREE WORDS THAT MEAN NOTHING.
AS IF SAYING THAT MIGHT EVER CHANGE SOMETHING.
IF WE KILL YOU, ANOTHER ASPECT OF YOURSELF WILL TAKE YOUR PLACE. THAT IS WHAT I LEARNED AT THE CONGRESS AT THE DAWN OF TIME.

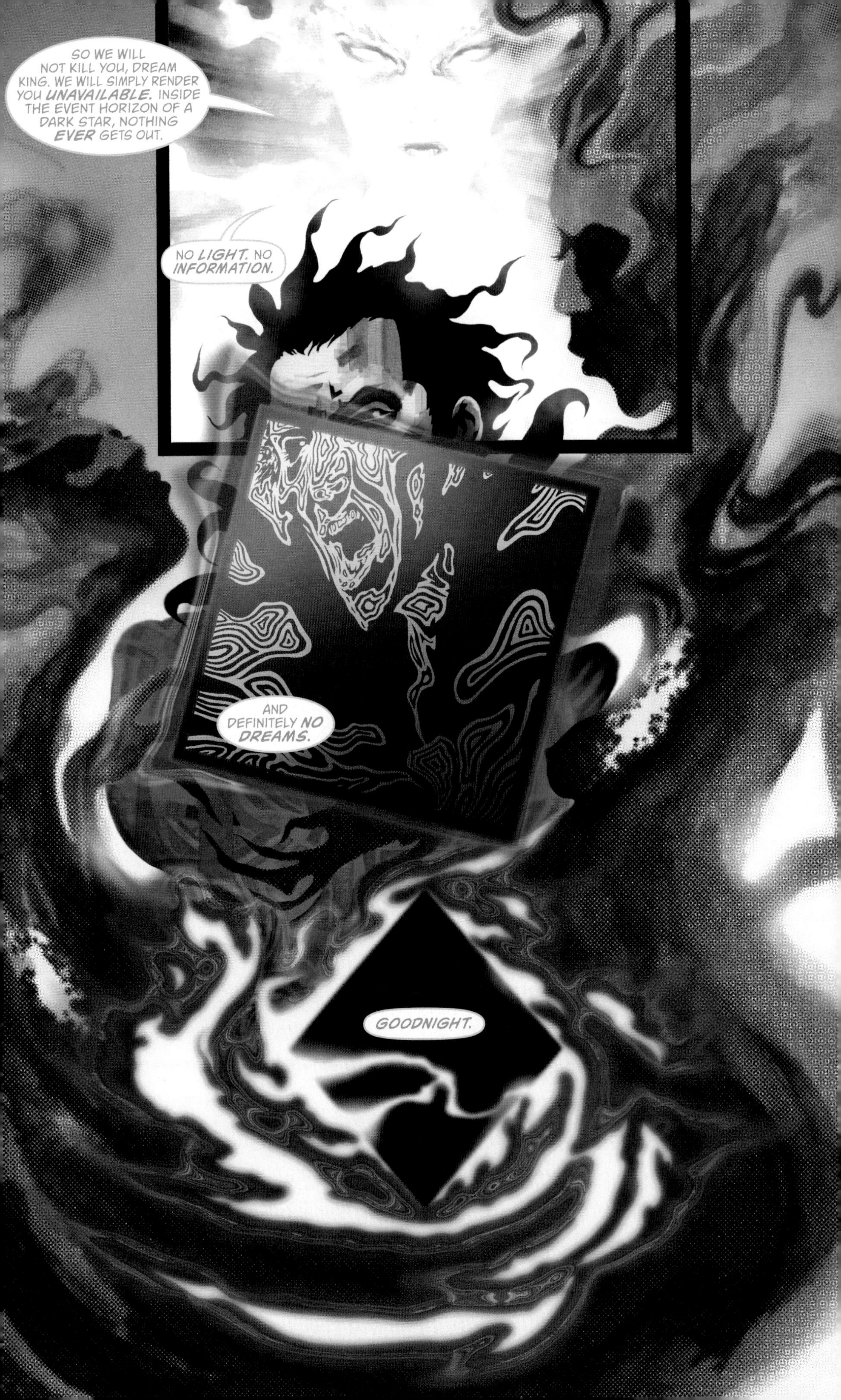
SO WE WILL NOT KILL YOU, DREAM KING. WE WILL SIMPLY RENDER YOU UNAVAILABLE. INSIDE THE EVENT HORIZON OF A DARK STAR, NOTHING EVER GETS OUT.
NO LIGHT. NO INFORMATION.
AND DEFINITELY NO DREAMS.
GOODNIGHT.

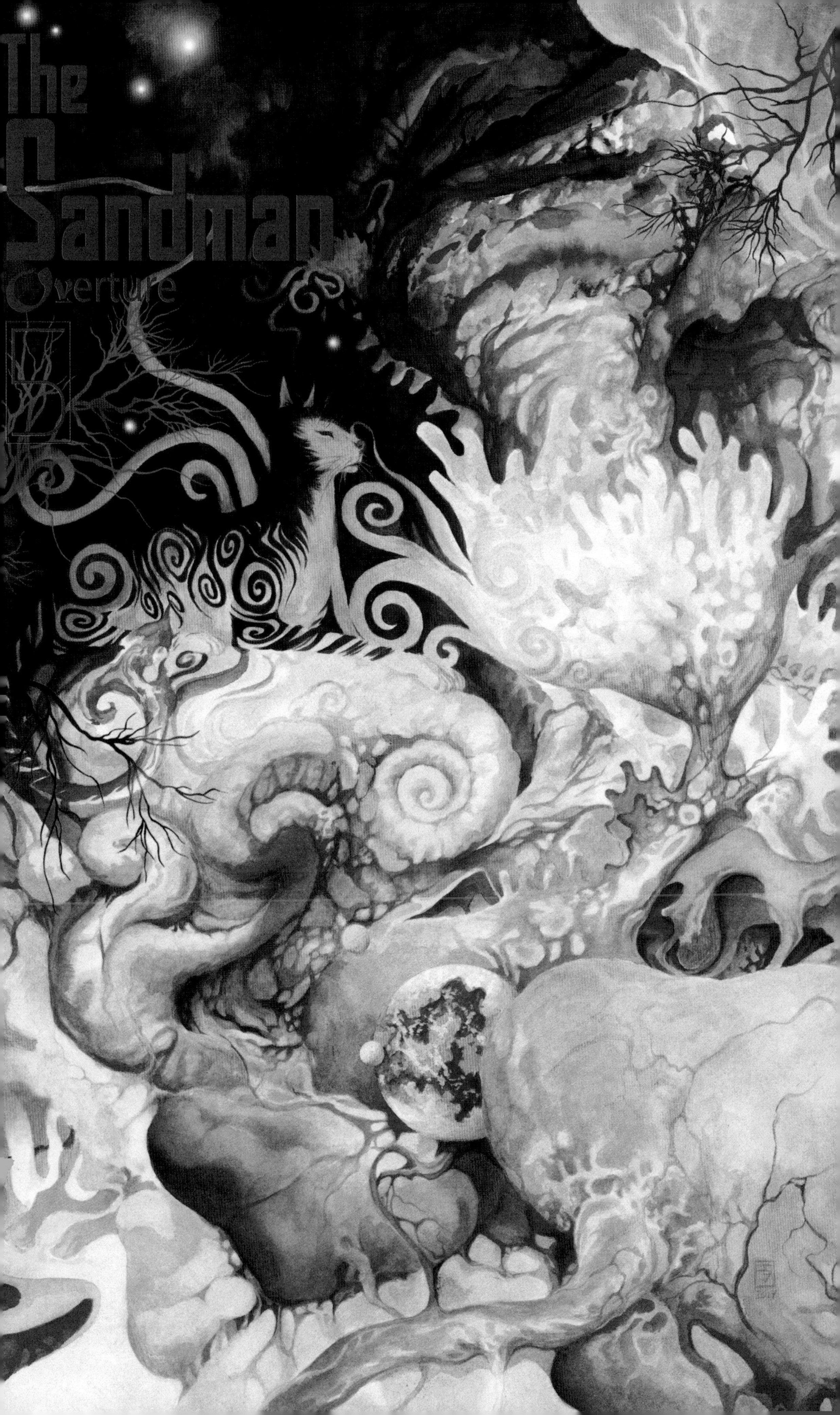
The Sandman
Overture
3

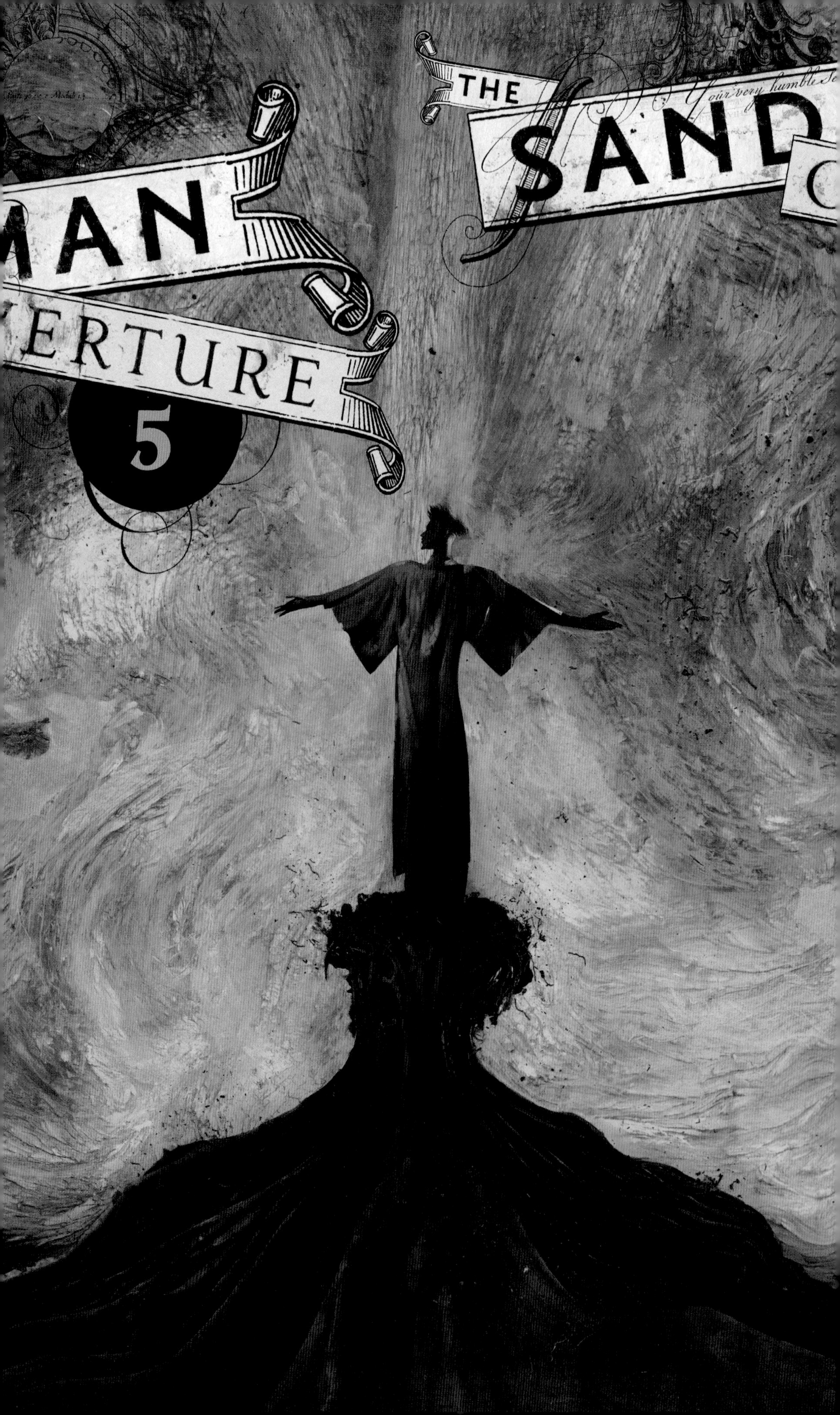
THE
SAND
MAN
ERTURE
5

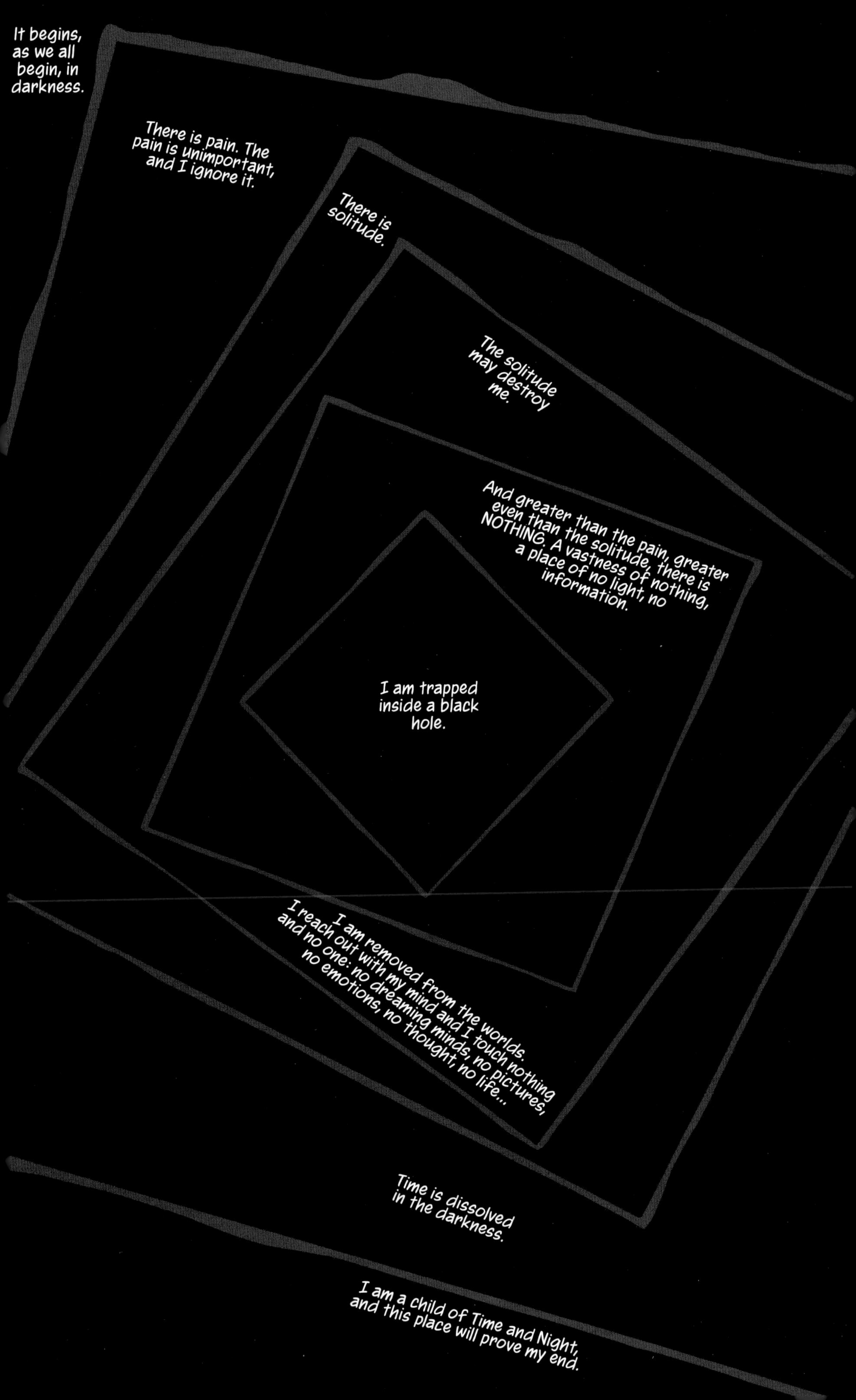
It begins, as we all begin, in darkness.
There is pain. The pain is unimportant, and I ignore it.
There is solitude.
The solitude may destroy me.
And greater than the pain, greater even than the solitude, there is NOTHING. A vastness of nothing, a place of no light, no information.
I am trapped inside a black hole.
I am removed from the worlds. I reach out with my mind and I touch nothing and no one: no dreaming minds, no pictures, no emotions, no thought, no life...
Time is dissolved in the darkness.
I am a child of Time and Night, and this place will prove my end.

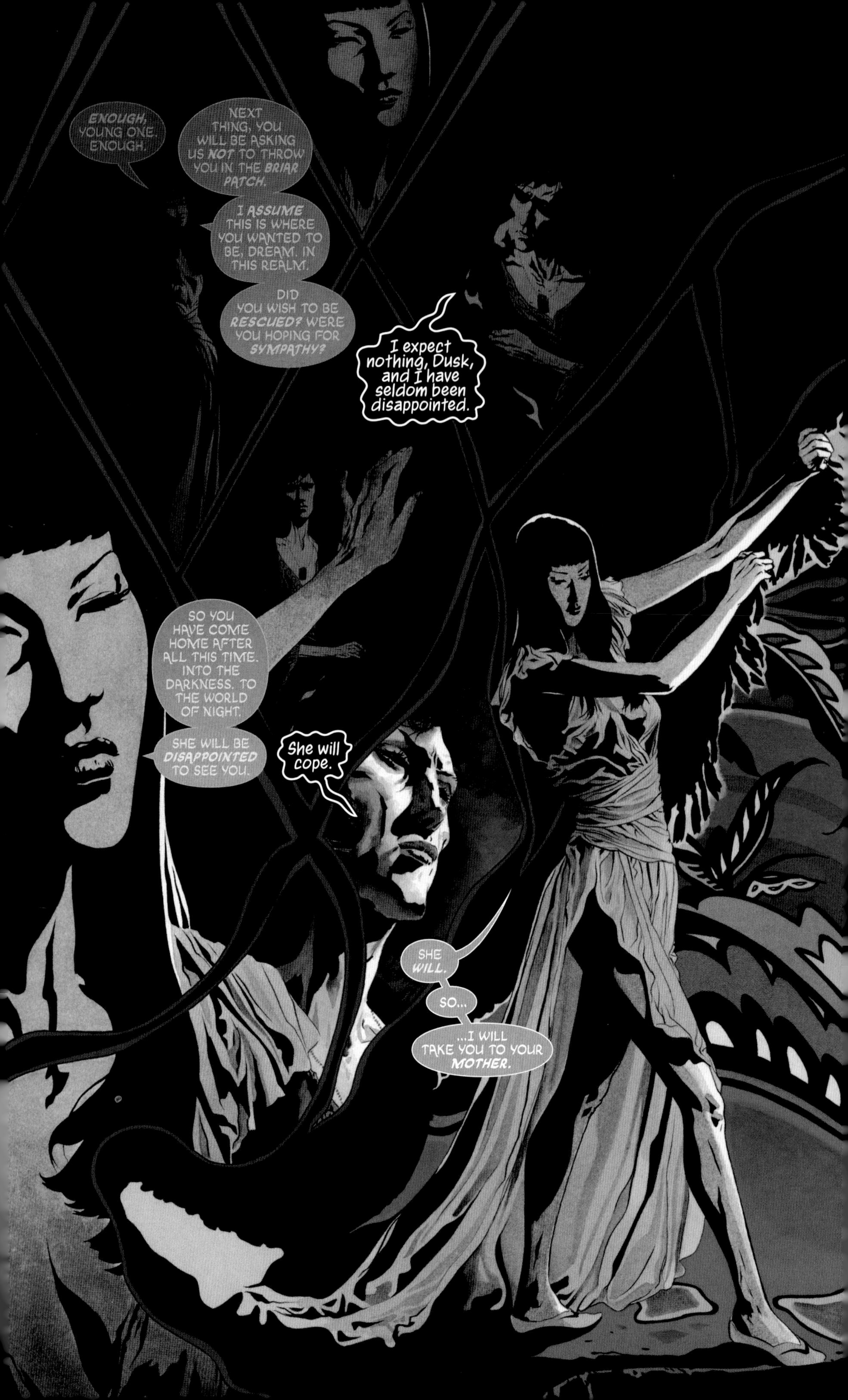
ENOUGH, YOUNG ONE. ENOUGH.
NEXT THING, YOU WILL BE ASKING US NOT TO THROW YOU IN THE BRIAR PATCH.
I ASSUME THIS IS WHERE YOU WANTED TO BE, DREAM. IN THIS REALM.
DID YOU WISH TO BE RESCUED? WERE YOU HOPING FOR SYMPATHY?
I expect nothing, Dusk, and I have seldom been disappointed.
SO YOU HAVE COME HOME AFTER ALL THIS TIME. INTO THE DARKNESS. TO THE WORLD OF NIGHT.
SHE WILL BE DISAPPOINTED TO SEE YOU.
She will cope.
SHE WILL.
SO...
...I WILL TAKE YOU TO YOUR MOTHER.

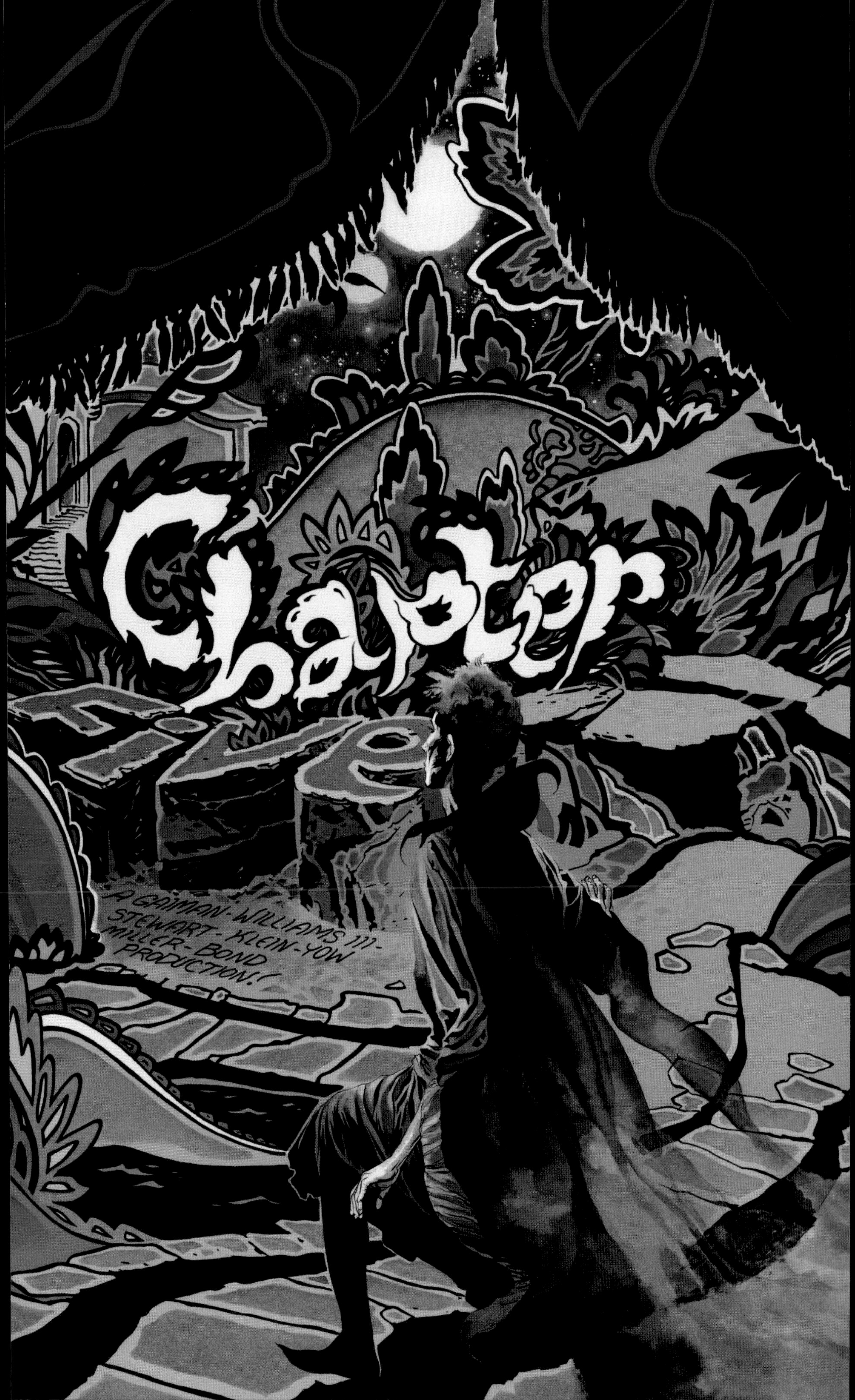
Chapter
Five
A GAIMAN - WILLIAMS III - STEWART - KLEIN - YOW MILLER - BOND PRODUCTION!

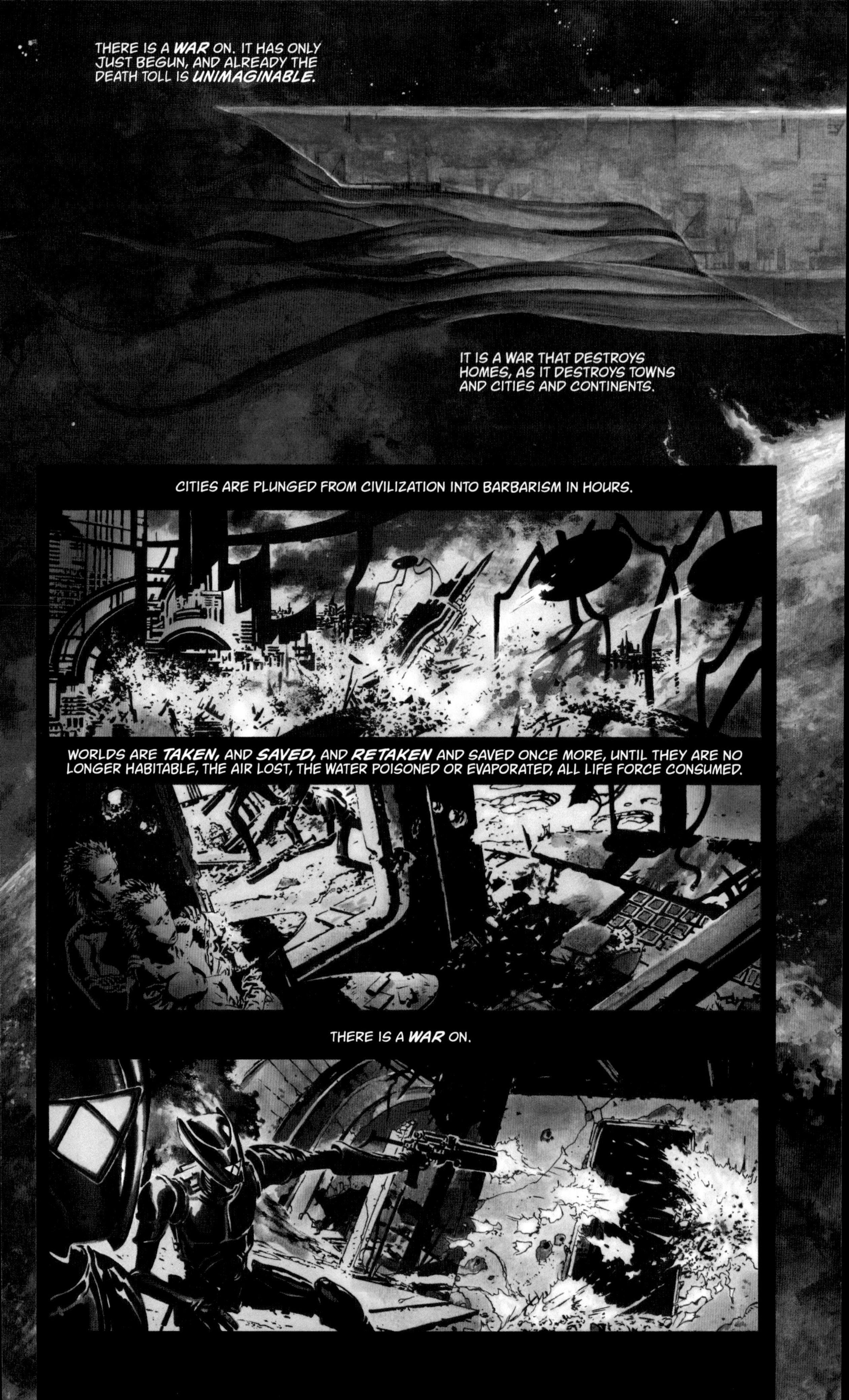
THERE IS A *WAR* ON. IT HAS ONLY JUST BEGUN, AND ALREADY THE DEATH TOLL IS *UNIMAGINABLE.*
IT IS A WAR THAT DESTROYS HOMES, AS IT DESTROYS TOWNS AND CITIES AND CONTINENTS.
CITIES ARE PLUNGED FROM CIVILIZATION INTO BARBARISM IN HOURS.
WORLDS ARE *TAKEN,* AND *SAVED,* AND *RETAKEN* AND SAVED ONCE MORE, UNTIL THEY ARE NO LONGER HABITABLE, THE AIR LOST, THE WATER POISONED OR EVAPORATED, ALL LIFE FORCE CONSUMED.
THERE IS A *WAR* ON.

IT IS SENSELESS, BLOODY, ABRUPT, AND IT IS ALSO UNAVOIDABLE--AT LEAST FOR THOSE AT THE RECEIVING END OF THE BULLETS OR THE BOMBS.

A RUMOR BEGINS, LITTLE MORE THAN A WHISPER. THEY SAY THERE IS SOMEONE WHO MOVES AMONG THE INJURED AND THE DYING, BRINGS COMFORT TO THE COMFORTLESS, WHO FEEDS THE HUNGRY.

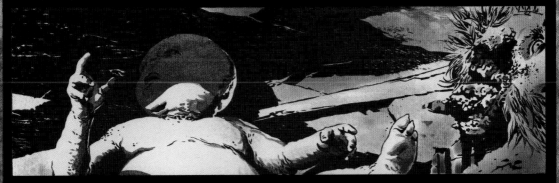

SOMEONE WHO OFFERS HOPE TO THE HOPELESS.

SOMEONE WHO, SOMETIMES, OFFERS *ESCAPE.*

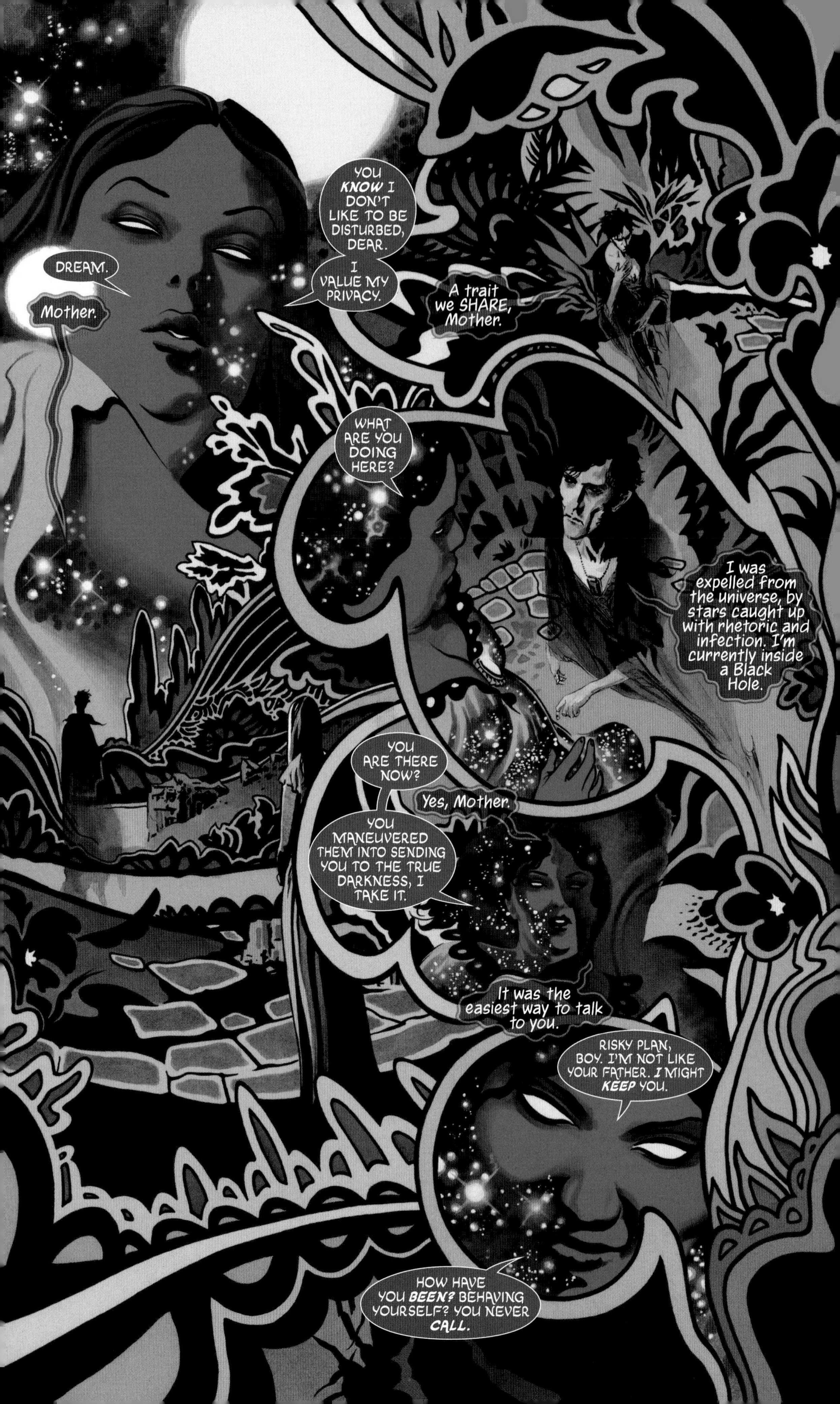
DREAM.
Mother.
YOU KNOW I DON'T LIKE TO BE DISTURBED, DEAR.
I VALUE MY PRIVACY.
A trait we SHARE, Mother.
WHAT ARE YOU DOING HERE?
I was expelled from the universe, by stars caught up with rhetoric and infection. I'm currently inside a Black Hole.
YOU ARE THERE NOW?
Yes, Mother.
YOU MANEUVERED THEM INTO SENDING YOU TO THE TRUE DARKNESS, I TAKE IT.
It was the easiest way to talk to you.
RISKY PLAN, BOY. I'M NOT LIKE YOUR FATHER. I MIGHT KEEP YOU.
HOW HAVE YOU BEEN? BEHAVING YOURSELF? YOU NEVER CALL.

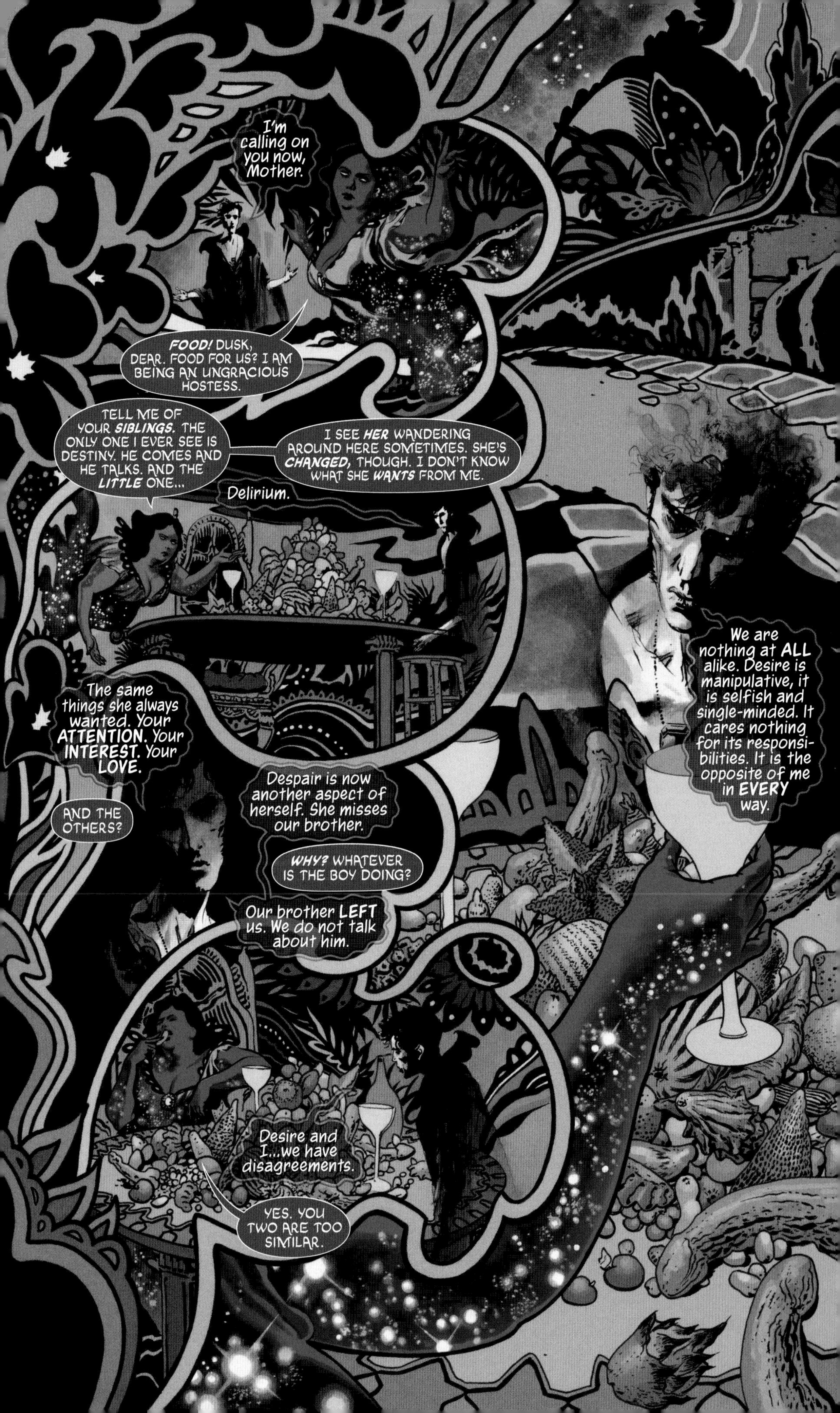

I'm calling on you now, Mother.
FOOD! DUSK, DEAR. FOOD FOR US? I AM BEING AN UNGRACIOUS HOSTESS.
TELL ME OF YOUR SIBLINGS. THE ONLY ONE I EVER SEE IS DESTINY. HE COMES AND HE TALKS. AND THE LITTLE ONE...
Delirium.
I SEE HER WANDERING AROUND HERE SOMETIMES. SHE'S CHANGED, THOUGH. I DON'T KNOW WHAT SHE WANTS FROM ME.
The same things she always wanted. Your ATTENTION. Your INTEREST. Your LOVE.
AND THE OTHERS?
Despair is now another aspect of herself. She misses our brother.
WHY? WHATEVER IS THE BOY DOING?
Our brother LEFT us. We do not talk about him.
Desire and I...we have disagreements.
YES. YOU TWO ARE TOO SIMILAR.
We are nothing at ALL alike. Desire is manipulative, it is selfish and single-minded. It cares nothing for its responsi-bilities. It is the opposite of me in EVERY way.

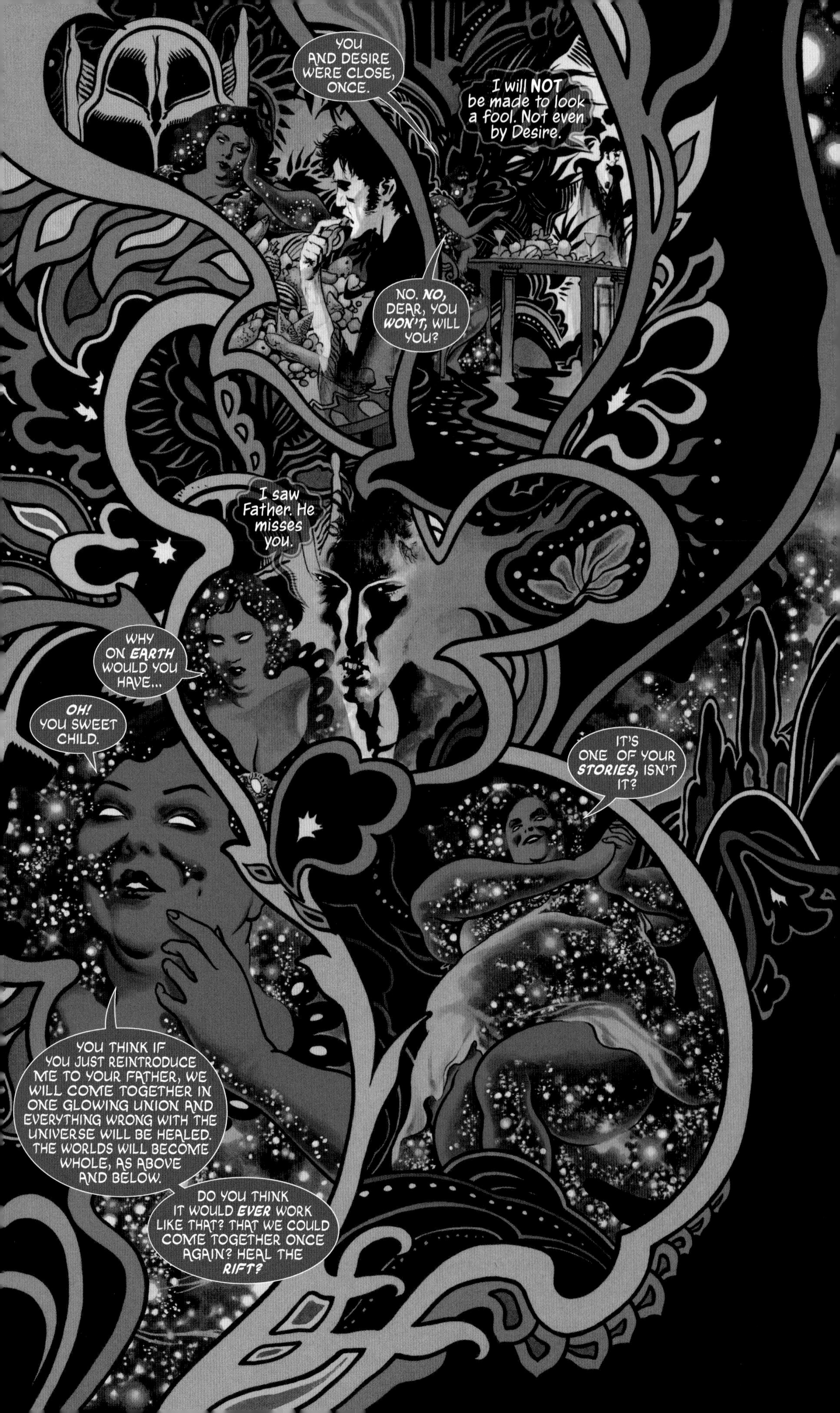
YOU AND DESIRE WERE CLOSE, ONCE.
I will NOT be made to look a fool. Not even by Desire.
NO. NO, DEAR, YOU WON'T, WILL YOU?
I saw Father. He misses you.
WHY ON EARTH WOULD YOU HAVE...
OH! YOU SWEET CHILD.
IT'S ONE OF YOUR STORIES, ISN'T IT?
YOU THINK IF YOU JUST REINTRODUCE ME TO YOUR FATHER, WE WILL COME TOGETHER IN ONE GLOWING UNION AND EVERYTHING WRONG WITH THE UNIVERSE WILL BE HEALED. THE WORLDS WILL BECOME WHOLE, AS ABOVE AND BELOW.
DO YOU THINK IT WOULD EVER WORK LIKE THAT? THAT WE COULD COME TOGETHER ONCE AGAIN? HEAL THE RIFT?

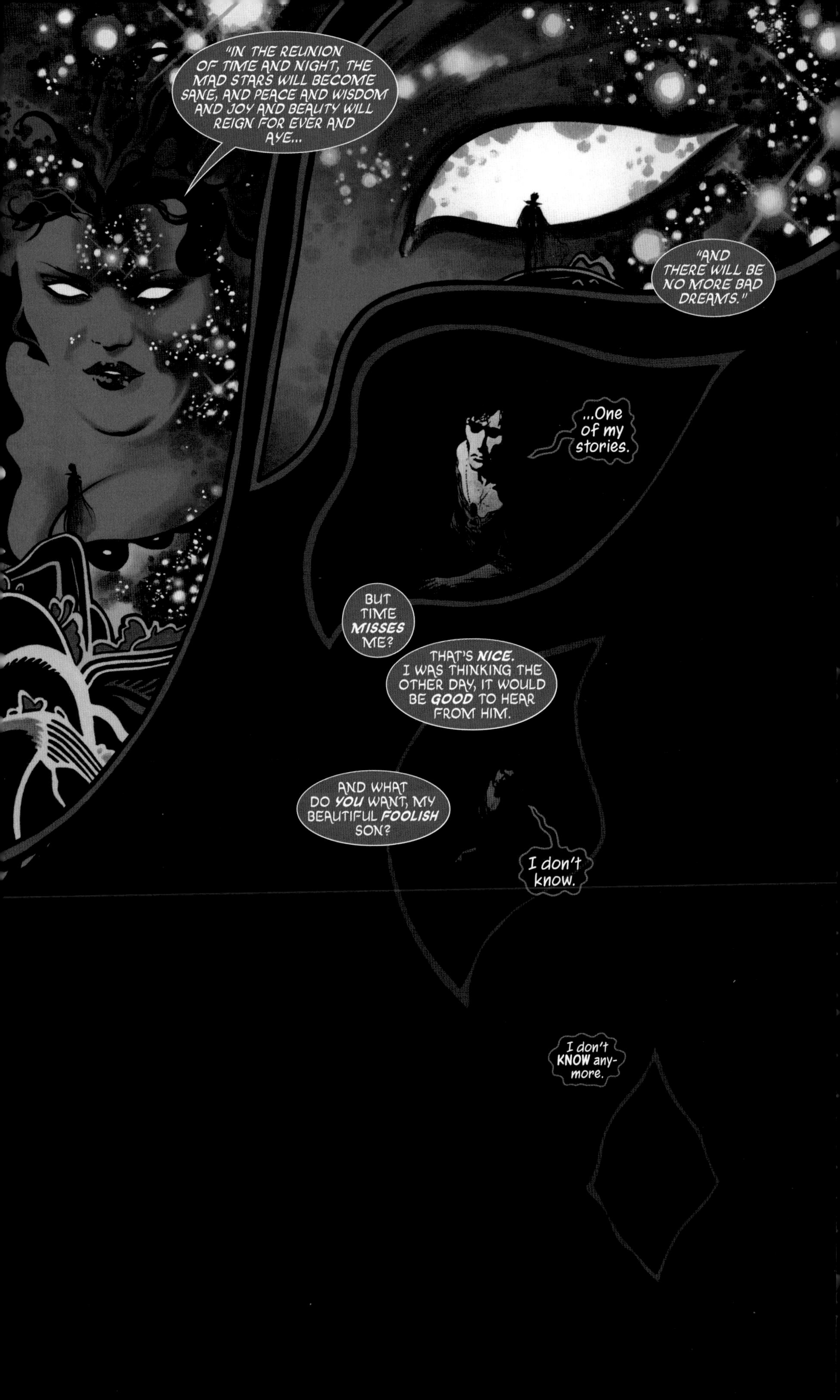
"IN THE REUNION OF TIME AND NIGHT, THE MAD STARS WILL BECOME SANE, AND PEACE AND WISDOM AND JOY AND BEAUTY WILL REIGN FOR EVER AND AYE...
"AND THERE WILL BE NO MORE BAD DREAMS."
...One of my stories.
BUT TIME *MISSES* ME?
THAT'S *NICE*. I WAS THINKING THE OTHER DAY, IT WOULD BE *GOOD* TO HEAR FROM HIM.
AND WHAT DO *YOU* WANT, MY BEAUTIFUL *FOOLISH* SON?
I don't know.
I don't **KNOW** any-more.

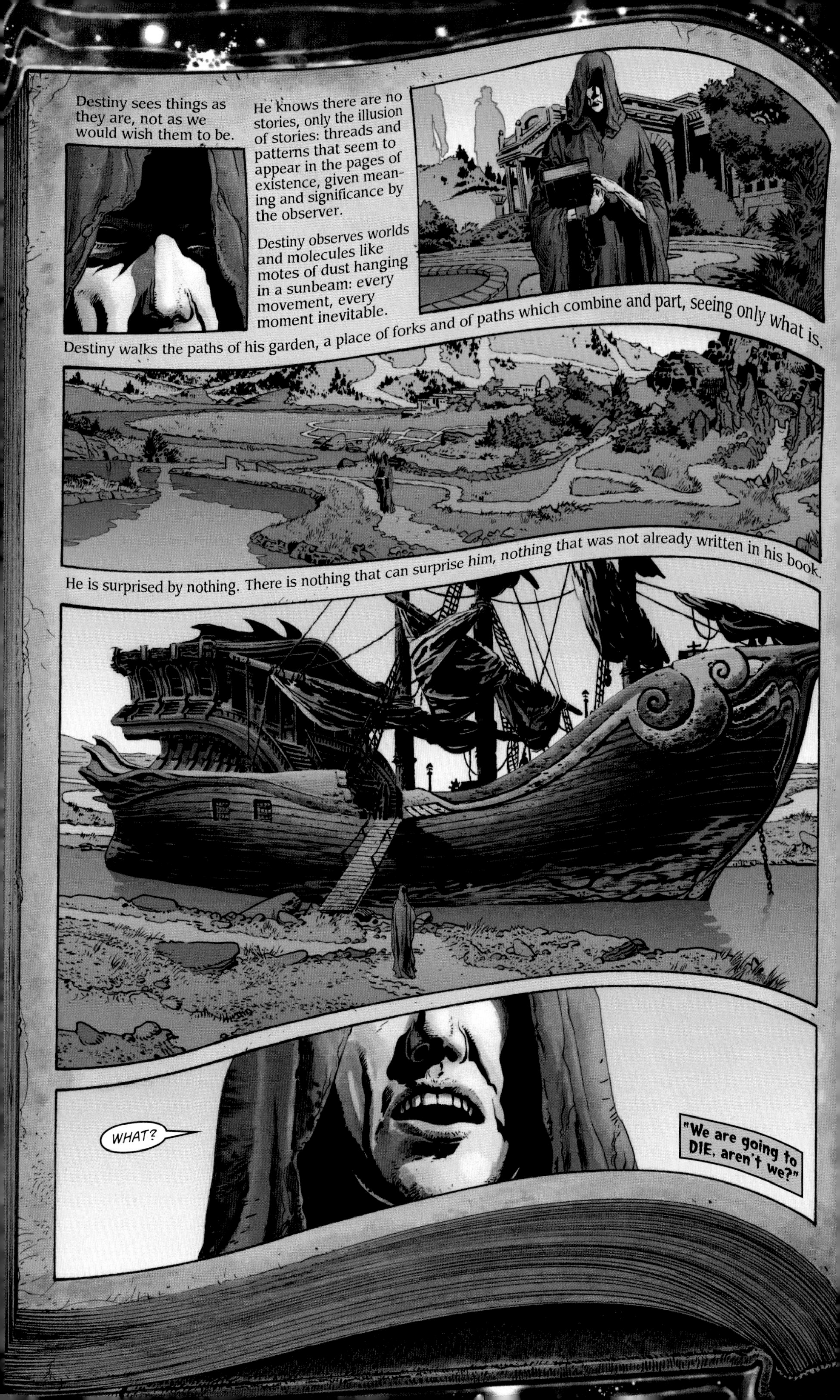

Destiny sees things as they are, not as we would wish them to be.
He knows there are no stories, only the illusion of stories: threads and patterns that seem to appear in the pages of existence, given meaning and significance by the observer.
Destiny observes worlds and molecules like motes of dust hanging in a sunbeam: every movement, every moment inevitable.
Destiny walks the paths of his garden, a place of forks and of paths which combine and part, seeing only what is.
He is surprised by nothing. There is nothing that can surprise him, nothing that was not already written in his book.
WHAT?
"We are going to DIE, aren't we?"

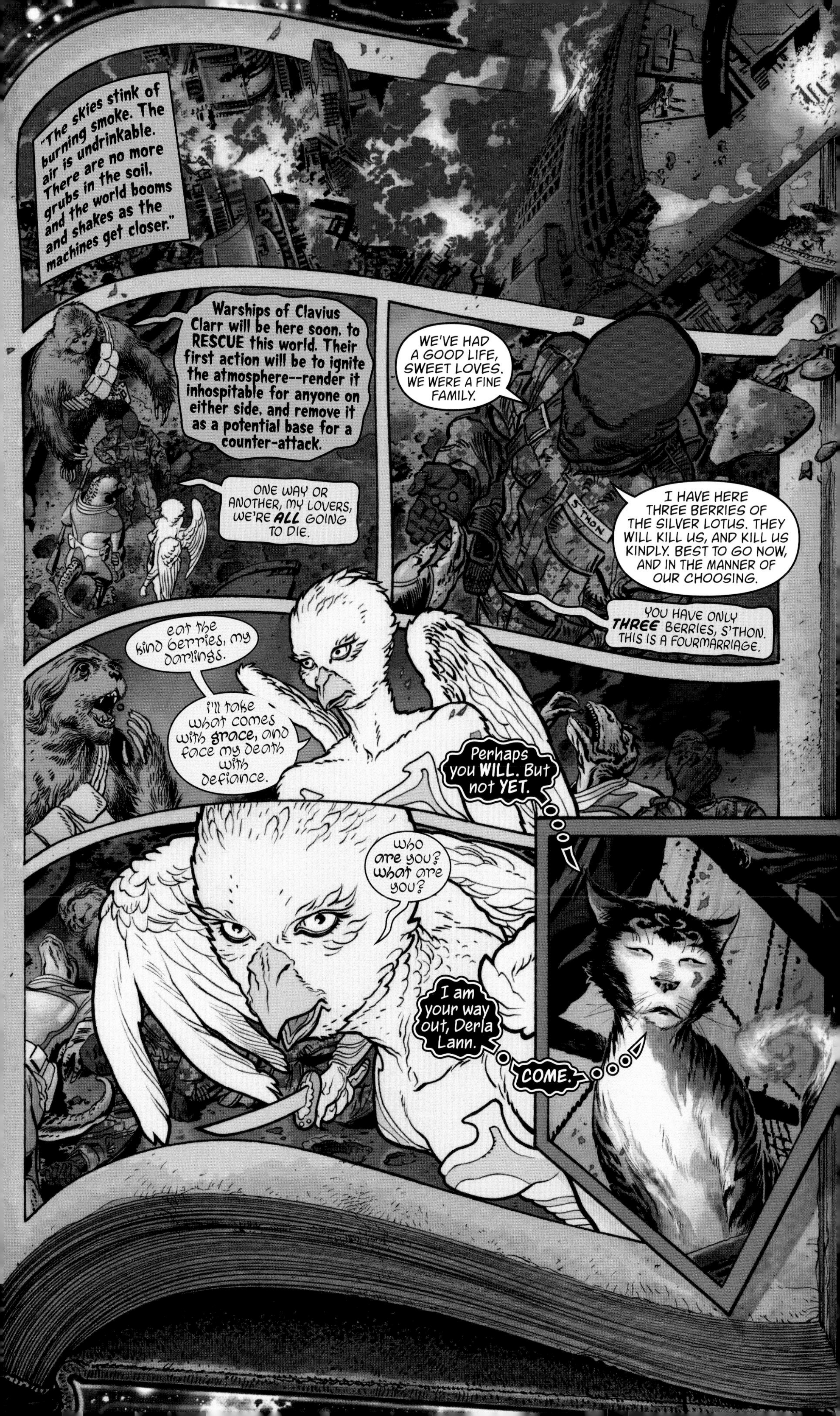
"The skies stink of burning smoke. The air is undrinkable. There are no more grubs in the soil, and the world booms and shakes as the machines get closer."
Warships of Clavius Clarr will be here soon, to RESCUE this world. Their first action will be to ignite the atmosphere--render it inhospitable for anyone on either side, and remove it as a potential base for a counter-attack.
ONE WAY OR ANOTHER, MY LOVERS, WE'RE ALL GOING TO DIE.
WE'VE HAD A GOOD LIFE, SWEET LOVES. WE WERE A FINE FAMILY.
S'THON
I HAVE HERE THREE BERRIES OF THE SILVER LOTUS. THEY WILL KILL US, AND KILL US KINDLY. BEST TO GO NOW, AND IN THE MANNER OF OUR CHOOSING.
YOU HAVE ONLY THREE BERRIES, S'THON. THIS IS A FOURMARRIAGE.
eat the kind berries, my darlings.
i'll take what comes with grace, and face my death with defiance.
Perhaps you WILL. But not YET.
who are you? what are you?
I am your way out, Derla Lann.
COME.

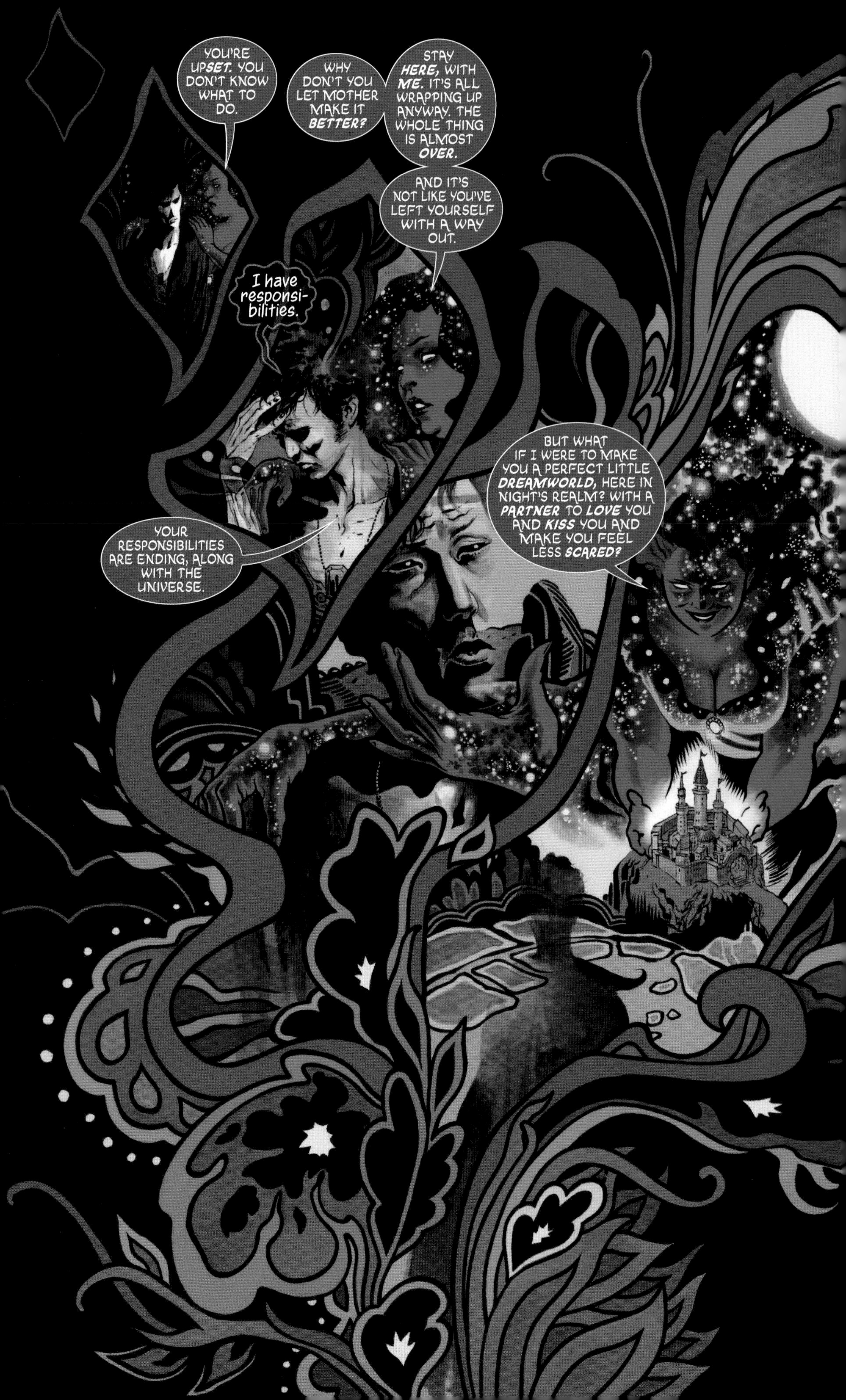
YOU'RE UPSET. YOU DON'T KNOW WHAT TO DO.
WHY DON'T YOU LET MOTHER MAKE IT BETTER?
STAY HERE, WITH ME. IT'S ALL WRAPPING UP ANYWAY. THE WHOLE THING IS ALMOST OVER.
AND IT'S NOT LIKE YOU'VE LEFT YOURSELF WITH A WAY OUT.
I have responsi-bilities.
YOUR RESPONSIBILITIES ARE ENDING, ALONG WITH THE UNIVERSE.
BUT WHAT IF I WERE TO MAKE YOU A PERFECT LITTLE DREAMWORLD, HERE IN NIGHT'S REALM? WITH A PARTNER TO LOVE YOU AND KISS YOU AND MAKE YOU FEEL LESS SCARED?

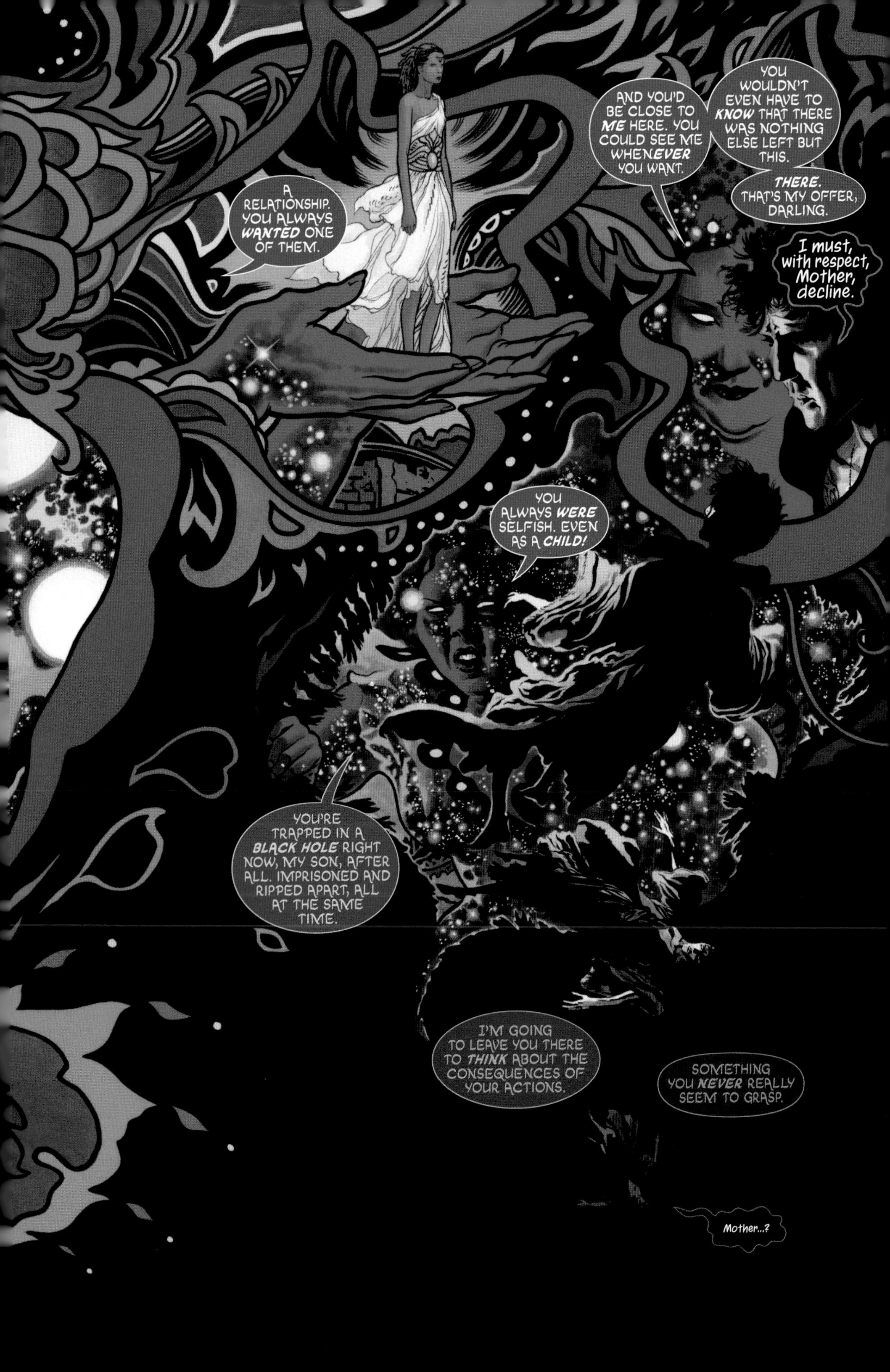
A RELATIONSHIP. YOU ALWAYS WANTED ONE OF THEM.
AND YOU'D BE CLOSE TO ME HERE. YOU COULD SEE ME WHENEVER YOU WANT.
YOU WOULDN'T EVEN HAVE TO KNOW THAT THERE WAS NOTHING ELSE LEFT BUT THIS.
THERE. THAT'S MY OFFER, DARLING.
I must, with respect, Mother, decline.
YOU ALWAYS WERE SELFISH. EVEN AS A CHILD!
YOU'RE TRAPPED IN A BLACK HOLE RIGHT NOW, MY SON, AFTER ALL. IMPRISONED AND RIPPED APART, ALL AT THE SAME TIME.
I'M GOING TO LEAVE YOU THERE TO THINK ABOUT THE CONSEQUENCES OF YOUR ACTIONS.
SOMETHING YOU NEVER REALLY SEEM TO GRASP.
Mother...?

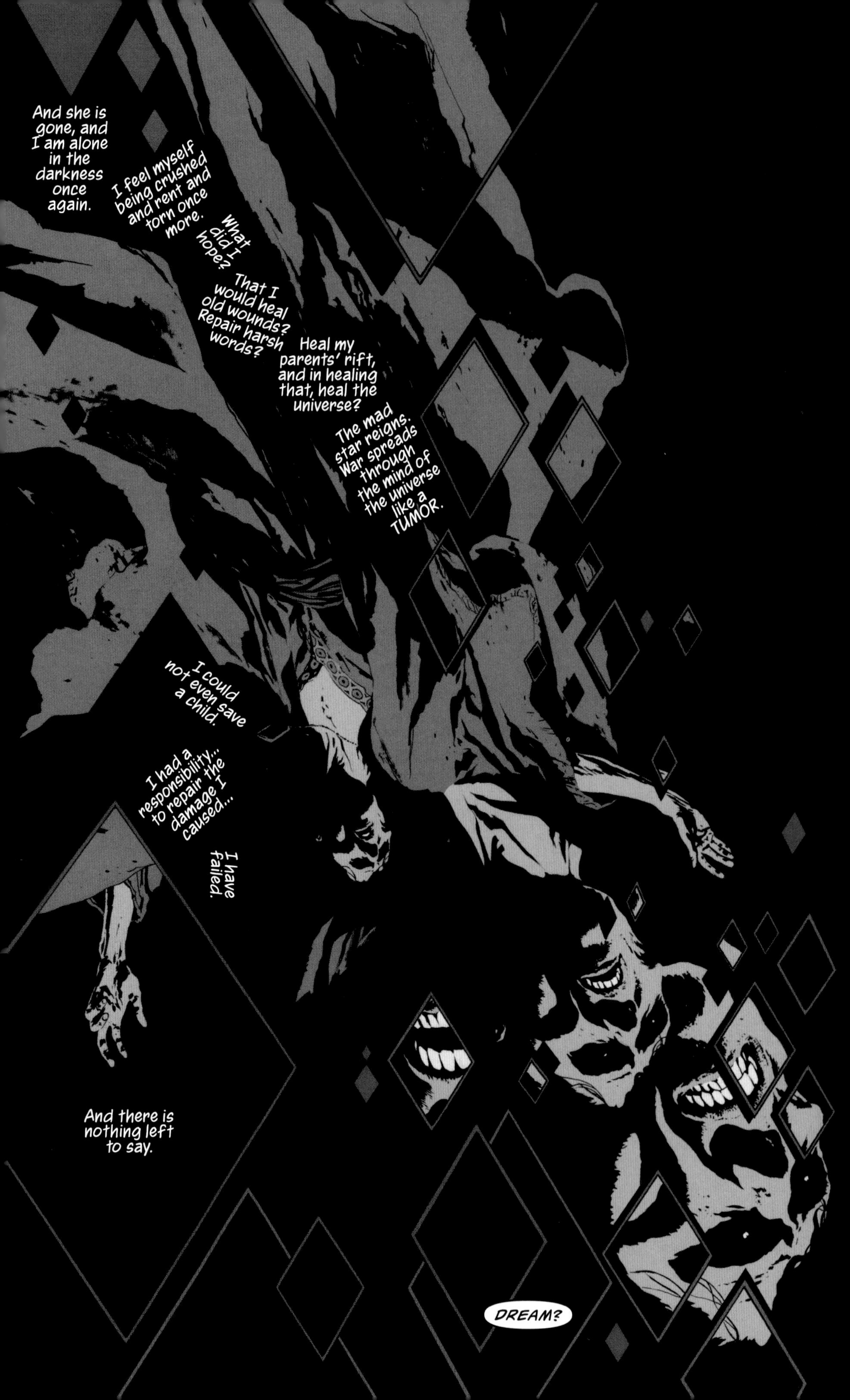
And she is gone, and I am alone in the darkness once again.
I feel myself being crushed and rent and torn once more.
What did I hope?
That I would heal old wounds? Repair harsh words?
Heal my parents' rift, and in healing that, heal the universe?
The mad star reigns. War spreads through the mind of the universe like a TUMOR.
I could not even save a child.
I had a responsibility... to repair the damage I caused...
I have failed.
And there is nothing left to say.
DREAM?

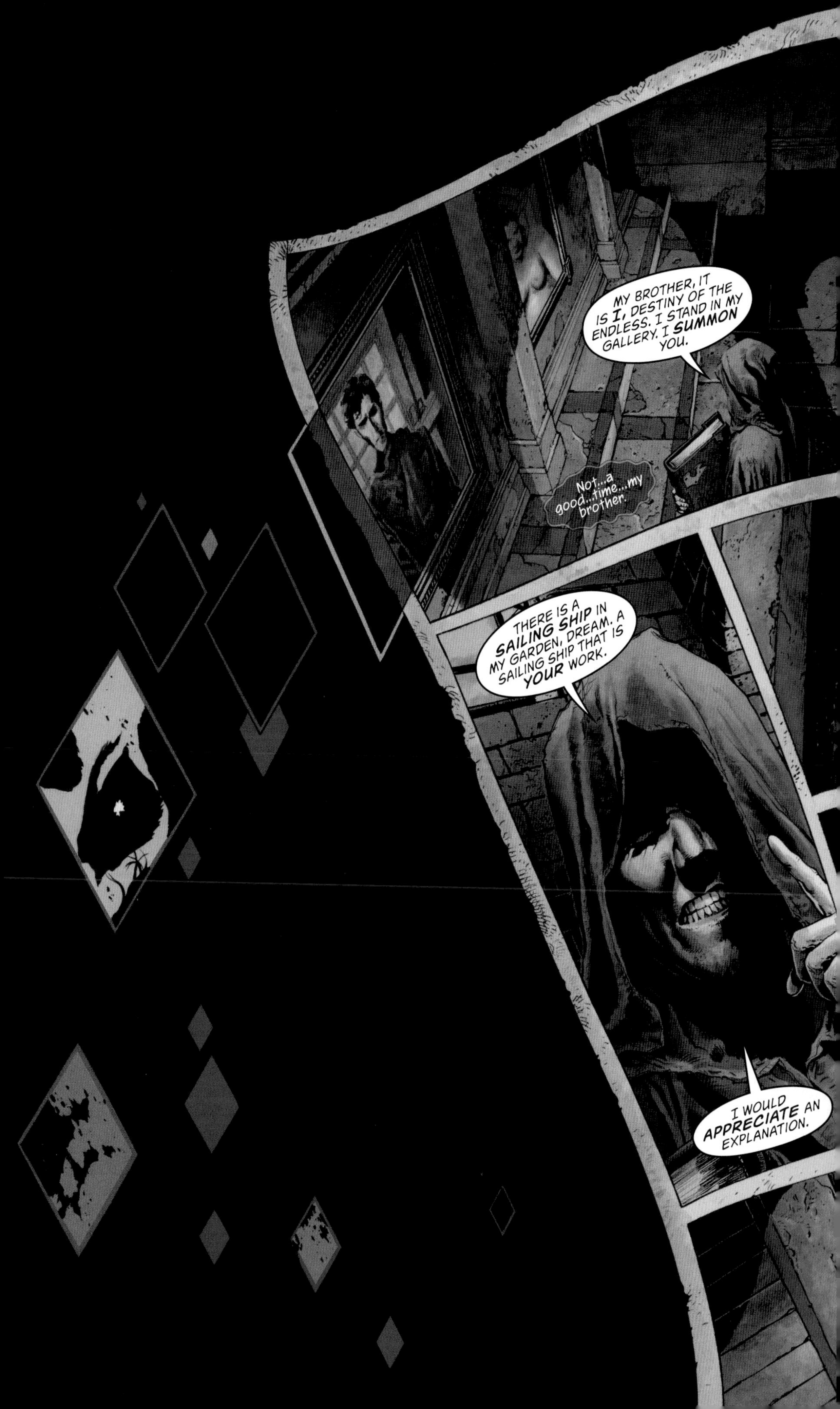
MY BROTHER, IT IS I, DESTINY OF THE ENDLESS. I STAND IN MY GALLERY. I SUMMON YOU.
Not...a good...time...my brother.
THERE IS A SAILING SHIP IN MY GARDEN, DREAM. A SAILING SHIP THAT IS YOUR WORK.
I WOULD APPRECIATE AN EXPLANATION.

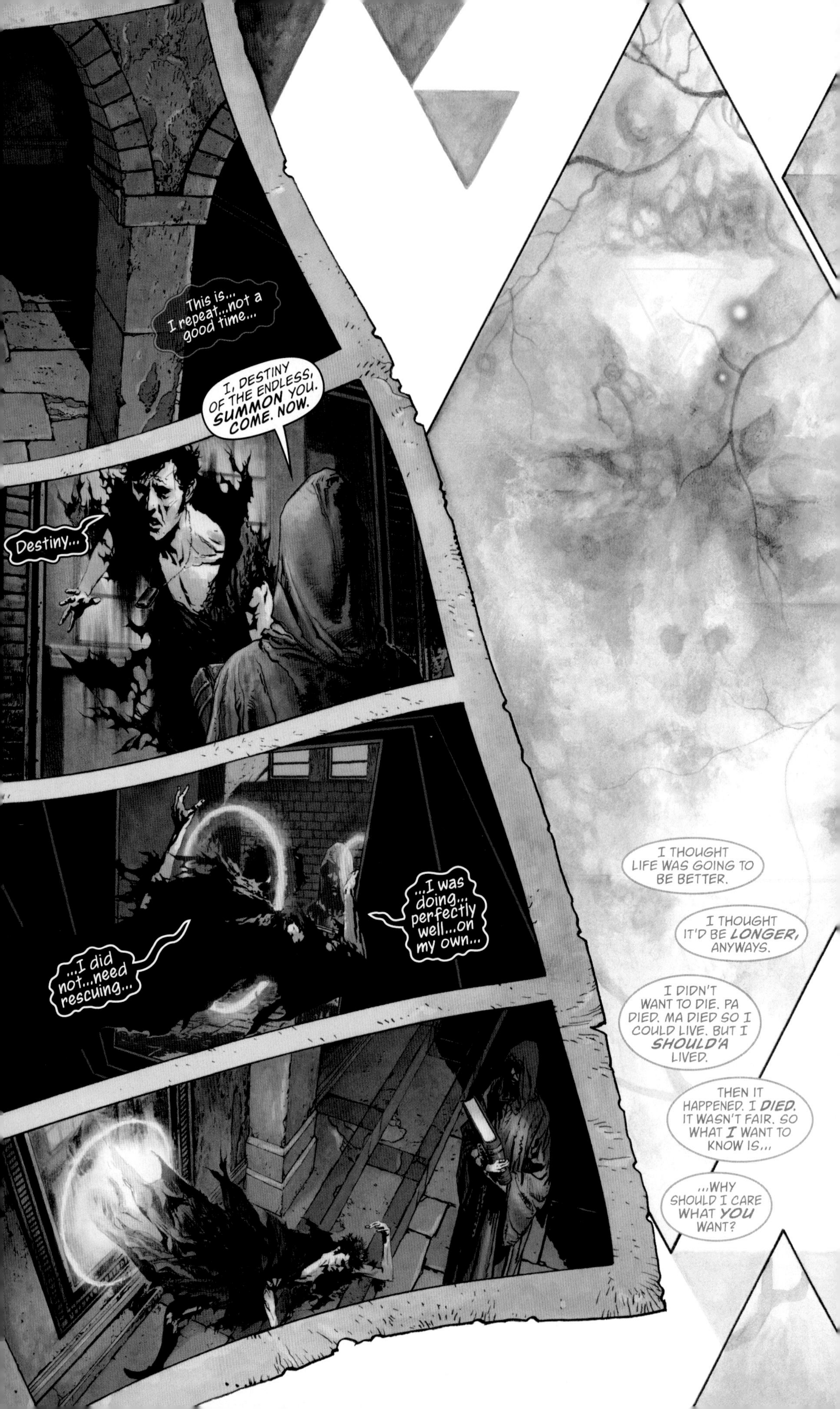
This is... I repeat...not a good time...
I, DESTINY OF THE ENDLESS, SUMMON YOU. COME. NOW.
Destiny...
...I was doing... perfectly well...on my own...
...I did not...need rescuing...
I THOUGHT LIFE WAS GOING TO BE BETTER.
I THOUGHT IT'D BE LONGER, ANYWAYS.
I DIDN'T WANT TO DIE. PA DIED. MA DIED SO I COULD LIVE. BUT I SHOULD'A LIVED.
THEN IT HAPPENED. I DIED. IT WASN'T FAIR. SO WHAT I WANT TO KNOW IS...
...WHY SHOULD I CARE WHAT YOU WANT?

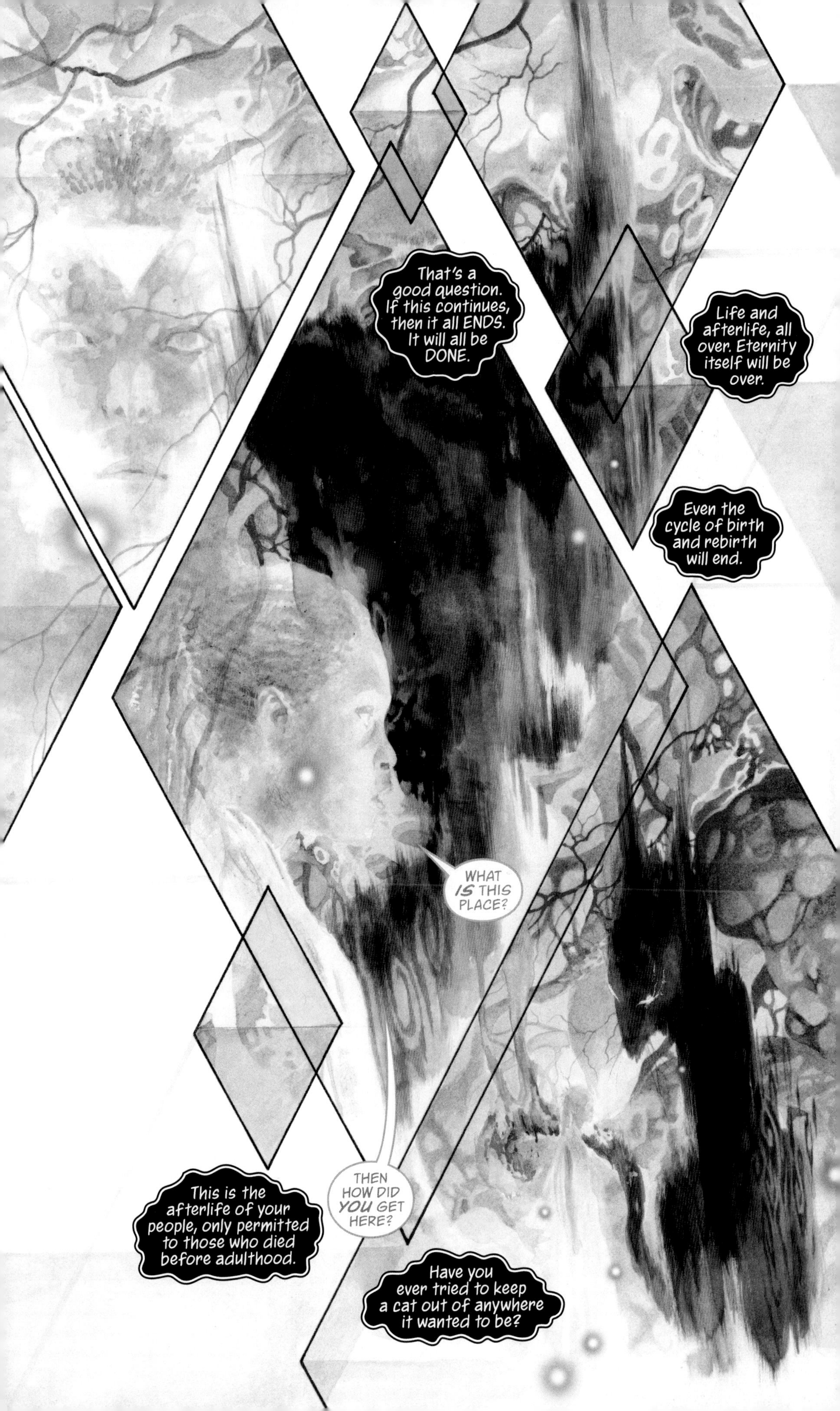
That's a good question. If this continues, then it all ENDS. It will all be DONE.
Life and afterlife, all over. Eternity itself will be over.
Even the cycle of birth and rebirth will end.
WHAT IS THIS PLACE?
This is the afterlife of your people, only permitted to those who died before adulthood.
THEN HOW DID YOU GET HERE?
Have you ever tried to keep a cat out of anywhere it wanted to be?

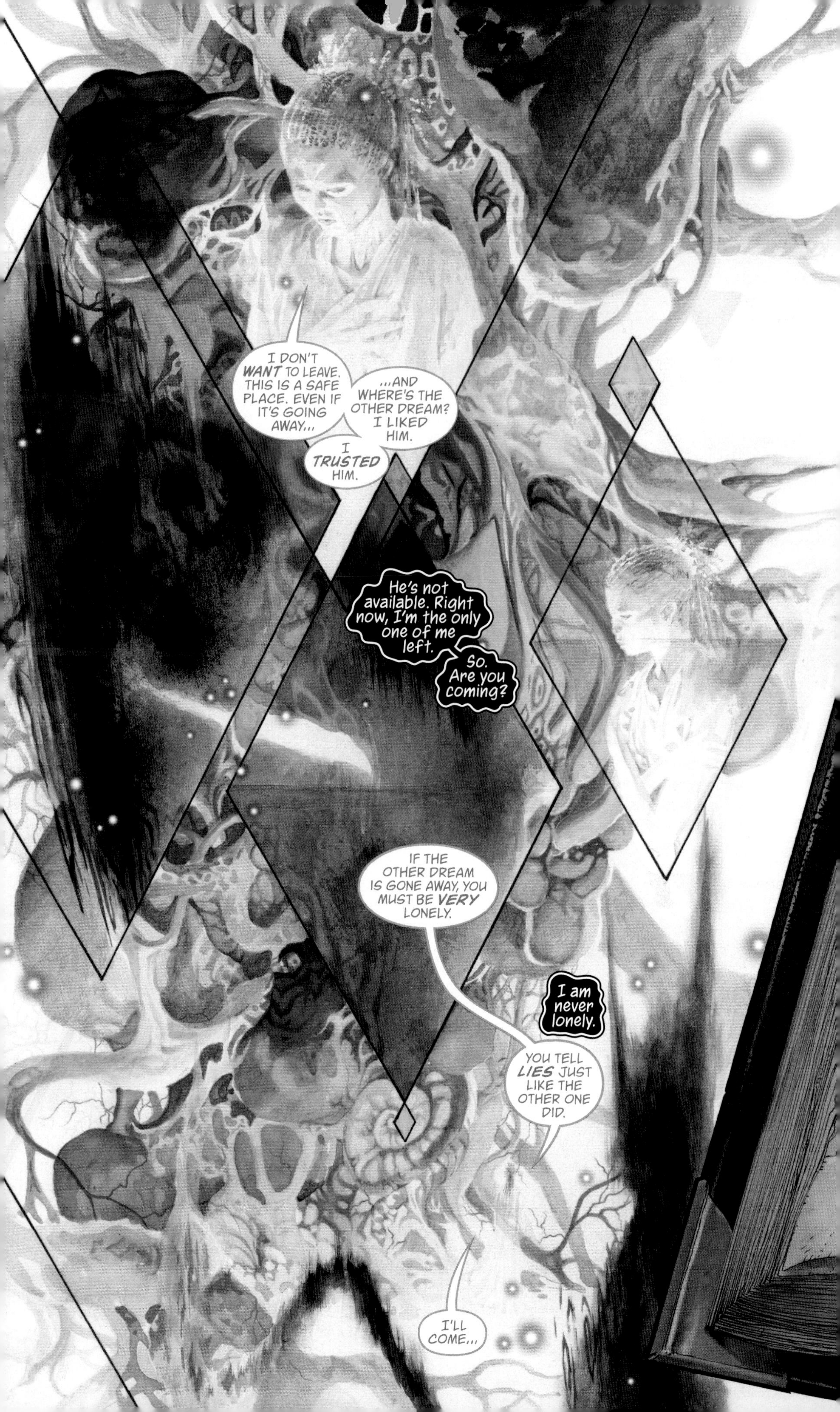
I DON'T WANT TO LEAVE. THIS IS A SAFE PLACE. EVEN IF IT'S GOING AWAY...
...AND WHERE'S THE OTHER DREAM? I LIKED HIM.
I TRUSTED HIM.
He's not available. Right now, I'm the only one of me left.
So. Are you coming?
IF THE OTHER DREAM IS GONE AWAY, YOU MUST BE VERY LONELY.
I am never lonely.
YOU TELL LIES JUST LIKE THE OTHER ONE DID.
I'LL COME...

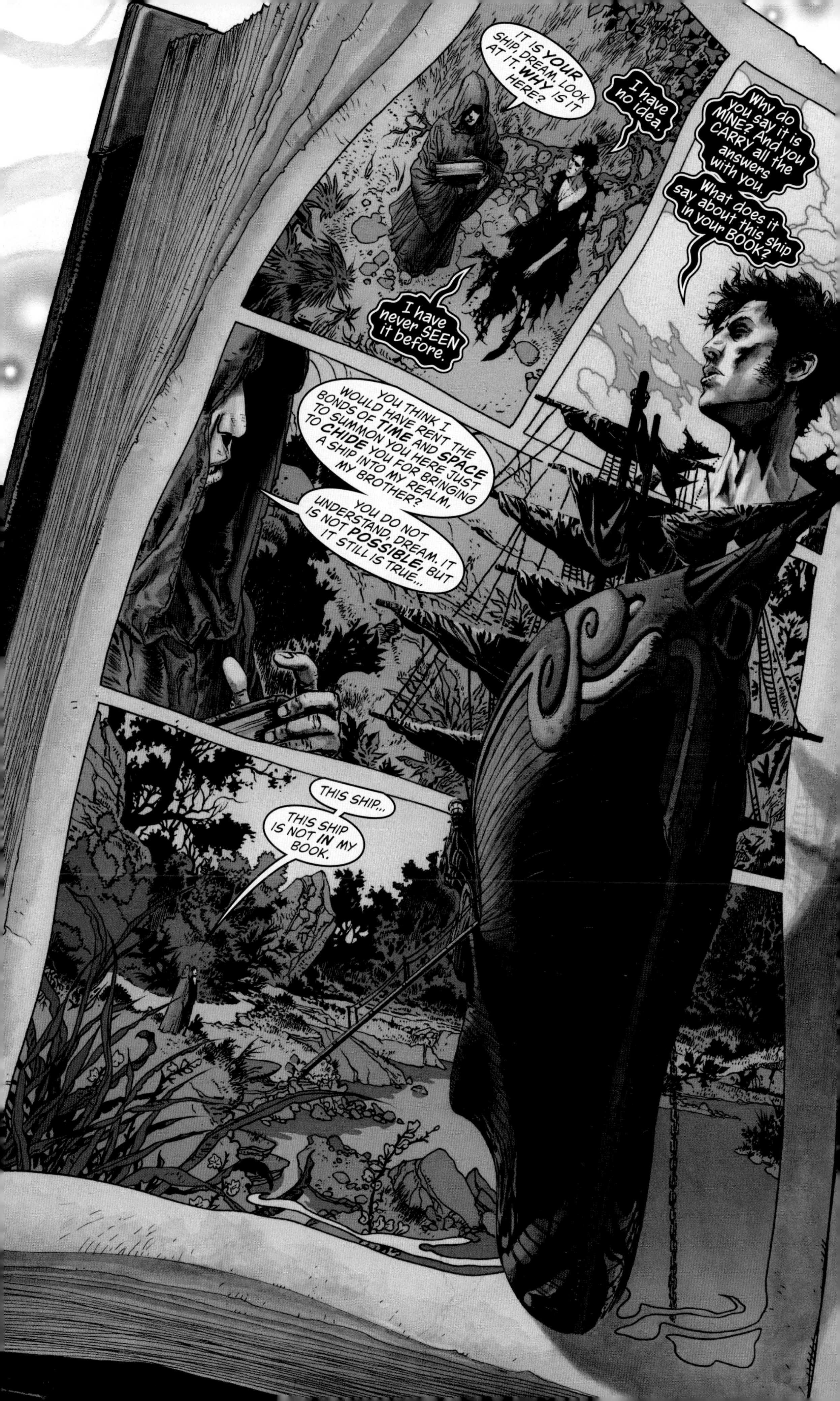
Why do you say it is MINE? And you CARRY all the answers with you.
What does it say about this ship in your BOOK?
IT IS YOUR SHIP, DREAM. LOOK AT IT. WHY IS IT HERE?
I have no idea.
I have never SEEN it before.
YOU THINK I WOULD HAVE RENT THE BONDS OF TIME AND SPACE TO SUMMON YOU HERE JUST TO CHIDE YOU FOR BRINGING A SHIP INTO MY REALM, MY BROTHER?
YOU DO NOT UNDERSTAND, DREAM. IT IS NOT POSSIBLE, BUT IT STILL IS TRUE...
THIS SHIP...
THIS SHIP IS NOT IN MY BOOK.

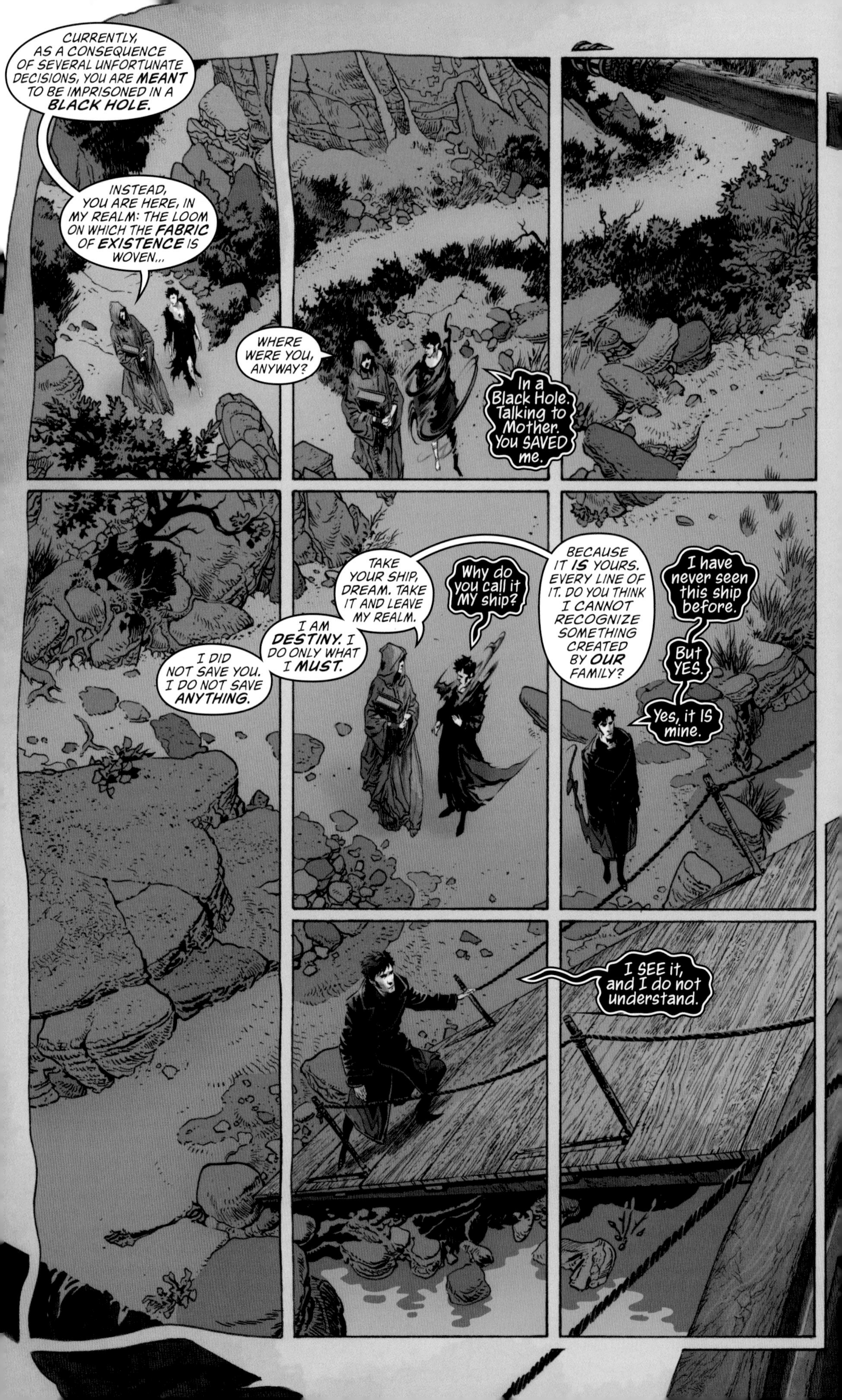
CURRENTLY, AS A CONSEQUENCE OF SEVERAL UNFORTUNATE DECISIONS, YOU ARE MEANT TO BE IMPRISONED IN A BLACK HOLE.
INSTEAD, YOU ARE HERE, IN MY REALM: THE LOOM ON WHICH THE FABRIC OF EXISTENCE IS WOVEN...
WHERE WERE YOU, ANYWAY?
In a Black Hole. Talking to Mother. You SAVED me.
I DID NOT SAVE YOU. I DO NOT SAVE ANYTHING.
I AM DESTINY. I DO ONLY WHAT I MUST.
TAKE YOUR SHIP, DREAM. TAKE IT AND LEAVE MY REALM.
Why do you call it MY ship?
BECAUSE IT IS YOURS. EVERY LINE OF IT. DO YOU THINK I CANNOT RECOGNIZE SOMETHING CREATED BY OUR FAMILY?
I have never seen this ship before.
But YES.
Yes, it IS mine.
I SEE it, and I do not understand.

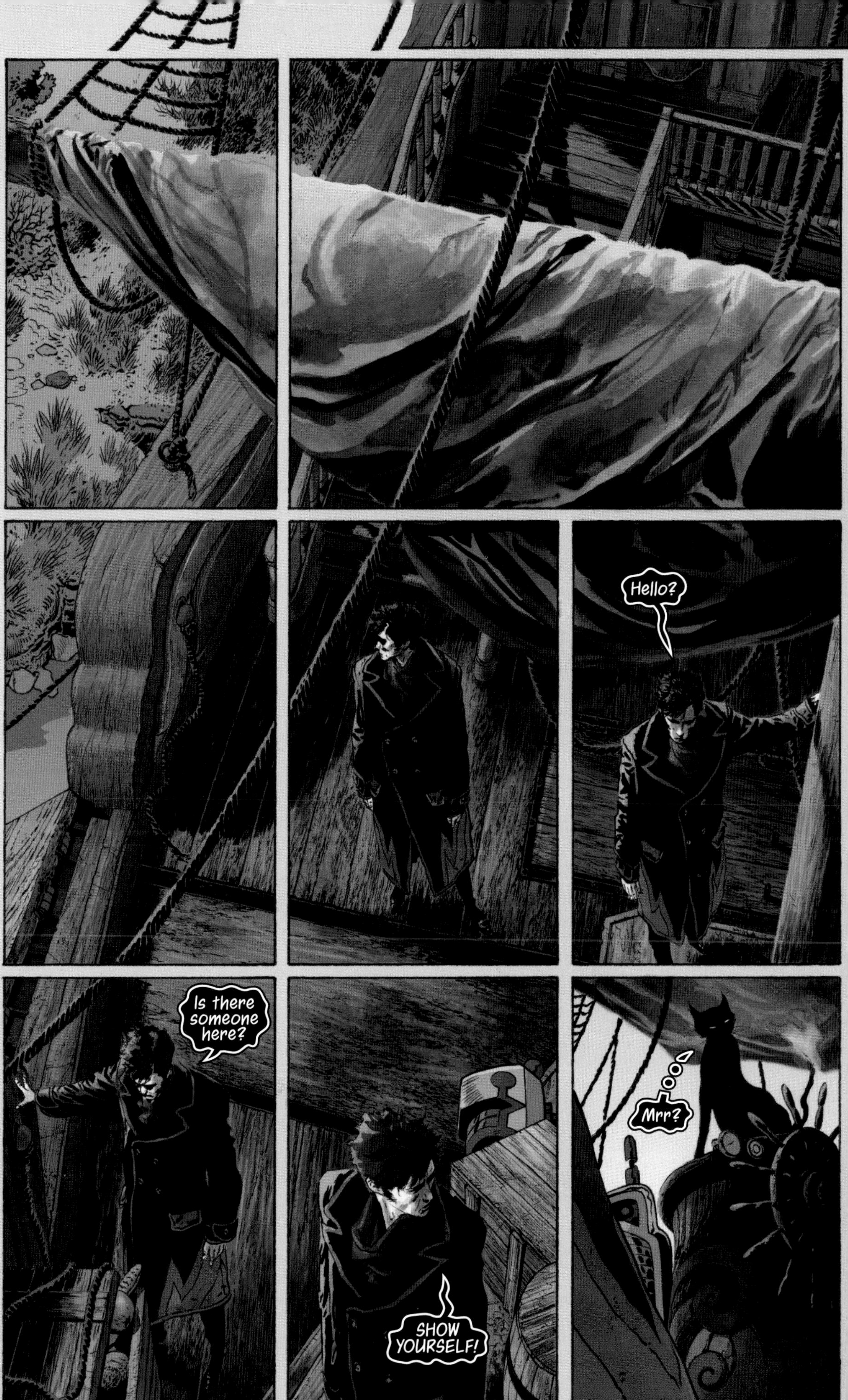
Hello?
Is there someone here?
SHOW YOURSELF!
Mrr?

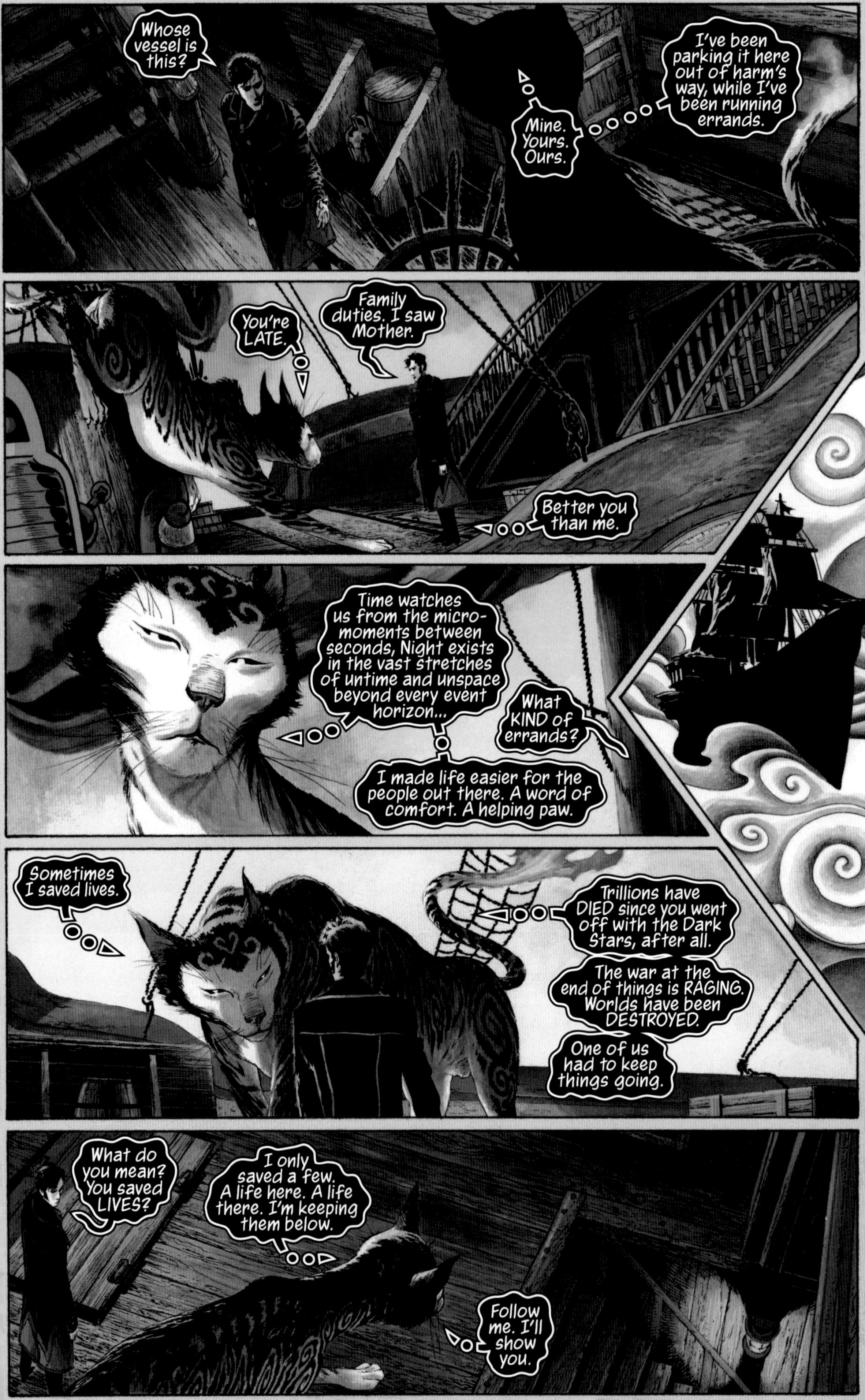
Whose vessel is this?
Mine. Yours. Ours.
I've been parking it here out of harm's way, while I've been running errands.
You're LATE.
Family duties. I saw Mother.
Better you than me.
Time watches us from the micro-moments between seconds, Night exists in the vast stretches of untime and unspace beyond every event horizon...
What KIND of errands?
I made life easier for the people out there. A word of comfort. A helping paw.
Sometimes I saved lives.
Trillions have DIED since you went off with the Dark Stars, after all.
The war at the end of things is RAGING. Worlds have been DESTROYED.
One of us had to keep things going.
What do you mean? You saved LIVES?
I only saved a few. A life here. A life there. I'm keeping them below.
Follow me. I'll show you.

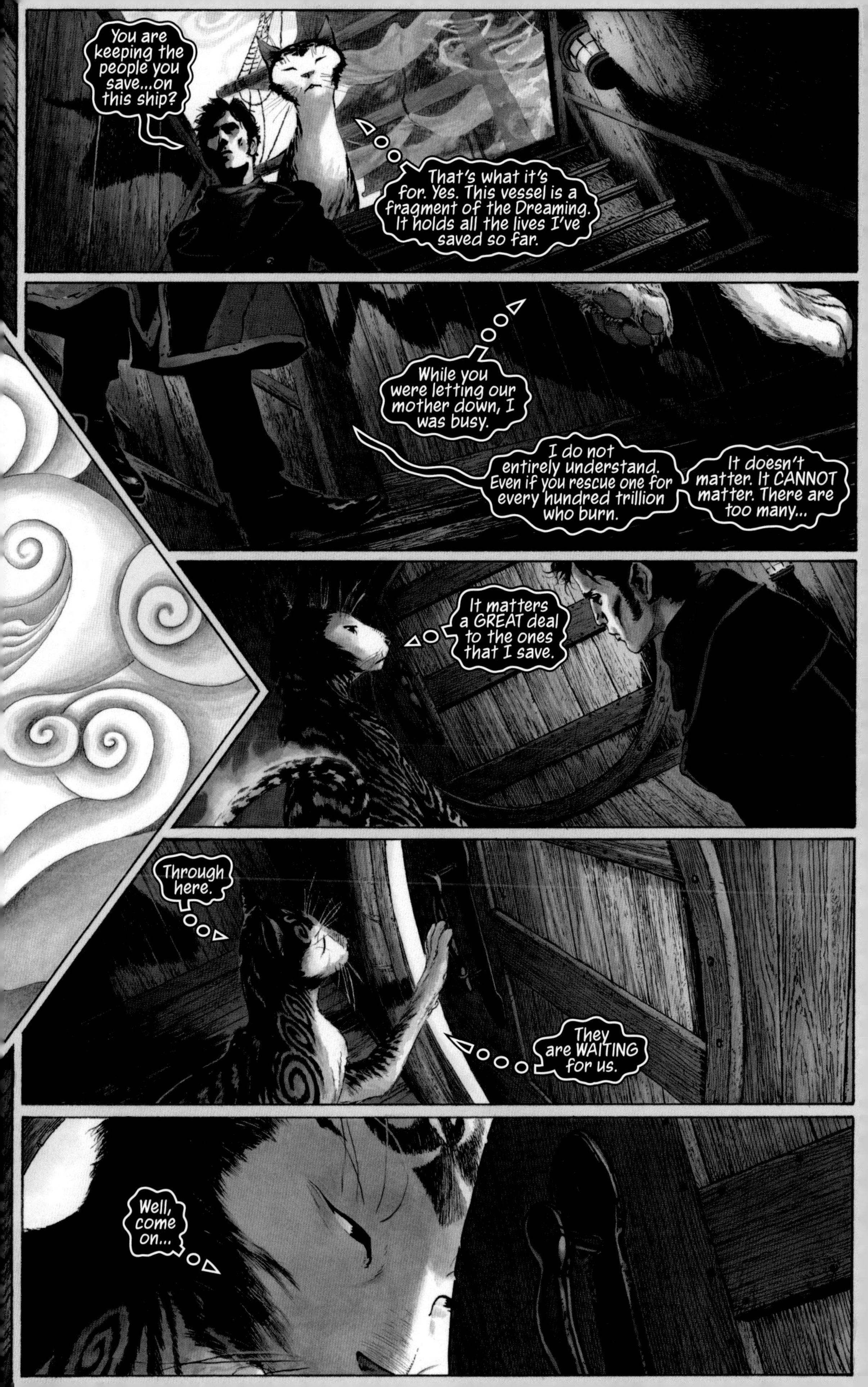
You are keeping the people you save...on this ship?
That's what it's for. Yes. This vessel is a fragment of the Dreaming. It holds all the lives I've saved so far.
While you were letting our mother down, I was busy.
I do not entirely understand. Even if you rescue one for every hundred trillion who burn.
It doesn't matter. It CANNOT matter. There are too many...
It matters a GREAT deal to the ones that I save.
Through here.
They are WAITING for us.
Well, come on...

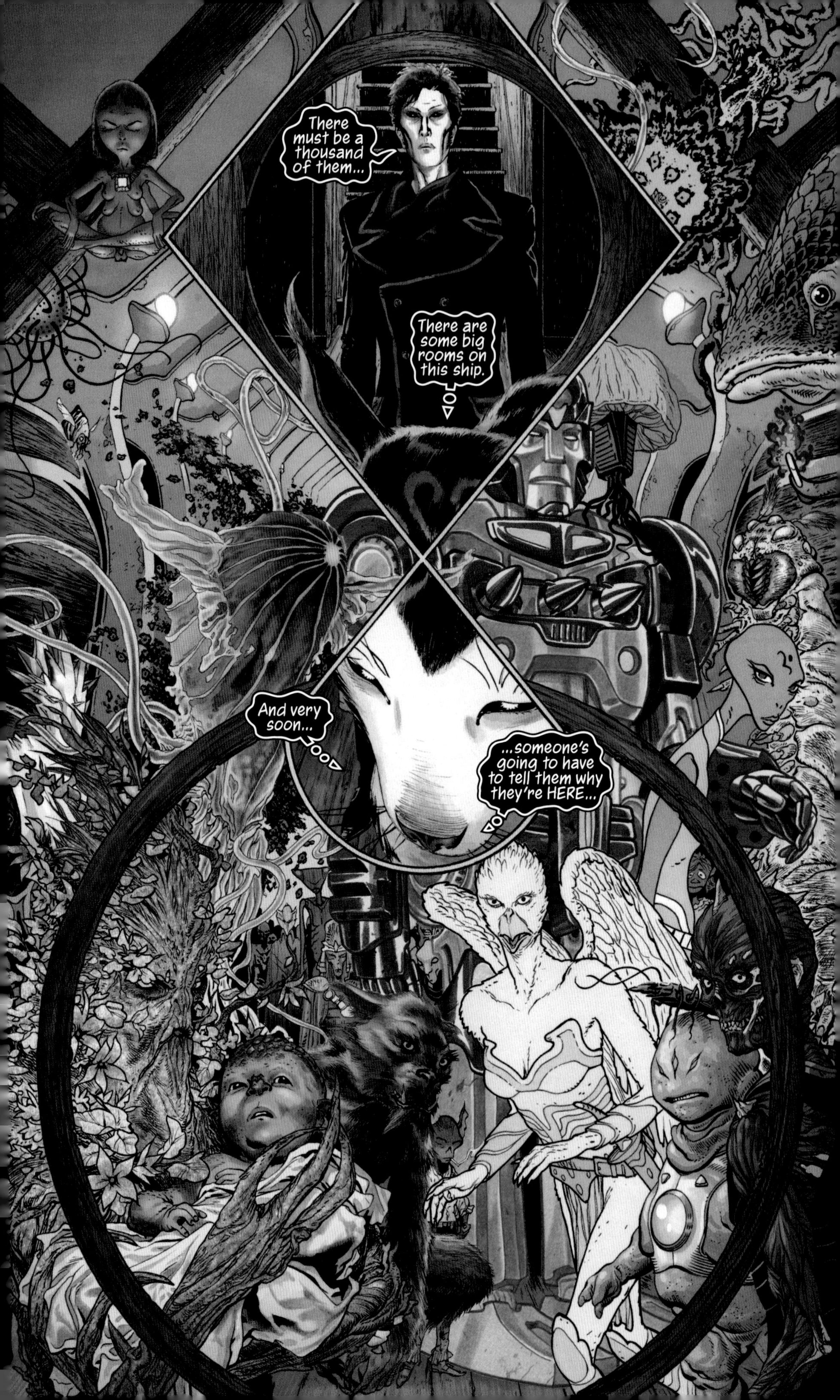
There must be a thousand of them...
There are some big rooms on this ship.
And very soon...
...someone's going to have to tell them why they're HERE...

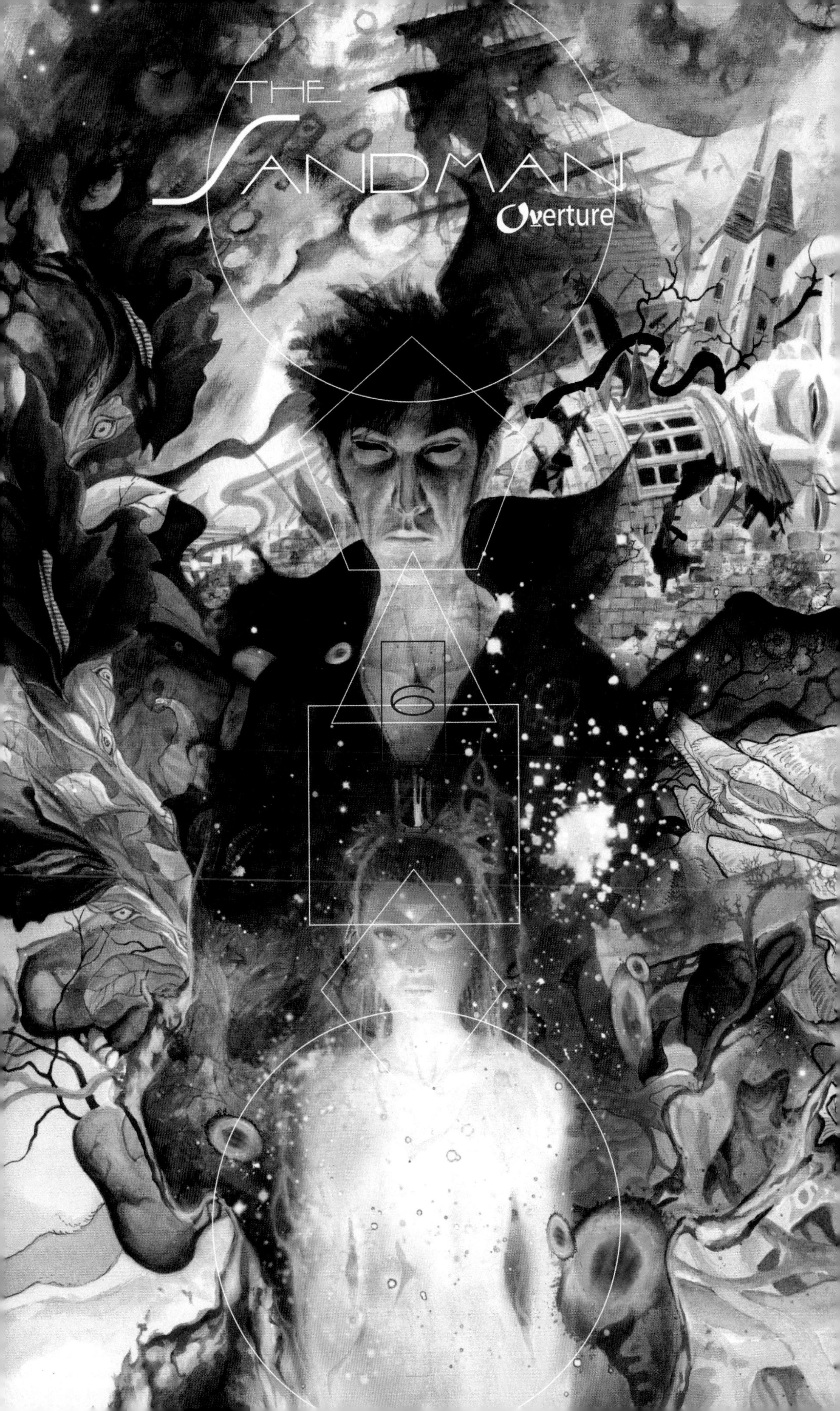
THE SANDMAN
Overture
6

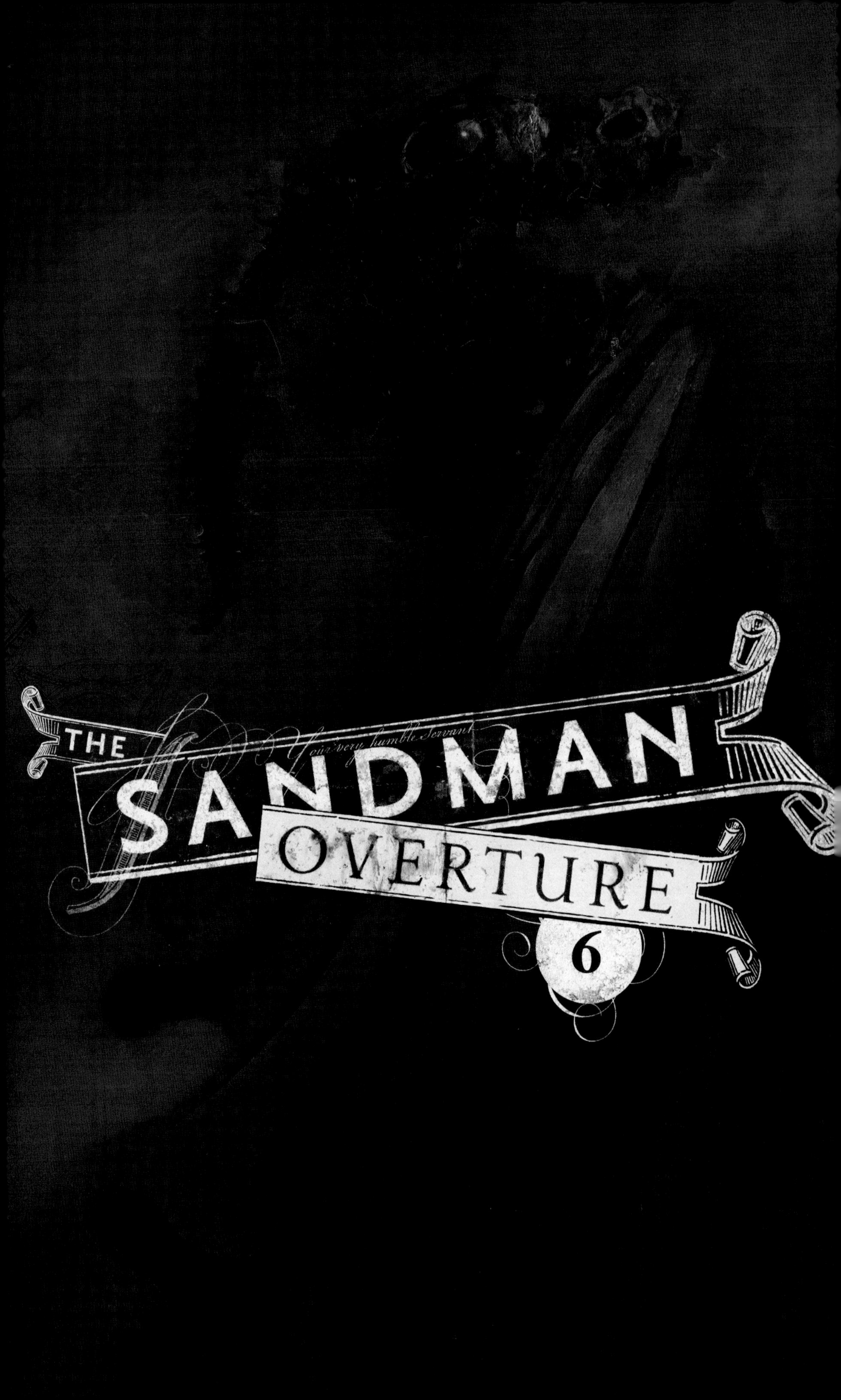
THE
SANDMAN
OVERTURE
6
Your very humble Servant

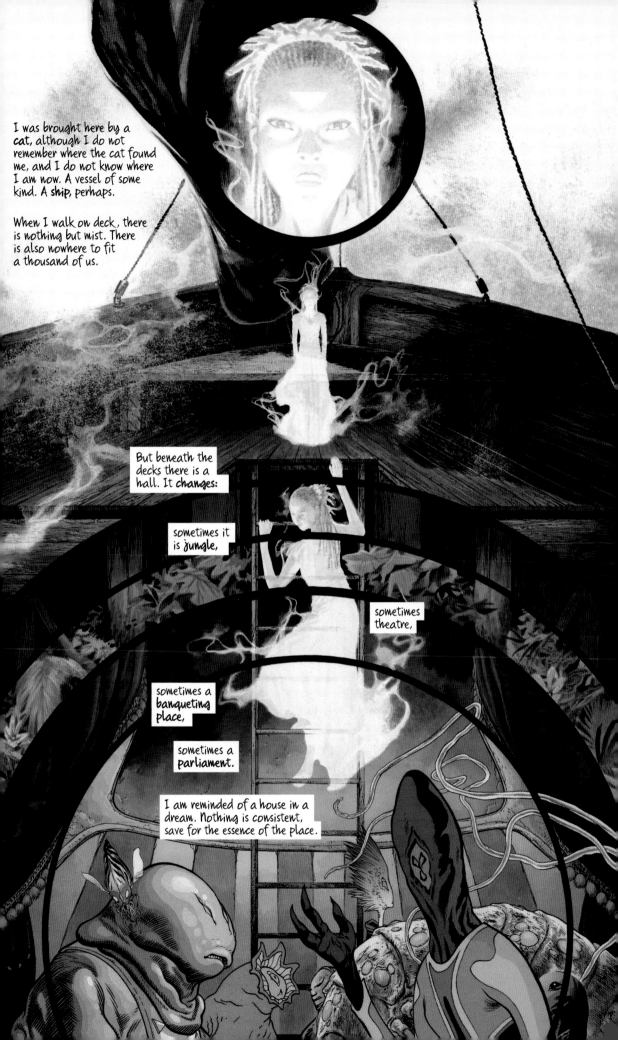

I was brought here by a **cat**, although I do not remember where the cat found me, and I do not know where I am now. A vessel of some kind. A **ship**, perhaps.

When I walk on deck, there is nothing but mist. There is also nowhere to fit a thousand of us.

But beneath the decks there is a hall. It **changes**:

sometimes it is **jungle**,

sometimes **theatre**,

sometimes a **banqueting place**,

sometimes a **parliament**.

I am reminded of a house in a dream. Nothing is consistent, save for the essence of the place.

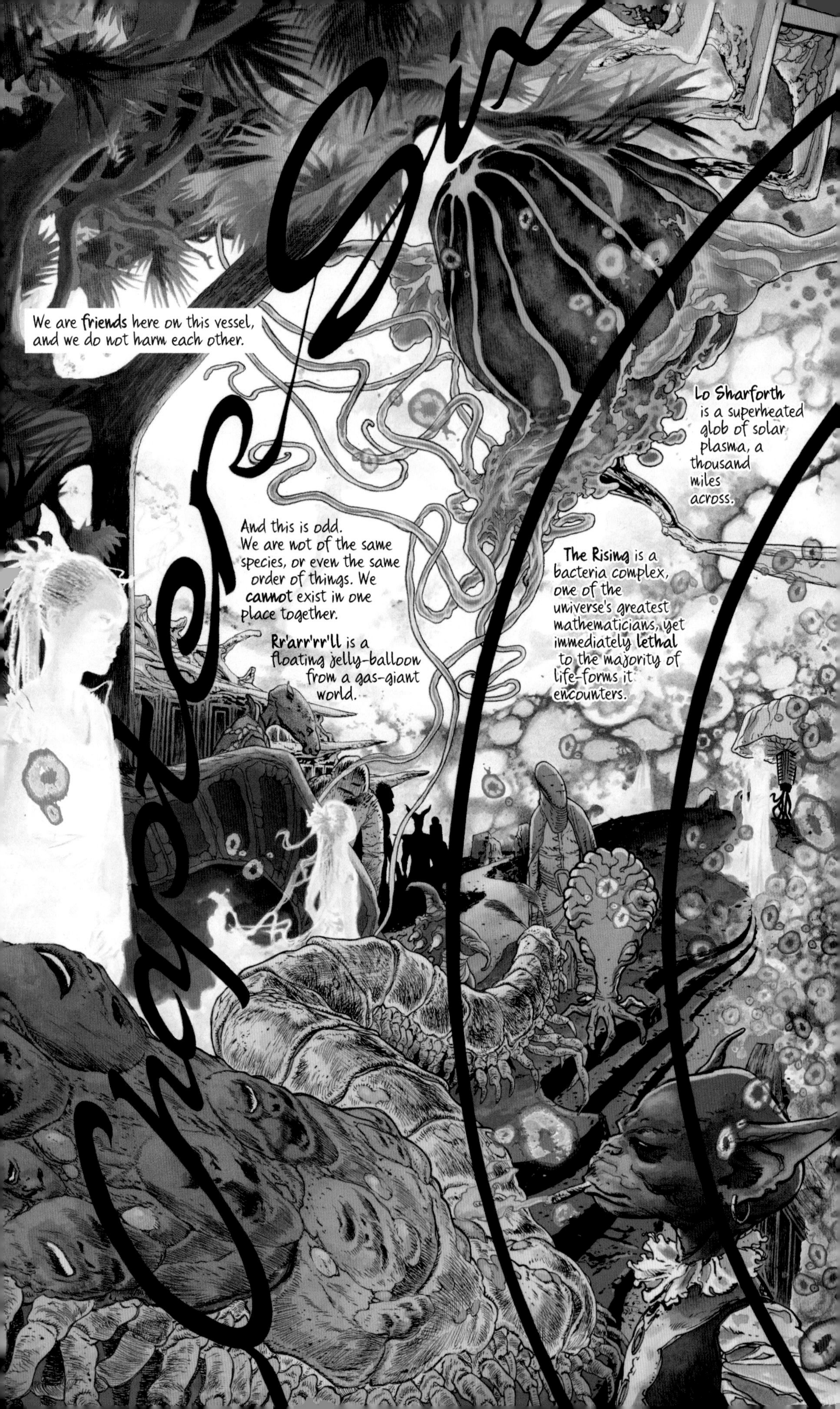
We are **friends** here on this vessel, and we do not harm each other.
And this is odd. We are not of the same species, or even the same order of things. We **cannot** exist in one place together.
Rr'arr'rr'll is a floating jelly-balloon from a gas-giant world.
Lo Sharforth is a superheated glob of solar plasma, a thousand miles across.
The Rising is a bacteria complex, one of the universe's greatest mathematicians, yet immediately **lethal** to the majority of life-forms it encounters.

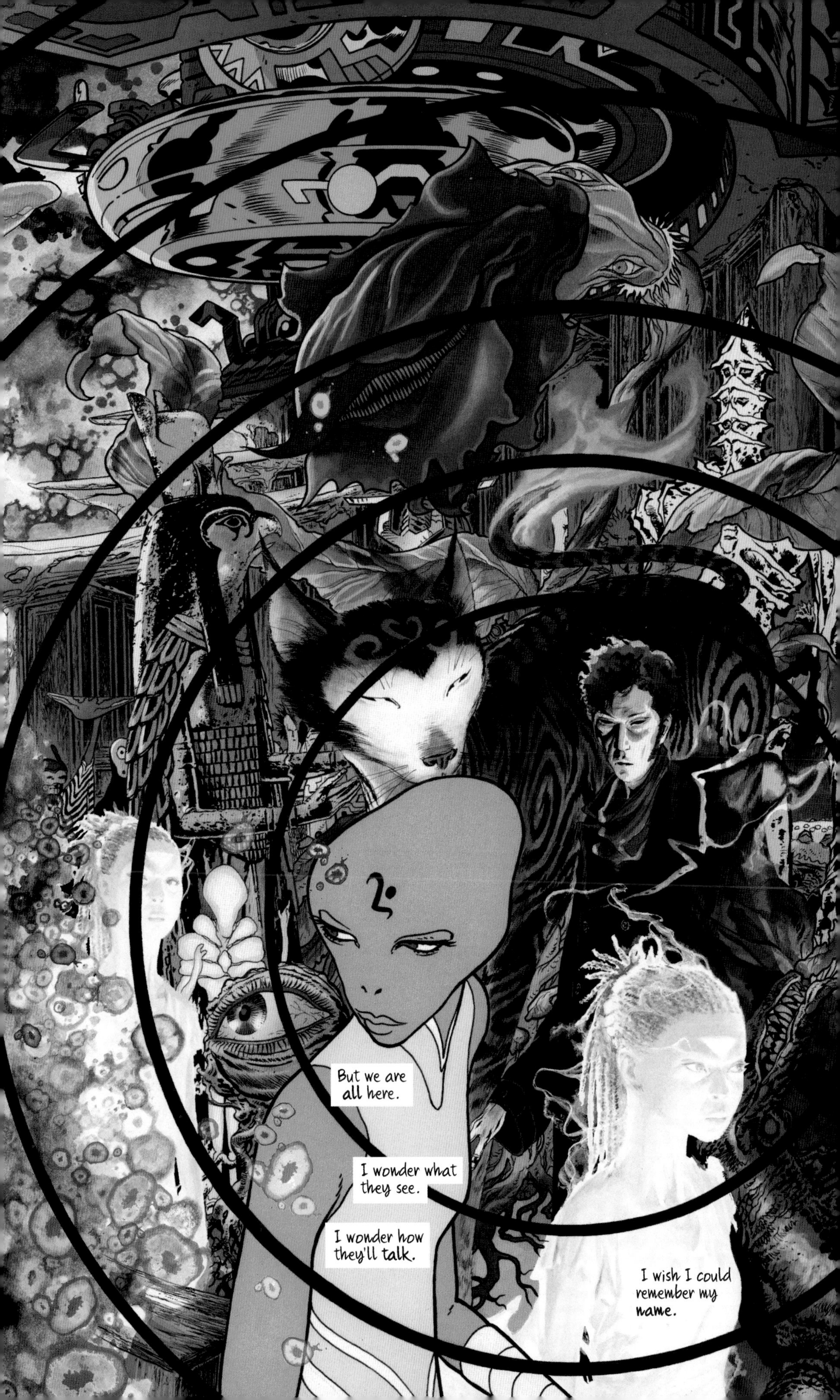
But we are all here.
I wonder what they see.
I wonder how they'll talk.
I wish I could remember my name.

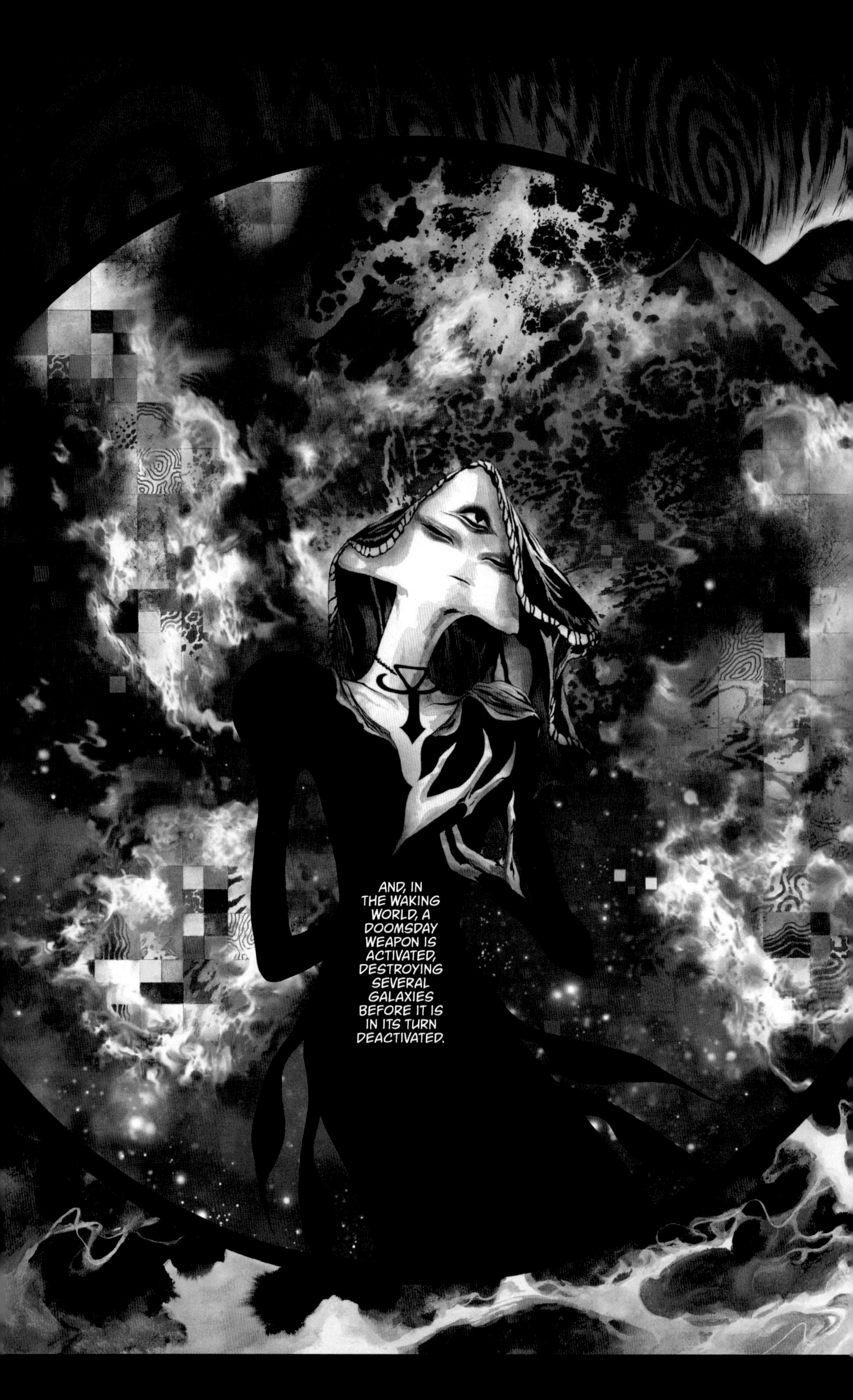
AND, IN THE WAKING WORLD, A DOOMSDAY WEAPON IS ACTIVATED, DESTROYING SEVERAL GALAXIES BEFORE IT IS IN ITS TURN DEACTIVATED.

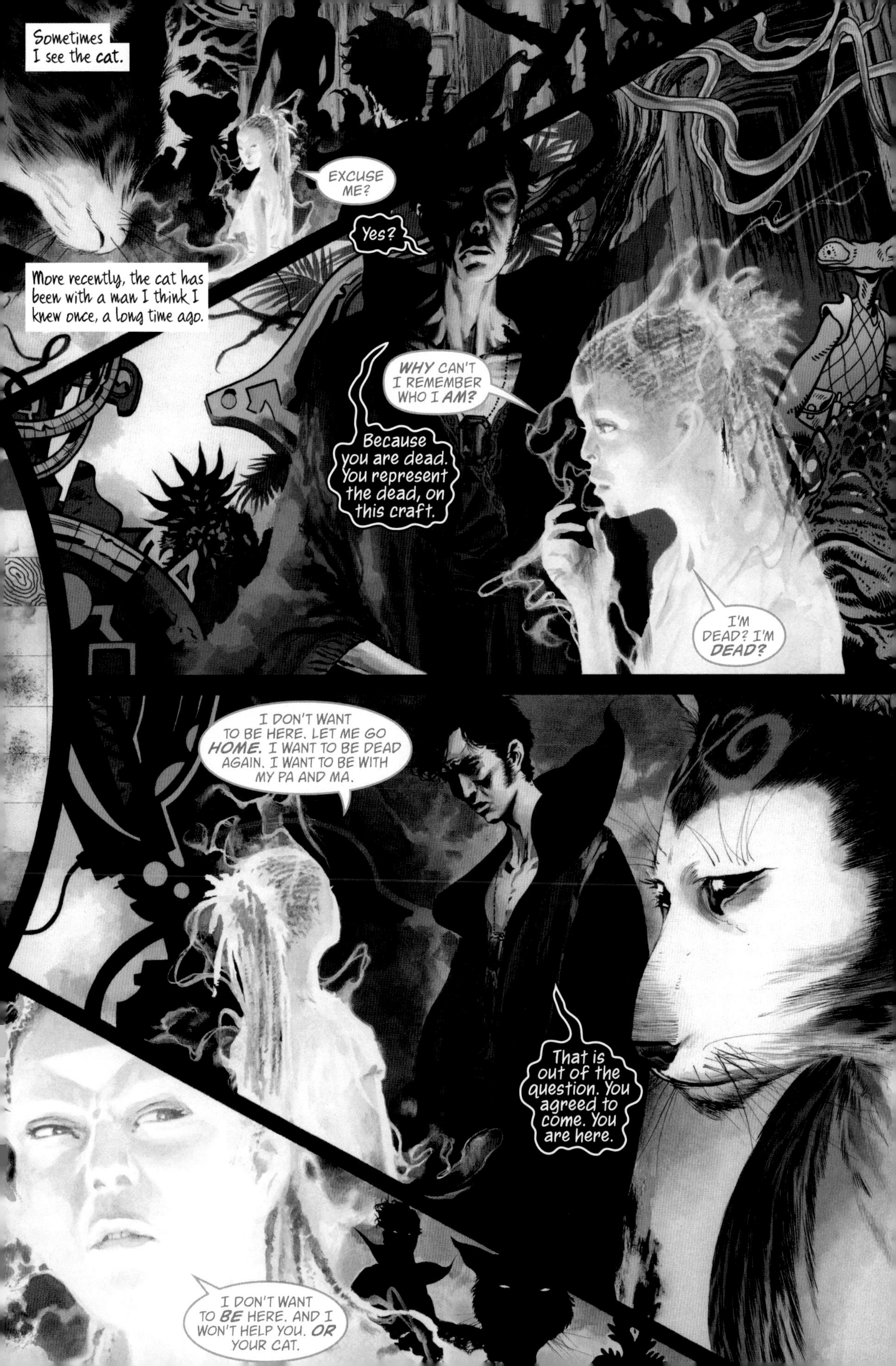
Sometimes I see the cat.
EXCUSE ME?
Yes?
More recently, the cat has been with a man I think I knew once, a long time ago.
WHY CAN'T I REMEMBER WHO I AM?
Because you are dead. You represent the dead, on this craft.
I'M DEAD? I'M DEAD?
I DON'T WANT TO BE HERE. LET ME GO HOME. I WANT TO BE DEAD AGAIN. I WANT TO BE WITH MY PA AND MA.
That is out of the question. You agreed to come. You are here.
I DON'T WANT TO BE HERE. AND I WON'T HELP YOU. OR YOUR CAT.

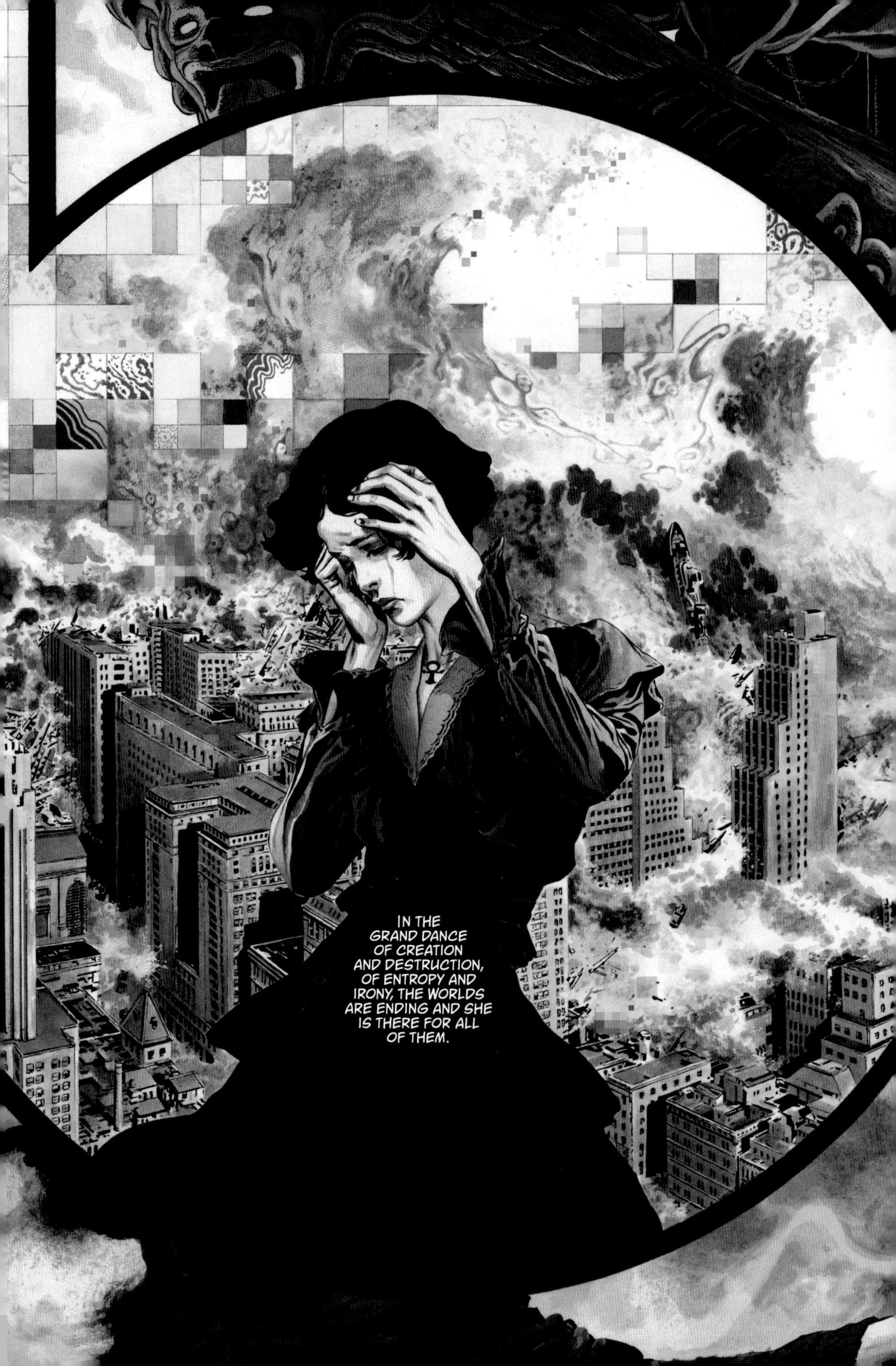
IN THE GRAND DANCE OF CREATION AND DESTRUCTION, OF ENTROPY AND IRONY, THE WORLDS ARE ENDING AND SHE IS THERE FOR ALL OF THEM.

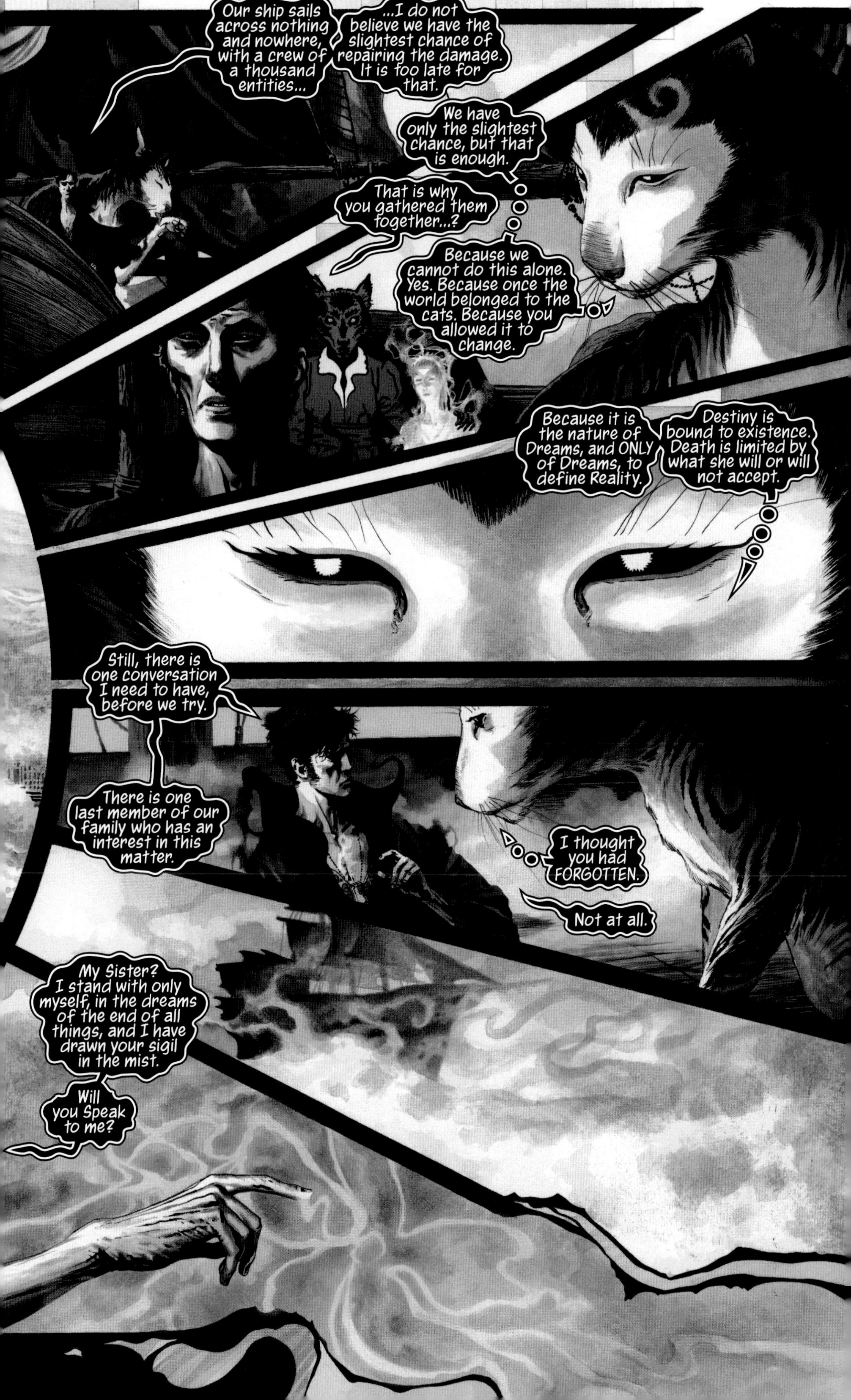

Our ship sails across nothing and nowhere, with a crew of a thousand entities...
...I do not believe we have the slightest chance of repairing the damage. It is too late for that.
We have only the slightest chance, but that is enough.
That is why you gathered them together...?
Because we cannot do this alone. Yes. Because once the world belonged to the cats. Because you allowed it to change.
Because it is the nature of Dreams, and ONLY of Dreams, to define Reality.
Destiny is bound to existence. Death is limited by what she will or will not accept.
Still, there is one conversation I need to have, before we try.
There is one last member of our family who has an interest in this matter.
I thought you had FORGOTTEN.
Not at all.
My Sister? I stand with only myself, in the dreams of the end of all things, and I have drawn your sigil in the mist.
Will you Speak to me?

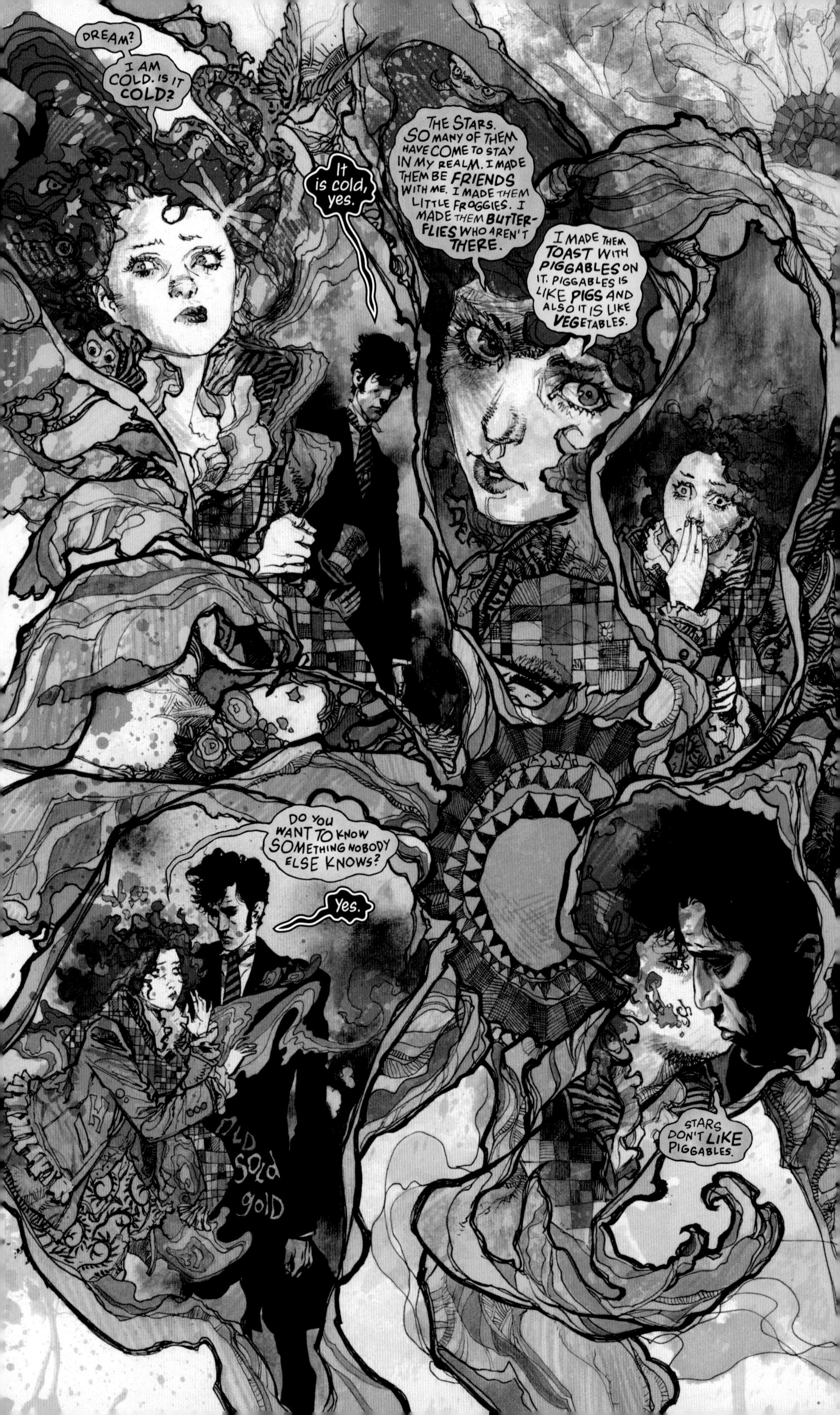
DREAM?
I AM COLD. IS IT COLD?
It is cold, yes.
THE STARS. SO MANY OF THEM HAVE COME TO STAY IN MY REALM. I MADE THEM BE FRIENDS WITH ME. I MADE THEM LITTLE FROGGIES. I MADE THEM BUTTER-FLIES WHO AREN'T THERE.
I MADE THEM TOAST WITH PIGGABLES ON IT. PIGGABLES IS LIKE PIGS AND ALSO IT IS LIKE VEGETABLES.
DO YOU WANT TO KNOW SOMETHING NOBODY ELSE KNOWS?
Yes.
STARS DON'T LIKE PIGGABLES.
Sold gold

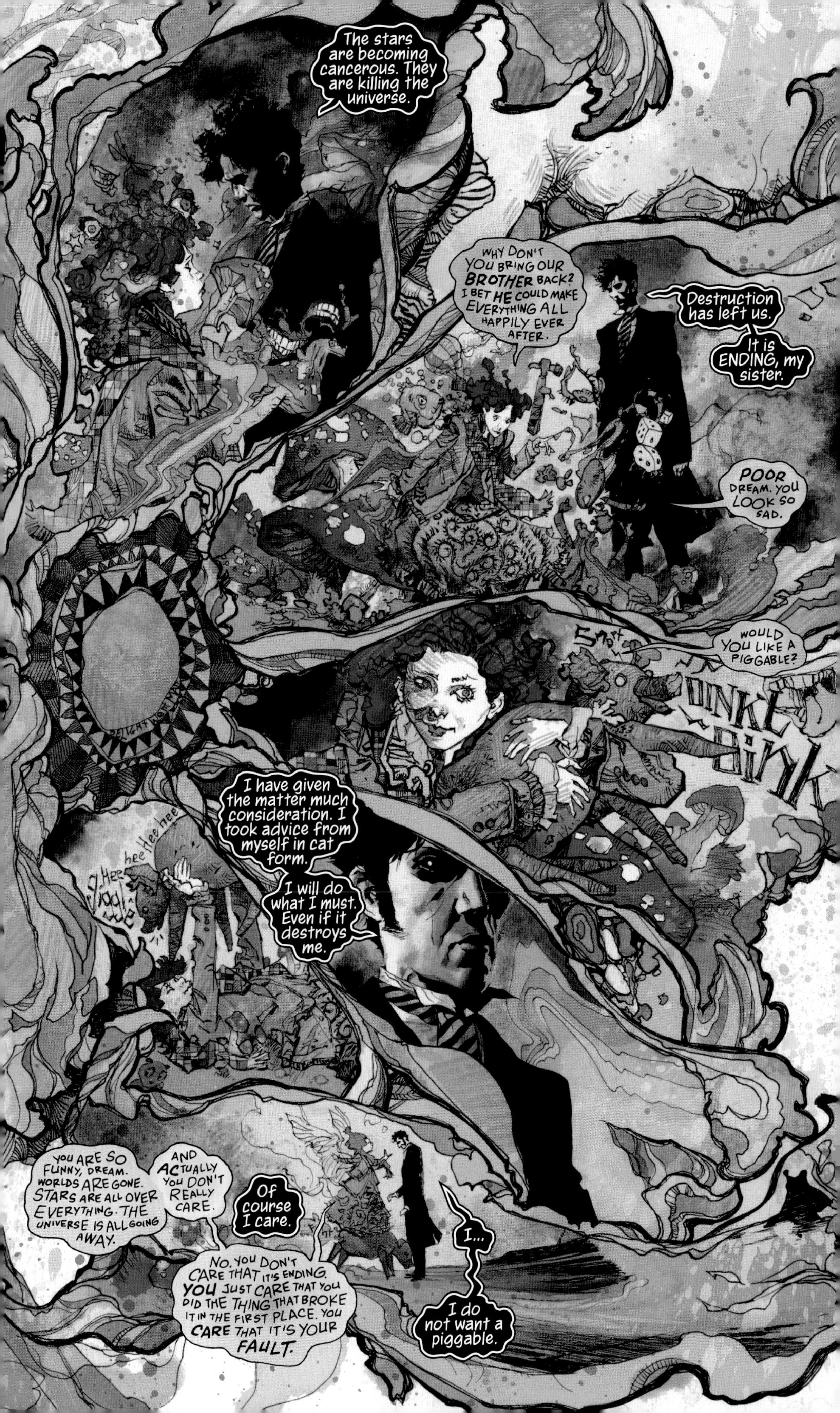
The stars are becoming cancerous. They are killing the universe.
WHY DON'T YOU BRING OUR BROTHER BACK? I BET HE COULD MAKE EVERYTHING ALL HAPPILY EVER AFTER.
Destruction has left us.
It is ENDING, my sister.
POOR DREAM. YOU LOOK SO SAD.
WOULD YOU LIKE A PIGGABLE?
I have given the matter much consideration. I took advice from myself in cat form.
I will do what I must. Even if it destroys me.
hee Hee hee
YOU ARE SO FUNNY, DREAM. WORLDS ARE GONE. STARS ARE ALL OVER EVERYTHING. THE UNIVERSE IS ALL GOING AWAY.
AND ACTUALLY YOU DON'T REALLY CARE.
Of course I care.
NO, YOU DON'T CARE THAT IT'S ENDING. YOU JUST CARE THAT YOU DID THE THING THAT BROKE IT IN THE FIRST PLACE. YOU CARE THAT IT'S YOUR FAULT.
I...
I do not want a piggable.

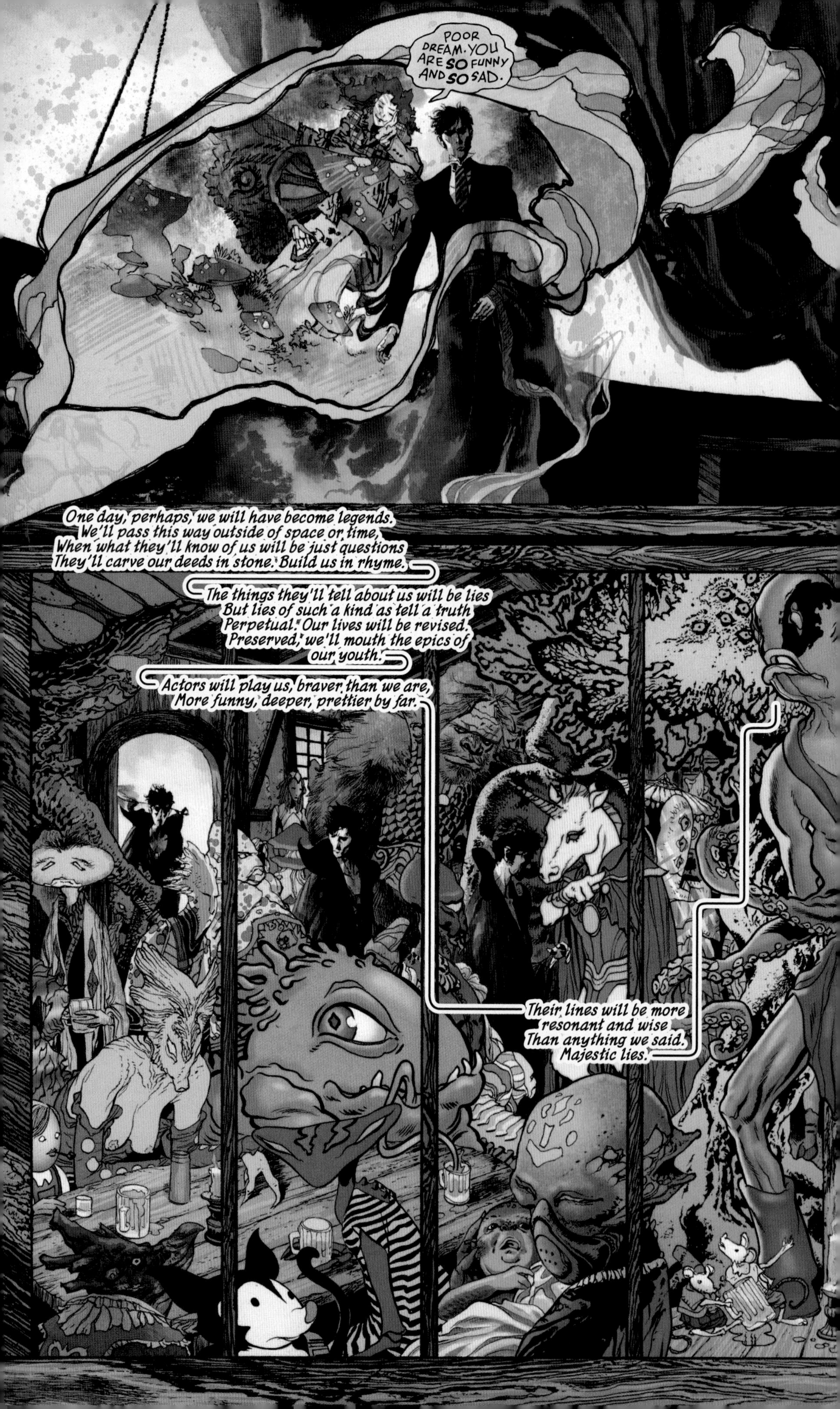
POOR DREAM. YOU ARE SO FUNNY AND SO SAD.
One day, perhaps, we will have become legends.
We'll pass this way outside of space or time,
When what they'll know of us will be just questions
They'll carve our deeds in stone. Build us in rhyme.
The things they'll tell about us will be lies
But lies of such a kind as tell a truth
Perpetual. Our lives will be revised.
Preserved, we'll mouth the epics of our youth.
Actors will play us, braver than we are,
More funny, deeper, prettier by far.
Their lines will be more resonant and wise
Than anything we said.
Majestic lies.

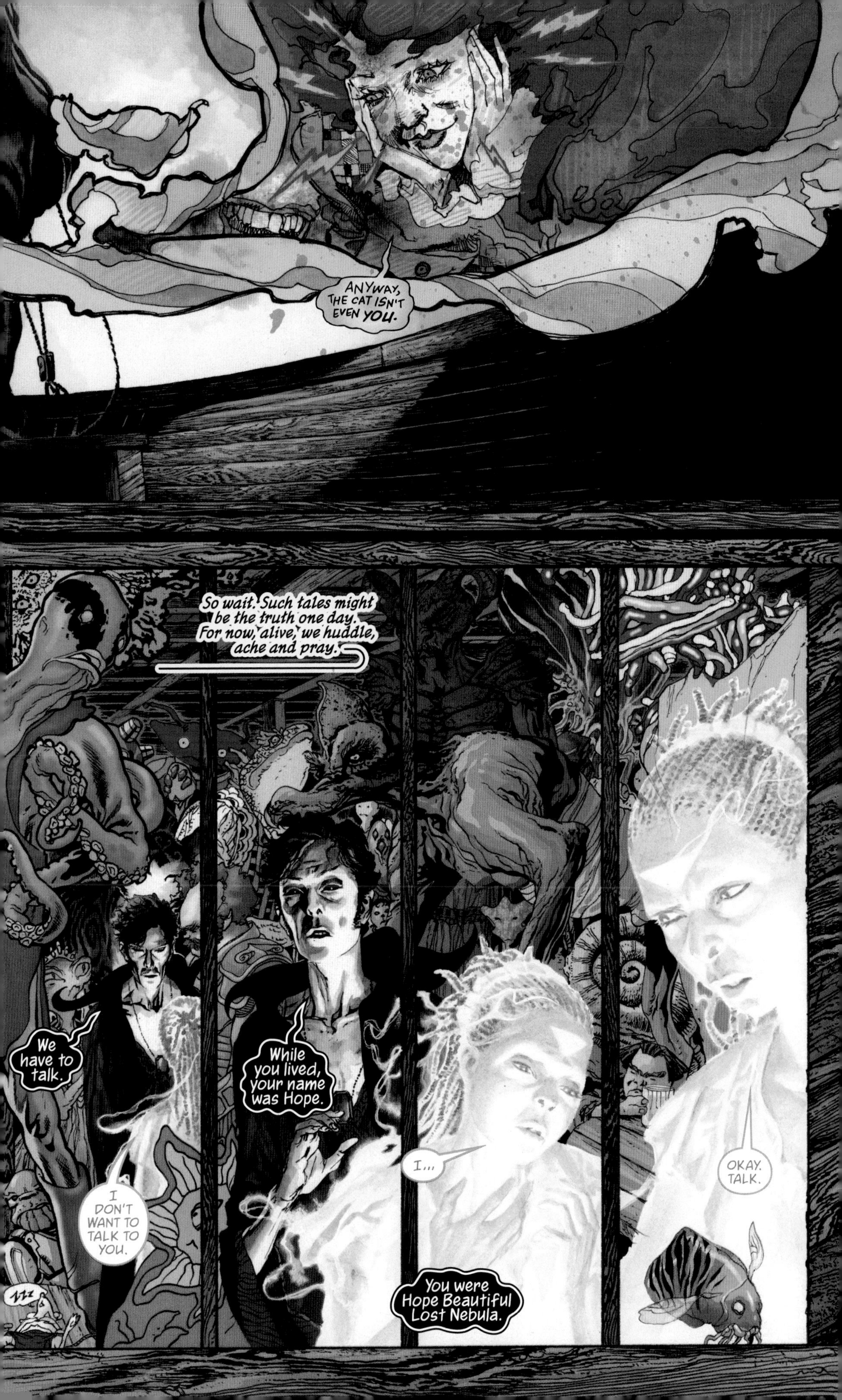
ANYWAY, THE CAT ISN'T EVEN YOU.
So wait. Such tales might be the truth one day. For now, alive, we huddle, ache and pray.
We have to talk.
I DON'T WANT TO TALK TO YOU.
ZZZ
While you lived, your name was Hope.
I...
You were Hope Beautiful Lost Nebula.
OKAY. TALK.

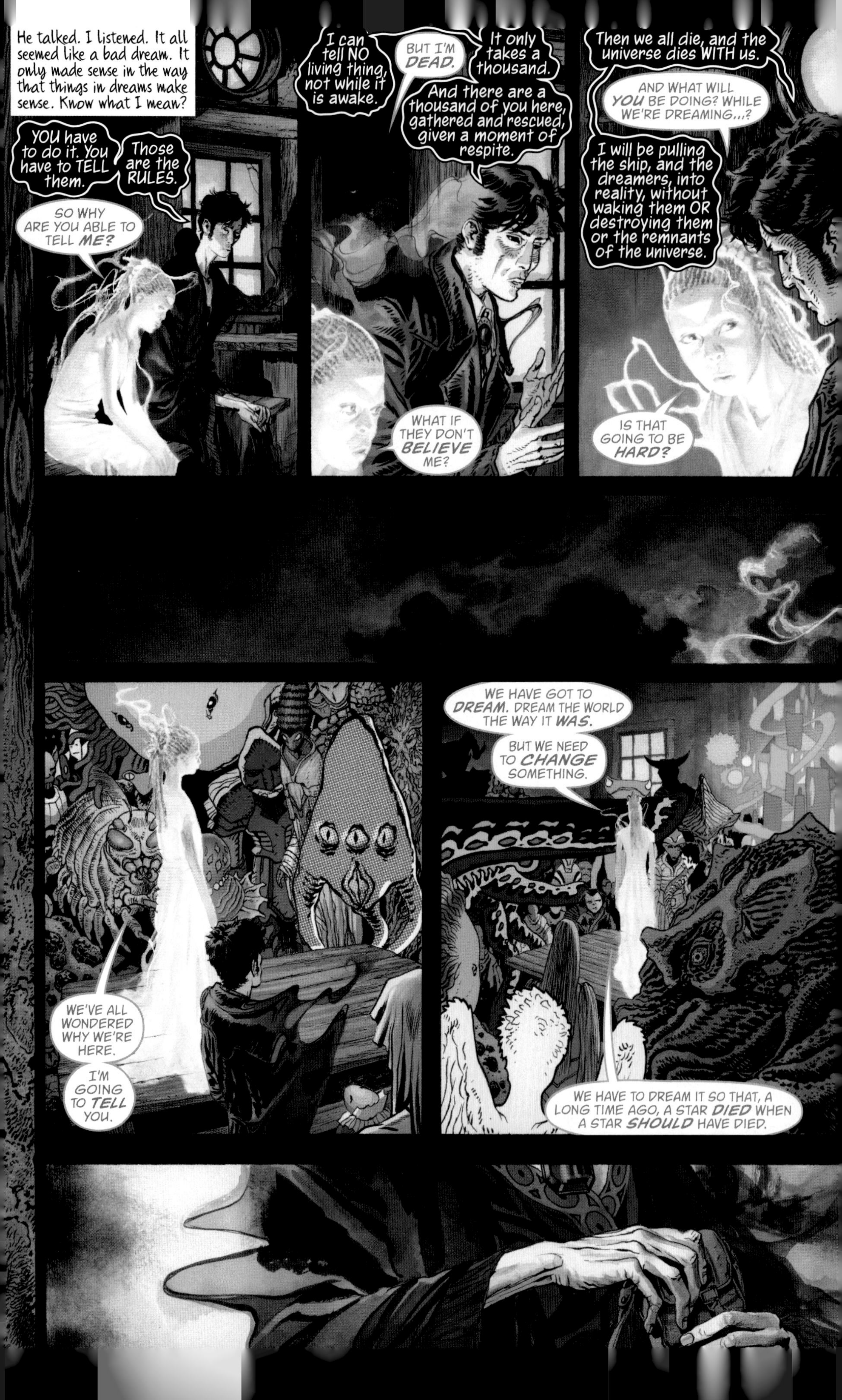

He talked. I listened. It all seemed like a bad dream. It only made sense in the way that things in dreams make sense. Know what I mean?
YOU have to do it. You have to TELL them.
Those are the RULES.
SO WHY ARE YOU ABLE TO TELL ME?
I can tell NO living thing, not while it is awake.
BUT I'M DEAD.
It only takes a thousand.
And there are a thousand of you here, gathered and rescued, given a moment of respite.
WHAT IF THEY DON'T BELIEVE ME?
Then we all die, and the universe dies WITH us.
AND WHAT WILL YOU BE DOING? WHILE WE'RE DREAMING...?
I will be pulling the ship, and the dreamers, into reality, without waking them OR destroying them or the remnants of the universe.
IS THAT GOING TO BE HARD?
WE'VE ALL WONDERED WHY WE'RE HERE.
I'M GOING TO TELL YOU.
WE HAVE GOT TO DREAM. DREAM THE WORLD THE WAY IT WAS.
BUT WE NEED TO CHANGE SOMETHING.
WE HAVE TO DREAM IT SO THAT, A LONG TIME AGO, A STAR DIED WHEN A STAR SHOULD HAVE DIED.

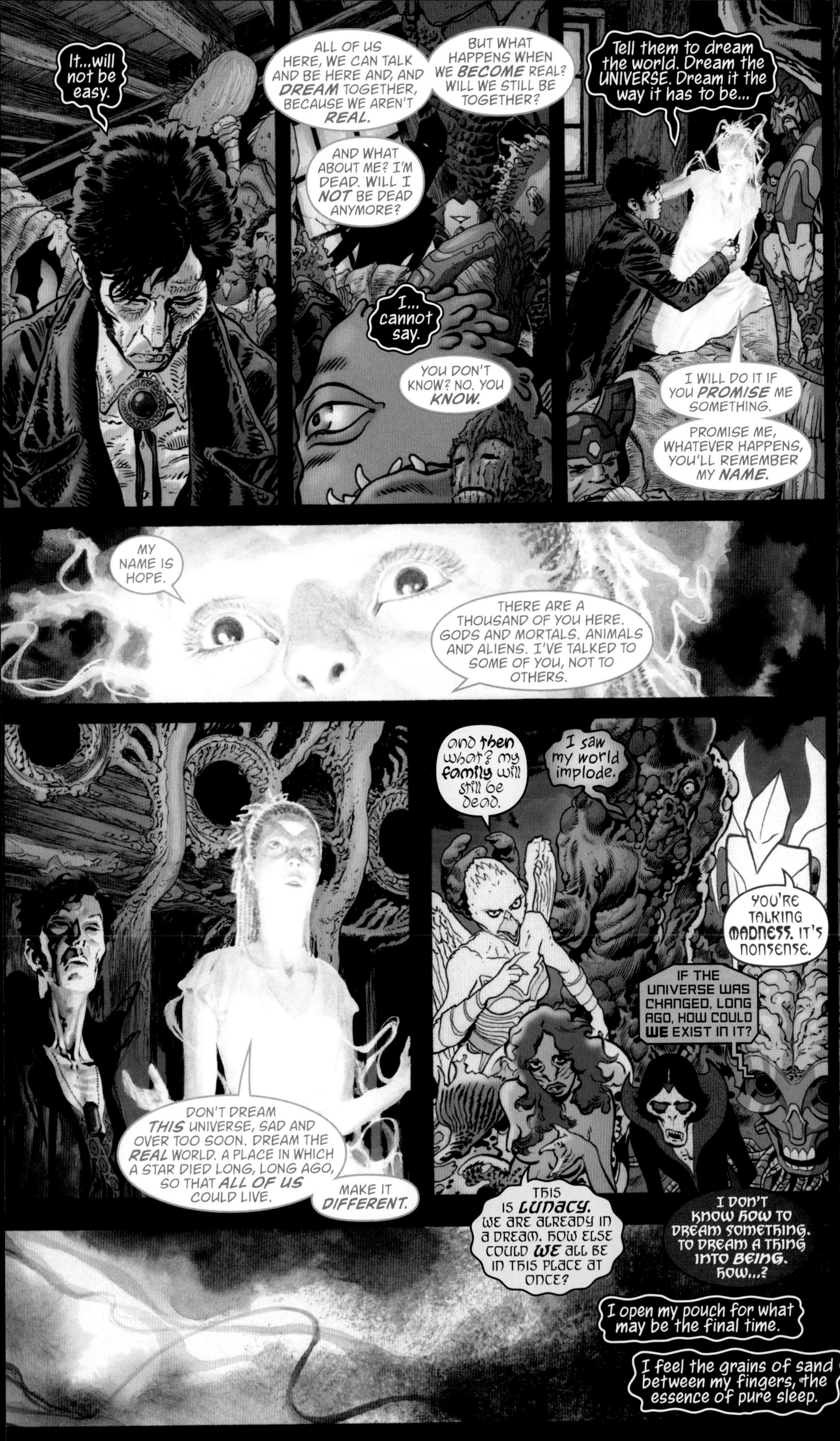
It...will not be easy.
ALL OF US HERE, WE CAN TALK AND BE HERE AND, AND DREAM TOGETHER, BECAUSE WE AREN'T REAL.
BUT WHAT HAPPENS WHEN WE BECOME REAL? WILL WE STILL BE TOGETHER?
AND WHAT ABOUT ME? I'M DEAD. WILL I NOT BE DEAD ANYMORE?
I... cannot say.
YOU DON'T KNOW? NO. YOU KNOW.
Tell them to dream the world. Dream the UNIVERSE. Dream it the way it has to be...
I WILL DO IT IF YOU PROMISE ME SOMETHING.
PROMISE ME, WHATEVER HAPPENS, YOU'LL REMEMBER MY NAME.
MY NAME IS HOPE.
THERE ARE A THOUSAND OF YOU HERE. GODS AND MORTALS. ANIMALS AND ALIENS. I'VE TALKED TO SOME OF YOU, NOT TO OTHERS.
DON'T DREAM THIS UNIVERSE, SAD AND OVER TOO SOON. DREAM THE REAL WORLD. A PLACE IN WHICH A STAR DIED LONG, LONG AGO, SO THAT ALL OF US COULD LIVE.
MAKE IT DIFFERENT.
and then what? my family will still be dead.
I saw my world implode.
YOU'RE TALKING MADNESS. IT'S NONSENSE.
IF THE UNIVERSE WAS CHANGED, LONG AGO, HOW COULD WE EXIST IN IT?
THIS IS LUNACY. WE ARE ALREADY IN A DREAM. HOW ELSE COULD WE ALL BE IN THIS PLACE AT ONCE?
I DON'T KNOW HOW TO DREAM SOMETHING. TO DREAM A THING INTO BEING. HOW...?
I open my pouch for what may be the final time.
I feel the grains of sand between my fingers, the essence of pure sleep.

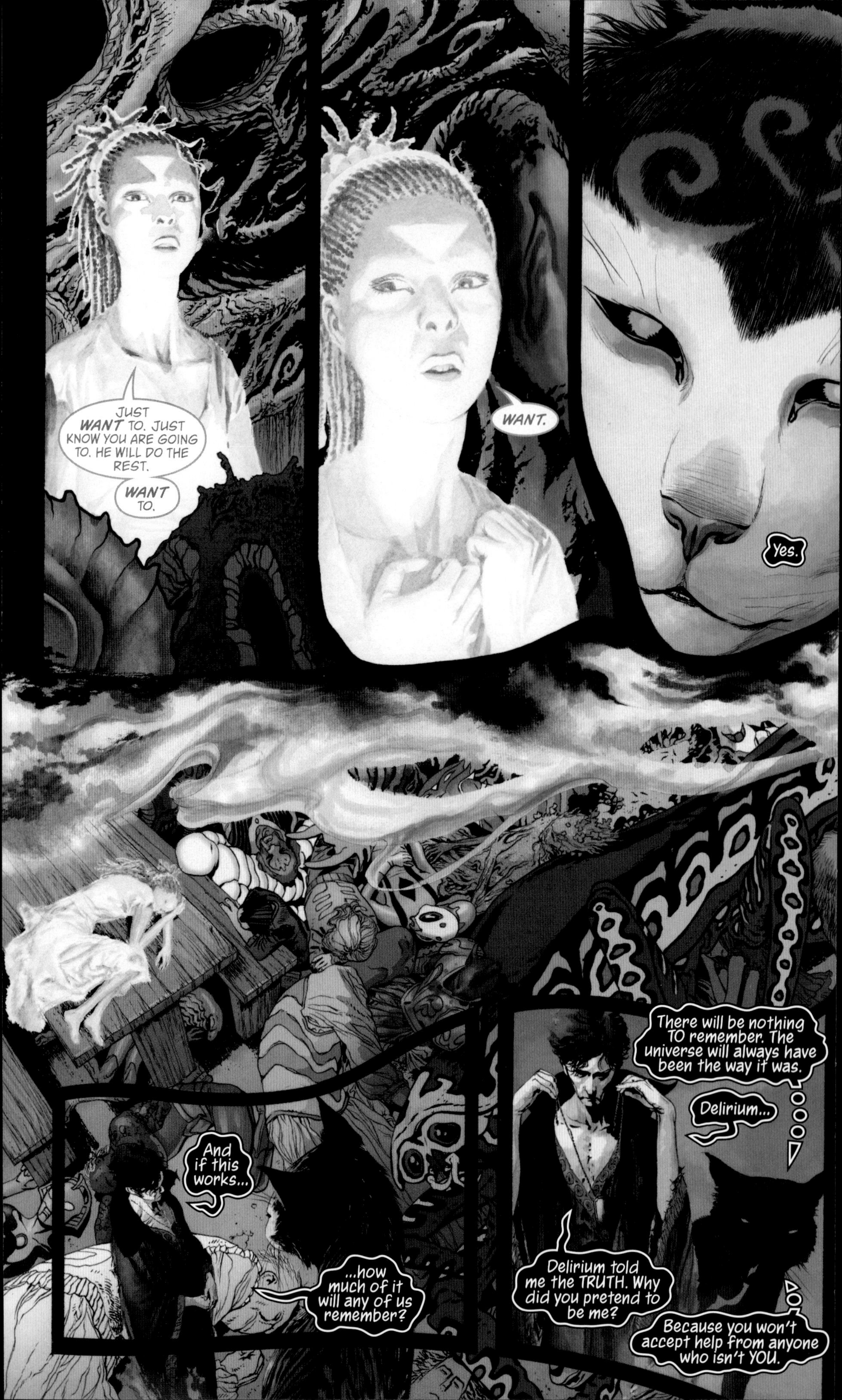

JUST WANT TO. JUST KNOW YOU ARE GOING TO. HE WILL DO THE REST.
WANT TO.
WANT.
Yes.
And if this works...
...how much of it will any of us remember?
There will be nothing TO remember. The universe will always have been the way it was.
Delirium...
Delirium told me the TRUTH. Why did you pretend to be me?
Because you won't accept help from anyone who isn't YOU.

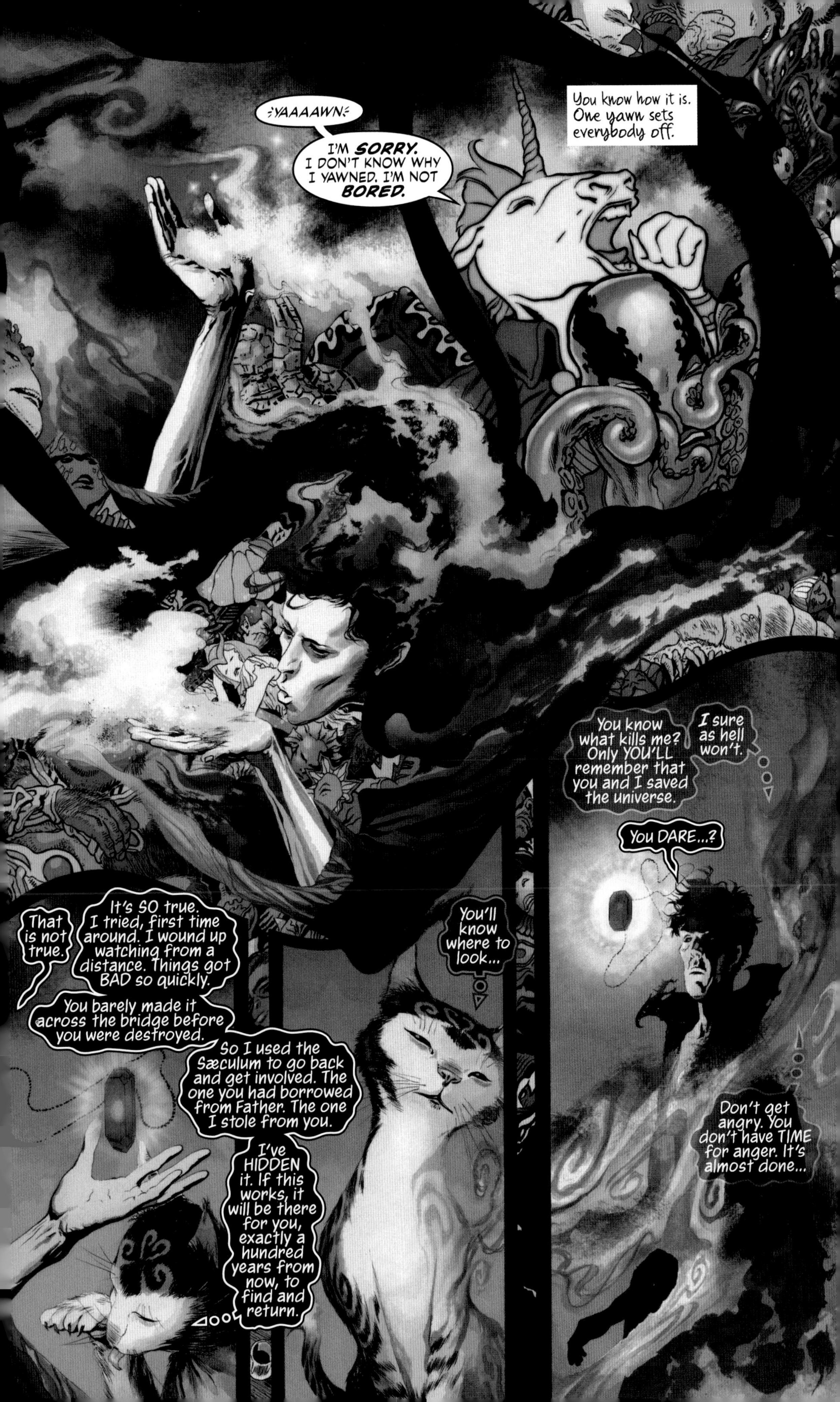
YAAAAWN
I'M SORRY. I DON'T KNOW WHY I YAWNED. I'M NOT BORED.
You know how it is. One yawn sets everybody off.
You know what kills me? Only YOU'LL remember that you and I saved the universe.
I sure as hell won't.
You DARE...?
That is not true.
It's SO true. I tried, first time around. I wound up watching from a distance. Things got BAD so quickly.
You barely made it across the bridge before you were destroyed.
So I used the Sæculum to go back and get involved. The one you had borrowed from Father. The one I stole from you.
I've HIDDEN it. If this works, it will be there for you, exactly a hundred years from now, to find and return.
You'll know where to look...
Don't get angry. You don't have TIME for anger. It's almost done...

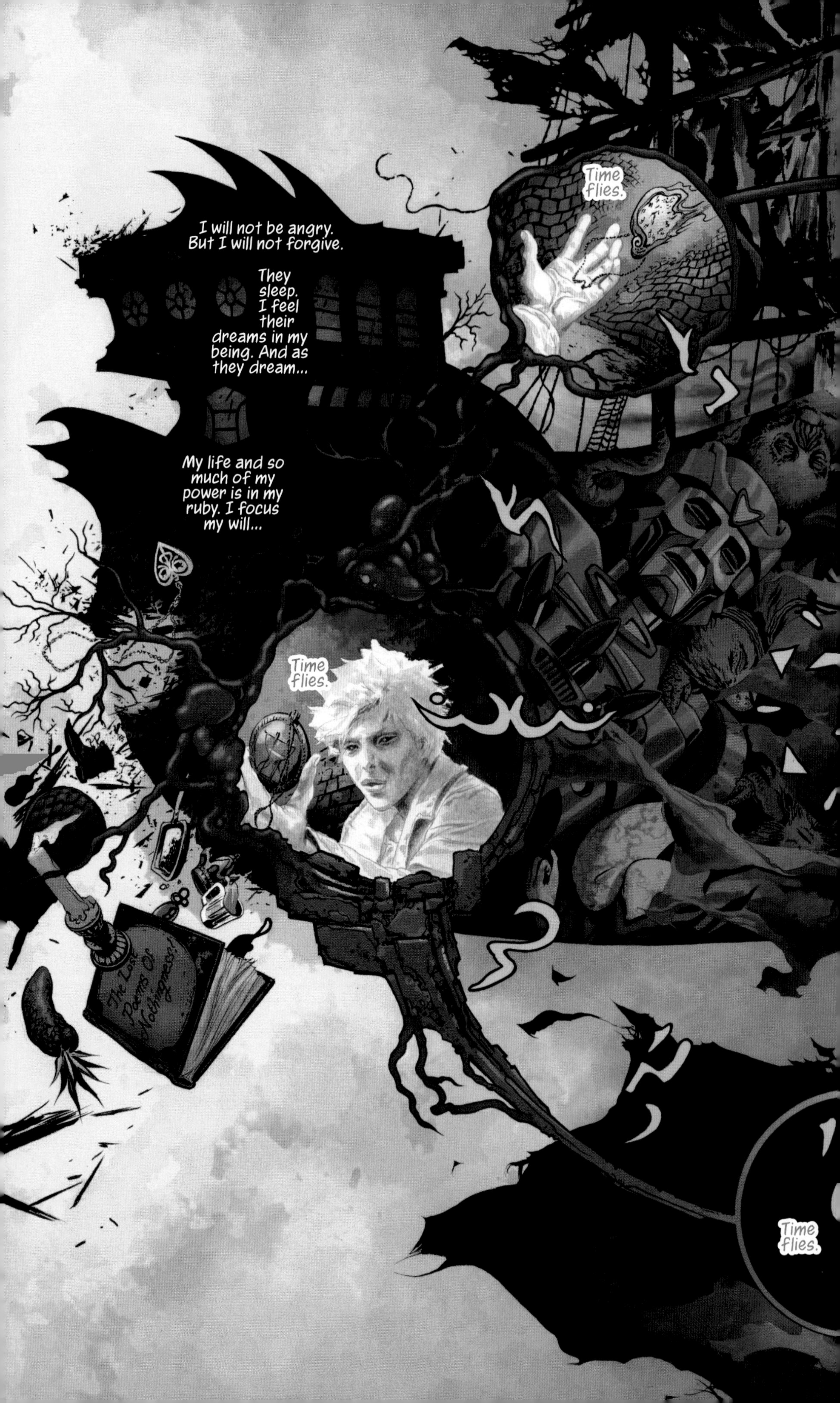
I will not be angry. But I will not forgive.
They sleep. I feel their dreams in my being. And as they dream...
Time flies.
My life and so much of my power is in my ruby. I focus my will...
Time flies.
The Lost Poems Of Nothingness?!
Time flies.

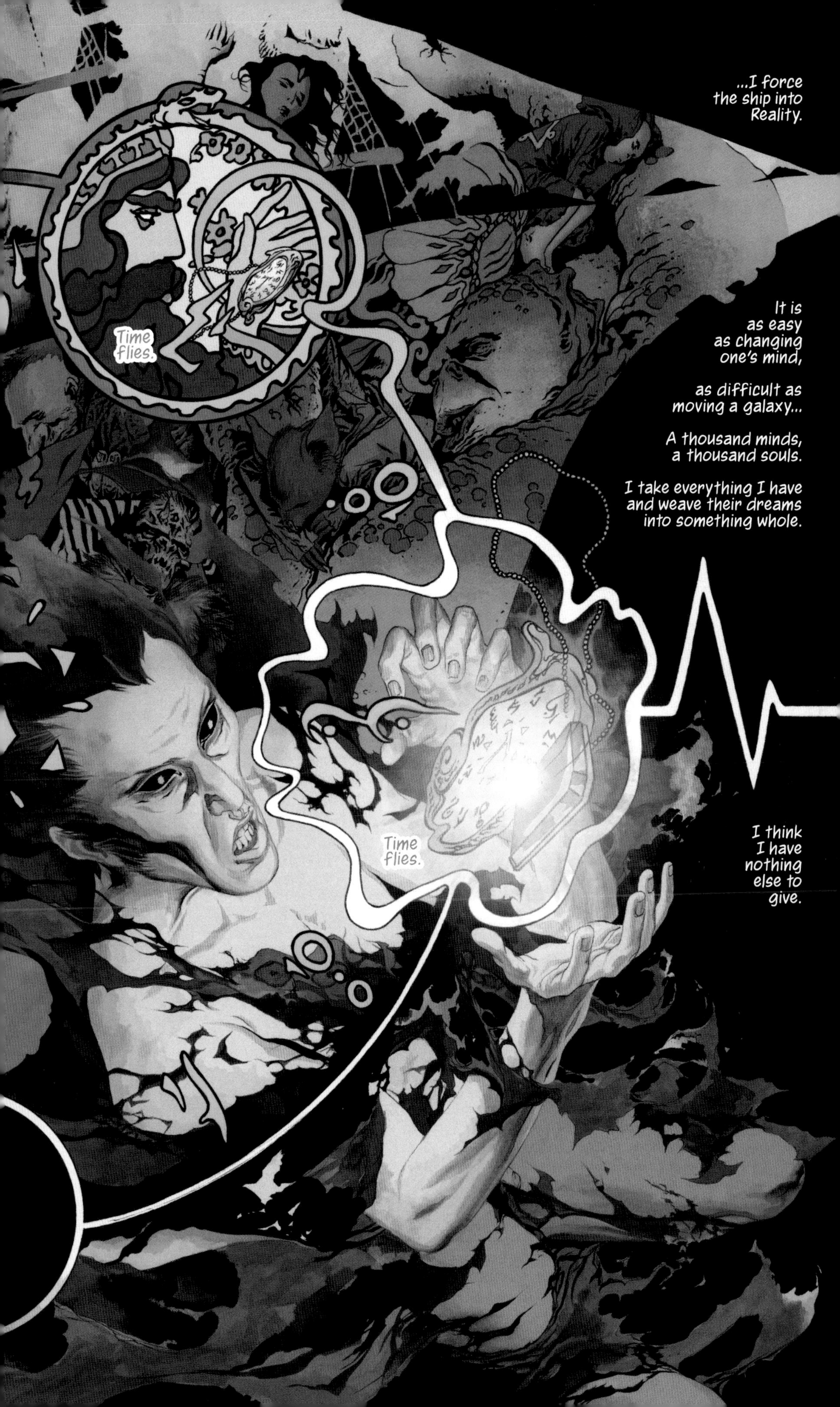
...I force the ship into Reality.
Time flies.
It is as easy as changing one's mind,
as difficult as moving a galaxy...
A thousand minds, a thousand souls.
I take everything I have and weave their dreams into something whole.
Time flies.
I think I have nothing else to give.

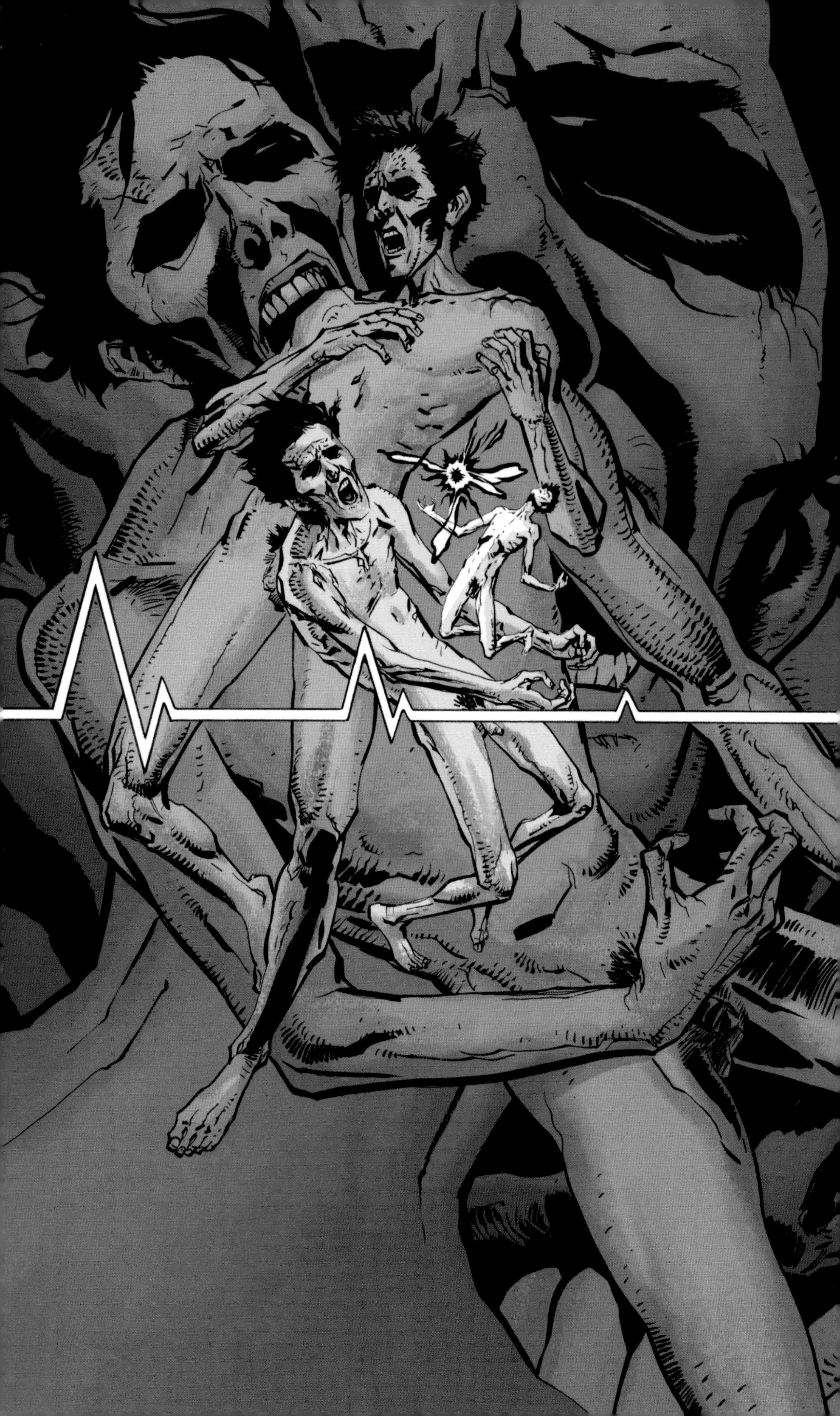

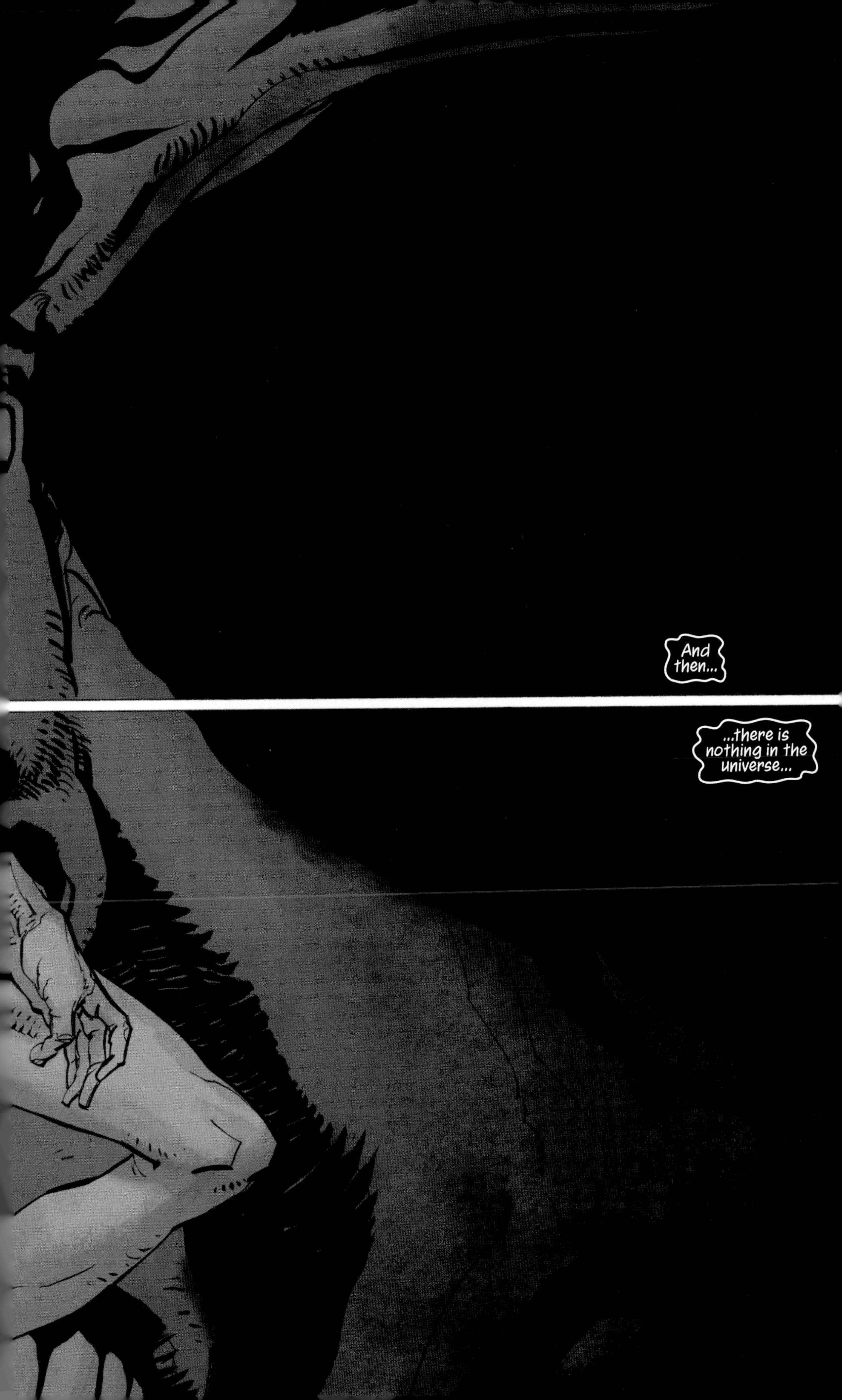
And then...
...there is nothing in the universe...

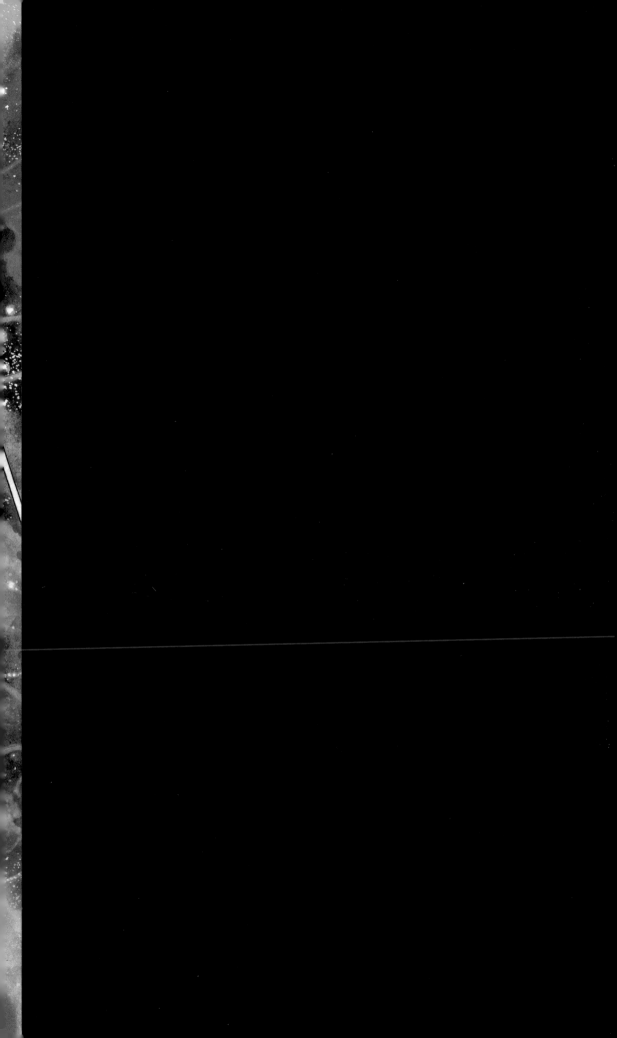

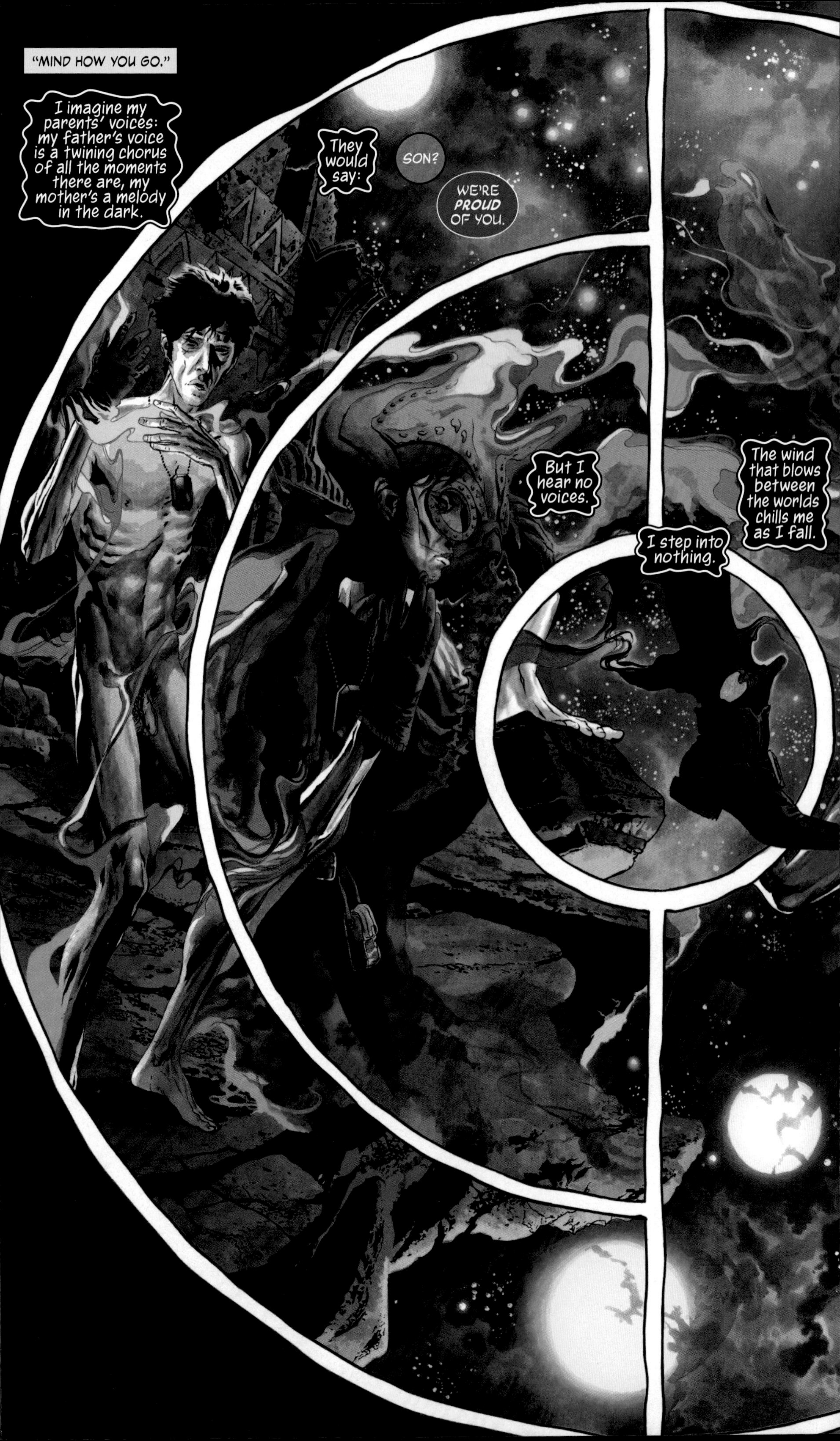
"MIND HOW YOU GO."
I imagine my parents' voices: my father's voice is a twining chorus of all the moments there are, my mother's a melody in the dark.
They would say:
SON?
WE'RE PROUD OF YOU.
But I hear no voices.
The wind that blows between the worlds chills me as I fall.
I step into nothing.

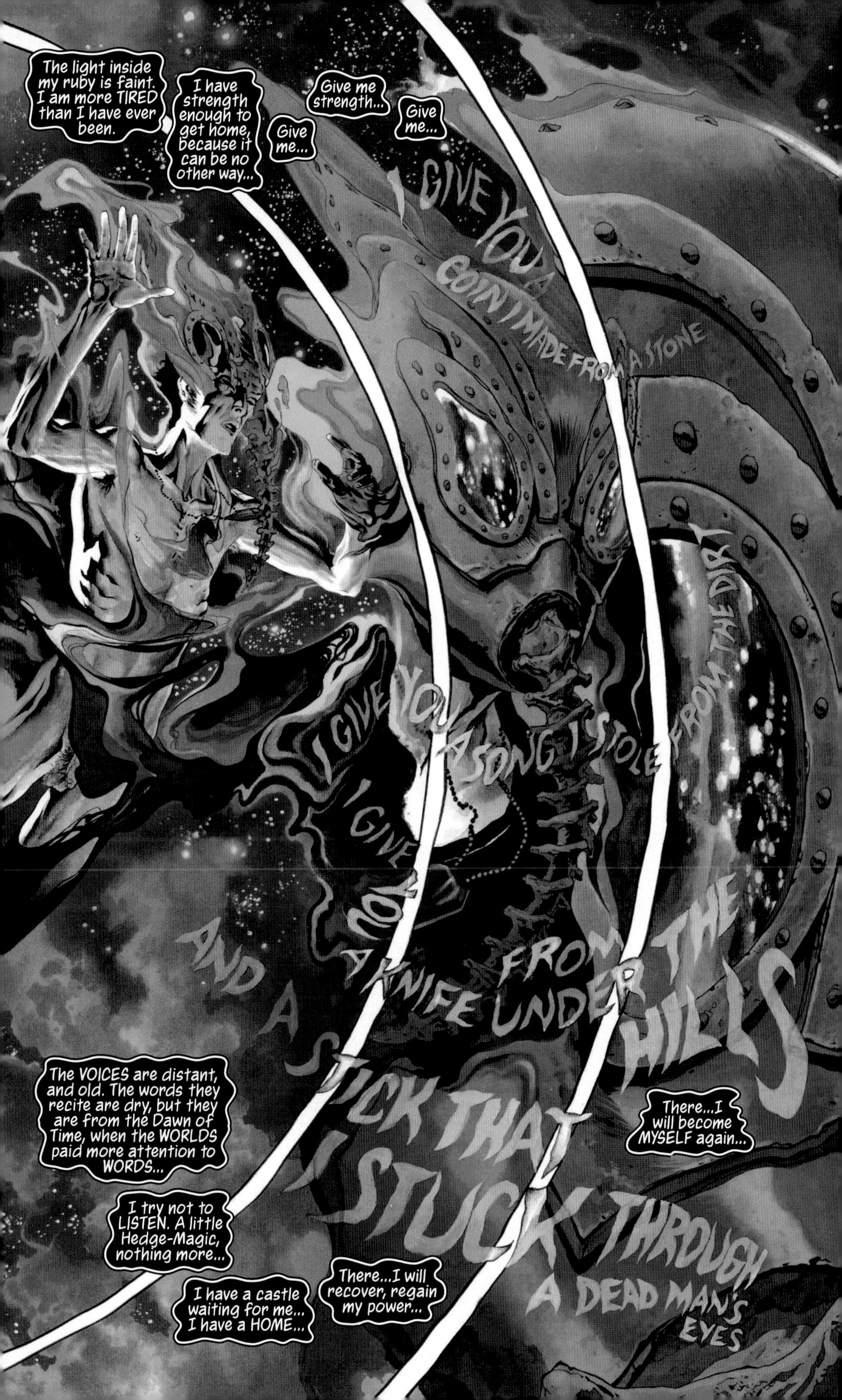
The light inside my ruby is faint. I am more TIRED than I have ever been.
I have strength enough to get home, because it can be no other way...
Give me...
Give me strength...
Give me...
I GIVE YOU A COIN I MADE FROM A STONE
I GIVE YOU A SONG I STOLE FROM THE DIRT
I GIVE YOU A KNIFE FROM UNDER THE HILLS
AND A STICK THAT I STUCK THROUGH A DEAD MAN'S EYES
The VOICES are distant, and old. The words they recite are dry, but they are from the Dawn of Time, when the WORLDS paid more attention to WORDS...
I try not to LISTEN. A little Hedge-Magic, nothing more...
I have a castle waiting for me... I have a HOME...
There...I will recover, regain my power...
There...I will become MYSELF again...

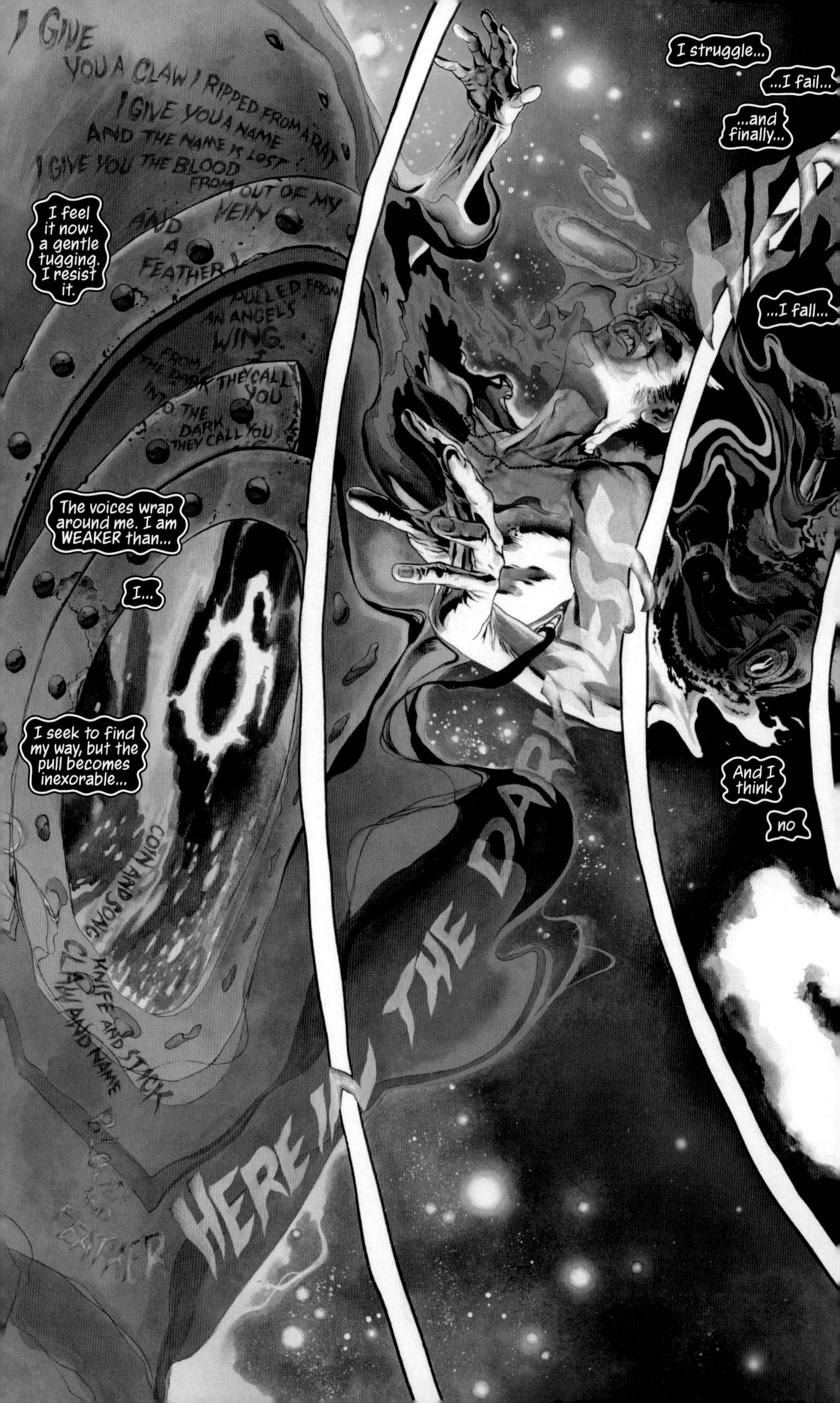

I GIVE YOU A CLAW I RIPPED FROM A RAT
I GIVE YOU A NAME AND THE NAME IS LOST
I GIVE YOU THE BLOOD FROM OUT OF MY VEIN
AND A FEATHER PULLED FROM AN ANGEL'S WING.
FROM THE DARK THEY CALL YOU
INTO THE DARK THEY CALL YOU
I feel it now: a gentle tugging. I resist it.
The voices wrap around me. I am WEAKER than...
I...
I seek to find my way, but the pull becomes inexorable...
COIN AND SONG KNIFE AND STICK
CLAW AND NAME
HERE IN THE DARK
I struggle...
...I fail...
...and finally...
...I fall...
And I think
no

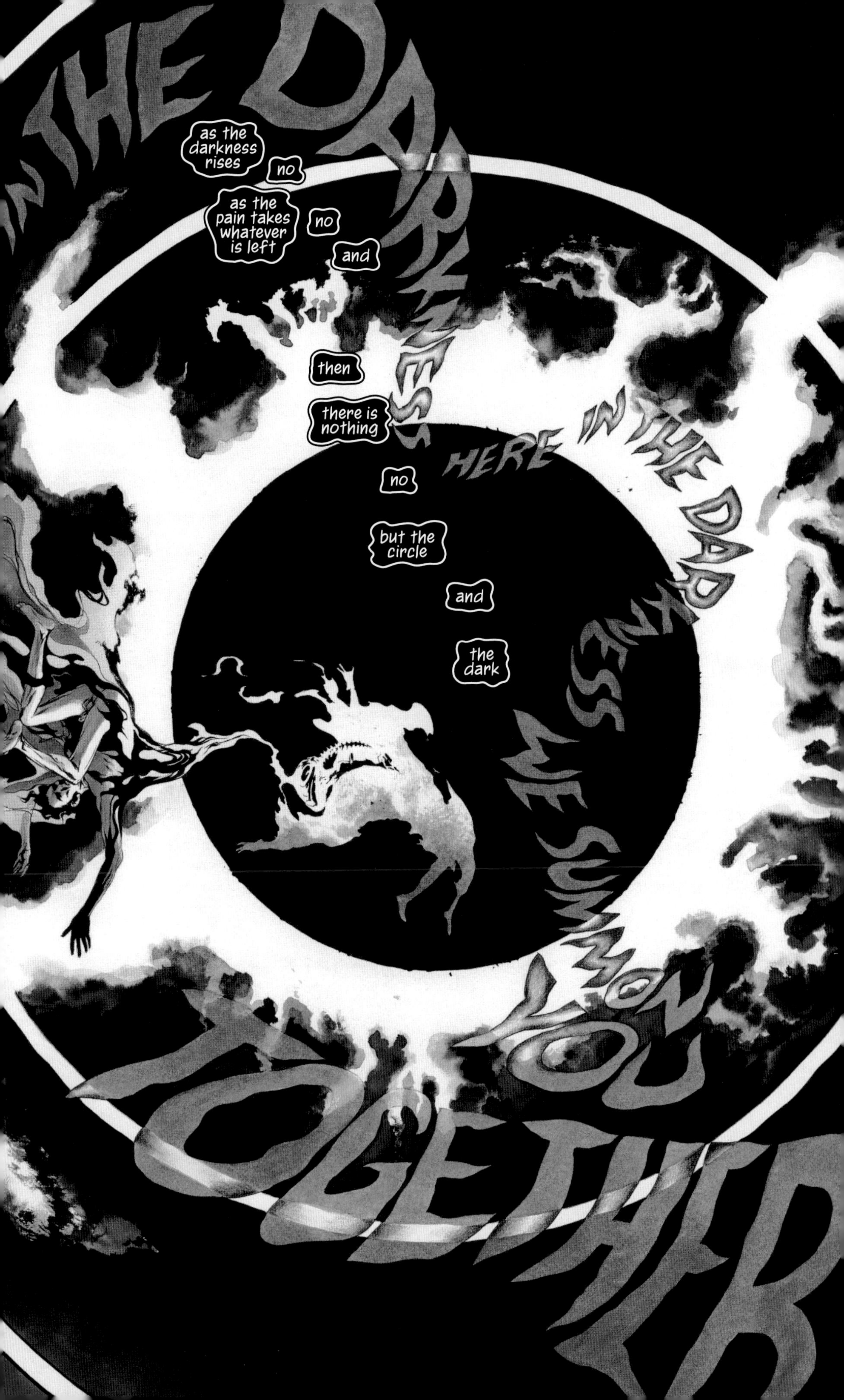
THE DARKNESS
as the darkness rises
no
as the pain takes whatever is left
no
and
then
there is nothing
no
but the circle
and
the dark
HERE IN THE DARKNESS WE SUMMON YOU
TOGETHR

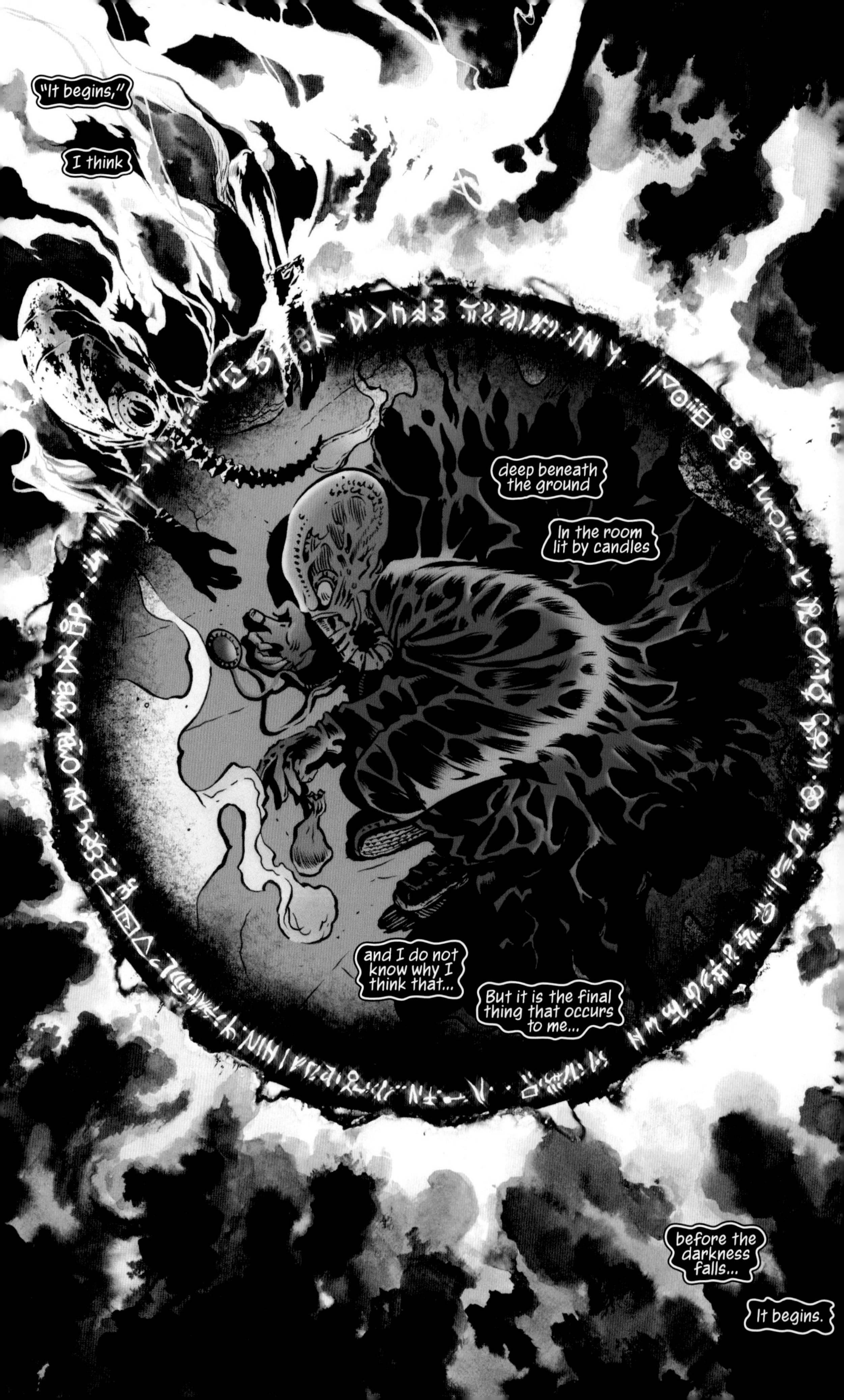
"It begins,"
I think
deep beneath the ground
In the room lit by candles
and I do not know why I think that...
But it is the final thing that occurs to me...
before the darkness falls...
It begins.

a Vertigo production by

Neil Gaiman
J. H. Williams III
Dave Stewart
Dave McKean (cover b)
James Jean (chase variant)
Todd Klein
Rowena Yow
&
Shelly Bond

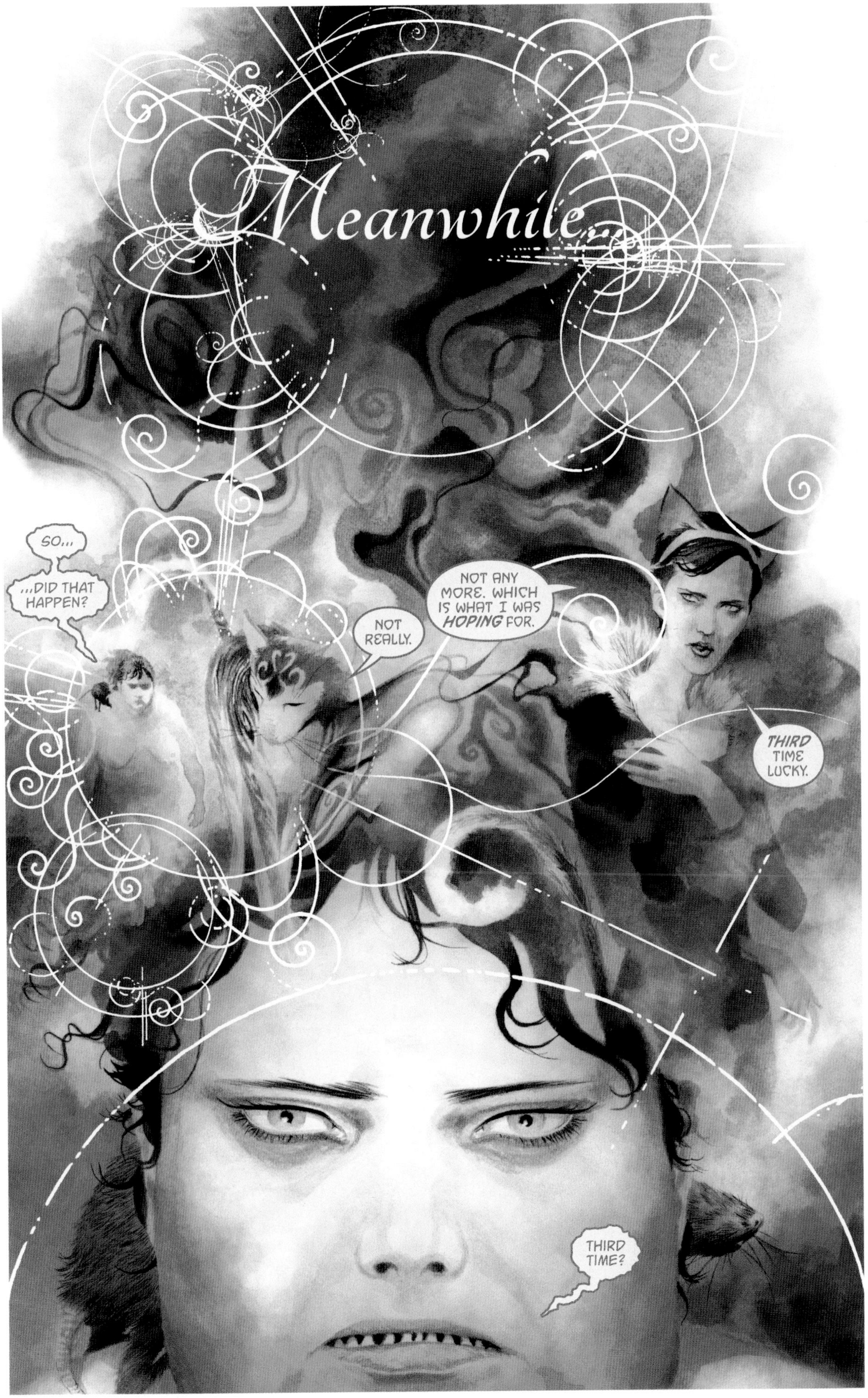
Meanwhile...
SO...
...DID THAT HAPPEN?
NOT REALLY.
NOT ANY MORE. WHICH IS WHAT I WAS HOPING FOR.
THIRD TIME LUCKY.
THIRD TIME?

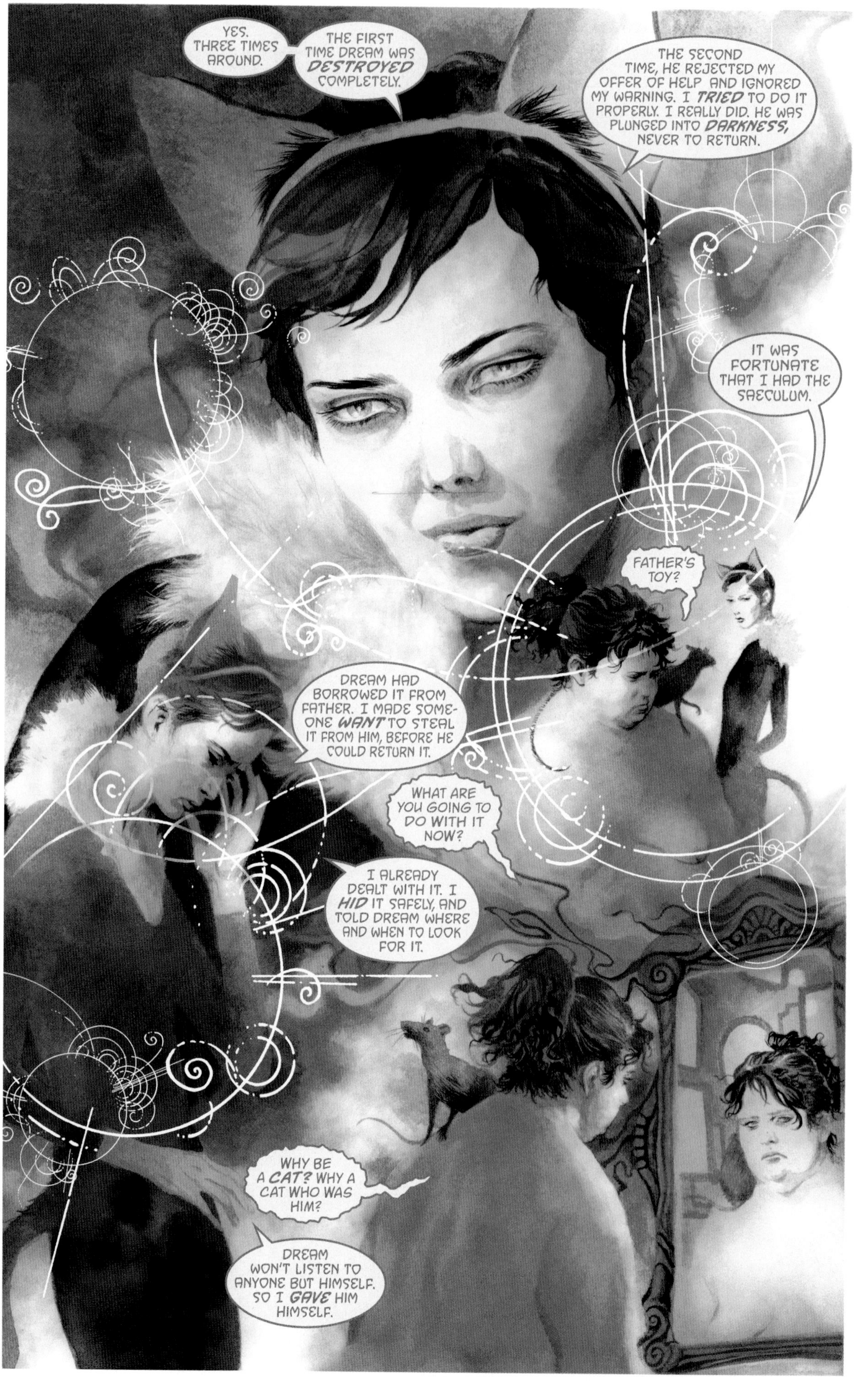
YES. THREE TIMES AROUND.
THE FIRST TIME DREAM WAS DESTROYED COMPLETELY.
THE SECOND TIME, HE REJECTED MY OFFER OF HELP AND IGNORED MY WARNING. I TRIED TO DO IT PROPERLY. I REALLY DID. HE WAS PLUNGED INTO DARKNESS, NEVER TO RETURN.
IT WAS FORTUNATE THAT I HAD THE SAECULUM.
FATHER'S TOY?
DREAM HAD BORROWED IT FROM FATHER. I MADE SOME-ONE WANT TO STEAL IT FROM HIM, BEFORE HE COULD RETURN IT.
WHAT ARE YOU GOING TO DO WITH IT NOW?
I ALREADY DEALT WITH IT. I HID IT SAFELY, AND TOLD DREAM WHERE AND WHEN TO LOOK FOR IT.
WHY BE A CAT? WHY A CAT WHO WAS HIM?
DREAM WON'T LISTEN TO ANYONE BUT HIMSELF. SO I GAVE HIM HIMSELF.

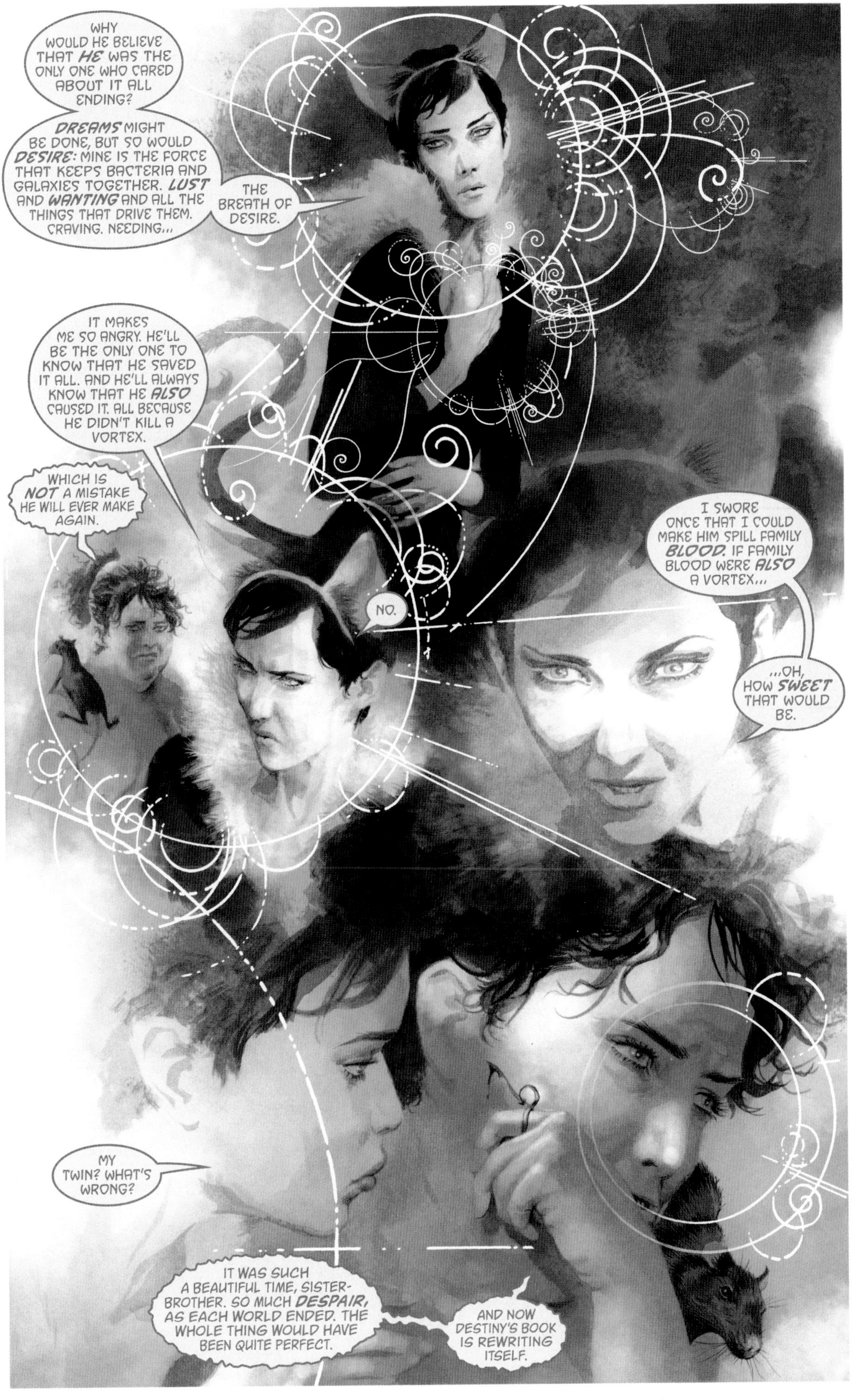
WHY WOULD HE BELIEVE THAT HE WAS THE ONLY ONE WHO CARED ABOUT IT ALL ENDING?
DREAMS MIGHT BE DONE, BUT SO WOULD DESIRE: MINE IS THE FORCE THAT KEEPS BACTERIA AND GALAXIES TOGETHER. LUST AND WANTING AND ALL THE THINGS THAT DRIVE THEM. CRAVING. NEEDING...
THE BREATH OF DESIRE.
IT MAKES ME SO ANGRY. HE'LL BE THE ONLY ONE TO KNOW THAT HE SAVED IT ALL. AND HE'LL ALWAYS KNOW THAT HE ALSO CAUSED IT. ALL BECAUSE HE DIDN'T KILL A VORTEX.
WHICH IS NOT A MISTAKE HE WILL EVER MAKE AGAIN.
NO.
I SWORE ONCE THAT I COULD MAKE HIM SPILL FAMILY BLOOD. IF FAMILY BLOOD WERE ALSO A VORTEX...
...OH, HOW SWEET THAT WOULD BE.
MY TWIN? WHAT'S WRONG?
IT WAS SUCH A BEAUTIFUL TIME, SISTER-BROTHER. SO MUCH DESPAIR, AS EACH WORLD ENDED. THE WHOLE THING WOULD HAVE BEEN QUITE PERFECT.
AND NOW DESTINY'S BOOK IS REWRITING ITSELF.

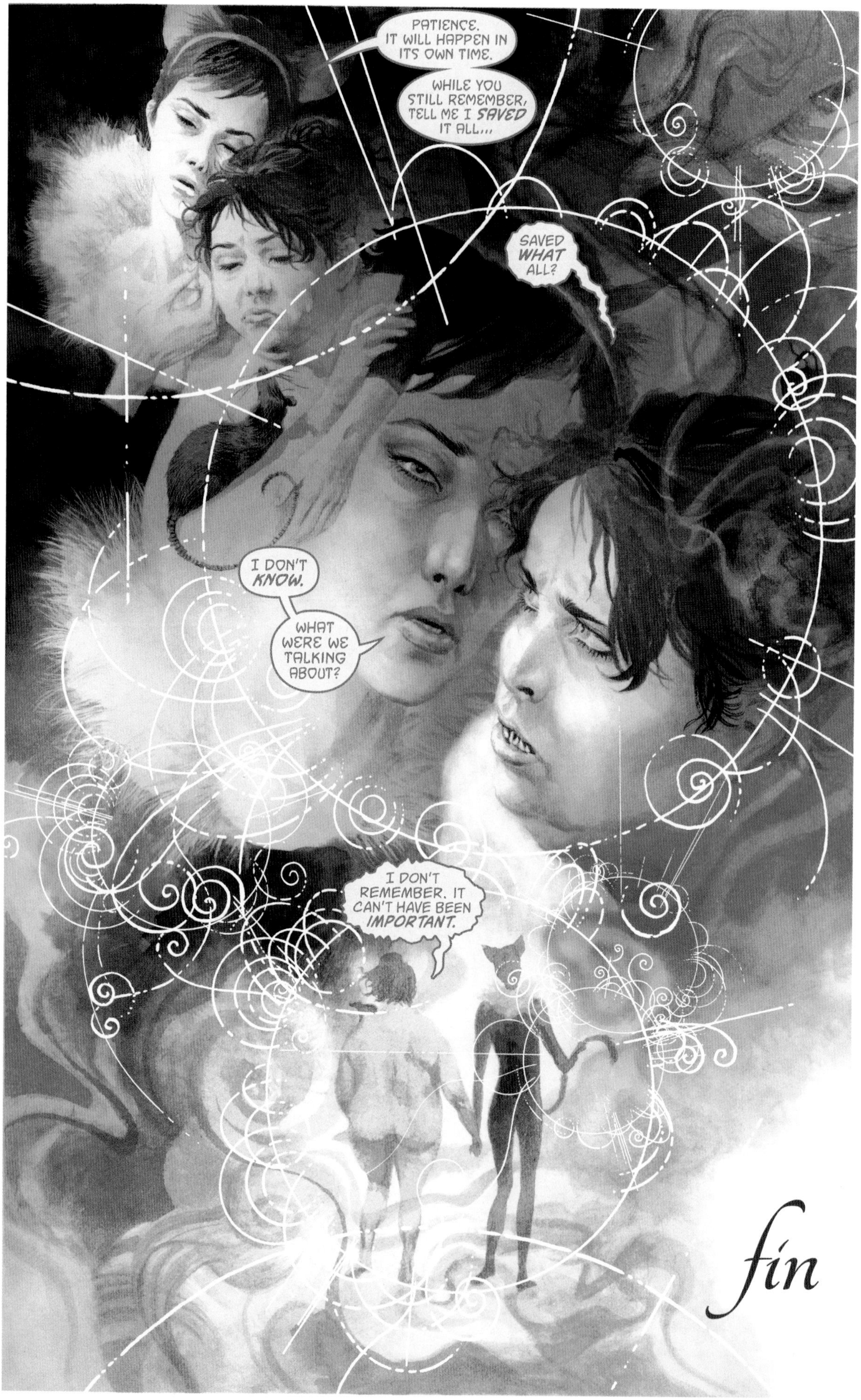
PATIENCE. IT WILL HAPPEN IN ITS OWN TIME.
WHILE YOU STILL REMEMBER, TELL ME I SAVED IT ALL...
SAVED WHAT ALL?
I DON'T KNOW.
WHAT WERE WE TALKING ABOUT?
I DON'T REMEMBER. IT CAN'T HAVE BEEN IMPORTANT.

fin

Accompaniments

Composing and Performing THE SANDMAN: OVERTURE

With Neil Gaiman, J.H. Williams III, Dave Stewart, Todd Klein, Shelly Bond and Sara Miller

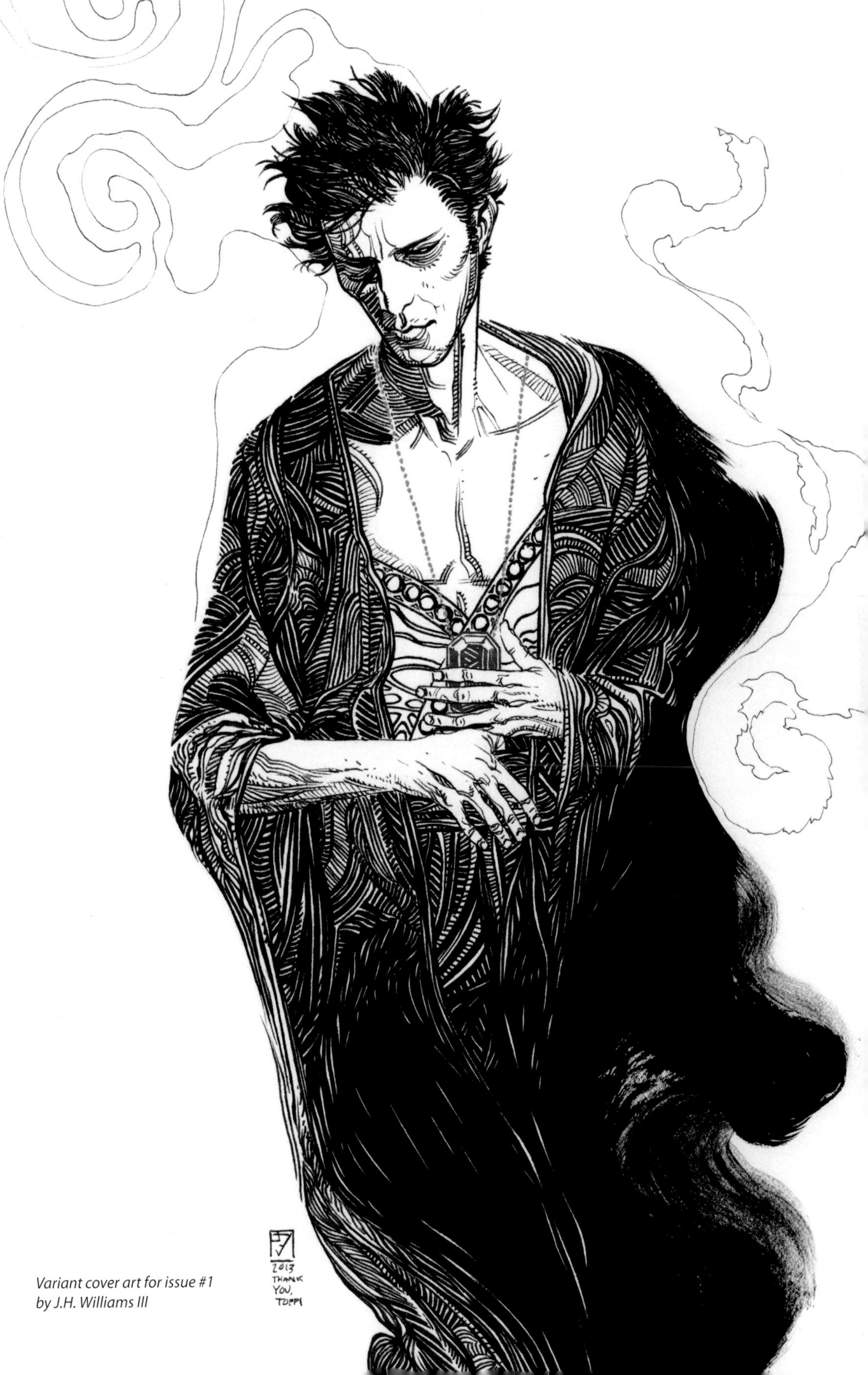
2013
THANK
YOU,
TOPPI

Variant cover art for issue #1 by J.H. Williams III

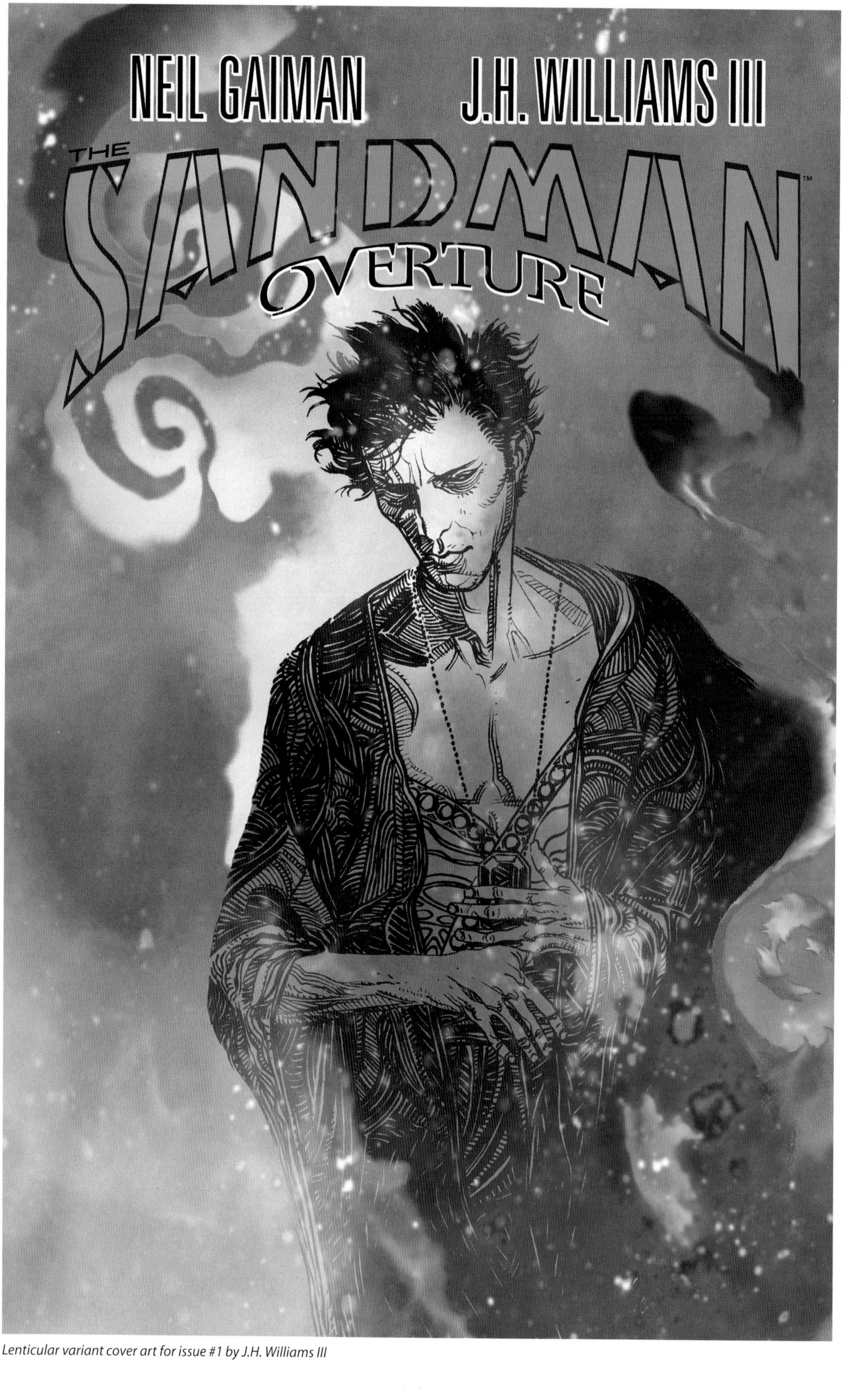
NEIL GAIMAN
J.H. WILLIAMS III
THE SANDMAN™
OVERTURE

Lenticular variant cover art for issue #1 by J.H. Williams III

ART PROCESS:
The Dreamscape Method

The art of J.H. Williams III is so complex, fantastical and awe-inspiring that it's sometimes hard to believe it comes from a human brain. The artist himself gives us an in-depth look at the magic that goes into the beautiful art of THE SANDMAN: OVERTURE.

Interview by Sara Miller

The style of Father Time's world stands out so differently from the rest of the places Dream goes in this series. Where did your inspiration for this style come from? What did you want it to reflect?

Well, this really stems from multiple notions. What sparked the initial aspect of finding the right style was when Neil wrote in Chapter 3 the scene involving Morpheus disappearing for an instant, but we don't get to see what happened, where he went. In our discussions Neil explained to me that Dream was being plucked out of the time-stream, or at least our understanding of it, and that where he ends up will be revealed in the next chapter, the opening sequence you refer to for issue #4, and we will be introduced to the father of the Endless, Father Time. This got me thinking on using a style that is not influenced by or based on comics, because it's as if Dream has been plucked out of the comic itself in chapter 3, outside of known time, outside of the story itself in a way.

It felt very appropriate to use something outside of comics as the basis for the visual of this scene, something that defied comics to a degree, or at least the notion of panel-by-panel comics storytelling. It needed to be something fluid, to capture the essence of Time being a fluid concept. Time, even though it is something that we measure, is a thing that the measurement does not follow our perception of it — "from when to when" can be fluid to our senses during our lives. The experience of time passing is very different from measuring it. And what Neil is portraying in the scene reflects this, that Father Time's age is never consistent, and not in chronological order, yet his intelligence remains constant. This all reinforced my thinking that there should almost be no real panels, as to be expected in a comic. This all takes place outside the construct of the narrative in a way, outside of measuring Time, outside of the typical comics storytelling structure. It needed to feel fluid. And I also wanted something very colorful, adding to the psychedelic experience of the fluidness, while contrasting against the heaviness of the main narrative that falls all around this particular sequence. Overall, we've been bold with color the entire series and wanted to see if we could push that beyond the usual range we've toyed with so far. So all that led me to basing the look of this scene on Peter Max as a starting point — one of the greatest pop artists. There is always this tremendous flow in his work, and very dreamscape in tone.

His earlier, flatter-in-feel works is where I wanted to derive from, rather than the later, more impressionist painterly works. This was important for a few reasons. I knew that other sections of this chapter were going to have painted work involved, so contrasting against that was key in making this feel very separated from everything else, maintaining that "outside of it all" aspect. I strongly felt that using the flatter aspect would allow it to feel like a place that is very disconnected from everything we've shown so far, the flatness sort of feeling like a defiance of what is expected to be a "reality." Hard to create that feeling in a comic, considering comics are already 2-D drawings. I think it is relatively successful in the goals set forth, even if not perfect. And I do enjoy the effect of the flat vividness vaguely reminding of stained glass, giving the scene an almost religious church window quality, while remaining pagan. And finally, the style allowed for the inclusion of symbolic aspects to integrate into the scene without feeling intrusive on what we are experiencing.

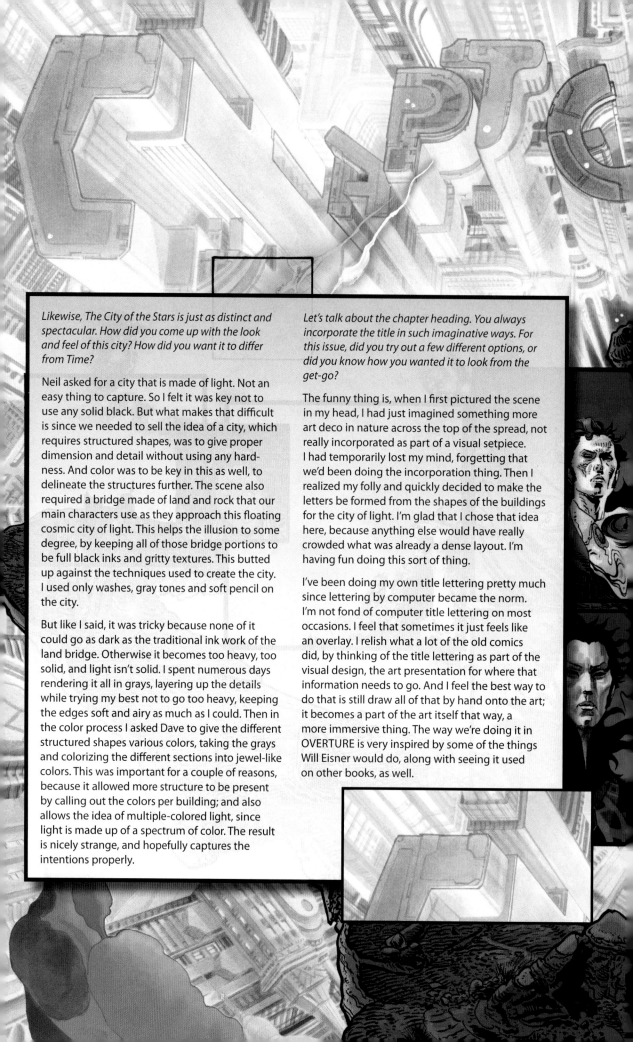

Likewise, The City of the Stars is just as distinct and spectacular. How did you come up with the look and feel of this city? How did you want it to differ from Time?

Neil asked for a city that is made of light. Not an easy thing to capture. So I felt it was key not to use any solid black. But what makes that difficult is since we needed to sell the idea of a city, which requires structured shapes, was to give proper dimension and detail without using any hard-ness. And color was to be key in this as well, to delineate the structures further. The scene also required a bridge made of land and rock that our main characters use as they approach this floating cosmic city of light. This helps the illusion to some degree, by keeping all of those bridge portions to be full black inks and gritty textures. This butted up against the techniques used to create the city. I used only washes, gray tones and soft pencil on the city.

But like I said, it was tricky because none of it could go as dark as the traditional ink work of the land bridge. Otherwise it becomes too heavy, too solid, and light isn't solid. I spent numerous days rendering it all in grays, layering up the details while trying my best not to go too heavy, keeping the edges soft and airy as much as I could. Then in the color process I asked Dave to give the different structured shapes various colors, taking the grays and colorizing the different sections into jewel-like colors. This was important for a couple of reasons, because it allowed more structure to be present by calling out the colors per building; and also allows the idea of multiple-colored light, since light is made up of a spectrum of color. The result is nicely strange, and hopefully captures the intentions properly.

Let's talk about the chapter heading. You always incorporate the title in such imaginative ways. For this issue, did you try out a few different options, or did you know how you wanted it to look from the get-go?

The funny thing is, when I first pictured the scene in my head, I had just imagined something more art deco in nature across the top of the spread, not really incorporated as part of a visual setpiece. I had temporarily lost my mind, forgetting that we'd been doing the incorporation thing. Then I realized my folly and quickly decided to make the letters be formed from the shapes of the buildings for the city of light. I'm glad that I chose that idea here, because anything else would have really crowded what was already a dense layout. I'm having fun doing this sort of thing.

I've been doing my own title lettering pretty much since lettering by computer became the norm. I'm not fond of computer title lettering on most occasions. I feel that sometimes it just feels like an overlay. I relish what a lot of the old comics did, by thinking of the title lettering as part of the visual design, the art presentation for where that information needs to go. And I feel the best way to do that is still draw all of that by hand onto the art; it becomes a part of the art itself that way, a more immersive thing. The way we're doing it in OVERTURE is very inspired by some of the things Will Eisner would do, along with seeing it used on other books, as well.

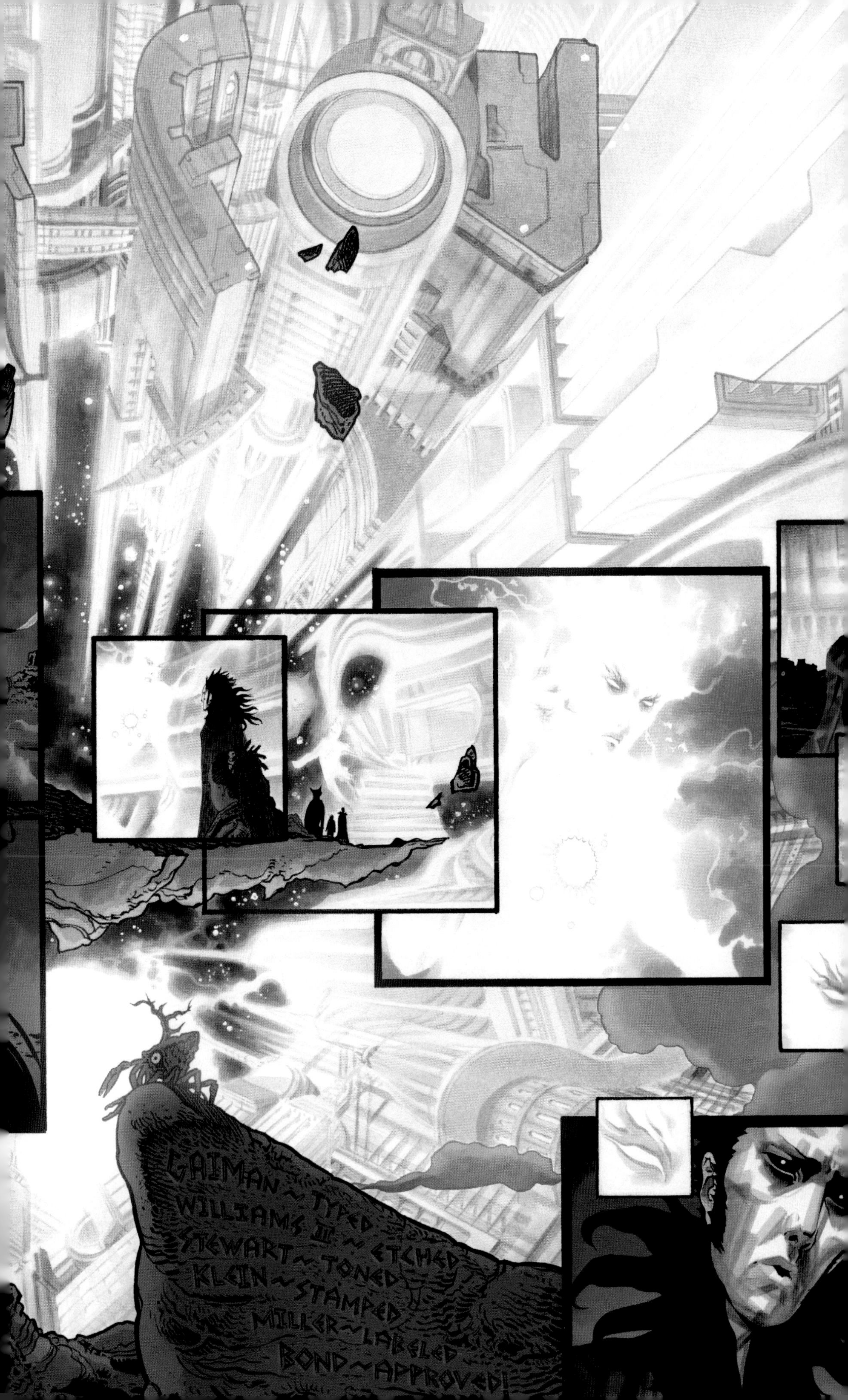
GAIMAN ~ TYPED
WILLIAMS III ~ ETCHED
STEWART ~ TONED
KLEIN ~ STAMPED
MILLER ~ LABELED
BOND ~ APPROVED!

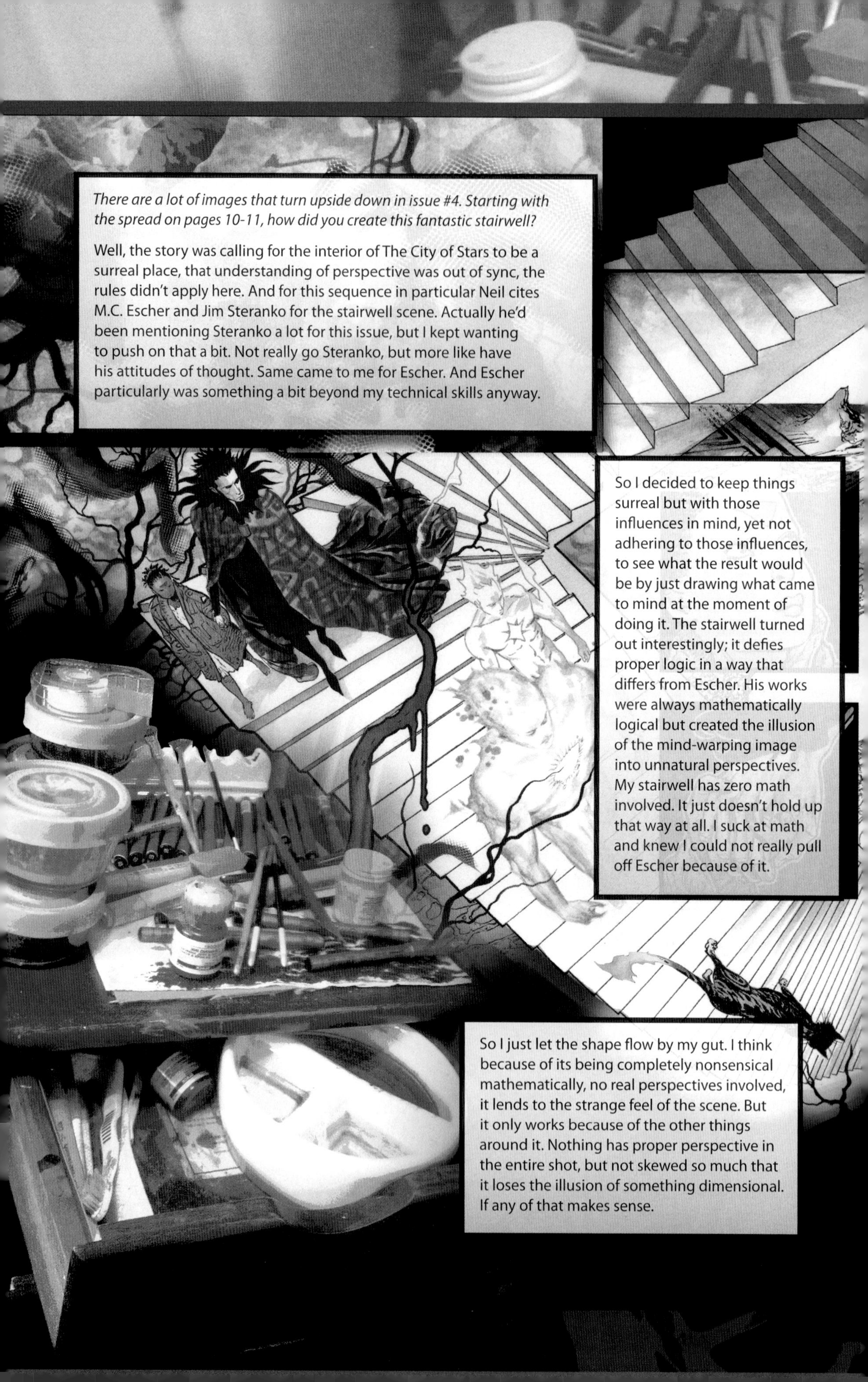

There are a lot of images that turn upside down in issue #4. Starting with the spread on pages 10-11, how did you create this fantastic stairwell?

Well, the story was calling for the interior of The City of Stars to be a surreal place, that understanding of perspective was out of sync, the rules didn't apply here. And for this sequence in particular Neil cites M.C. Escher and Jim Steranko for the stairwell scene. Actually he'd been mentioning Steranko a lot for this issue, but I kept wanting to push on that a bit. Not really go Steranko, but more like have his attitudes of thought. Same came to me for Escher. And Escher particularly was something a bit beyond my technical skills anyway.

So I decided to keep things surreal but with those influences in mind, yet not adhering to those influences, to see what the result would be by just drawing what came to mind at the moment of doing it. The stairwell turned out interestingly; it defies proper logic in a way that differs from Escher. His works were always mathematically logical but created the illusion of the mind-warping image into unnatural perspectives. My stairwell has zero math involved. It just doesn't hold up that way at all. I suck at math and knew I could not really pull off Escher because of it.

So I just let the shape flow by my gut. I think because of its being completely nonsensical mathematically, no real perspectives involved, it lends to the strange feel of the scene. But it only works because of the other things around it. Nothing has proper perspective in the entire shot, but not skewed so much that it loses the illusion of something dimensional. If any of that makes sense.

And for the actual flip on pages 17-19, did you have to do any preemptive work to accomplish this effect?

The flipping that occurs in this issue is intended for the reader to sort of feel like what Morpheus is feeling. Unfortunately for those who read digitally, it means a very frustrating moment, but oh well. Morpheus is frustrated as well. This place does not play by rules of common-sense understanding, emotionally or logistically.

And that Morpheus has difficulty in having proper judgment because of it. I think the hardest bit was getting the lettering placement to defy expectations, to use it to get the reader to slowly turn, not just promptly flip the book. If you just promptly flip it, the lettering becomes hard to follow in a spot or two. You to have ease into it, and ease out of it through rotation, not abruptly flip it. But this meant that when coming out of it you had to read some of the dialogue balloons in an almost backward reading direction than normal.

For me, I felt this enhanced how uncomfortable this place is. We also needed the reader to want to turn the pages in the proper direction once the thing is now upside down for the first rotation. I had to take a printed book and define clearly what was right-hand and left-hand pages while being upside down, and figure out rotation movement.

So by the last rotation that returns the book to the correct way up, the last panel falls on the right-hand page for that natural turning of the page. As with anything that asks the reader to alter their trained reading perspective, it can only be partially successful. Because not everyone will rotate the book as it really requires; some will, and some won't. You will have an imperfect result of a perfectly warranted experiment. But what is grand about that is the brief story narrative flow distortions that come from that. It makes for a disconcerting experience no matter what, and in so doing, it reinforces the lack of logical rules that the interior of The City of Stars has, especially because of the warped influence over this place that the Mad Star clearly has. It gives us a hint of what it is like for Morpheus and the others to be here.

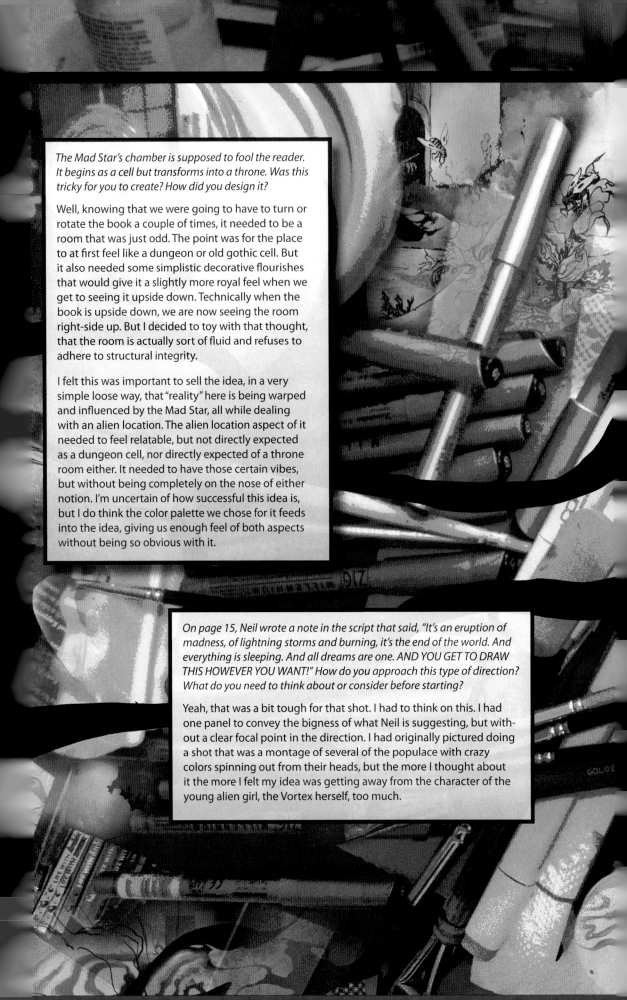

The Mad Star's chamber is supposed to fool the reader. It begins as a cell but transforms into a throne. Was this tricky for you to create? How did you design it?

Well, knowing that we were going to have to turn or rotate the book a couple of times, it needed to be a room that was just odd. The point was for the place to at first feel like a dungeon or old gothic cell. But it also needed some simplistic decorative flourishes that would give it a slightly more royal feel when we get to seeing it upside down. Technically when the book is upside down, we are now seeing the room right-side up. But I decided to toy with that thought, that the room is actually sort of fluid and refuses to adhere to structural integrity.

I felt this was important to sell the idea, in a very simple loose way, that "reality" here is being warped and influenced by the Mad Star, all while dealing with an alien location. The alien location aspect of it needed to feel relatable, but not directly expected as a dungeon cell, nor directly expected of a throne room either. It needed to have those certain vibes, but without being completely on the nose of either notion. I'm uncertain of how successful this idea is, but I do think the color palette we chose for it feeds into the idea, giving us enough feel of both aspects without being so obvious with it.

On page 15, Neil wrote a note in the script that said, "It's an eruption of madness, of lightning storms and burning, it's the end of the world. And everything is sleeping. And all dreams are one. AND YOU GET TO DRAW THIS HOWEVER YOU WANT!" How do you approach this type of direction? What do you need to think about or consider before starting?

Yeah, that was a bit tough for that shot. I had to think on this. I had one panel to convey the bigness of what Neil is suggesting, but without a clear focal point in the direction. I had originally pictured doing a shot that was a montage of several of the populace with crazy colors spinning out from their heads, but the more I thought about it the more I felt my idea was getting away from the character of the young alien girl, the Vortex herself, too much.

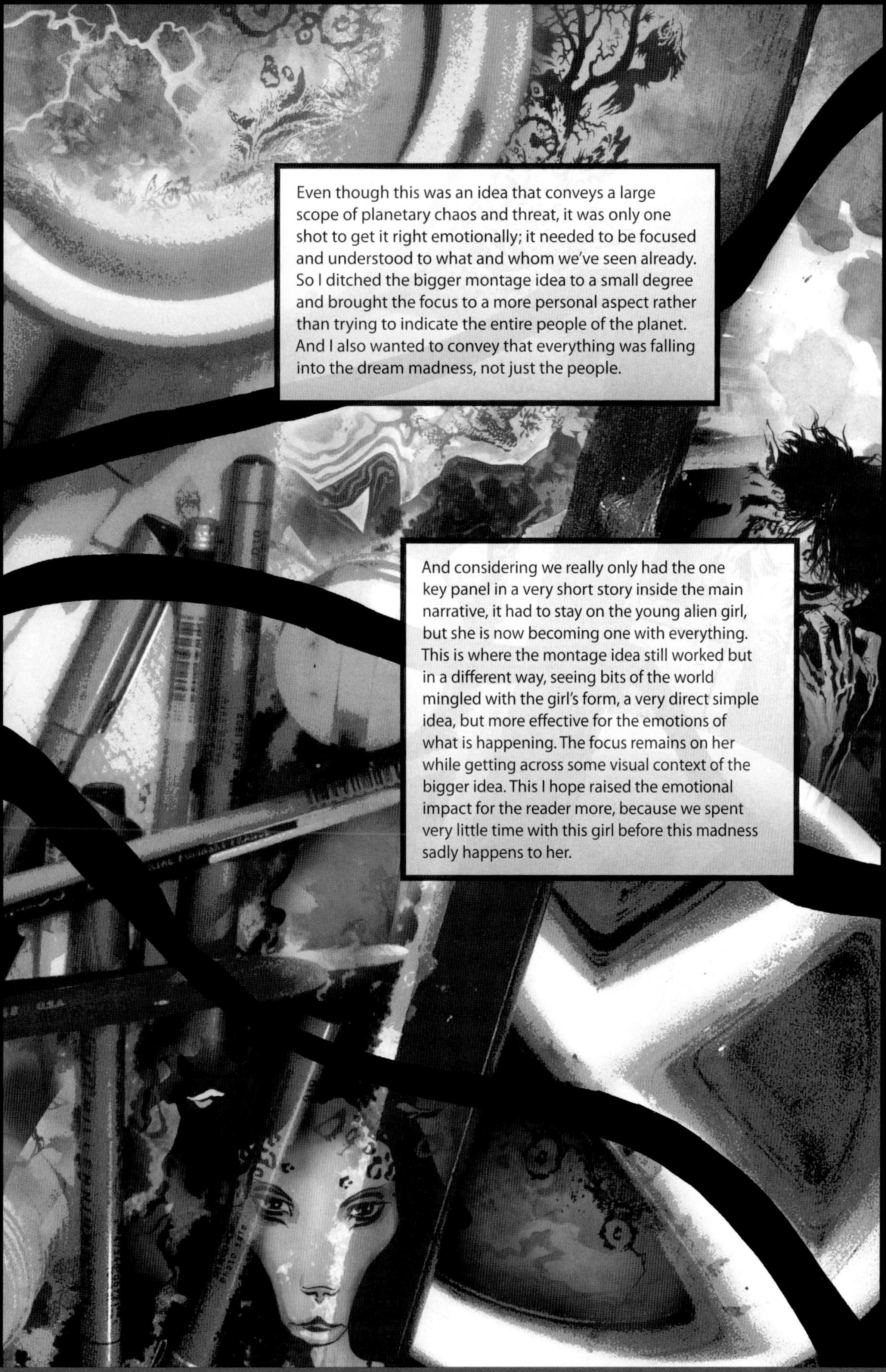

Even though this was an idea that conveys a large scope of planetary chaos and threat, it was only one shot to get it right emotionally; it needed to be focused and understood to what and whom we've seen already. So I ditched the bigger montage idea to a small degree and brought the focus to a more personal aspect rather than trying to indicate the entire people of the planet. And I also wanted to convey that everything was falling into the dream madness, not just the people.

And considering we really only had the one key panel in a very short story inside the main narrative, it had to stay on the young alien girl, but she is now becoming one with everything. This is where the montage idea still worked but in a different way, seeing bits of the world mingled with the girl's form, a very direct simple idea, but more effective for the emotions of what is happening. The focus remains on her while getting across some visual context of the bigger idea. This I hope raised the emotional impact for the reader more, because we spent very little time with this girl before this madness sadly happens to her.

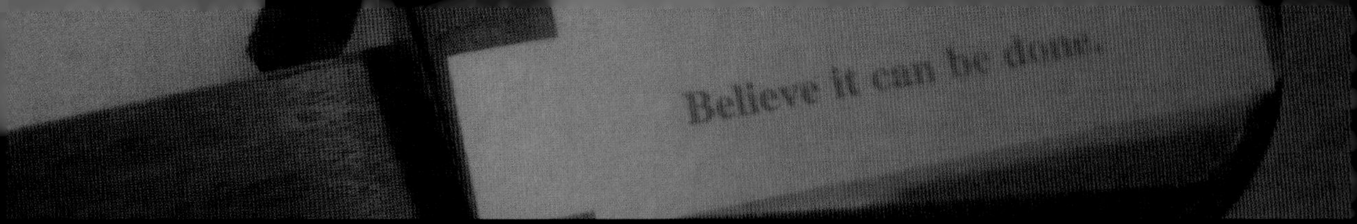
Believe it can be done.

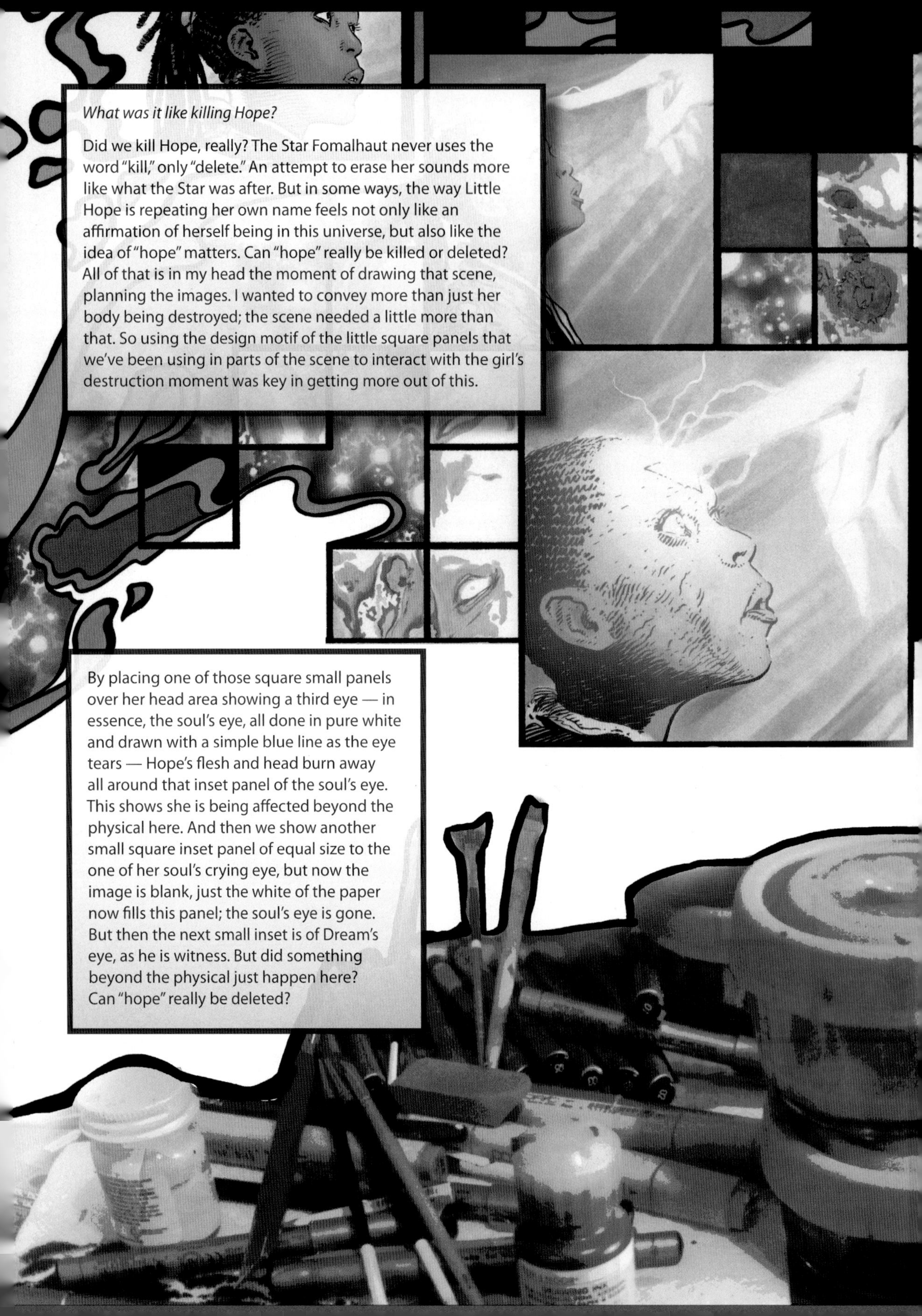

What was it like killing Hope?

Did we kill Hope, really? The Star Fomalhaut never uses the word "kill," only "delete." An attempt to erase her sounds more like what the Star was after. But in some ways, the way Little Hope is repeating her own name feels not only like an affirmation of herself being in this universe, but also like the idea of "hope" matters. Can "hope" really be killed or deleted? All of that is in my head the moment of drawing that scene, planning the images. I wanted to convey more than just her body being destroyed; the scene needed a little more than that. So using the design motif of the little square panels that we've been using in parts of the scene to interact with the girl's destruction moment was key in getting more out of this.

By placing one of those square small panels over her head area showing a third eye — in essence, the soul's eye, all done in pure white and drawn with a simple blue line as the eye tears — Hope's flesh and head burn away all around that inset panel of the soul's eye. This shows she is being affected beyond the physical here. And then we show another small square inset panel of equal size to the one of her soul's crying eye, but now the image is blank, just the white of the paper now fills this panel; the soul's eye is gone. But then the next small inset is of Dream's eye, as he is witness. But did something beyond the physical just happen here? Can "hope" really be deleted?

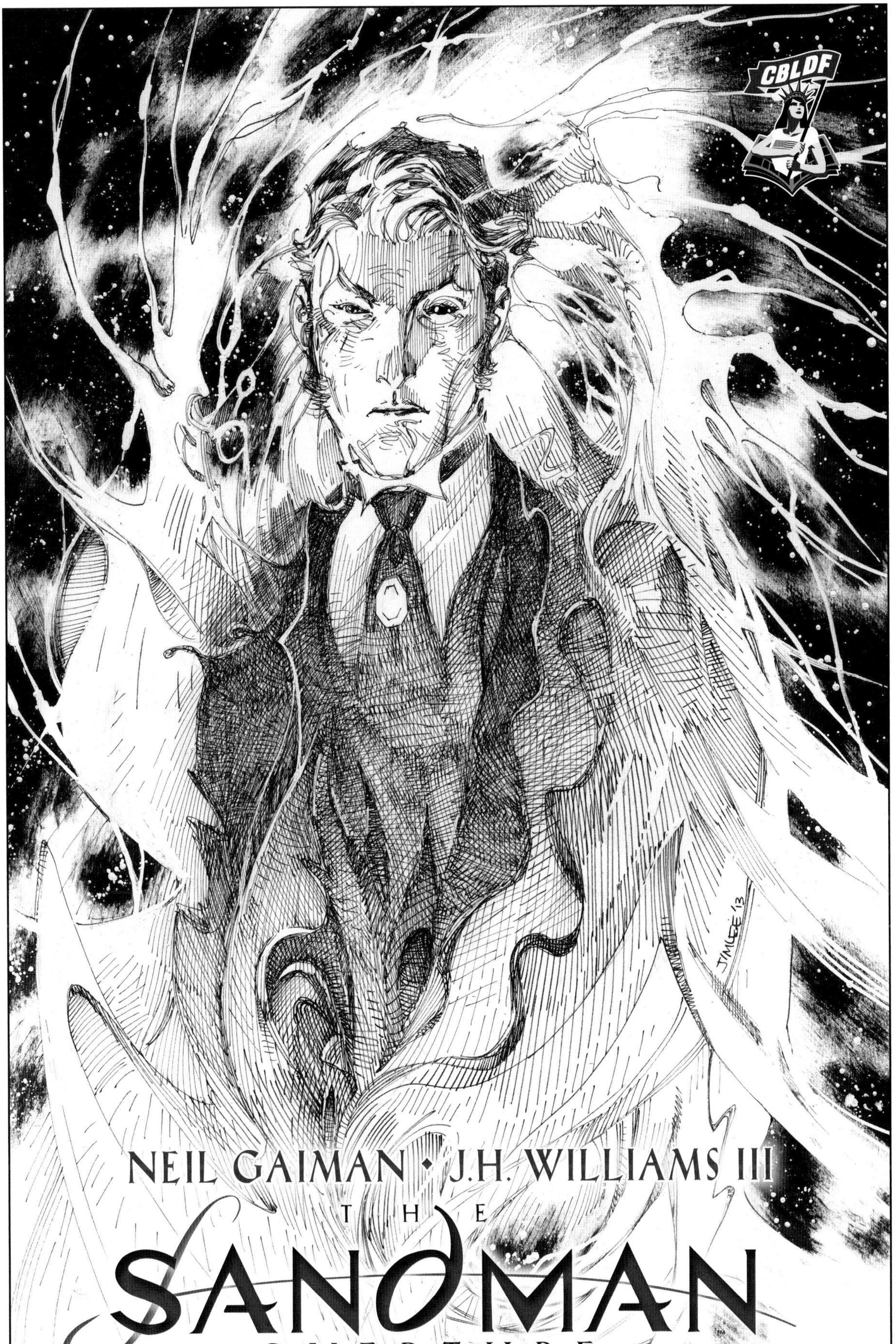
CBLDF
NEIL GAIMAN • J.H. WILLIAMS III
THE
SANDMAN
OVERTURE

Variant cover art for issue #1 by Jim Lee, in support of the Comic Book Legal Defense Fund

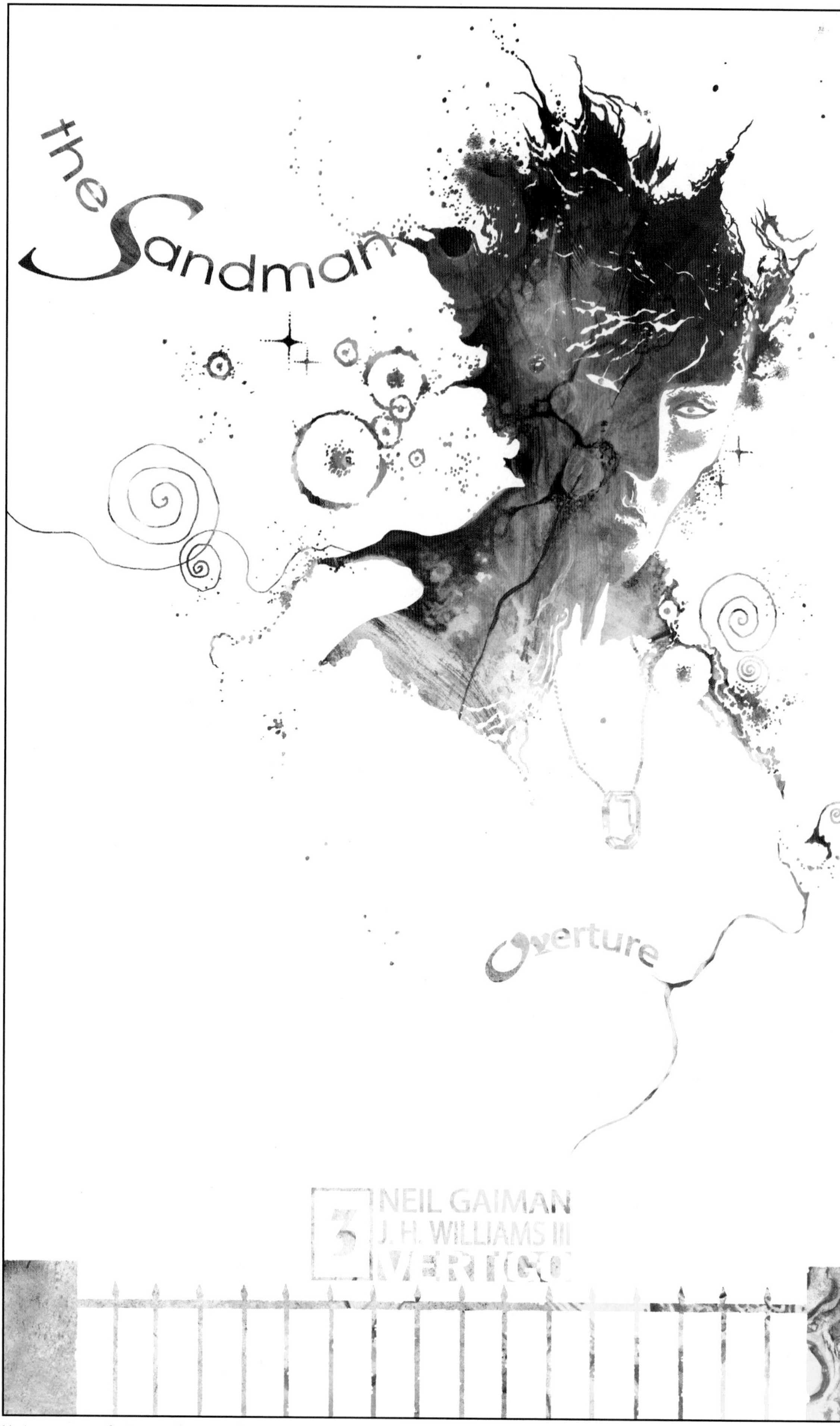
the Sandman
Overture
3
NEIL GAIMAN
J. H. WILLIAMS III
VERTIGO

Variant cover art for issue #3 by J.H. Williams III

COLOR PROCESS: FROM THEORY TO EXECUTION

by Dave Stewart

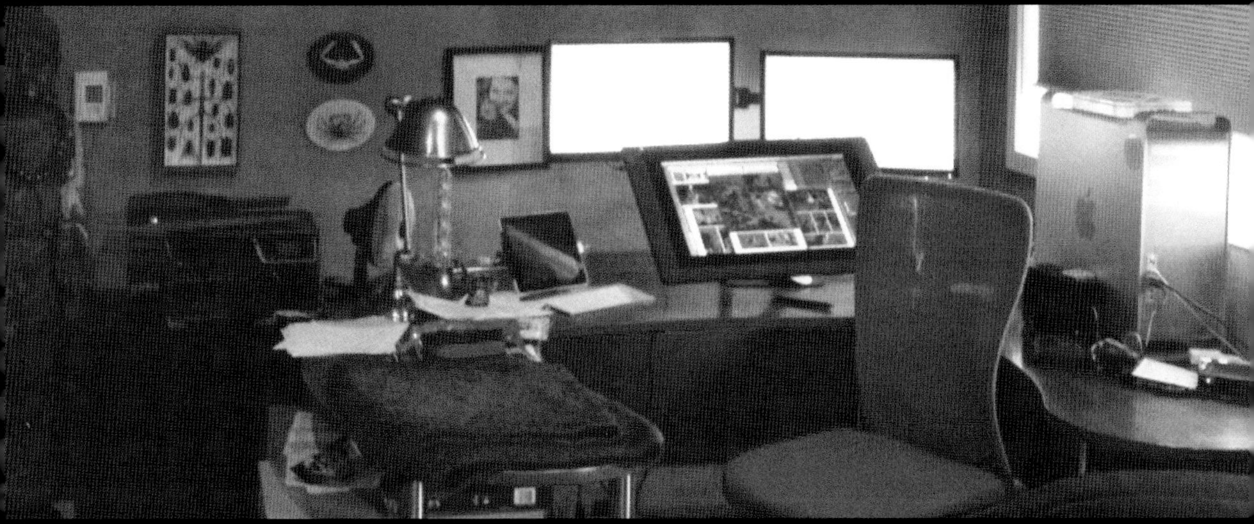

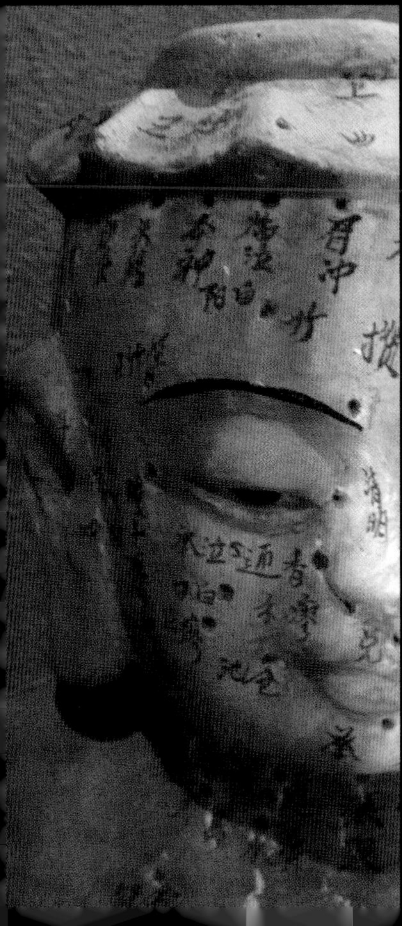

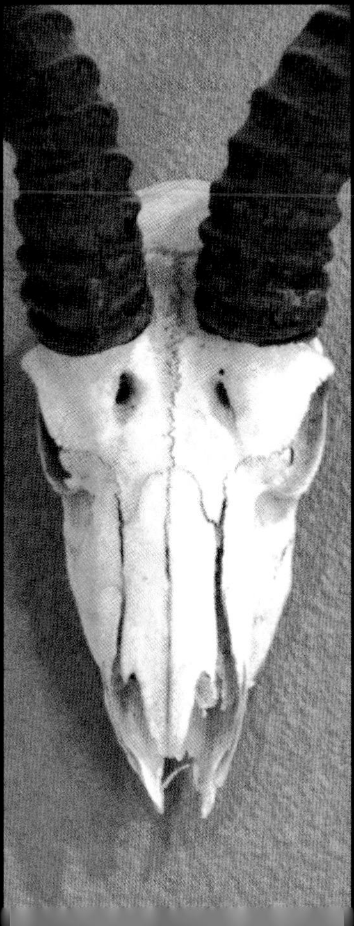

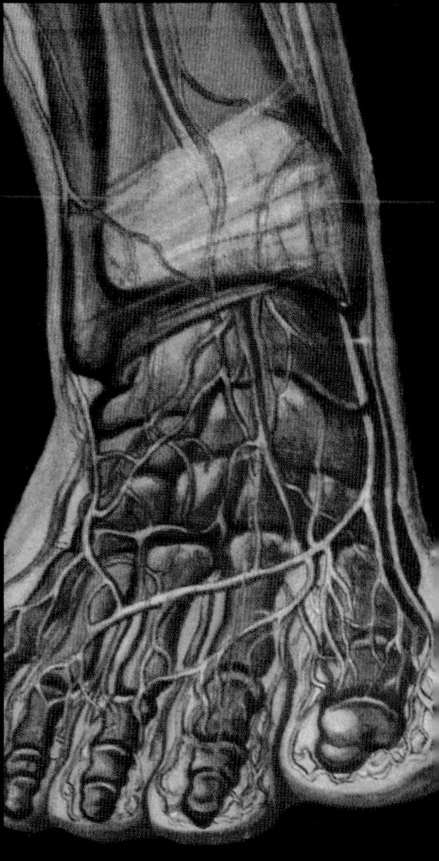

First I get the line art digitally. The file is sent to a flatter, in this case Dee, who breaks up all the basic shapes so I can easily drop in color and make selections for rendering.

Line Art

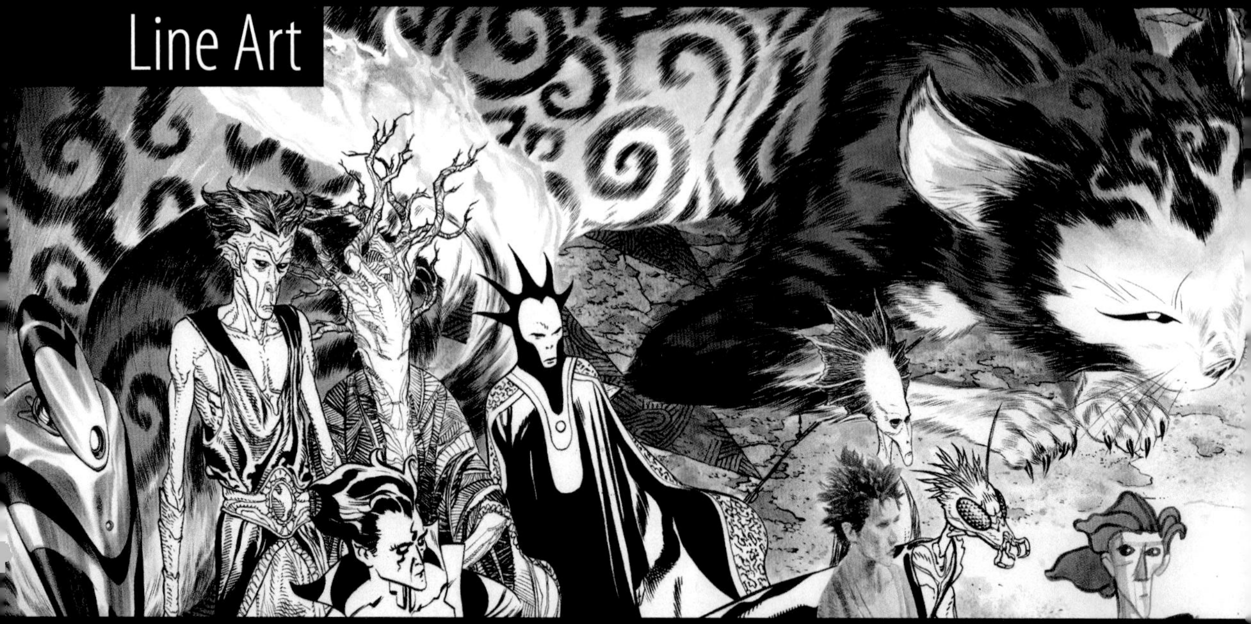

J.H. writes notes included in the file that give me an idea of the direction he is heading in. Here's an example of J.H.'s notes from THE SANDMAN: OVERTURE #1:

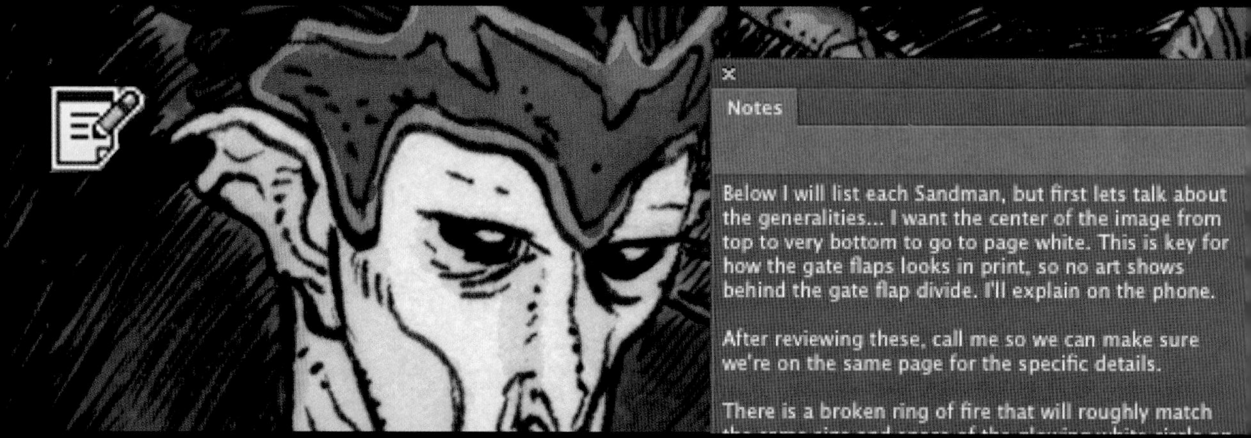
Notes
Below I will list each Sandman, but first lets talk about the generalities... I want the center of the image from top to very bottom to go to page white. This is key for how the gate flaps looks in print, so no art shows behind the gate flap divide. I'll explain on the phone.
After reviewing these, call me so we can make sure we're on the same page for the specific details.
There is a broken ring of fire that will roughly match

All the work I do is digital on a Cintiq that allows me to color directly onto the monitor.

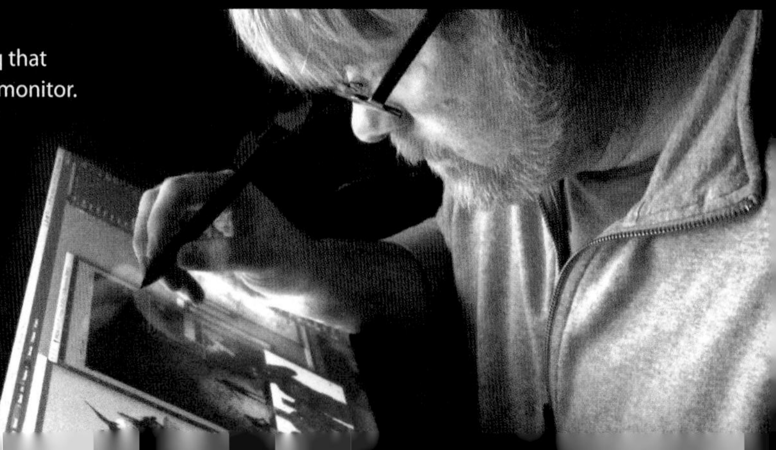

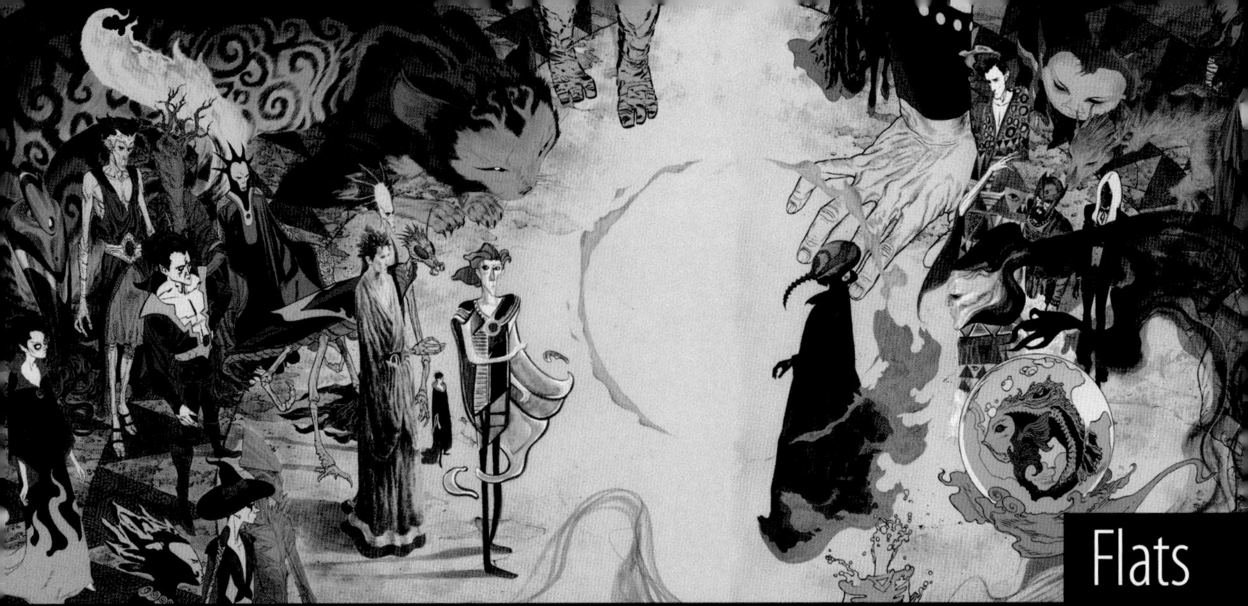

Flats

I add my base colors to the flats, and then jump into rendering.

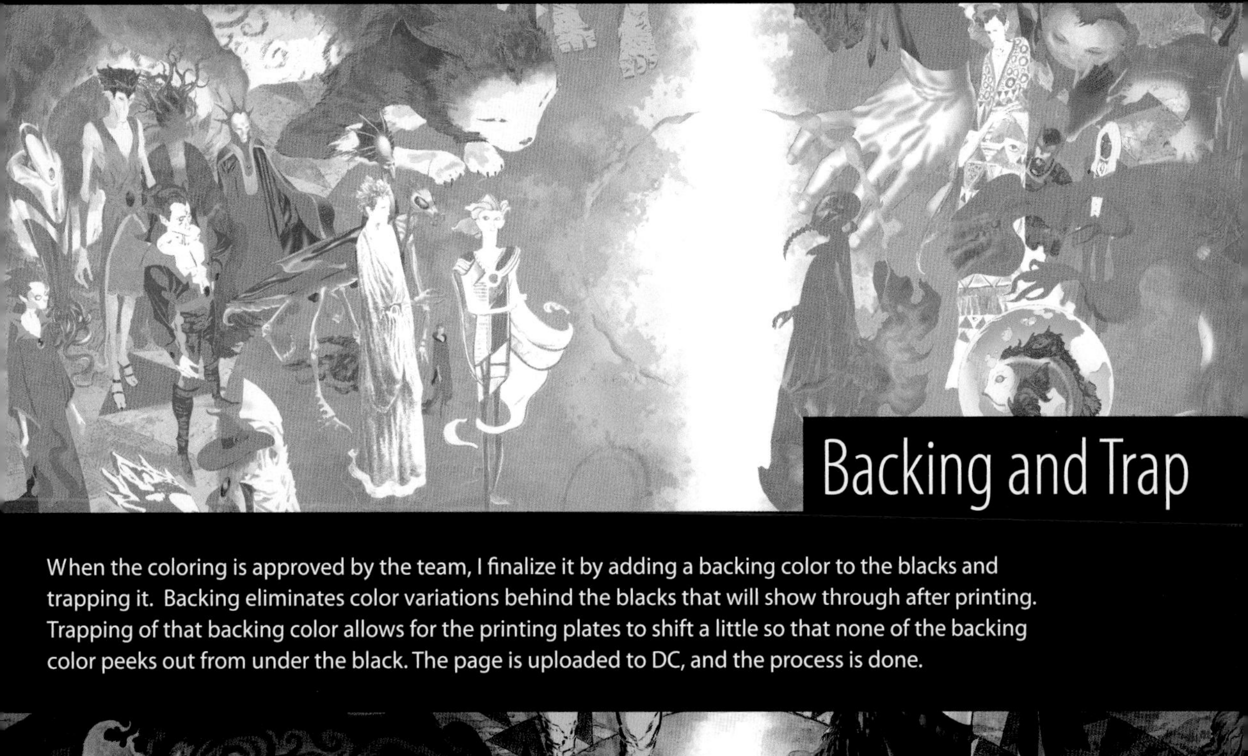

Backing and Trap

When the coloring is approved by the team, I finalize it by adding a backing color to the blacks and trapping it. Backing eliminates color variations behind the blacks that will show through after printing. Trapping of that backing color allows for the printing plates to shift a little so that none of the backing color peeks out from under the black. The page is uploaded to DC, and the process is done.

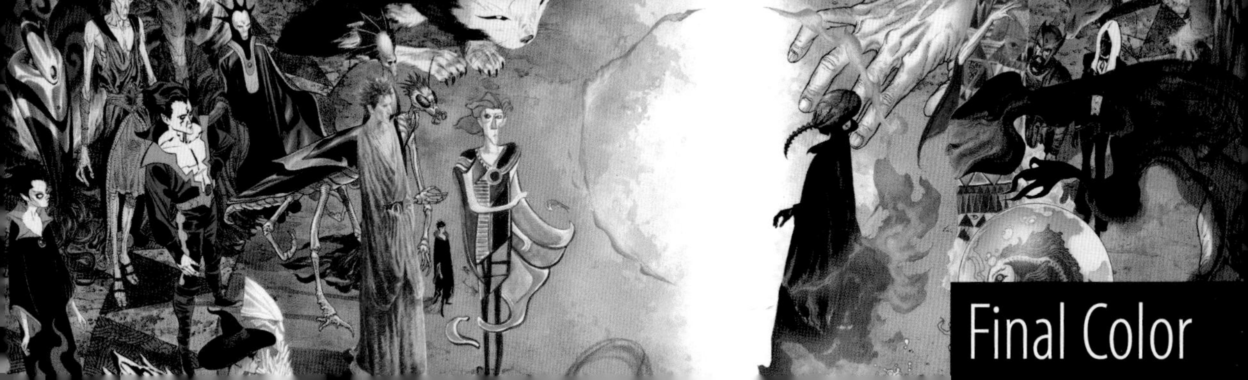

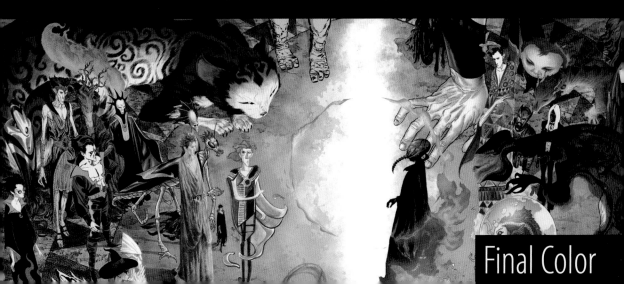

Final Color

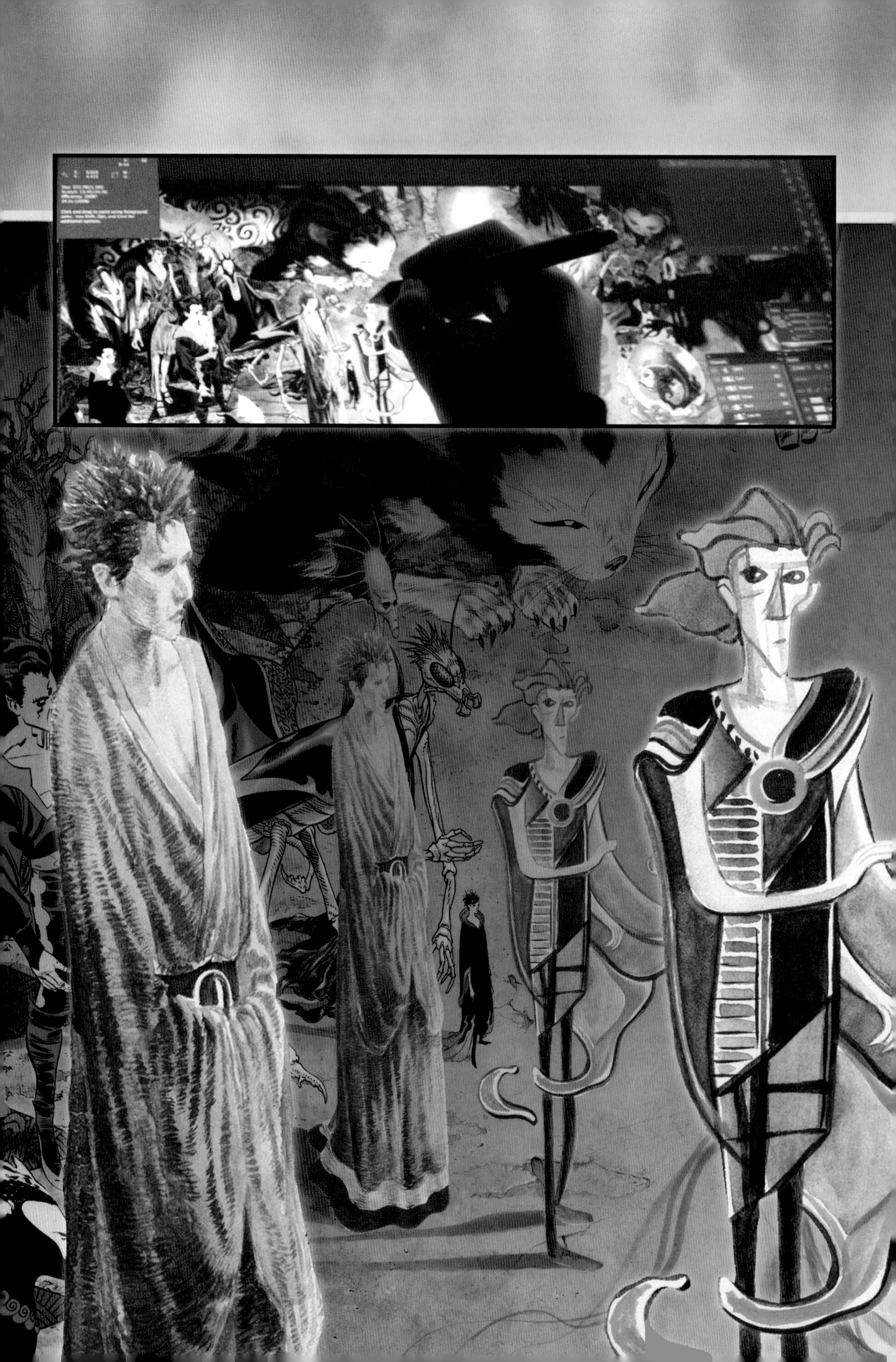

On this four-page spread, J.H. hand-painted a few of the characters who needed to be seamlessly added to the image. J.H. often has me approach color and rendering with a specific mood and storytelling idea in mind, and that varies quite a bit in one book. Hope you enjoyed a close-up look at my coloring process.

Dave Stewart

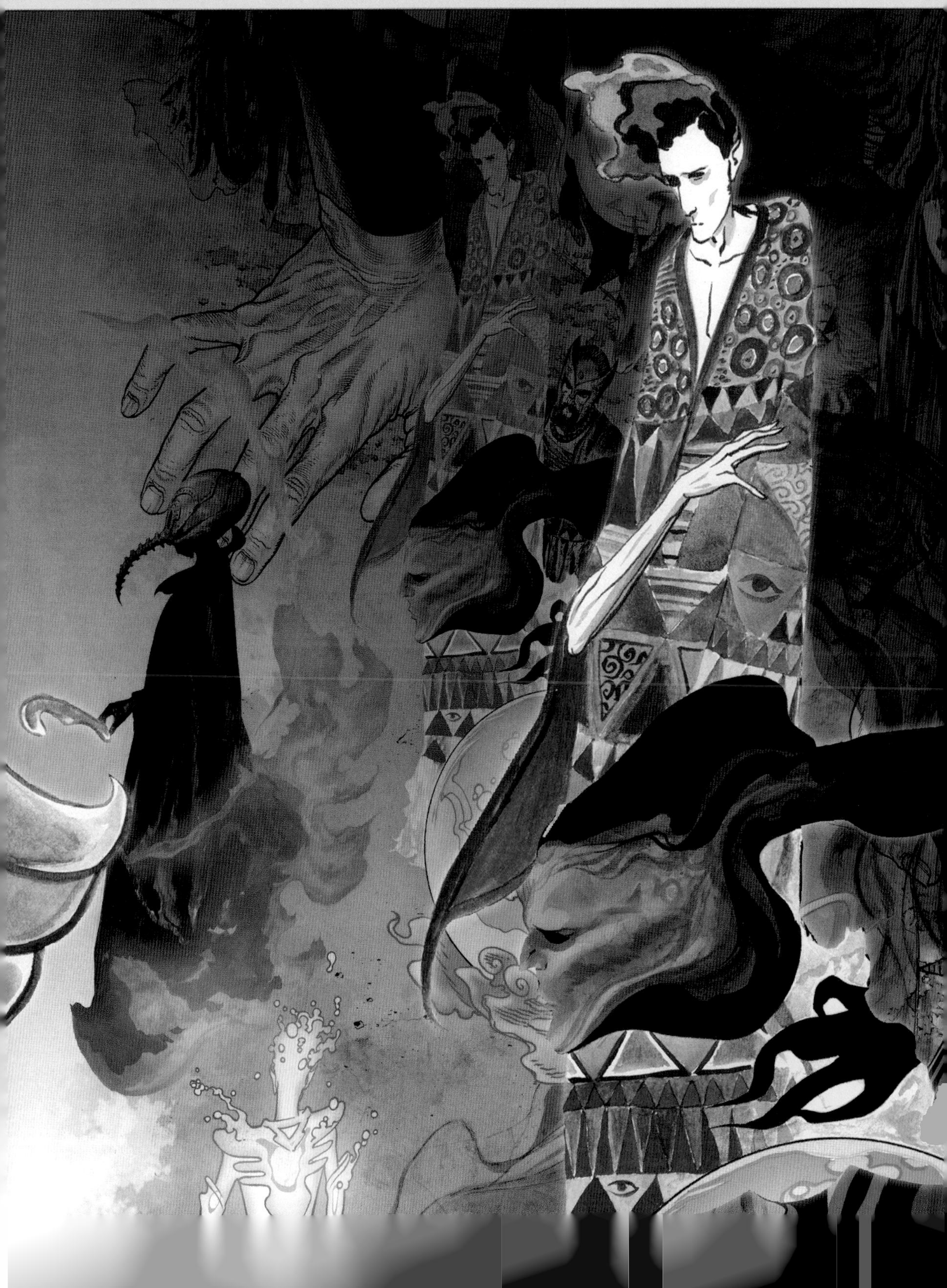

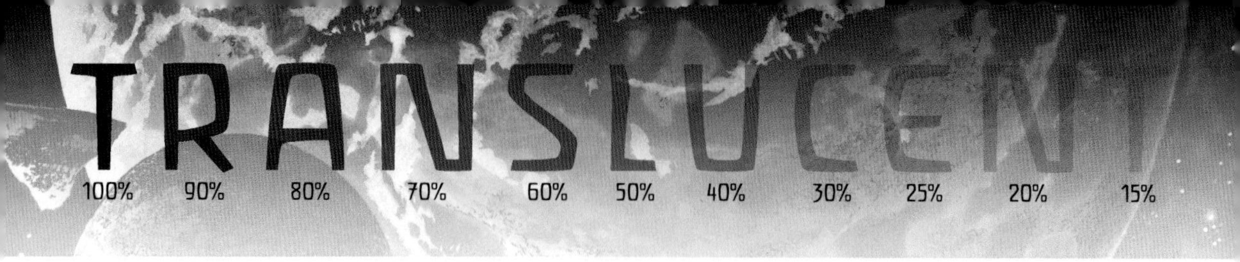
TRANSLUCENT
100% 90% 80% 70% 60% 50% 40% 30% 25% 20% 15%

Lettering THE SANDMAN has long been one of my favorite assignments, and one of the most challenging. I love Neil's writing, and the series concept has so much depth and scope, able to encompass a vast variety of story types, settings and characters. Toward the end of the first issue, when we finally see Morpheus speak, Neil and editor Karen Berger requested a special lettering effect for that: white letters on a black balloon shape.

It was 1987-88 and I was doing all my lettering by hand (in fact the entire original run of THE SANDMAN was lettered by hand, except for issue #74), so the only way to achieve this was through a production trick. I would letter Dream's balloons normally, with black ink lines on white paper. Once the art was finished and turned in to DC Comics' production department, negative prints of the lettering were made on their photostat camera, white letters on black. Then each of the Sandman balloons was carefully cut out and pasted over the original lettering to achieve the desired look. It worked, more or less well, depending on the exposure of the negative and the accuracy of the cutting and pasting. Beyond that trick, I gave Dream a nonstandard style: upper and lower case rather than the usual (for comics) all upper case letters, and an amorphous balloon shape, kind of like an amoeba.

Thus began what became a regular feature of the series. Around issue three, Neil asked if it was okay to request more nonstandard lettering styles for certain characters. I was up for the challenge, and they were soon coming thick and fast. Neil developed an extensive pantheon of gods, demons, fairies, animals, and of course the brothers and sisters of Morpheus, The Endless, many with unique lettering styles. This is something that can easily be overdone, and I don't advise using special styles unless there's a valid reason for it in the story. Neil's reach was wide, and he kept finding plenty of valid reasons!

I mean, if your character is an Egyptian cat goddess, surely she would speak in a unique way, right? In the run of the series, I believe I came up with over 50 different character and caption styles.

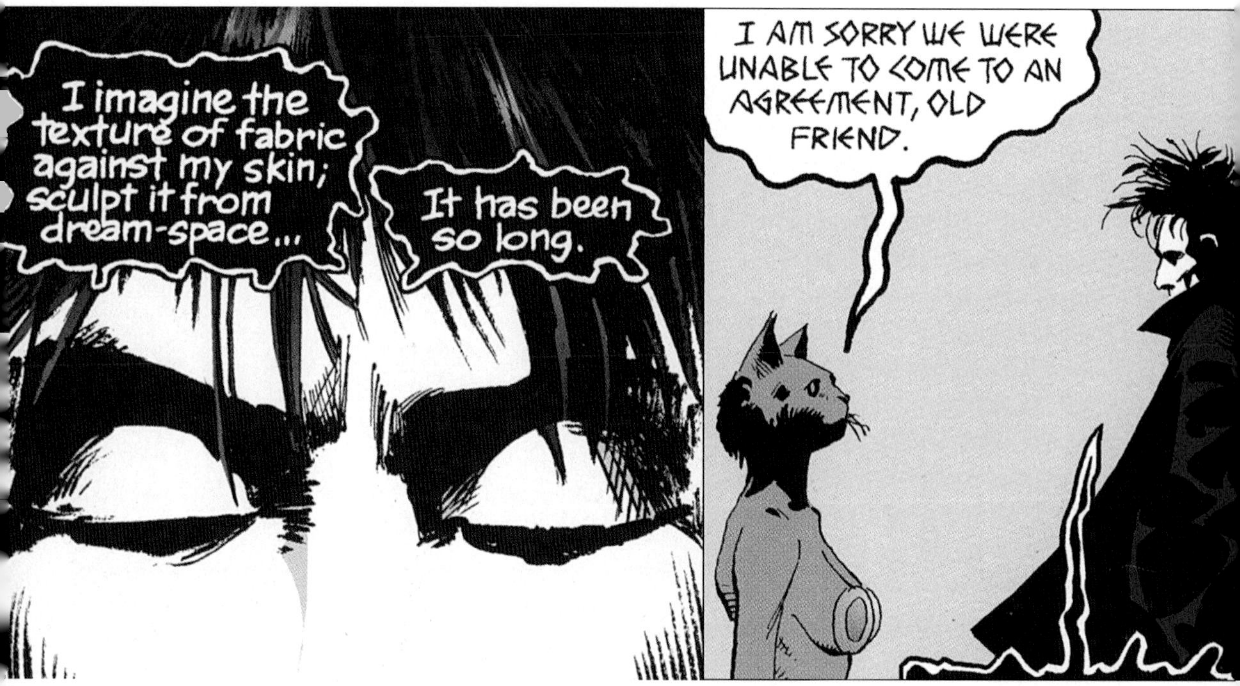
I imagine the texture of fabric against my skin; sculpt it from dream-space...
It has been so long.
I AM SORRY WE WERE UNABLE TO COME TO AN AGREEMENT, OLD FRIEND.

Years passed, and Neil wrote a new collection of Sandman stories that became THE SANDMAN: ENDLESS NIGHTS hardcover, published in 2003. By that time I was doing nearly all my comics lettering on my Apple computer, using Adobe Illustrator and Photoshop, and creating fonts from my hand-lettering with programs like Fontographer. The comics industry had changed, and digital lettering was now the requested style at DC Comics. While some of the ENDLESS NIGHTS stories were hand-lettered ("Death and Venice" with art by P. Craig Russell and "Endless Nights" with art by Frank Quitely), most were done on the computer. I was able to get pretty close to my hand-lettered styles with one exception: Dream's sister Delirium.

LETTER PROCESS BY TODD KLEIN

Her lettering, which constantly changes size in rolling waves, was beyond my computer skills, and had to be lettered by hand, then scanned and incorporated into the computer files. One nice thing about digital: It gave me control over the lettering and balloon colors. I was now able to create Dream's reversed white-on-black style myself, and more consistently than in the past.

While there are some inherent limitations in digital lettering, there are also advantages and options unavailable to me previously, and I'm always ready to experiment with new techniques. One of those came on another series, PROMETHEA, specifically issue #7 published in 2000. That story had a sequence where the characters became much more realistic than usual,

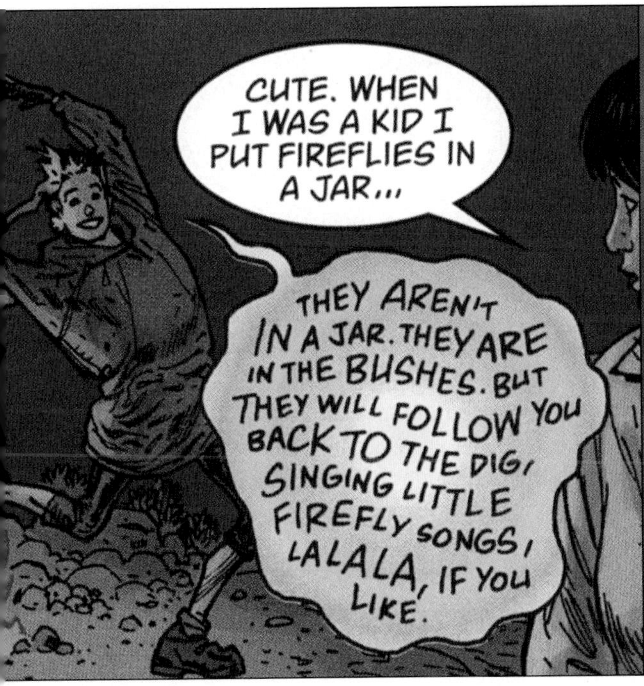

CUTE. WHEN I WAS A KID I PUT FIREFLIES IN A JAR...
THEY AREN'T IN A JAR. THEY ARE IN THE BUSHES. BUT THEY WILL FOLLOW YOU BACK TO THE DIG, SINGING LITTLE FIREFLY SONGS, LALALA, IF YOU LIKE.

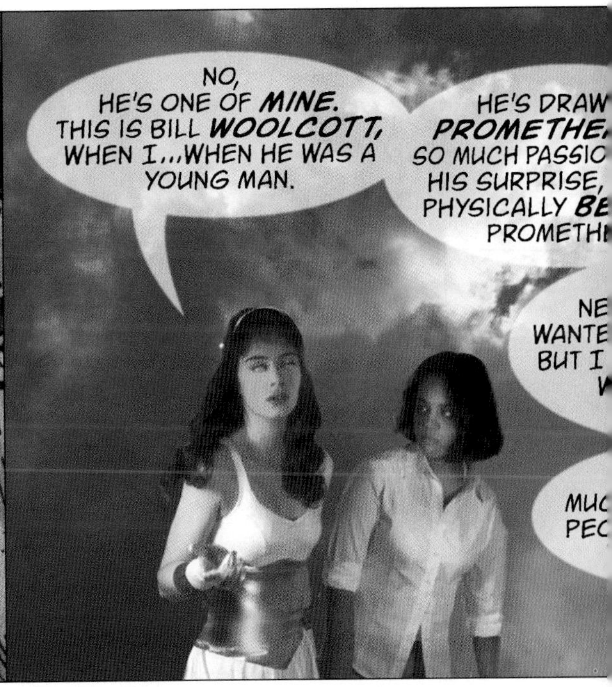

NO, HE'S ONE OF *MINE.* THIS IS BILL *WOOLCOTT,* WHEN I...WHEN HE WAS A YOUNG MAN.

an effect achieved by using actual photographs of people by artist José Villarrubia. To enhance that, I used a translucent effect on the balloons. You could partially see the art through them. Not enough to make the lettering hard to read, but sufficient so that the balloons seemed to become part of the photographs rather than sitting on the surface.

Transparency effects had already been available for some years in Adobe Photoshop, but were not yet easily achieved in other programs, so what I did there was to letter in Illustrator, as usual, then move the lettering and balloon shapes directly onto the art files in Photoshop, adding about 70% transparency on the latter. Everyone was happy with the way it turned out, including regular series artist J.H. Williams III.

When the concept for the Special Editions of THE SANDMAN: OVERTURE came forth from editor Shelly Bond, each one to be printed the month after the regular edition and intended to show off J.H. Williams' superb artwork, J.H. remembered the effect from PROMETHEA and suggested it be used on the lettering here. Shelly called me.

"J.H. says you can make the lettering transparent," she said.

"Well, if it was ***really*** transparent, you couldn't see it at all," I pointed out. "The correct term would be translucent."

Shelly laughed and agreed, and not long after that I was amused to see a *Wall Street Journal* blog article about the series describing the lettering effect to be used as "Todd Klein's translucent word balloons." The word had stuck.

Okay, the plan was set, but what would it actually look like?

While the art for issue #1 of THE SANDMAN: OVERTURE was still being drawn, I created some samples of the translucent lettering to show to J.H.,

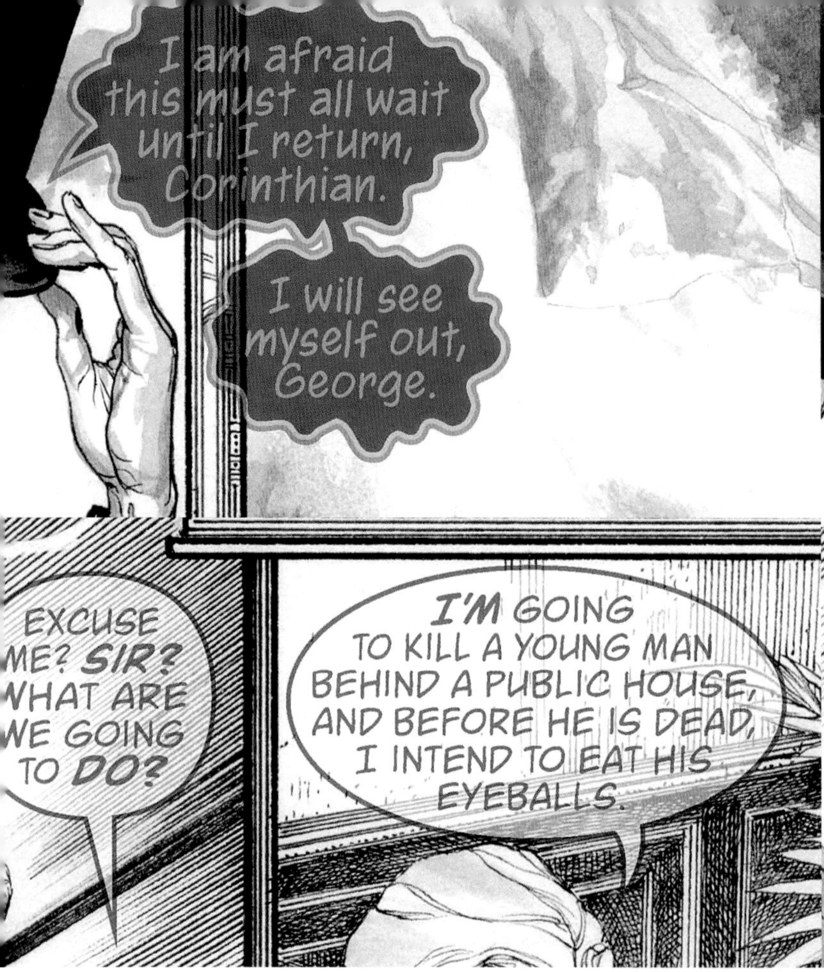
I am afraid this must all wait until I return, Corinthian.
I will see myself out, George.
EXCUSE ME? SIR? VHAT ARE VE GOING TO DO?
I'M GOING TO KILL A YOUNG MAN BEHIND A PUBLIC HOUSE, AND BEFORE HE IS DEAD, I INTEND TO EAT HIS EYEBALLS.

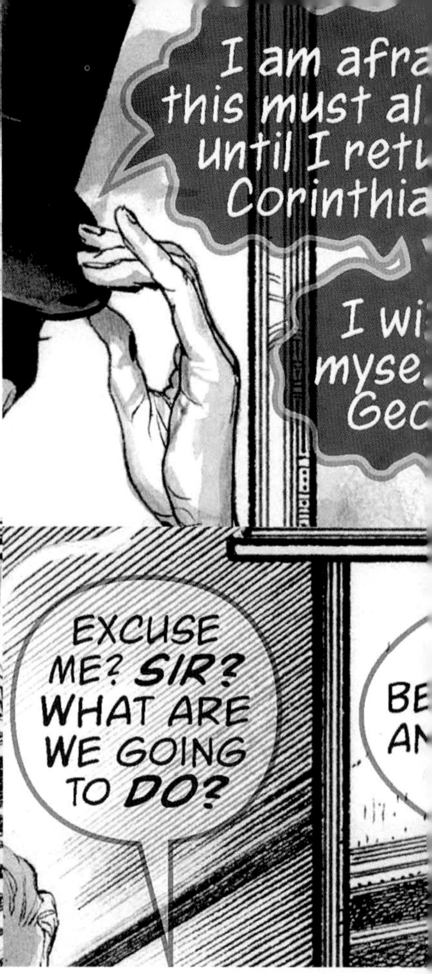
I am afra this must al until I retu Corinthia
EXCUSE ME? SIR? WHAT ARE WE GOING TO DO?

Shelly and Neil. The idea was to allow as much of the art to show through as possible while permitting the words to remain readable, but I felt they didn't have to be ***easily*** readable. It was unlikely that many readers would be coming to this version of the story before the regular edition. One thing that was easier now than in 2000: Adobe Illustrator has transparency effects built in. I could experiment easily without a lot of moving things from one program to another.

In this first example above I tried a transparency level of 60% on the standard balloons and its black lettering, about as much translucency as I thought I could use. Even then, the dark grays of the letters and the line work behind it were fairly close. You would think that having just 40% of the line art showing would be plenty of distance from the 60% letters, but it's more complex than that. The letters use only black, but the line art is a rich black that includes a good deal of blue, magenta and yellow tones in addition to the solid black, so when it's reduced by the transparency algorithm, it's still darker than merely black lines would be. For the Morpheus balloon, I had been using a rich black fill already, so that color was denser and I was able to use a 40% transparency effect as shown here. The art was showing through, but was it a look that would carry the idea across 28 pages of story? I polled J.H. and Shelly and they had the same doubts I did.

We were not really happy with the first test, and J.H. suggested we keep the letters 100% black (or in the case of Morpheus, 100% white) and just use transparency on the balloons and captions. That's what you see in this second example, and we all felt it worked much better. With that change, I was able to go further with the translucency and still have the text be readable. Everyone liked this. In fact, it's what I did on PROMETHEA, though I hadn't looked at that until gathering reference for this article. Here the regular balloon transparency is about 50% and the Morpheus balloons are at about 35%. It's a little hard to read at the bottom of the last balloon, but the more visible line art is worth the tradeoff.

I could have stopped there, but I thought it was worth exploring the possibility of going even further with the transparency effect on the balloons and captions. I did one more sample of this panel, which you can see on the next page.

Here the normal balloon is down to 45% and the Morpheus one at a mere 30%. Still worked, everyone thought. The road forward was clear, though I knew that I would have to test each individual balloon and caption to find the right transparency level, and make adjustments accordingly. This was particularly true for the brand-new unique character styles you'll find

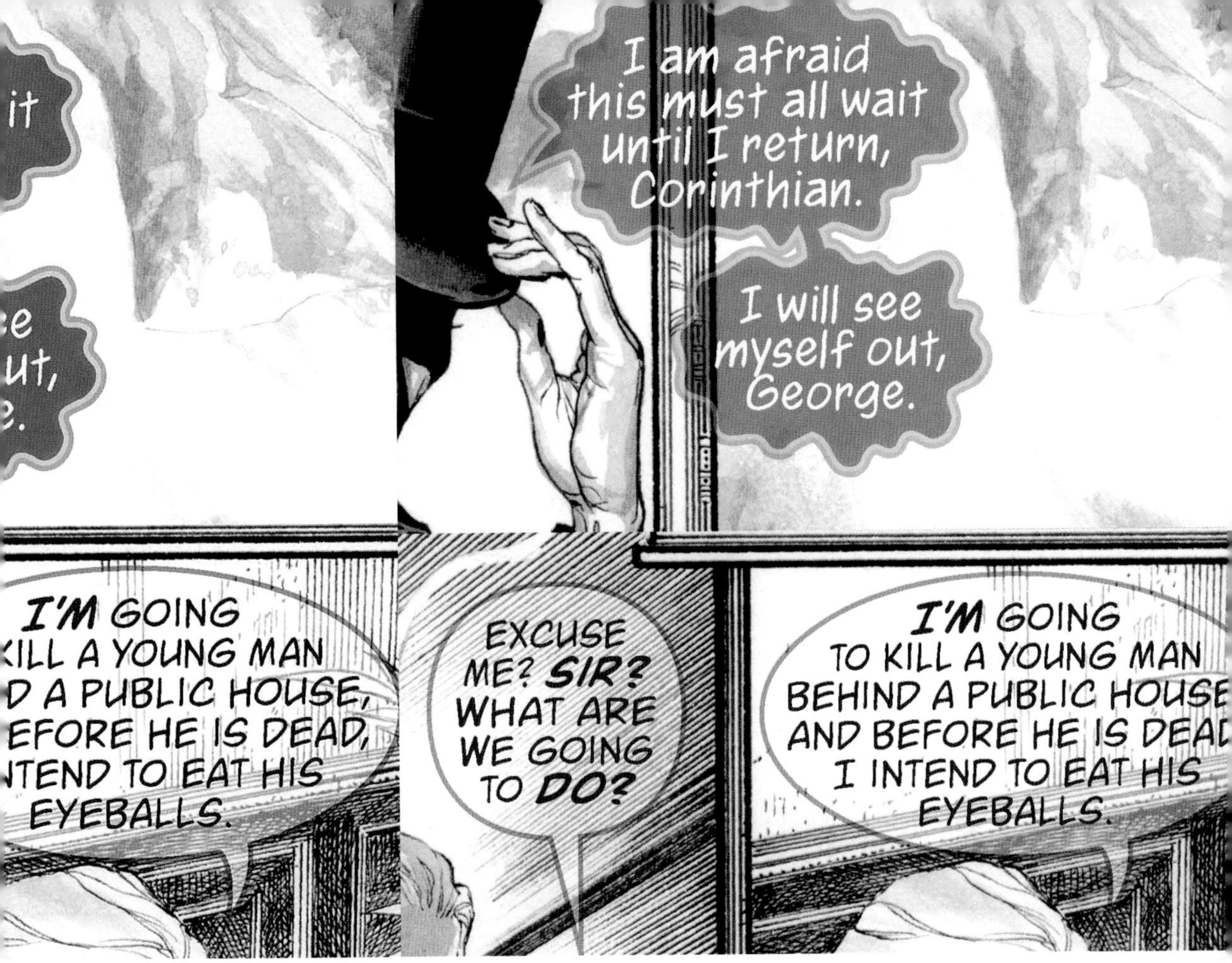

I am afraid this must all wait until I return, Corinthian.
I will see myself out, George.
I'M GOING KILL A YOUNG MAN D A PUBLIC HOUSE, EFORE HE IS DEAD, NTEND TO EAT HIS EYEBALLS.
EXCUSE ME? SIR? WHAT ARE WE GOING TO DO?
I'M GOING TO KILL A YOUNG MAN BEHIND A PUBLIC HOUSE AND BEFORE HE IS DEAD I INTEND TO EAT HIS EYEBALLS.

inside the double gatefold! I did that fine-tuning, and the result is on the following pages. Only the balloons and captions are translucent, with one exception. See if you can find the place where parts of the lettering are translucent, too.

Once I had transparency levels set on everything, I sent out new proofs of the entire story. Everyone felt it worked. J.H. wrote in an e-mail, "Looks really cool. It's quite interesting actually."

When I had final approval, I still had to create art files that included the translucent lettering on the artwork. I felt it would be safest to do it that way rather than combining the Illustrator lettering files with the Photoshop art files in the usual way: compositing them in layers in Adobe InDesign. By giving the printer final art files with the lettering embedded, there was less chance of anything going wrong once it left my hands. Therefore, I know that what you'll see here is exactly the way I intended it to look, for better or worse.

Okay, enough of my blathering — go look at the story. Thanks to translucency, I hope you enjoy being able to see a little more of J.H. Williams' incredible art!

Todd Klein

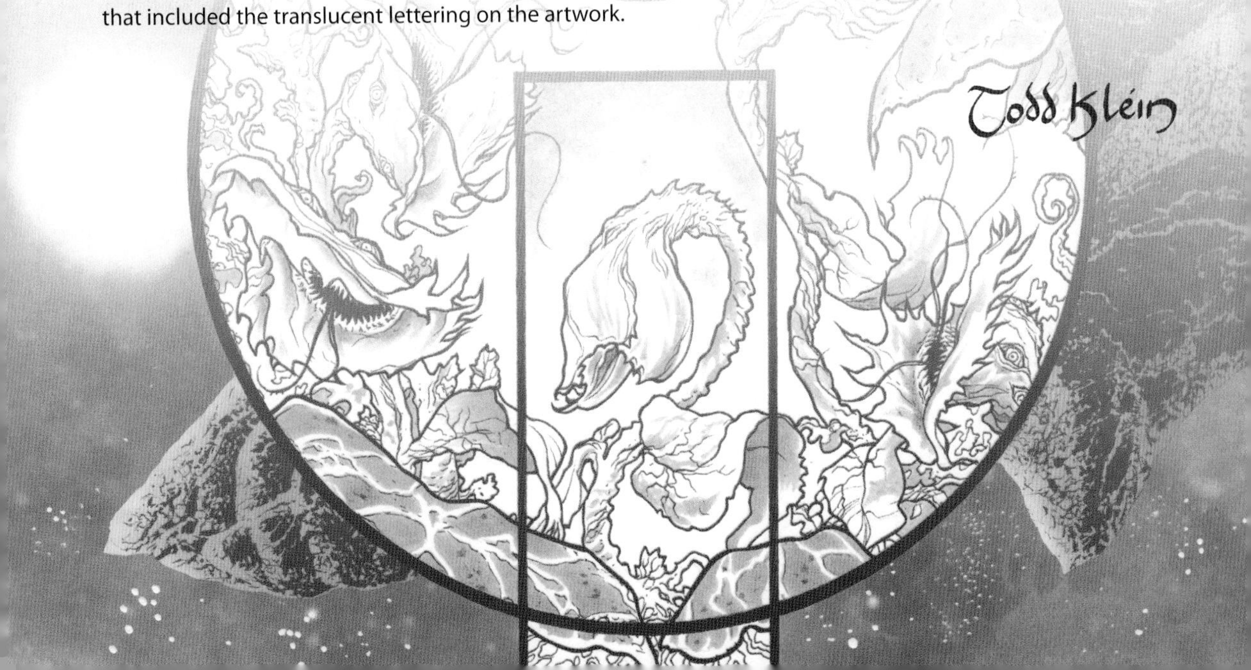

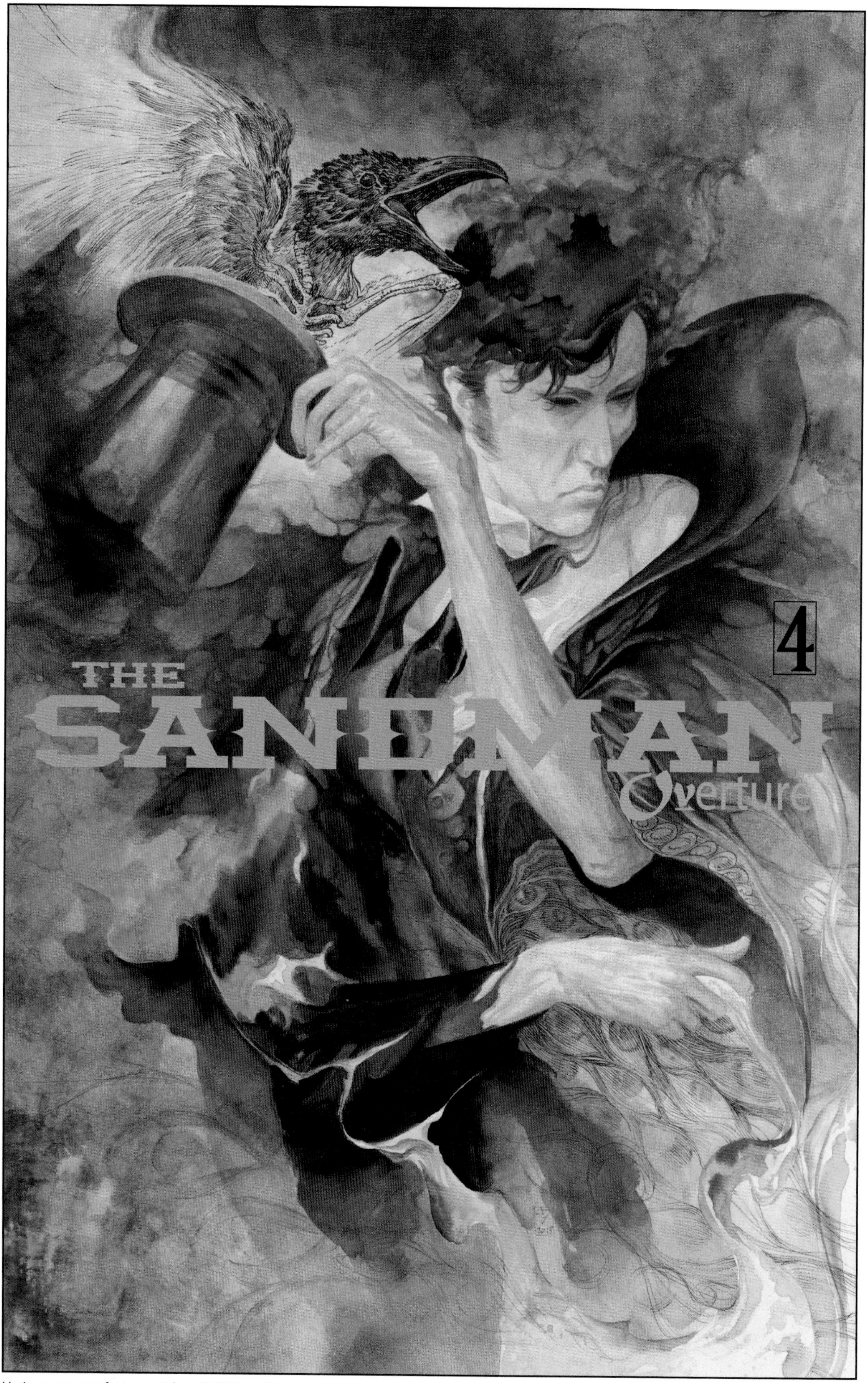
4
THE
SANDMAN
Overture

Variant cover art for issue #4 by J.H. Williams III

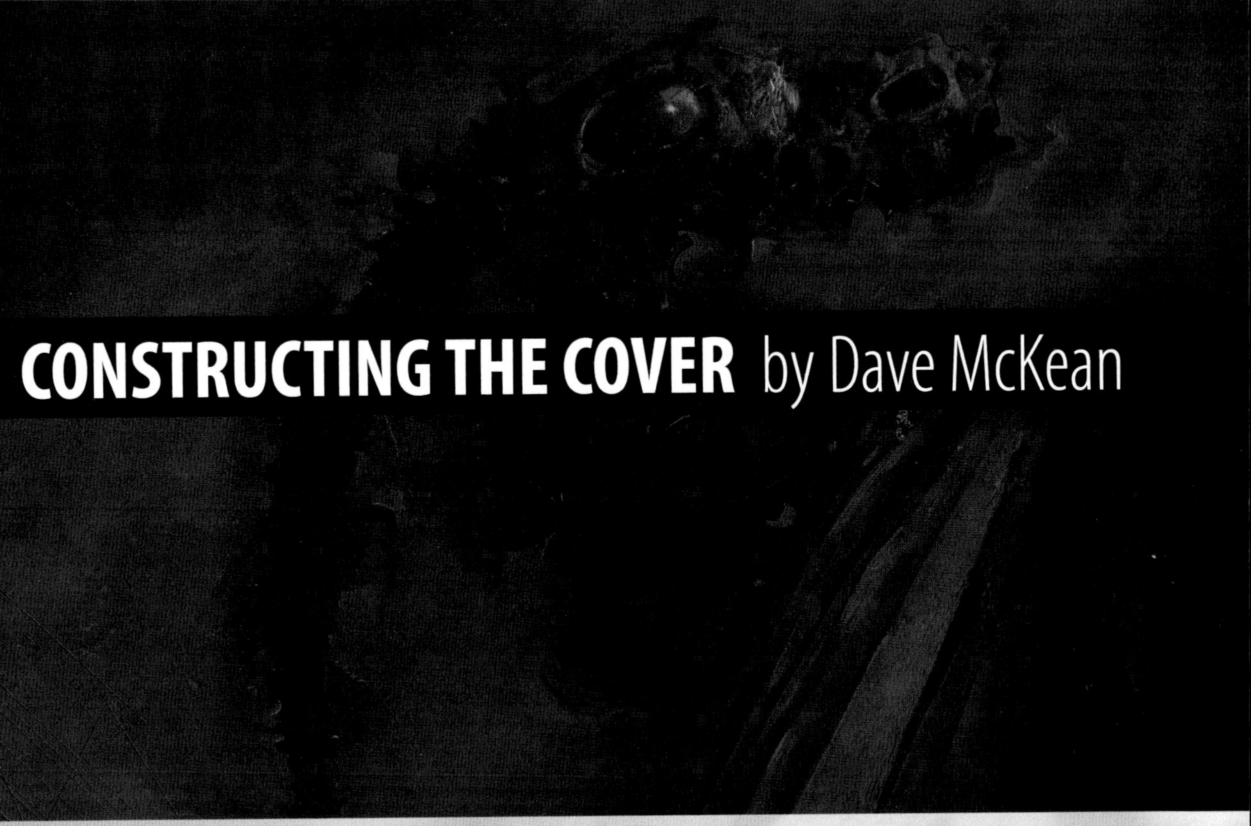

CONSTRUCTING THE COVER by Dave McKean

I DON'T LIKE LOOKING BACK AT THE WORK I DID LAST YEAR, LET ALONE A SERIES THAT STARTED 25 YEARS AGO.

So revisiting the past for these SANDMAN: OVERTURE covers has been a rather daunting experience. I did the original covers over a six-year period, when they functioned very much like a monthly diary entry. When I look at them now, I remember where I did them, the music I was listening to, the influences I was absorbing, the various conversations with Neil around each storyline, and the other work I was doing at the time. They were done without expectations, fear or much of a master plan. I responded to Neil's story outlines and did whatever I fancied doing at that moment. I had no editorial input, art direction or guidance. After the first year I didn't even do roughs, and the only imposition was that of a Vertigo design sidebar that appeared about halfway through the run.

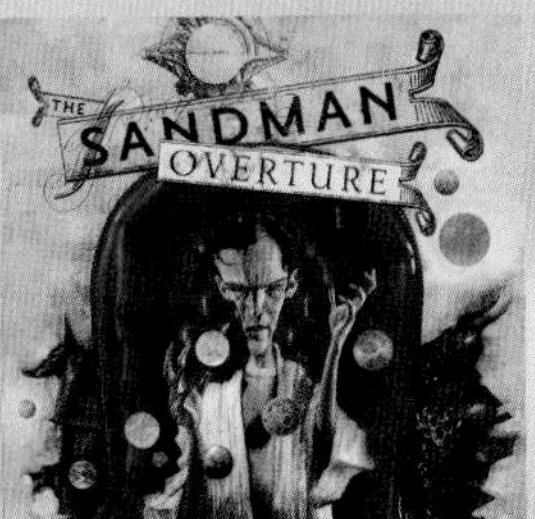
THE SANDMAN OVERTURE
NEIL GAIMAN
J.H. WILLIAMS III

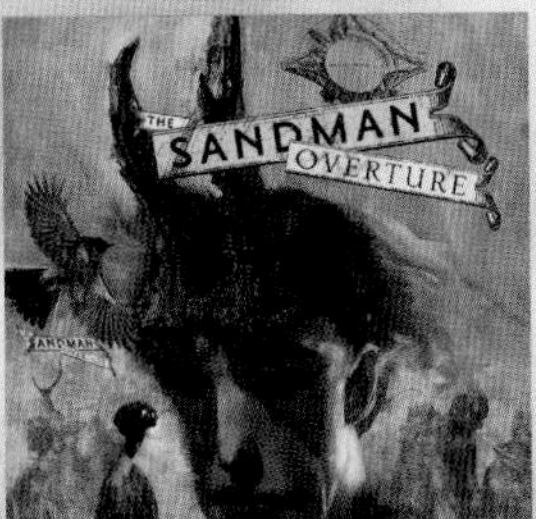
THE SANDMAN OVERTURE
NEIL GAIMAN
J.H. WILLIAMS III

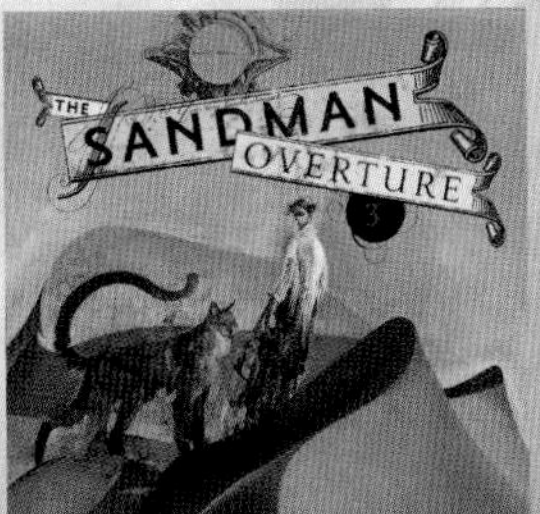
THE SANDMAN OVERTURE
NEIL GAIMAN
J.H. WILLIAMS III

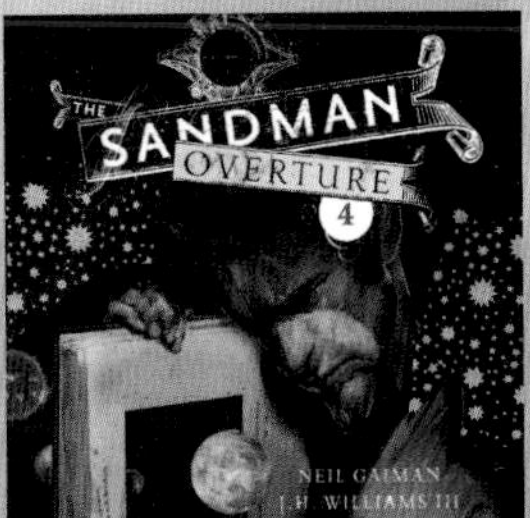
THE SANDMAN OVERTURE
4
NEIL GAIMAN
J.H. WILLIAMS III

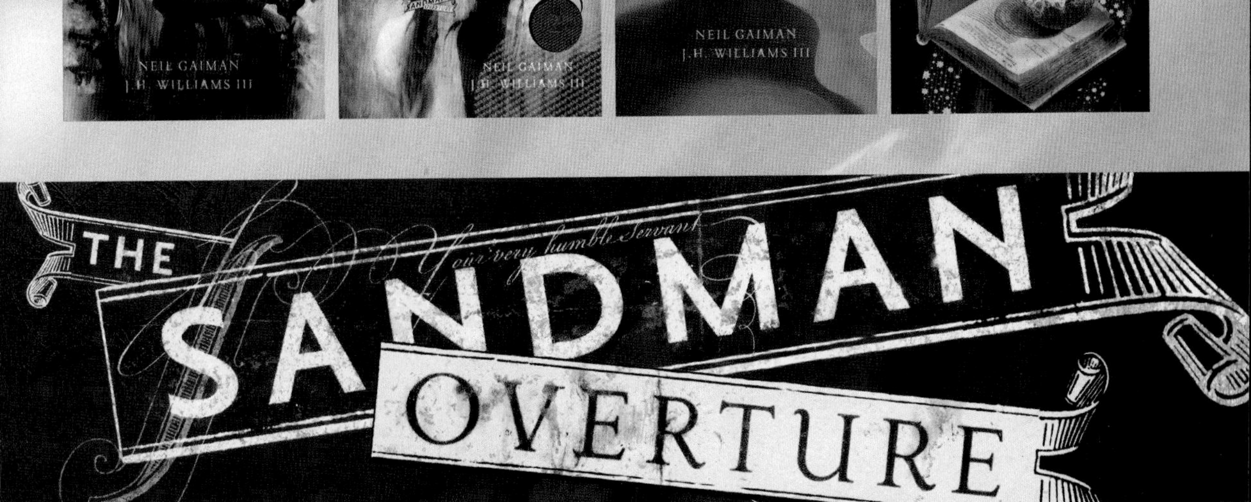
THE
Your very humble Servant
SANDMAN
OVERTURE

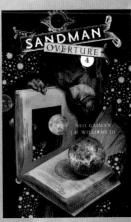

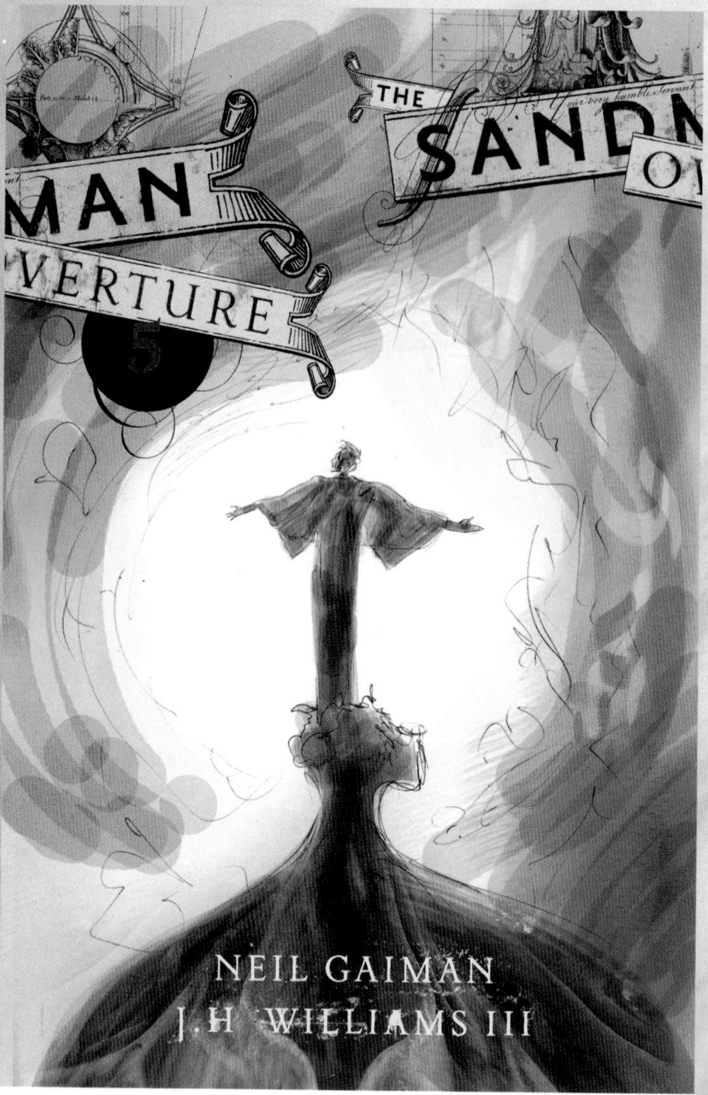
THE
SAND
MAN
VERTURE
5
NEIL GAIMAN
J.H WILLIAMS III

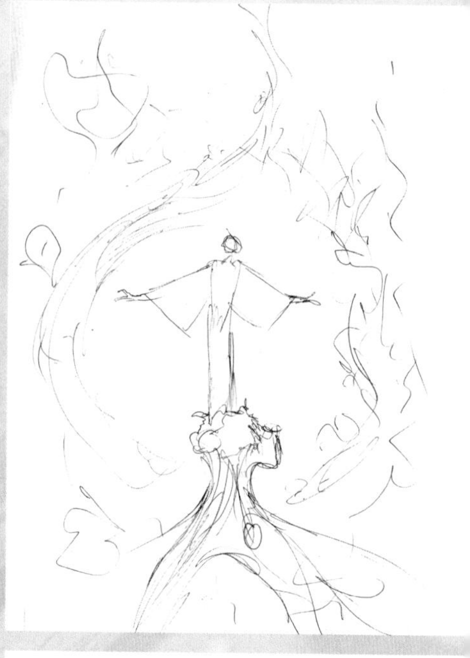

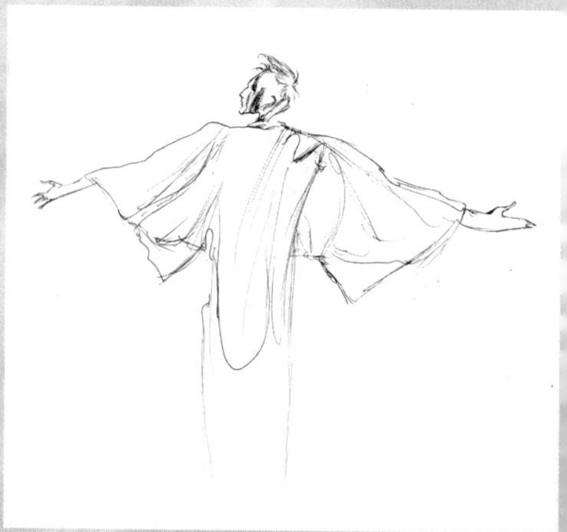

Twenty-five years later, THE SANDMAN is something of a classic moment in mainstream comic history, with a rather reverential reputation. Coming back to the character, and to DC Comics after so much time and with such expectation, I felt stage fright for the first time in years. It also happened to be Apple's 30th anniversary last year, and they used my work on THE SANDMAN to represent the year 1995: the year after I bought my first Mac Quadra — the year I started to use it to reinvigorate my interest in doing the monthly SANDMAN gig, which had taken a bit of a dive around the Worlds' End storyline. Nothing to do with the book; I was just getting more out of doing other things. Photoshop came to the rescue, and I really started to enjoy having this monthly diary in which to make note of my current digital experiments.

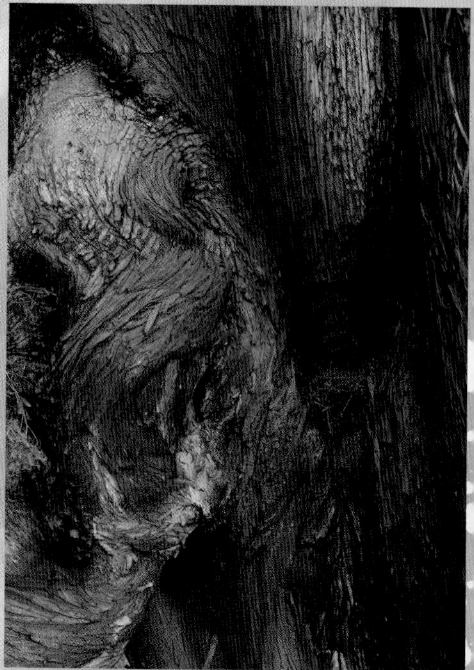

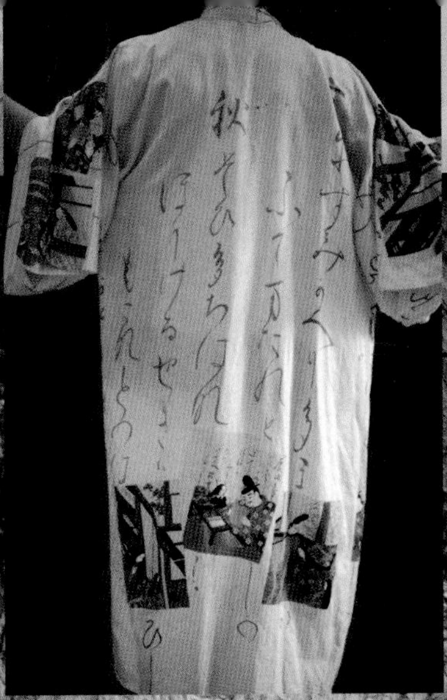

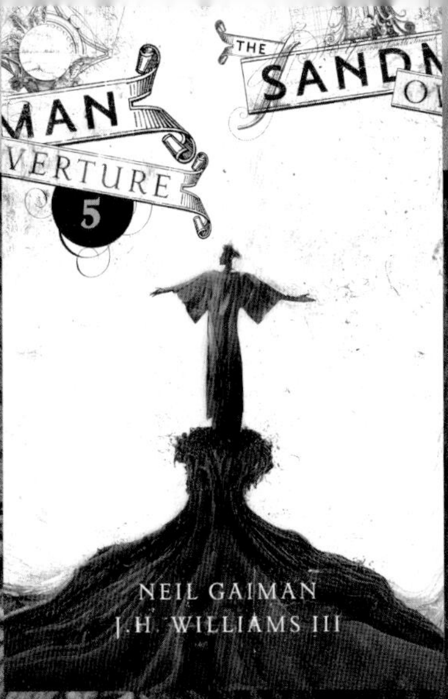
5
NEIL GAIMAN
J.H. WILLIAMS III

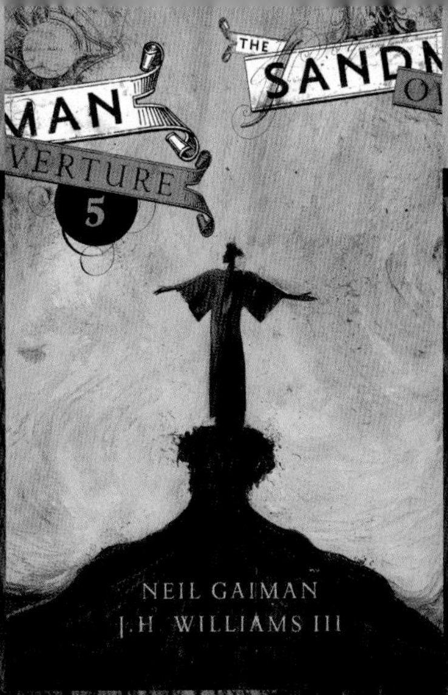
5
NEIL GAIMAN
J.H. WILLIAMS III

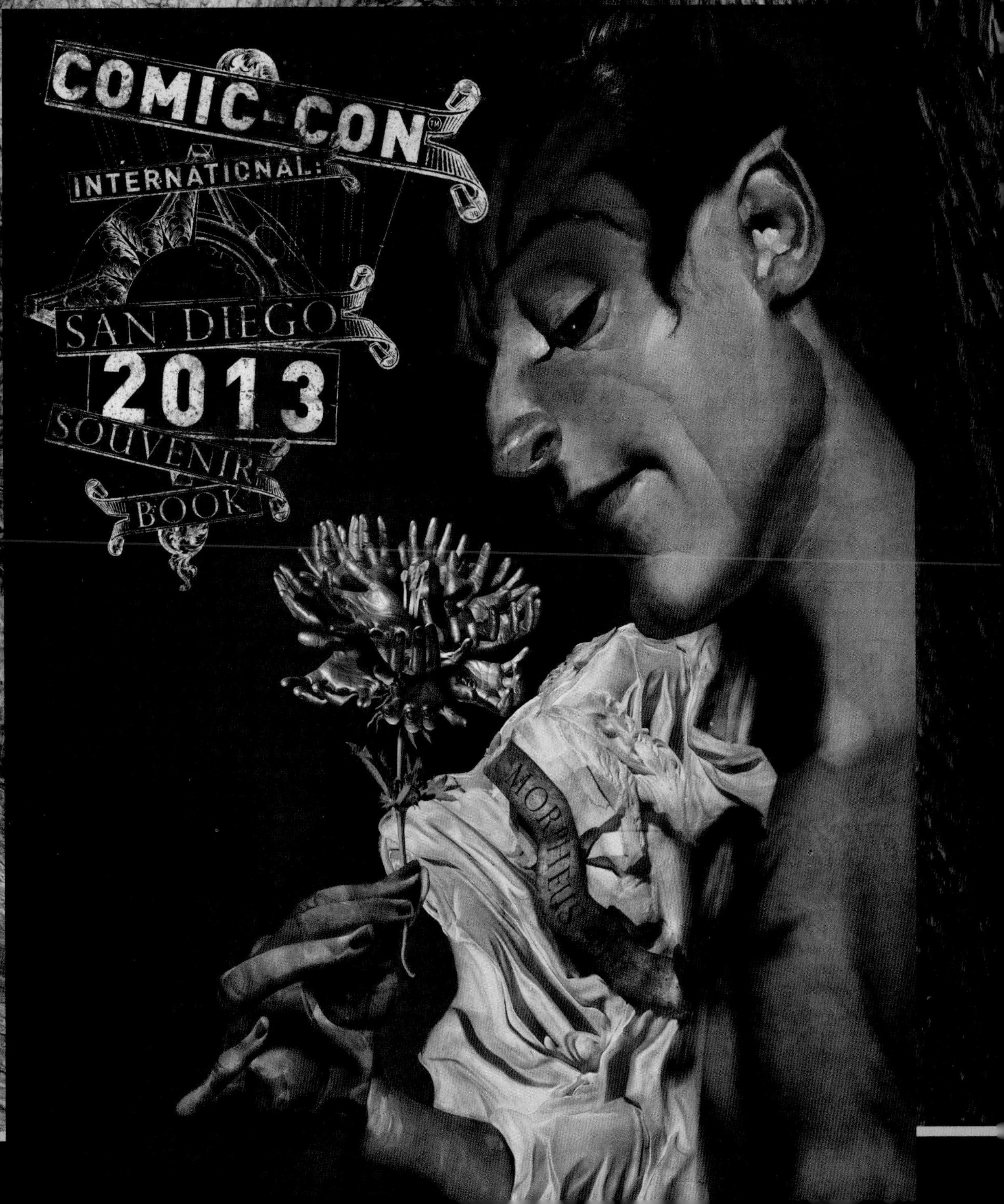
COMIC-CON
INTERNATIONAL:
SAN DIEGO
2013
SOUVENIR
BOOK
MORPHEUS

So, I thought the covers for THE SANDMAN: OVERTURE could be about my to-and-fro relationship with analog and digital media. I wanted to use Photoshop somewhere in the process, and I wanted the covers to end up as physical objects that could be exhibited.

I had lunch with Neil and managed to squeeze out of him just about enough information to think about each of the covers. I think Neil had a sense of the overall story, but very little of it was written down at that point.

So I started with pen-and-ink workings-out as usual. I composited very rough color sketches for Shelly Bond to approve. I then made Photoshop files that included key textures and occasional images. For #5, I used photographs I took of some extraordinary trees while visiting Sydney's Botanical Park in October 2013. The swirls of cracked bark seemed to provide an interesting starting place for the

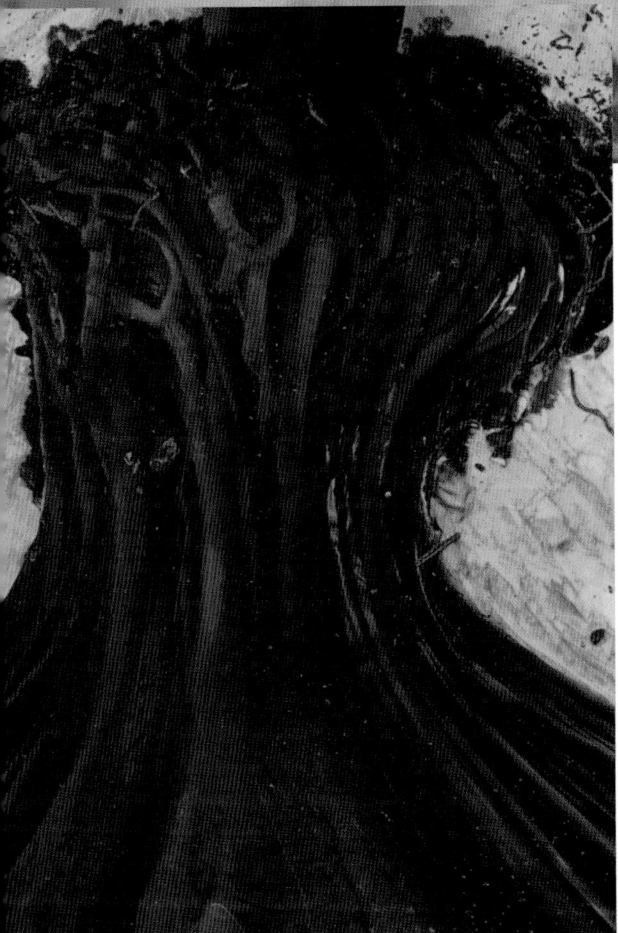

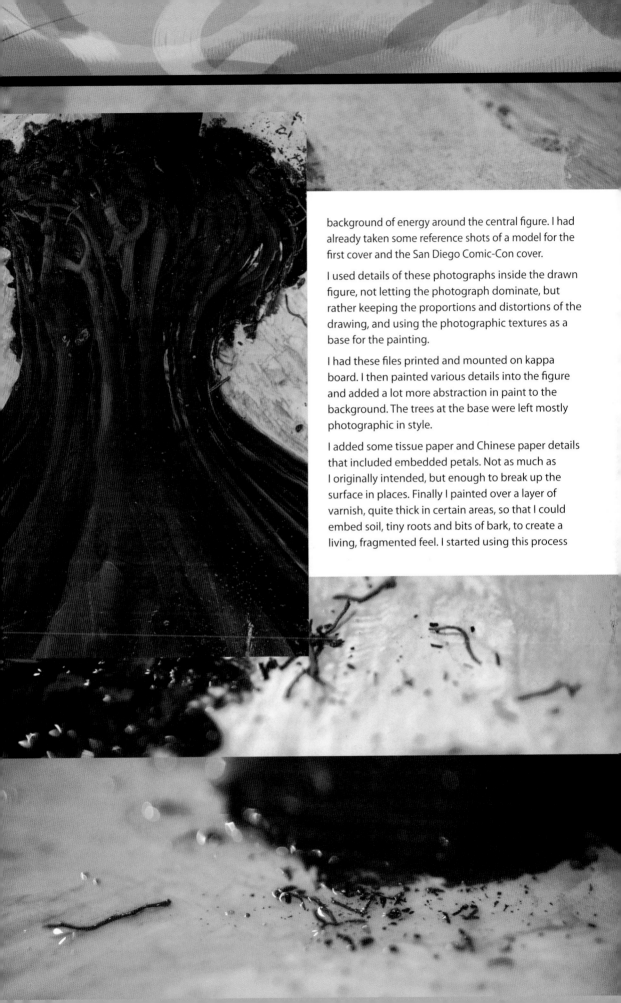

background of energy around the central figure. I had already taken some reference shots of a model for the first cover and the San Diego Comic-Con cover.

I used details of these photographs inside the drawn figure, not letting the photograph dominate, but rather keeping the proportions and distortions of the drawing, and using the photographic textures as a base for the painting.

I had these files printed and mounted on kappa board. I then painted various details into the figure and added a lot more abstraction in paint to the background. The trees at the base were left mostly photographic in style.

I added some tissue paper and Chinese paper details that included embedded petals. Not as much as I originally intended, but enough to break up the surface in places. Finally I painted over a layer of varnish, quite thick in certain areas, so that I could embed soil, tiny roots and bits of bark, to create a living, fragmented feel. I started using this process

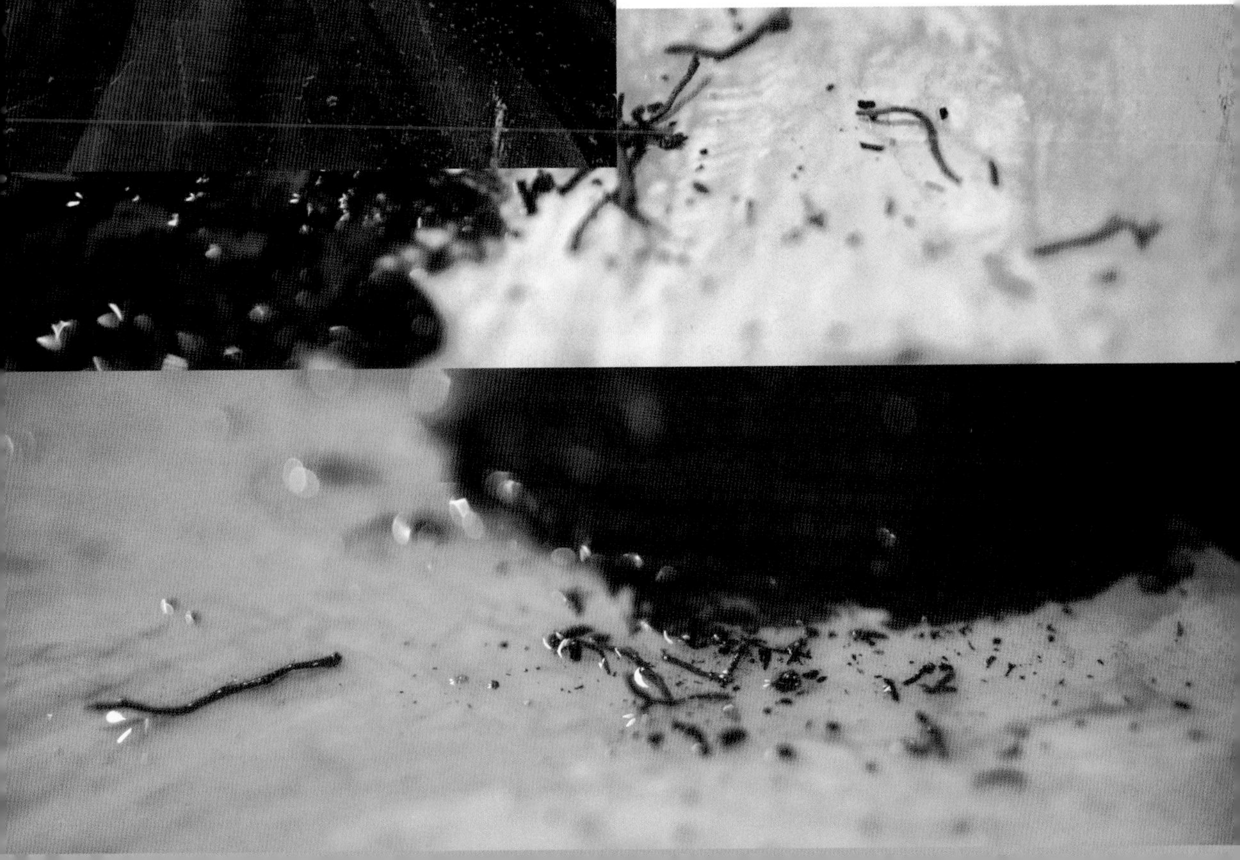

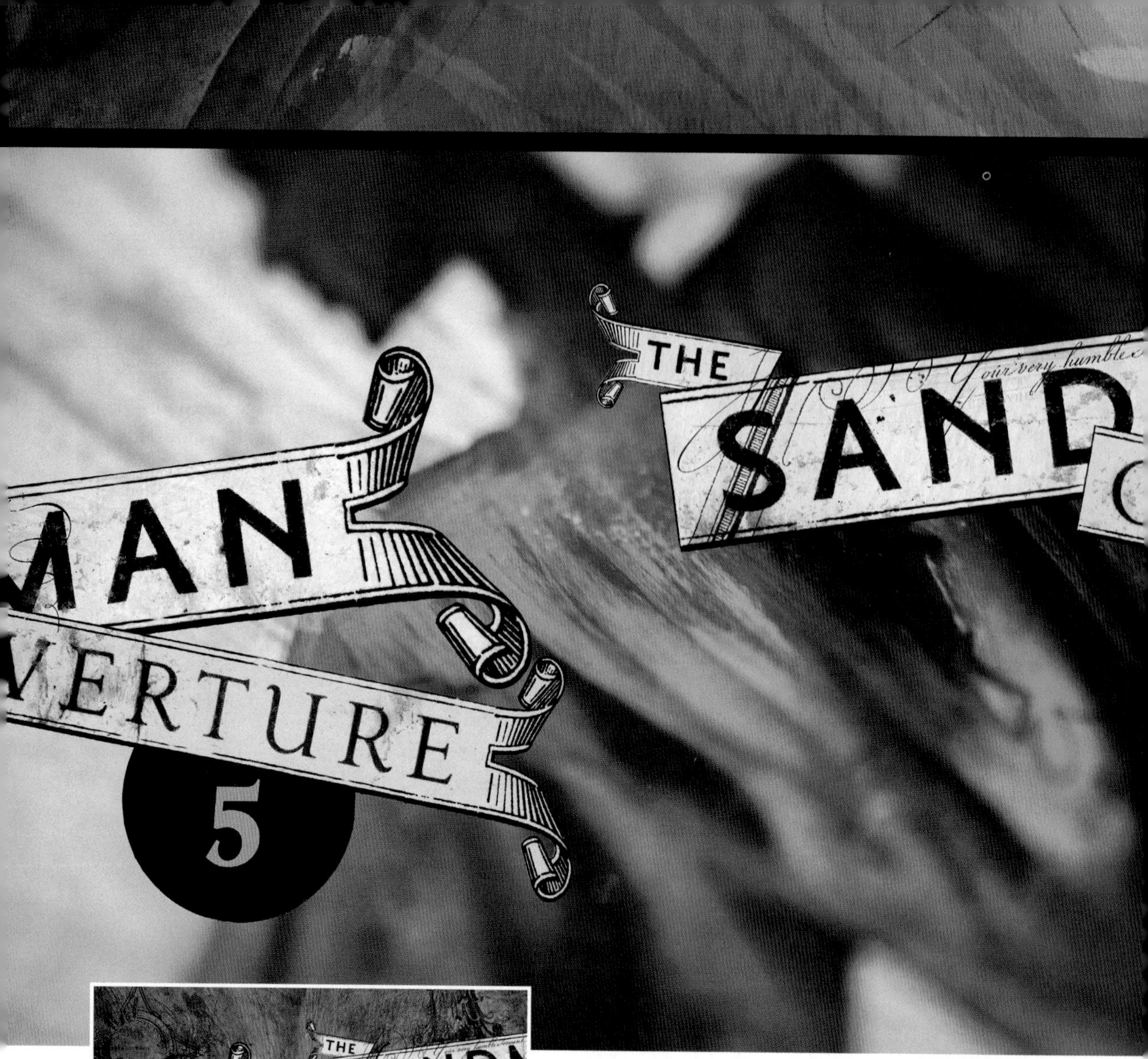
THE
SAND
MAN
VERTURE
5

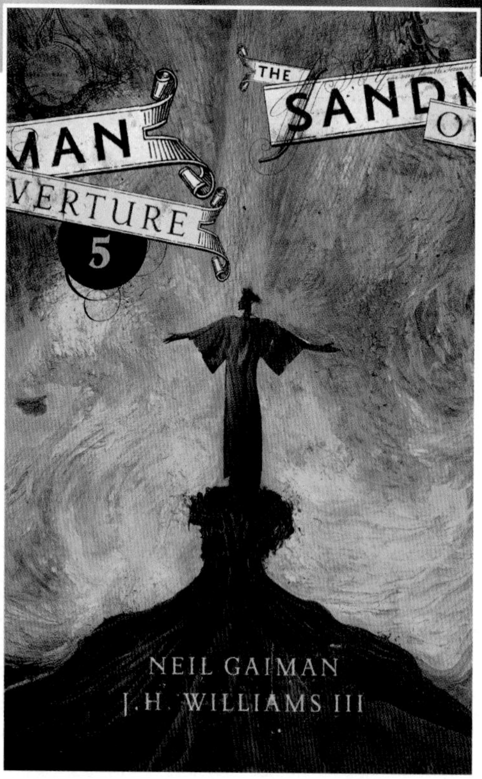
THE
SAND
MAN
VERTURE
5
NEIL GAIMAN
J.H. WILLIAMS III

in order to mimic the easy addition of dust, scratches and surface noise that you can achieve in Photoshop for the paintings I wanted to exhibit in gallery shows.

I decided to keep the design elements of all the covers essentially the same, but with a few changes each time. With its turbulent background, I felt that the logo could be almost blown off the cover, hence this slightly more playful placement. I've always presumed there's a large degree of visual awareness among SANDMAN fans — I have no doubt they will find the latest issue or book collection, no matter how hard I make it for them with the design.

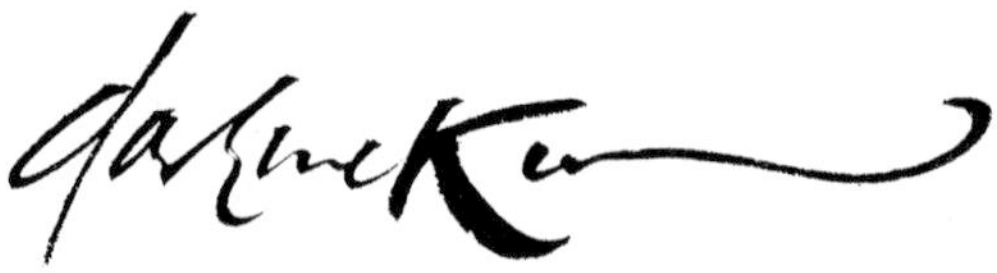

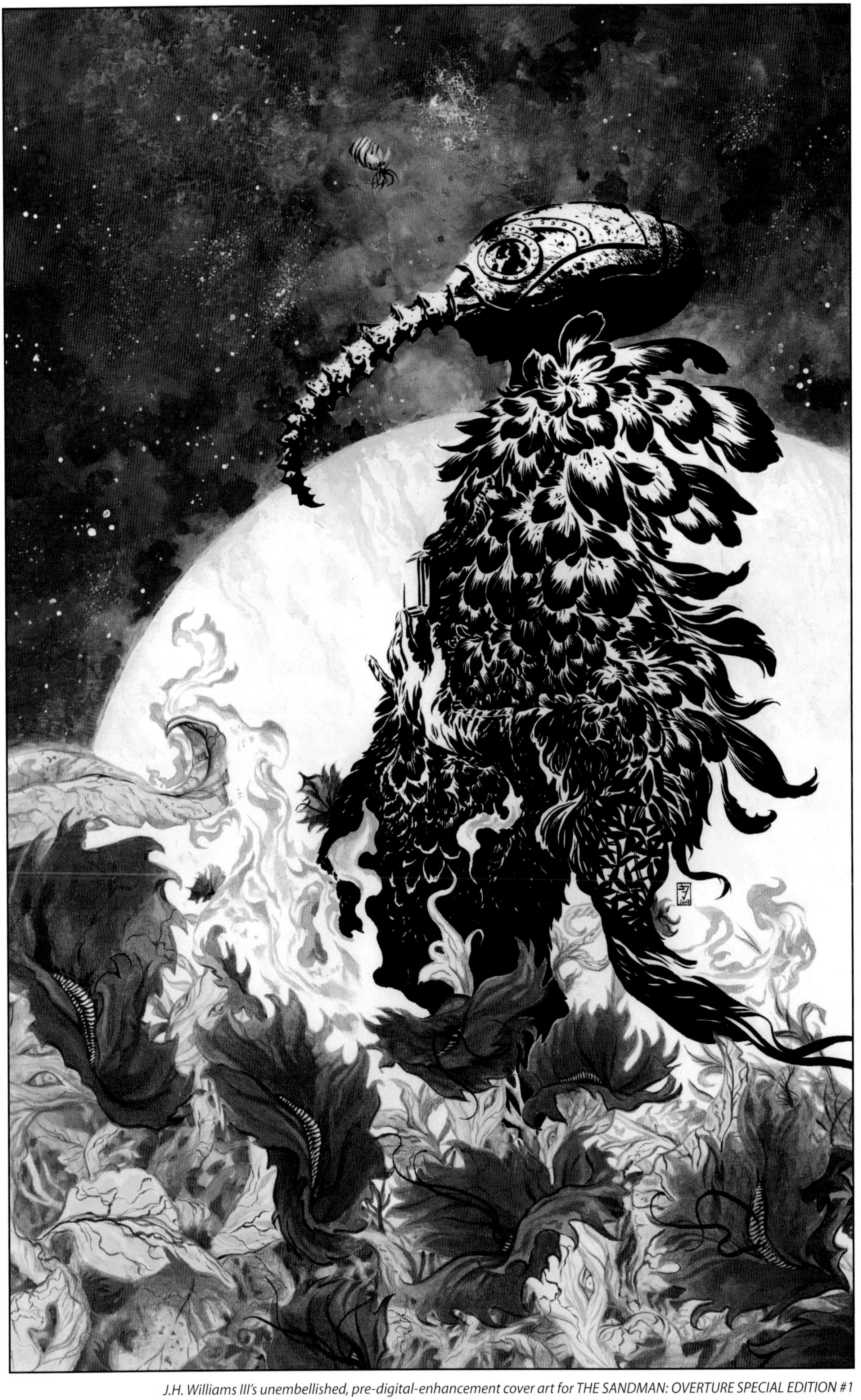

J.H. Williams III's unembellished, pre-digital-enhancement cover art for THE SANDMAN: OVERTURE SPECIAL EDITION #1

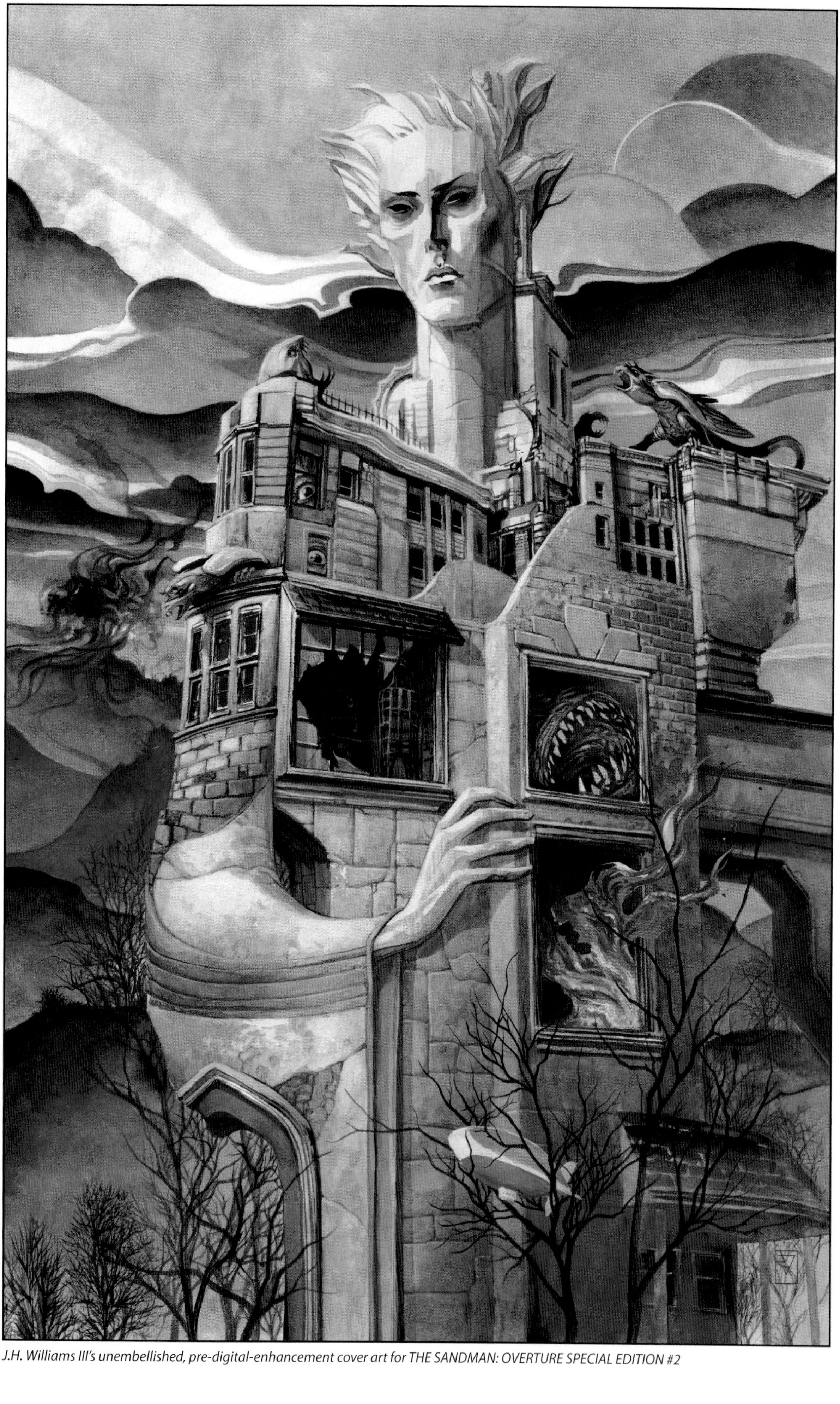

J.H. Williams III's unembellished, pre-digital-enhancement cover art for THE SANDMAN: OVERTURE SPECIAL EDITION #2

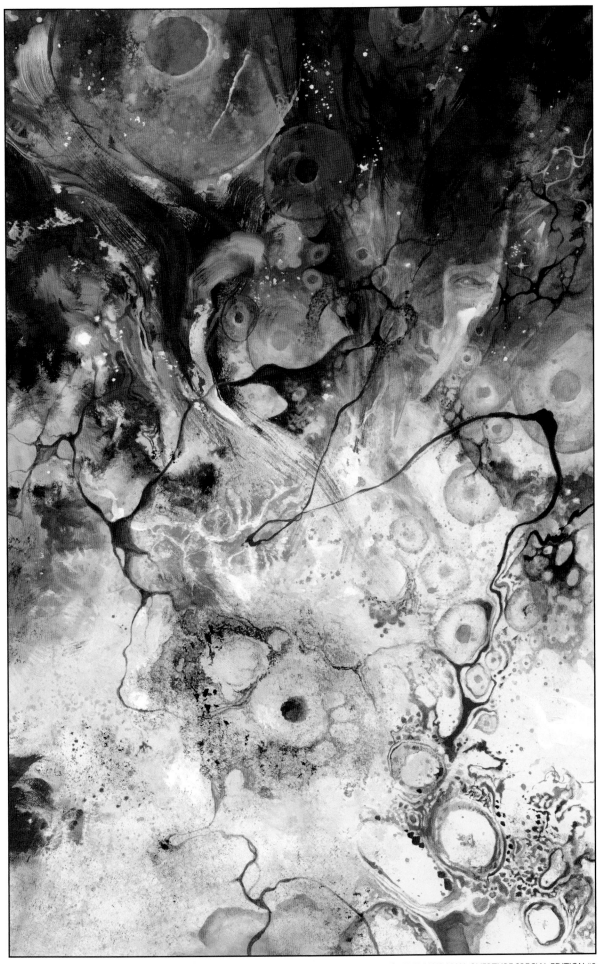

J.H. Williams III's unembellished, pre-digital-enhancement cover art for THE SANDMAN: OVERTURE SPECIAL EDITION #3

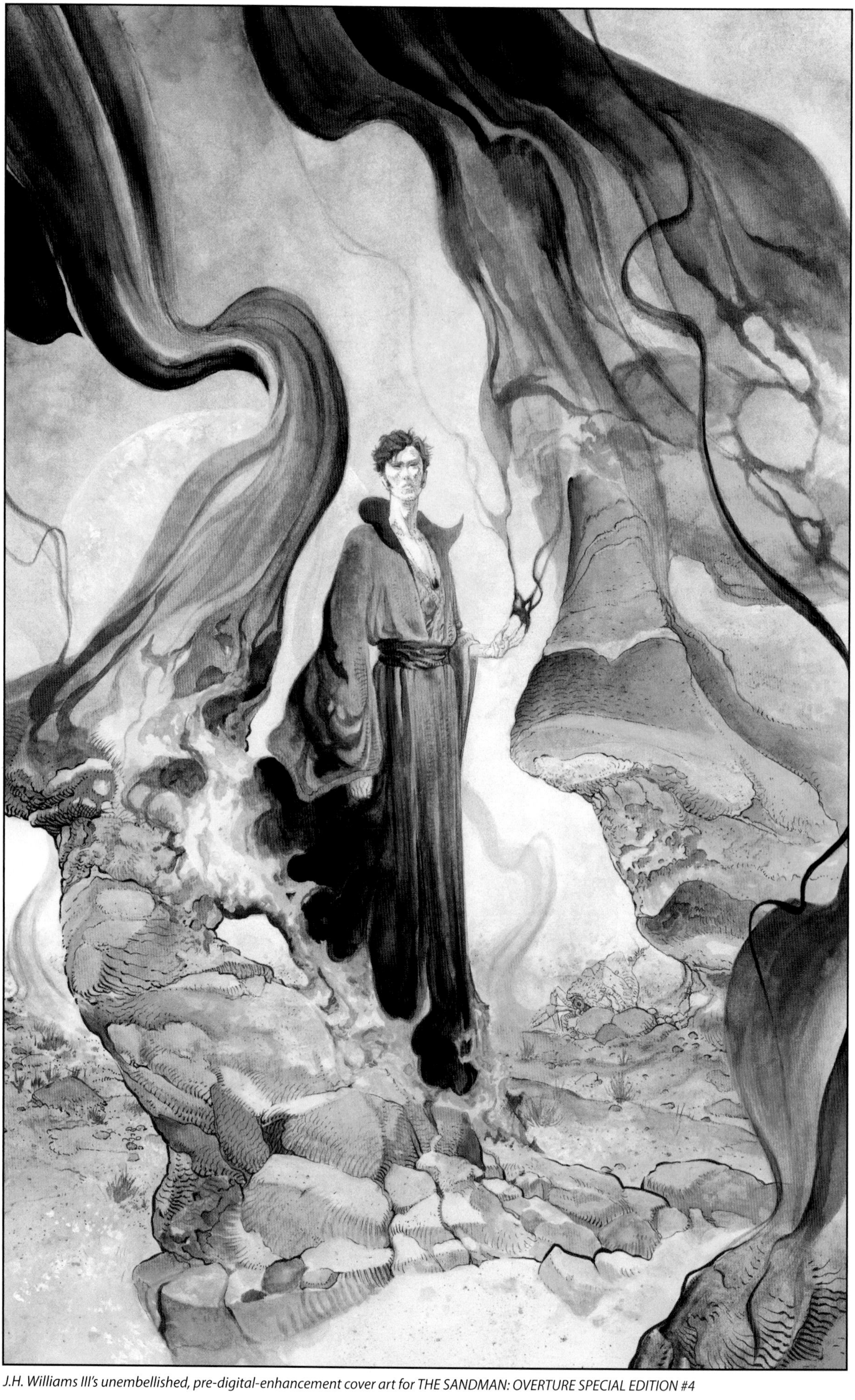

J.H. Williams III's unembellished, pre-digital-enhancement cover art for THE SANDMAN: OVERTURE SPECIAL EDITION #4

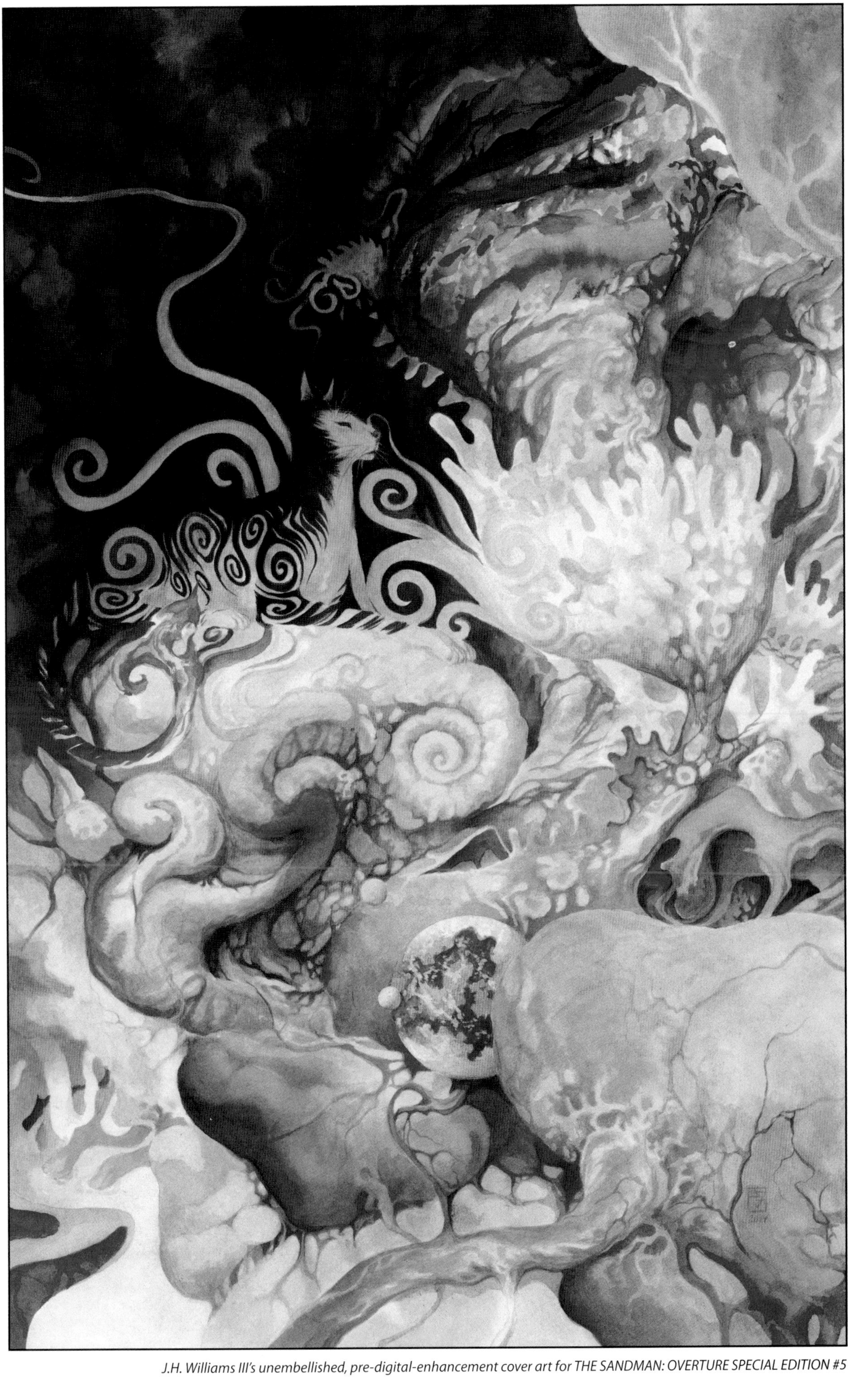

J.H. Williams III's unembellished, pre-digital-enhancement cover art for THE SANDMAN: OVERTURE SPECIAL EDITION #5

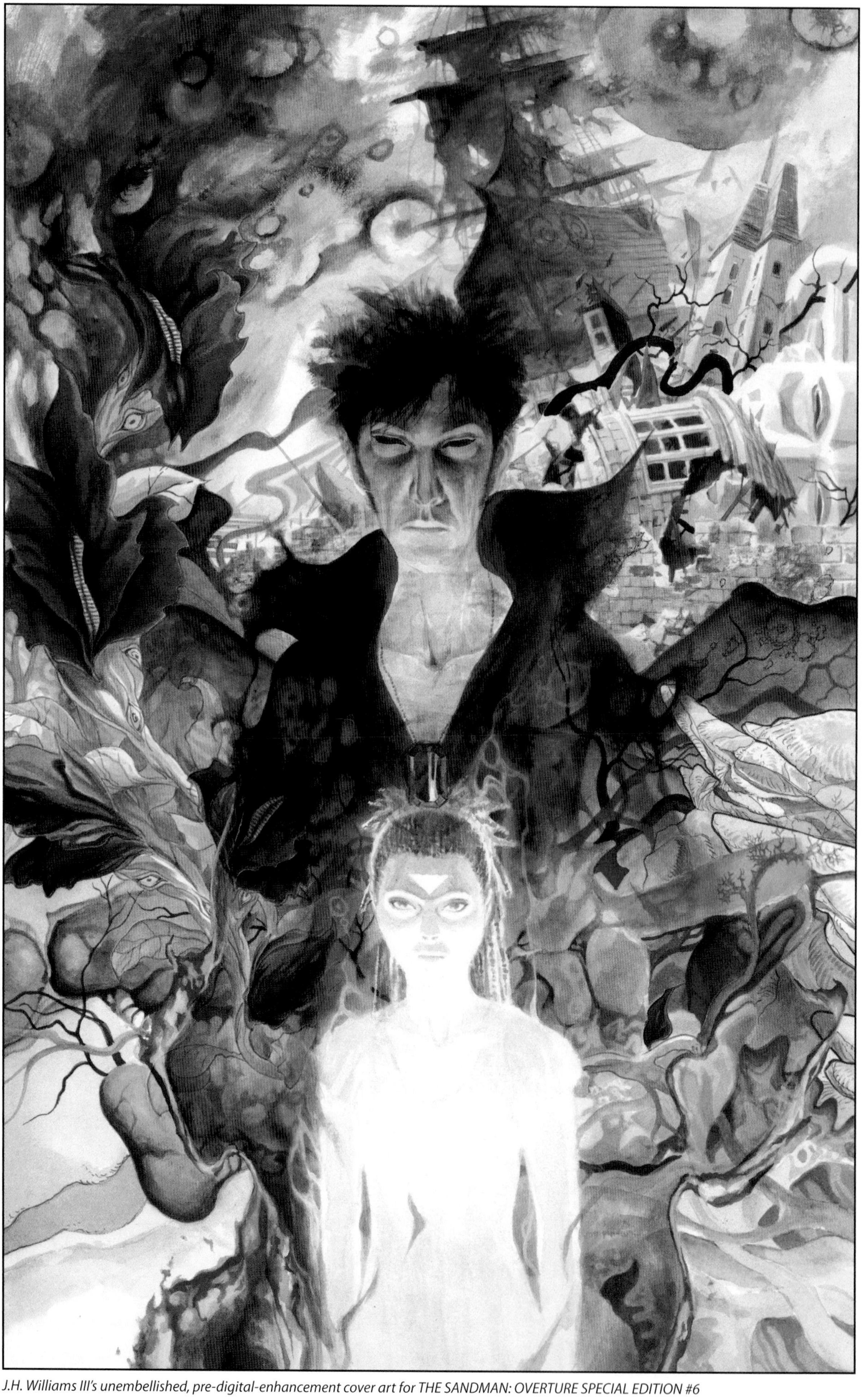

J.H. Williams III's unembellished, pre-digital-enhancement cover art for THE SANDMAN: OVERTURE SPECIAL EDITION #6

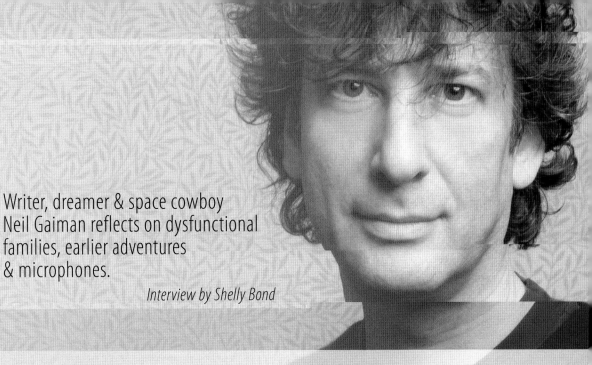

Writer, dreamer & space cowboy Neil Gaiman reflects on dysfunctional families, earlier adventures & microphones.

Interview by Shelly Bond

When did you start writing? When did you start writing for a living?

I started writing for a living when I was 22. I thought I was so old.

What's currently on your nightstand, and does it dream?

I do not own a nightstand. I shall start saving up for one now.

Is Dream's origin story in OVERTURE something you determined when you were writing the original SANDMAN series or did it evolve over time?

It's not really an origin story, is it? All of SANDMAN evolved. There were lots of odd stories that weren't easy to tell in the structure of SANDMAN. This is a way of telling some of them.

Is it fair to call The Endless the first dysfunctional family?

That's what we in the U.K. always used to call a family, isn't it? I've not yet met a functional one.

What was your greatest surprise in working with J.H.?

The beauty.

Three _____ you'd take with you into outer space:

comics: The Years Have Pants, The Bojeffries Saga, The Complete Will Eisner Spirit

albums: Coney Island Baby, Boys For Pele, 69 Love Songs

items of clothing: black T-shirts, black jeans, space jacket

keepsakes from the eighties: Kathy Acker, The Cafe Munchen (a long-gone pub), sunglasses

refreshments: an infinite supply of sustainable space-sushi

Time of day you're most creative:

SANDMAN was all written at night, but these days I fall asleep.

What's your intended soundtrack for OVERTURE?

Bowie's *The Next Day* and Alvy & Rubin's Argentinian album of Magnetic Fields covers are what I've been playing most...

Do you prefer reading comics on paper or plastic?

Paper. But I dream of a huge piece of intelligent paper that weighs nothing but has all the comics I want on it.

Issue #3 of the series is a western in space. Is there any genre you haven't conquered? What's your favorite to read? To write?

I like stories better than genres.

What song does Death sing in the shower?

"Happy Talk." And "Spread a Little Happiness."

We've seen Dream laugh. Will we ever see him dance?

No. Not even for you, my editor.

How do you know when to call a page a finished page?

When you start begging me to let it go so Jim can draw it.

As a young journalist, what was your most embarrassing moment when interviewing a celebrity?

I was 16, my first interview, interviewing artist Roger Dean, and at the end of the interview realizing the tape recorder batteries had run down. And nothing had taped.

What does a microphone dream of?

Electric words.

Artist extraordinaire J.H. Williams III waxes philosophic on discovering THE SANDMAN, the perfect playlist and paper vs. plastic. *Interview by Shelly Bond*

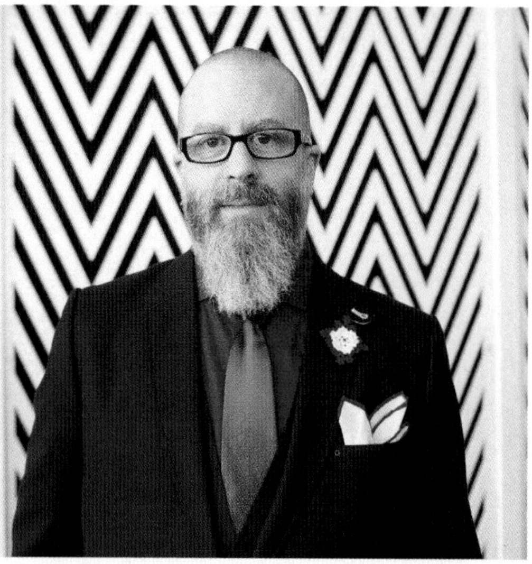

SB: What's your first memory of discovering SANDMAN in the late '80s? (Note: If you reveal precisely how much black you were wearing at the time, you may score extra points.)

JH3: Ha, pretty funny about the black wardrobe. But in all honesty, black is what I wore. I was certainly an introverted, morose teenager. And I tend to still wear a lot of black to this day, but with more pizzazz. THE SANDMAN was one of those books that came along for me at a time when I was hungry for something out of comics other than brightly clad heroes. It came at a time when you saw that what was on the average store shelf was changing dramatically, feeding off successful sophisticated works such as *Watchmen* or *V for Vendetta,* among others. I think there became an eagerness among comics readers to discover and broaden their/our perspectives. THE SANDMAN was a perfect fit for this mindset. And Neil was the perfect writer to bring this to everyone. And now that we have a mass resurgence of comics in a variety of genres, much stronger than ever before in the types of content to be found, there is no better time for THE SANDMAN to return for this strangely grand new story.

SB: Do you have a defining storyline/moment/character?

JH3: I know a lot of people revere the "Midsummer Night's Dream" chapter (THE SANDMAN #19) as the one that really set things afire, which was fantastic. But for me it was "A Dream of a Thousand Cats" (Issue #18). That was the point where pure brilliance came through, in my opinion. This is where I knew I was reading a series made of magic. It remains one of my favorites to this day.

SB: When did you start drawing? When did you start drawing for a living?

JH3: I've been drawing all my life, I can't remember ever ***not*** drawing. And I attempted to make a living from it right out of high school, but didn't find much success until later. So the work was able to start paying the bills around the beginning of the '90s.

SB: Your work is so strongly focused on the horizontal. From a mood and design perspective, it's been compared to such cinematic masters as Peter Greenaway in ambiance and presentation. Stylistically, one could cite many examples such as Lempicka, Mucha and traditional Art Nouveau. Who and what are your specific influences in art and design and photography?

JH3: I have no specific influences, but I feel I'm influenced by everything I come in contact with in life. Sure, I can recite many artists or novels or films that have impacted me, but there is too much to narrow it down in overly specific terms. So things tend to come out of whatever it is I've been exposed to or excited about recently from numerous sources. But I do seem to have standard things that live with me all the time, such as old pulp ideas, or fantasy concepts, or science fiction. I always gravitate toward those things, almost subconsciously.

SB: What's your perfect playlist for the original 10-volume SANDMAN series?

JH3: Now that's a loaded question! I don't know how perfect it would be either, but it would have to have an appropriate amount of dark, light, heavy, metaphysical, humor and a little cheese…

The Cure — *Disintegration* and the second half of *Pornography*

Blondie — "Sound-A-Sleep," "Angels on the Balcony," "Do the Dark," maybe "Atomic"

The Sisters of Mercy — *Afterhours*

Fields of the Nephilim — "Psychonaut," "Sumerland (What Dreams May Come)," among others, I'm sure

Roxy Music — "In Every Dream Home A Heartache"

Hawkwind — "LSD"

Gary Wright — "Dreamweaver" (I mean, how could we pass that up, right?)

Brian Eno — Just about anything could work

Anyway, if I had an entire day to think about this properly, then I'm sure I could have better choices — some more current choices.

SB: What's your intended soundtrack for the new series?

JH3: Well, with barely being into the production of the story, I can't really pin that down: an appropriate amount of dark, light, heavy, metaphysical, humor and a little cheese, again…

SB: On working with Neil so far, what's your… Greatest surprise?

JH3: Not really a surprise, but more of a noting of his warmth and enthusiasm, and an immediately personable quality to our first real conversations. But I was mildly surprised that he fondly remembered my abrupt interruption of a conversation he was having with some other people years ago one day outside of a hotel in San Diego, where I rudely interjected myself just to say hello and insisted that I had to shake his hand. You see, I had seen him as I was walking by and just lost all sense of proper etiquette, and in doing so, telling him I'd love the opportunity to work with him someday. And apparently, even through my rudeness, I must have left some sort of positive impression, enough that he hadn't forgotten after all these years. And now here we are working on THE SANDMAN together — certainly a dream come true for me (yes, a poor blatant pun).

SB: Greatest challenge?

JH3: Not to disappoint Neil on his expectations, or my own, to do the story justice with my scribblings.

SB: Do you prefer reading comics on paper or plastic?

JH3: Paper, always paper — the same for books of all sorts. It's all about the tactile experience for me. I feel an important part of the experience of reading a story, whether it be comics or novels, comes from what it feels like to hold it in your hands, the design of it, the weight of it, the shape of it, the paper texture between your fingers as you turn the page for that next little discovery that awaits you. There is nothing more or equally as satisfying in my opinion.

SB: How do you know when to call a page a finished page?

JH3: When it's at the point that if I add anything more it will be overwrought, becoming ruined and a drag.

SB: Three _____ you'd take with you into outer space.

comics:
JH3: Love and Rockets (or anything by the Hernandez brothers), Strangers in Paradise, THE SANDMAN, and anything by Jack Kirby. I know, more than three, but I'm selfish.

albums:
Now this is almost impossible. But let's say for now, Autoamerican by Blondie, Mourning Sun by Fields of the Nephilim, 2112 by Rush. These answers most likely would change daily.

items of clothing:
Socks! I can't imagine the deep cold of space without socks. Especially socks with goofy patterns, like my Dalek socks for example.

keepsake from the eighties:
My autographed Jim Steranko poster that lives in my studio office.

refreshments:
Coffee, and banana bread with walnuts.

Colorist extraordinaire DAVE STEWART
waxes kaleidoscopic on killer combinations,
rendering styles, depth & demons.

Interview by Shelly Bond

SB: When did you start coloring? When did you start coloring for a living?

DS: I started coloring in college. I was interested in comic art and my professor, Mark Conahan, and I figured out how to color line art in Photoshop. We scanned in a black and white *Aliens* story by Kilian Plunkett. This was just when tint prep was adopted and the Image coloring revolution started. I was ahead of the game when Photoshop started to take over as the coloring program of choice.

SB: What's your favorite color?

DS: They're all my babies. How can I choose?

SB: What's your favorite color combination?

DS: I enjoy the way color combinations work more than individual colors. Certain rusty red, yellow green, and mustard yellow hues in combination make me pretty happy.

SB: How did you get into coloring comic books?

DS: Design internship through Portland Community College at Dark Horse Comics. That turned into trying out for a full-time colorist position. At that time, hand-painted guides created by the colorist were interpreted into computer vector graphics by separators. I didn't get the colorist/guide painter position, but I got the separator's position that opened when he was promoted to colorist.

SB: If you weren't a colorist, what would you be?

DS: Well, I'm sure I'd want to do some other artistic job. Photography, painting? I've been thinking what I would want to do outside of a creative job. Maybe a backwoods guide. Using downtime to paint what I see.

SB: Advice for aspiring colorists?

DS: Work on mastering several different styles of rendering. Once you master that, you'll have a lot more to offer a publisher. Put a lot of focus initially on depth in your work. Color can work against the line by flattening out the image.

SB: Last comic or novel you couldn't put down?

DS: I read the last *Prophet* trade in one sitting. The last novel I read was *The Demonologist: The Extraordinary Career of Ed and Lorraine Warren.*

SB: What's your greatest pleasure in working with artist J.H. Williams III?

DS: J.H.'s art is so fantastic. I think he's pushing the comics medium into new territory. It's always amazing to see the new pages and the mindblowing layouts. And he's my friend. Love the guy!

SB: Greatest challenge?

DS: Some of the stuff we're doing requires a new technical approach: Figuring out how *not* to trap portions of ink wash, add scans of his hand-painted work and replace blacks with the four-color black we're printing with. The detail can be a bit overwhelming. A lot to remember sometimes!

SB: How do you know when to call a page a finished page?

DS: Sometimes deadlines help determine that :) Well, I like to bring a page to a finished stage and let it sit a day if I have time. That finished stage checks off all the boxes: detail all filled in, colors all dropped in. That extra day lets me distance myself and critically look at what I've done. Does everything separate well? Does all the rendering read correctly? Do all the scene changes separate nicely?

SB: Do you prefer reading comics on paper or plastic?

DS: Well, paper still. I like the look of digital, but I just haven't made the jump.

SB: Three _____ you'd take with you into outer space:

SB: comics

DS: *Hellboy, Secret History of DB Cooper*, Kirby Cap

SB: albums

DS: *Hunky Dory, Highway to Hell, Junior Kimbrough: Sad Days, Lonely Nights*

SB: items of clothing

DS: My old Ecco boots (best boots I had), Carhartt pants, and my W.A.S.P. (not the comic character) T-shirt

SB: keepsakes from the eighties

DS: Battletech board game, Rambo knife, Warhammer 20k figures

SB: refreshments

DS: Barbara's jalapeño cheese puffs, Whirly Pop popcorn, and a kale shake to even it all out

Dave Stewart is a nine-time Eisner Award-winning colorist:
2003, 2005, 2007, 2008, 2009, 2010, 2011, 2013, 2015

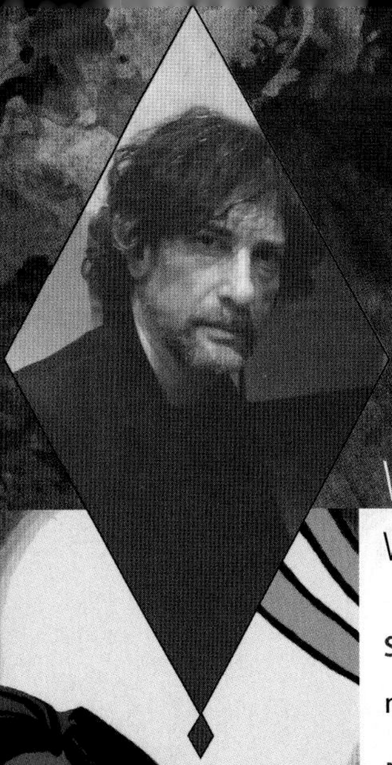

WAXING PHILOSOPHIC on family matters with NEIL GAIMAN and SHELLY BOND

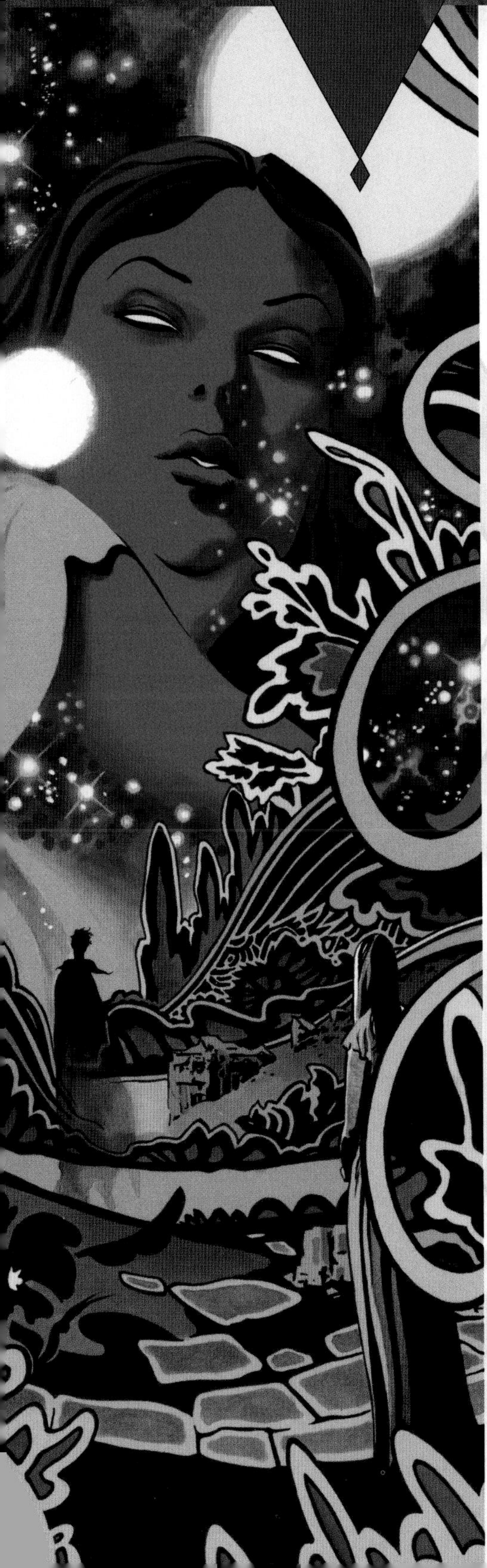

SB Does Night treat all her children in the same manner in which she treated Morpheus in issue #5?

NG *No, she plays favorites. Some of the Endless she adores, some she ignores, but then, she wants to be left alone as much as she wants to be paid attention to.*

SB What's your surefire cure for writer's block?

NG *Shelly Bond's tears. Werewolves. Werewolves carrying vials of Shelly Bond's tears.*

SB When do you know a page is a finished page?

NG *When they clutch it from my twitching hands. Or when I want to know what happened next.*

SB What's on the Sandman's iPod?

NG *The music of the spheres. Soul music with real souls. Every song ever dreamed of that was never written or recorded.*

SB What could the Sandman learn from *The Art of Asking* by the amazing Amanda Palmer?

NG *How to care. How to ask for help. Except he wouldn't. Or mostly wouldn't.*

BONUS: Neil's Notes

Take a real backstage tour of THE SANDMAN OVERTURE by reading the notes Neil prefaces his scripts with. They'll give you more insight, laughs and Britishisms than anything else in comics!

CHAPTER ONE

Hullo everyone,

I'm not 26 anymore, am I? I don't think I've ever felt less 26 in my life. I'm wearing computer-writing glasses, and feeling like I'm re-forming a beloved supergroup, and the only thing I can be certain of is that the world will buy the story and grumble that it's not as good as they remember.

But then, that always happened with SANDMAN, from about issue 6 or 7 on, when the reviews started coming in, people lamented the lost golden age of SANDMAN, now passed away.

I've started this and thrown away what I started a half-dozen times now, but it's really time to grit my teeth, stiffen my sinews, imitate the action of a tiger — well, of a tiger who can, fortuitously, not only write but also write comics — and just keep going.

This was how I always used to start, with me talking about what was going on in my head. That's good to remember.

So. I'm in my writing gazebo, accompanied by two large white dogs and an enormous monarch butterfly perched on a set of antlers now sitting above the door. I do not know how the butterfly got in.

CHAPTER TWO

So. Chapter One is done and being drawn and the art is amazing. I've thrown out a whole grand opening scene for much the same reason I threw away a grand opening scene in SANDMAN 24. (And I just, curiously, went and looked at it to see if there were any bits I could lift.) (There weren't.)

We need to throw down a few more cards onto the table before we get to that point. And I want to see a J. H. Williams III Daniel.

I'll write this as 24 pages, assuming that's what we'll get.

I keep expecting the stage fright to lift on this, to get comfortable, to not feel like the whole world is staring over my shoulder. So far it's just getting worse.

So.

We're bringing Daniel in for an opening scene (and he'll be back in the final part). He's younger than Morpheus: Morpheus tends to appear in his late 20s or early 30s. Daniel's in appearance about 19 or 20. His skin and his hair are white, his eyes are still dark pits with distant stars in them, and he wears white robes, normally patterned. If they were real, they would be priceless, woven from white silk and white thread by lacemakers and silkmakers and the like.

He's gentler. Softer. And in terms of body language, he touches things. Nothing ever touches Morpheus unless he wishes it, and he does not touch things or people except with a purpose. But Daniel does.

Also, he is the same being: he is Dream of the Endless, with all the majesty and magic that implies.

CHAPTER THREE

Right. This pretty much entirely exists in note form, but now I'm going to turn it into comics, by god.

Jim, I love what you're doing. We both have to do it faster, obviously, and to stop looking over our shoulders and to stop thinking, and to trust our fingers and our eyes, which know what they are doing. That's what I think. I hope I speed up...

Here goes.

CHAPTER FOUR

Dear Jim,

You know, the art you are making is, hands down, the finest periodical comics work I've ever seen. It's reason enough to come back and tell this story. The biggest challenge for me is making it big enough and beautiful enough for you.

So. Issue 4. I'm taking your initial suggestions in mind, and keep thinking about Steranko, and what he did right — the way he took a limited drawing ability, but all the design sense in the world, and beautiful storytelling. The way he'd make things into a silent movie of tiny panels, and then you'd turn the page to a panel the size of a page and it would make your head explode. The way that he was pop art at a time when fine art was staring at comics and trying to figure out what they were stealing.

Barry Windsor Smith and Jim Steranko fascinate me — they both started out as Kirby clones, and then they each rapidly went their own way, Barry into the Pre-Raphaelite Brotherhood, Jim into Madison Avenue, Design, Op Art, Pop Art, making a virtue of all his weaknesses. SANDMAN's always had a lot more to do with the BWS side of things (I've told people over the years who couldn't figure out how to draw Dream to just starve BWS's early Conan) but I love the idea of an issue that's Sterankoesque: Pan Galactic, huge, and consists of silent sequences and splashes.

And conversations. And revelations. And one tragic Death.

CHAPTER 5

Hi JH, hullo world.

Sorry about this. I wrote a lot, and then I threw it out when I realised it would wind up doing that thing I do where we get to the last episode and either have to make it double-sized, or add an extra issue. I figure that might break the universe if I did it on this.

So I've gone back to the drawing board a bit, and am trying to trim it here.

Visually, we will want to echo some of the things we've done before (you'll see, it's like we're on the downward slope). I also like the idea that we'll find new things to do, but classically, as if we've moved from the futuristic spatter of #4 to something contained and very human.

Everything in this issue should be about making people care, not about spectacle. Even where it calls for spectacle, if you see what I mean. It's all about the emotion. Make us feel, make us cry…

That's all.

CHAPTER SIX

So here we are. The end of the beginning, which is also the end of the end, because this is a beginning which will mean more if it is read after reading all of SANDMAN, and will make re-reading SANDMAN afterwards a slightly different experience, I hope.

I've sighed in e-mail that this last issue is going to be like trying to fit four elephants into a small car: we can do it somehow, two in the front, two in the back. It's going to be a tight squeeze, though. The main reason for the delay and rewrites and throwing out and rewrites of Chapter 5 was having to cut strands and not let them expand. (SANDMAN itself was never meant to go for more than 50 issues, and I was pretty sure it would be done by about #36. It wasn't. The story grows in the telling.)

What I have to do here is:

Finish the story. Does the universe end? Does Morpheus save the day? What about Time and Night, and the mysterious chronos device that Daniel returned to Time in part 2? Where is Delirium in all this? How will the mad star be dealt with?

How do the events change him?

And, once it's done, and Morpheus is exhausted beyond all imagining, and returning, will he be captured?

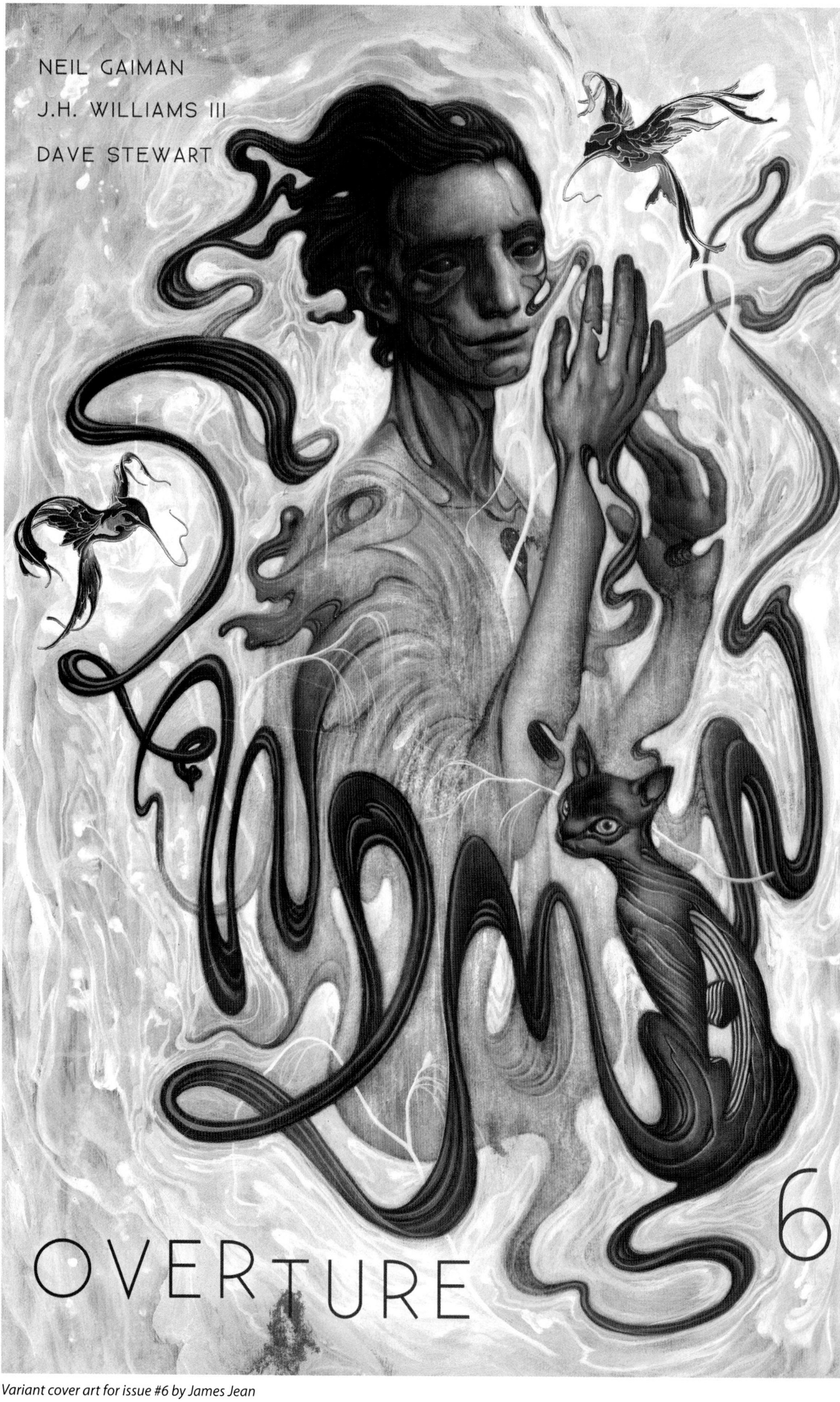
NEIL GAIMAN
J.H. WILLIAMS III
DAVE STEWART
OVERTURE
6
Variant cover art for issue #6 by James Jean

PRELUDES

Sketchbook and Annotations by J.H. Williams III

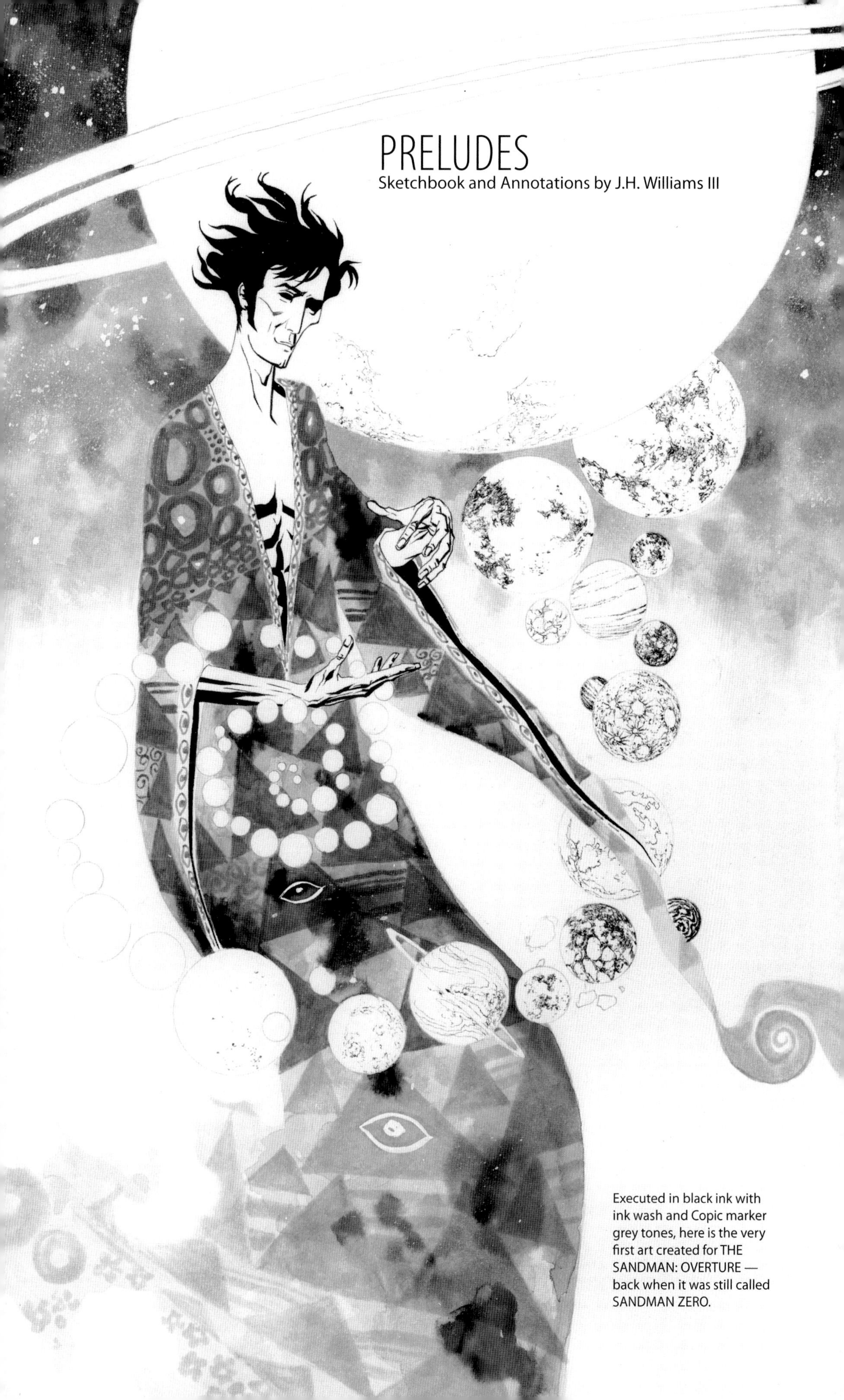

Executed in black ink with ink wash and Copic marker grey tones, here is the very first art created for THE SANDMAN: OVERTURE — back when it was still called SANDMAN ZERO.

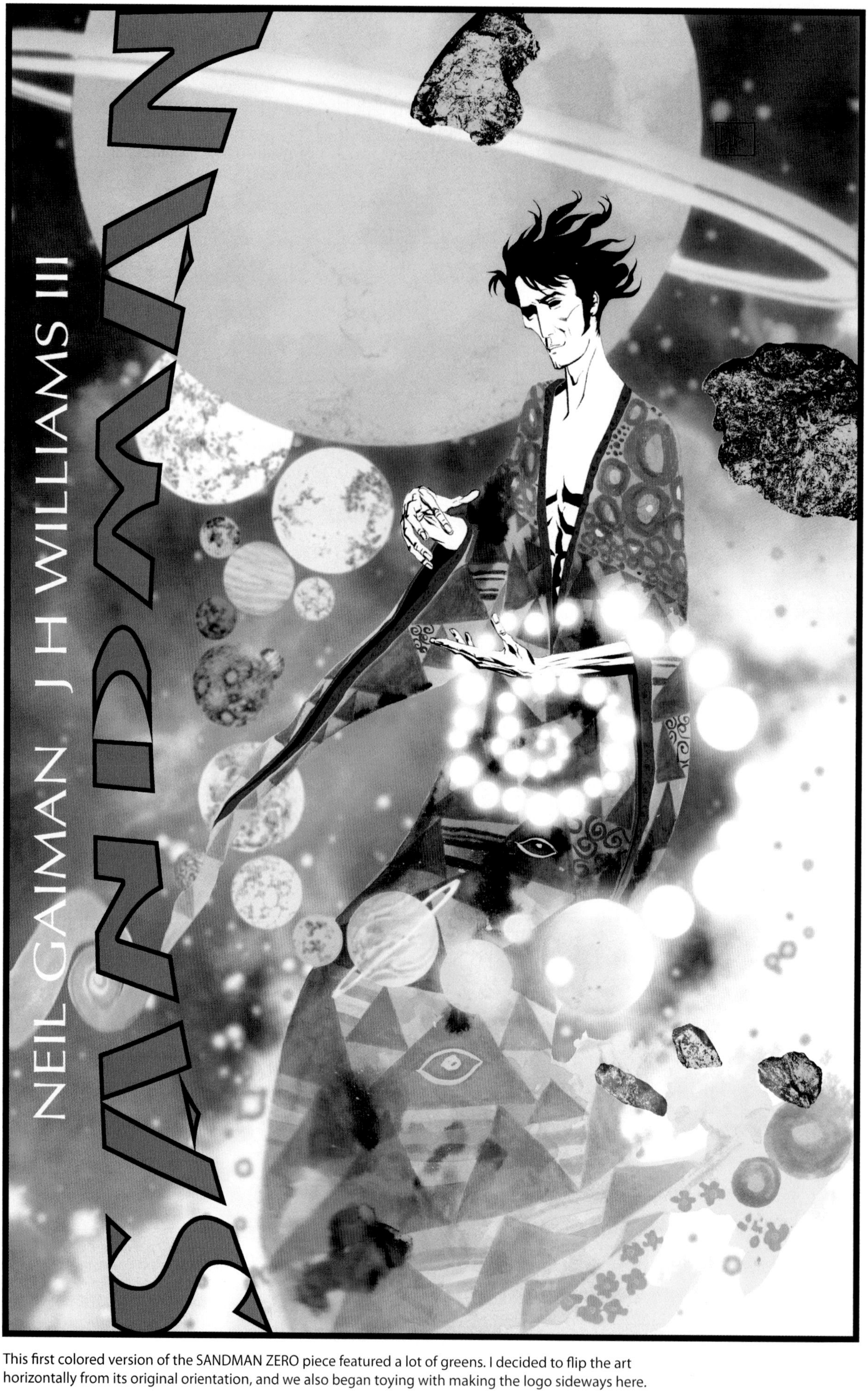
SANDMAN
NEIL GAIMAN J H WILLIAMS III

This first colored version of the SANDMAN ZERO piece featured a lot of greens. I decided to flip the art horizontally from its original orientation, and we also began toying with making the logo sideways here.

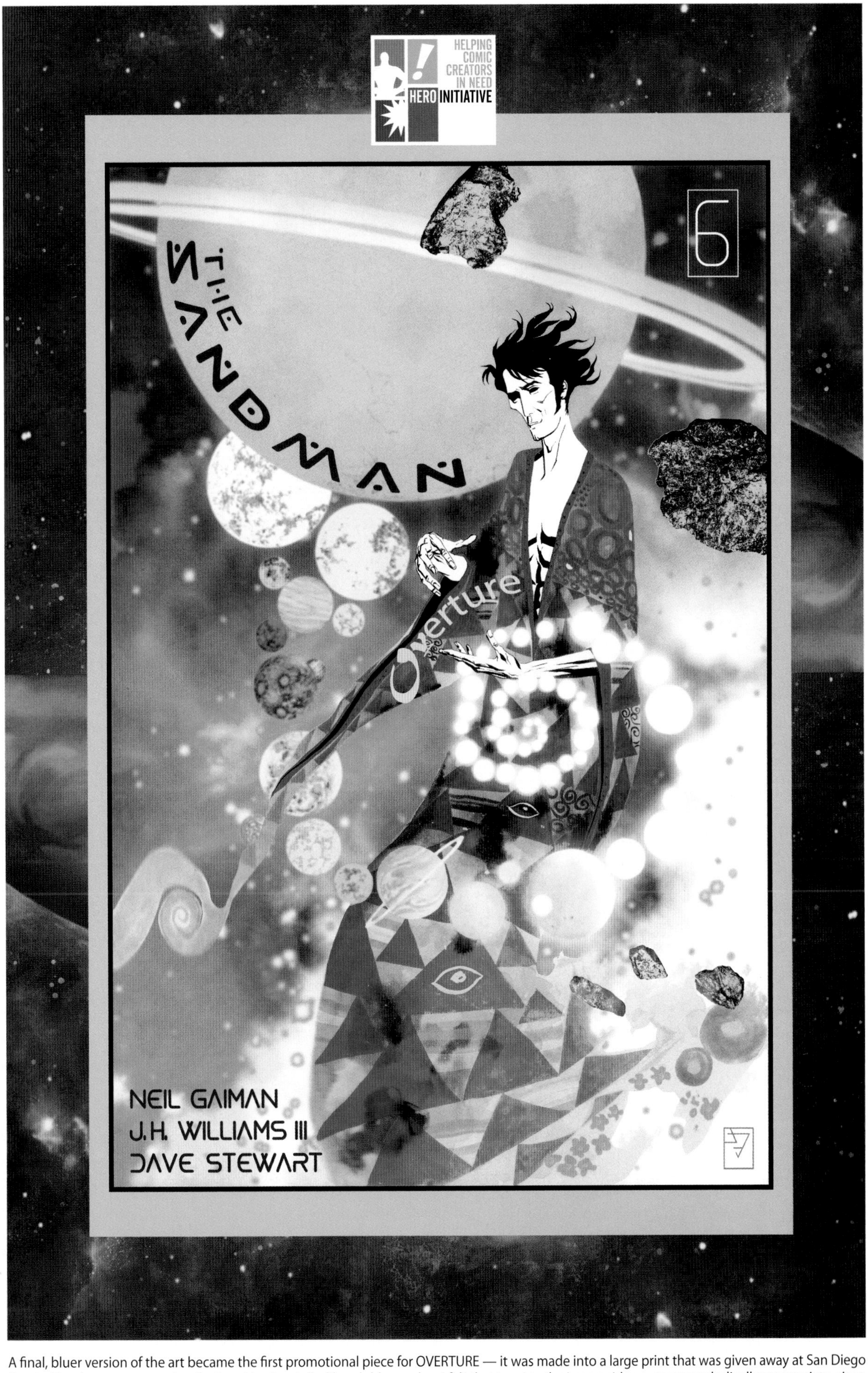

HELPING COMIC CREATORS IN NEED
HERO INITIATIVE
THE SANDMAN
6
Overture
NEIL GAIMAN
J.H. WILLIAMS III
DAVE STEWART

A final, bluer version of the art became the first promotional piece for OVERTURE — it was made into a large print that was given away at San Diego Comic-Con. It was meant to be displayed horizontally, like a lobby card — I felt that turning the image sideways was symbolically appropriate, since OVERTURE would be turning what we know about the Sandman on its end. Fast forward several years to the final issue of the series, for which I wanted to create a variant cover in support of the Hero Initiative, a charity close to my heart as a comics professional. Once again, this piece seemed symbolically appropriate — here at the end, we return to the beginning: the circle is complete.

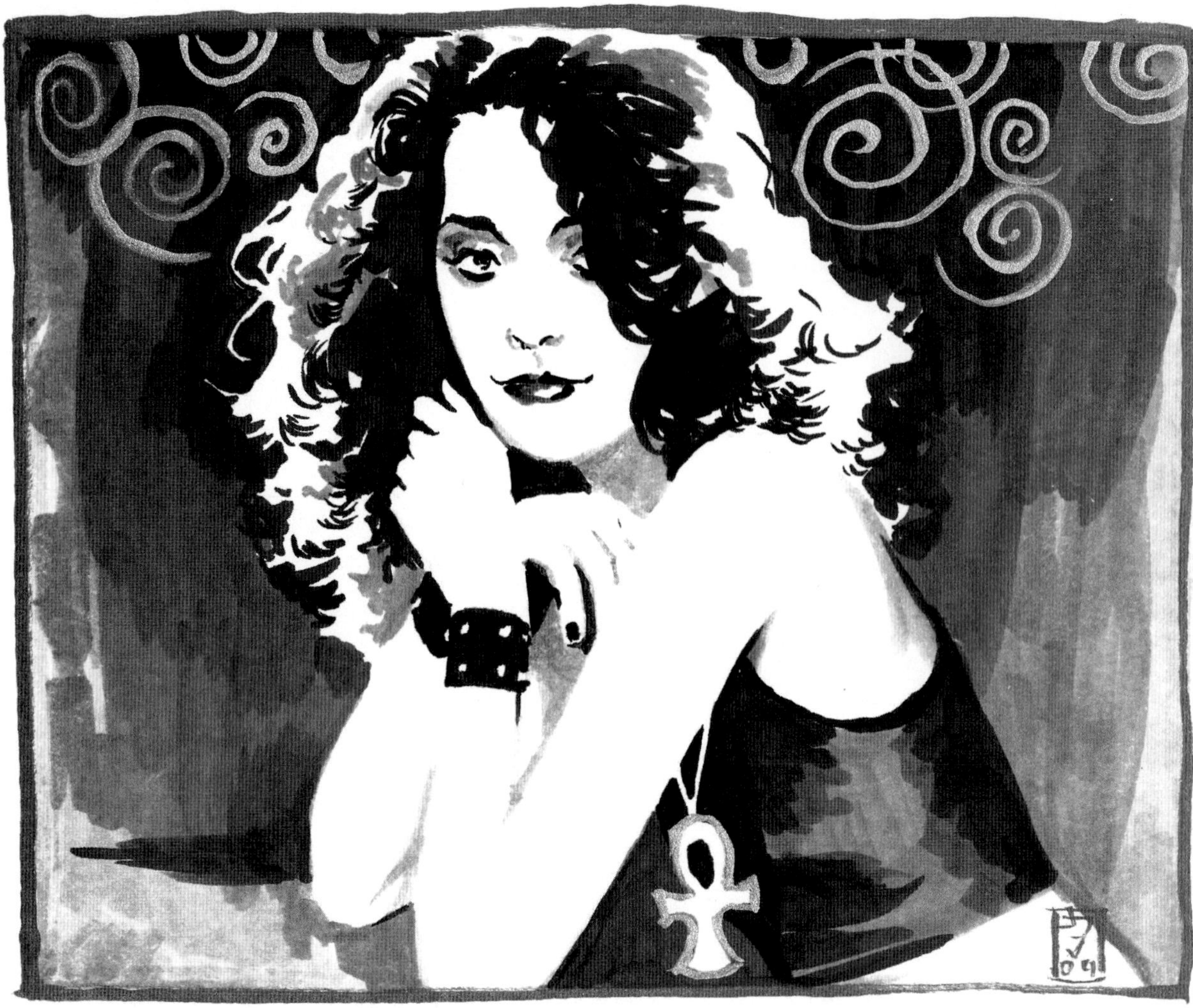

A more loosely styled Death piece from 2004, near the time I first met Neil — it turns out that I was prepping for OVERTURE long before I even knew such a story existed.

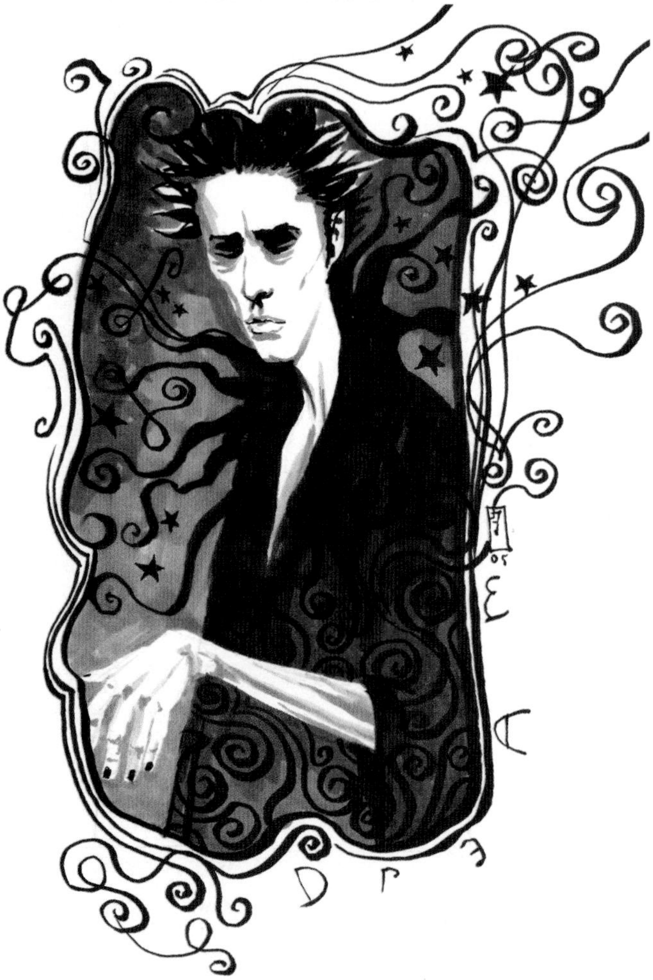

A rather unfortunate, but amusing, 2005 sketch of Morpheus.

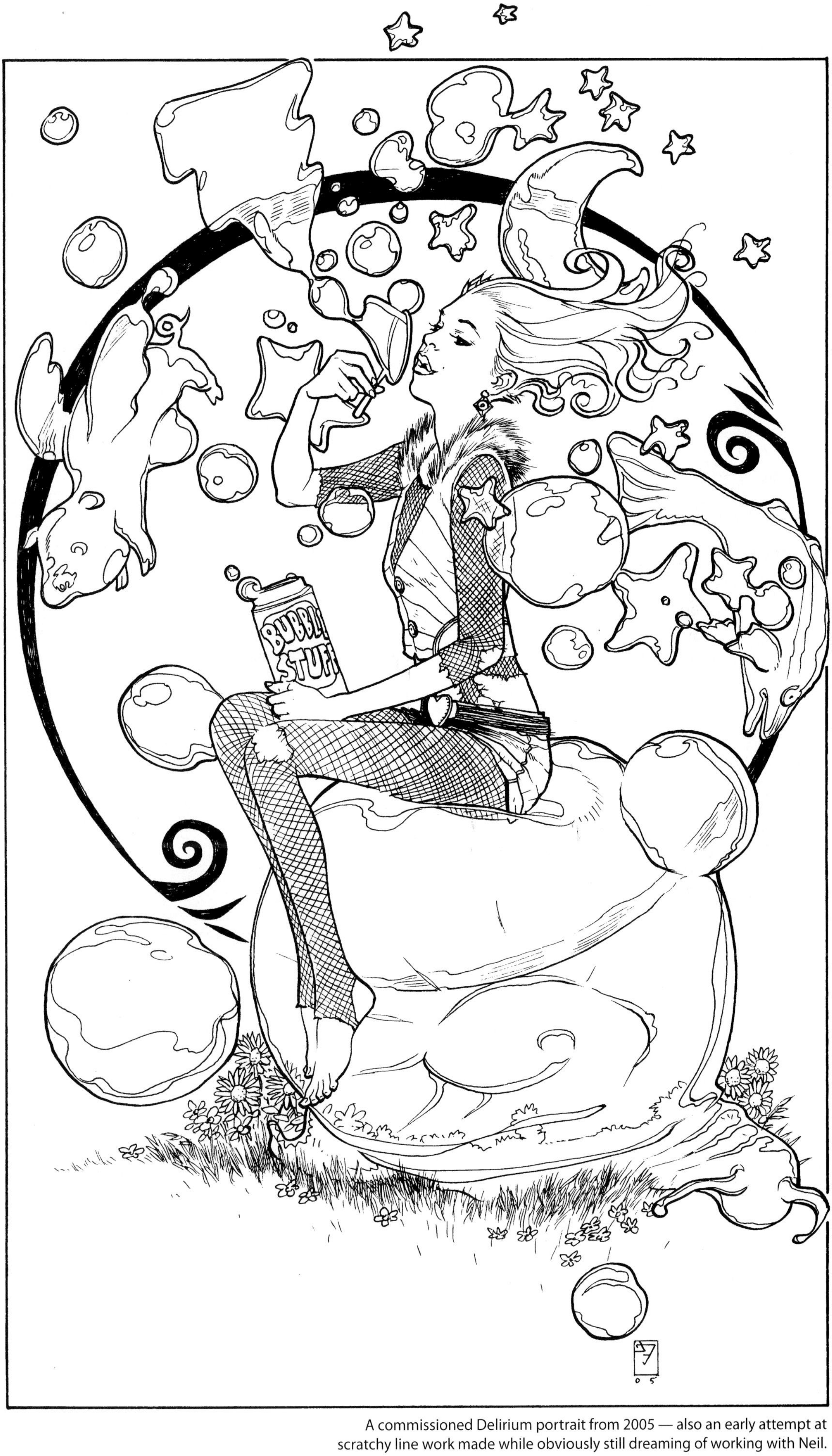
BUBBLE
STUFF

A commissioned Delirium portrait from 2005 — also an early attempt at scratchy line work made while obviously still dreaming of working with Neil.

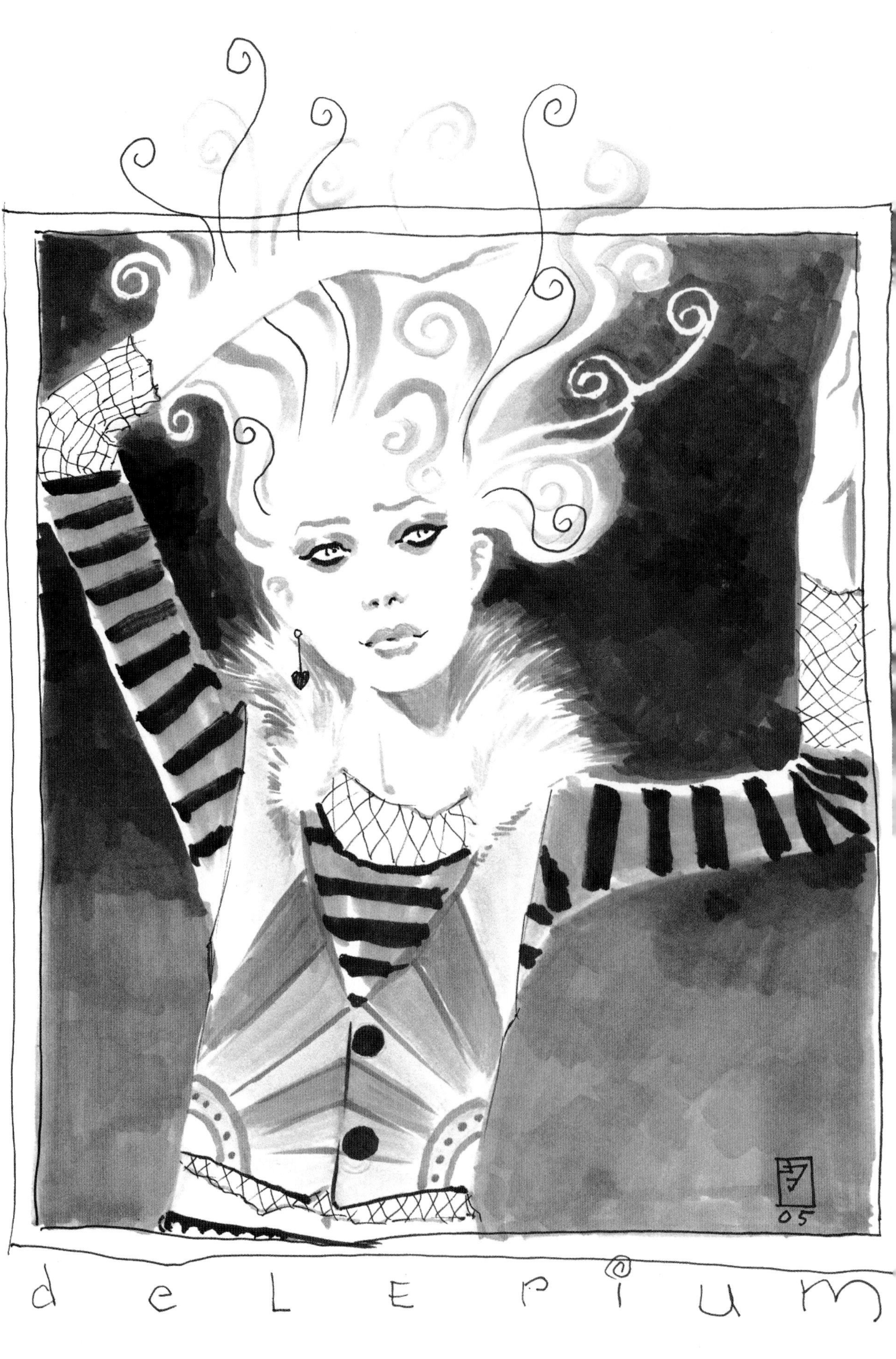
05
deLErium

Another loose sketch from 2005, with "Delirium" awkwardly misspelled — or was she toying with my mind?

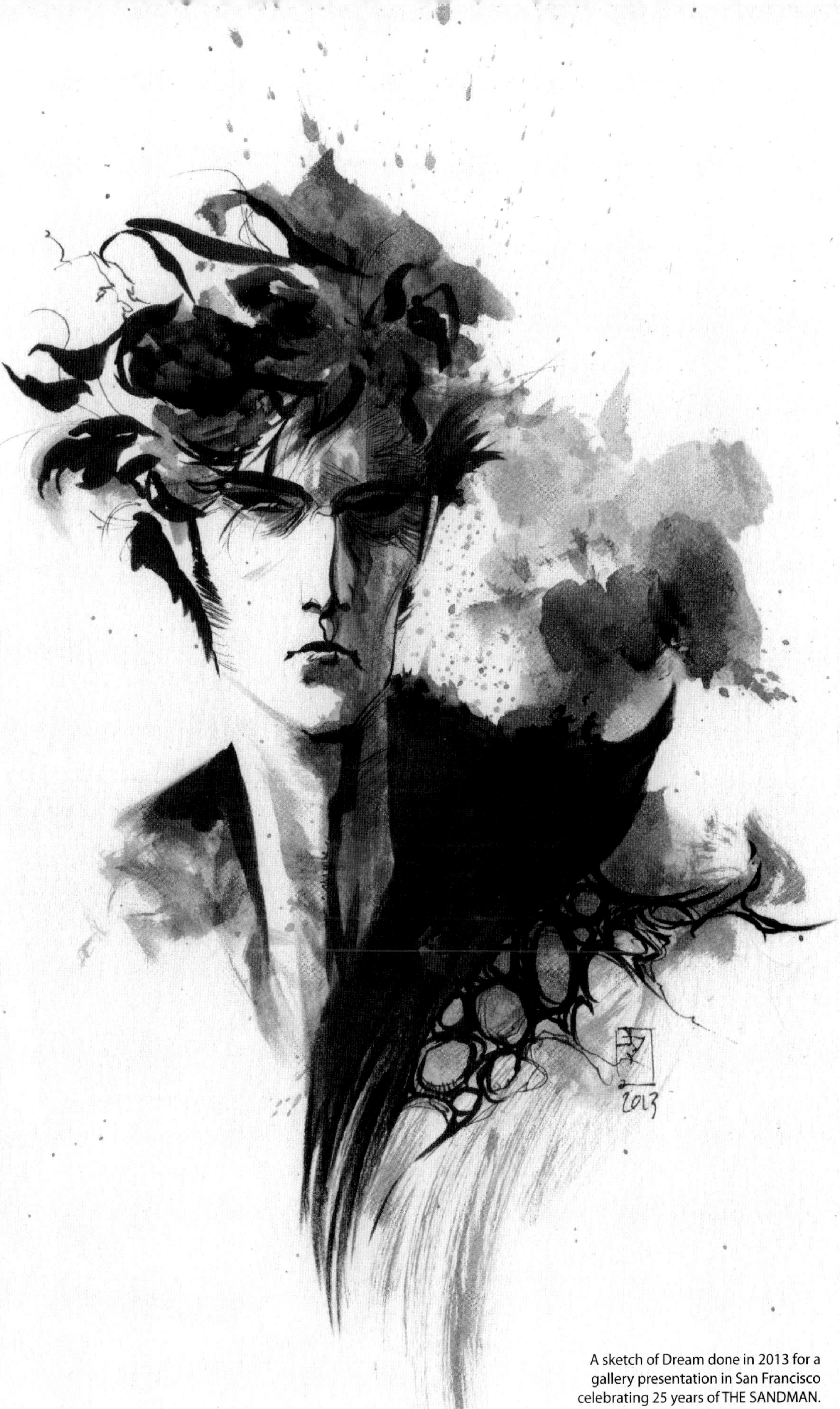
2013

A sketch of Dream done in 2013 for a gallery presentation in San Francisco celebrating 25 years of THE SANDMAN. I like the somewhat alien quality of his features here — in fact, I'd like to draw a Sandman story in this style sometime.

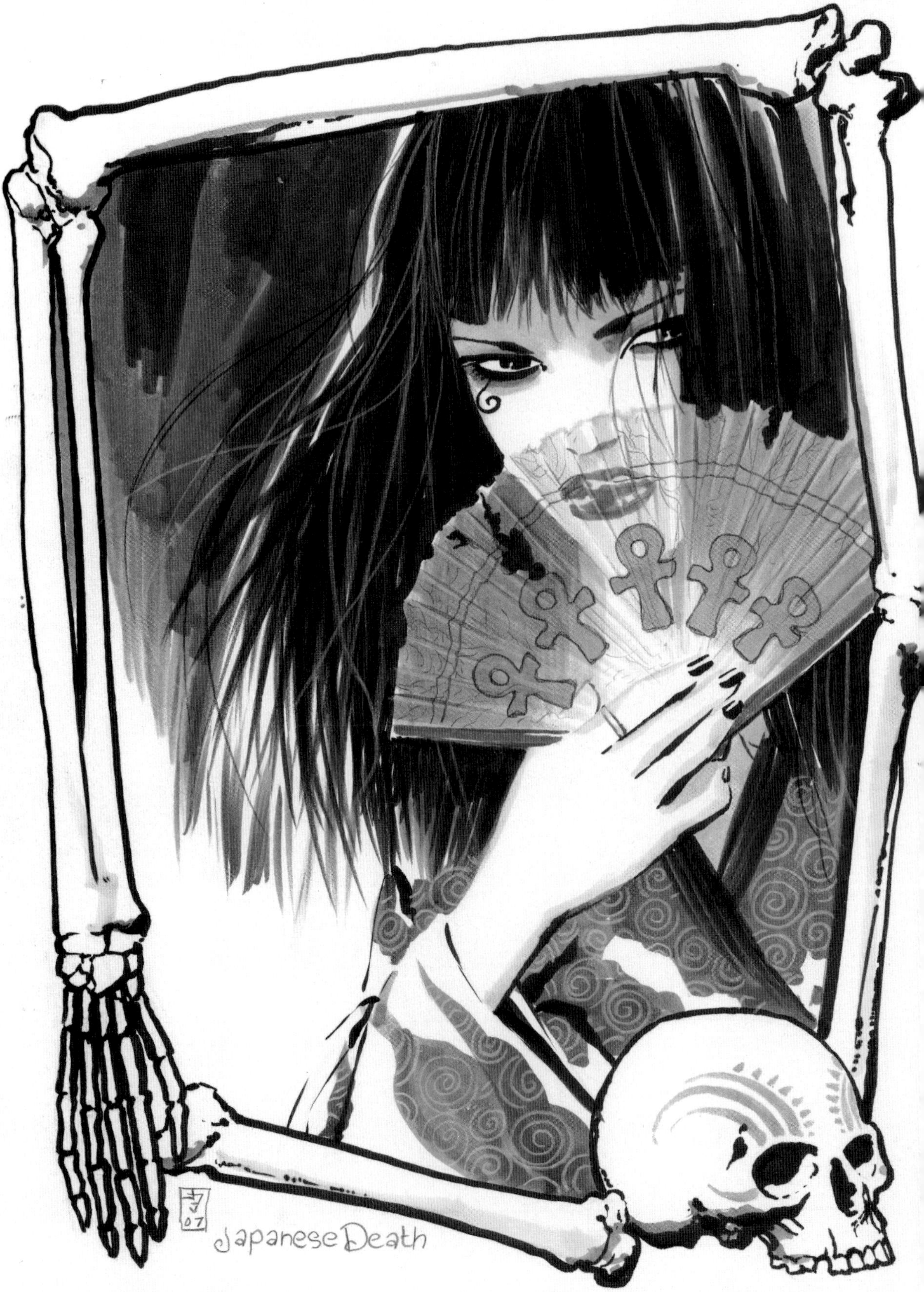
JapaneseDeath

A Japanese Death from 2007 — time is
marching forward toward OVERTURE!

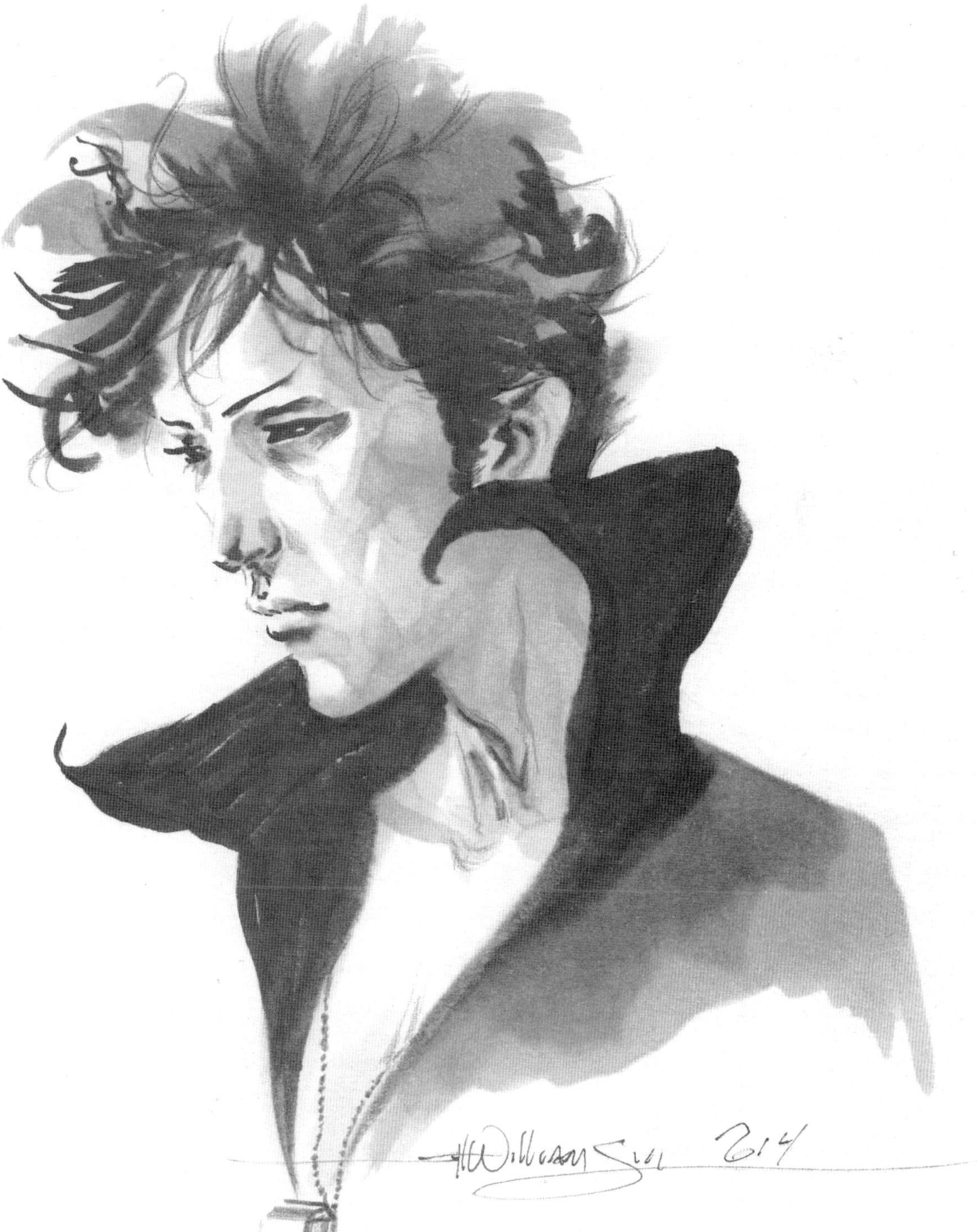

A decent sketch of Morpheus I did in 2014 for the very talented Brandon Graham when he and his *Inkstuds* podcast crew visited for a day.

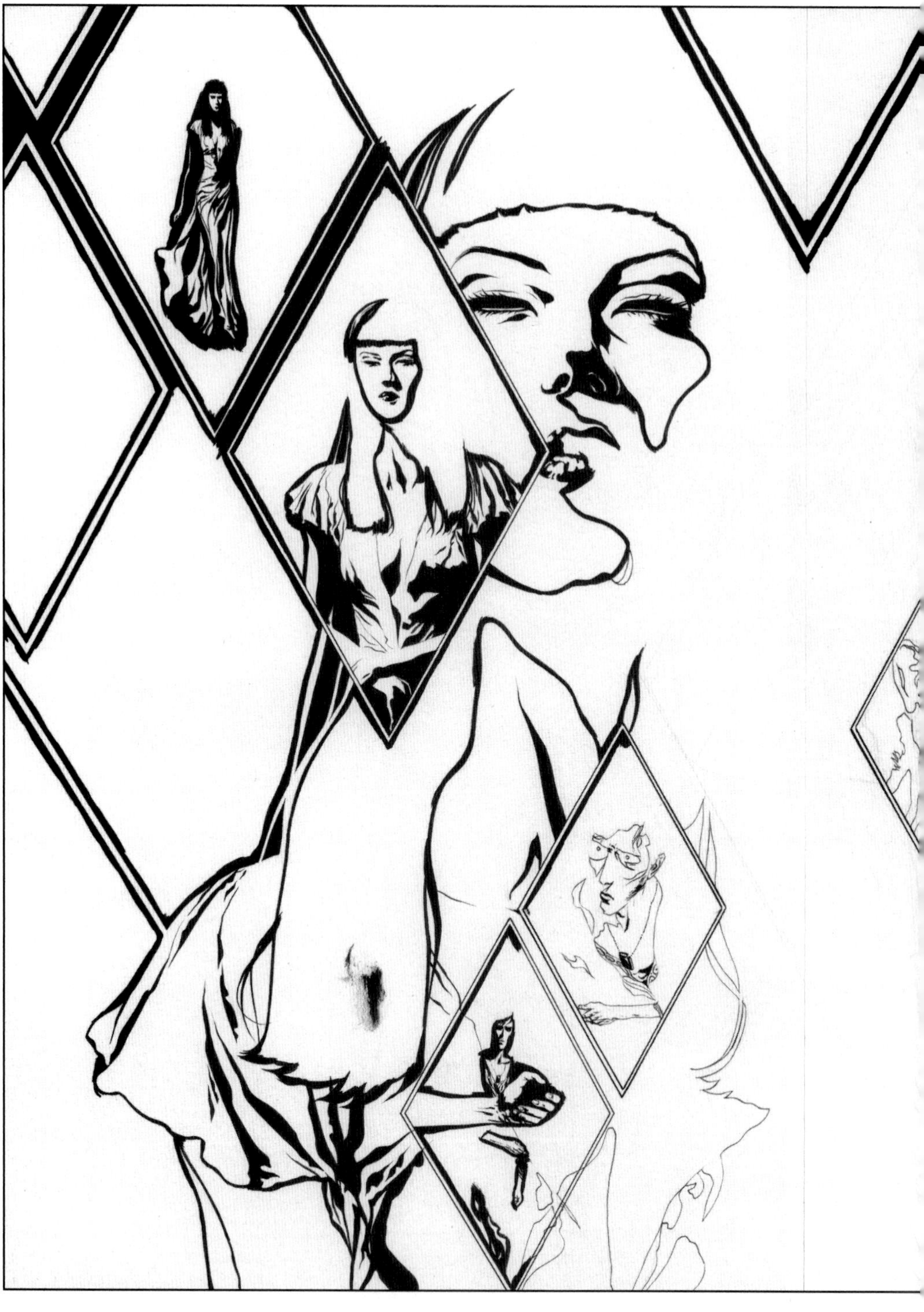

I almost never throw out a page that I'm already working on and start over from scratch — I've only done it maybe three times throughout my career. This incomplete spread from issue #5, pages 2 and 3, is such a time. The script called for Dusk to open a door out of the blackness, and what I have here wasn't working at all. There wasn't any movement. So I asked Neil if we could change the door into a giant black curtain, and have it become the veil of darkness being lifted. And so we did. The final result is to the right, shown for comparison.

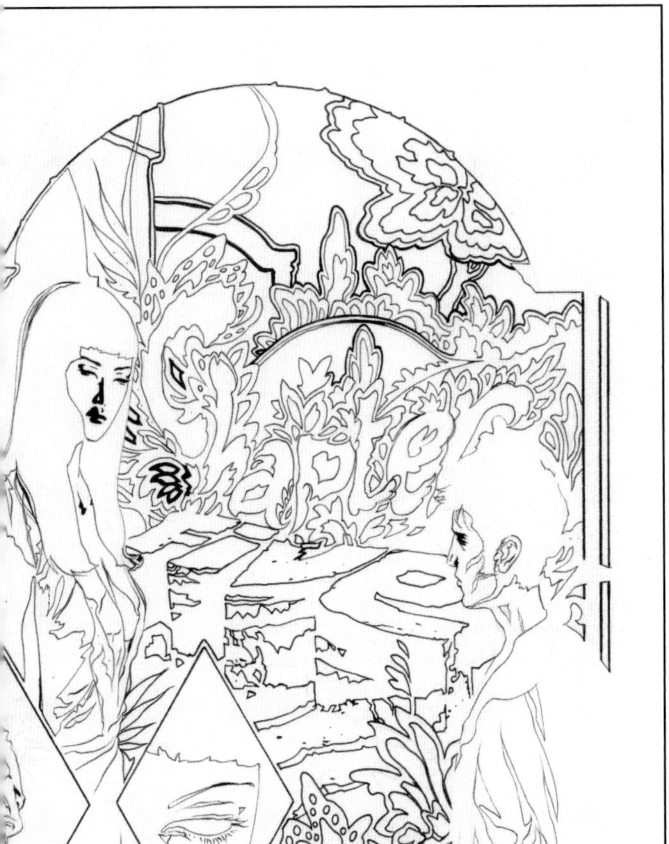
A
GAIMAN · WILLIAMS III · STEWART · KLEIN · MILLER · BOND PRODUCTION!

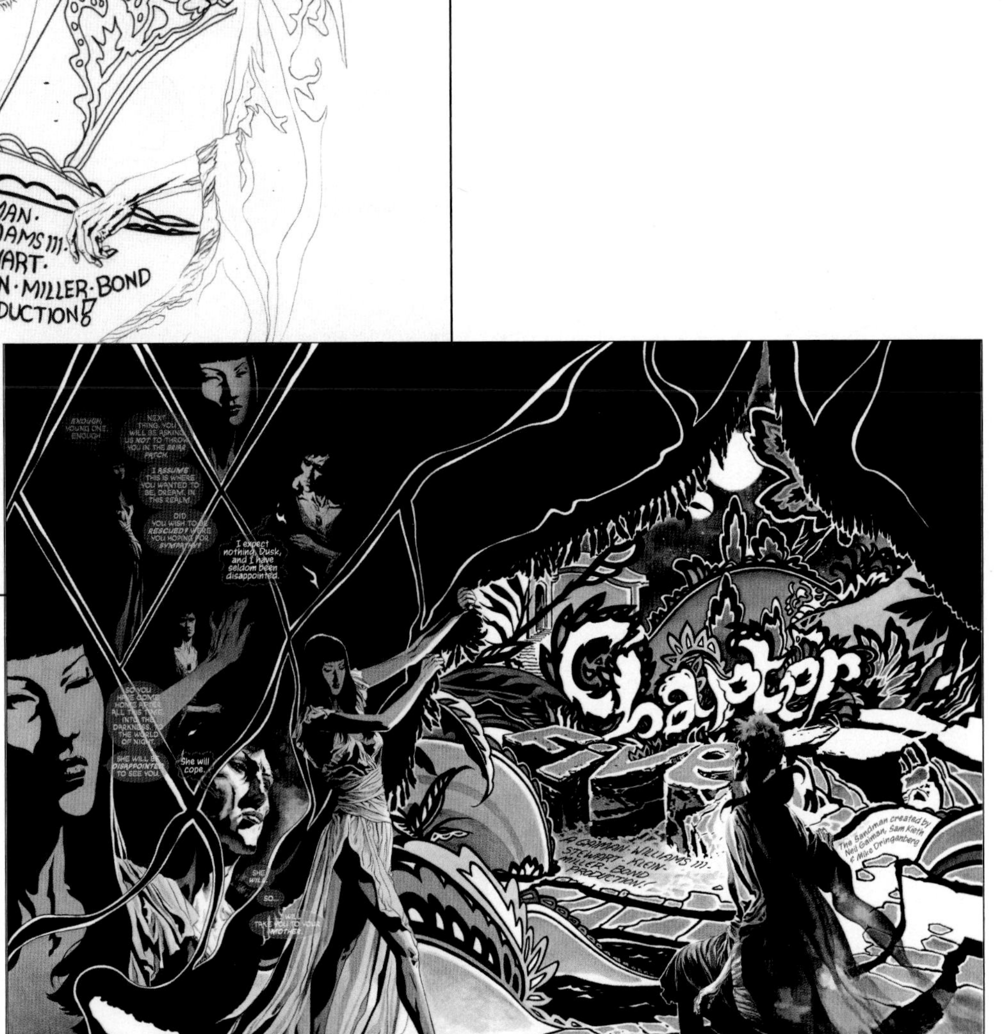
ENOUGH, YOUNG ONE. ENOUGH
NEXT THING, YOU WILL BE ASKING US NOT TO THROW YOU IN THE BRIAR PATCH.
I ASSUME THIS IS WHERE YOU WANTED TO BE, DREAM. IN THIS REALM.
DID YOU WISH TO BE RESCUED? WERE YOU HOPING FOR SYMPATHY?
I expect nothing, Dusk, and I have seldom been disappointed.
SO YOU HAVE GONE HOME AFTER ALL THIS TIME. INTO THE DARKNESS. TO THE WORLD OF NIGHT.
SHE WILL BE DISAPPOINTED TO SEE YOU.
She will cope.
SHE WILL...
SO...
I WILL TAKE YOU TO YOUR MOTHER.
Chapter Five
A GAIMAN · WILLIAMS III · STEWART · KLEIN · MILLER · BOND PRODUCTION!!
The Sandman created by Neil Gaiman, Sam Kieth & Mike Dringenberg

BIOGRAPHIES

Creator and writer of the internationally acclaimed comics masterpiece THE SANDMAN, **Neil Gaiman** is also the *New York Times* best-selling author of *The Ocean at the End of the Lane*, *Coraline* and the Newbery Medal-winning *The Graveyard Book*. His other books include the novels *Anansi Boys*, *Neverwhere*, *American Gods* and *Stardust* (winner of the American Library Association's Alex Award as one of 2000's top novels for young adults) and the short story collections *Fragile Things*, *M Is for Magic* and *Smoke and Mirrors*. Among his many awards are the Eisner, the Hugo, the Nebula, the World Fantasy and the Bram Stoker. Originally from England, he now lives in the United States.

J.H. Williams III is a multiple-award-winning creator known for his fine work on a wide array of titles, including THE SANDMAN: OVERTURE, BATMAN, STARMAN, CHASE, SON OF SUPERMAN, SEVEN SOLDIERS OF VICTORY, JONAH HEX, DESOLATION JONES (co-created with Warren Ellis), the revered PROMETHEA (co-created with Alan Moore), DETECTIVE COMICS (with writer Greg Rucka) and a celebrated run on BATWOMAN (as writer and artist). He has also provided art and designs for music releases, including the albums *Apocryphon* by The Sword and *Ghosts of Download* by the legendary Blondie, and he occasionally dabbles in fashion. J.H. and his wife, Wendy, live in the ethereal.

Dave Stewart began his career as an intern at Dark Horse before moving on to coloring comics. An artist in his own right, Stewart's stunning and versatile work has made him one of the industry's most sought-after color stylists. His credits include BATMAN, SUPERMAN, BATMAN/THE SPIRIT, *Conan*, *B.P.R.D.* and *Hellboy*. His industry awards include nine Eisners and five Harveys. He currently resides in Portland, Oregon with his wife, Michelle, and three black cats.

Dave McKean has illustrated nearly fifty books and comics, including *Signal to Noise*, *The Wolves in the Walls*, *Coraline*, and *The Graveyard Book*, all written by Neil Gaiman, *The Magic of Reality* by Richard Dawkins, *The Fat Duck Cookbook* by Heston Blumenthal, and *What's Welsh for Zen* by John Cale. He has written and illustrated the multi-award-winning *Cages*, *Pictures That Tick 1* and *2*, and *Celluloid*. He has also directed several short films and three features: *MirrorMask*, *The Gospel of Us* with Michael Sheen, and *Luna*, which premiered at the Toronto Film Festival in 2014. He lives on the Isle of Oxney in Kent, UK.

One of the industry's most versatile and accomplished letterers, **Todd Klein** has been lettering comics since 1977 and has won numerous Eisner and Harvey Awards for his work. A highlight of his career has been working with Neil Gaiman on nearly all the original issues of THE SANDMAN, as well as BLACK ORCHID, DEATH: THE HIGH COST OF LIVING, DEATH: THE TIME OF YOUR LIFE and THE BOOKS OF MAGIC.

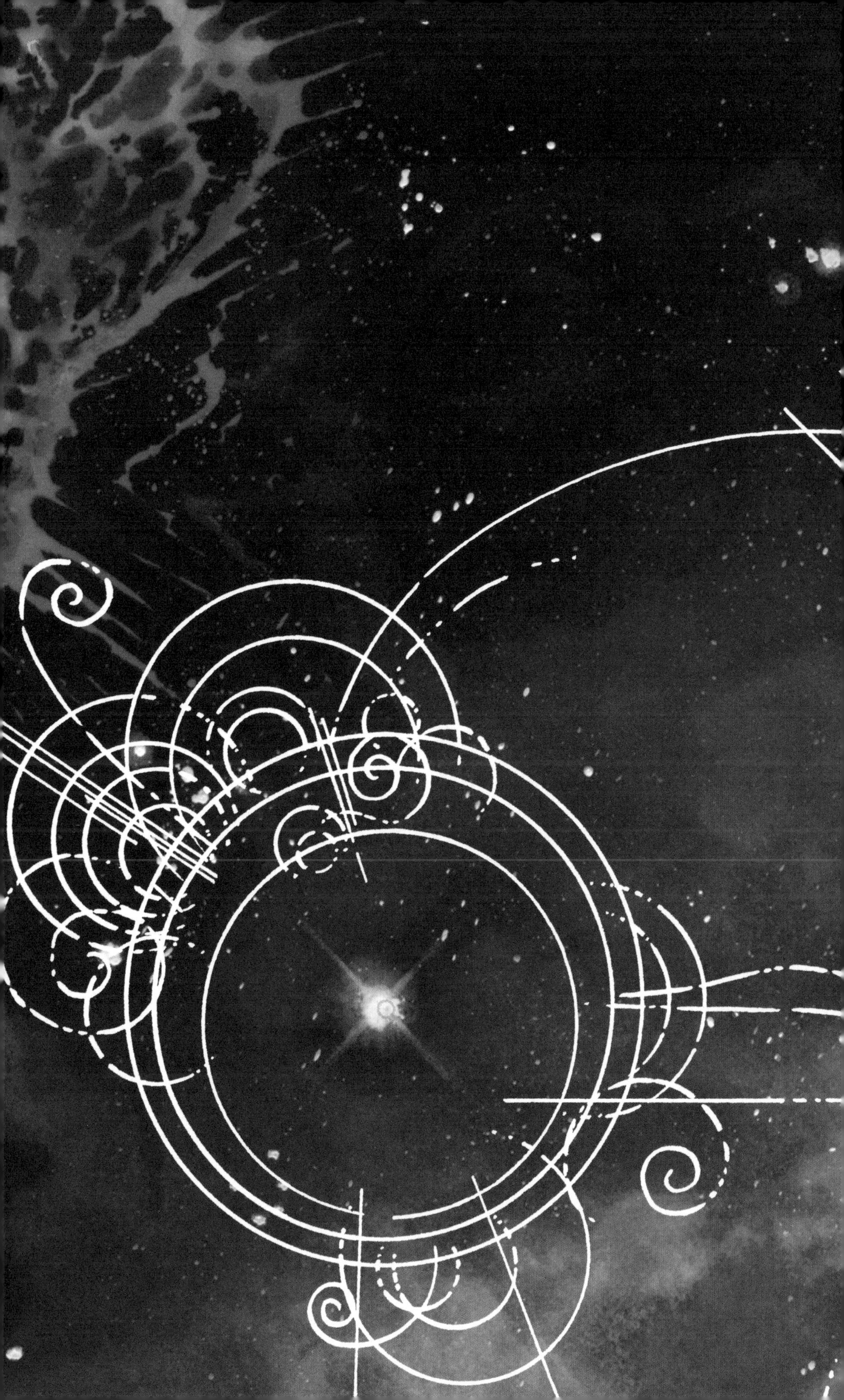

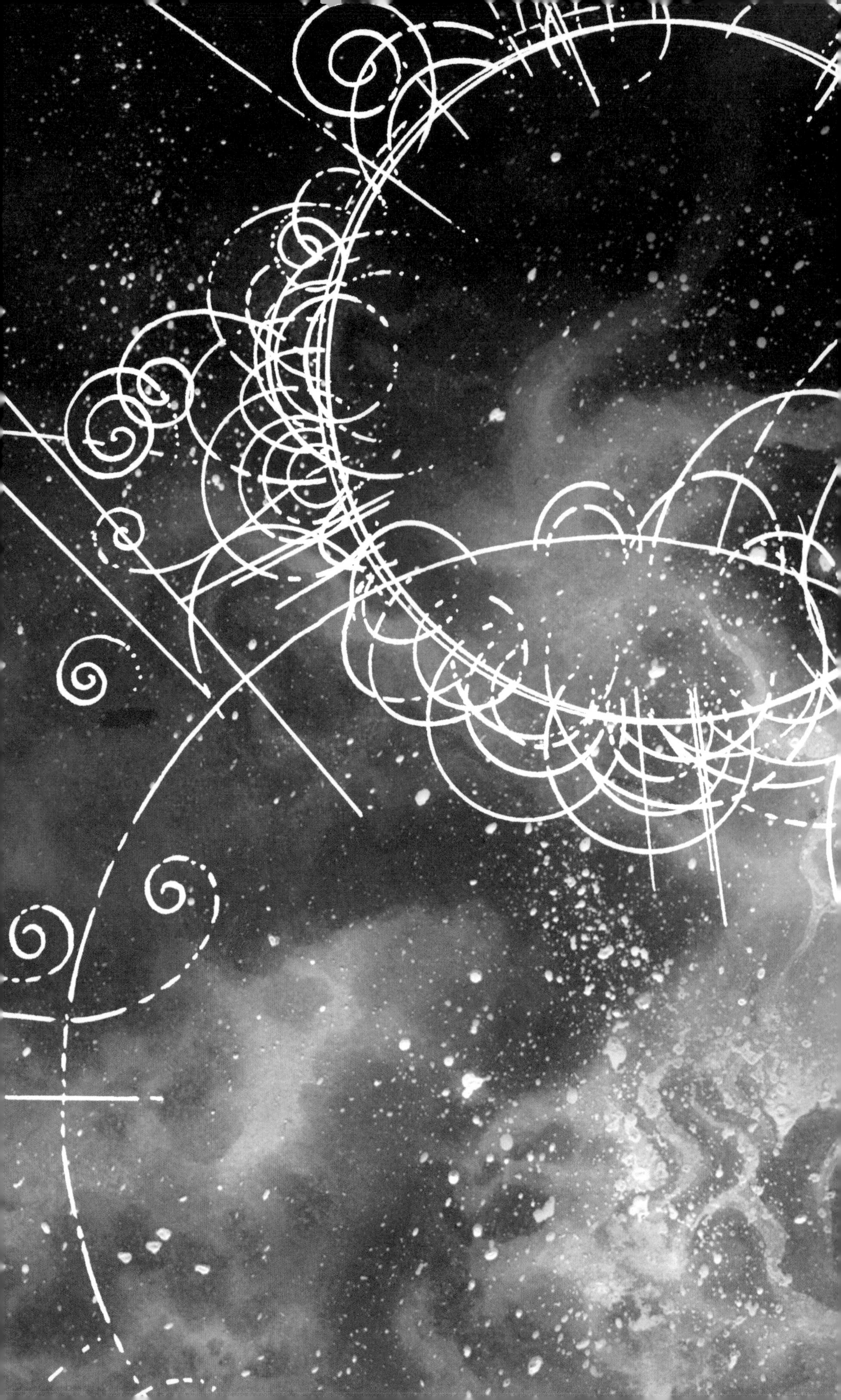